Experiences in Language

Third Edition

Experiences in Language

Tools and Techniques for Language Arts Methods

Walter T. Petty

Dorothy C. Petty

Marjorie F. Becking

Allyn and Bacon, Inc.
Boston, London, Sydney, Toronto

Series Editor: Margaret Quinlin

Production Editor: Joanne Dauksewicz

Library of Congress Cataloging in Publication Data

Petty, Walter Thomas, 1918–
    Experiences in language.

    Includes bibliographies and index.
     1. Language arts (Elementary) I. Petty, Dorothy C., joint author. II. Becking, Marjorie F., joint author.
III. Title.
LB1575.8.P47 1981   372.6′044   80-21449
ISBN 0-205-07176-7

Printed in the United States of America.

10 9 8 7 6 5 4 3 2 1   85 84 83 82 81

Photo on page 129 is by Christopher Morrow/Stock, Boston, Inc.
Photos on pages 15, 19, 28, 30, 218, 307, 331, 365, 409, and 418 are by Talbot D. Lovering, Allyn and Bacon staff photographer.
Photo on page 136 (bottom) and photos on page 305 (top right and bottom) are also by Talbot Lovering.
Photos not otherwise credited are by Peter Walders, Ellicott Road Elementary School, and the author.

Contents

Chapter 15   *Literature for Children*   360

Chapter 16   *Reading and Study Skills*   393

Chapter 17   *Children and the Library*   428

Preface

This book is dedicated, first, to Michelle—and to all the children who are or will be in elementary classrooms. Second, it is written for and dedicated to all of you now teaching in classrooms or preparing to teach.

In this third edition we again stress our strong belief that the language arts are the core of the elementary school program, that they provide the foundation for essentially all of the activities of the classroom and serve as the means for interrelating the many areas of the curriculum. If this premise is sound, then effectively teaching the language arts is crucial to each child's learning and vital to the entire program of the school.

Thus, we again present a complete language arts program. We focus on practicality by providing specific teaching suggestions, yet neither research nor sound theory has been ignored. The ideas and suggestions presented in the following pages are based upon many years of experience, an examination of research evidence, and the examples and suggestions of many creative and inspiring teachers.

The organization of this edition, changed somewhat from that of earlier ones, reflects an increased emphasis on the foundational aspects of effective programs—including those of planning, integrating the teaching of all of the language arts, recognizing differences among children as to abilities and needs, building readiness, and fostering positive attitudes. Again we have chapters on speaking, listening, written expression, reading, literature, handwriting, spelling, vocabulary building, grammar and usage, study skills, and using the library. Each of these suggests content that should be taught as well as activities for its teaching. It should be emphasized, however, that these activities are only suggestions. We hope that they will be helpful in tailoring activities to the particular personalities and needs of specific children in specific classrooms.

Many inservice teachers, as well as graduate students with teaching experience, have helped us with this book. We especially want to thank Peter Walders, a teacher at Ellicott Road Elementary School, Orchard Part, New York, for many of the photographs. We are also appreciative of the courtesy shown us by Robert Horvath, principal, and the teachers and children of the Ellicott Road Elementary School.

W. T. P.
D. C. P.
M. F. B.

Experiences in Language

I

Foundations

of

Language

Arts

Programs

The effectiveness of a language arts program depends to a great extent on how well the program has been planned. Planning requires knowledge—knowledge about the children to be taught, the nature of language and how language is learned, what communication skills and abilities children need to learn, and teaching procedures that work. Part I provides a foundation of the knowledge needed and describes how planning may be done.

In chapter 1 we discuss the nature of language and language learning and briefly describe the language arts and ways that they are interrelated. Chapter 2 focuses on planning—both long- and short-term—and includes discussions of planning principles, the identification of pupil differences, and organization for instruction. In chapter 3 we discuss classroom climate, learning principles, and beginning language arts activities.

The final two chapters in Part I are concerned with children who have handicaps or disorders that require special teaching attention and the perennial issue of grammar and usage teaching.

We hope that these chapters will help you formulate your individual beliefs about language and the teaching of language skills to children and will serve as a guide to your reading and study of the remaining chapters.

1

The Language Arts and Language Learning

Language is such an integral part of our lives that we tend to take it for granted —to use it in our everyday activities without giving thought to the miracle that it really is or even to its importance in our lives. Yet today the exchange of ideas and knowledge is increasingly crucial to each person's social, economic, political, and psychological well-being. At the same time, the vocational and personal environments of all of us are becoming more and more specialized, with the result that specialized vocabularies and ways of using language are developing within these environments. These factors surely limit the exchange and may lead to or increase class and status barriers that result in a loss of the give-and-take essential to democracy. Thus developing in each child his or her full capabilities for using language maximizes the possibilities for eliminating the barriers we already have and for avoiding the establishing of others. Beyond this, such development should foster a respect for the rights, privileges, and responsibilities of every human being.

THE NATURE OF LANGUAGE

Webster's *Third New International Dictionary* defines language in a number of ways. Some appear to limit language to speech and to human beings, while others are more inclusive, including "signs, sounds, gestures, or marks" and even "the means by which animals communicate or are thought to communicate." The latter definitions imply that the waving of an arm or the furrowing of a brow is language, as is writing, and perhaps the chattering of a frightened squirrel or the tail-wagging of a favorite dog. For school purposes we ordinarily think of language as verbal symbols that are associated with ideas and objects and that are produced in systematic patterns to convey meaning from one person to another. The symbols may be graphic (letters and combinations of letters) or they may be vocal (separate sounds or combinations of sounds).

Characteristics of Language

The systematic arrangement of symbols is a key characteristic of language. The systematic nature of any language is shown by interwined and interrelated principles that cause the language to operate in regular ways. Each language has its own system—a system peculiar in at least some respects to no other language—but every language is systematic and every language has arbitrarily attached vocal (and generally graphic) symbols to the ideas and objects that are a part of the culture it serves.

Thus, arbitrariness is a part of language related to its systematic nature. The people of every culture have simply designated a sound or set of sounds to represent something that they need to talk about. The French say *le chien,* the English say *dog*; both are arbitrarily designated symbols (both in sound and graphic forms) that represent the same object, and they do so regularly and systematically. Those who use a language also make it as complete as necessary for their culture. We have the term *nuclear physics*; an American Indian language of the year 1600 had no need for such a term. This difference makes neither language any less "advanced," complete, or systematic than the other. Each is a social instrument facilitating communication between people about the things they want to communicate about.

Still another characteristic of language is that it changes. Evidence of the change in English is apparent, for example, if one compares pages from the King James version of the Bible, a Shakespeare play, a Hemingway novel, and an issue of *Time*. These changes in language occur in many ways. We readily think of new meanings being attached to words and of new words or combinations of words being used for new or changed objects or ideas. Perhaps we can think of pronunciation changes or spelling changes, though the latter tend to take longer to occur, and we may not be aware of them until we read something written a hundred or so years ago. And if we look back far enough we can even find changes in word order.

System in Language

The way language operates is described in terms of sounds, groups of sounds arranged as words and word parts and their classification as to function, and the ways words can be arranged or ordered in sentences or parts of sentences. These terms are defined and briefly discussed in the remaining paragraphs in this section.

The basic sounds of a language are called *phonemes.* Phonemes are defined as the smallest units of sound by which different meanings may be distinguished. A phoneme is actually not a single significant sound, but a class of sounds heard by the typical native speaker as the same sound. For example, the sounds represented by *p* in *pin, spin,* and *lip* are actually articulated slightly differently, but for all practical purposes they are the same. On the other hand, the differences between the sounds represented by *b* and *p* in *bit* and *pit* are also slight, but they are differ-

---

Characteristics of Language

1. Language is symbolic.
2. Language symbols are arbitrary.
3. Language is systematic.
4. Language is a form of human behavior.
5. Language is a social instrument.
6. Language continually changes.

The Alaskan natives of the North Slope are said to know more than 80 different kinds of snow—and have words for all of them.

New Words

backlash
bionic
centrism
guru
macho
pixel
troika

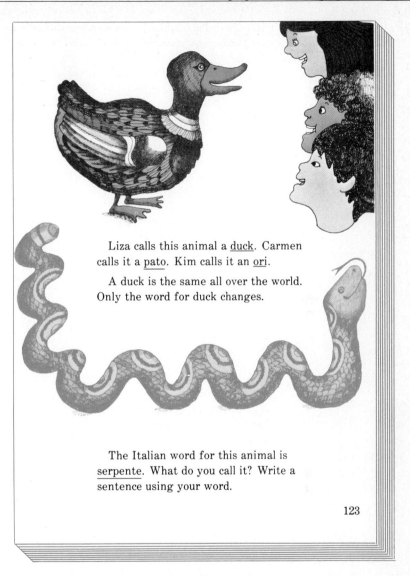

Liza calls this animal a <u>duck</u>. Carmen calls it a <u>pato</u>. Kim calls it an <u>ori</u>.

A duck is the same all over the world. Only the word for duck changes.

The Italian word for this animal is <u>serpente</u>. What do you call it? Write a sentence using your word.

123

Language textbooks for children are increasingly giving attention to aspects of language study. (USING OUR LANGUAGE, 1977 edition; copyright © by BOWMAR/NOBLE PUBLISHERS, INC., Los Angeles, California 90039.)

ences that we all recognize and they distinguish meaning.

Phonemes, of course, are not letters of the alphabet. The same phoneme may be represented by different letters of the alphabet or even combinations of letters. The /s/ phoneme is represented by *s* in *send*, *c* in *cent*, and *sc* in *scent*. Conversely,

Phonemes are represented in written form by using virgules, in order to distinguish between letters and the sounds they represent. For example, to show the sounds in mat, *the linguist writes* /m/ /a/ /t/.

a letter of the alphabet may represent different phonemes. For instance, the *g* is the graphic form of the initial sound in *gun* and *gene* and the medial phoneme in *regime*.

Linguists differ as to the number of phonemes that are called segmental—that is, through simple voicing and articulation, the continuous stream of sound is divided into segments that are recognizable as meaningful units. The differences are relatively minor—the numbers ranging slightly greater and slightly less than 40—and are due to differences in classification systems used.

In addition to the segmental phonemes, there are suprasegmental features which also describe the language we use. These include four degrees of *stress* in the flow of language, three levels of *pitch* in the voice, and four *junctures* or interruptions in the stream of speech. The degrees of stress are similar to the familiar accent, but they go beyond this—each syllable is identified as having a relative degree of emphasis in comparison to others. Pitch, of course, is the relative voice height in speech.

The smallest units in language that cannot be divided without eliminating meaning or changing it drastically are called *morphemes.* Morphemes may be thought of as the building blocks of the language. They relate sound and structure aspects of language to meaning. Morphemes may be *free* or *bound.* A morpheme is often a word, as in such lexical items as *cat, walk*, and *laugh.* These are free or lexical morphemes. A bound or grammatical morpheme is one that must be combined with another morpheme— *-s, -ed, anti-* Thus, *cat* is one morpheme (three phonemes) and *cats* is two morphemes (four phonemes).

Words may be classified into four large *form* classes or parts of speech (nouns, verbs, adjectives, and adverbs). Placement in these classes in most present-day descriptions of language is determined by four basic considerations, none of which give particular emphasis to meaning or function in the traditional sense (for example, that a noun is the name of a person, place, or thing). The considerations used include affixes, word order, particular structures or function, and the sound stress given. Thus, a noun is a word that will take the inflectional endings *-s* or *-es, -'s*, and *-s'*; it will take derivational suffixes such as *-er, -or, -ment, -ness, -ism,* etc.; it may be signaled or marked by such words as *the, a, each, some, many, my;* or it receives major stress on the beginning syllable (for example, *sus'pect* is a noun while *suspect'* is a verb). Of course, a word can be classified as a noun by applying only one of these criteria; there are few instances in which all can be applied. The other form classes—verbs, adjectives, and adverbs—also use word order, signal words, and affixes to determine classification.

In addition to the four form classes, our language has *structure* or *function* words. These include the signal words, qualifiers (*very, rather, quite,* etc.), prepositions (*on, in, after,* etc.), and conjunctions (*but, and,* etc.). The structure words relate words of the form classes to each other and provide an essential structure so that our language has fluidity and cohesion.

The meaningful arrangement or order of words in sentences or parts of sentences is the fundamental aspect of system in language. This is known as *syntax,* which may also be defined as the grammar or description of a language. There are several approaches to describing word ordering in English sentences (see chapter 5). The arrangement or order of words is particularly important in English, since it is a major way of expressing grammatical ideas and it is essential in making meaningful sentences. For example, the words *"selected book the quickly girl the"* ex-

Function or Signal Words

Noun markers–my, some, two, the, an
Verb markers–am, is, were, had, will
Phrase markers–into, above, down, up, out
Clause markers–because, that, if, why, how
Question markers–who, when, what, where, why

press grammatical meanings by structure signals and endings, but the meaning is not clear until they are arranged into *"The girl quickly selected the book."*

Variety in Language

Any language is an entity only in a limited sense. The language each person uses is largely a matter of his early environment, his education, and the social situation in which he expresses himself. The variation in language that is most obvious is in the dialects. Dialects, like the language of which they are a part, are systematic, adequate for communication among their users, and to a large extent predictable in structure and use. In general, dialects differ in matters of pronunciation and vocabulary to a greater extent than they do in grammatical features. Some dialects are also identifiable by the rate of speech and variations in pitch. The slow drawl associated with the South and Southwest and the nasality in the southern hills are familiar examples. Most of us know that *Mary, marry,* and *merry* are pronounced identically by most natives of the northern midwestern United States, whereas in New England the natives pronounce these words differently. We also know that groceries are placed in a *bag* in some sections of the country but in a *sack,* or perhaps a *poke,* in others. There are many other examples of differences in pronunciation and vocabulary and some paralanguage differences. Sentence structure, on the other hand, remains essentially the same in most English-speaking communities.

Of course, even though everyone speaks a dialect (and not just people in the South or Brooklyn or Boston), each person's language varies from one expressional situation to another, particularly after one becomes an adult; these variations may be thought of as levels or styles. Each of us uses a colloquial or homely language in speaking with close friends and family. This language is certainly less formal than that used in giving a speech or writing an article. One may also use particular words and expressions—localisms—in his or her own town or neighborhood that would probably be avoided in another geographical location. Thus, although we may say that a person speaks *a* dialect, there are variations in this just as there are variations among dialects. Certainly any dialect is an adequate means of communication for its users, but if it deviates from the community's belief as to what is "standard English" (discussed in chapter 5) there may be an instructional problem. Although some linguists—and some other persons, including some teachers—believe that all dialects are equally "good," there is evidence that the public generally expects teachers to teach "good" English, meaning that of an "acceptable" standard (as difficult as that is for anyone to define).

How Do You Say?

creek
greasy
roof
wash
stomach
hog

LANGUAGE LEARNING

Children generally learn to talk without much difficulty. This learning begins at birth, with the first sounds a child hears seeming to trigger a propensity to communicate. The fact that language is systematic facilitates this learning, as does the desire of persons around the child to communicate with him. The child's experimenting, trying to communicate, leads rather quickly to a discovery of how the language works, what the system is. Of course not everything about the system is discovered at once. In fact, some aspects of it are still being learned well into the elementary school years, but the essentials for talking are learned by most children by about age two.

Controversy as to how this learning occurs has led to several theories being advanced. The differences among these center largely on the extent to which the ability to learn language is innate as opposed to its being learned by imitation. There is agreement that a child must have some interaction with a speaker, and this seems to imply that imitation is the basis of the learning. However, not every word, pair of words, or sentence a child utters is one he has heard. Accounting for this seems to imply an inborn ability.

Language Acquisition Theories

Essentially there are two basic language acquisition theories. One point of view, the empiricists' position, holds that language is learned entirely through experience. Children learn the language of the persons around them when they are born and during their infant years. According to this theory, the infant in the babbling stage is rewarded by a smile, pat, or tone of voice for uttering an appropriate sound (part of a word in the language of the persons around him), and as this experimenting and reinforcing continue language is acquired. Significant to this theory is the fact that this acquisition is of the sounds, patterns, and system of the language the learner has heard. The fact that children produce patterns of language that they have not heard is explained either as attempts to imitate that have gone awry or as examples in language production of children's tendency to experiment.

A second theory holds that language acquisition is innate, that it is as natural for children to learn language as it is for them to learn other human abilities. This position is based on the existence of language universals; that is, all languages consist of sets of sounds, these sounds are combined into meaningful units, and these units are arranged in a particular order. Advocates for this theory cite as evidence the consistency with which children develop language. This theory, of course, does not deny a role for experience with language to activate this ability, just as contact with humans is necessary to learn other human abilities.

Related to this latter theory is one which holds that humans are born with a capacity that allows them to process language and intuitively formulate rules for using it. This capacity at any time is affected by the learner's cognitive capacity and, again, experience in a language setting is needed for the processing to occur.

While theories about how language is acquired are interesting, and are important to many language researchers, acceptance of one theory by teachers is not necessary. What is significant to teachers is the rapidity of the child's learning, the naturalness of this learning, the importance of experience with language in the early learning, and the fact that how language works is largely understood when children enter school.

Language Development

Children begin at birth to experiment with their vocal organs, to make sounds. This experimenting progresses through cries and cooing, some of which are detected as expressing pain, fear, anger, or joy. These early vocalizations show little system or little relationship to the language spoken by those caring for them. At about four months of age the infant shows signs of responding to human sounds—turning the head and eyes to look for the speaker. Shortly thereafter the cooing will change to babbling, which with increasing practice shows considerable mastery of the basic elements of the vocal mechanism. The child does more ''practicing,'' gaining a great deal of control of volume, pitch, and articulation as shown by the ability to repeat sounds he hears. By the time the normal child has reached his first birthday, he is producing sounds to which his listeners can genuinely attach meaning. Usually these first ''words'' are consonant-vowel in form— ''ma-ma,'' ''da-da,'' ''bye-bye''—with the child possibly not attaching the same meaning to them as the adoring father and mother, although the experimenting will soon cause him to relate the sounds to the adult meanings.

At around eighteen to twenty months of age most children begin to put words together. The experimenting in doing this is similar to that done with words. The first combinations of words tend to follow the pattern of a few words in a particular utterance position joined with a variety of other words (''bye bye daddy,'' ''bye bye mommy,'' ''bye bye doggie''). The experimenting continues with more of these singled-out words being tried out with other words and combinations of words. Gradually, then, the child perceives the notion of word order—that some words belong first and some words second. Sometimes this early perception is faulty in respect to the language system. More, often, though, word order is satisfactory, but frequently some words are omitted. The child says ''I see car'' for ''I can see the car.'' This is *telegraphic speech* (as in telegrams) and is simply further experimenting. All such experimenting is a normal stage in development, a stage in learning how the language works.

By the time most children are two years of age they will have a fund of words that represent objects and actions and will be able to use them in ways that are understood. They test hypotheses about noun and verb endings, frequently overgeneralizing about the rules by saying *foots, goed,* and *mines.* This ''sorting out'' continues for some time (in some aspects of syntax to about age nine and perhaps beyond), but by the time the average child reaches kindergarten age he speaks in sentences, the complexity of which depends on his mental maturity, language aptitude, and experiences.

From the very beginning the child's use of language is purposeful, not perfunctory. The child who has learned to talk enough to use language for satisfying immediate physical needs soon becomes absorbed in making the acquaintance of a great variety of things. He asks, ''What's that?'' over and over. Asking questions is the characteristic type of language activity at this stage of preschool language development. As a two- to five-year-old he struggles to identify the many objects in his environment; he seeks to bring order into a wide world of sight, sound, smell, and feeling. The responses to this exploring are very important to language development. Thus narrow experiences and limited responses result in language development that is less than that of the child who has had broad experiences and has secured responses to these expressions of curiosity.

The family environment is the most important factor other than the child's maturity pattern in determining the language facility he develops and the speed with which it is developed. For instance, an only child may have closer association with adults than one who has brothers and sisters. This closeness may result in the development of a larger vocabulary and more maturity in expression. Simi-

See Language Arts, *March 1975, Nov./Dec. 1974 for readable articles on language acquisition and development*

A Note to Parents

Work daily to help your child acquire language.

Use expansions in your speech of the language the child uses.

Ask questions which require more than one word in answers.

Help the child give labels to everything in the environment—from apples to sun, car, geese, and taxi.

Remember that your language is the model.

Talk to the child and *listen.* Encourage but do not push!

larly, the child whose parents talk with him a great deal develops language facility earlier than one who grows up in a family in which he is ignored or told to "be quiet." In addition to providing the child with language experiences, the family provides the language model—the kind of language he is going to imitate.

A child's mental development and his progress in using language move along together, both thoroughly interwoven through the experiences of his life. Every experience a child has bears upon his development, especially his intellectual and language development. Each new experience or enrichment of an earlier one results in his gaining greater knowledge and understanding. A child soon learns that language is important to the gaining of knowledge and understanding, and he makes use of it as he explores things around him.

The things children encounter in this exploration determine the language they use, the words they learn, and the meanings they attach to those words. A preschool child living in a city apartment house certainly has different experiences from those of the farm child. One will certainly know the words *woods, pasture, hedge,* and *pig,* and the other will as certainly know *taxi, curb, lobby,* and *elevator.* Of course, each may know some words in both lists, or they may have different meanings attached (e.g., an *elevator* is used to store grain, and in street parlance a police officer may be called a *pig*) since words, lexical units, have meaning only as they are used in context.

What Are the Language Arts?

The Language Arts

RECEP-TIVE	←→t←→	EXPRES-SIVE
	h	
	i	
listening	n	speaking
	k	
	i	
reading	n	writing
	g	

The language arts are the *receptive* language activities of reading and listening and the *expressive* activities of speaking and writing. Involved in both reception and expression is *thinking,* which is sometimes called the fifth language art.

Although "language arts" is the most widely used term, there are other names given to the portion of the school program devoted to teaching language communication skills. "English," of course, is the historical term, but "the communicative arts," "the English language arts," and simply "language" are also used. It is also true that many teachers think of reading, spelling, composition, and the like rather than thinking more broadly of the language arts; hence they use no inclusive term.

The "language arts" seems to be the designation that best describes the activities of speaking, writing, listening, and reading and recognizes their interrelatedness. It focuses upon language, as opposed to the more narrow and traditional elements of writing, grammar, and literature associated with English or to the broad aspects of communication involving sound, sight, feel, and smell without the use of language.

Elements of the Language Arts

The use of the term "language arts" aids in focusing on the interrelatedness of the four aspects of language communication. If we are to use an all-inclusive term, however, we must define the various elements and know how they are related to one another.

Parents are sometimes confused by school terminology, particularly as it is used on report cards. Many parents have their own ideas as to the meanings of spelling, grammar, etc., but they do not realize that "language" or "language arts" includes much of what they think should be taught.

Writing includes the skills of spelling, penmanship, punctuation, capitalization, and, most importantly, composition—the putting together of ideas and information in a coherent and appealing manner. The major element in speaking is also composition, but the skills of articulation, pronunciation, and voice projection, as well as those related to physical posture and manner, are also included.

Reading and listening have common characteristics. Both are concerned with perception of either graphic or oral symbols, with the identification of unknown words and terms, and with the use of these, along with one's experience, to gain meaning.

All of the language arts involve thinking and have the common base of language. Therefore, how the language is put together, how it works, how it influences our thinking, and how it is used in this thinking add the elements of grammar, vocabulary, dialect, and usage.

The language arts also include the study skills involved in using a dictionary, locating information, and using the library, as well as proofreading and editing of composition and conventionality of writing and speaking forms.

Furthermore, the language arts include attitudes toward language usage, communication activities, and the aesthetic components of these activities. For example, reading is more than merely gaining meaning, for the literature of mankind is a part of this aspect of the language arts. In a like sense, listening is done both for useful purposes and for pleasure, and writing may be both "practical" and "creative."

Interrelationships among the Elements

At the elementary school level the language arts program may sometimes be separated into particular facets—spelling, handwriting, reading, etc.—for instructional purposes. Yet it is not possible to keep the various segments from merging, since even the most superficial examination of language arts instruction will lead to the conclusion that rarely does any language skill function independently.

The interrelationships among the language arts are many and varied, as will become even clearer in the chapters that follow. At the heart of the interrelationships is the presence of language in each element of expression or reception and the fact that an experience affecting one facet will usually affect others. For example, if you seek to teach a child to read without recognizing his desire to write and the importance of listening and speaking skills to readiness for reading instruction, you will meet with frustration. Similarly, listening and speaking skills require knowledge of vocabulary, writing requires spelling and penmanship, both oral and written expression require language organizational skills, and so on. A teacher who is sensitive to interrelationships will not wait until confronted by a problem to note the commonness of elements, but will keep the carry-over effects in mind when teaching any of the facets.

The sequence of development of the language skills is listening, speaking, and later—in our culture, usually at school—reading and writing. Although the infant's cries, gurgles, and related sounds are language in its broadest sense, an infant's first contact with language as most of us think of it is through hearing it. Thus, even though hearing is the only language ability he has for much of the first

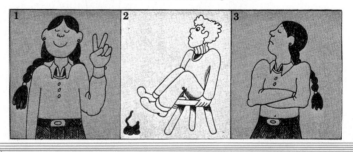

A smile can show happiness. A frown can show anger. But we have many other feelings. Our body language tells a lot about us.

Look at the pictures below. Can you tell how the people feel? Does their body language help you guess what they might say? Write what you think they could say. Number your paper from 1 to 3 because there are three pictures.

Not all communication is verbal. (USING OUR LANGUAGE, 1977 edition; copyright © by BOWMAR/NOBLE PUBLISHERS, INC., Los Angeles, California 90039.)

year of his life, the interrelated nature of the language arts soon becomes evident. At an early age he learns to relate his vocalizing to sounds that he hears, and soon he develops skill in saying the speech sounds he has heard and practiced; the fact that deaf children do not learn to speak during this early period provides evidence of the close relationship between speech and listening.

Listening and reading both entail receiving messages. Thus, there is considerable similarity in the skills needed for determining what these messages are. Ability in reading varies significantly with language development and proficiency in oral expression—an interrelationship of great importance to elementary school teaching. What is read or listened to is often the substance of or motivation for writing—and writing is done for someone to read. Writing and speaking are, of course, interrelated in a similar manner to that of listening and reading.

All children come to school with patterns of speech based on what they have heard, speech that they have used in whatever environments they come from. The speech that a child uses is of basic importance in any effort to instruct him or her in learning to use language as effectively as possible. Every child also comes to school with habits of listening, and many even have some ability in writing and reading. Practically all children certainly have observed and "practiced" writing and reading and have developed attitudes toward the language skills and their importance. All of these abilities, habits, and knowledge must be considered in instruction, and there must be recognition that growth in one language arts area often reinforces the others and that all language activities need to be rich and varied in order to assure optimum growth in each facet of the language arts.

Language learning results from experiences and talking about them.

A Final Word

Because language is the major means by which ideas are shared, it is basic to all living and learning. For this reason, the language arts are the foundation of the school curriculum, and the teaching of the language arts is perhaps the teacher's most important task. To accomplish this task requires a knowledge of language—the way it works, the way it grows and changes, how children learn it, and the way it affects the lives of all of us. It also requires that a teacher know what to teach, when to teach it, and the best procedures for teaching. The intent of the chapters that follow is to help you accomplish this task.

References

Books

Alexander, Henry. *The Story of Our Language.* New York: Doubleday, 1969.

Cazden, Courtney B. *Child Language and Education.* New York: Holt, Rinehart and Winston, Inc., 1972.

Brown, Roger. *A First Language: The Early Stages.* Cambridge: Harvard University Press, 1973.

Dale, Philip S. *Language Development,* 2nd ed. New York: Holt, Rinehart and Winston, Inc., 1976.

Malmstrom, Jean. *Understanding Language.* New York: St. Martin's Press, 1977.

Pflaum, Susanna W. *The Development of Language and Reading in the Young Child.* Columbus, OH: Charles E. Merrill Publishing Company, 1974.

Reed, Carroll, ed. *The Learning of Language.* New York: Appleton-Century-Crofts, 1971.

Films

Development of the Child: Language Development. Harper and Row (20 min.).

Regional Variations. Stuart Finley (28 min.; for teachers).

Social Variations. Stuart Finley (27 min.; for teachers).

Discovering Language Series. Coronet (5 color films; for grades 4–9).

Recordings

Our Changing Language. National Council of Teachers of English (record).

Culture, Class, and Language Variety. National Council of Teachers of English (cassette to accompany book with the same title).

Americans Speaking. National Council of Teachers of English (cassette).

The Changing English Language. Folkway Records (middle grades).

ACTIVITIES FOR PRESERVICE TEACHERS

1. Investigate theories of language development. Do you accept any one theory? Why or why not?

2. Recall your language arts experiences in the elementary school as a student. What did the teachers seek to teach you? What was your opinion of this? What do you recall about their teaching procedures related to this content? Did you react favorably? Why or why not?

3. Visit a classroom for approximately half a day and observe one child specifically. What can you say about his or her language? Can you make any judgments about the child's early language experiences?

4. Look up the pronunciations of *aunt, brooch, dais, orange, garage, root, route, suite,* and *stoop* in several dictionaries. Report to the class what you found.

5. Examine the treatment of the following in a number of other language arts methods textbooks:
   a. Elements of the language arts.
   b. Interrelationships among the language arts.
   c. Language acquisition theories.
   d. Language development of children.

6. With which regions of the country and why do you associate with them each of the words or phrases in these pairs: string beans, snap beans; pail, bucket; sweet corn, roasting ears; porch, stoop; cherry pit, cherry seed; pavement, sidewalk.

7. Visit a classroom and talk with children who did not begin their schooling in the school they are now attending. Find out the reason for the child having moved. As the children talk, listen for variety in language patterns and usage. What might any or all of this mean to you as a language arts teacher?

ACTIVITIES FOR INSERVICE TEACHERS

1. Prepare a booklet for parents of young children, stressing the importance of experience and language development as they are related to success in school. Include activities for parents to share and discuss with their child, such as reading a story.

2. Survey the professional materials available to you in your school. What is in them related to the content of this chapter? Report to the class.

3. What evidence do you have that the differences in language abilities among children in your class

are reflections of their family environments? List your observational evidence for four of your children.

4. Which of the four areas of the language arts receives the least attention in your classroom? Write a paragraph telling why this is so.

5. Think about what things concerning our language and how it is learned might interest children. Categorize these by age and grade levels and then for one level outline what you might teach and how.

6. Investigate non-verbal language (often called *body language* or *silent language.* See such sources as Edward Hall, *Silent Language* (Doubleday, 1959) and Julius Fast, *Body Language* (Evans, 1970). Also observe the uses of this type of communication by the children in your class.

2

Planning for Teaching and Learning

Do you remember when you were in the elementary school? What do you remember about the language arts? What was good or bad about spelling lessons? Did you do much writing? What did you write about? Did you give talks? Oral reports? Did the teacher tell stories? Read to you? Did you consider what you were learning about language and how to use it to be important? Part of "real" life?

Your reflections about what you remember, particularly as to what was good or bad, what was useful and relevant and what was not, can be very important to your teaching. Using your common sense in regard to these reflections can tell you a great deal about what to teach and how to teach it. Think about these things as your read this chapter—and, in fact, as you read all of the book.

The purpose of this chapter is to give you an overview of effective language arts teaching and the planning and organizing that is so important in maximizing children's learning. The content of this chapter has application in each of the chapters that follow—and you may find yourself referring back to it as you study them.

PRINCIPLES OF PLANNING

Planning is not something that can be done once and then dropped. Planning needs to be done for the long-term, for intermediate periods of time, and for daily lessons. While long-term planning (what should be accomplished this year, this term, this month) is crucial, plans need to be made, changed, dropped, and remade as events change and as children learn. Thus, the principles suggested here are just as applicable to daily planning as they are to long-term planning. Of course the amount of time given to daily planning will be less than that given for more extensive planning. One reason for this is that daily plans are simply portions of

Planning together is important to children.

Who are the children?

What are their needs?

What differences are there among them?

those for longer amounts of time.

The basic element in all planning is the children—the children who are actually in your class. You need to know what knowledge, skills and abilities, and attitudes they have and what their needs are. Determining all of this is a big task and one that has to be worked on all year long (see the section Planning for Pupil Differences later in this chapter). To start, though, before meeting the children and having personal contact with them, review their school records so that you have some idea of their abilities and needs.[1] But this is only the beginning since no person can be put on paper.

In addition to knowing the children, you also need to know the curriculum content generally identified for their age and ability level, including the range of this content required to care for the differing needs and abilities of a typical group of such children. Furthermore, it is helpful to have your own philosophy fairly well defined, as well as to know what the administrative and supervisory personnel in your school believe about children, what should be taught, and how it should be taught.

Determination of Content

What should be taught is important to organizing a language arts program, but how content is selected—on what premises and by what principles—is of utmost concern if teaching effort is to accomplish anything worthwhile. The findings of research, the contents of curriculum guides and textbooks, and the policies and standards of the school provide guides, but the responsibility for determining what is taught is primarily the teacher's. Sometimes teachers say this is not true—that the principal tells them what to teach or that the textbooks and other materials structure the program for them—but this belief is too often an easy way to avoid planning and exercising personal initiative. The teacher presents whatever is presented in his or her classroom for the children to learn; the teacher is the major controlling force.

Guiding principles for exercising this responsibility include the following:

Basic principles to observe

1. The content of the program should be selected after a consideration of statements of objectives formulated by the school or district. If objectives have not been stated, are too general or not clear, or are simply thought to be understood, then the formulation of objectives is a necessary first step. For this formulation basic reliance should be on research evidence rather than upon custom, the opinion of some school authority, or the resources available.
2. The emphasis in teaching should be on using the skills of communication rather than on learning subject matter. In other words, it is more important for a child to have the skills necessary for effective expression and reception of ideas and information than to know rules about language structure, punctuation, etc.
3. The selection of content should take into account the communication needs of the children in the classroom—their experiences and development, the types of communication they can and cannot handle, the things they will need to have mastered before progressing further in school, and the ongoing activities that develop from day to day in the classroom.

In deciding what knowledge, skills or abilities, and attitudes are to be taught, ask yourself these questions:

1. How frequently is this needed and used in the life activities of children and adults? For example, writers use colons much less frequently than they use commas, people do more storytelling than choral speaking, and seldom does one need to identify the adverbs in a sentence.
2. How important is this when the need for it arises? Will the need arise? For instance, many people do not write business letters frequently, but when the need arises, it is usually important that the letter be well written.
3. How universally is this skill or ability encountered in the various life activities? For example, giving a book report is a school activity for most people, but conversing is something everyone does.
4. What evidence is there that this will meet a permanent need? For example, some of the first words a child should learn to spell are the same words adults use frequently in their writing.
5. Which children, if any, in my classroom are ready to learn this? In other words, attention must be given to the needs of the children, the experiences they have had, and what they have already learned. Dictionary instruction will have little value for the child who has not learned alphabetical order.

Making Instruction Systematic

How the content selected is to be taught is also important. This "how" includes the techniques for the specific teaching of the content, but the key element in the "how" is the overall instructional plan to be followed. This plan should be a systematic one to be most effective, not one that deals with the content incidentally or perhaps accidentally. Systematic instruction is really not complicated; it simply means that all teaching effort is directed at the content decided on by the criteria stated above.

While events occur in every classroom that cannot be foreseen and planned for, without systematic attention to the content that has been selected after considerate and careful thought, too much is left to chance. Such incidental teaching may result in no attention to some experiences that develop language ability, the overlooking of skills that should be taught for their later importance, and a waste of time through needless repetition and interference with instructional objectives in other curriculum areas or at other instructional levels.

Systematic instruction, on the other hand, does not preclude taking advantage of a "teachable moment" or working into plans those unforeseen events that will further the objectives. Actually, a truly well-planned program provides for using the ongoing activities of a classroom—including many of those that cannot be foreseen—for the meaningful teaching of the knowledge, skills, and attitudes that have been selected.

Neither does systematic instruction imply a nonintegrated program. If the principles and guide questions suggested above are adhered to, genuine integration of language arts with other areas of the curriculum will be fostered when such integration furthers children's learning.

Cooperative Planning

The most important kind of planning involves the children, since they will learn more effectively from the participation. This planning should be done on various levels and throughout the year—overall planning for the year, planning a unit of work, and planning for a particular activity that may take place in a single day or a short segment of a day.

The ability to plan is not equally developed in all teachers, and it certainly varies from child to child. Nor is the ability to plan in conjunction with others equally developed in all of us. We have to *learn* to respect the rights and ideas of others—it does not just happen. However, cooperative planning can be learned by doing. Below are some suggestions for involving children; you will discover others for yourself as you continue to plan with them.

First, do not abdicate your responsibility. The amount of responsibility that pupils should assume or can assume varies according to their maturity and their experiences with planning. Second, make sure that some genuine choices are open to the children. If the pupils are really to feel that they have participated in the planning, there must be some options open. If you intend to have things done your way, planning by the class is a waste of time and may do far more harm than good. Third, when plans are made, try to stick with them. If the plans were bad, learning this fact may result in better planning the next time. Of course, plans sometimes have to be changed, so be realistic. Finally, make certain that the planning is not being done by only a few members of the class. Children can be as unmotivated by the authoritarianism of their classmates as by that of the teacher.

PLANNING IN ACTION

Using the principles for the selection of content, and with the involvement of the children as appropriate, a decision needs first to be made regarding the objective or objectives of a teaching-learning effort—a day's lesson, a unit of work, or an activity requiring an even larger time segment. Sometimes this only means the clarification of an idea for the activity or unit of work—one that may come from you, from the children, from previous events, or from a textbook or curriculum guide—but this clarification is important and means stating the goal in terms that are understandable to all.

The next step is to decide on the scope of the objective in terms of specific problems to be solved. This should be done rather broadly at first so that refinement in scope will naturally follow later. For example, suppose the class is about to begin a unit on colonial America. After a discussion with the children of what they might expect to learn from this unit, these questions are decided on and written on the board:

> What famous people lived during that period? Why are they famous?
> What events occurred during the period that are important to us today?
> How did the people of that time live?

Finding answers to these questions becomes the broad objective of the unit.

After the objectives have been clearly defined, decide on a number of ways the objectives might be accomplished. From this decision, further decisions can be made as other factors are considered and a definite plan of action evolves. Suppose that you have decided to concentrate first on the third question above and have chosen several avenues for discovering the manner of living in colonial times:

- Using the textbook and other references that have been assembled in the room.
- Visiting the library to find other helpful books.

- Visiting a museum, an old fort, or some other historical site.
- Inviting a local antique collector to show items in his collection and tell about them.
- Viewing films about colonial times.

At this point you and the children should think together about materials that may be needed in order to utilize the suggested means for accomplishing the objectives. These should be listed and consideration given to any problems related to getting or using them. Obtaining library books, for example, might entail learning about or reviewing library procedures and how to find information in books. Materials brought by the antique collector would require making arrangements for displaying them and perhaps discussing how a person should be introduced and interviewed.

The next step is to identify some of the problems that may be encountered in achieving the objective and discuss how these problems may be overcome or avoided. In the sample unit, one problem might be arranging transportation for the museum trip.

One important consideration is the needs of the class members and what each can contribute to attaining the objective. This calls for assessment of individual abilities, interests, and possible assignments. Might a shy child be ready to introduce a speaker or perhaps help display materials? Might a child who is reticent about speaking build a model and show it to the class?

When all possibilities have been considered, the scope can be refined, specific means and materials selected, and assignments decided on. Perhaps the class might be divided into groups, each choosing a particular aspect of colonial life to study and report on (clothing, transportation, food, etc.). You could work with each group to decide on the best way of reporting to the class—demonstration, oral reports, dramatization, etc. It is important that the children participate actively in the planning, but as coordinator you can guide them in providing variety in the presentations.

Once these specifics have been decided on, a tentative time schedule should be set up for the activity and for segments of it as it progresses, allowing time each day, or at regular intervals, for children to work on their projects.

The final step is to decide how the activity will be evaluated. This should include plans for determining whether the objectives have been achieved and what to do if an objective has not been accomplished. It is important that the children be included in this step as well as in the others. Let them help to set standards for conducting the work planned, for guiding individual performance, and for evaluation.

Purposeful use of the Language Arts—genuine motivation for learning

Although the steps here focus on an example from social studies, the same kind of planning is needed if the focus is science, health, language change, or whatever. The significant point is that effective communication is a second center of attention. This is integration of subject areas, and it is through such integration that language skills are most effectively taught. For this particular unit of study to achieve its objectives, children may need to use library skills, take notes, and organize material; they may need to introduce speakers, listen courteously, and discuss what has been heard; they may write and present reports, produce dramatizations, and perhaps even do some creative writing. Some of the skills needed may already have been mastered; others will have to be introduced or reviewed.

A Basic Instructional Approach

The diagram below illustrates a basic plan for teaching the skills needed in such expressional activities as those suggested in the preceding section. The plan calls for two types of lessons; one in which the emphasis is on the communication and one in which the emphasis is on improving the specific skills used in that communication. The plan has several parts and operates in a cyclical fashion; that is, an expressional activity is followed by an instructional lesson which is followed by another expressional activity, another instructional lesson, and so on.[2] The effectiveness of the communication should improve with each subsequent expressional activity.

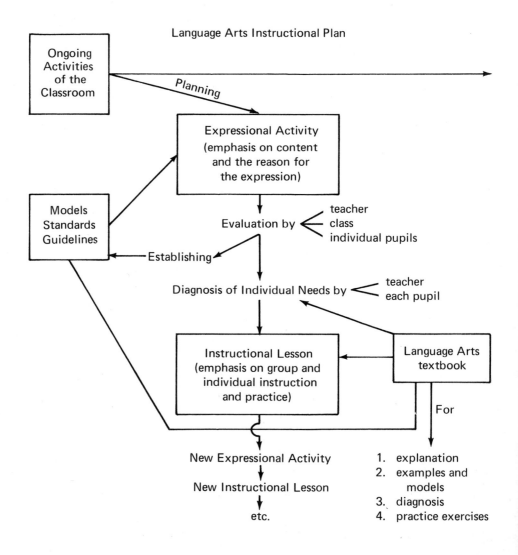

Language Arts Instructional Plan

The plan is essentially for one type of expressional activity at a time—giving reports, participating in a discussion, writing stories, etc.—although any activity will involve a multiplicity of skills. Sometimes the activity takes more than a day; sometimes it is completed in a day—one class period. Fundamentally it makes use of activities in the classroom that call for children to express themselves. For example, children may talk about a TV program, discuss playground behavior, write letters to chambers of commerce for social studies materials, tell stories they have heard, keep records of the feeding and watering schedule of a classroom plant, write imaginative stories, and introduce their parents to you. These situations—and many more—are natural activities that require expression and may be utilized.

The expressional activity should focus on the communication itself and the purpose for it as well as the role of the audience in the process and the use of models, standards, or guidelines as aids in making the expression effective. The standards or guidelines should be flexible; that is, they should get progressively (from activity to activity throughout the year) more stringent and precise. They should be formulated by the class, but the textbook may provide suggestions that will be helpful.

The final aspect of the expressional activity should be that of evaluation by you alone, by you in conjunction with the class members, and by each pupil individually. As is suggested later, most evaluation should be informal and directed at learning rather than at giving grades or comparing children with one another. It should result in identifying for you and for each child the level of development he or she has achieved in skills and abilities needed for a particular language activity. A further element of the evaluation is the identification of a limited number of items for emphasis in instructional lessons. For example, evaluation of an activity in which the children wrote reports might result in the determination that organizational skills need instructional attention. Later, a similar activity might show a need for attention to handwriting improvement.

Evaluate Yourself

How might this have been a more successful lesson?

The instructional lesson should focus on both group and individual needs but, as suggested above, it should not be so extensive that you dissipate your instructional effort by trying to teach too many things. The objective is to make the next expressional activity more effective and the key to the plan really lies in the immediacy of the instruction that is given and the fact that it is based on genuine needs. The expressional situation provides motivation; this is lost when instruction is directed at errors made last month or those which may be made next month.

The instructional lesson should conclude with practice activities or exercises designed to establish the learning and reduce or eliminate the same faults or errors in the next expressional activity.

The textbook may be used at several stages in this instructional plan, as the diagram shows and as is suggested later in this chapter. The textbook is only one instructional resource, however. Others include the library, reference books, audiovisual materials, people, and community institutions.

While this approach is idenitified as a plan for teaching the expressional language arts, the essentials of it may be used in teaching the receptional ones. For example, there are many activities that require listening; standards for listening may be established, the effectiveness of the listening may be evaluated, and instructional lessons may focus on what the evaluation and diagnosis show is needed. Reading, too, is done for specific purposes, the success of which can and should be evaluated and instruction provided for deficiencies found.

PLANNING FOR PUPIL DIFFERENCES

We know that each person is unique. Yet aside from observing obvious physical differences, a teacher may not really recognize the range of differences that exist among the children in his class. In terms of pupil achievement, only about one-third of a typical class achieve at or near the norm for that grade level on a standardized achievement test. The other two-thirds are usually about equally divided above and below the norm, with the range (distances from the norm) increasing as the grade level advances. For example, a classroom of sixth graders may show 40 percent at grade level, 20 percent at seventh grade level, 10 percent at eighth grade level or above, 20 percent at fifth grade level, and 10 percent at fourth grade level or below. And since the achievement test does not measure many of the language skills, we can assume that the range among all pupils for all skills, abilities, and attitudes important to language communication is even more startling.

Teacher Identification of Differences

A teacher must be a careful observer.

To determine the specific differences among pupils and hence determine their instructional needs, it is necessary to carry on a continuing program of evaluation. The following are specific evaluative devices you might employ:

1. Observe and record on a note or checklist the speech performance of each child, including his or her speaking skills, mannerisms, and behavior as a member of an audience.
2. Make observational notes on individual pupils at regular intervals with respect to usage problems, difficulties in organizing expression, and lack of ease in speaking.
3. Use checklists or inventory forms to note achievements and deficiencies in specific language activities such as conversations, discussions, letter writing, or story writing. (Examples of these evaluative techniques are given in later chapters.)
4. Construct tests to determine each pupil's knowledge and abilities in choosing correct expressions, punctuating and capitalizing properly, and constructing sentences.
5. Tabulate the writing errors each pupil makes.
6. Use standardized tests in a planned program to measure growth and achievement in language arts.
7. Make recordings of speech and oral reading activities and analyze them for particular problems.
8. Keep anecdotal records of information for special teachers, parents, etc.
9. Keep samples of children's written expression for comparison at intervals throughout the school year.
10. Discuss with children their problems in expression.

Record keeping is a chore, but it is necessary if you are truly going to provide for differences and help individual pupils to overcome their difficulties. The task can be simplified by varying procedures throughout the year, by using checklists wherever possibile, and particularly by keeping records up to date. A few minutes at the end of each day will save hours at the end of the month—as well as enabling you to attack problems as they arise rather than at some later date.

Pupil Self-Appraisal

Stimulating a pupil to identify his or her own language needs—the knowledge, skills, abilities, and attitudes needed for effective communication—is a basic motivational procedure that will pay rich dividends if you can do it successfully. Below are some methods teachers have used successfully to help pupils identify their own needs. With patience on your part every child can learn to do some of the following:

1. Use checklists, preferably ones that the child has helped to devise or that are based on standards he or she has helped to develop.
2. Proofread and edit his or her own work. A proofreading checklist is usually helpful (see chapter 12).

3. Check his or her own work as much as possible; for example, children can check their own spelling tests. (Having pupils exchange papers for checking does not help the child to discover his or her own problems.)
4. Write in a notebook things that need to be worked on—spelling words, new vocabulary, usage errors.
5. Keep charts of errors, such as those made in handwriting.
6. Compare his or her work with models (business letter form, for example) and scale examples (handwriting).
7. Look at the materials in a folder that contains samples of the child's work and records of his or her achievement.
8. Work as one of a pair or as a member of a small group in identifying areas in which improvement is needed.
9. Plot or record his or her own standardized test scores and compare them with the results of previous testing.
10. Participate in class discussions of needs, efforts to attain class-established standards, and plans for learning activities.
11. Meet with you to discuss problems and needs.

ORGANIZING FOR TEACHING AND LEARNING

There are many ways of organizing the programs of an entire school or of a classroom. The intent of each plan is to facilitate teaching and learning—the interaction of teachers and learners. Apparently, however, no one plan of organization of a school or of a class of youngsters is the ideal, one that research or practice has shown to be the most effective. Each plan is affected by many factors, including the number of children involved, the characterestics of the children as a group, the community and traditions related to it, legal regulations, fiscal and space requirements and limitations, curriculum decisions that have been made, and the philosophies of school board members, administrators, and teachers.

It is not our intent to review all possible organizational plans nor to discuss any in great depth. There are published resources that do both.[3] However, we do believe that every language arts teacher needs to know something about school organizational plans and how he or she may best organize a classroom of children for the maximum learning of each individual to occur.

Working in pairs.

Grouping into Classes

Children attending an elementary school are most frequently identified with and grouped at grade-levels (usually those of approximately the same age together in a grade), although sometimes instead of the identification being with a grade it is with an ability level (usually from reading or mathematics tests or from both). In schools where there may be several classroom groups at each grade level, the children to be in each of the several rooms will often be determined in this way. Thus, in this type of grouping there is an attempt at achieving greater homogeneity in the abilities of the children in a classroom, and this is the principal advantage claimed for it.

Sometimes children are grouped heterogeneously. This may mean that ones of the same age level are randomly assigned to classes, or it may mean that children of different levels of ability (and usually different ages) are deliberately grouped together. The latter classrooms are called *ungraded*. Very similar is a plan, often called *multi-level*, in which children of several grade levels (first, second, and third, for example) may be grouped together in a classroom. The advantage claimed for this type of grouping is that it allows children to learn from each other and leads to greater individualization of instruction.

Schools may be organized into *self-contained* classrooms in which a teacher and a group of children (however grouped) are together for the entire day. Another familiar form of organization is *departmentalization*. In this plan children move from teacher to teacher (and room to room) for teaching in subject areas of specialization that the teachers have. *Team teaching* is somewhere in between self-contained and departmentalized classrooms. Children are assigned to several teachers (and rooms—or an extra large room). The advantages claimed for this are that teachers may teach their specialized areas and that more flexibility in in-class grouping is permitted. For example, one or more teachers might supervise a large group of children in an activity, while another teacher instructs a small group needing remedial aid.

There are also various combinations of these plans. For example, one is that children are with one teacher for half of the school day but are in a departmentalized program the other half. Sometimes, too, the basic school program may be one of self-contained classrooms but with pupils leaving these classrooms for instruction in some curriculum areas.

Classroom Grouping

For much instruction in a classroom—and generally too much—the children are taught as a single group. Storytelling, reading aloud, dramatic activities, choral speaking, discussion, and written expression are examples of aspects of the language arts for which total-class instruction may be appropriate. On the other hand, all of these activities may be equally appropriate for smaller groups. If there is need for specific instruction in regard to skills or knowledge not needed by the entire class, or for which some pupils are not ready, then small group or individual instruction may be mandatory.

Grouping and individualizing instruction are discussed in many other chapters.

Most teachers do at least some teaching of groups within the classroom. The children may be grouped according to abilities, skills, interests, needs, and so on. In fact, children will often get together in groups of their own accord if given the opportunity—and they certainly should be given such an opportunity. Grouping does not have to be limited to the traditional three reading groups; abilities and interests vary in all things children do. Neither does grouping need to be so lacking in flexibility that a child is always in the (so-called) "dumb group."

Keep parents informed about your classroom organization and management.

Grouping is not easily done by many teachers, as observation of a number of classrooms soon forces one to conclude. However, a teacher who has confidence in the children and feels that he or she can rely on them seems to have much greater success with grouping than does that teacher's counterpart who is more authoritarian or less inclined to involve children in the planning and conducting of activities. In addition, recognition of the limitations of evaluative instruments in pinpointing needs should not result in failure to use the instruments we do have and to devise others to supplement them. Furthermore, grouping for instruction is easier when objectives are clearly defined.

In addition to the need for your objectives to be clear, you need to think about the children's needs and interests and their personalities, the materials available to work with, how the groups will operate, and how you will handle time and space needs. Keep in mind that no grouping should be set in concrete. Sometimes plans just don't work out. Sometimes you learn more about individual children and their needs. Sometimes they take spurts in learning.

Individualizing Learning

There are many ways for providing instruction to meet individual needs. The organization plans and related activities suggested below are only a few. As you read other chapters and think further about the importance of individualizing learning opportunities you will add to the ideas presented in this section.

There has been considerable interest expressed in recent years for the "open" or "informal" classroom. While descriptions about how such a classroom is organized and operates vary considerably, the basic idea is to focus on individual child needs, with children themselves identifying these needs in relation to their interests. Independent learning in good open classrooms occurs as children largely work by themselves on individual tasks and at their individual rates in learning centers. These centers may be simply tables, areas of a room partly screened off, or whatever; the idea is to have opportunity for independent work. Frequently there are centers for writing, listening, reading, science experimenting, research in books, mathematics projects, etc. In the following paragraphs we suggest ways in which assignments and special interests may be worked on individually or in small groups. Many suggestions for making this concept a reality are given in the chapters that follow, and at the end of each chapter are specific examples of independent learning activities. Like all other activities suggested in this book, these are only samples. If activities are to meet specific needs of individual children, they *must* be designed with those needs and those children in mind.

Regardless of the school or classroom organizational plan or plans, it is possi-

Children reading the books they have chosen is genuine individualized learning.

ble to provide individualized practice on specific skills for children who need such work. For example, some children can profit from exercise materials that require them to make decisions about which words should be capitalized. On the other hand, it is obvious that many language skills cannot be practiced with paper-and-pencil exercises. In fact, one of the big errors made by many teachers (and encouraged by some textbooks) is the use of written practice exercises as a means of changing the way children speak. However, discriminating use of practice materials, in ways such as those suggested below, may be helpful. For example:

- Practice exercises can be secured from workbooks, old textbooks, and clippings from teachers' magazines. These materials should be cut up so that the exercises that apply to a particular skill can be filed together.
- Often it is profitable to have two copies of workbooks that you intend to use in this manner so that the material on both sides of a page can be used. These exercises can be placed in clear plastic envelopes in order to keep them clean and to permit children to write on them with crayon that can be washed off. Answers to the exercises should be provided (perhaps on the back of the excercise page) so that pupils can check their own papers.
- Since many commercial materials (e.g., the pages of a workbook or textbook or a card in a kit) may either provide unrealistic and useless practice or try to give practice on more than one skill, exercises that you make yourself may be the most helpful.

Integration of the language arts with other areas of the curriculum provides many opportunities for individualization of instruction not only in the subject matter areas but also in the language arts. Integration with social studies (as in the example in the Planning in Action section) is relatively easy since both the receptive and expressive language arts are essential to most social studies activities. The same is true for several other curriculum areas, and even in science instruction—which tends to be highly structured by textbooks and other commercial materials—integration which may foster individualized instruction is possible. For example, if a class of third graders is studying the use of water by plants, there would be a need for children to be given library research to do—and to report orally to the class. Individual children could be assigned to list and assemble materials needed for the several experiments (plants watered and not watered, tracing absorption of water by a plant, how water gets out of plants, etc.) the activity would call for, while other children could keep records (of water levels, times needed for absorption, etc.). Children could write descriptions of the experiments, with the difficulty of these adjusted for individual pupil ability. Vocabulary words would need to be looked up in a dictionary and possibly written on a chart. All of the children would be involved in conversations and discussions about the activity.

Note the similarity to the Basic Instructional Approach on page 24.

Related to the above procedure is one in which children enter into "contracts" to do specific tasks. These contracts usually develop from pupil-teacher conferences in which previous work is evaluated in terms of objectives agreed on earlier. Since children vary in their capacities to plan and in their abilities to assess their own capabilities and interests, it is appropriate for the teacher to provide alternatives that may be contracted for. Suggestions may also be made regarding pacing, although it is important for each child to discover his or her own working speed. Decisions will also need to be made regarding the way the product of a contract will be evaluated.

Children may need help in organizing for contract work.

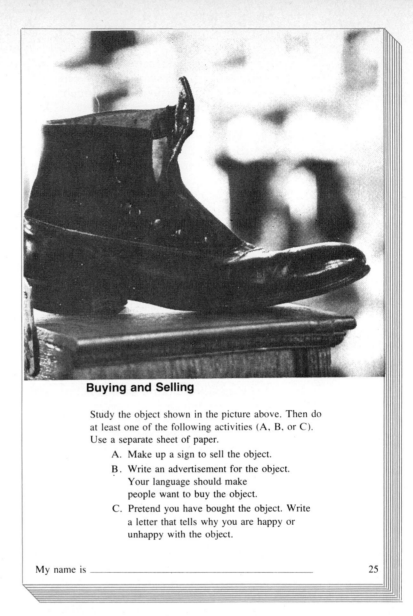

Buying and Selling

Study the object shown in the picture above. Then do
at least one of the following activities (A, B, or C).
Use a separate sheet of paper.

    A. Make up a sign to sell the object.

    B. Write an advertisement for the object.
       Your language should make
       people want to buy the object.

    C. Pretend you have bought the object. Write
       a letter that tells why you are happy or
       unhappy with the object.

My name is _____ 25

Commercial materials often provide for individualizing activities. (From THE WORLD OF
LANGUAGE—Activities and Evaluation, Book N, Revised Edition. Copyright © 1970, 1974
by Follett Publishing Company, a division of Follett Corporation. Used by permission of the
publisher.)

Other suggestions for individualizing include the following:

- Children who finish assignments or activities before their classmates may be encouraged to make copies for the bulletin board of something they feel they have written well.
- A child who does good work in a particular area may help others who are having difficulty.

- Each child may keep a notebook for unassigned writing of a personal nature, and should have the option of showing it to the teacher only if he or she wishes.
- Children who finish assignments early may be permitted to browse in the library, work on special reports, listen to recordings, etc.

TEACHING RESOURCES

Anything in the children's world—in the classroom and outside of it—may be a teaching resource. However, in a more narrow sense, the principal resources are the textbook and materials intended to supplement it, or those materials—films, cassettes, cards, and so on—intended to be used as a replacement for the textbook.

Textbooks

Virtually every classroom has textbooks. They are the most readily accessible instructional aid a teacher has, but they are *aids,* not directors or regulators. To begin the instruction for the year on the first page of a textbook and to continue throughout the year in a page-by-page manner fails to take into account the language abilities and needs of a particular class, to say nothing of the varying needs and abilities of individual children in that class.

The language arts textbook can be an important aid to teaching, but it is not a teacher, not can it do everything. It can serve several functions if properly used as suggested earlier in the Basic Instructional Approach section. However, not every textbook will provide for those aspects of the approach identified for it. In general, though, language textbooks present a point of view about the teaching of skills, attitudes, and information that should be useful to you in objectifying your own philosophy. They also identify skills and content the authors believe to be suitable for a particular grade level, thus serving as a reminder and a base against which the instructional program may be evaluated. In addition, textbooks suggest methods for teaching many language skills, provide practice materials and suggest activities for establishing the learning of the skills and abilities taught, provide evaluation materials, and suggest other materials and techniques.

The limitations of most language textbooks are many, particularly if the textbooks are relied on too heavily. In the first place, the presentation of the program is likely to be too formal. In addition, the emphasis in many textbooks is on aspects of language study that children either already know or have no valid reason for learning. The suggested activities are for a hypothetical class and may not be suitable for a particular group of children. The practice exercises and activities suggested are usually inadequate in number and type because of being directed at a hypothetical class, and because of limitations in the size of the textbook. Also, many language activities need to be oral ones, and textbooks simply can't adequately take care of that need. Further, the teaching suggestions in the textbook and sometimes in the teacher's manual may be too brief because of space limitations, or they may be too detailed and fail to recognize knowledge that many teachers (or pupils) already possess. Finally, the evaluation aids are also limited by space and by the inability to focus on evaluating a particular class.

The important thing to remember is that innumerable occasions for genuine language teaching occur as a teacher and children work, play, and study together. The textbook may help you to take advantage of these occasions in several ways. First, suggested settings for language activites, such as an imaginary conversation pupils might have or a hypothetical occasion for reporting orally, may be altered so that they apply to current work in a classroom or they may be used as a guide for taking advantage of similar settings. In addition, the textbook provides information regarding communication activities (for example, what should be included in giving directions, procedures to follow in conducting an interview or writing a radio script) that is useful in taking full advantage of natural situations. The textbook also may provide models of letters, outlines, and reports, which may be used in discussing the content, organization, and mechanics needed for effective writing in each situation; and it may provide examples supporting the explanation and suggestions you give regarding punctuation and capitalization items, choices of words, construction of sentences, and so on.

Other Resources

An effective language arts program regards virtually everything and anything as a teaching resource. Children are interested in the world and want to communicate about it. They learn outside the classroom as well as inside—in many ways they learn more outside. Thus we lose touch with much of the child's world if we limit our teaching resources to just that which is within the walls.

Parents should be told and shown how you will use the textbooks and other resources.

There are, however, many resources other than the textbook that can be made a part of the resources inside the walls, and bringing these into teaching often puts the textbook in proper perspective. These resources include trade and reference books, displays, art work, puppets, bulletin boards, films, recordings, cassettes, filmstrips, transparencies, and visual slides. Because of their importance in attaining an effective language arts program, at the end of each chapter we have listed many resources that you should bring into your planning and instruction.

These resources are often referred to as audiovisual aids, but they are more than aids. When used in a well-planned program, they will heighten motivation for learning, provide for better retention of what is learned because of their concreteness and multisensory aspects, give the program freshness and variety, provide reinforcement for other learning, encourage active participation of pupils, widen the range of experience in a manner that has special attraction, and appeal to varied abilities and interests.

EVALUATION AND GRADING

Too often evaluation is equated with giving a grade, but evaluation is much more than this. Evaluation is a process, an essential component of the larger process of instruction. It is directly related to instructional goals and to the attainment of these goals. Evaluation determines what has not been effectively taught—what else needs to be taught. Grading, on the other hand, is done for the purpose of reporting to pupils, to parents, and to school authorities. Grading should be based on evaluation; therefore, evaluation is necessary for grading. However, the converse is not true—grading is not required for evaluation.

The Role of Evaluation

Evaluation is a process that includes all the procedures used by the teacher, the children, the principal, and other school personnel to appraise the outcomes of instruction. As a process it includes formulating goals in terms of behavior that can be measured or appraised, securing evidence from representative situations regarding the extent of the achievement of the objectives, summarizing and recording the evidence, interpreting or analyzing the evidence in terms of the objectives and the instructional procedures, and using the interpretation to extend and improve instruction.

In relating these steps to a particular aspect of an instructional program (perhaps a writing activity, the giving of an oral report, or learning to use the dictionary), begin by giving an inventory test or by using some other appropriate means for appraising what the learner already knows or can do that is specifically related to what you plan to teach. Then teach the skills, knowledge, or attitudes needed by the learner as shown by this appraisal. Provide motivation for learning the things taught by designing situations in which they are actually needed and used; this will establish learnings firmly. Next, give a test or make an appraisal similar in content and form to that used during the inventory stage, using the results of this appraisal to determine the extent of learning and discover specific deficiencies. And finally, reteach for these deficiencies, giving practice as needed; if necessary, continue the process by retesting, reteaching, and so forth.

Techniques and Instruments

As suggested earlier, instruments and procedures for evaluation vary widely in type, structure, and function. The procedures include the administration of tests, questionnaires, inventories, checklists, and observation forms, as well as conferences, examination of biographies and folders of pupils' work, and oral or written questioning. Tests vary, too—they may be oral or written, standardized or teacher-made, essay or short-answer. In addition, there are models, statements of standards, progress charts, logs and diaries, and scales.

Many of the instruments and procedures are discussed in later chapters where specific reference is made to their use. At this point the emphasis is on the importance of evaluation and the fact that there are many instruments and procedures available. It is also important to recognize the imprecision in commercial materials for evaluating oral and written language abilities—a fact reflected in the paucity of tests available for evaluating many important objectives. Thus, it is necessary to do much informal evaluation—to make use of checklists, records, charts, and inventories; to collect pupils' work in folders; to keep logs and diaries; to have conferences; and to help pupils develop models, scales, and statements of standards.

Reporting Progress

A teacher must observe the reporting policies of the school and district, of course, and in many cases this means putting letter or numerical grades on a report card.

You can go further than this, though, by sending home samples of children's work, evaluative statements and explanations, and the results from using various instruments and procedures. While some teachers think doing these things is too time consuming and others simply don't know what to say in evaluative statements (often due to their having done too little evaluating), the value of more adequate reporting cannot be denied. In addition to better and more detailed written reports, you should arrange to confer with parents about their children's progress and needs more often than once a year.

Children should also be reported to, but again this does not mean that every paper or activity has to be marked with a grade. Pupils will appreciate talking with you about their progress, seeing your marks on checklists and observation forms, and participating in interpreting data obtained through testing, using scales, etc. This kind of active participation, along with helping to establish criteria before activities are begun, will help children to learn habits of self-evaluation and to understand what is expected of them.

All reports—to parents, to pupils, and to school authorities—should be based on evidence that can be shown and understood; they should be made in consideration of the child and the effect of the report on the child and his or her learning; and they should be as accurate an assessment of achievement or progress as is possible and without subjective bias of any sort—or as nearly so as possible.

A FINAL WORD

This chapter gives only a brief overview of the organizing and planning needed to teach language arts effectively; suggestions will be expanded on in the chapters that follow. Principles for selecting content and guidelines for planning become operational only when you consider the particular children in a classroom, how well they speak and write, and what problems they seem to have. In the same manner, the instructional plan suggested and the means for implementing it can become truly meaningful only when considered in connection with specific content and procedures for teaching speaking, listening, reading, and writing.

ENDNOTES

1. Recognize, however, that school records sometimes present a biased picture of a child's potential and possible problems. Test scores, teachers' comments, and even "confidential" information may give an accurate picture, but they may also reflect personality conflicts, cultural differences, and judgments made hastily.

2. See also suggestions given later in this chapter regarding individualizing instruction, using the textbook, and evaluating and grading.

3. Especially balanced discussions are in John I. Goodlad and Harold G. Shane, eds., *The Elementary School in the United States*, the 72nd Yearbook of the National Society for the Study of Education, Part II; and Daniel L. Duke, ed., *Classroom Management*, the 78th Yearbook, Part II of the Society.

REFERENCES

Books

Blake, Howard E. *Creating a Learning-Centered Classroom.* New York: Hart Publishing Co., 1977.

Blitz, Barbara. *The Open Classroom: Making It Work.* Boston: Allyn and Bacon, 1973.

King-Stoops, Joyce. *The Child Wants to Learn.* Boston: Little, Brown, 1977.

Klugman, Edgar. *Teaching in the Elementary School: A Guide to Planning.* San Francisco: Fearon Publishers, 1970.

Petty, Walter T., ed. *Curriculum for the Modern Elementary School.* Chicago: Rand McNally College Publishing Co., 1976.

Shiman, David A.; Culver, Carmen M.; and Lieberman, Ann. *Teachers on Individualization: The Way We Do It.* New York: McGraw-Hill, 1974.

Thomas, George I., and Crescimbeni, Joseph. *Individualizing Instruction in the Elementary School.* New York: Random House, Inc., 1966.

Waskin, Yvonne. *Teacher-Pupil Planning for Better Classroom Learning.* New York: Pitman Publishing Corp., 1967.

Films

Charlie and the Golden Hamster: The Non-graded Elementary School. Melbourne, FL: Institute for Development of Educational Activities (13 min., color).

Team Teaching in the Elementary School. Melbourne, FL: Institute for Development of Educational Activities (22 min., color).

ACTIVITIES FOR PRESERVICE TEACHERS

1. Interview an elementary school teacher, asking about the range of intellectual abilities and academic aptitudes of the children in his or her classroom. Also ask about the principal means used to give instructional attention to the differences.

2. Obtain copies of your state or district syllabi for language arts. Study these to determine what children are expected to learn at each grade level.

3. List the advantages and disadvantages of subject-matter departmentalization teaching in the elementary school. Indicate the sources you used for determining these.

4. Use syllabi, texts for the grade level of your choice, and/or methods textbooks to prepare a learning activity for social studies, science, or some other area, giving particular emphasis to interrelating the language arts with your planned lessons.

5. Make an appointment with the individual in your local school system who is most involved with the testing program and ask to see and discuss the tests used for language arts evaluation. Report your findings.

6. Visit an elementary school and ask the teachers how they group for instruction in different subjects. See how many different grouping designs you can find and what teachers believe to be the strengths and weaknesses of each.

7. Make an appointment with an elementary school principal or assistant principal and ask to be shown the different types of records that are found in a child's cumulative folder.

8. Read articles from professional journals about varying organizational plans and/or designs for grouping. List advantages and disadvantages of each and decide which you would like to try.

9. Go through a year's issues of such journals as *Instructor, Learning,* and *Teacher* for ideas about special weeks and days. These journals indicate where kits for observance of these special events can be obtained (for example: The American Bar

Association, 1155 East 60th St., Chicago 60637, has material on Law Day U.S.A. and Lutheran Brotherhood, 701 Second Avenue South, Min-neapolis, MN 55402, has a kit for fire prevention week).

ACTIVITIES FOR INSERVICE TEACHERS

1. Plan an informal meeting with other teachers in your school or district who teach at your grade level and make an outline of the major subjects that should be covered. You might want to include such topics as materials (including media), sharing of materials, interrelating all of the language arts, teacher-pupil planning, and evaluation.

2. Examine a number of language arts texts designed for your class's level. Select an area of interest to you, such as letter writing. Compare the way different texts introduce and develop this topic. Which text or combination of texts would you prefer to use as a guide? Why? Select another topic and go through the same process.

3. Plan an *interesting* program for parents designed to explain the language arts: teaching goals, importance, evaluation, and how parents might help at home or as volunteer aides in your room. Discuss the program with your administrator before presenting it.

4. Evaluate a commercial kit purported to provide basic or supplemental instruction in a language arts area (i.e. spelling, composition, listening). Base your evaluation on the curriculum planning principles in this chapter.

5. Make several individual, self-correcting practice exercises for reinforcing a specific language arts skill. Report to the class how you would use these.

6. Prepare a card file of the audiovisual material available in your district that you have previewed and believe to be useful to you in your language arts program. Each card should tell how the material can be obtained, its major use, the time it requires, a synopsis of its content, and a brief evaluation of its value to your program.

3

A Foundation for Language Growth

As we discussed in chapter 1, a child's language development begins long before he enters school. Ideally, before a child enters kindergarten he or she will have had a wide variety of experiences related to the vocabulary and concepts that the school seeks to teach. He will have talked with adults and other children, watched *Sesame Street*, *The Electric Company*, and other television programs directed specifically at children, had stories read to him, and had the opportunity to look at and handle many books. Some may have attended nursery school or some other type of preschool program. Realistically, however, many children have had limited experiences with language—particularly the language of the school. Thus a kindergarten class will usually represent a wide range of abilities in language because the children will have had a wide range of experiences. Some will have had so few contacts with others in groups that they may have difficulty expressing basic needs; others will be very much at ease and will already be showing creativity in expressing themselves. Despite these variations, there is much that a teacher can do to help each child learn to express himself naturally, interestingly, and creatively.

In chapter 2 we discussed things a teacher might do in order to care for the differences among children, the importance of planning and organization, the selection of curriculum content, and a basic teaching approach—all directed at creating the best possible classroom learning situation for each child. This chapter continues that discussion, focusing on how children learn, the importance of experience, and ways of building readiness for children to move into direct and specific learning activities in each of the language arts areas. The general thesis of this readiness is that since young children have not yet acquired to any extent the skills of reading and writing, beginning activities must be largely oral in nature. The emphasis is on creativity, spontaneity, and providing experiences that call for the use of language. The activities suggested here are not specifically designed to further growth in a particular area of the language arts; rather, they are intended to promote familiarity with and ease in the use of language itself and thus to help lay a foundation for growth in all the language arts.

How Children Learn

The planning procedure advocated in the preceding chapter, as well as the instructional suggestions that were made, reflects an attention to the issue of how children learn. In this section we extend this to learning principles and other factors important to facilitating learning.

Principles of Learning

Just how any of us learn something is complex, and knowledge of the process is in many ways superficial. However, observations of the results of learning provide evidence as to how learning may be expedited. This evidence can be stated in several principles—principles that every teacher needs to heed.

Learning Is Individual.   Children differ from each other in many ways, including the ability to learn. This difference is shown in learning capacities and rates in the effectiveness of various modes. Further, in addition to differences in inherited and intellectual and physical endowments, children differ from one another in terms of emotions, previous experiences, and motivation and may differ in age, sex, maturation, and physical condition. Thus, children's participation in a classroom activity will reflect these factors. A teacher can do something about some of the factors but not about others, yet all have to receive consideration in teaching.

Learning Is an Active Process.   While much of what we know seems to have been learned subtly—possibly because the human mind is much like a constantly running computer ready to take in data—learning is a seeking process. An individual's environment almost constantly presents the need for that individual to transact with it, to try to overcome any disequilibrium felt. The school environment needs to take into account children's backgrounds and needs in such a way as to facilitate many of their transactions even while presenting tasks that establish disequilibrium. That is, if the learning tasks are challenging rather than frustrating, the seeking process will be encouraged.

Learning Is Developmental.   Anything learned is built on and added to previous learning. Learning will not occur without readiness; therefore it is important to determine what children know, their maturation levels, and their learning rates and capacities as well as to plan for the proper sequencing of their experiences.

Learning Is Motivated.   The disequilibrium that an individual's environment may cause him or her to feel is a motivation for reacting, for learning. As suggested, this may be a very subtle process. However, for much learning—particularly much of that in the classroom—there is more than a simple reaction. There will be a conscious drive established if the challenge, the motivation, is strong enough.

Learning Requires Reinforcement. Anything learned but not used moves rather quickly out of the conscious mind. It may be forgotten. If it is used, on the other hand, it becomes established. Thus, those things we want children to learn in school need to be practiced. This practice, of course, needs to be meaningful and satisfying to the children. Reinforcement does not occur if what is learned is separated from its use.

Learning May Transfer. Ordinarily, transfer of learning takes place from one situation to another to the extent that there are identical elements in both. In language arts teaching, transfers in learning may be facilitated if proper attention is given to what is taught (as suggested in chapter 2), when it is taught, and whether children are helped to see the similarity of the situations.

The Role of Experience

An effective language arts program recognizes in three ways the importance of experience in the development of children's ability to use language. First, the program is based on an awareness that every child entering school, whether he or she comes from a white middle-class neighborhood or from a highly diversified socioeconomic and ethnic one, has a background of many experiences. While these experiences—including the language ones—may not have been used as learning tools and built upon to the extent that is desirable, they are important. Second, an effective program provides experiences that build vocabulary and concepts, develop multiple meanings of words, and familiarize children with the kinds of sentence patterns and ways of expressing themselves that they will encounter in school. Third, an effective program provides these experiences in settings that focus on genuine, lifelike communication activities that have meaning for the children involved and provide motivation for learning.

Awareness that every child has a language background developed prior to entering school—one which continues to be developed outside of the classroom—means more than overcoming any bias about a "disadvantaged" or "deprived" child having had little language experience or being "nonverbal." Children's language backgrounds are simply different, and to assume a background of experience on the basis of family economic conditions, race, ethnicity, or anything else is a fallacy. It is important, though, to try to determine just what the experiential background of each child is and to find out which experiences important to the school curriculum are lacking. To take for granted a background of experience and an understanding of concepts is dangerous. For example, teachers frequently report that inner-city children do not have a concept associated with the word *pet*, yet reading readiness books and first primers usually have pets in their stories. One teacher recently told one of the authors that children (and these were not "deprived" children) in her class had difficulty choosing a picture of a writing *pen* as a word which rhymes with *hen*. They apparently knew *pen* as the name of an enclosure for the chickens, but they did not know another meaning for the word. Probably their parents write either with a pencil or with something called a "ball point." Another teacher found an entire class of sixth graders who could not verbalize a definition of *physician*. It is possible, of course, that they would have known *doctor* or *pediatrician*—we must remember that language is constantly

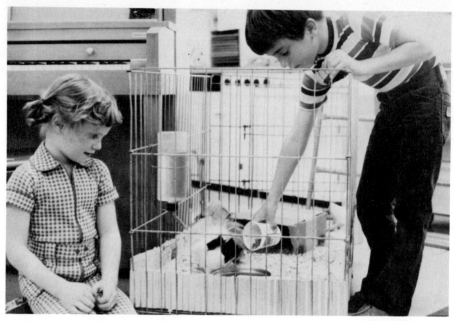

Talking about things that are real and important.

growing and changing.

There is a need in language arts programs to build on children's experiences, and for the focus of this building to be on developing language ability; experiences of children both inside and outside of the classroom are opportunities for this to happen. An experience is simply any occurrence, but more importantly it needs to be thought of as the reaction and feeling of the participants about the occurrence. Thus the activities in a classroom provide differing experiences to different children, and some may provide little to any of them. The key is the quality of the activity—the experience—how the activity is planned, how it relates to the learning objectives, its realism, children's interest in it, and the guidance given by the teacher toward achieving the objectives.

Providing Input

Because of the differences discussed, there should be provision for diversity in children's school experiences. At the same time, a teacher should attempt to provide a common core of experiences because of the similarity of many children's needs. Children will be limited in their use of language by the experiences that they have had. A child will hardly express his feelings about "early morning on the farm" if he has never been on a farm and arisen early. In the same way, a child will not react with feeling about the dazzling wonders of the snowflake if he or she has not seen snow—or even if snow has only been something to contend with rather than to appreciate (though the opportunity may be present to help this child discover the wonder and beauty that accompany the hardships of snow).

A Few Awareness Books

Rain Drop Splash—Alvin Tresselt (Lothrop, Lee and Shepard)
Find Out by Touching—Paul Showers (Thomas Y. Crowell)
What Is Your Favorite Smell, My Dear?—Myra Gibson (Grosset and Dunlap)
I See the Winds—Kazue Mizumura (Thomas Y. Crowell)

Take Time to Observe

• the swooping of a swallow
• the chugging and blinking of a helicopter
• a bird's nest in a tree fork
• the swaying of a tall pine
• the ripple on the water caused by a fallen leaf
• waves creeping up a sandy beach
• the bouncing run of a rabbit

Children must have an abundance of opportunities to gain new ideas, new impressions, and new feelings, and to relate these to the experiences that they have had. The number of ways to give children these experiences is almost infinite: reading aloud from a variety of materials; talking with them about news events and other things of interest; providing for interesting visitors to the classroom; making available television and radio programs, recordings, films, and still pictures; providing books in profusion and the opportunity to read them; and giving special attention to expressive words and apt phrases and how they may be used. Particularly important are excursions or field trips. These may be merely excursions into the school yard or another part of the building, they may be visits to various points of interest in the neighborhood, or they may entail more extended trips.

Helping children be more aware of their senses is particularly needed and will result in input that builds language growth. Children, like most adults, often are not good observers, although too often time for observing is simply not provided for in a crowded school day—and this is sometimes the case on a field trip or some other experience building activity. While various observation games are available or can be created—such as displaying a number of objects, removing one, and asking what is missing—the observation of natural phenomena is more helpful. Taking time to observe cloud formations, how the wind has drifted the snow, a flock of geese overhead, or the spread of the roots of a sprouting bean seed will interest children, cause them to use language, and facilitate the learning of new ideas and words.

Children themselves can provide much input. With very little encouragement they will bring butterflies, leaves, worms, rocks, and innumerable other objects to the classroom.

Activities such as the following are all useful to adding to children's knowledge, and are things they will communicate about.

• Keeping an aquarium or terrarium.
• Noting temperature differences in sunshine and shade.
• Watching flying formations of birds.
• Collecting leaves of different kinds or colors.
• Collecting kinds and shapes of rocks.
• Tasting particular substances, such as pickles, berries, fruits, spices, or nuts.
• Feeling various materials, such as velvet, fur, aluminum foil, sand, wool, and silk.
• Caring for a classroom pet.
• Observing the growth of different kinds of seeds.
• Keeping a weather chart.
• Bringing in pictures of things of interest, such as a new baby at the zoo.
• Feeding birds or squirrels in winter.
• Observing soil erosion.
• Listening to stories and recordings.
• Participating in singing games.

CREATING THE CLIMATE

Children's growth in language depends on many things—as suggested earlier in this chapter and in the preceding ones—but not the least of these is the atmosphere or climate in a classroom. The importance of this is stressed not only here but in each of the remaining chapters.

The climate desired is one that fosters goodwill, respect, and friendliness on the part of all concerned. It is one in which an effort is made to have each child feel relaxed, at ease, and accepted as an important member of the group. Such a climate respects each child's personality, heritage, and the social and emotional effects of his or her out-of-school environment. Creating the climate for developing each child's potential is largely your responsibility, and it will evolve chiefly from the children's feelings of acceptance, freedom, and shared responsibility.

Teacher Attitude

While there are differences among teachers (and who would want it otherwise?) every teacher ought to be a vital, interesting person, one who is sensitive and encouraging. These qualities are reflections of attitude, and your attitude can be shown in many ways. These include the following:

1. Show each child that he or she is an accepted and important member of the classroom group.
2. Encourage an attitude of friendliness and mutual respect among the children—including respect for differences as well as likenesses.
3. Talk with and listen to children individually and in groups, and encourage them to exchange ideas and experiences.
4. Be receptive to ideas and interests expressed by the children.
5. Show appreciation of each child's efforts at expression.
6. Be enthusiastic—and allow the children to be—about the activities of the classroom.
7. Show sensitivity to and awareness of the world about you—encourage children to notice the way things look, sound, smell, and feel.
8. Let children see your own enjoyment of the stories you read, the way words sound, and the images they create.

Other Personnel

Classroom climate is also affected by the general learning environment or climate of the school. The principal, office workers, lunchroom helpers, custodians, bus drivers, and teacher aides are all involved in setting the learning conditions in classrooms. The principal is a key person in this. He or she must understand children, know the curriculum and materials, and see the importance of a busy and interesting classroom, one in which the children are active participants. If a teacher has an aide, this person certainly should share the teacher's feelings about children and seek to develop the same attitudes that the teacher has or is developing. A custodian needs to be interested in what a class is doing and be willing to accept possible personal inconveniences such as a disarranged classroom. Other school personnel should also appreciate children's curiosity and enthusiasm. You cannot control the actions and reactions of these people, but you can do much to influence their attitudes by talking with them about what the children are doing and why they are doing it. Try inviting each of them to be a special guest of the class for a particular activity or program. Also, try having them become involved in a class activity—making something, telling about something, giving their opinion on something, etc.

Physical Environment

Physical materials in the classroom are also important. Little stimulation of language growth or creativity will come from drabness. Wall and bulletin board decorations, displays, pictures and objects to handle and talk about are all important. And, of course, there must be language: signs, titles, and name plates to show the use of words; records, tapes, and tables and shelves of books to show the delight and knowledge they can bring. Further, a classroom where language growth is taking place is one that shows evidence that the children themselves have taken part in planning, preparing, and arranging the decorations and displays and that many activities are taking place there. This does not necessarily mean neatness, though children must learn that materials left strewn around the room are not easily found when needed or may not be in condition to be used again. Nor does it mean that absolute peace and quiet must reign; children learn as they share their experiences, discuss their activities, and help each other with problems.

BEGINNING ACTIVITIES

From the moment children enter a classroom there are opportunities for developing their language abilities. Most children will talk together naturally as they engage in activities of interest to them. Your program should capitalize on this ability and interest, both at this beginning stage of children's school years and as they progress beyond it.

Materials and Expression

A tub of water makes a good beginning. There's no question that it is a sloppy thing to have in a classroom, but playing in water is fun and the children become so involved that they forget about themselves and their shyness and begin to chatter like chipmunks. There are any number of activities that can result from water play, all of which encourage language development. Discussing what will float, what won't, and why is one; others are washing toy dishes and doll clothes, talking about animals that live in water and those that don't, and "painting" the school sidewalk. (The children will talk about what they are doing and what happens to the water.) Adding bubbles and letting the children just play and talk about the bubbles can also be successful.

Sandboxes are also guaranteed to be messy, but they do help to promote the freedom of expression and thought so necessary for school success. Pretending to be a truck driver hauling sand or building roads and lakes creates an opportunity for a child to talk with others and leads to other conversations.

Manipulation of objects helps children to know and understand them. For example, objects as simple as balls and building blocks of different sizes can lead to discussions of likenesses and differences, concepts such as small, large, round, square, etc., as well as vocabulary associated with these.

A bulletin board display of materials that children may handle will bring about new understanding of words, as well as awareness of everyday things in our world. Remember to encourage discussion of how things look, feel, and smell, as well as of likenesses, differences, and uses of materials. The display might consist of burlap, cotton, suede, velvet, wool, and nylon. The amount needed for a bulletin board is small and can be obtained easily and inexpensively from a fabric shop.

One of the most important factors to remember when developing language through sense awareness is to start with items that are fairly certain to be in the children's environment. Build on their knowledge and encourage them to talk about what they know. Encourage expansion of creative expression and thought through discussion of other ways to use the objects and materials.

Another simple way to start discussion is to ask every child in the room to bring in the top from a jar or bottle. Each child may show his or her top to the other children, who handle it and ask questions. For example, a discussion may begin with "Is this from a catsup bottle?" "What do you use catsup for?" "If I put mustard on my hamburger, why isn't the top of the catsup like the top of the mustard? They are used for the same purpose." "Could we put a catsup cap on mustard?" Such a discussion might lead to the discovery that differences may be very slight or not immediately obvious. For example, though the consistency of both *appears* much the same, catsup will pour, whereas mustard will not.

To expand this discussion you might bring in catsup, mustard, and a variety of relishes and onions. The children may taste these and discuss the differences in the way they taste, the ones they like, those they don't like, and why. This lesson is more enjoyable if hamburgers or hot dogs can be served, but that is not always easy to arrange.

Things that can be smelled provide a way to begin a discussion that should bring about some interesting statements. Encourage the children to describe and discuss different smells they have encountered in their young lives, which ones they liked and why, and which ones they didn't like. This may lead to a discussion of what smells tell us and the recognition that not all liquids that look like water are indeed water. In fact, using water, rubbing alcohol, and white vinegar is a good way to begin a discussion of the difference between looks and smells. Such a discussion can lead to further vocabulary development, of course, as well as inducing discussion and concept building.

Physical and Rhythmic Activities

Often a message—a thought, an idea, a feeling—comes from someone's eyes, a bodily stance, the way a head is held, or the extension of a chin. These bodily movements are expressive, just as language is expressive; both provide opportunity for communication.

The physical activity of children often seems to be expressed in perpetual motion. A child sways, bends, skips, runs, prances, and jumps. He screws up his mouth; she wrinkles her nose and sticks out her tongue. These are natural movements and they express feelings and reactions. These natural and expressive movements and gestures are communicative; many occur as children are talking. The fact that they are natural to children can and should be capitalized on in beginning language arts programs. Particularly important are rhythmic activities. Each child posesses an individual rhythm in speech, walk, and other movements, and these movements are expressive of a personality, background of experiences, and physical and mental maturation. But a little observation will show very real differences among the children in their coordination and their abilities to make fundamental movements. Make allowance for these differences instead of expecting the children to perform like a ballet group. In addition, take note of those children who appear to have particular difficulty with bodily control and coordination and plan additional ways to help them.

A fundamental way to get children to express themselves through body movement is for them to listen to music and react to it. Children enjoy improvising to music or to rhythm instruments by running, walking, galloping, trotting, hopping, jumping, bending, stretching, swaying, crawling, creeping, and so on. The emphasis in such activities is on responding to the mood of the music, which should be highly rhythmic with definite contrasts in mood—particularly in beginning activities. First have the children listen to the music and then let them begin their movements spontaneously and individually. As they become more skilled in interpreting music, they can respond in a more designed fashion.

Fundamental rhythmic activities include the following:

- Walking to a rhythm tapped by you.
- Clapping in unison.
- Walking and clapping to a beat.
- Walking to music.
- Walking and running to changing rhythmic tempos.
- Moving from walking to running with an increase in the beat of the rhythm.
- Skipping rope.
- Hopping to a musical rhythm.
- Combining a leap with other movements.
- Galloping, tip-toeing, swaying, etc., to rhythm.
- Creating a repetitive pattern of movement (e.g., walking, running, hopping—walking, running, hopping).

Finger Plays and Other Action Verses

Finger plays and other action verses call for bodily movements, coordination, and rhythm. They teach children new words and unison speaking, and they are fun to do. The fun is in the action and the repetition of familiar favorite verses. Demonstrate to the children using the entire verse; then, doing a line at a time, have one or two children join in.

The verses and the directions below are only suggestions. The children will have many of their own—perhaps nursery rhymes that they know or verses that they make up. They should be allowed to express their creativity in the verses they make up and in the variations they give to the words and actions.

My Fingers

I stretch my fingers way up high,
Until they almost reach the sky.
I lay them in my lap, you see,
Where they're as quiet as can be!

Little Leaves

Little leaves fall gently down,   (*Raise hands and lower them,*
Red and yellow, orange and brown;   *fluttering fingers like*
Whirling, whirling round and round,   *falling leaves*)
Quietly without a sound;   (*Repeat above motions*)
Down—and down—and down—and   (*Lower bodies gradually to the*
    down!   *floor*)

Stretch, Stretch

Stretch, stretch, way up high;	*(Reach arms upward)*
On your tiptoes, reach the sky.	*(Stand on tiptoe and reach)*
See the bluebirds flying high.	*(Wave hands)*
Now bend down and touch your toes;	*(Bend to touch toes)*
Now sway as the North Wind blows;	*(Move body back and forth)*
Waddle as the gander goes!	*(Walk in waddling motion back to seats)*

Ten Little Finger Men

Ten little finger men,	*(Hold up ten fingers)*
Who will clap for me today?	
"I will, I will," all my fingers say.	*(Clap hands on "I will")*
Ten little finger men,	*(Hold up ten fingers)*
Who will write for me today?	
"I will, I will," all my fingers say.	*(Draw circles in the air)*

Five Little Rabbits

Five little rabbits under a log;	*(Hold up fingers of one hand)*
This one said, "Sh! I hear a dog!"	*(Point to little finger)*
This one said, "I see a man!"	*(Point to ring finger)*
This one said, "Run while you can!"	*(Point to middle finger)*
This one said, "I'm not afraid!"	*(Point to index finger)*
This one said, "Let's hide in the shade!"	*(Point to thumb)*
A man and his dog went hurrying by,	
And you should have seen these rabbits fly!	

This Little Boy

This little boy is just going to bed.	
Down on the pillow he lays his head,	*(Palms together at side of face)*
Wraps himself up in his blankets tight,	*(Hands folded across chest)*
And this is the way he sleeps all night.	
Morning comes. He opens his eyes.	*(Sit up tall)*
Back with a toss the cover flies.	*(Spread arms apart quickly)*
Soon he is up and dresses for play,	
Ready for school and a bright new day.	

Houses

Here is a nest for the robin;	*(Cup both hands)*
Here is a hive for the bee;	*(Fists together)*
Here is a hole for the bunny;	*(Finger and thumb make a circle)*
And here is a house for ME!	*(Fingertips together to make a roof)*

Three Little Witches

One little, two little, three little witches	*(Hold up fingers one by one)*

Ride through the sky on a
  broom; — (*Clasp hands together in front as though grasping broomstick*)
One little, two little, three little
  witches — (*Repeat action in line one*)
Wink their eyes at the moon. — (*Wink one eye while making circles with arms*)

This Little Clown

This little clown is fat and gay; — (*Hold up thumb*)
This little clown does tricks all day; — (*Hold up index finger*)
This little clown is tall and strong; — (*Hold up middle finger*)
This little clown sings a funny
  song; — (*Hold up ring finger and wiggle it*)
This little clown is wee and small, — (*Hold up little finger*)
But he can do anything at all!

Riding the Merry-Go-Round

Ride with me on the merry-go-round,
Around and around and around. — (*Move hand in circles*)
Up go the horses, up! — (*Raise arms in the air*)
Down go the horses, down! — (*Lower arms*)
You ride a horse that is white; — (*Point to neighbor*)
I ride a horse that is brown; — (*Point to self*)
Up and down on the merry-
  go-round, — (*Raise and lower arms; then move one hand in circles*)
Our horses go round and round.

The Angel on My Christmas Tree

Two small hands that touch in prayer, — (*Touch hands in prayer*)
A golden halo in her hair, — (*Make a circle above head with one hand*)

On her back, two silver wings; — (*One hand on each shoulder*)
Once each year my angel brings
The Christmas story back to me,
While she rests upon my — (*Touch hands again in prayer*)
  Christmas tree.

Five Little Goblins

Five little goblins on Halloween night
Made a very spooky sight.
The first one danced on his
  tippy-tiptoes; — (*Hold up first finger*)
The second tumbled and bumped
  his nose; — (*Hold up second finger*)
The third one jumped high up in the
  air; — (*Hold up third finger*)
The fourth one walked like a fuzzy
  bear; — (*Hold up fourth finger*)
The fifth one sang a Halloween song. — (*Hold up thumb*)
Five goblins played the whole
  night long!

The Wind

The wind came out to play one day.
He swept the clouds out of his   (*Make sweeping motion with*
   way;   *arms*)
He blew the leaves and away they   (*Make fluttering motion*
   flew.   *with fingers*)
The trees bent low and their branches (*Lift arms and then lower*
   did, too.   *them*)
The wind blew the great big ships   (*Make sweeping motions*)
   at sea;
The wind blew my kite away from me.

Mr. Duck and Mr. Turkey

Mr. Duck went out to walk   (*Hold up thumb*)
One day in pleasant weather.
He met Mr. Turkey on the way,   (*Hold up other thumb*)
And there they walked together.   (*Move thumbs together*)
"Gobble, gobble, gobble,"   (*Move one thumb back*
                                            and forth)
"Quack, quack, quack."   (*Move other thumb back*
                                            and forth)
"Good-by, good-by."   (*Nod both thumbs*)
And they both walked back.   (*Move thumbs apart*)

Counting Action Rhyme

One, two; sit up. Please do.   (*Children sit tall*)
Three, four; feet flat on the floor.   (*Feet on floor*)
Five, six; stir and mix.   (*Motion of stirring*)
Seven, eight; close the gate.   (*Clap*)
Nine, ten; make a pen for a hen.   (*Interlace fingers*)

Ready to Listen

Let your hands go clap, clap, clap.   (*Clap hands three times*)
Let your fingers snap, snap, snap.   (*Snap fingers three times*)
Let your lips go very round,   (*Make lips round*)
But do not make a single sound.
Fold your hands and close each eye;   (*Follow action indicated*)
Take a breath . . . and softly sigh.
Ah———!!   (*Follow action indicated*)

Stand Up Tall

Stand up tall,   (*Stand*)
Hands in the air.   (*Raise hands*)
Now sit down
In your chair.   (*Sit*)
Clap your hands.   (*Clap three times as words*
                                            are said)
Make a frown.   (*Knit brows*)
Smile and smile,   (*Smile*)
And flop like a clown!   (*Relax with arms dangling*)

A Readiness Game

Make one eye go wink, wink, wink;
Make two eyes go blink, blink, blink.   *(Suit actions to words)*
Make two fingers stand just so;
Then ten fingers in a row.
Front and back your head will rock;
Then your fists will knock, knock,
    knock.
Stretch and make a yawn so wide;
Drop your arms down to your sides.
Close your eyes and help me say
Our very quiet sound today.

Talking about Things

Many primary teachers start the day with a "Talking Time" in which anything of interest to the children is discussed. This provides an opportunity to help children practice amenities in conversation and discussion and to work on speaking skills. During this time children can practice taking turns, listening carefully, sticking to the topic, telling events in sequence, articulating and pronouncing clearly, and constructing good sentences.

Sometimes the morning "Talking Time" takes the form of a "newspaper" for which the children report items, with the teacher writing them on the board or on a chart. Some decisions usually need to be made about what are suitable items for the newspaper or even for the more informal "Talking Time." Things that everyone knows need not be reported, nor should items that have limited interest. The children can help decide these matters.

Teachers sometimes put the newspaper on a sheet of newsprint twenty-four by thirty-six inches in size. The upper half may be left for a picture, and children can take turns illustrating the "news." Special events such as birthdays may mean a departure from "turns," with the one who has the birthday drawing a picture of his cake or a present she received.

The newspaper provides an opportunity to teach the names of months and their abbreviations, punctuation of dates, and capitalization skills. However, the emphasis should be on the content and on making the experience bring forth oral expression from the children.

Many other opportunities will present themselves throughout the day for talking things over and discussing and clarifying concepts. For example, a new word used may lead to a considerable exchange of ideas, or some knowledge gained in science that needs clarifying may result in much talking.

Talking may be fostered by providing occasions in which children may meet together in groups or four or five children. Much "sharing" may occur in such groups, particularly by children who are shy or less verbal.

Creative Play

From the time children first walk around the house in their parents' slippers, role playing and other forms of dramatic play are an exciting part of their lives. Young children love to live in a land of make-believe. Early in life they begin to play "house," "school," and other games based on aspects of life about them. Much of children's emotional and social growth occurs through this form of creative experimentation and expression; therefore schools should foster opportunities to continue this growth. Using activities throughout the school day to provide children with opportunities to pretend and dramatize events informally will make oral language lessons both enjoyable and instructive.

Children may experiment with adult words as they play in the housekeeping corner, build roads and houses in the sandbox, shop for bargains in the classroom grocery store, or carry on imaginary telephone conversations. In a more structured type of situation, children may act out what they will do when the principal comes to visit them or play at introducing themselves or each other to a class guest.

Other opportunities for informal dramatizations may be suggested by conversations or situations that occur on the playground or in the classroom. Suppose children playing a game get into an argument about the rules. Later, the situation could be dramatized, and the children themselves could work out a solution to the problem. Naturally, the focus should be on discovering a better way to resolve the disagreement, *not* on placing any child or children in an awkward or embarrassing position. This will not occur, of course, if the classroom is one in which every child feels that he or she is an accepted and important individual.

Dramatizing Stories and Rhymes

An activity liked by young children that is also helpful in developing abilities in all of the language arts is that of hearing and saying rhymes. Many colorful and attractively illustrated nursery rhyme books are available in book stores and libraries and every primary classroom should have several. Choose one or two rhymes that the children in your class will particularly enjoy. Then establish listening purposes by telling the children to listen to the rhyme as you read it so that they can tell you what happened. You may need to read the rhyme several times, asking them to listen for the answer to a specific question each time. Next, one child may relate the sequence of events in correct order. (The child need not march to the front of the room to do this.) Once the children know what happened, they may act the rhyme out as you read. It is sometimes helpful to select the most extroverted children to participate first, as they will generate enough enthusiasm to encourage others to try.

The next step is to encourage the children to act out the rhyme using the words they want to say. Particular attention should be given to whether or not children use the rhyme when they are speaking. If no child mentions that the words sound alike at the end, this may be pointed out after the dramatization. Read the rhyme once again, asking them to listen for the rhyming words. Or, if you wish, do this the first time you read the rhyme.

Children know much about rhyming and they may pick up the wording of the rhyme, but memorization should not be required. Keep in mind that spontaneity of expression and ease with language are the goals. Some children, particularly those who are extremely self-conscious, may not readily respond to these activities and to do some of them may take months, even with six-year-olds. Gently encouraging these children will help. Patience and knowledge of the particular children involved are the keys in planning such activities.

Some suggested Mother Goose rhymes to dramatize are these:

This Is the Way the Ladies Ride	Three Little Kittens
Rock-a-bye-Baby	Baa Baa, Black Sheep
Jack Be Nimble	Simple Simon
One, Two, Buckle My Shoe	Old King Cole
Jack and Jill	Polly, Put the Kettle On
Georgie Porgie	Old Mother Hubbard
Humpty Dumpty	Wee Willie Winkie
Little Miss Muffet	

Many others are as suitable as those listed. Always be on the lookout for poems well suited to dramatization or to pure enjoyment.

Once the children have had experience with dramatizing simple rhymes, move on to the dramatization of stories that have more plot and a greater variety of actions—but do continue to use rhymes. Simple, brief stories of a repetitive nature but with much action are good to begin with in teaching young children. Try these:

The Three Billy Goats Gruff	Millions of Cats (Wanda Gag)
The Three Little Pigs	The Little Brown Hen (Martin)
The Three Bears	Cinderella
The Elves and the Shoemaker	Chicken Little
Peter Rabbit (Beatrix Potter)	The Snowy Day (Keats)

If the children express considerable interest in dramatizing a specific story or rhyme, you may want to discuss with them ways to make their dramatization effective. The discussion may center around such questions as these:

1. What part of the room shall we use?
2. What shall we use for props and costumes? (*Note:* simple and readily available materials minimize problems.)
3. What is the sequence of the story?
4. How many scenes will we need?
5. What characters are in this story?
6. What other people do we need?

Dramatization is an excellent way to extend creative language and develop oral skills. Working in a group and being a person other than one's self help to eliminate self-consciousness. Thus, attention can be given to speaking loudly and clearly; using appropriate gestures, voice tone, and facial expression; and choosing words that are suitable to the character and the occasion.

At the primary level, formal dramatization is seldom desirable. Rehearsing and preparing costumes, properties, and scenery are time-consuming in proportion to the values gained, and children are apt to "freeze" when they forget lines—which they will, however well rehearsed they may be. If you wish to plan a program for parents or another class, it is better to do a simple type of choral reading (see chapter 6 for a discussion of this) or the type of informal dramatization discussed in the preceding paragraphs. The story should be one with which the children are very familiar and which they have dramatized a number of times in class, preferably with different children taking the parts (in case of absences on the day of performance). Emphasis should be on getting the story in the correct sequence and making the characters seem real rather than on remembering specific words and actions. If certain words or expressions are particularly colorful or often repeated, children will remember them readily, provided the story is well known to them.

Showing and Telling to an interested audience.

Reporting Orally

Children Can Show and Tell About

· a colorful rock
· seashells
· a bird's nest
· a photograph
· a self-drawn picture
· foreign stamps
· toys
· books

Oral reporting in the primary grades takes place under the names "Show and Tell" and "Sharing." Both are a good deal more informal than the oral reporting in later grades since the focus is on spontaneity of expression—that is, on helping the child tell his or her thoughts and ideas.

Show and Tell has a great advantage over Sharing or simply talking about things. In the Show and Tell activity the child shows something—a new sweater, colorful leaves, a new toy—on which he can focus his attention and thus keep from thinking about himself and any reluctance he may feel about talking. Too, the act of showing something and telling about it tends to be more organized than other forms of talking, since there is no need to ramble on when something has been shown and talked about.

Showing and sharing need not involve having children come to the front of the room. Much very informal sharing and showing can be done in small groups. For many children this is helpful; it may also be easier for you to deal with only a group at a time.

Keep in mind that you should strive to develop each child's creativity—his spontaneity and personalization of oral expression. In doing so you can also give attention to other matters important to oral reporting. Helpful principles to observe are the following:

1. Urge children to talk to the group rather than to you.
2. Encourage questions and comments on reports.
3. Insist upon attention and good listening.
4. Practice good listening yourself.
5. Limit the number of reports given on a single day, thus eliminating boredom and providing adequate time for each child.
6. Do not formalize "taking turns" too much.
7. Remember that informal seating will promote expression.
8. Do not force any child to share or show.
9. Take special care to praise the efforts of shy children.
10. Include the children in the planning and management of the sharing period.
11. Take advantage of the opportunity provided by the sharing period to note children's interests, possible speech defects or articulation difficulties, and nonstandard usages that may need teaching attention.
12. Encourage variety in the types of objects children show and talk about.

Telling Stories

Beginning storytelling experiences include the telling of stories a child has heard or has had read to him, the relating of imaginative stories created by the child himself, and the telling of stories derived from personal experiences. The latter represents for the younger child the most potent approach to more advanced and creative forms of storytelling.

After children have listened to a wide variety of stories—and the responsibility for their having listened to many stories is yours—they will reproduce many in dramatic form and, finally, will begin to tell ones they know. Storytelling is discussed more completely in chapter 15; at this point it is sufficient to remember that storytelling helps to develop such language skills as recalling events in proper sequence; using descriptive words and phrases; speaking loudly and distinctly enough for all to hear; avoiding poor sentences; using gestures, facial expressions, and voice changes; and speaking easily and without self-consciousness.

Storytelling should be done informally. Often sitting on the floor in a circle is the best way. There should be no feeling of a standardized way of doing things and no emphasis on technicalities and memorization of details. Remember that a child tells a story because he or she is enthusiastic about something interesting and wishes to share it with others, and that an audience listens to a story for enjoyment.

Experience Stories

An experience story is a story dictated by a pupil or pupils to the teacher. The teacher records what a child or group of children say on the chalkboard or on a large sheet of chart paper. The story is usually based on some experience—most often something the entire group has experienced. Recording directly on chart paper is usually more practical than recording on the board. It saves time and avoids the possibility that the story will be erased inadvertently.

First experience stories are not written for children to read. The dictation simply serves to help the children understand that written symbols stand for spoken words. It also gives children a new reason for expressing their ideas and helps to develop feelings of self-confidence and status.

The sharing period, dramatic play activities, materials and objects in the classroom, and the class events the children participate in can all become subjects for experience stories. The arrival of a gerbil in class, which necessitates a discussion of what it eats and what kind of cage it should have, may serve as the basis for a three- to five-line story, depending on the maturity level of the children. A schoolyard walk, the planting of seeds, or an educational film can also serve as the basis for a story. With the exercise of a little imagination and effort the possibilities are endless.

Unless the children have developed a good deal of spontaneity, you will need to use guiding questions to help them formulate ideas for an experience story and to aid them in organizing these ideas. Such questions should lead children to recall the experience in sequence, to avoid leaving out important details, and to state what they really mean to say.

As children mature, attention can be given to written expression skills as suggested in chapters 8 and 9.

A Final Word

Beginning school language activities must build on the experiences children have had and the language abilities they bring to the classroom. Since the experiences will be varied and the abilities different, the language arts program must be built around individual needs and differences from the very start. Emphasis should be upon broadening knowledge, developing understanding of new concepts and words to describe them, and helping children to express themselves with ease and imagination. Success in achieving these goals depends both on the activities you plan for the children and on the climate you create in the classroom.

REFERENCES

Books

Carkhuff, Robert R., et al. *The Skills of Teaching: Interpersonal Skills.* Amherst, MA: Human Resources Development Press, 1976.

Edwards, Charlotte. *Creative Dramatics.* Dansville, NY: Instructor Publications, Inc., 1972.

Forte, Imogene, and Mackenzie, Joy. *Nooks, Crannies and Corners.* Nashville, TN: Incentive Publications, Inc., 1972.

Hoover, Kenneth H., and Hollingsworth, Paul M. *A Handbook for Elementary School Teachers.* Boston: Allyn and Bacon, 1973.

Lowndes, Betty. *Movement and Creative Drama for Children.* Boston: Plays, Inc., 1971.

McIntyre, Barbara M. *Creative Drama in the Elementary School.* Itasca, IL: F. E. Peacock Publishers, Inc., 1974.

Spodek, Bernard. *Teaching in the Early Years.* Englewood Cliffs, NJ: Prentice-Hall, Inc., 1972.

Stewig, John W. *Spontaneous Drama, A Language Art.* Columbus, OH: Charles E. Merrill Publishing Co., 1973.

Films

Dance Your Own Way. Los Angeles: Bailey-Film Associates (10 minutes; color; primary and intermediate).

Magic Moments, A Visual Language Experiences Series. Chicago: Encyclopaedia Britannica (Primary; a series of 20 short—3 to 9 minutes—films).

Ready, Set A of *Ready-Set-Read* Program. New York: Learning Corporation of America (Set of 12 three to four minute color film loops).

Sharing Time in Our Class. Urbana, IL: Visual Aids Service, Division of University Extension, University of Illinois (Rental; 10 minutes; color; primary).

The Learning to Look Series. New York: McGraw-Hill (Color; primary; titles include "Let's Find Some Faces," "On Your Way to School," "Learning to Look at Hands").

Filmstrips

Developing Cognitive Skills in Young Learners. Valhalla, NY: Stanley Bowmar Company, Inc. (Set of 7 strips; primary).

I Hear a Rhyme. Jamaica, NY: Eye Gate House (8 sound-color strips; primary).

Primary Language Arts Kit. Chicago: Encyclopedia Britannica Films (8 strips and 4 records; primary).

Sensory Awareness. New York: Teaching Resources Corp. (4 filmstrips with records and guide).

Visual Efficiency Filmstrip Set. Huntington Station, New York (10 filmstrips).

Talking Time Series. New York: McGraw-Hill Films (2 sets of 8 strips each; primary and intermediate).

Recordings

The Art of Learning Through Movement. Valhalla, NY: Bowmar Records (Record with games and dramatic play ideas).

The Talking Storybook Boxes. Glenview, IL: Scott Foresman and Co. (Books and records; elementary).

Talkstarters. Glenview, IL: Scott Foresman and Co. (Books and records; primary).

Other Aids

Early Childhood Discovery Materials. New York: Bank Street College of Education (Pictures, books, puzzles, and teacher's guide).

Wagner, Guy, et al. *Games and Activities for Early Childhood Education.* New York: Teachers Publishing Corp., 1967.

Grayson, Marion F. *Let's Do Fingerplays.* New York: David McKay, 1972.

Peabody Language Development Kits. Circle Pines, MN: American Guidance Service, Inc. (Puppets, stimulus cards, and recordings).

Simple Games for Primary Grades. Darien, CT: Teachers Publishing Corp.

ACTIVITIES FOR PRESERVICE TEACHERS

1. Visit a preschool or kindergarten class. Make a note of differences among the children in size, physical coordination, willingness and ability to express themselves orally, and extent of vocabulary.

2. Watch a television program for children, such as *Captain Kangaroo, Sesame Street,* or *Mister Rogers's Neighborhood.* Would this program help to develop a child's experience background, vocabulary, and/or interest in learning? How?

3. Read one of the following books and report to the class how you would use what you learned for helping with movement and dramatization: *If You were an Eel, How Would You Feel?* (by Mina and Howard Simon, Follett Publishing Co.); *The Snow and the Sun* (by Antonio Fransconi, Harcourt Brace Jovanovich); *Little Toot* (by Hardie Gramatky, Putnam); *Whistle for Willie* (by Ezra Jack Keats, Viking).

4. Visit the children's section of a library and begin compiling a list of books that would possibly be useful in helping children better use their senses. For each entry include enough information so that you could both find the book and know how it might be used.

5. Prepare a bibliography of good stories to read to primary children. See recent publications of the American Library Association, International Reading Association, National Council of Teachers of English, and the Association for Childhood Education International for assistance.

6. From your observations in classrooms and talking with teachers, add to the list of activities in the *Input* section of the chapter.

7. Observe children on the playground or during a physical education period. Select several children and compare their coordination with that of the other children. If you notice a child who seems to be particularly lacking in coordination, ask the teacher how he compares with the others in articulation, handwriting, spelling, and reading.

8. Use chart paper or shelf paper to write an imaginary experience story on a topic such as "Our Fish," "Dirt," or "Flowers." On a separate sheet, outline the steps you would use in helping children to write such a story. Be sure to include a description of the motivating experiences.

ACTIVITIES FOR INSERVICE TEACHERS

1. Prepare a monthly environment notebook or card file. Leave room to add ideas. Include sketches of bulletin boards, lists of physical materials and media, and ideas for trips—everything that will add interest and stimulate discussions. Old copies of *The Instructor* and *Grade Teacher* magazines may give you ideas for the notebook.

2. Prepare a listening, speaking, and motor-skills coordination checklist for use with young children. As the children participate in activities suggested in this chapter, evaluate them in terms of the criteria you have established for their age level. Then, based on your observation, prepare a card for each child listing his or her strengths and

weaknesses. Include a brief statement about how you plan to adjust the curriculum to meet these needs.

3. Describe steps that might be taken to help a shy child participate more in classroom activities.

4. Write on the board or ask the children the following questions: "Do you like to pretend? What would you like to pretend you are? Can you draw a picture about your pretending?" After pictures have been drawn, ask for volunteers to tell about their pictures. This activity may be either for the whole class or for small groups.

5. Evaluate a skit, film, filmstrip, or recording purported to be related to the content of this chapter. Report to the class.

6. Collect other finger plays. You might ask your fellow teachers—many of them will have ones that will be new to you.

7. Make a surprise box filled with objects that are interesting to touch. Include such items as a smooth pebble, a piece of sandpaper, satin cloth, tree bark, and a feather. Use this with your class to develop concepts and/or vocabulary.

8. Make a box similar to the one described above, but use objects to be smelled (children can wear blindfolds). Items might include a piece of orange peel, a cinnamon stick, a coffee bean, an evergreen twig, and a piece of leather.

9. React to the learning principles stated in this chapter in terms of your experiences.

INDEPENDENT ACTIVITIES FOR CHILDREN

1. Provide a box of old clothing, shoes, etc. for children to use in creative dramatics.

2. Discuss "news items" with the children and then provide newsprint for them to individually illustrate these "items."

3. Prepare paper bags, each containing a single object. The objects should be of varying shapes, sizes, and textures. Have a child reach into the bag and feel the object and describe it to a second child. The objective is for the first child to describe the object well enough for the second one to guess what it is.

4. Following a vacation or trip, a child could make a series of pictures illustrating highlights of the trip in sequential and left-to-right order. He or she may then use these pictures as illustrations for reporting orally to other children.

5. A child can choose materials from an "odds and ends" box to make "pretend" animals. These may be shown to the class, stimulating a discussion which the child who made the animal would lead.

6. Collect sets of pictures from magazines for individual children to place in sequence for a story. The pictures may be mounted on cardboard with flannel patches on the back so that the child can place them on a flannel board.

4

Children with Special Needs

While every child is special and has special needs, there is a history in the United States of identifying some children as "special" or "exceptional." This history began more than 150 years ago with a concern for educating blind children.[1] Later special attention was given to children with other handicaps or disorders. Parents and teachers prompted much of this attention over the years and were largely responsible for the establishing of special schools and classes for these children. However, even with these special arrangements, there have always been "special" children in classrooms waiting to be identified or to be placed, as well as many other children considered to be "borderline." Authorities estimate that "seventy-five percent of hearing-impaired children, 80 percent of emotionally disturbed children, and about 40 percent of visually impaired children were not being adequately served as of 1975."[2]

Now the situation with respect to these special children has changed. With the passage of The Education for All Handicapped Children Act (P. L. 94–142) many children who have been in special schools and classrooms will be "mainstreamed." That is, they will return to the classrooms populated with children not identified as "special."[3] Thus, the range of differences among children in the average classroom has increased or will soon do so.

In addition to those children historically defined as special, there are thousands of children entering classrooms each year who are unable to speak English and are unprepared by their cultural backgrounds for the environment of the school. Still other children enter school speaking a dialect different from that used by the teacher and found in textbooks. Both of these groups of children are also special and add to the range of differences among children.

It is important, though, that this increase in the extent of differences not be overemphasized. In most classrooms there is a rather wide range of differences in the intellectual abilities of children, and even with a narrow range, children differ in learning rates and styles. There are also children who are undernourished, fatigued, or with anxiety or health problems—any or all of which may or may not be temporary. Thus, in the preceding chapters, as well as those that follow, we stress the importance of a teacher giving each child as much individual attention as possible. This chapter simply seeks to provide as much help as can be given in a limited space for the teaching of children who perhaps need a bit more individual attention than most do. However, since this book is intended for teachers in regular classrooms, we will not attempt to discuss all "exceptional" children. There are some children so severely handicapped mentally, physically, emotionally, or by some combination of these that they will seldom if even be in regular classrooms—even with mainstreaming. Too, the proliferation of categories of children within the rubric of "learning disabled" will not receive the attention some readers might desire.[4]

Teaching the Slow Learner

Mentally retarded children have many of the same needs as other children. Like all children, they want and need to explore and extend their environment. They need firsthand experiences—the concrete more than the abstract. Children commonly labeled mentally retarded now in regular classrooms or likely to be in mainstreaming programs are "borderline" or mildly retarded. They are slow learners; their development is slower than average. They have short- and long-term memory deficits greater than normal children, along with more problems in focusing and maintaining attention. Yet they can learn many of the things taught to other children if the teaching respects their limitations.

Planning Instruction

Try to help parents adjust to their children's limitations and yet recognize their potential.

Teaching techniques and procedures proven by research and practice to be effective with so-called normal children are generally effective with children identified as slow learners. Modifications do need to be made, largely in terms of the rate of learning and in the reinforcement of perception and retention, but such modification—caring for individual differences in attitudes, interests, needs, and abilities—is the essence of all good teaching.

The instructional planning described in chapter 2 is appropriate for use in planning for the slow learner, particularly if the following suggestions are kept in mind:

1. Utilize short-range goals, and be sure the child understands them.
2. Break up the content of the material to be taught into smaller units than usual.
3. Make the child aware of his successes—by making progress charts, by showing him he has met standards and objectives he has helped to set, by complimenting him on gains, and by encouraging him to strike out in new directions.
4. Have the child compete with his own record rather than with others in the class.
5. Provide books and other materials the child is capable of using.
6. Make instruction systematic and orderly.
7. Talk to the child directly and calmly. Ask him to repeat directions and assignments.
8. Be patient and understanding; show interest in him and in his needs and interests.

Activities and Suggestions

Concepts fundamental to much learning are frequently difficult for slow learners to attain. Although the teaching focus should be on the concrete rather than the abstract, with extra teaching effort the abstract can also be taught. For example, a bulletin board displaying pictures of houses might be used to show *big* and *little*, *same* and *different*, etc. Such words as *next, near, far, last, first, second, third, above, below, under, over, between, high, low,* and many others fall into the category needing special attention. You can help these children develop understanding by working with them throughout the school day for several days or weeks on no more than two or three words at a time. Reinforcement should be provided several times during the year.

Words like *up* and *down* can be taught in connection with a study of weather—for example, the thermometer can be the basis for learning *up* and *down.* Weather study also permits a slow student to learn concepts: high humidity, low temperature, below normal rainfall, etc. These concepts and others very basic to understanding much that children hear and read—*up, down, tall, short, round, corner, loud, soft,* etc.—can be shown in concrete fashion in many ways.

Many of the suggestions made in chapter 3 concerning readiness are particularly needed by slow-learning children, and the length of time devoted to such readiness may need to be greatly extended. Such things as eye-hand coordination, color awareness, and arithmetic concepts can be developed through the use of peg boards and other objects that can be seen and handled. Finger-hand coordination can be improved through the finger plays that were suggested.

Sandpaper or felt letters are often useful in teaching the slow reader. These can be traced by the child with a finger as he or she says the letter names. This activity is helpful in both reading and spelling instruction. A variation is to use a felt pen to print or write a letter or word on oaktag or a 5 × 8 card. Have the child pronounce the letter or word, saying each letter name—not sound—as he traces it on the card. (Some teachers feel that all handwriting of these children should be cursive with little or no manuscript taught. They believe that cursive writing helps the child to continue his or her thought, whereas manuscript stops and starts.)

Still another variation is for you to write a word in sand (the sand might be in a relatively small container such as a cigar or shoe box) and have the child trace it with a finger.

After several tracings the child may feel that he is ready to write the word. He then dumps some of the sand from his box onto a brightly colored 12 × 18 sheet of construction paper on his desk. He spreads the sand out, says the word, and then uses his finger to write the word so that the construction paper shows through the sand.

Words to use in the sand activity can be placed on cards so that the child can check a word letter by letter after he has written it in the sand. When he has learned to spell a word, he can file the card and start learning another. If he does not spell the word correctly in the sand, he should start the process again. This activity takes time, effort, and much encouragement, but it will help the child learn to spell and will probably give his reading a boost as well.

Letter identification—both name and shape—may be taught by using a teacher/pupil-made book. For the book cut both capital and small letters from sandpaper, felt, leather, or any textured material and paste each pair of letters on a 12 × 18 sheet of construction paper with a picture of an object that begins with the particular letter. For example, for the letter B the picture might be of a bird, ball, or boy. Then from magazines cut out the letter B (both large and small) and add these B's to your chart. (You will discover that printers use a great variety of sizes and forms of letters.) Again, the purpose of this activity is for the child to learn to recognize the letter, know its name, and associate it with words representing ideas or objects he knows, regardless of the size or form of that letter.

In general, the focus in teaching the slow learner should be on one or only a few items at a time. The activities suggested above for teaching a word or a letter should not be rushed. Teach one letter, then move to another. In the same way, have the child practice one letter or movement in handwriting at a time, learn one new vocabulary word at a time, learn to write a short report before moving on to another form of written expression, or learn to give a simple oral explanation rather than simply working on oral expression generally.

There are suggestions for activities and teaching situations that should be used with slow learners in most of the chapters in this book. For example, in chapter 12 we suggest that the number of words in the spelling list be reduced for the slow learner and that extra effort be given to teaching both auditory and visual perception skills and memory. Chapter 14 contains a discussion of reading readiness that applies directly to the needs of most slow learners. In chapters 8 and 9 we suggest some writing activities that are not taxing to the extent that they would frustrate the slow learner.

TEACHING GIFTED CHILDREN

Children with unique abilities or talents are frequently not thought of as children with special needs. A general point of view is that the extremely bright among these children will learn almost regardless of conditions; likewise, the ones with special talents are considered either to be maturing lopsidedly or to be stubborn and arrogant. As a consequence of these and other misconceptions, programs in language arts and other curriculum areas have generally not provided for gifted children in systematic and continuing ways.

Identifying the Gifted

The U. S. Office of Education estimates that 3 to 5% of the population is gifted or talented.

Various definitions have been advanced for the gifted and talented. Possibly the most practical one is that these children are ones who show outstanding ability in a variety of areas—general intelligence, specific aptitudes, creativity, leadership, artistic skill, or athletic prowess. The identification of children as gifted or talented should be done by professionals—teachers, psychologists, and others. The identification should *not* be based solely on the typical intelligence tests. In the first place, an intelligence test is subject to considerable error, particularly group tests as they are often administered. In the second place, such tests measure verbal aptitude and ability more than anything else. Finally, there are many areas of giftedness or talent not necessarily highly correlated with intelligence.

Instructional Suggestions

Keep in mind that an individual may be gifted and also handicapped. The best known example is Helen Keller.

Gifted children are children and not adults. They generally have many of the same interests and needs as other children. However, many of them also have broader interests than their so-called normal peers. This is particularly true for those with high general intelligence and academic-related aptitudes. A major school question regarding these children is whether their movement through the normal school curriculum should be accelerated or whether the curriculum should be enriched at each level to better accommodate their needs and interests. There is no one answer to this question, but our general assumption is that most gifted children will not exceed the abilities of their age peers to the extent that curriculum enrichment could not meet their needs. Thus, the suggestions in this section (as well as in many other chapters) apply to teaching the gifted in regular classrooms.

If the classroom experiences of gifted children are to meet their needs, the extension of the curriculum should not be "more of the same." Gifted children don't need longer lists of spelling words, more questions to answer, more book reports, and the like. They do need more stimulating ideas, more opportunities to extend their interests, and most of all a teacher who is neither threatened by their intellects and talents nor prone to be too demanding of them. The teacher should share interests with these children, discuss things with them—particularly abstract ideas—and permit a good deal of independence in their classroom activities.

You may want to contact

American Association for Gifted Children, 15 Gramercy Park, New York, NY 10003.

There are, of course, many ways for gifted children to extend their learning. Because of their abilities they may be given many leadership roles in the classroom—for example, small group discussions, planning activities, writing dramatics scripts, and conducting interviews. Frequently, too, many of these children are interested in and capable of taking photos; making films, filmstrips, and slides; and preparing other materials for the use of the class. Books should be available in quantity—books about almost anything and everything, particularly informational ones: almanacs; encyclopedias; an unabridged dictionary; field guides on birds, trees, animals, etc.; biographies; sports and hobby. Since most of these children will be good readers and zealous ones, informational type reading will foster interest in fiction beyond the interests of many of their peers; therefore, these need to be available. Perhaps these children may be given more freedom and time for library visits than that given their peers.

CHILDREN WITH VISUAL DISABILITIES

Children who are visually impaired may, depending on the severity of the handicap, present particular teaching problems in most areas of the language arts. Children who are blind or nearly so generally will not be in a regular classroom, although with mainstreaming they may be for a portion of the school day. There are now in classrooms, however, a good many children who have visual problems of a less severely handicapping nature. These children often have difficulty seeing the board, charts, and/or the print in books. They may also reflect such handicaps in their writing.

Identifying the Children

Symptoms of possible visual problems include losing one's place while reading, avoiding close work, poor posture while reading, holding the reading material closer or farther away than normal, holding one's body rigid while looking at distant objects, rubbing the eyes, tilting the head to one side, frowning, blinking, scowling while reading or writing, excessive head movement while reading, inflamed eyelids, and frequent headaches. Children in the primary grades who have difficulty learning their colors may be suspected of having color "blindness."

Most schools make some provision for screening children's vision. Usually the screening is done with the Snellen Chart, a procedure that checks vision at 20 feet but does not check near-point vision, nor measure fusion ability, muscular imbalance, and other visual abnormalities. A lesser number of schools also screen with a chart held at a distance of 14 inches from the eye, which does adequately screen near-point vision.

There are other testing instruments sometimes used in schools (such as the Keystone Telebinocular), usually by a school nurse or some other specialist rather than the classroom teacher. The classroom teacher can check on symptoms by having material on the chalkboard read and by close questioning about letters and words in near-point reading. All children suspected of having problems seeing properly should be referred to specialists.

For help or information write:

National Society for Crippled Children and Adults, 2023 W. Ogden Ave., Chicago, IL 60612
Council for Exceptional Children, 1920 Association Drive, Reston, VA 22091
National Association for Visually Handicapped, 305 E. 24th St., New York, NY 10010

Instructional Provisions

When referred to a specialist, a child who has a vision problem usually receives attention, glasses, supervised muscle training, and so on. However, the attention needed may take most of the school year to materialize. And even if a child does receive the kind of special assistance he needs, there are still some ways a teacher can help. These include the following:

1. Seat the child so that he or she can see the board as well as possible.
2. Arrange the child's desk to avoid glare.
3. Prevent the child from facing sharp contrasts in the amount of direct or reflected light.
4. Use reading materials that are not "slick" or glossy.
5. Remove the glossy finish from the top of the child's desk.
6. Use a typewriter with large type to make materials for the child.[5]

Assignments can be given orally, the child can be read to by other children, and the answers to questions can be given orally rather than in writing. Information, directions, and even literary selections can be recorded on tape for the child to listen to, particularly if other pupils are enlisted to aid in preparing the tapes. Extra attention should be given to teaching listening skills, since the child with a vision problem must depend more heavily on his ears than does the child with normal vision.

Children with Speech Disorders

It is estimated that 5 to 10% of children have speech disorders.

The number of children in any classroom with speech problems, those that may be called speech disorders—ones that require extended training by specialists—may be small, but it is important that a teacher identify these children and provide for their instruction. It is also important for a teacher to know which child's speech borders on the unintelligible and who needs instructional attention.

Normal Speech Problems

Normal Speech Development

By age 4½ the child should be able to produce all speech sounds except the following:

f–as in *four, five, foot*
l–as in *lamp, lamb, letter*
r–as in *rabbit, run, race*
s–as in *sun, soap, sail*
v–as in *valentine, van, vase*
z–as in *zip, zebra, zoo*
th–as in *then, this, them*
th–as in *think, thin, thumb*
zh–as in *television, treasure*
sh–as in *should, sugar, mission*
wh–as in *why, whale, where*

By age 7½ or 8 normal speech development should have led to the ability to produce these sounds.

When a child first enters school, his or her speech may retain vestiges of "baby talk." Estimates indicate that over 40 percent of kindergarten children and 25 percent of those in the first grade show such retention.[6] The speech of many of these children is characterized by one or more of the following: reversals (for example, *aminal* for *animal*), inability to articulate some blends (*st, th, str,* etc.) and individual speech sounds, mispronunciations, and divergencies in pitch and loudness.

A child with any of these speech characteristics may be referred to a speech correctionist, who will probably simply wish to observe the child's maturation but may suggest activities similar to those in this chapter.

The child of eight or nine (and often younger) certainly should be able to produce all of the speech sounds unless he or she has a genuine speech handicap. The child may, of course, have certain speech habits (saying *deese* for *these,* for example) that need attention and may continue to have problems of voice quality and control.

Speech handicaps that go beyond the speech characteristics of many young children, with the exception of those associated with a psychological disturbance, are discussed below.[7] Most of these problems call for the services of a speech correctionist either directly or in giving the classroom teacher suggestions or assistance. However, since speech specialists are not always available, these suggestions may be useful.

Types of Abnormal Speech

Speech problems may be manifested in a variety of forms. These can be grouped, though, in four major categories: (1) articulatory, or pronunciation disorders; (2) voice disorders—malfunctioning of the sound-producing mechanism; (3) linguistic, or language disorders; and (4) disorder of speech rhythm.[8]

Articulation Disorders.   Probably as much as 70 percent of all speech problems found in the normal elementary school classroom are those in which the speaker cannot make certain speech sounds either in isolation or within blends with other speech sounds. Most frequently these articulation problems are those of sound substitutions, omissions, reversals, and additions, in the speech of children older than eight years. This persistence of common speech characteristics of young children is called "infantile perseveration" and may be caused by poor muscular coordination, illness, retarded physical maturation, low intelligence, short auditory memory span, poor auditory discrimination, or various environmental factors (overprotection by a parent, desire for attention, jealousy of a younger sibling, etc.). There are other articulatory disorders identified by speech specialists—the most common of which is probably lisping—but they are also manifested in problems with specific individual speech sounds.

Voice Disorders.   Voice disorders are those in which speech sounds are articulated acceptably but the voice has a quality that is unpleasant to the hearer. Few children have this problem beyond the primary years. The most common voice disorder is nasality, usually caused by a physical problem, the most serious of which is a cleft palate. Other voice disorders include hoarseness, an unnaturally high or low pitch, and excessive loudness or softness.

Write to:

Alexander Graham Bell Association for the Deaf, 3417 Volta Place, N. W., Washington, DC 20007, for material on speech problems.

Language Disorders.   Language disorders are the result of physical, environmental, or psychological problems which have interfered with language learning. The language disorders most often found in the elementary school are delayed speech and childhood aphasia. Delayed speech may mean that a child does not know some sounds or has a very limited vocabulary. Delayed speech varies from a mild delay in the appearance of a few sounds to reaching the primary grades with the ability to say only three or four words. When seriously delayed language development is shown, the cause is usually a brain damage; the condition is known as aphasia.

Rhythm Disorders.   The principal speech disorder of a rhythmic nature is stuttering. Some stutterers block on producing sounds; some repeat sounds, syllables, or words; some speak very slowly or very rapidly; some prolongate sounds; and others have spasms of the speech mechanism. There may be combinations of the above in the speech of a stutterer, and there are usually times when there is no evidence of stuttering. Speech specialists generally state that there is no definite cause of stuttering, and no certain cure.

Teaching Considerations

Never display impatience with a child who has faulty speech. The child must feel accepted and secure.

Children suspected of having a speech problem or disorder should be referred to a speech correctionist for diagnosis and remediation. Usually the speech specialist will contact the parents after seeing the child and will involve a physician, the school psychologist, and others if the problem is a serious one. Unless the child is removed from his regular classroom, the teacher will be brought in on planning the remediation. As suggested in chapter 6, a warm, calm, and receptive classroom atmosphere is important in getting a child with a speech handicap to want to talk. This child should be encouraged to talk; his classmates should not be permitted to make fun of him. *Do not* cut his speech off, finish an expression or sentence for him, have him start over, or tell him to think before he speaks. Give special attention to how you speak to him. Looking directly at him and speaking in a well-modulated voice and in an unhurried and pleasant manner will help.

Cooperate with the speech correctionist by sending the child to appointments on time, keeping the correctionist informed of classroom activities that may be capitalized upon for speech exercises, and making certain you understand what the correctionist is trying to do.

Activities

Working relationships between teachers and parents are important to teaching all special children.

Activities that may modify or remedy speech defects should be used to meet specific needs; they should not be used indiscriminately. It is much more important for children—including those who have speech handicaps—to engage in genuine communication situations than in speech exercises. Speech activities, such as those suggested here, are certainly important and necessary when speech correction is needed, but they are only part of a total speech improvement program.

Relaxing exercises such as falling completely relaxed into a chair, dropping the head and letting the arms dangle, shaking the hands and arms, and rotating the head on the chest and shoulders may help a child whose speech problem is related to tenseness. Breathing exercises, such as taking short quick breaths, inhaling deeply, taking in a quick breath and exhaling slowly (by counting), and doing specific acts (smelling a flower, saying "ah" for the doctor, showing surprise) may also be helpful. To correct excessive nasality, try such activities as yawning, panting, and "blowing out" vowel sounds (or blowing out a candle, blowing a pinwheel, etc.).

Ear training exercises are also important, since good speech depends on aural acuity and the ability to discriminate between correct and incorrect production of a sound. These exercises include discriminating among sounds (the ringing of a small bell, the sound of a triangle), telling when two words begin with the same sound (or end, or have the same middle sound), and selecting objects whose names contain a particular sound.

In helping the child who retains vestiges of baby talk, the first task is to identify the particular sounds the child does not produce correctly. Then attempt to have the child distinguish between words correctly and incorrectly said: *fadder— father, wittle—little, thithter—sister.* It may be necessary for him to use a mirror so that he can watch his lip and tongue movements. Tape recording these efforts may also help. Another useful technique is to have the child say poems and sing songs containing the sounds that are troublesome.

Tongue exercises are helpful with simple articulation problems. These should be done individually with the aid of a mirror. They include stretching the tongue out and down, up toward the nose, inside the lips, etc. There are also activities suitable for groups, such as saying the following rhymes:

>Little kitty laps her milk,
>   Lap,lap,lap!
>Her tongue goes out,
>Her tongue goes in,
>   Lap,lap, lap!
>
>Little kitty likes her milk,
>   Lap, lap, lap!
>Oh, see her tongue
>Go out and in,
>   Lap, lap, lap!
>("Make your tongue go like kitty's.")
>
>Tick! Tock! Tick! Tock!
>The clock goes ticking all the day.
>Tick! Tock! Tick! Tock!

It has no other words to say.
Tick! Tock! Tick! Tock!
It ticks all night; it ticks all day.
And when I sleep, or when I play,
The clock goes on the same old way.
Tick! Tock! Tick! Tock!

Exercises for correcting the production of specific sounds may be used when particular faults have been identified. For example, for the sound represented by *s* the following might be done.

1. Say lists of words.

see	pencil	nice
sit	answer	dress
sun	dressing	house
soup	insect	base
salt	groceries	tennis

2. Repeat "s" sentences.

   My sister is sick.
   We ate soup, salad, roast, and carrots.

3. Say contrasting words.

some—thumb	sick—thick	so—though
seem—theme	thin—sin	

THE HEARING IMPAIRED

The incidence of hearing losses among the children in schools is not known, since these losses range from very slight ones to total deafness. Hearing losses and learning difficulties are not necessarily related, but the fact that so much instruction is on an aural–oral basis means that there may be problems. Most children with hearing losses that are less than total deafness can be successful in the regular classroom if sensitivity is shown for their handicaps and instructional adjustments are made.

Screening for Hearing Losses

The best procedure for a school to use to determine whether a child has a hearing loss is to test the child with an audiometer. This test requires a competent operator for the equipment, so often every child is screened on a systemwide, regional, or statewide basis. If such a testing service is not available, a child with a suspected hearing loss should be referred to a physician.

Children can be tested informally to determine the need for audiometric testing or referral by having them listen to a ticking watch or to whispering. The watch should have a fairly loud tick, one that would be heard at about four feet from the ear by a child with normal hearing. Each ear should be tested separately; the actual testing is done by holding the watch near the ear and moving away until the child signals that it can no longer be heard. The whispering testing is done by whispering directions (e.g., "raise your left hand," "close your fist," etc.) at increasing distances from the ear being tested.

A teacher also needs to be alert to children's behavior or habits that indicate a hearing impairment or an impending difficulty with hearing properly. These conditions include recurring earaches, the tendency to favor one ear in listening, rubbing an ear, headaches, head noises, and dizziness. Excessive inattention, reflected in poor achievement and the failure to follow directions, may also signal a hearing problem. Sometimes, too, faulty pronunciation, heavy breathing through the mouth, and an unnatural pitch of voice are signs of hearing impairment.

Children with hearing losses often need professional treatment. The teacher is usually informed about the diagnosis and treatment, particularly if there is a responsibility the physician thinks the school should assume. For example, if a child is given a hearing aid, he or she has to be helped in getting accustomed to using it. If a child is receiving instruction in lip reading, the teacher should know this. Likewise, if there is medication prescribed, this should be known. Do not hesitate to inquire of parents or the school physician about these matters.

Helping the Child

Children don't like to be too different. The child with a hearing loss should be given the consideration needed to aid learning without calling excessive attention to the problem. For example, when directions are given or other talking is done with this child, he or she should be faced as directly as possible. The child will learn to watch faces (some children even learn to read lips). Do not shout or exaggerate lip and facial movements. Try looking in the mirror sometime while reciting "Mary Had a Little Lamb" with exaggerated facial expression and a shouting voice. Who would want to look at such efforts all day? Hands and books should be held away from the face when speaking to a child with a hearing loss. And if the child does not understand, rephrasing or restating is better than repeating what was said.

Seating arrangements should be such that a child with a hearing loss has his back to the light (actually a good idea for seating all children). With the light off the child's face he or she will be better able to watch the speaker.

It is also important to keep in mind that lip reading requires constant attention and concentration (try it for half an hour; ask a friend to whisper while you watch his lips). Thus the child who depends heavily on lip reading will get tired and need time to rest.

Because hearing loss often affects speech and confidence in oral language situations, particular attention should be given to structuring activities that the child can engage in successfully. Others in the school—special teachers, clerks, etc.—should be aware of the child's hearing loss so that they can cooperate with you in your efforts. A child with a hearing loss often needs to develop skill in auditory discrimination. Although not every child who has a hearing loss has undeveloped auditory discrimination skill, nor is every child who needs auditory discrimination training suffering a hearing loss, being able to discriminate among speech sounds is important to success in using language. Listening and readiness activities such as those suggested in chapters 5 and 14 will help children develop this ability.

OTHER PHYSICAL HANDICAPS

Children who are physically handicapped can usually be taught in the regular classroom if sensible adjustments are made to care for their handicaps so that learning problems do not develop or are not aggravated. In working with any physically handicapped child, a teacher must help him acquire a common sense viewpoint in regard to his strengths and limitations and to life itself and must provide experiences that are realistic but can be handled with the particular handicap.

Types of Handicaps

There are many types of physical handicaps other than hearing and vision losses, and some speech problems have a physical base. Many of these physical handicaps are manifested in slight impairments of movement. Children with severe handicaps, such as serious cardiac conditions, will usually not be in regular classrooms. But many children with serious physical problems, such as epilepsy or the loss of a limb, have learned to function in a group setting like the classroom. In general, doctors seek to let physically handicapped children be with their peers in normal settings. There are also many borderline "special" children—children with a rather minor physical defect or a temporary or permanent crippling condition. These children are generally in the regular classroom, and they may be especially sensitive to their physical problems, even though these may not be of a serious nature. Certainly whenever the child regards himself as handicapped, he must be treated as a "special" child.

Instructional Provisions

Special classroom arrangements must be made for a child who is in a wheelchair or who otherwise needs help in moving about. Special tables, desks, and other work areas will need to be arranged, and usually changes will need to be made in schedules and routine activities of the classroom.

Many children with physical defects have gaps in their experiential lives. They have missed some of the so-called normal experiences that much of the school curriculum is built upon. Thus, special provision may need to be made for extra films, excursions, and demonstrations. These extra activities can be the basis for many language arts activities—and physically handicapped children can engage in most language activities.

Attention often needs to be given to the child's special social needs—his relationships with parents, peers, and personnel of the school. The child may need social contacts that he has not had, physical activity that has been avoided, and the general opportunity to extend himself as a person. Certainly physical limitations and any special problems related to them must be known before efforts are made in these areas. This means that the teacher must have some contact with the child's physician, parents, and other specialists who are also working with him.

A physical handicap often brings about an emotional condition that is reflected in behavior and learning problems. Helping the child to overcome such problems and to adjust to conditions that cannot be overcome is often the teacher's most important task, and there is no easy way to do this. Certainly a teacher must extend himself as a sensitive human—this is a broad concept, one that includes the very best of teaching practices and true attention to needs, interests, and abilities. The basis for the teaching that needs to be done is often in providing a means for the child to recognize his own problem and to work on it himself.

The Issue of Learning Disabilities

Sometimes there are children in classrooms who apparently experience extreme difficulty in maintaining "grade level progress" (most often in reading, but also in language expression and mathematics), who are not known to have "physical, emotional, or motivational difficulties which could account for their problems."[9] These children are frequently said to have "learning disabilities."

Labeling children has too often been an educational diversion used to avoid facing up to the teaching problems some children present. The process of labeling has tended to fragment teaching efforts into dealing with the "fortunate and unfortunate, can do and can't do, normal and abnormal."[10] Yet there is hope that the new "learning disabilities" movement may result in new approaches to instructional tasks rather than extending the stigmatizing of children or providing an excuse for poor teaching or parental neglect.

Children from other cultures and those economically or socially handicapped may have emotional and/or motivational problems in some school settings. This does not mean that these children are disabled learners. Of course, some may be.

Definitions and Labels

A learning disability may be defined as a condition that prevents an intellectually and physically normal child from absorbing knowledge, organizing experience, and expressing the synthesis of these in ideas and actions at the level of his or her true potential. This is a broad definition—and deliberately so, since there tend to be almost as many definitions as people doing the defining. However, the common element in all the definitions—and in the terminology applied to specific types of disabilities—is that learning achievement is highly unsatisfactory when compared to the apparent learning potential.

Some educators prefer the term *learning disorder* to learning disability, since disorder implies that something is out of order that can be fixed. Others point out that learning disabilities may have their bases in brain injuries, perceptual handicaps, or minimal brain dysfunctions.

A related term increasingly being used is *dyslexia.* It has also been variously defined. One definition is that it is "one type of reading, spelling or writing disability which is not caused by low intelligence per se."[11] The source of this definition adds that the disability is not primarily caused by such factors as emotional disturbances and organ deficits, but that children with low intelligence, emo-

Possible Symptoms of Learning Disabilities

inattentiveness
aggressiveness
impulsiveness
shyness
lack of organization
overexcitability
speech irregularities
perceptual difficulties
lethargy

tional problems, etc., may have dyslexia. However, the same author classifies "primary emotional communication causes," "minimal neurological dysfunction," "genetic dyslexia," and "social, cultural or educational deprivation" in a table listing the "causes and types of dyslexia."[12]

We have not meant to confuse you by these definitions—if for no other reason than that the professional confusion should not be added to. Our purpose is to make you both concerned about children who have learning disabilities such as those described and cautious about the application of labels. We also think you should be reminded that labeling—or even identifying children's problems—does not remedy the learning difficulty. It is a fact that there are children who seem to be genuinely disabled in their learning ability by a disablement or disorder that is not easily explained or determined. However, the number of children identified as having a learning disability—of whatever nature—has increased as the literature on the subject has increased, which may indicate better identification being done. On the other hand, the more skeptical will say that the number of children so identified has increased as the commercial materials and programs prepared for them have become more abundant.

For materials write:

Association for Children with Learning Disabilities, 4156 Library Road, Pittsburgh, PA 15234

U. S. Office of Education, Bureau of Education for the Handicapped, Suite 4030, Donohoe Bldg. 6th and D streets, S. W., Washington, DC 20202

Instructional Provisions

Many techniques and procedures have been suggested for working with children who have special disabilities. However, as one book on the subject reports, "There is very little evidence of research which indicates static procedures or techniques" for teaching disabled children.[13] This source goes on to indicate that "Some things work for some children and some things work for other children." Surely this suggests that attention should be given to children's individual needs and that individual readiness for learning must be observed—to repeat a theme of much of this book.

In most cases, a child who is regarded as having a learning disability needs to develop patterns of behavior that he or she uses without conscious thought. Such a child needs to be taken back to the foundational levels of visual, auditory, and motor learning skills that were not acquired in previous learning experiences. In the following chapters, factors involved in the initial learning of various language skills are listed, along with suggestions for identifying deficiencies and developing skills. These suggestions are applicable to teaching children with learning disabilities, particularly if they are applied to specific disorders and what is to be learned is presented in a graduated sequence of small steps. Teachers should also stress the social value of what is to be learned and, of course, each child must be respected as an individual.

THE EMOTIONALLY AND BEHAVIORALLY MALADJUSTED

As with learning disabilities, how one defines the emotionally or behaviorally disturbed child depends largely on who is doing the defining. Many teachers, at one time or another, have considered a child who misbehaves more than the other children in a class to be emotionally disturbed. The same feelings have surely also been experienced by some parents.

In considering emotional and behavior problems, one must recognize the fact that every child is growing, changing, and developing in a nonstatic world and that so-called normal behavior in that world is difficult to describe. What is acceptable behavior at one time and place may not be in another. Definitions such as those which say the emotionally disturbed child is "one who cannot emotionally, intellectually, and socially function in a manner that is acceptable to his peers, teachers, parents, and legal authorities within his school, home, and community environment"[11] are less than helpful, since they bring to our minds the question "Who can?"

It is true that there are children with psychoses, neuroses, and personality disorders—just as there are such people in the adult population. A physical or intellectual handicap may bring about emotional maladjustments. Similar maladjustments may arise from the child's size, appearance, or degree of social maturity. The child who is careless, lazy, spoiled, or immature has a learning maladjustment. So does the one who displays an antisocial attitude, emotional instability, or hyperactive behavior.

On the other hand, many children manifest transient and situational behaviors that do not warrant their being identified as emotionally disturbed. Too often labeling is a rationalization by the school and the home for improper attention to the needs the children have shown. We think that the increase in the number of children considered emotionally disturbed and the refuge into treatment by drugs should cause all teachers to think about whether the roots of many of the problems of these children are in the teaching practices and the school program. Identifying children's particular problems is not providing the teaching they need. Of course, the determination of a child's specific problems and needs should lead to more effective instruction; the question is whether or not this is happening.

A child with a behavior problem—an emotional handicap—does not respond positively to prodding or coercing. Such procedures will usually reactivate or reinforce his rebelliousness, negativism, or escapism. To gain any rapport at all with many of these children requires a great amount of patience. This patience needs to be shown in understanding, sympathy, and friendliness, but it also needs to be shown in firm controls and fair limitations. The child needs to feel accepted, but he also needs to learn that you accept all the other children and respect their rights as well as his. Above all, you should not retreat from attempting to teach him, and he should understand that you have expectations that he will learn.

Children are often unaware that they possess an undesirable trait or an unhealthy attitude, and telling them that they have it is not effective. However, if the child meets someone in a story who is like himself, the situation is different. It is helpful, therefore, to use stories and books about particular handicaps, behavioral traits, and personality problems as much as possible. Many teachers have developed files of such books and stories (include title, short summary, reading level, and where the book or story can be found) because of the number of these children in normal classrooms. In the following chapter we suggest some books that are helpful in building the self-image of disadvantaged children. Books related to other possible learning handicaps are suggested at the close of this chapter. These are only suggestions; there are many other useful books available.

A teacher should know if a child is receiving medical or psychological treatment. If you do not know, but suspect that this may be the case, ask the parents.

CHILDREN WITH LANGUAGE DIFFERENCES

Who are the children?

- Black children who live in the ghettos of cities or in poor rural areas.
- Children without English language backgrounds, especially Puerto Ricans and immigrants from eastern and southern Europe and Mexico.
- Children of poor whites in the South, the Appalachian mountain regions, and the city locations to which these people have moved.
- American Indian children.
- Children of migrant workers.

A child with a speech or hearing impairment may also be a ''quiet one.''

Education has always been a major road to social advancement and economic success in society; thus it is something of a blow to most of us to realize that the school itself often complicates and adds to the problems of teaching some children. In the past the schools dealt reasonably well with the majority of immigrants' children, but today the schools are not experiencing similar success with the children of the poor, minority racial groups, and many more recent immigrants. Perhaps one difference is that the ''melting pot'' concept of America is being replaced by one of cultural pluralism, with the result that not all children are eager to imitate the teacher and learn the language of the school. Perhaps also, the earlier ''success'' was not really as complete as it appeared, because some children either dropped out of school or never attended.

Today, since fewer and fewer jobs are available to the young, the unskilled, and the uneducated, educators and governmental groups are attempting to discover and eliminate the causes of students dropping out of school. And more and more people are demanding an education—not just enough to meet minimal literacy standards but secondary and higher education as well. This is bringing about a wider range of individual differences among students in the schools, particularly in language abilities, and a greater demand for effective instructional procedures to deal with these differences.

Understanding the Child

Since the use of language is fundamental to the task of the school, a child who knows that his or her language (or dialect) is different from that of other children in the classroom will often not talk very much. Possibly such directions as ''Hang up your wraps'' or ''Wash after you go to the lavatory'' may be met with what is interpreted by the teacher as defiance or inattention, but the problem might actually be a lack of understanding.

A second possible cause of withdrawal and seeming inattention may well be hunger and fatigue, for these children often come from poor homes—and these are conditions usually associated with poverty. Undernourished children do not learn as efficiently as well-fed ones; therefore, such a child should receive extra patience and encouragement.

Finally, the child who feels alien to the school environment may well develop feelings of insecurity and inferiority; thus he or she will almost certainly need help in building a stronger self-image. This child needs understanding and assistance in overcoming inferiority feelings and in becoming a contributing member of the group. At the same time he needs to get this help in a manner that does not single him out as being particularly different from or inferior to the other children in the class.

Building the Child's Identity

When teaching a child the English of the school it is basic to truly believe that neither a child's thinking abilities nor any other of his qualities as a human being are being "improved." We do believe that it is important for a child to speak English in a dialect that will not later be handicapping to him if he is to be educated in the school as it is presently structured (and this is a structure that is not likely to change substantially). But this child must be respected in the same way a teacher respects other children who show deficiencies in skills or knowledge important to their future success in school.

As has been pointed out in many other sections of this book, family and cultural ties are important to every person and must be given prime consideration in instruction. A child's earliest thoughts are of home and family, and his native language or dialect is a very important part of this background. A child's personal dignity is inseparable from his early background—a fact that every teacher should remember. To abuse or dishonor a child's heritage by condemning his language in any way degrades the child and shows a lack of sensitivity to humankind. Beyond that, there is the very practical fact that the desire of a child to learn a new language depends heavily upon the attitude he has about his own worth as an individual.

A first step in helping the non-English-speaking child retain his identity while he learns the language of the school is to understand his heritage. Learn as much as possible about the child's native country, its customs and history, its values and traditions, and its language. Although it may not be possible to learn the language, some expressions—greetings, school and home words, and other words that are used often—can be learned.

Perhaps the child can be encouraged to teach the other children words and customs that have been and still are important to him. Someone from the child's native land—possibly one of his parents, if they speak English—can be invited to the classroom for a special program or as a resource person when the child's homeland is being studied. Since all children are interested in the dress, art, music, customs, and food of a country, this is a good opportunity not only to enhance this child's self-image but also to make all the children knowledgeable about and appreciative of other cultures.

In a similar manner, children who speak non-standard English can be made to feel that their identities are important. This will not be as difficult as some might imagine, since we are a mobile people, each of us retaining at least some elements of his or her heritage. Exchanging information about words and expressions, customs, favorite foods, etc., can enrich all the children.

In addition to having a positive feeling about himself or herself, the child needs a similar attitude toward school and the language used in school. Thus the child needs affirmation not only of his or her identity as a person but also of the ability to achieve success in this new world. Whether he is in the kindergarten or a higher grade, he needs to participate in classroom activities—games, duties, projects—that he is capable of handling and that are enjoyable. He needs to gain new confidence about this strange place before tasks are made difficult for him.

Self-images are not built in a few months or even a few years; the feelings a child has about himself are the result of all his experiences, including his environment, his family, and his observations of others. But working for even a short time (e.g., the year a child is in your class) on helping a child build a more positive feeling toward himself is worthwhile and is fundamental to teaching the skills and knowledge he needs.

Build the child's self-concept

1. By taking pictures of him and things he has done.
2. By listening to him tell about himself and sometimes writing accounts of his experiences for him.
3. By having objects or pictures related to his race or culture in the classroom.
4. By making him the leader in games and other activities he does well.
5. By respecting him as a person at all times.

A catalog listing materials, objects, and symbols related to the Chicano experience can be obtained from Bilingual Education Services, P.O. Box 669, 1508 Oxley St., Pasadena, CA 91030.

Dialects and Teaching

The teaching of acceptable language usage is discussed in the following chapter. There is also reference to it in the following section since teaching standard English to children whose dialects are substantially different from that standard is not unlike teaching English to native speakers of another language. A nonstandard dialect and standard English differ at specific interference or contrast points, and these are the points that must receive particular instructional attention. On the other hand, there are differences between learning a second language and learning a second dialect. Probably the most important of these is that it is more difficult to motivate the learning of a second dialect. Also, a speaker of a nonstandard dialect has little or no trouble understanding most speakers of standard English—or at least grasping their fundamental meaning (though the opposite is less likely to be true). But the level of understanding may suffer considerably as standard English is met in print.

Points of interference or difference between standard and nonstandard English have been identified by linguists.[15] These features or points of interference can serve as the bases for teaching standard English using foreign language teaching procedures.

Teachers themselves can determine in a nontechnical way the features of two dialects that are different. Both phonological and grammatical differences should be noted if they appear consistently and are such that their use would sound out of place in conversation among educated Americans.

In essence, the strategy for teaching a second dialect "amounts to teaching the smallest possible number of vitally significant items—and *teaching each of them hard.*"[16] Implementing this strategy successfully requires a long-term teaching effort that helps children recognize that the dialects are different, understand the reasons for language differences between people, and know the social situations in which it is appropriate to use the second dialect rather than the first. Although children can be taught to hear phonological differences and to recognize grammatical ones and can be drilled so that they repeat phrases and sentences in the second dialect, the new dialect will not be used effectively if the children do not have a favorable attitude toward it.

It is important for a teacher to be fully aware of the implications of the fact that we all speak in different ways as we engage in different activities. Not only do well educated, partly educated, and uneducated people speak the dialects of their geographical regions and societal settings, but they all speak different varieties of those dialects. In addition, almost everyone has differences in levels of style or formality in speaking and writing.

Educators have increasingly come to accept the point of view that it is educationally unsound to attempt to obliterate a child's native dialect and to replace it with standard English. This has led to stressing functional bidialectalism, in which the speaker uses the dialect appropriate to the situation in which he finds himself. Yet even this viewpoint has come under attack by those who insist that in a pluralistic society, the child's language should not be tampered with at all.[17] However, it is fair to ask, as one prominent linguist has done, "whether dialect switching is essentially different from the style shifting characteristic of most of us as we go from a formal to a casual situation."[18]

The issue is largely one of the extent to which a nonstandard dialect is stig-

---

For help and information write:

National Committee on Education of Migrant Children 145 E. 32nd St., New York, NY 10016

National Advisory Council on the Education of Disadvantaged Children 1717 H St., N.W., Washington, DC 20009

Black Child Development Educational Center 1028 Connecticut Ave., N.W., Suite 601, Washington, DC 20036

Additional sources of information:

Association of American Indian Affairs, Inc. 432 Park Avenue South, New York, NY 10016

Institute of American Indian Arts, Bureau of Indian Affairs, U.S. Department of Interior, Cerillos Road, Santa Fe, New Mexico

Inter-Tribal Indian Ceremonial Assoc., P.O. Box 1029, Gallup, New Mexico 87310

matizing to an individual (although some persons argue that grammatical and phonological differences impede a child's ability to learn to read), since there seems to be no doubt that people do use at least features of more than one dialect. In fact, Bailey reports on children " . . . shifting from black English to the standard and back. . . .," citing as an example the speech of the child who said, "I ain't had my play clothes on" and "I did not" in one situation and, "No, that's not cash money" and "That ain't no cash money" in another.[19]

TEACHING ENGLISH AS A SECOND LANGUAGE

A variety of methods for teaching a new language to children have been suggested and tried in schools, with varying degrees of success. Some teachers have felt that children can best learn a second language by exposure to it—a "catching" process. Others have stressed learning vocabulary or grammar. Some programs have segregated the non-English-speaking pupils, thus ignoring the motivation that comes from attempts to communicate with peers. However, the most successful procedure seems to be one that focuses upon imitation and memorization of basic elements of oral communication as they are used by native speakers. The essence of the procedure is the identification of the points of difference or interference between the two languages, followed by the development of an aural–oral program for dealing with these points.[20]

The teacher does not need to assume total responsibility for teaching the non-English-speaking child; the children in the class who speak English can help. Although children are naturally accepting, they can also be cruel, so they must be shown how to give this help. First, like the teacher, they must learn to respect the child's native language and his or her culture. Imitation of teacher attitudes and general classroom atmosphere are factors here, but it is also a good idea to plan a study of the country, language, and customs of each non-native child early in the year.

Even before that, though, a child who speaks English can be asked to serve as a "special friend" for a non-English-speaking one. This special friend will be particularly helpful, since the two children will soon learn to communicate with one another. Children assigned as "special friends" can be given some quick coaching, but they will usually take their assignments seriously and may do more for the non-English-speaking child than you can.

Principles

The aural–oral method is generally recognized as the most effective procedure in teaching English as a second language. This approach stresses the importance of hearing and speaking with purpose and understanding. It avoids many of the problems that arise when emphasis is given to grammar study and to writing and reading the new language. The following are recommended guidelines for teaching English as a second language:

1. The focus should be on oral activity. Specific English expressions should be listened to and spoken.

2. The language forms or patterns taught should be taken from the natural English speech of children. Attention should be given to the conversational speed, intonation patterns and stress, and idiomatic uses of the native child speaker of English.
3. The tape recorder provides a good means for gaining samples of speech, for listening to the forms being taught, and for allowing the child to listen to himself. Other audiovisual aids are particularly helpful in teaching meanings of words and expressions through pictures and actual objects.
4. The teacher sets a model for quality of speech, so he must actually be this model or provide the model by means of tapes and records.
5. The child should not be pushed into reading. Not only does he have a language handicap, but he has had a different experiential background from that of native speakers of English. Attempting to teach a child to read before he has the language and experiential readiness for it is an inexcusable waste of both your time and the child's.
6. The basic procedure should be one of drill on language patterns selected on the basis of a contrastive analysis of English and the child's native language. The emphasis in the drill should be on the language patterns known to be the most difficult to learn.
7. Language drills should be related as closely as possible to actual classroom experiences. The emphasis in the drill is on imitation of the model, including the pronunciation the model gives to words. Some separate drill on making particular sounds will probably be needed.
8. Making the sounds of English is difficult, so a sympathetic noncritical climate in the classroom is important. Overcorrecting a child's pronunciation, accent, or speech patterns should be avoided.
9. The child's native language should not be used during the teaching or drill sessions, since translation interferes with the automatic responses that are necessary.

Techniques

There are many techniques for presenting English to a nonspeaker that are based on the aural–oral approach. A number of these are suggested below. Each one can lead to teaching situations made unique by the personalities, attitudes, and interactions of the individuals involved. That is, these are not "patterns" or "the way to do it" but are suggestions that may be useful in developing procedures for a specific classroom.

Suggested Items for an Object Box

knife	mirror
fork	comb
spoon	hairbrush
plate	watch
glass	button
chalk	eyeglasses
notebook	purse
scissors	string
key	hammer
soap	nail
money	shoelaces

Teaching Vocabulary and Language Structure Directly.   Direct instruction is essentially a drill procedure in which an object, a specific action, or an idea is associated with the word or expression that names, describes, or explains it. A very useful tool to have is an "object box." Objects can be selected from the box and identified by a simple sentence—for example, "This is a spoon." At first, the teacher should select the object, but later a child can select objects or two children can use the box for a game (one should be a native speaker of English). The child should always repeat the entire sentence, usually while handling the object.

For direct teaching of action words and expressions, objects will not be helpful (except in the teaching of words such as *cut*, in which case scissors, a knife, etc., would be needed). Many actions can be demonstrated by the teacher, an aide, or other children.

Ideas can be directly shown by placing something *in* a box, holding an object *above* a desk, taking a book *from* a shelf, etc. Of course, more complicated ideas are difficult to show directly because they involve several concepts. Some of these—for example, "helping one another"—can be demonstrated in the class-

Motivating language learning with games.

room if time is taken to do so.

Using Media.   Pictures can be used in somewhat the same way as objects to show actions and ideas. Pictures can be the basis for stories and games in which the idea or action is pointed to and appropriate sentences are constructed for the child to repeat. Pictures can also be used as the basis for questions that require the beginning speaker of English to formulate responses. A picture file (added to regularly) is of course helpful to every teacher, whether he has non-English speakers in class or not. The file should be organized by major topics—communications, sports, animals, ways people live, bodies of water, foods, etc.—with subdivisions for each and perhaps some cross-referencing so that pictures can readily be found and related to the vocabulary and structures that need to be taught.

In a similar way, other materials can be used for children to talk about and as a basis for the construction of drill sentences. These include advertisements, news items, comic strips, games, and books.

Stories and poetry can also be used to present new vocabulary and structures. The selection should be read and reread—possibly only one section at a time—until the children show understanding by their ability to answer specific questions. Using several readings will also help lead children into understanding new concepts by relating them to known ones, and will aid them in memorizing many structures. If this memorization does not occur from the repetition of the reading, memorization drills may be used for teaching the most important structures.

Using Pattern Drills

Pattern drills are used to teach structures basic to communication in standard English. The procedure is basically one of constant repetition until the structures have been learned. The drills should be simple and easy so that children have the

See chapters 5 and 9 for further suggestions and examples.

opportunity to use language successfully, and they should focus upon the stress and intonation given to commonly used English expressions. They should include sentence patterns in which a substitution is made for one of the words in the pattern (This is a *ball*, This is a ____ ; John runs fast, John ____ fast); questions that force a response of a particular pattern (Are you going to the store? *Yes, I am*); and sentences that call for a response in which the order is changed (Joan has a torn dress, *Joan's dress is torn*), the sentence is expanded or reduced (There is a box on the table, *There is a big red box on the center table*), or two sentences are combined into one (Bill has a bicycle. The bicycle was lost. *Bill's bicycle was lost*).[8]

Perhaps the most important type of drill is that in which specific contrasts in pronunciation are emphasized. The drill material may be words, phrases, or sentences, but in each case the entire context is the same except for one sound. Following are some samples.

bat	my bell	We will shop here.
hat	my ball	We will stop here.

A FINAL WORD

Since most classrooms include children with some of the impairments, disabilities, handicaps, or problems identified in this chapter, careful planning of language arts programs and sensitive and informed teaching is necessary. With the increased "mainstreaming" of children formerly segregated into special education classrooms, as well as the increasing elimination of racial and social/economic segregation of children, a good many schools need to look at their curriculum and teaching practices. But, as we try to stress throughout this book, there is no substitute for good teaching. Good teaching means acceptance of all children, diagnosis of their needs and interests, and direct and individualized attention to these needs and interests.

ENDNOTES

1. Bernard G. Suran and Joseph V. Rizzo, *Special Children: An Integrative Approach* (Chicago: Scott, Foresman, 1979), p. 15.

2. Ibid., p. 439.

3. A point that is often not clear is that mainstreaming not only involves placement of handicapped children in classrooms with their nonhandicapped peers but also requires that supportive services for these children be supplied so as to ensure that they have successful educational experiences. See Suran and Rizzo, *Special Children*, p. 444.

4. The authors recognize that the educational literature abounds with conflicting descriptions and definitions of many of the terms used in this chapter. We have used terms that we believe to be most acceptable, and we do not think that attempting to define such fine points as the many aspects of neurological impairment or learning disabilities—for example—warrants the use of the space it would take.

5. A fully annotated booklist by Thomas Horn and Dorothy Ebert, *Books for the Partially Sighted Child*, is available from the National Council of Teachers of English, Urbana, IL.

6. Alan W. Huckleberry and Edward S. Strother, *Speech Education for the Elementary Teacher*, 2nd ed. (Boston: Allyn and Bacon, Inc., 1972), p. 285.

7. See also Jon Eisenson and Mardel Ogilvie, *Speech Correction in the Schools*, 2nd ed. (New York: The Macmillan Co., 1969) and other references at the end of this chapter.

8. Virgil A. Anderson and Hayes A. Newby, *Improving the Child's Speech*, 2nd ed. (New York: Oxford University Press, 1973), p. 23.

9. James F. Winschel and Elizabeth A. Lawrence, "Learning Disabilities: A Critical Exposure" in *Orientation to Language and Learning Disorders*, Mitchell R. Burkowsky, ed. (St. Louis: Warren H. Green, Inc., 1973), p. 10.

10. Ibid., p. 4.

11. Alexander Bannatyne, *Language, Reading and Learning Disabilities* (Springfield, IL: Charles C. Thomas Publisher, 1971), p. 16.

12. Ibid., p. 18.

13. William R. Van Osdel and Don G. Shane, *An Introduction to Exceptional Children* (Dubuque, IA: Wm. C. Brown Company, Publishers, 1974), p. 203.

14. Ibid., p. 229.

15. See Kenneth R. Johnson, "Standard English and Disadvantaged Black Children: Teaching Strategies," in William W. Joyce and James A. Banks, eds., *Teaching the Language Arts to Culturally Different Children* (Reading, MA: Addison-Wesley Publishing Co., 1971), p. 123; and Roger W. Shuy, "Nonstandard Dialect Problems: An Overview," in James L. Laffey and Roger Shuy, eds., *Language Differences: Do They Interfere?* (Newark, DE: International Reading Association, 1973), pp. 8–9.

16. Virginia F. Allen, "Teaching Standard English as a Second Dialect," *Teachers College Record* (February 1967), pp. 355–370.

17. The most detailed—and yet cautious—statement on this position is "Students' Right to Their Own Language," which has appeared in numerous National Council of Teachers of English publications since it was first published in a special fall 1974 issue of *College Composition and Communication*.

18. Albert H. Marckwardt, "The Nature of Language and of Language Learning," in Robert P. Fox, ed., *Teaching English as a Second Language and as a Second Dialect* (Urbana, IL: National Council of Teachers of English, 1973), p. 29.

19. Beryl Loftman Bailey, "Some Principles of Bilingual and Bidialectal Education," in Fox, *Teaching English as a Second Language*, p. 113.

20. Since there is great variety in approaches to teaching English as a second language—and many books written about it—we suggest that you may want to contact one or all of these organizations for information and suggestions: American Council on the Teaching of Foreign Languages, 62 Fifth Avenue, New York, NY 10011; Teachers of English to Speakers of Other Languages, School of Languages and Linguistics, Georgetown University, Washington, DC 20007; and National Council of Teachers of English, 1111 Kenyon Road, Urbana, IL 61801.

REFERENCES

Books

Bailey, Richard W., and Robinson, Jay L., eds. *Varieties of Present-Day English*. New York: The Macmillan Co., 1973.

Cheney, Arnold B. *Teaching Children of Different Cultures in the Classroom, A Language Approach*, 2nd ed. Columbus, OH: Charles E. Merrill, 1976.

Dunn, Lloyd M., ed. *Exceptional Children in the*

Schools: Special Education in Transition. New York: Holt, Rinehart, and Winston, 1973.

Fox, Robert P., ed. *Teaching English as a Second Language and as a Second Dialect.* Urbana, IL: National Council of Teachers of English, 1973.

Gallagher, James. *Teaching the Gifted Child,* 2nd ed. Boston: Allyn and Bacon, 1975

Huckleberry, Alan W., and Strother, Edward S. *Speech Education for the Elementary Teacher,* 2nd ed. Boston: Allyn and Bacon, Inc., 1972.

Joyce, William W., and Banks, James A. *Teaching the Language Arts to Culturally Different Children.* Reading, MA: Addison-Wesley Publishing Co., 1971.

Knight, Lester N. *Language Arts for the Exceptional: The Gifted and The Linguistically Different.* Itasca, IL: F. E. Peacock Publishers, 1974.

Mainstreaming Series. Boston: Teaching Resources (15 paperbound books with such titles as *Mainstreaming Exceptional Children, Managing the Hyperactive Child in the Classroom, Mainstreaming the Mentally Retarded Child,* etc.).

Meyen, Edward L., et al., *Instructional Planning for Exceptional Children.* Denver: Love Publishing Co. 1978.

Suran, Bernard G., and Rozzo, Joseph V. *Special Children: An Integrative Approach.* Chicago: Scott, Foresman, 1979.

Books about Gifted Children*

Barne, Kitty. *Barbie.* Boston: Little, Brown, 1969.

Fitzhugh, Louise. *Harriet the Spy.* New York: Harper and Row, 1964.

Books about Mentally Retarded Children

Byars, Betsy. *Summer of the Swans.* New York: Viking Press, 1970.

Little, Jean. *Take Wing.* Boston: Little, Brown, 1968.

Wrightson, Patricia. *A Racecourse for Andy.* New York: Harcourt Brace Jovanovich, 1968.

---

* There are many books for children related to the content of this chapter, and new ones are coming out each year. The lists on these pages merely suggest some that you may want to examine.

Books about Children with Physical Handicaps

Angelo, Valenti. *Hill of Little Miracles.* New York: The Viking Press (Crippled).

Beim, Jerrold. *Sunshine and Shadow.* New York: Harcourt Brace Jovanovich (Paralyzed).

Branfield, John. *Why Me?* New York: Harper and Row (Diabetic).

Burnett, Frances H. *The Secret Garden.* Philadelphia: J. B. Lippincott Co. (Crippled).

Canty, Mary. *The Green Gate.* New York: David McKay (Blindness).

Cunningham, Julia. *Burnish Me Bright.* New York: Pantheon (Mute).

De Angeli, Marguerite. *Door in the Wall.* Garden City, NY: Doubleday and Co. (Crippled).

Frick, C. H. *Five against the Odds.* New York: Harcourt Brace Jovanovich (Lameness).

Garfield, James. *Follow My Leader.* New York: Viking Press (Blindness).

Killilea, Marie. *Wren.* New York: Dodd, Mead (Cerebral palsy).

Little, Jean. *Mine for Keeps.* Boston: Little, Brown (Cerebral Palsy).

Robinson, Veronica. *David in Silence.* Philadelphia: J. B. Lippincott Co. (Hearing).

Southall, Ivan. *Let the Balloon Go.* New York: Martins (Spastic).

Books about Children with Behavior and Personality Problems

Beim, Jerrold. *Just Plain Maggie.* New York: Harcourt Brace Jovanovich (Social immaturity; intermediate).

———. *Taming of Toby.* New York: William Morrow and Co. (Self-control; primary and intermediate).

Boutwell, Edna. *Red Rooster.* New York: E. P. Dutton and Co. (Self-image; primary).

Calhoun, Mary. *The Nine Lives of Homer C. Cat.* New York: William Morrow and Co. (Show-off; primary).

Eichenberger, Rosa K. *Bronko.* New York: William Morrow and Co. (Immigrant adjustment; intermediate and upper).

Estes, Eleanor. *The Hundred Dresses.* New York: Harcourt Brace Jovanovich (Superiority; intermediate).

Fern, Eugene. *The Most Frightened Hero.* New York: Coward-McCann, Inc. (Timidity; primary).

Forbes, Esther. *Johnny Tremain.* Boston: Houghton Mifflin Co. (Arrogance; upper).

Friedman, Frieda. *Janitor's Girl.* New York: William Morrow and Co. (Snobbishness; intermediate and upper).

Harrison, Crane Blossom. *The Odd One.* Boston: Little, Brown and Co. (Antisocial; upper).

Henry, Marguerite. *Geraldine Belinda.* New York: Platt and Munk. (Selfishness; primary).

L'Engle, Madeline. *Meet the Austins.* New York: Vanguard Press. (Spoiled; upper).

Lexau, Joan. *Benjie.* New York: Dial (Shyness; primary).

Lord, Berman. *Rough Ice.* New York: Henry C. Walck, Inc. (Procrastination; intermediate).

Miller, Jane. *The Ill-tempered Tiger.* Philadelphia: J. B. Lippincott Co. (Bad manners; primary).

Schlein, Miriam. *The Way Mothers Are.* Racine, WI: Whitman Publishing Co. (Anxieties; primary).

Tunis, John. *Highpockets.* New York: William Morrow and Co. (Conceit; upper).

Wilson, Christopher B. *Hobnob.* New York: The Viking Press. (Sharing; primary).

Books about Children with Appearance Problems

Barr, Catherine. *Little Ben.* New York: Walck (Undersize; primary).

Beim, Jerrold. *Smallest Boy in the Class.* New York: William Morrow and Co. (Undersize; primary).

Felsen, Gregor. *Hepatica Hawks.* New York: The Macmillan Co. (Fat; upper).

Godden, Rumer. *The Fairy Doll.* New York: The Viking Press (Short, fat and clumsy; upper).

McGinley, Phyllis. *Plain Princess.* Philadelphia: J. B. Lippincott Co. (Plain; primary).

Meader, Stephen. *Spark Plug of the Hornets.* New York: Harcourt Brace Jovanovich (Undersize; intermediate).

Stanek, Muriel. *Tall Tina.* Chicago: Albert Whitman and Company (Large size; intermediate).

Books about Puerto Rican Children

Anderson, Mary. *Just the Two of Them.* New York: Atheneum, 1974.

Bouchard, Lois. *The Boy Who Wouldn't Talk.* New York: Doubleday, 1969.

Buckley, Peter. *I Am from Puerto Rico.* New York: Simon and Schuster, 1971.

Edell, Celeste. *Present from Rosita.* New York: Julian Messner, 1967.

Keats, Ezra Jack, and Cherr, Pat. *My Dog Is Lost.* New York: Thomas Y. Crowell Company, 1960.

Lewiton, Mina. *Candita's Choice.* New York: Harper and Row, 1959.

Mann, Peggy. *How Juan Got Home.* New York: Coward-McCann, 1972.

Mohr, Nicholasa, *Nilda.* New York: Harper and Row, 1973.

Sonneborn, Ruth A. *Friday Night Is Papa Night.* New York: Viking Press, 1970.

Weiner, Sandra. *They Call Me Jack.* New York: Pantheon, 1973.

Books about Chicano Children*

Agnew, Edith J. *Treasure for Tomas.* New York: Friendship Press, 1964.

Buffler, Esther. *Rodrigo and Rosalita.* Austin, TX: The Steck Company, 1949.

Bulla, Clyde Robert. *Benito.* New York: Crowell-Collier Press, 1961.

Clark, Ann Nolan. *Paco's Miracle.* New York: Farrar Straus and Co., 1962.

Ets, Marie Hall. *Gilberto and the Wind.* New York: Viking Press, 1963.

Krumgold, Joseph. *And Now Miguel.* New York: Crowell-Collier Press, 1953.

Lampman, Evelyn S. *Go Up the Road.* New York: Atheneum, 1976.

Lecht, Jane. *Two Surprises.* New York: American Book Company, 1965.

Politi, Leo. *Rosa.* New York: Charles Scribners Sons, 1963.

Schweitzer, Byrd Baylor. *Amigo.* New York: The Macmillan Co., 1963.

Books about Native Americans

Baker, Alex W. *The Picture-Skin Story.* New York: Holiday House, 1968.

Baker, Betty. *Little Runners of the Longhouse.* New York: Harper and Row, 1962.

---

*Write to the Commission for Mexican Affairs, 1514 Buena Vista Street, San Antonio, Texas 78207, for a catalog containing lists of books, posters, films, magazines, journals, etc., related to the Chicano experience.

Beatty, Hetty B. *Little Owl Indian.* Boston: Houghton Mifflin Company, 1951.

Brewster, Benjamin. *The First Book of Indians.* New York: Franklin Watts, 1950.

Bulla, Clyde Robert. *Indian Hill.* New York: Thomas Y. Crowell, 1963.

Clark, Ann Nolan. *Sun Journey.* Washington, DC: U.S. Government Printing Office, 1945.

Clymer, Eleanor. *The Spider, the Cave and the Pottery Bowl.* New York: Holt, Rinehart and Winston, 1973.

Floethe, Louise Lee. *Sea of Grass.* New York: Charles Scribner's Sons, 1963.

Kirk, Ruth. *David, Young Chief of the Quileutes: An American Indian Today.* New York: Harcourt Brace Jovanovich, 1967.

Lampman, Evelyn S. *The Potlatch Family.* New York: Atheneum, 1976.

Louis, Ray Baldwin. *Child of the Hogan.* Provo, UT: Brigham Young University Press, 1975.

Momaday, Natachee Scott. *Owl in the Cedar Tree.* Flagstaff, AZ: Northland Press, 1975.

Showers, Paul. *Indian Festivals.* New York: Thomas Y. Crowell, 1969.

Waltrip, Lela, and Waltrip, Rufus. *Quiet Boy.* New York: David McKay, 1961.

Worthylake, Mary M. *Children of the Seed Gatherers.* Chicago: Melmont, 1964.

Yellow Robe, Rosebud. *An Album of the American Indian.* New York: Franklin Watts, 1969.

Books about Children of Other Nationalities

Bulla, Clyde Robert. *Johnny Hong of Chinatown.* New York: Crowell-Collier Press, 1952 (Chinese).

Estes, Eleanor. *The Hundred Dresses.* New York: Harcourt Brace Jovanovich, 1964 (Polish).

Greene, Constance. *The Unmaking of Rabbit.* New York: Viking Press, 1972. (Polish).

Hunt, Mabel L. *Stars for Christy.* Philadelphia: J. B. Lippincott Co., 1956 (Italian).

Judson, Clara I. *The Green Ginger Jar.* Boston: Houghton Mifflin Co., 1949 (Chinese).

Molnar, Joe. *Sherman: A Chinese-American Child Tells His Story.* New York: Franklin Watts, 1973.

Oakes, Vanya. *Willy Wong, American.* New York: Julian Messner, 1951 (Chinese).

Bibliographies and Sources of Books*

Carlson, Ruth Kearney. *Emerging Humanity: Multi-Ethnic Literature for Children and Adolescents.* Dubuque, Iowa: Wm. C. Brown Company Publishers, 1972.

Dreyer, Sharon S. *The Bookfinder.* Circle Pines, MN: American Guidance Service, 1977 (Categorizes 1,031 current children's books by psychological, behavioral, and developmental topics).

Griffin, Louise. *Multi-Ethnic Books for Young Children.* Washington, DC: National Association for Education of Young Children, 1970.

Information and Materials to Teach the Cultural Heritage of the Mexican American Child. Austin, TX: Dissemination Center for Bilingual Education, 1972.

Kircher, Clara J. comp., *Behavior Patterns in Children's Books: A Bibliography.* Washington, DC: Catholic University Press, 1966 (Organized by behavior/personality headings).

Rolleck, Barbara, selector. *The Black Experience in Children's Books.* New York: New York Public Library, 1974 (Annotation of 900 titles).

Tanyzer, Harold, and Karl, Jean (eds.). *Reading, Children's Books, and Our Pluralistic Society.* Newark, DE: International Reading Association, 1972 (Ethnic related bibliographies since 1967).

Films†

The Child Few People Understand. Pittsburgh: Association for Children with Learning Disabilities (For adults; 20 min.; color; dyslexia).

Circle of the Sun. New York: McGraw-Hill (29 min.; color; middle grades and up).

The Exiles. New York: McGraw-Hill (72 min.; b/w; Indians in urban areas).

Films for Special Education. Del Mar, CA: CRM/ McGraw-Hill (Several films in series dealing with learning disabilities, retarded, blind, and cerebral palsy).

How Come It's Thundering—You Don't See the

---

* See chapters 15 and 17 for additional assistance.

† Films, filmstrips, recordings, kits, etc., exist in abundance for children identified as "special." In addition, materials listed at the close of other chapters are often useful with these children.

Moon? New York: Brandon Films, Inc. (13 min.; color).

School Is for Children. Hollywood, CA: AIMS Instructional Media Services (17 minutes; color; for teachers/parents).

The Tenement. Mass Media Ministry (40 min.; b/w).

What Color Is the Wind? Los Angeles: Allan Grant Productions (27 minutes; color).

Whistle for Willie. Weston, CT: Weston Woods (6 min.; primary).

Filmstrips

The American Indian: A Study in Depth. Pleasantville, NY: Warren Schloat Productions 1961 (Six records and six filmstrips).

Approaches to Mainstreaming. Boston: Teaching Resources Corp. (2 sets of 4 filmstrips each with cassettes and guides; for teachers).

Beginning Fluency in English as a New Language. Los Angeles: Bowmar/Noble (5 sets of filmstrips, cassettes, records, booklets).

Children of Courage. New Rochelle, NY: Spoken Arts (4 color filmstrips and cassettes or records; ethnic tales).

Five Children. Englewood Cliffs, NJ: Scholastic Book Services (Children visit a ranch, a Puerto Rican family, a fisherman, a Southern farm, and a Chicago suburb).

Five Families. Englewood Cliffs, NJ: Scholastic Book Services (Children visit San Francisco Chinatown, pinata party in Phoenix, a New York apartment, a Navajo family, and a circus family).

Mainstreaming. Pasadena, CA: SFA James Stanfield Film Associates (6 sound filmstrips on hearing, visual, orthopedic handicaps, development disabilities, learning disabilities, behavior disorders; for teachers).

On Our Block. New York: McGraw-Hill Films, 1970 (Color; 5 strip series for primary and above).

The Skyline Series. New York: McGraw-Hill Films (6 strips; disadvantaged children in urban areas).

Why Billie Couldn't Learn. Pittsburgh: Association for Children with Learning Disabilities (40 min.; color; adults).

Recordings

American Indian Tales for Children. New York: CMS Records (Told by Anne Pellowski).

Anthology of Negro Poetry for Young People. Englewood Cliffs, NJ: Folkways Scholastic Records (One 10″ LP; intermediate).

Chinese Fairy Tales. New York: Caedmon Records, 1973 (33-1/3 rpm).

Folk Tales of the Tribes of Africa. Paramus, NJ: Educational Reading Service (Told by Eartha Kitt; intermediate and upper).

Indian Music of the Southwest. Englewood Cliffs, NJ: Folkway Records (Primary).

Raven: Creator of the World. New York: Caedmon Records, 1973 (Eskimo Legends; 33-1/3 rpm).

ACTIVITIES FOR PRESERVICE TEACHERS

1. Record the voices of several elementary school children. Play the tape to the class and have your colleagues note speech problems.

2. Visit a school when hearing-loss screening is occurring. Report your observations to the class.

3. Examine materials used in schools for testing children's vision. Familiarize yourself with the way these are used.

4. With others in the class, plan a panel discussion in which the issues involved in "special learning disabilities" are presented. Make certain you deal with the apparent increased incidence of learning disabilities and the influx of commercial materials presumed to attack learning disorders.

5. Visit special classrooms for mentally retarded children. Note the basic language arts emphasized in these classrooms.

6. Find out if the schools in your local community are teaching English as a second language. If they are, what procedures are being used?

7. If you have not observed in schools in ghetto or slum areas, do so in connection with reading this chapter. What differences do you note

among the children? How do the classroom conditions and activities compare with those you have observed located in more prosperous areas?

8. Visit an Indian reservation and/or a migrant labor camp to observe the environment of the children living there.

9. Develop a plan for learning songs, stories, customs, and the history of a particular country whose emigrants you might sometime have in class. Begin the execution of your plan.

10. Prepare a bulletin board directed at building interest in some of the children's books suggested in the references for this chapter.

ACTIVITIES FOR INSERVICE TEACHERS

1. Write to your county health association to request names of agencies and clinics where children with problems identified in this chapter may be referred. Also request a list of free or minimum-charge films that you can use to acquaint parents with problems that may exist. Prepare a program for parents and teachers to expand their knowledge.

2. As you look at your class, identify in your mind children who may be "special" as described in this chapter. Search through all records (test results, etc.) that you can find. Confer with parents. Then plan changes in your program to better meet the needs of these children.

3. Record sentences for a child to listen to and repeat, recording his effort at repeating. He can then listen to your sentence and his, making his own comparison.

4. If there is no speech therapist in your school system, write to a nearby university or another school system to ask for an appointment with the therapist. Take a tape recording of the speech of those children in your class with possible speech problems to the meeting. Ask this person to evaluate the children's speech and give you suggestions of things you might do.

5. Prepare activities "special" children can do individually to learn language skills. Those suggested in the following section will give you a start.

6. Give special attention to possible vision problems in your classroom. Begin with a visual screening as suggested in this chapter, then institute as many of the adjustments as appropriate.

7. Let two children work together with a tape recorder—one who has always spoken only English and a second who has not. The first child makes a statement and the second repeats it. Then the second child says the same thing in his native language and the first one repeats it. After repeating this procedure a number of times, they may listen to the tape. This will help both children to understand the problems involved in learning a new language—the native-born child will be less critical, and the non-English-speaking child will, hopefully, feel less frustrated in his attempts at speaking English.

INDEPENDENT ACTIVITIES FOR CHILDREN

The Slow Learner*

1. Slow learners will profit from many kinds of readiness games, such as matching objects of the same shape, size, or color; putting pictures in sequence for a story, etc.

* Each chapter has activities for children that can be used or adapted for the children in this chapter.

2. Provide many recorded or taped stories for the children to listen to; these will help build vocabulary and concepts for reading and writing.

3. Obtain an old book of flocked wallpaper samples from a wallpaper store. Let individual children use them to trace and cut out letters. They can use these letters to become more familiar with letter shapes and to put together spelling words.

4. Let the slow learner make captions for pictures or write titles for stories in the class newspaper so that he or she will feel a part of the class activities.

The Gifted

1. These children can make spelling and vocabulary charts, design bulletin boards, design and make games, and do many similar tasks that interest and challenge them.

2. Provide time and a place for them to write stories, scripts, reports, etc. Encourage them to write to favorite authors, TV producers, etc.

The Visually Handicapped

1. Provide recorded and taped stories and poems for the visually handicapped child to listen to as a substitute for at least a part of the independent reading other children do. He or she can report on these as others report on their reading.

2. Let the child make a special bulletin board illustrating his view of things about him. For example, he might draw a picture of the way a familiar object or scene looks to him without his glasses, the way small print looks, the size letters that are comfortable for him, etc. This will help the other children to be more aware of his problem and therefore more understanding. It will also make him feel important if he is helped to recognize that only he can provide this understanding for the others. (A child who is unwilling should not be forced, however.)

3. Utilize activities suggested in chapter 7 to increase the child's listening skills.

Children with Speech Handicaps

1. Prepare tapes directed at the specific speech sounds the child has difficulty with so that he or she can listen to them and practice the sounds.

2. Provide short selections that the child can read aloud on tape. He can then listen to the recorded speech, practice needed corrections, record again, and compare the two readings.

3. Consult the speech therapist for specific activities that might help the child.

Children with Hearing Impairment

1. Provide the child with reading material containing the information provided in oral reports given by other children—children speaking before a group are often difficult to hear.

2. This child will frequently not participate in discussions, since he will not hear everything that is said and thus may be hesitant to comment. In order that he does not become withdrawn from class activities, appoint him to perform special functions, let him prepare oral and written reports, and capitalize on any special talents he has to make him feel important.

Children with Physical Handicaps or Personality Maladjustments

1. Make it a special point to provide stories for independent reading that may help these children. Learning that others, too, have problems may help them to adjust to theirs.

2. Seek out the special talents which these children have and provide opportunities to use them. For example, the child who likes to draw might illustrate a story the class has written or design the cover for a creative writing booklet; a very shy child could tape a story for individual listening activities; a hyperactive one might be put in charge of keeping library books shelved; etc.

Children Speaking a Divergent Dialect or Other Language

1. Children may make alphabet books with words in their own language as well as in English for each letter.

2. Have a child make a bulletin board centered around the country of his or her origin. This might include a picture of the flag of that country, pictures of its people and their homes, a map, a list of principal occupations and products, etc.

3. Let a child prepare for the class a program of folk songs, stories, and/or poems from his native land or culture.

4. A child may invite a speaker to talk to the class about his native country. He will be responsible for introducing the speaker and providing any

audiovisual aids or other articles that might be needed (a table for displaying handiwork, a projector and screen, etc.).

5. Children working in pairs with a simple camera can take pictures of one another. Each child can then use his pictures, examples of his classwork (stories, pictures drawn, etc.), and pictures from magazines of things he is interested in to make a booklet about himself.

6. Materials suggested above might also be used by individual children to make bulletin boards about themselves. Perhaps a bulletin board could be marked off into quarters and entitled "Our Class." When a child has gathered the particular objects he would like to display, he could arrange them in one of the sections to make a picture story about himself.

7. Provide materials for a child to read and record so that he can listen to his own speech; have short stories and poems that he can listen to for cadence and word order, record questions for him to answer, etc.

8. A child who speaks a nonstandard dialect might prepare a story for the class using particular idioms or expressions that are peculiar to that dialect. This may be used in connection with a study of dialects to help children understand the many variations that are present in speech even within the same country.

5

Grammar and Language Usage

Traditionally, authors and publishers of language textbooks for elementary school children have given a large amount of space and attention in their books to teaching grammar. This is still true in many, if not most, of the more recently published textbooks—although the grammar in these books may be different from that in books published about twenty years ago, and the proportion of the textbook devoted to grammar is likely to be less. Still, there is often page after page of explanations, rules (now usually called "generalizations"), and exercises far removed from children's writing and speaking needs and interests. Both the grammar and usage material seem to be directed at teaching children to speak and write "correctly"—generally disregarding research evidence about what children already know, how they learn, and what they need to know and practice if they are to speak and write effectively.

In this chapter we define terms whose meanings are often confused, briefly describe several grammars, discuss dialects and usage, and suggest what aspects of grammar and usage should be taught and how it should be done.

GRAMMARS: OLD AND NEW

In everyday language, and often in school as well, the word *grammar* means the rules for speaking and writing correctly and is considered to be synonymous with the term *usage*. However, *usage* properly refers to the form of expression—the choice of words one makes in structuring speaking and writing. Saying "It is me" or "We was going" instead of "It is I" and "We were going" are usage choices. *Grammar,* on the other hand, refers to the system of word structures and word arrangements in expression. All the sentences above are grammatical ones, but expressions such as "Were going we" or "All the boy and girls are going" are ungrammatical. Since the term *grammar* refers to the language system—how it works—there can be different descriptions of this system (see below—and there are others).

The mechanics of expression, more properly called *conventions* (see chapter 10), are no more a part of grammar than usage is, although they are often included as items of grammar in textbooks. The layman usually also includes spelling and penmanship in grammar when complaining about the schools "not teaching grammar any more."

Traditional Grammar

Traditional grammar is a description of the English language that is based on the system of the Latin language. Historically it has simply been called *grammar* and only recently has the adjective been added. The description arose some 400 years ago in an effort to explain why certain words were used or certain sentences constructed rather than others. The fallacy in this description was the assumption that all languages have the same system (although all do have system) and the failure to recognize that language grows and changes.

Another problem with traditional grammar is that it has generally been taught formally. Rules, definitions, and diagrams for showing relationships have been emphasized, with little or no attempt to relate these to students' actual speaking and writing. Most classroom time has been spent conjugating the forms of verbs, naming the parts of speech in sentences, and memorizing rules. The focus in traditional grammar teaching has been on teaching the system as the basis for prescribing what is "correct" in expression.

Structural Grammar

Structural grammar is the product of linguists' scientific study of the way we speak. Structural grammar does not prescribe what is "correct" but simply reports the language as it exists, including its growth and changes. In structural grammar, the ways words are put together into utterances have been categorized, and from this categorization certain principles and patterns of the language system have emerged. One difficulty with this grammar is the problem of determining how people actually do speak, a matter that is basic to the categorization that produces the patterns. Not everyone speaks the same way; that is, there are social and regional differences in usage and pronunciation. Then there is the problem of completeness. How large a sample of language must be examined to determine whether or not all possible patterns and principles of the system have been discovered? Of course, both of these weaknesses are of no greater importance to structural grammar than to any other, except that since the basis of this grammar is its scientific determination, they introduce some limitations to generalizing about the completeness of its patterns as a description of the language system.

Structural grammar identifies basic sentence patterns in English and describes the form and function of words in those patterns. In traditional grammar a word is described in terms of meaning: "A verb is a word that expresses action" or "A noun is the name of a person, place, or thing." In structural grammar a word is a noun because it has a particular function or is signaled in a particular way. In addition, the levels given to the parts of speech in structural grammar are somewhat different from those of traditional grammar. For example, words such as *a, an, the,* and *some* are called determiners or noun markers; they signal that a noun is to follow: "*My* mother went to *the* store." There are also verb markers (can, could, might—also called auxiliaries), clause markers (because, if, how), and phrase markers (in, down, toward), as well as intensifiers or qualifiers (very, just, less) and connectors or conjunctions (and, but, for); but the four major classes are the well-known noun, verb, adjective, and adverb.

Transformational Grammar

Transformational grammar came into being after the development of structural grammar, as a result of the recognition by some structural grammarians of the impossibility of securing factual information on all possible sentences the speakers of the language may use. This grammar has a theoretical base rather than the empirical (observable or factual) base of structural grammar. To overcome the problem of examining actual utterances, transformational grammar assumes a *deep structure* system that leads to a *surface structure* (the sentences actually said and written). There are two basic types of sentences: kernel and transformed. Kernel sentences, of which there are a relatively small number, are the core of the system. They are sentences that cannot be derived by analysis from other sentences (e.g., The children ride bicycles.). All other sentences are transformed sentences. They can be constructed by transforming kernel sentences (Bicycles are ridden by the children, Do the children ride bicycles?, "Don't the children ride bicycles?", etc.). Sentences can also be constructed by expansion of the noun phrase of a kernel sentence (The children *in the fifth grade* ride bicycles) or the verb phrase (The children ride bicycles *all day long*), by the coordination of kernel sentences (The children and their parents ride bicycles), or by subordination of one or more sentences to another (Since parents have other activities, they do not ride bicycles all day as their children do).

This grammar makes use of terminology similar to that used in structural grammar. Like structural grammar, it is not prescriptive, except in the sense of indicating whether or not an utterance is grammatical. There is no prescription as to correctness of the words used. However, transformational grammar (sometimes called *generative* or *transformational-generative*) can be taught as formally as was traditional, and this often is the case. Teaching it can have much of the same emphasis on rules, relationships of words and phrases to one another (usually by a new kind of diagraming), isolation of the study from the expression of children, and activities that have little interest for or little meaning to children. Of course, the same can be said for structural or any other grammar.

USAGE AND DIALECTS

As was discussed in chapter 1, the language that any of us use is largely a matter of our early environments—although by the time a person is an adult he or she has learned a great deal about choosing language appropriate to the communication situation. Such choosing does not mean that we always change some pronunciations of words and the use of expressions that we learned in childhood, but we do learn the jargons of our professions and social groups and in some situations we avoid language that might be labeled "nonstandard."

The above suggests that there are levels of language, and a few years ago differences in usage were labeled as being on different levels. These levels were often termed *formal, informal,* and *colloquial* and sometimes—in an attempt at finer distinctions—*illiterate, homely, informal standard, formal standard, literary,* and *technical.* There was also the idea that an individual used the language of one of these levels—apparently all or most of the time. We now know that each person's language usage varies. However, usage is still largely termed as standard and nonstandard, even though these terms are difficult to define.

Acceptable Usage

Deciding what the school should do about usage teaching is a major problem. In the first place determining what items of usage are unacceptable is difficult at best. A textbook is only a partially satisfactory guide, as it is directed at a hypothetical classroom rather than an actual one. Also, too often the authors are unrealistic about which language usages are acceptable and which ones are not. Language scholars for some years have recommended that only a very few usage items should receive instruction or attention in the elementary school. In support of this attitude one authority says,

> (1) the constant repetition of a relatively small number of deviations constitutes over 90 percent of the nonstandard usage problems in the elementary grades [and] (2) a large number of "errors" listed in textbooks and language workbooks are not errors at all but standard colloquial English appropriate to the speech and writing of children and adults alike.[1]

The reluctance of many teachers to accept certain usages as standard or acceptable is the major reason that the number of usage items that receive teaching attention is not more limited. A 1949 study showed that teachers were only about half as accepting of *"Can* I have another helping of dessert, please?", "Everyone put on *their* coat and went home," "Go *slow,*" and "It is *me*" as were a group of editors and writers.[2] A decade later, another study showed continuing objection to the items of the earlier study as well as to many more (for example, *"Who* are you waiting for?", "Americans *have got* to make democracy work," "He *fixed* the clock," and "The swimmers *dove* into the pool".

As recently as 1968, a study of five items identified as acceptable by linguists showed that a large majority of the teachers questioned regarded these usages as incorrect (particularly in writing, but also in most cases in speech). This study dealt with the following examples of "incorrect" usage:

1. Everyone put *their* name in the upper left corner of the paper.
2. I *will* go to the store tomorrow.
3. The *reason* the page is missing *is because* Johnny tore it out.
4. They invited my friends and *myself.*
5. *Who* did you see?[4]

Even more startling, this research also showed that 99 out of the 100 teachers in the study actually used at least one of the "incorrect" usages in either their own writing or speech, or both!

Idiolect is a term used to refer to the language of an individual. Although each of us speaks a dialect (and possibly can speak more than one) our language does show individual differences.

The list below is intended as a guide to the kinds of usages that should receive attention in the elementary school.[6] It is not likely that the children in any one class will use all of them—and of course they should not be attacked unless the need is present. In no case, however, should all of them receive direct teaching effort in a single year. If a large number of them are used by the children, it is best to select those which occur most frequently and concentrate on them so that teaching effort is not dissipated.

ain't or *hain't*	my brother, *he*
yourn, hern, ourn	*her* and *me* went
hisen, theys	there *is* four
youse	there *was* four
onct	they *knowed*
hisself, theirselves	I, they *growed*
hair *are*	haven't *no,* isn't *no*
a orange	*leave* for let
have *ate*	haven't *nothing*
they *eats*	that's *mines*
was *broke*	where *it* at?
he *brung*	where is she *at?*
he *come*	he *run*
clumb	have *saw*
had, have *did*	I *says*
she, he *don't*	he *seen*
it *don't*	*them* books
didn't ought	*this here*
hadn't ought	*that there*
he *give,* he *walk*	*us* boys went
me and Mary went	we, you, they *was*
she *taken*	with *we* girls
I *likes* him	have *went*
I *drunk, drunks*	have *wrote*
can't hardly	the *mens*
does we have	*learn* me a song

Since language does change and since the studies cited earlier suggest that teachers and textbooks are often slow to recognize this change, aid may be needed in deciding what to teach. One way to obtain this aid is to listen to the speech of educated people and to read current newspapers and magazines; doing this with particular usages in mind can be very revealing. Another way is to check the appropriateness of words and expressions in reference books about usage, although sometimes these are not really current, and they may largely reflect the point of view of their authors.

Dialect Differences

It is certainly true that the pronunciations, vocabulary, and language structures of some children are such wide departures from the standard language or prestige dialect of the community that they cannot be ignored in classrooms. On the other hand, the dialects of other children may differ from the prestige dialect, yet they do not depart widely from the variations in language that one hears and reads in the community. Thus, the attention given to these usages may be minimal, since many of the differences will cause no real communication difficulties and will add color and individualism to expression.

However, dealing with dialect differences becomes very important if other children laugh at the way a child speaks or say "He talks funny," if the dialect is of such low prestige and differs so markedly from "school" language that a genuine problem exists, or if understanding the child is difficult. If a youngster pronounces words such as *pin* and *pen* or *cheer* and *chair* the same way, there is a possibility that he or she will have difficulty with phonic analysis in reading— that is, a lack of sensitivity to a child's language may create a reading problem. Similar kinds of problems may appear in spelling instruction, but in neither of these language arts areas, or in any others, should it be assumed that the youngster's pronunciation must be changed or that the child should be told he or she is speaking incorrectly. All that is needed is to know the child's dialect and be able to reinforce learning when necessary. This is the only way to avoid mistakes like that of the teacher who asked the child what "canal" meant, was told what sounded like "a dish of water," and then proceeded to give an elaborate explanation of the concept of "canal."[5]

Grammatical differences from the standard or prestige dialect of a community are often indices of the dialects of the disadvantaged. The following are the principal types of grammatical differences that may be found:

1. Absence of inflectional endings [*s, es, 's, s', en, ed, ing*] for noun plurals, noun genitives, third-singular present indicative, past tense, present participles, and past participles.
2. Analogical forms such as *hisself* or *theirselves* and the absolute genitives *ourn, yourn, hisn, hern, and theirn.*
3. Double comparatives and superlatives, such as *more prettier* and *most lovingest.*
4. Omission of the copula *be*[usually *is*, e.g., "He a cop"] with predicate nouns, predicate adjectives, and present and past participles.
5. *Be* as a finite verb ["He *be* fast" for "He runs fast"].
6. Differences in the principal parts of verbs, such as *growed, drawed, taken* as a past tense, *rid* as the past participle of *ride,* and *clum* or *clim* as the past tense or past participle of *climb.*[6]

These differences in grammatical features result in such expressions as the following:

He be absent yesterday.
She come to school every day.
He ax me can I go.
She had three sister.
Daisy is more taller than Eileen.
I drawed the picture.

It is important to recognize that a child using such expressions is not being careless. Careful listening will reveal that there is a system to the sentence construction as well as to the pronunciation and the vocabulary used. The child is using language that is familiar and that has worked well in meeting his or her communication needs.

In addition, no teacher should overlook the fact that his or her speech may

A Various Language: Perspectives on American Dialects, edited by Juanita V. Williamson and Virginia M. Burke (Holt, Rinehart and Winston, 1971), is a readable compilation of articles dealing with various dialects.

Do you get water from a *tap*, a *faucet*, or a *spigot*? Do you carry the water in a *pail* or a *bucket*?

not be fully understood by a child. Not only may the teacher use words unfamiliar to the child, but the pronunciations or the names given to objects or actions may be new as well.

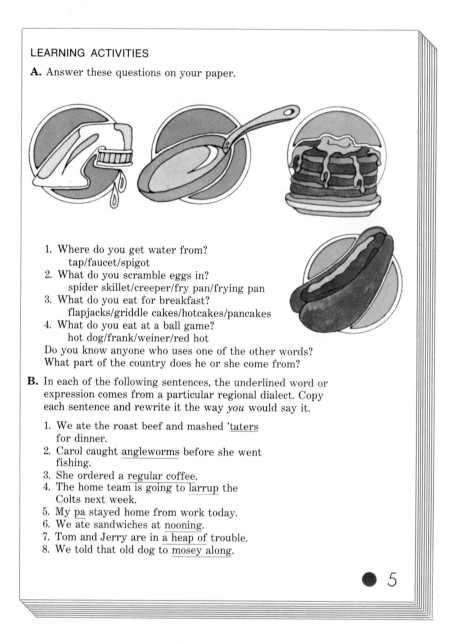

LEARNING ACTIVITIES

A. Answer these questions on your paper.

1. Where do you get water from?
   tap/faucet/spigot
2. What do you scramble eggs in?
   spider skillet/creeper/fry pan/frying pan
3. What do you eat for breakfast?
   flapjacks/griddle cakes/hotcakes/pancakes
4. What do you eat at a ball game?
   hot dog/frank/weiner/red hot

Do you know anyone who uses one of the other words?
What part of the country does he or she come from?

B. In each of the following sentences, the underlined word or expression comes from a particular regional dialect. Copy each sentence and rewrite it the way *you* would say it.

1. We ate the roast beef and mashed 'taters for dinner.
2. Carol caught angleworms before she went fishing.
3. She ordered a regular coffee.
4. The home team is going to larrup the Colts next week.
5. My pa stayed home from work today.
6. We ate sandwiches at nooning.
7. Tom and Jerry are in a heap of trouble.
8. We told that old dog to mosey along.

5

Children are interested in dialect differences. (LANGUAGE BASICS PLUS, Level E. Copyright 1979 by Harper and Row, Publishers. Used by permission of the publisher.)

Standard English

Parents and others in our society expect schools to teach "good English," meaning that they want children to learn the English that "important" people in the community use. This is the "standard English" referred to earlier that is so difficult to define. In fact, it simply cannot be defined in terms of specific words or pronunciations. However, it can be thought of as expression that is appropriate to the purpose of the speech or writing, that is consistent with the system of the language, and that is comfortable to both the expressor and the audience. It is language that is natural and uncramped by rule, reflecting custom that is widely accepted by society because it serves the needs of society. It is never static but changes with the communication needs and other changes in society.

This definition is based on criteria that the National Council of Teachers of English has long urged teachers to observe: acceptable usage (1) is determined by the living language of today; (2) recognizes dialect, geographical, and vocational variations; (3) is judged by its appropriateness for the purpose intended; (4) recognizes that there are situational levels of speech; and (5) takes into account the historical development of the language.

THE TEACHING DILEMMA

Previous sections of this chapter have tried to define and show the distinction between grammar and usage and have suggested that some matters of usage need to be given instructional attention. We have not suggested how this instructional attention should be given, nor what an elementary teacher should do about the teaching of grammar. Suggestions concerning the teaching of usage are made in the final part of the chapter; this section is directed to the question of grammar teaching.

Grammar teaching has long been a tradition in elementary schools. In an earlier day, elementary schools were called *grammar* schools, and even today a parent occasionally talks about the "grammar" school his child attends. Also, as was mentioned earlier, the content of many textbooks is largely grammar explanations, terminology, and exercises. Thus an elementary school teacher is faced with a problem if he or she is a true professional who knows that the research evidence shows that grammar teaching does not change children's usage or aid them in either speaking or writing more effectively. Tradition, pressures, and materials simply have to be dealt with, though, and what to do must be given serious thought.

Values Attributed to Grammar Teaching

There are several reasons proponents of grammar teaching give for including it in the curriculum. Traditionally, many thought that only through an understanding of the grammar of the language could anyone learn to write and speak effectively. It is true, of course, that an understanding of language contributes to effective communication, but this understanding is gained from experience in com-

See *Research in Teaching English* 10 (1976), pp. 5–21; and *English Journal* 66 (Dec. 1977), pp. 86–89; for reports of grammar studies.

municating rather than from the ability to verbalize facts about the language system. However, even though repeated studies have shown that studying grammar (including any of the "new" ones) does not result in improved speech and writing, many people have been slow in accepting this overwhelming evidence.[7]

Closely akin to the argument that teaching grammar improves skill in communication is the belief that a knowledge of grammar is necessary for success in later education. For years elementary teachers have been prodded into teaching grammar by the complaints, both real and imagined, of secondary school teachers that pupils come to them unable to identify the parts of speech or to tell a subject from a predicate. Secondary school foreign language teachers frequently express the same concerns. However, there is no evidence that grammar teaching in the secondary school has any more bearing on writing and speech than it does in the elementary school. Furthermore, there has been evidence for about forty years that the teaching of English grammar—of whatever type—has no bearing on the learning of foreign language.

Perhaps the most valid reason given for teaching grammar is that advanced by many linguists, who believe that an understanding of the way language works is valuable in and of itself. They argue that language is the thing that sets man apart from the animals, that it is a uniquely human thing, and that children therefore ought to know about their own language. It is important to remember, however, that few linguists advocate the teaching of grammatical systems in the elementary school, nor that grammar be taught in a formal or prescriptive manner. They generally believe that grammar teaching should be done in an eclectic and empirical way; the teacher should select only those items that are appropriate to the children and help them to discover *about* language through much experience, observation, and practice.

Although linguists vary in their opinions about how much—and when—grammar should be taught, most believe that any intensive study of grammar should be postponed until the secondary school, and some believe that even then it should be done on an elective basis. An important distinction too lies in the fact that, in general, they speak of helping children to discover "about *language*," not "about grammar." This is certainly a more inclusive term and may include many things that are not strictly grammar: word histories and derivations, the use of the dictionary, how style and structure can contribute to meaning, and more. In light of this interpretation, every good elementary language arts program includes much study "about language."

A Functional Approach

What can teachers do to break away from the traditional emphasis on grammar teaching, even though they are supposed to use textbooks that have this emphasis? The answer is that they must know the research evidence, understand and be able to explain the difference between grammar and usage, and know the kinds of things that can be done to improve youngsters' speaking and writing. They must also know a good deal about language study that will appeal to children.

Children are not likely to generate much enthusiasm if the program is centered around a textbook that insists that it is wrong to say "Don't go *in* the house" and that it is normal and proper to say "The team is *we*, the athletes."

Neither will they have much interest in exercises calling for identifying the nouns, verbs, adjectives, etc., in sentences; for underlining the "complete" predicates; for categorizing common and proper nouns; and so on. Children like to talk and they like to write; they want to tell what they have discovered and what they think about something.

Children come to the kindergarten and even to the nursery school with much basic knowledge of their language and how it operates. They are not yet literate as we think of literacy, but they understand sentences when they hear them and they know if a part of a sentence has been omitted or is in the wrong order. They speak in sentences and phrases that reflect their knowledge of language patterns. They know many words, and they know the language system well enough to realize that structural changes can be made in them to achieve particular purposes and meanings (e.g., adding inflectional endings such as -s, -es, -ed, -er, -ing). Certainly some children will occasionally mix up word order, add the wrong ending or not add one, or have a problem in holding to a tense or person. But the basic understanding of the system is present and developing—if it were not, the child would not have been able to communicate during his or her early years.

We suggested earlier that any grammar can be taught in a formal manner or a functional one. In functional teaching the focus is on expression and its purpose; thus, there is the implication that the grammar taught is of value—is functional—in making expression more effective. There is little evidence to support this, but if grammar is taught (for any of the reasons suggested) it seems to make sense that an effort should be made to relate it to expression rather than to teach it as something entirely separate from the natural expression that occurs as children communicate.

It is natural for children to learn the names of parts of sentences as they construct and reconstruct their own sentences and as they learn how to make their sentences more effective. Attention should be given to the terminology of the language system only as it relates to the children's expression and to the improvement of that expression in terms of its purpose.

If children construct sentences well and thus convey the message they intended, there is no need to teach grammatical items. On the other hand, if a child says, "The boys is going," the opportunity *may* be present to teach about agreement of subject and verb. Certainly the child may be taught that *is* is a verb, not just something referred to as "this word." In a similar way, if a child describes the black bear in a film the class has viewed as simply a "black bear," there is a functional situation for teaching about using other adjectives—*big, lumbering, awkward,* etc.—to give a better word picture of what the child has seen.

Teaching about language functionally means that teaching about nouns cannot be allocated to the fourth grade, nor can it be done in a series of isolated lessons. Functional teaching requires that understanding be developed from the very first contacts teachers have with children. The kindergarten or first grade teacher who says, "Who can give me another sentence telling about one thing we saw at the bakery?" is teaching grammar. So is the fifth grade teacher who says, "Let's see how we can make this sentence more exact. Have we used the best adjectives to describe the carts the natives use for hauling grain?"

There is no need to avoid using grammatical terminology when it is natural to use it. A verb is more properly called a verb than an "action word," and "verb" is no more difficult to learn than many other words that children readily use. We

Chapter 9 has many suggestions about sentence construction and sentence combining.

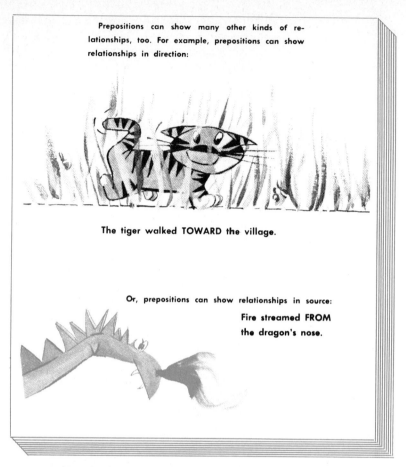

Prepositions can show many other kinds of relationships, too. For example, prepositions can show relationships in direction:

The tiger walked TOWARD the village.

Or, prepositions can show relationships in source:

Fire streamed FROM the dragon's nose.

Functional teaching of grammar emphasizes the uses of parts of speech rather than dwelling upon definitions, diagrams, and rules. (Mary E. Platts, *Grammar with Glamour.* Stevensville, MI: Educational Service, Inc., 1967. Used with permission.)

don't call a television a "box that shows pictures" or a wheel "something that goes around," and children have no trouble with these words or the basic concepts which they represent.

Functional language teaching should be done informally and always in relation to actual expression. The Basic Instructional Plan suggested in chapter 2 can be the framework for such teaching. This plan does not leave the teaching of language skills to unplanned or incidental occasions; with careful planning opportunities arise that require the use of particular language skills and hence provide situations for functional teaching.

Activities

In thinking about ways in which the normal activities of a class may be structured so that interest in language, its variety, and its structure are furthered, consider again the "black bear" illustration used in the preceding section. In addition to merely thinking of adjectives to describe the bear, the children might learn to make sentence structures more complex and varied by experimenting with turning the adjectives into phrases, clauses, verbs, or adverbs. For example "the awkward, lumbering black bear" might become "the awkward black bear with the lumbering gait," "the black bear who lumbered toward us with an awkward gait," or "the black bear lumbered awkwardly toward us." This kind of activity can also lead to a discussion of how words change form and position when they are used differently and, if it is done often, should lead to much greater variety in children's sentences.

An understanding of word order and form is also encouraged by the use of sentences made up of nonsense words, and children will have a great deal of fun while they are learning. A sentence such as "Ra slishy glugged ra rigit" immediately initiates the discovery that *ra* must be a noun marker—an article or determiner—and therefore *slishy* and *rigit* have to be nouns. Similarly, *glugged* is probably a verb in past tense because of its position and the *-ed* ending. Ask the children what would happen to *slishy* and *glugged* if their positions were exchanged, and see what kind of discussion ensues.

For word order, present simple sentences in jumbled order: "had many about airplanes Joe read books." Children will have little trouble putting this sentence in order, but try adding phrases and clauses (in his younger years, while he was growing up, which were used in World War II), and they will soon discover that word order is important to sentence sense. This kind of exercise should be helpful also for children who tend to misplace modifiers or use danglers. Using some of the children's own sentences will also help them to see how the way a sentence is put together can contribute to meaning and effectiveness.

A similar activity that encourages an understanding of sentence parts and sentence completeness involves using strips of tagboard on which are printed noun phrases and verb phrases. Distribute these to the children; then ask each child to see how many mates he or she can find that will make meaningful, complete sentences. As the children advance in sentence mastery, add coordinating conjunctions—*and, but,* etc.—and subordinating or adverbial conjunctions—*if, because, when,* etc. In this case, one child might be chosen to begin a sentence, with others volunteering to continue and complete it. The class would judge whether the resulting sentence was a good one and possibly experiment with revisions. This activity could also be done with teams, points being given for finishing first, having the greatest number of parts to a sentence, and, of course, having a well-constructed sentence.

Another excellent way to help children discover the importance of word order and structure is to use the overhead projector to show a paragraph in which all sentences are simple ones and the words are in natural order (i.e., subject, verb, object). To demonstrate the need for variety, have them try altering each sentence in the same way. Depending on the maturity of the children, they might invert order and make every active verb passive, add an adjective before each noun in the subject position, begin each sentence with a prepositional phrase, make all sentences compound by connecting each pair with the word *and,* etc. After doing this in several ways, have the children select one sentence from each rewrite to make a new paragraph, perhaps experimenting with several different combinations. Then evaluate the results by determining which paragraph is most interesting. (Reading the paragraphs aloud is a good way to demonstrate monotony in structure.)

In the upper grades the need for variety in structure can be illustrated by revising a famous speech such as Lincoln's Gettysburg address or Patrick Henry's "Give me liberty, or give me death," keeping vocabulary the same, insofar as is possible, but structuring all sentences in the same way.

In the middle and upper grades, children often have difficulty with tense sequence, agreement, and staying in the same person as they write. Activities such as those suggested above can be structured to develop a better understanding of the way language works in these areas as well. For example, if you are using the tagboard strips, include various tenses of the same verb, both singular and plural forms of nouns, or a selection of pronouns (definite and indefinite, singular and plural, all persons). Or play a game in which no one is allowed to use plurals, past tense, or a particular pronoun for a certain period of time. This could be done in several ways; one is similar to "Ghost," with a child becoming one-third of a ghost the first time he uses the forbidden construction, two-thirds the second time, and so on. Obviously, some badly constructed sentences will result, but the children will become more aware of the grammatical need for different kinds of constructions.

These are only a few suggestions; obviously, the activities selected for a particular class must be chosen according to the needs and maturity of the children. The important point to remember in planning activities is that they should be directed at helping children see how the structure of language works for them to make expression more effective and more meaningful.

Combine these sentences:

My dog is named Susie.
She is a German shepherd.
Susie likes dog biscuits.
She likes to eat lying down.

How many ways could they be combined?

Teaching Usage

Judgments about people are frequently made on the basis of the language they use. Fair or not, this is a fact. Thus, even though the way a child uses language at home and in his or her neighborhood may be useful for immediate communication needs, it may not serve lifetime needs, and the child may later feel cheated if the school has not attempted to teach a more widely acceptable dialect. It is important, then, to help each child to see the advantage of learning and using standard English, but it is equally important to do this without condemning his or her original dialect.

Procedures for teaching language usage are not as well defined by either research or established practice as we would like. However, the following sections suggest instructional principles and practices that appear to have the best foundation in research evidence and learning theory and to have received the greatest acceptance by teachers. These should help teachers who are frustrated by the failure of efforts they have made to bring about changes in the language children use. Many teachers do not modify their procedures in spite of being aware that what they have been doing is often fruitless—possibly because they do not know how these procedures might be changed. Possibly also they do not really appreciate the fact that language habits are really that—habits—and that habits are not easily changed.

To expect children to change their language habits because a teacher or a textbook says they should be changed is unrealistic. What is realistic is to recognize that the daily program in every classroom abounds with opportunities for children to use a more generally acceptable language for genuine communication purposes. What is also realistic is to realize that pupils learn to do what they do. If pupils are to speak and write a standard dialect they must have practice in speaking and writing it. Rules and exercises are too far removed from genuine communication to have much value.

Analysis of Usage Problems

It is not possible to indicate the specific items of usage that you may need to teach, since the language backgrounds of children vary widely. The usage items suggested earlier in this chapter are a guide (as are those in language textbooks), but specific needs of children in a specific class must be determined by a survey of the oral and written usage of the children in that class. The example below shows how a survey form may be used to record usage items that need instructional attention. Listening to the children in the classroom and on the playground and observing their writing will provide the usage items. Note language patterns (grammatical structures) as well as individual words.

Another form that may be useful is the one shown on page 104, which focuses on items previously selected and provides a simple means for noting particular improvements by pupils.

	Usage survey for _____			
	verb forms	pronouns	redundancy	illiteracies
Bill	he growed			yourn
Harry			John he	
Dennis			this here	
Pearl	be tall			yourn
Lucy	axt			
Cynthia				
Roy		it's		
Walter	has took			

Basic Instructional Procedures

The most vital factor in teaching acceptable usage is motivation. Therefore, every possible device must be utilized to relate the activities of the classroom to the basic goals of each pupil. Children must be made to feel that standard English is actually in widespread use (thus, as suggested earlier, the items taught must be realistic ones) and that learning it will benefit them personally. They must be shown that their communication is, at least in many situations, more effective when they use standard English.

Acceptance of children and the language they use is most important in teaching usage. Finding fault doesn't work; this is a fact that all adults recognize in their own experiences. And acceptance means more than simply recognizing that children can and should use their own dialect when it is appropriate—on the playground, for example. It means also accepting each child's cultural heritage—family, neighborhood, style of living, and so on. It means encouraging children to talk and write about their experiences and the things that are important to them.

Begin by surveying your class early in the year and at intervals throughout the following months. From these surveys choose only a few usage items for concentrated teaching effort. A few items will probably apply to the entire class, and these may receive total class instruction. Items needed by only a few may be worked on individually or in small groups. Only the most frequently used and grossest departures from acceptable usage should be selected for teaching–perhaps by comparing the children's speech with lists of divergent dialect features or mis-

	Louis	Tom	Fannie	Henry	Marjorie	Dorothy	Dick	Mary	Linda	Barbara
I goes	✓		✓	✓				✓		
brung	✓	✓		✓						✓
he don't				✓		✓	✓			
hisself	✓	✓								
me and _____			✓		✓		✓			
drawed	✓	✓				✓				
he be late	✓		✓	✓						
he a tall boy	✓									
rid for rode		✓								

used words such as those presented earlier in this chapter. After these have been selected, identify them for the children, along with the reason for their selection, without making a child feel inadequate because he or she employs a particular usage.

These items may be attacked in two ways. First, and most important, opportunities must be provided for the children to use the particular items being emphasized in natural communication. The focus should always be on the communication rather than on the usage, but teaching directed toward the particular items need not be minimized by this focus. Simply see to it that the children use the accepted forms of the items selected, and do so without fault-finding or placing undue stress upon them. Second, specific practice activities may be used (as suggested in the succeeding section) if more than a relatively few usage habits need attention.

Along with these activities, continue to work toward building interest in words and expressions—and in language generally. This is done principally through providing many experiences with language of many kinds. Read to children often from prose and poetry, imaginative and factual materials; call attention often to the pictures created by words, as well as to the emotional reactions they call forth. Particular attention should be given to variations in language used for different purposes—for example, a science lesson and a story containing conversation.

This kind of activity can be combined with discussions about dialect, colloquialisms, and differences in situational usages. Children might collect sentences heard on the playground and revise them into language appropriate for an assembly announcement and for a social studies report. Activities such as those suggested earlier in this chapter for teaching grammatical concepts can also be adapted for usage practice. For example, tagboard strips containing noun and verb phrases can be combined, with children saying sentences aloud as they are formed. Both seeing and hearing the accepted forms will help to provide reinforcement.

As much as possible, the children themselves should assume the responsibility for making changes. Encourage them to work independently, both individually and in groups, with the children keeping their own lists of individual problems and charting progress they make in learning new forms. This will help to focus their attention on their own particular problems and provide motivation by concentrating on improvement.

Practice Activities

Although the provision of many language experiences will provide the fundamental basis for eradicating some usages for many children, those whose language is considerably different from an acceptable standard may need a more direct teaching approach. In selecting what to teach, attention should be given at specific points of difference between the standard and nonstandard dialects.[8] Teachers generally can determine in a nontechnical way these key differences. Both phonological and grammatical differences should be noted if they appear consistently and are such that their use would sound out of place in conversation among educated Americans.

As stated in chapter 4, the basic principle for teaching a second dialect "amounts to teaching the smallest possible number of vitally significant items— and *teaching each of them hard*."[9] Such teaching requires a long-term effort that helps children recognize dialect differences, understand the reasons for these differences, and know when it is appropriate to use standard English rather than the native dialect. Certainly, children can be taught to hear phonological differences and to recognize grammatical ones, they can be drilled so that they repeat phrases and sentences in the second dialect, but the new dialect will not be used effectively if the children do not have a favorable attitude toward it.

The sentences below illustrate the kind of repetition of patterns of standard usage that may be appropriate. These may be supplied directly by the teacher or by the use of recordings. The children simply repeat the sentences after the teacher or the recorded voice; the concept behind this procedure is that with enough repetition a new dialect will be learned. The evidence on the success of the procedure is mixed, but many linguists support this approach, basing their support on the analogy that may be made with teaching a second language.[9]

She carry me home (the language pattern of the child).

| She
He
John
Mrs. Rock
The teacher
Mother | } takes me home. | You
They
The ladies | } take me home. |

There is virtually no end to the sentences that can be used for repetition exercises; however, any drill can become monotonous unless some variety is injected into the program. Keep practice periods short, make them into a sort of game, use both your own voice and recordings, make the sentences as interesting as possible, and give lavish praise for improvement. This will help to provide motivation, and motivation is of the utmost importance if such activities are to produce improvement.

The abilities of a child who does not speak English or who speaks a nonstandard dialect should not be underestimated. Since many judgments in school are based on intelligence tests, it is important to remember that such tests are related to a particular culture and that even nonverbal tests retain the cultural basis. A low score on an intelligence test, therefore, may reflect only a different cultural background rather than a degree of mental inability.

Further, time spent on pattern practice and other teaching techniques may curtail or supplant other activities in which English can be learned. Such activities are important to the child who is seeking to become an accepted member of the group. Therefore, an *overemphasis* on activities that have characteristics of formality and/or predictability should be avoided.

A Combined Approach

If the usage problems of the children are few in number, activities such as those suggested above are probably unnecessary. In many classrooms, however, it is likely that the best approach is to use both specific practice and language enrichment activities. Certainly practice activities alone would become tedious and result in only a limited amount of language growth. On the other hand, utilizing natural communication situations to promote the use of standard English also has some limitations. It is difficult to limit oneself to teaching specific usage items in a direct and systematic manner without interfering with the content of the communications.

In addition to using both practice activities and language enrichment, it is necessary to ensure that children consistently hear acceptable usage. They also need to hear and see their own usage that differs from acceptable forms and to see and hear the acceptable forms.

In short, then, providing for much use of language (both oral and written) in meaningful situations, presenting many opportunities for children to see and hear language that is well used (through books, records, films and filmstrips, and your own language), and including frequent, *brief* drill on a limited number of items that have been selected for your particular pupils should result in some measure of success in teaching children to use language effectively.

A FINAL WORD

Teaching children to make changes in their language is a task that requires a great deal of planning and preparation. It should begin with a careful analysis of what the children know about language and language usage, along with a determination of what they most need to learn. A multitude of language experiences through listening, reading, writing, and speaking are essential to provide purpose and opportunity for learning about language. These should be planned in conjunction with the ongoing activities of the classroom in such a way that interest is maintained and children can see the need for learning the desired concepts, structures, or forms. Some practice activities will be needed to establish learnings, particularly in matters of usage, but these too should be related to meaningful situations, and drill periods should be kept short so interest will not lag.

As in all other areas—and perhaps even particularly so in matters of usage—children need a great deal of encouragement, and they need to feel a sense of achievement. Teacher attitude is of prime importance and can be supplemented by having the children keep folders of their own work, as well as charts showing individual progress.

Above all, the program must be varied and alive, filled with opportunities for children to learn from language and to communicate what they have learned to others.

ENDNOTES

1. Robert C. Pooley, *The Teaching of English Usage* (Urbana, IL: National Council of Teachers of English, 1974), pp. 182–183.

2. Norman Lewis, "How Correct Must Correct English Be?" *Harper's Magazine*, March 1949.

3. Thurston Womack, "Teachers' Attitudes Toward Current Usage," *The English Journal* 48 (April 1959): 186–190.

4. Robert S. Johnson, "A Comparison of English Teachers' Own Usage with Their Attitudes

Toward Usage," Ph.D. dissertation, Teachers College, Columbia University, 1968.

5. John K. Sherk, Jr., "Dialect—The Invisible Barrier to Progress in the Language Arts," *The Allyn and Bacon Reading Bulletin,* Number 131.

6. Raven I. McDavid, Jr., "The Sociology of Language" in *Linguistics in School Programs,* The Sixty-ninth Yearbook of the National Society for the Study of Education, Part II (Chicago: University of Chicago Press, 1970), pp. 96–97. Examples in brackets added by authors.

7. See pp. 88–89 in Constance Weaver, *Grammar for Teachers* (Urbana, IL: National Council of Teachers of English, 1979).

8. See Kenneth R. Johnson, "Standard English and Disadvantaged Black Children: Teaching Strategies," in William W. Joyce and James A. Banks, eds., *Teaching the Language Arts to Culturally Different Children* (Reading, MA: Addison-Wesley Publishing Co., 1971), p. 123; and Roger W. Shuy, "Nonstandard Dialect Problems: An Overview," in James L. Laffey and Roger Shuy, eds., *Language Differences: Do They Interfere?* (Newark, DE: International Reading Assn., 1973), pp. 8–9.

9. Virginia F. Allen, "Teaching Standard English as a Second Dialect," *Teachers College Record* (February 1967), pp. 355–370.

REFERENCES

Books

Cazden, Courtney B., ed. *Language in Early Childhood Education.* Washington, DC: National Association for the Education of Young Children, 1972.

De Stafano, Johanna S., ed. *Language, Society and Education: A Profile of Black English.* Worthington, OH: Charles A. Jones, 1973.

Joos, Martin. *The Five Clocks.* Bloomington, IN: Indiana University Press, 1962.

Malmstrom, Jean. *Understanding Language, A Primer for the Language Arts Teacher.* New York: St. Martin's Press, 1977.

Pooley, Robert C. *The Teaching of English Usage.* Urbana, IL: National Council of Teachers of English, 1974, especially Chapters 9 and 10.

Reed, Carroll E. *Dialects of American English,* rev. ed. Amherst, MA: University of Massachusetts Press, 1977.

Shuy, Roger. *Discovering American Dialects.* Urbana, IL: National Council of Teachers of English, 1967.

Trauger, Wilmer K. *Language Arts in the Elementary Schools.* New York: McGraw-Hill Book Co., 1963.

Filmstrips

Fundamentals of English. New York: McGraw-Hill, 1964 (6 color strips).

Learning About Our Language Series. New York: McGraw-Hill (4 sets of 6 each; primary).

Using Language Correctly. Jamaica, NY: Eyegate House (Color; intermediate).

Words We Need. Niles, IL: Filmstrip House (Grades 2–4; 4 filmstrips, 4 LP records, 4 scripts).

Recordings

Instructional Record for Changing Regional Speech Patterns. Urbana, IL: National Council of Teachers of English (by Ruth I. Golden; Folkways record).

ACTIVITIES FOR PRESERVICE TEACHERS

1. Find several children's books which provide sentences that would appeal to children and can be used for sentence combining activities. Plan combining exercises that will both appeal and teach.

2. Read "Sense and Nonsense about American Dialects" by Raven I. McDavid (*PMLA* LXXXII, No. 2, May 1966, pp. 7–17) and be prepared to report to your classmates on it.

3. Present arguments for and against teaching grammar in the elementary school. Be specific about your definition of the grammar and the grammatical items you are teaching.

4. Observe a particular class and make a record of usages that need to be worked on by most or all of the class, by small groups, and by individual children. Use resources suggested in this chapter to determine which usages should be attacked.

5. Plan a lesson that will bring about practice in one of the forms selected in question 4.

6. Compose a paragraph using only simple sentences (as suggested on p. 101) and plan the kinds of revisions a particular class might be asked to make.

7. Prepare a set of tagboard strips for teaching a particular grammatical concept or a particular usage.

8. Examine an elementary school language arts textbook for its grammar content. Does the book attempt to teach *about language* or *about grammar?* Be prepared to report to the class.

9. Compare definitions in textbooks and articles of grammar, usage, linguistics, and the several parts of speech.

ACTIVITIES FOR INSERVICE TEACHERS

1. Ask teachers in your school to define "standard English." Compare these definitions with those you find in textbooks similar to this one.

2. Find out from secondary school English teachers in your district their views as to how much grammar should be taught by elementary school teachers. Evaluate these views in terms of the content of this chapter.

3. Listen to and watch television programs that demonstrate dialect differences. List these programs and assign pupils to watch and listen; then plan class discussion around the language differences noted.

4. Prepare a checklist similar to the ones in this chapter. Evaluate your class, then contract with them to eliminate usage errors, one or two at a time.

5. Review the language teaching activities in this chapter and select several to use with your class. Keep a record of the use, including the planning.

6. Evaluate your own ability to identify parts of speech. Assess this knowledge in terms of the degree to which you use this knowledge in writing and speaking. React to this assessment and to the exercises and practice material commonly given to children.

INDEPENDENT ACTIVITIES FOR CHILDREN

1. Let a child make his own checklist of expressions he needs to work on in his writing. For example, he might list these in two columns:

Words I Use with Friends	*Words I Use in Writing*
I ain't gonna do it.	I am not going to do it.

Only a few expressions should be worked on at a time. When these have been mastered, the child can add others.

2. Prepare exercise materials that ask the child to change a given expression to standard English. Expressions that might be used in such an exercise include these:

have ate   *he brang*

he give   was broke
have went   them books

3. Write on cards sentences in which the child is to substitute phrases that he thinks of. For example, a sentence such as "He wanted to go to the store" might be used with directions to the child to substitute other phrases after the first *to* (e.g., ride around the block, play ball, go to the circus).

4. Prepare a set of cards with a two-word sentence on each (Boy walked. Dog barked. Snow fell.). Adding one or a few words at a time, the child is to expand each into a series of sentences. For example:

> *Snow fell.*
> *Snow fell steadily.*
> *Snow fell steadily all day.*
> *Snow fell steadily all day long.*

5. To help individual children with word order, make cards with simple instructions, such as the following:

Write a simple sentence. Then add an adverb to make your sentence more specific. Tell how, when, or where. For example:

> *The horse jumped.*
> *The horse jumped* suddenly.

Rewrite the sentence with the adverb in another position. Keep your adverb list for your free writing time.

6. Prepare cards or ditto sheets from which the child can select sentence exercises such as the following:

Put in missing words.

> *The* _____ *man* _____ *scolded the* _____ *boy.*
> *There was a* _____ *storm* _____ *night.*

Directions may include listing as many words as possible for each blank that would "make sense."

7. Give the child tagboard strips containing noun and verb phrases. Have him see how many he can match so that they make meaningful sentences. An extension may be to provide coordinating conjunctions—*and, but,* etc.—and subordinating conjunctions—*if, because, when,* etc.—on other strips for forming compound sentences.

8. Using a compartmented tray or box, place in separate compartments cards containing determiners, nouns, verbs and verb phrases, adjectives, adverbs, prepositional phrases, and conjunctions or clause markers. Use ink or marking pencil of a different color for each category. The child may experiment with word order and structure by making sentences from these. At the upper levels, gerunds and participles may be added.

II

Teaching Language Expression

Our concern in Part II is with teaching speaking, listening, and writing. There are three chapters on writing, plus one each on spelling and handwriting. The beginning focus in Part II is on oral expression since much of the communicating we do both in school and out, as children and adults, is done orally. Further, much of a child's success in learning to read and write is based on the effectiveness of his or her ability in oral expression and the companion activity of listening.

Writing involves many different skills—the organization of ideas and thoughts into sentences, paragraphs, and compositions; the mental–physical act of forming letters and words; the spelling of words; the punctuation of discourse and the capitalization of words; and a knowledge of form and custom. It also involves saying something of value in a way that is interesting and original. Learning to write well is an elusive goal; thus it is a basic concern of this section.

6

Developing Speaking Abilities

Children entering school for the first time ordinarily will have developed a speaking ability adequate to meet their needs at the time. They will not, however, have developed the speaking skills and the knowledge of speaking situations that are necessary for meeting their school and adult needs. In chapter 3 we discussed how a foundation for effective speaking can be laid in beginning school experiences. Children with speech handicaps were discussed in the following chapter, as well as some instructional procedures to use with them. In this chapter we extend the focus on oral expression, stressing in this focus the importance of building on children's early school experiences, fostering their inclination to talk with others, and providing speaking activities that are genuine and purposeful.

The Speech Skills

Skill in oral expression results from practice in the various situations in which an individual needs to speak. The instructional program, then, must provide many speaking situations, and it must utilize these situations to direct attention to speech skills, to behavioral attitudes and habits, and to content.

Naturally *what* is said is of primary importance. Closely related to this are the vocabulary used and the organization and development of that content. These aspects of speaking are discussed later in this chapter, and since they apply to all of the language arts, they are also discussed in chapters 8, 9, 13, and 16. The skills discussed in the following section are those peculiar to speech activities: (1) control and use of the vocal mechanism, (2) use of facial and bodily expression, and (3) development of audience-speaker rapport.

Vocal Control

Effective speech is pleasing to the ear. It is produced with ease and confidence. It is rhythmic and free from hesitations, repetitions, and interruptions. The tempo and volume are suitable to the content and the audience, and all sounds are clearly articulated and distinctly enunciated. To aid children in developing this kind of fluency the teacher must do three things: help each child to feel confident and secure in speaking situations, help each child discover his or her own weaknesses and have the desire to improve them, and help each child learn to speak as clearly and distinctly as is physically possible.

A person's emotional state is often indicated by voice quality, tone, pitch, and tempo. This is especially true of children. A child who is upset, tense, or worried shows it in his or her voice. A self-reliant, alert child shows confidence by a pleasing voice. An eager, happy child is usually friendly and talkative. A diffident child who is emotionally and socially insecure is unable to express himself in fluent, articulate speech. A child who is overly aggressive, perhaps also reflecting emotional insecurity, is apt to speak in a strident voice and insist on monopolizing speaking situations.

You cannot, of course, be expected to solve all of your children's personal and social problems, but you can create a classroom atmosphere in which children feel secure and free to speak. You can work on building each child's self-concept (including the loud child who talks too much). And you can help children to overcome weaknesses that may cause insecurity.

Choral speaking, which is discussed more fully in a later section of this chapter, is an excellent beginning activity for shy children, since they can find security in being part of a group. Possibly such a child could even be assigned a solo part, particularly in a selection where other children also have solo lines. Another value of choral speaking is in helping children develop an understanding of the importance of rate, pitch, rhythm, stress, use of pauses, etc. Experimenting with different ways of reading lines helps them to see how these factors contribute to effective speech.

Few of us really listen to our own voices except through artificial means. Therefore, one of the best ways to help children discover their individual needs with respect to pitch, volume, and rate of speaking is to record their voices and have them listen to the recordings. This may be done individually, in small groups, or with the entire class participating. The clearly established purpose of the listening, of course, should be to seek ways to improve, not to find fault. Listening to recorded speech may also be helpful in formulating standards; these should not be unrealistic, but they are not likely to be if the children participate in setting them. They can then be posted and referred to in evaluating each new effort—and refined as the children progress in speaking abilities.

One fourth grade set these standards

1. Don't talk too fast.
2. Speak clearly and loudly enough so everyone can hear.
3. Be sure you know how to pronounce all the words.
4. Don't use too many *and's*.
5. Look at the audience.
6. Use facial expressions and gestures.
7. Be interested in what you are saying.
8. Try to look relaxed; don't fidget.

Articulation

As stated in chapter 4, children just entering school frequently have problems articulating some sounds. These problems, however, are eliminated by most children before they reach the middle grades. If not, they may need to be referred to a speech therapist. On the other hand, some children simply may not have learned to make certain sounds correctly. In such cases you may attack the problem by doing the following:

1. Showing the child how the sound is made as he or she listens and observes the movement of your lips and tongue.

2. Having the child imitate you and examine his or her attempts by watching in a mirror.
3. Having the child repeat the sound several times.
4. Having the child say syllables and words that include the sound.

Try asking the noisy, aggressive child to work with one who needs practice in articulation or enunciation. Tell him to listen carefully to see whether sounds are produced clearly and correctly. This may help build his self-image while the other child gains needed practice.

In teaching the production of speech sounds, time should not be wasted in drilling on those that present only minor difficulties, since to be motivated to improve, a child must feel that proper production of the sound is important to communication and not just something to be done during a practice period. The child, of course, will readily recognize that minor speech faults do not interfere with communication.

Individual attention is usually more effective than teaching a given sound to the entire class. The instruction should be as close as possible to the time when the difficulty with the utterance occurs. Finally, throughout the instruction make your own speech an example of good articulation, distinct enunciation, and correct pronunciation.

Gestures and Bodily Expression

Children need to be aware that oral communication often includes more than speech. It is virtually impossible for a person to express things orally without using some body movements, and these movements should be natural and in harmony with the speech activity and the content of the communication. The rhythmic activities, finger plays, and action verse suggested in chapter 3 are both fun for children and a means for developing the harmony between speech and physical movements. Children may, though, develop annoying mannerisms such as fidgeting, head jerking, hand twisting, exaggerated facial expressions, and other undue physical movements. The avoidance of their development is usually accomplished by the elimination of self-consciousness; this can be accomplished through careful planning and participation in speaking situations that have real meaning.

In the primary grades, the activity of showing an object while telling about it may relieve a child's nervousness by taking his attention away from himself. Similarly, the middle or upper grade child might use a map, chart, or other aid in giving a report; this will also encourage natural gestures and more purposeful body movement. Group and individual pantomimes, discussed below, as well as creative dramatics can also teach the value and proper use of gestures and body movement. And, of course, you are a constant example; just as you try to set a model in speaking, so you should also be aware of your own use of facial expressions, gestures, and body movements throughout the school day.

Pantomime

Pantomime follows rather naturally and easily the rhythmic activities and creative play described in chapter 3. It also is basic to fostering children's creativity. It should be a part of every language arts program, both because of the relation of body movements to oral expression and the discussion that will occur both before and after pantomimes are done.

Beginning Pantomimes

A boy who has ripped his
   pants
A tree being pruned
Someone walking an unruly
   dog
A shopper with an armload
   of packages
Building a snowman
Getting dressed in the
   morning
A girl washing her hair
A football fan watching a
   game on TV

Individual Pantomime

Practicing the violin
Being a school crossing
   guard
Roller skating
Getting gum from a
   machine
Opening birthday presents

Group Pantomime

Playing catch
Doubles ping pong
A mouse is loose in the
   room
Building a campfire
Raising the flag
Putting up a tent

Pantomime is expression. It tells something. It is imitation. The familiar is easy for children to show by pantomime. Therefore, start with simple ideas. Encourage children to work their pantomime from the inside out, to use their own thoughts and feelings, and to pantomime both in groups and individually. Children may imitate a parent driving a car, caring for a baby, shopping for groceries, or playing golf, or they may imitate the look on someone's face when that person is happy, surprised, angry, or sad. Other actions they may want to mimic are swimming, watching television, vacuuming a rug, playing with a dog or cat, or building a snowman.

The entire body is brought into pantomime when children pretend to be one of the following (add your own suggestions or have children add theirs): a rag doll, a tin soldier, a runaway horse, an angry dog, a dish of jello, a monster, a tree on a windy day. Or perhaps a fat lady trying to tie a shoe, a man who just sat on a tack, a fireman climbing a ladder, or even a coffee pot perking.

Pantomime activities can also be used to develop sense awareness. For example, a child might pretend to put a foot in a tub of ice water, or may look at an apple, think how good it will taste, bite into it, chew it, and—find half a worm. Another might act out putting a finger into a hot pie, eating a hamburger, smelling something burning on the stove, hearing noises in the night, etc. While one child does the imitation or pantomime other children will enjoy guessing who this child is or what he is doing. These pantomime activities, which appear to children to be a game, provide many opportunities for language development. Encourage questions and responses that go beyond one word. That is, when a child asks, "Why?" it may be appropriate to ask, "Why, what?" in order to get a good question. In the same manner, one word answers may be changed to sentences.

A full-length mirror in the classroom will give children the opportunity to practice their pantomimes and try out variations before an audience of only one. It can prove to be an invaluable aid in many other oral activities as well, in addition to providing an opportunity to talk about good grooming and discuss why we should look clean and neat.

Audience-Speaker Rapport

An individual speaks because he or she has something to say—the person needs to express an opinion, wants to present facts or information, or seeks answers to questions. This person has something to say to *someone*—that is, an individual is usually speaking to an audience. The audience may be one person or many, but the audience is very much a part of any oral expression activity.

It is important for a speaker to establish and maintain a relationship with this audience in which there is interplay, in which there is genuine communication. The people in the audience will show that this communication is taking place by their posture, their eyes, their facial expressions, their courtesy in listening, the incisiveness of their questions, and their voiced reactions. The skilled speaker shows a sensitivity to the audience in his or her response to their reactions. For the child this is often difficult; it is only learned through experience and careful planning.

Am I a Good Listener?

1. Do I pay careful attention and not distract the speaker by doing something else?
2. Do I use facial expressions to show that I do not understand or that I am interested in what is said?
3. Do I show appreciation without calling attention to myself by commenting or laughing too loudly?
4. Do I jot down questions or notes for discussion after the speaker has finished?

The first requisite in establishing rapport is to select a subject and a method of presentation that will appeal to the audience. Children should learn that, even when talking to one person, they should talk about something that will interest that person. In planning a report for the class, the child should use the kinds of examples, reasons, etc., that will be interesting and appropriate; choose vocabulary that is colorful and will be understood by the listeners; select visual aids that will add meaning and interest; and, of course, use the speaking skills discussed in the preceding sections.

The second step is difficult and requires much experience, but it will be easier if a presentation has indeed been planned with the audience in mind. This step is to think about the audience rather than oneself. Children will learn to think of the audience if the classroom atmosphere is one of cooperation and sharing. Again, example is the best teacher. When you present information, explain a problem in mathematics, or tell a story, ask yourself this question: "Am I sharing this with the children, or am I performing for them?"

Point out to children (and show by example) that watching for audience reaction will aid them in doing a better job. A puzzled frown may indicate that a word needs explanation or a point needs clarification. A shake of the head may imply that an argument needs further support, whereas a smile or nod shows appreciation and affirmation. Such reactions show that the audience is listening, and responding to them results in a better experience for both the speaker and the listeners.

The audience, of course, is a vital part of any speaking activity, and children should learn to be good listeners as well as good speakers. Allowing an opportunity for questions and discussion following a presentation will encourage listening, as will class-formulated standards. And make sure that you observe these standards yourself—*never* grade papers or work on records while a child is speaking. In fact, it is a good idea for the teacher to sit in the back of the room and become a physical part of the audience; this will help children to avoid talking to the teacher instead of to the class.

OPPORTUNITIES FOR ORAL EXPRESSION

Natural situations—the class discussing a problem, a small group working on a project, two or three children conversing—should be the basis for much of the instruction in oral expression. In addition, the teacher must plan other opportunities in connection with the ongoing activities and studies of the class—reports, dramatizations, etc. Genuine and meaningful activities that are truly concerned with communication provide the best opportunities for giving attention to specific speech skills, to behavior related to speech activities, to the content of the speech, and to listening abilities.

The school day abounds with such natural situations, since oral language is basic to teaching and learning in every subject area; therefore, activities calling for the use of oral language are found in virtually every chapter of this book. This section is devoted to the kinds of oral activities that are not adequately discussed elsewhere and for which particular skills and attitudes need to be taught.

Conversation

A wise teacher shows interest in his or her students by being available to talk with the children when they first come to school in the morning. This "chatting time" before school should not be considered a waste, since many children have no one in the home who will listen to or talk with them. To develop favorable self-concepts, children need to know that others are interested in them and their interests.

The desire to communicate thoughts and ideas to others continues throughout the school day. Whether it is a discussion of the room arrangement, a future assembly program, a social studies or science project, or current news events, certain habits and courtesies must be agreed on and practiced by those involved.

Decide on some conversation topics and then divide the class into two's or three's to talk about the ones they choose.

For effective conversation, the listener must be attentive in order to react to what the speaker is saying, the topic must be of mutual interest, and both participants must be polite (even when angry) and tactful (especially when being truthful). A good conversationalist will be friendly and remember that a conversation is not a battle of wits in which one attempts to disarm another. A good conversationalist will also be enthusiastic about what he or she has to say and about what others say. Being enthusiastic requires being informed and knowing about many things that become the subjects of conversations—books, movies, television, political and social events, and the like.

Many behaviors in conversational situations are suitable for dramatization by pupils or for discussion in large and small groups. The first week of school is a good time to discuss conversational abilities and courtesies, with a review

Provide places and time for conversations.

whenever it seems appropriate.

It is important to remember that conversing is an activity of some intimacy and that the necessary intimacy is difficult to achieve in a formal physical setting with a classroom of children. A shy child who will not talk from his or her seat may find it easier to talk in a conversational group of four or five children where it is possible to talk in a low voice and to feel secure in the physical nearness of others. However, even in a small group setting, it may be necessary to have one or more self-confident children included in order to keep the conversation rolling and to foster the participation of the other children.

Telephoning

Tips on Telephoning

1. Formulate messages, orders, and other detailed information as concisely as possible before starting a call.
2. Identify yourself to the person being talked to clearly and courteously when making or receiving a call.
3. Explain clearly and courteously the purpose of a call.
4. Speak as courteously as in a face-to-face conversation.
5. Allow the person who made the call to close the conversation.
6. Ask permission to use another person's telephone.
7. Place calls at times convenient to the persons called.
8. Avoid monopolizing a party line or the telephone in your home.

Using the telephone is an activity that provides its own motivation and opens the door for numerous language arts activities. Though many schools do not encourage children to use the telephone in the building, a telephone is found in a vast majority of homes, and it is wise to plan to teach or review its use. If possible, actual situations involving the use of the telephone that arise either at school or at home should be used. Such situations might include telephoning the mother of a child who is ill to give information about assignments or class activities, phoning to make arrangements for an interview, using the telephone to ask someone to come and speak to the class, or calling to inquire about suitable dates for a trip to a museum or another place of interest.

Some teachers plan a telephone unit for a time when there is a lull in activities and overall enthusiasm about school. This is a helpful idea, since such times call for an activity that both you and the children will enjoy. Contact your local telephone company for a kit of materials including posters, the film *We Learn About the Telephone,* the filmstrip *How We Use the Telephone,* and two colored telephones which plug into a box called a Teletrainer. From this Teletrainer one can press buttons that ring the telephone and give busy signals. Be certain to request these materials several weeks in advance, as they are in heavy demand.

The American Telephone and Telegraph Company has prepared a very helpful booklet, "Communications and Telephone Programs for Lower Grades"; this is usually a part of the kit. In an area serviced by another telephone company, you may obtain these materials by asking your company to help you obtain the materials from the American Telephone and Telegraph Company. If all else fails, write to the New York office of AT&T.

How We Discuss a Topic

1. Everyone thinks before speaking.
2. Only one person talks at a time.
3. Everyone listens carefully.
4. Everyone is given a chance to talk.
5. We keep to the subject.
6. We are polite.

Discussion

Many of the problems that arise in the daily activities of the classroom lead to discussions among the pupils. With guidance, these discussions can lead to the development of skill in critical thinking, reasoning, problem solving, and expressing ideas orally in a rational and organized manner. Through discussion children gain information, learn to stick to the point of the topic being discussed, and develop the ability to express themselves effectively.

Discussion differs from conversation in that it ordinarily has a topic that was at least somewhat agreed upon and a more purposeful goal, but it is similar to conversation in the need to take turns, to be courteous, to avoid repetition, and to speak so that all can hear. Discussion is not the same as arguing, although some arguments may occur as a discussion progresses. Arguments, however, arise from an attempt to defend a point of view, whereas a discussion seeks to arrive at an answer or a solution to a problem.

To teach discussion skills, direct attention should be given to helping the children discover what needs discussing, define the topic accurately, explore various viewpoints, and agree on rules or limits (such as the time to be spent discussing, the number of times an individual can speak, and how a conclusion will be reached). Keep in mind that many topics are more suitable for discussion by a group of a half-dozen or so of the children than by the entire class.

Debate

Debating is ordinarily considered a secondary school or college speech activity. However, some children in the upper grades of the elementary school can be attracted to the idea of a "formalized" argument. If there are children in a class who are so attracted, and if they are mature enough, the research that goes into preparing the arguments is good practice for using reference skills and doing logical thinking.

Debating calls for two children to present one side of the debate topic and two children to present the other. Each speaker makes a presentation and a rebuttal, with a time limit set for each turn at speaking.

An entire class can become involved in a debate through the listening they must do in order to judge which team won the debate. How to judge a debate usually should be a discussion topic for the class, with the discussion leading to standards for judging.

Announcements and Directions

Giving announcements has become a part of school life, and many schools have regular opening announcements that come over a speaker system. A few schools allow children to make some of these announcements, as well as some of their own. In addition, there are many opportunities in classrooms for children to make announcements. Outside school, children may make announcements at Scout meetings, club meetings, and parties.

Announcements should be given in a clear, brief, and friendly manner. The announcement usually has "who, what, when, where, and how" qualities. Standards for announcements should be developed by the class in consideration of these qualities and manner of presentation. The standards can then be used as the basis for instruction and as a guide for the preparation and delivery of announcements that members of the class make.

Children also have many opportunities to give and follow directions during a school day. They may give directions for playing a game, participating in a scavenger hunt, performing a science experiment, or getting to their homes. Standards for giving directions should also be established by the class as a group; they should stress accuracy and sequence, as well as delivery.

The skills and abilities necessary for making announcements and for giving directions are similar to those needed in most oral language situations. The language used must be organized and presented in terms that will be understood by the audience. Acceptable language should be used, but greatest attention should be upon the conciseness and clarity of the message and its appropriateness for the particular audience.

Meetings

Intermediate grade children are of the "let's form a club" age. When this interest is expressed it is time to teach parliamentary procedure. The name and type of club as well as the desire for it should come from the children. It is possible, for example, to have science, book, and class clubs all at the same time with different members and officers. A fair amount of guidance will be needed, since children sometimes become quite cliquish within clubs and may hurt others' feelings.

Interest in forming a club does not automatically mean interest in parliamentary procedure. You may need to initiate a discussion of the importance of learning how to operate a club effectively prior to starting one. The children need to be taught the purpose of rules for conducting a meeting as well as the rules to be followed. Although rules should not be too detailed or formalized for beginning groups, a chart of the rules agreed on could be posted and referred to during meetings.

As the children become more experienced with clubs and their meetings they will need to develop some understanding of parliamentary procedure and its vocabulary. What is a *motion*? How do you make a motion? What does it mean to *amend* a motion? What do we mean when we say that only one person may *have the floor* at a time? What are the possible omissions, additions, or corrections that are asked about following a secretary's or treasurer's report?

The following is a guide to making motions and voting upon them that may be useful.

1. The individual who wishes to make a motion stands and says, "Mister (or Madam) Chairman."
2. The chairman replies, "The Chair recognizes Tommy Blank."
3. Tommy then says, "Mister Chairman, I move that we be permitted to have a morning and afternoon snack in our room." (Note that correct wording is "I move," *not* "I make a motion that . . .")
4. Another child says, "I second that motion." (Remember that a motion must be seconded before it can be voted upon.)
5. The chairman then says, "It has been moved and seconded that we be permitted to have morning and afternoon snacks in our room. Is there any discussion?"
6. After discussion the chairman may need to repeat the motion. He then calls for a vote by saying, "All in favor say 'Aye.' Those opposed say 'No.' " (If there is doubt about the outcome of a voice vote, a member may say, "Mr. Chairman, I call for a show of hands.")
7. The chairman announces, "The motion has been carried" (or defeated). Once a motion has been voted upon there need be no further discussion of it in the meeting.
8. Members of the club need to keep in mind that only one motion may be on the floor at a time and that a motion must be voted upon before a second motion may be made.

Basic Elements of Parliamentary Procedure

1. The chairman calls the meeting to order.
2. The secretary reads the minutes of the last meeting.
3. The chairman asks for corrections or additions to the minutes.
4. The minutes are approved by vote. In most clubs, the chairman, instead of taking a vote, says, "If there are no objections, the minutes stand approved as read" (or corrected). Should someone object, of course, a vote must be taken. The same procedure may be followed with the treasurer's report.
5. The chairman asks for the treasurer's report.
6. He asks for corrections to or questions concerning the treasurer's report.
7. The treasurer's report is approved by vote.
8. The chairman asks for committee reports.
9. The chairman asks for old business to discuss. If there is any, it is discussed and proper motions are made and voted upon.
10. The chairman asks for new business. New business is discussed, committees are appointed, and motions are made, discussed, and voted upon.
11. The chairman asks for a motion to adjourn. The motion is made, seconded, and voted upon.
12. The meeting is adjourned.

The above is a simplified list, but it should be quite adequate for the needs of most groups of either children or adults. If several children—or the entire class—become particularly interested in studying the fine points of parliamentary procedure, obtain a copy of *Robert's Rules of Order*.

Parliamentary procedure should *only* be taught when children have the desire and need for this procedure. If the children are not interested in clubs, or only in quite informal ones, it is not necessary to teach these procedures. However, some form of organization is important in even an informal group activity.

In addition to learning how to conduct and participate in club meetings, the children should also learn that meetings will be more orderly and fewer arguments will arise if a simple set of bylaws or standing rules is agreed upon. These might include such items as the number of officers, the length of their terms of office, whether they can succeed themselves, the time and place of meetings, the amount of dues (if any), etc.

Interviews

An interview is a good method of securing information and provides the interviewer with the opportunity to use speaking skills, organize his or her thinking, and develop listening ability.

Teach outlining and note taking along with interviewing (see chapter 16).

Many situations occur that give children the opportunity to conduct interviews. Intermediate grade children studying a foreign country may wish to talk with someone who has lived in or visited that country. The children themselves may know of such a person, possibly a parent, a friend, or even a child in another class. If not and if you are new to the community, you may have difficulty in locating interviewees. Try one or all of the following:

1. Talk with other teachers or the principal, who may know someone who has spent time in that country.
2. Contact the local Chamber of Commerce office or a senior citizens' group to obtain a speakers' bureau list.
3. Send letters to parents with a list of countries the class will be studying during the year and invite any of them who have knowledge of a country to talk with the group.

Interviewing parents and other adults about their occupations or hobbies will also enrich the curriculum. In planning for these interviews, emphasize their importance to the community, their uniqueness, or their relation to subjects being studied. It is amazing how unaware both children and adults are of services that are provided in communities. For instance, when children drop money into a juke box or soft-drink machine, do they think about how it got there or who keeps it running? Have they ever thought that someone earns his living this way?

What is necessary for an interview experience? First, preplan by listing questions that the class or individual would like answered. Develop enough knowledge of the topic that sensible questions can be asked. This often means that the children may need to do some library research. Above all, it is important that an interview have some purpose other than simply giving the child experience in interviewing.

Some people will be able to come to school for an interview, but others will not, and plans will need to include arrangements for these interviews. In addition,

Information from Interviews

Books, newspapers, and magazines are not the only sources of information that you can use for a report. People are also sources. Perhaps you know someone who has a good knowledge of the subject on which you wish to report. If so, you may wish to interview this person.

There are three steps to holding an interview: making an appointment, preparing questions in advance, and taking notes.

Making an Appointment

Kathie had long been interested in becoming a doctor. She decided to write a report on "A Career in Medicine." She knew that the woman who lived next door, Dr. Robinson, would be a good person to interview.

Kathie asked Dr. Robinson for an appointment on Saturday morning. She told her why she was asking for an interview and what the topic of the interview would be. She mentioned one or two questions she would ask and said she would like to stay about fifteen minutes.

Preparing Questions in Advance

Before the interview, Kathie wrote in a notebook all the questions she wanted to ask, with space left for the answers. Here is her list of questions:

1. Are there any special subjects that help prepare you for medical school?
2. How many years must you attend medical school?
3. What is an "intern"?
4. What is a "resident"?
5. Can a medical doctor have a career in medicine besides private practice? If so, what are some examples?

Now Kathie was ready for Saturday's interview.

127

Proper planning and preparation are necessary if language activities are to be meaningful.
(From LANGUAGE FOR DAILY USE, Explorer Edition (Purple) by Mildred A. Dawson et al., copyright © 1978 by Harcourt Brace Jovanovich, Inc. Reprinted and reproduced by permission of the publisher.)

plans should include ways the information gained may best be utilized. Children may want to use a cassette recorder for an interview if one is available. They should know, however, that if an interview is to be recorded, permission should be obtained from the person being interviewed. Nonprofessional speakers are sometimes frightened by the thought of having their words recorded.

Standards that could be developed for interviewing include the following:

1. Introduce yourself and state the purpose of the interview.
2. Avoid sentences like "The teacher says we have to ask you about _____ ."
3. Remember that the interviewer should open and close the interview.
4. Have the questions to be asked firmly in mind or on paper so that you stick to the topic.
5. If it seems advisable, give the person to be interviewed a list of the questions to be asked. This can be done when the appointment is made, thus giving the person time to consider his answers.
6. Discover appropriate times for an interview appointment.
7. Give the person being interviewed some idea of the amount of time the interview is to last.
8. Take notes during the interview (see chapter 16).
9. Find a way to end the interview other than "Well, our time is up so we have to quit."
10. Always be courteous, listen carefully, and express appreciation for the information.

Don't forget the writing of "thank-you" notes.

Reports

The giving of oral reports is an extension of the Show and Tell activity of the primary grades and should have many of the same characteristics. That is, the content of the reports should be organized and be limited in scope rather than being rambling accounts, but many should also be given because the children want to give them. Children beyond the primary grades will volunteer to show something or to tell about personal interests and events. This volunteering if encouraged can lead to effective reporting on social studies and other content area topics, even if these report topics are assigned.

Good reports don't just happen—they need to be motivated and planned. A good report must communicate something to an audience that is important to them. Thus children will need to develop the ability to select material appropriate to the topic and to the audience, the ability to collect and organize material (this will require skill in reading critically, taking notes, summarizing, and outlining), and the ability to face the group and give the oral report with accuracy, interest, and avoidance of "ah–hmm–well a–you know" and the like.

If topics are assigned to children, there should be some choice of topics so that each child can select one that interests him or her. Children should not have to give reports, however, if they need to develop more security in speaking through some other situation first. Instruction is generally needed in location of information, preparation of notes, and the avoidance of plagiarism. Children will also need help in judging the amount of time available for the report, developing good beginnings and endings, and selecting visual aids.

A bulletin board with steps for children to follow in preparing reports may be useful. At the top of the next page is one example:

STEPS IN PREPARING A REPORT

6. Develop good opening and closing sentences.

5. Think: Is this report too long? Should it be cut?

4. Choose interesting vocabulary and illustrations.

3. Review your notes and outline the report.

2. Check the encyclopedia and other references—take notes to answer your questions.

1. What questions might be asked about this topic? List them.

Oral reporting can be fun.

Decide what opportunities there are for genuine and useful reporting. Here are some suggestions:

1. Topics related to social studies or science are suitable. See the end of each chapter in textbooks or in teacher's editions.
2. Reports may be an extension of reading. Perhaps the class has read a story about a Scottish family and the children want to know more about Scotland. The more able readers could be asked to give reports on Scotland to the class after they have consulted additional resources.
3. New plans or rules of the school can be determined and reported upon.
4. Extensions of current events topics may be the subjects of reports. For example, events as they are discussed in different newspapers would furnish excellent topics for reports during a study of propaganda techniques—detecting bias in a writer's viewpoint, the use of "loaded" words, etc.
5. Other opportunities for group or individual reports include interviews, trips to places of interest, and reviews of movies, books, or television programs.

As the children give their oral reports, make certain you are aware of individual weaknesses in usage, organization of the material, eye contact with the group, and the like. Give attention to criteria established by the children themselves. Such questions as these might be included: Did I get the attention of the class before I spoke? Did I select a topic of interest to the class? Was I sufficiently organized and prepared so that the talk moved along smoothly? Did I keep my talk in order; was it sequential? Did I have a good ending?

Children should be encouraged to set up criteria and to evaluate their individual reports. There is some danger that children will tend to set their standards too high, so you will want to participate too. Group evaluation of a talk should be carefully guided; children are sometimes cruel to one another. However, if your criticism is helpful and constructive, the children are likely to follow suit.

Storytelling

The telling of stories by children should begin when they are in the primary grades. It is an activity that they enjoy, both as tellers and as listeners, and this enjoyment can continue throughout their lives.

Storytelling is discussed in chapter 15, particularly the storytelling that teachers should do as a part of the literature program. Children's storytelling begins with their telling about personal experiences since storytelling is essentially an act of sharing. These first experiences in sharing can be followed by encouraging the children to tell stories that they've heard and liked, and later ones that they've read. The best encouragement comes from the frequent telling of stories by the teacher. Not only does this show that storytelling is "approved of," but the teacher is the model; the techniques that he or she uses are those the children adopt.

Storytelling is more informal than most other oral expressional activities, but the speech skills are still those that are needed for these others. A pleasing voice is needed, and the projection of the voice must be appropriate to the story, audience, and setting. Likewise, gestures and facial expressions must be appropriate and not exaggerated as is sometimes the case.

Storytelling is natural for children if informality is maintained.

Jokes and Riddles

When children are about eight they develop a real interest in telling jokes and riddles that may last for years. This interest can be utilized to develop oral language skills. Begin by having joke and riddle books on the library table and occasionally reading a joke or a riddle to the class.

Using jokes and riddles is often good for a time when you and the children are experiencing a letdown. One way to overcome such doldrums is to cover a bulletin board with black paper, cut out white stars, and use a red marking pen to write a riddle on each star. Use another star for the back, since the marking usually goes through the paper. This second star, which has the answer printed on it, should be fastened to the one with the question. The bulletin board title could be "The Answer Is in the Stars" or "The Stars Know—Do You?"

After the bulletin board has been made and used, the children have listened to you read jokes and riddles, and they have looked at the joke and riddle books on the library table, they should be sufficiently motivated to want to tell jokes themselves.

A class discussion is in order to establish rules for telling jokes and the types of jokes to tell. The discussion may be used to bring out the point that jokes should never hurt another person's feelings or make fun of him in any way. Children may want to tell jokes about nationalities, races, or religions because they have heard their parents or friends tell these jokes and know that people have laughed. A child may say, "My Dad tells jokes about _____ all the time." There is no good answer to this; however, you might say that when his Dad was growing up such jokes were common, but now they are disappearing. If interest is present and the class sufficiently mature, you might even go into the changes that have taken place in comedy—the disappearance of the blackface comedian, the shift-less Negro servant, the Irish cop, etc. But it is vital to avoid being critical of the child's family, or even giving the impression of being critical.

From the class discussion, lead the children to set up rules for telling jokes. The following are good:

1. Tell the joke to the teacher first to be certain that it is good joke for the class.
2. Look at the audience when telling a joke.
3. Know the order in which events happen in the joke so you don't have to say, "No, wait a minute; I forgot; let's see—ah—then he went. . . ."
4. Don't laugh at your own joke until it is over.
5. Remember the punch line. Use your voice to lead up to the punch line, and then deliver it quickly.

A good way to begin is to let the children take turns telling jokes or asking riddles as a part of the daily opening exercises. Later, extend the class time for telling jokes and riddles to an assembly program. For such a program each child in the room might dress as a clown or wear another costume of his or her choice. The entire program could consist of jokes, riddles, funny songs, and funny dances. Many or all of the children in the class should know all of the jokes so that if one child is ill there is not a crisis—his spot can be filled.

Watching a comedian on television can help children learn about such things as expression, timing, and mannerisms when telling a joke. Children can *report* to the class what they have learned about telling jokes from watching a particular individual. Work on listening skills at the same time by asking each child to re-member one joke a comedian told and to tell it to the class.

The telling of jokes and riddles is a good way to develop many oral language skills. It is especially useful with a class that has negative ideas toward school and learning, since it will develop interest and may cause them to decide that school can be fun. Reading is also taught, as children turn to books for jokes and riddles. For a child to remember a joke it is essential that he comprehend and remember what was read and understand the sequence of events. Children with negative at-titudes toward reading will generally read a book of riddles or jokes.

The telling of jokes and riddles can also be related to daily handwriting les-sons through having the children work on their handwriting problems by copying riddles from the board or writing their own. These handwriting papers can be col-lected and later made into a riddle book. Saving answers to the riddles until the end of the day will promote class conversation as children try to guess answers.

Choral Speaking

Choral speaking is a most enjoyable way to interpret literature orally. Experience with choral reading helps children learn to sense mood development, to understand the role of rhythm in speaking, and to realize the importance of volume, tone, and quality of voice. Fluency, clarity of enunciation, and speaking with expression are improved through choral speaking.

Children who are too shy to speak tend to lose their shyness when they are just members of the group in choral speaking. Children who never seems to close their mouths learn to discipline themselves when they become a part of the group. Children who hate to read may develop more positive attitudes toward reading while engaged in this activity. As with everything else in the classroom, your enthusiasm will be the factor determining whether children enjoy choral speaking and profit from it. Types of choral speaking are described below.

Refrain.   A selection such as *Poor Old Woman* appeals to children, for this is a form of choral speaking in which a soloist reads the narrative and the others join the refrain. When introducing this poem to the class you can make it more appealing by showing pictures of each bug or animal as it is mentioned. These pictures can make a delightful bulletin board and certainly sharpen imagery and highlight meanings.

Give each class member a copy of the selection. Ask the class to follow with their eyes while listening to your reading of the selection, paying particular attention to the expression. Read it again with the children joining in on the refrain.

Poor Old Woman

SOLO:	There was an old woman who swallowed a fly.
ALL *(dramatically)*:	Oh, my! Swallowed a fly!
(slowly)	Poor old woman, I think she'll die.
SOLO:	There was an old woman who swallowed a spider.
(slowly)	Right down inside her, she swallowed a spider. She swallowed the spider to kill the fly.
ALL *(dramatically)*:	Oh, my! Swallowed a fly!
(slowly)	Poor old woman, I think she'll die.
SOLO:	There was an old woman who swallowed a bird.
(said in an aside)	How absurd to swallow a bird!
(more quickly)	She swallowed the bird to kill the spider, She swallowed the spider to kill the fly.
ALL *(dramatically)*:	Oh, my! Swallowed a fly!
(slowly)	Poor old woman, I think she'll die.
SOLO:	There was an old woman who swallowed a cat.
(slowly and deliberately)	Fancy that! Swallowed a cat!
ALL:	She swallowed the cat to kill the bird, She swallowed the bird to kill the spider, She swallowed the spider to kill the fly. O, my! Swallowed a fly! Poor old woman, I think she'll die.

SOLO:	There was an old woman who swallowed a dog.
(as if telling a secret)	She went the whole hog! She swallowed a dog!
ALL:	She swallowed the dog to kill the cat,
	She swallowed the cat to kill the bird,
	She swallowed the bird to kill the spider,
	She swallowed the spider to kill the fly.
	Oh, my! Swallowed a fly!
	Poor old woman, I think she'll die.
SOLO:	There was an old woman who swallowed a cow.
(slowly and carefully)	I don't know how, but she swallowed a cow.
ALL:	She swallowed the cow to kill the dog,
(with increasing momentum)	She swallowed the dog to kill the cat,
	She swallowed the cat to kill the bird,
	She swallowed the bird to kill the spider,
	She swallowed the spider to kill the fly.
(slowly and deliberately)	Oh, my! Swallowed a fly!
	Poor old woman, I think she'll die.
SOLO:	There was an old woman who swallowed a horse.
ALL:	She died, of course.

Poems with a refrain include:

"Hoppity" by A. A. Milne.
"Hickory, Dickory, Dock," "To Market, to Market," "This Is the Way the Ladies Ride," and "A Farmer Went Trotting" (Mother Goose)
"The Wind" by Robert Louis Stevenson.
"The Mysterious Cat" by Vachel Lindsay.
"The Lamb" by William Blake.

Antiphonal.   Antiphonal choral speaking contrasts light voices with heavier ones. For example, boys may read questions and girls answers, or poems containing dialogue may be used. Poems of contrast are also excellent, with heavier voices taking parts that contain long vowels. Middle and upper grade children do well with this type of choral reading.

Give the children copies of the selection and have them follow as you read aloud to give the pattern for the children to imitate. Have several children try parts of the selection until class agreement is reached on voice quality, inflection, and timing. One good selection is Christina Rossetti's "Who Has Seen the Wind?"

HEAVY VOICES:	Who has seen the wind?
LIGHT VOICES:	Neither I nor you:
HEAVY VOICES:	But when the leaves hang trembling
	The wind is passing thro'.
LIGHT VOICES:	Who has seen the wind?
HEAVY VOICES:	Neither you nor I:
LIGHT VOICES:	But when the trees bow down their heads
	The wind is passing by.

Of course this poem could also be done with one group asking the question in each stanza and the other responding, but the above division is a bit more unusual and gives each group an opportunity for creativity in reading the lines. Other poems that can be used in this way include "Baa, Baa, Black Sheep" (Mother Goose), "Little Boy Blue" (Mother Goose), "Night" (Sara Teasdale), "It Is Raining" (Lucy Sprague Mitchell), "The Little Elf" (John Kendrick Bangs), "Father William" (Lewis Carroll), and "What Is Pink?" (Christina Rossetti).

Line-a-child.   In the line-a-child choric form small groups of two to four children or a single child speak a line or couplet. The selection is continued by another child or group, then another, and so on until the end. It is necessary that the selection have lines or couplets that are naturally separated from one another—possibly marked off by semicolons or periods.

A bulletin board display or individual pictures may serve as an introduction to the selection. Each child should have a copy of the poem, and you should point out where each line or couplet ends. (*Note:* combine this oral language activity with a written language lesson on thought units and punctuation.) Read the selection with the children listening to get the feeling of the poem and to determine which words or expressions need emphasis. Discuss these and then place the individuals or groups according to the order in which they speak so that they can remember their turns. Speaking on cue is essential for the continuity of the poem.

A good poem to try is "Jump or Jiggle" by Evelyn Beyer.

GROUP I:	Frogs jump.
	Caterpillars hump.
GROUP II:	Worms wiggle.
	Bugs jiggle.
GROUP III:	Rabbits hop.
	Horses clop.
GROUP IV:	Snakes slide.
	Sea gulls glide.
GROUP V:	Mice creep.
	Deer leap.
GROUP VI:	Puppies bounce.
	Kittens pounce.
GROUP VII:	Lions stalk.
	But
ALL:	I walk!*

Other poems for line-a-child speaking are "The Little Turtle" (Vachel Lindsay), "The Barnyard" (Maude Burham), "My Zipper Suit" (Mary Louise Allen), "The End" (A. A. Milne), "Only One Mother" (George Cooper), "Merry-Go-Round" (Dorothy W. Baruch), "Mice" (Rose Fyleman), "Someone" (Walter de la Mare), "The Wind" (Robert Louis Stevenson), "Spring Rain" (Marchette Chute), "Very Lovely" (Rose Fyleman).

* From *Another Here and Now Story Book* by Lucy Sprague Mitchell. Copyright 1937 by E. P. Dutton & Co., renewal © 1965 by Lucy Sprague Mitchell. Reprinted by permission of the publishers, E. P. Dutton & Co., Inc.

Try these:

"There Was a Crooked
  Man" (Mother Goose)
"Galoshes" (Rhoda W.
  Bacmeister)
"Silver" (Walter de la Mare)
"Snow" (Dorothy Aldis)
"The Sun" (John
  Drinkwater)
"Someone" (Walter de la
  Mare)
"The Monkeys and the
  Crocodile" (Laura E.
  Richards)

Unison.   Teachers are often surprised to discover that unison speaking is the most difficult of all choral work. Lower elementary children have great difficulty in coordinating their voices, and this precision is essential for quality unison speaking. This form also requires the greatest skill by the director. If you wish to see whether young children can do unison speaking, try Mother Goose rhymes, as they are easily interpreted and can serve as a beginning for pantomime and dramatics.

A wealth of poems are suitable for unison speaking in the intermediate and upper grades. One example is "The Purple Cow" by Gelett Burgess:

> I never saw a purple cow,
> I never hope to see one;
> But I can tell you anyhow,
> I'd rather see than be one!

Choral reading or speaking has advantages as an assembly presentation. First, all the children in the class become involved and are on stage. Second, all children will learn the selection; then if the child selected as soloist comes down with measles on the day of the production, others know the part. Those who have been involved with the trauma of having a sick child on the day of a program will appreciate this advantage of choral speaking.

Creative Dramatics

The dramatic play that has long been an essential part of the language arts program in the primary grades is essentially the same as creative dramatics, which is now advocated as an important aspect of the oral language program in the middle and upper grades—and beyond. Creative dramatics has many advantages over formal dramatization, the most obvious being that it requires no scenery, props, costumes, or memorization of lines. Beyond this, however, it has many more important values.

First, of course, it helps to develop creativity in language, in thinking, in use of the voice, and in body movement. Since the essence of creative dramatics is improvisation, children are inspired to use imagination in choosing words and actions that will convey the desired impression. They can experiment with tone, rate of speaking, use of gestures, and even bodily stance as they try to create a believable mood or character. All of these require creative thinking.

In addition, the use of creative dramatics promotes both personal and social growth. Children release energy and express emotions as they respond to music or some other stimulus and as they create characters and scenes. A shy child can gain confidence through pretending to be someone else, as well as through working in a group. The aggressive child learns to work as a part of a group, and all children learn how important cooperation and planning are to achieving a desired outcome. And, finally, children gain a better understanding of themselves and others as they "become" other people and discover the commonality of human emotions.

If the children have not had a background of experience in dramatic play and other oral activities, it would probably be best to start at the beginning of the year with activities similar to those used in the primary grades: rhythmic response to

A Checklist for Actors

Did I

1. Speak clearly?
2. Speak loudly enough for everyone to hear?
3. Look at the person I was talking to?
4. Follow the story sequence?
5. Feel and act like my character?

A Checklist for the Audience

1. Was I a good listener?
2. Was I polite to the actors and the rest of the audience?
3. Could everyone be heard?
4. Was the story in sequence?
5. Did the characters seem real?

music, pantomime, and re-creation of incidents from literature. Dramatizing an incident such as Charlie's visit to the chocolate factory or Tom Sawyer conning his friends into whitewashing the fence is not difficult, yet it presents an opportunity for creativity. From there you might graduate to using a different ending to a story or to creating another incident involving the same characters (e.g., "What do you think might have happened if Tom's friends had decided to turn the tables on him?").

Children may also react bodily to music, expressing through motion the way the music makes them feel. They may portray moods, such as happiness, sorrow, pain, etc., with or without words. They may dramatize endings for a story beginning; this could be only a sentence, or it could be a partially developed plot. (Many of the suggestions in chapter 9 for starting creative writing are adaptable to creative dramatics.)

Creative dramatics can also be used to add understanding and depth to almost any area of the curriculum. A child who has helped to create a rhythmic dance based on a mathematical concept (e.g., a square, subtraction, etc.) will not find arithmetic dull. Similarly, dramatizing a day spent traveling across Kansas in a covered wagon will give students a deeper understanding of the hardships of the westward expansion.

All the skills required for any oral activity can be developed through creative dramatics. Like any other activity, it should not be overdone, but do make it an integral part of your language arts program.

Puppetry

Puppets and marionettes can be useful tools for teaching oral expression. Besides they are fun! Puppets are more helpful than marionettes, unless a teacher is experienced with marionettes. A marionette is usually operated from above by strings, which often isn't easy for children to do, whereas a puppet is operated by hand from below. Interest in puppets may first be developed when a child brings a hand puppet for "Show and Tell." Children may wish to use this puppet to recite a favorite Mother Goose rhyme. Talking for a puppet instead of one's self tends to bring out a shy child rather easily. Once interest has been generated you will want to encourage each child to make his or her own puppet. Making puppets and putting on a play is an excellent way to teach children to follow directions and to strengthen language skills. And the children will have a delightful time while they are learning.

When making puppets, start with simple ones such as the cut-out stick puppets, empty-bag puppets, or vegetable and fruit puppets.

Cut-out Stick Puppets. To make stick puppets figures or faces may be drawn, colored, and cut from cardboard, or paper dolls may be used. Coloring books often have outlines of figures or faces that can be pasted on cardboard. Tongue depressors or ice cream sticks can be glued to the bottoms for the children to hold. If a puppet needs support up the back, a longer stick will be needed—one long enough so that the hand holding it will not show if the puppet is used in a puppet stage. Stick puppets can be clothed, either with cloth or paper. Old wallpaper, leftover gift wrap from Chrsitmas, or even colorful shelf paper can be useful for making attractive paper clothes, and remnants or scraps from mothers' sewing bags can provide materials for cloth garments.

Empty-bag Puppets.   Children can make and use empty-bag puppets if the bags are not too large for them to handle. Place the bag flat, with the folded bottom part

Puppets, puppets, puppets! And creativity and talk!

up. Draw or paint the upper part of a face on the bottom of the bag and the lower part of the face on the side. If you want the puppet to have a moving mouth, the upper part of the mouth should be on the bag bottom, and the lower lip on the side. If the eyes are to move, the lashes should be on the bottom, with the lower part of the eyes on the side. The puppet is operated by placing fingers in the bag so that the folded-down bottom can be moved up and down to show a mouth moving (or eyes, eyelashes, or eye brows). Yarn, crepe paper, or cotton can be glued on for hair.

Vegetable and Fruit Puppets.   Potatoes, carrots, beets, radishes, apples, and oranges are a few of the vegetables and fruits that can be mounted on sticks and used as other stick puppets are used. Faces can be made in a variety of ways: they can be cut out with a vegetable peeler, drawn on with paint or a felt-tip pen, or made from paper or felt and pasted on. Or thumb tacks or paper stars may be used for eyes, with other features added in one of the above ways.

More Advanced Puppets.   At a little more advanced level are *sock puppets.* These are simply socks with buttons sewed on for eyes and with crayons or paint used to make other features. The *stuffed-bag puppet* is an extension of the empty-bag puppet. The bag is filled about halfway with crumpled paper. (This simply fills out the bag, which is used in about the same way as described above.) If the bag is large, it can be partly drawn together with a string to represent a neck and shoulders below the face. Usually stuffed-bag puppets are decorated or dressed more than the simpler puppets.

Puppets you and children can make.

The Stage.   You will need some kind of stage to use puppets for dramatization. Of course, hand puppets are good for storytelling, getting children's attention, and just talking, but to get full value from the puppets children make, dramatization is needed.

The stage should be inexpensive and easy to make. Tip a card table on its side; the children can sit behind it and raise puppets above the table edge. A large box or carton—the kind refrigerators or stoves are shipped in—also works well. Part of a side is cut out and the part visible to the audience is painted. The children sit inside and raise their hand puppets to the "stage floor" level.

The Story.   Almost any situation can be dramatized with puppets. Here are some ideas:

1. Accepting responsibility for tasks at home and at school, such as cleanliness of a room or completion of a task. Let the children plan their own dialogue for this.
2. Good sportsmanship on or off the playground.
3. Correct behavior in social situations.
4. Stories from literature. Try these:

See chapter 15 for criteria for choosing stories to read or tell.

Amiable Giant (Louis Slobodkin)
The Three Bears
Andy and the Lion (James Daugherty)
Hansel and Gretel
Snipp, Snapp, Snurr (Maj Lindman)
Pet Show (Ezra Jack Keats)

SPECIAL CONSIDERATIONS IN TEACHING

Look into Tape Clubs
(exchanges like Pen Pals)

World Tapes for Education
  P.O. Box 9211
  Dallas, TX 75221
International Tape Worms
  P.O. Box 215
  Cedarhurst, NY 11516
The National Tapespinners
  Box 148
  Paoli, PA 19301

The sections that follow emphasize special concerns in teaching oral communication. These are important to oral situations and should receive attention in many teaching activities.

Social Amenities

Social amenities are best taught when the situation demands their practice. Many teachers undoubtedly would like to think that these are taught in the home, but most of us know that often they are not.

Your attitude toward teaching and toward each child and the atmosphere in your classroom are of prime importance in teaching social behavior. Since nearly every classroom has at least one child who is disliked by the other children, or perhaps several children who come to school so dirty that you may hesitate to touch their papers (to say nothing of their bodies), the need for teaching social amenities is readily apparent. The basis for such teaching is acceptance and mutual respect among all concerned—you and each child.

If you are having difficulty getting children to accept a particular child, talk with the librarian about a bibliotherapeutic book that may help bridge the gap. These books are designed to improve a child's attitudes toward himself or toward adjusting to a difficult situation. Reading a book about such a situation to the class may help the children to develop understanding and acceptance. Hopefully, the children will follow your lead and become pleasant and accepting of each other. Social amenities that children particularly need to learn are making introductions and extending and responding to greetings. Children need to learn the conventions followed in these amenities and this is best done through the many genuine occasions that arise in every classroom. For example, visitors who come into the room

Making Introductions

Have you ever had to introduce two strangers to each other? If so, did you have any trouble deciding how to do it?

Read what Manuel says.

1. "Dad, this is Alan Johnson. Alan plays on my team. Alan, this is my dad, Mr. Ruiz."
2. "Jill, this is my neighbor Tim Thomas. Tim, this is my friend, Jill Levine. She just came home from a camping trip."
3. "Ms. McCarthy, my name is Manuel Ruiz. My sister Amy won't be able to come to tumbling practice today. She has the flu."

To Discuss

1. When Manuel introduced a younger person to an older person, which name did he say first?
2. Why did he tell Tim that Jill had gone camping? What would you say to Jill if you were Tim?
3. Could Manuel have given Ms. McCarthy the message without telling her his name? Why do you think he introduced himself?

Practice

1. Select two classmates. Decide on a situation like one of those above. Practice introducing them the correct way. Check the rules before you begin.
2. Act out your introduction.

9

Children should learn social amenities as part of the program. (From LANGUAGE FOR DAILY USE, Explorer Edition (Orange) by Mildred A. Dawson et al., copyright © 1978 by Harcourt Brace Jovanovich, Inc. Reprinted and reproduced by permission of the publisher.)

may be greeted by a room host or hostess, who introduces them to the teacher and the other children. Good practice can also occur during an open house, parents' night, or similar occasion. In addition, there are many situations in which these amenities can be taught through dramatization.

In making introductions children should learn to say, "Mrs. Smith, this is Sue" or "Mary, I'd like you to meet Jimmy." The first name mentioned should be the person honored—an older person, a woman, or a special guest.

Children should also learn how to respond: "I'm very glad to meet you, Sue" or "How do you do." Encourage them to shake hands firmly (but not too firmly) and to look at the person they are being introduced to.

Rules that are helpful include these:

1. Speak each person's name clearly (if a name is not understood ask that it be repeated).
2. Use an introduction to start a conversation, with the person making the introduction beginning the conversation.
3. When introducing yourself to another, be certain to give your name clearly and add some identifying remark.
4. Speak the name of a person you are introduced to and use it when speaking to him to help remember it.

Discuss with children the awkwardness of a situation in which two people are talking and are joined by a third person, known to one of the first two but not to the other. The person who knows the one who has joined them does not introduce him because of having forgotten his name. This should be no excuse; the person should simply apologize, ask his name, and then introduce him. Children will be eased by knowing that many people feel shy and embarrassed in this situation—that this is natural but needs to be overcome.

Other situations to discuss with children might include the following:

1. What can be said to make a new child feel welcome?
2. What words should be used in such situations as thanking an aunt who has given a boy a shirt that he thinks is ugly? What can he say about the shirt without lying or hurting the aunt's feelings?
3. What might be said and done if a group of children are playing ball and notice some strange children watching? What do you do?
4. Suppose you are having dinner at a friend's house. What do you do and say after dinner?
5. What do you say if you want a person to sit in a particular place?
6. A friend invites you to a movie. What do you say?
7. What are some situations in which you should offer assistance? For example, in removing a coat, what do you say?
8. Suppose the teacher asks, "Who discovered America?" and a child replies "George Washington." Is it polite to laugh?
9. How do you respond to courtesies shown you?
10. Someone knocks at the door. How do you greet this person?

Classroom Courtesy

Manners and courtesy are essential if people are to get along in a pleasant atmosphere. It might help to begin the year with a discussion of "What we need to do to make our room a pleasant place in which to live and work."

This may also be the time to discuss the ways in which courtesy and safety work together. The discussion of classroom behavior might well lead to a unit on courtesy and the necessity for obeying the rules on school buses, in the lunchroom, or on the playground.

You can get help with such units from several sources. For example, an excellent aid in teaching bicycle safety and courtesy is *Bicycle Safety Program Handbook* (4H Club Leaders' guide L-2-1A), which can be acquired from the New York State College of Agriculture, Cooperative Extension Service, Cornell University, Ithaca, New York. Other materials related to safety and courtesy may often be obtained from insurance agents, since many insurance companies provide a wealth of materials on these subjects. For example, write to Public Relations, Kemper Insurance Company, 4750 Sheriden Road, Chicago, Illinois 60640, for free material on several aspects of school safety.

Also, by the same author, What Do You Do, Dear? *and* Dear Dragon *(New York: Harcourt Brace Jovanovich).*

The library is important in teaching courtesy; there are numerous books, films, and filmstrips available on this topic. You might want to read to your class *What Do You Say, Dear?* by Sesyle Joslin. Magazine pictures may also be used to promote discussions of good manners; use these on a bulletin board or show them to a group using an opaque projector.

After discussing courtesy in the room and the importance of courtesy and safety when coming to or going from school as well as on the playground, discuss courtesy and safety in the school building—the corridor, cafeteria, auditorium, and office. Perhaps the principal will be able to come to the room to discuss the importance of courtesy and how the children can help by being polite and following school rules (or a child may interview the principal). Teachers are often hesitant about asking school administrators to talk with their classes, but many are flattered to be invited. Other people who work in the school building may be willing to discuss their jobs with the children and tell how good manners make their work easier. Or a patrol boy or crossing guard may discuss why good manners and following directions are essential for safety.

Children may also discuss correct behavior and courtesy in public places such as stores, museums, libraries, zoos, parks, restaurants, pools, movies, or ball games. Courtesy and behavior on escalators, elevators, streets, and public buses should also be discussed. It is essential that children learn appropriate physical and verbal behavior, since there really is no excuse for rudeness by people of any age.

Through dramatization—actually playing roles—children can learn many social amenities that will be useful to them. In fact, teaching the amenities provides an opportunity to use a variety of oral language experiences. Discussion, role playing, telephoning, interviewing, committee work, puppet plays, making announcements, and giving directions can all be used to further children's understanding of behavior that shows concern for others.

The Role of Parents

It is the sharing of experiences that broadens children's knowledge of the world about them, increases their vocabulary, and develops their ability to express themselves. Most teachers agree that it is from a child's experiences and his or her discussion of them that concepts necessary for future learning are developed. Yet schools are not able to provide all the experiences that a child needs—much is the job of the parents. Consider planning a program for parents with the purpose of informing them of the role of experience in learning. Include in such a program an explanation of the importance of talking with and to children at every age level. If a program is not possible, perhaps the school might place an article in the local paper or you might send a list of suggestions home to parents. Caution is needed in wording such a message, as most parents do not want to be *told* how to raise their children. Yet parents do want their children to do well in school. The following type of suggestion for encouraging a child's oral language development might work:

1. Is it possible for most or all of your family to eat meals together? Mealtime conversation can help children to know that you are interested in them and to talk more freely.
2. Answer children's questions when you can. If you don't know the answer, perhaps you can help them to find it.
3. Instead of trying not to use words that children do not understand, explain the meanings of new words to them.
4. Encourage children to talk in sentences, but do not be so demanding about this that they stop talking at all.
5. Remember that children will model their speech after that of adults who live around them.
6. Discourage baby talk; help children learn to talk so that they can be understood by strangers as well as by the family.
7. Stories, poems, nursery rhymes, and records should be a part of every child's life. Read to your child as much as you can, and talk about the stories and the people in them.
8. A child's experiences contribute to his or her school work. The more people, places, and things a child sees, the better prepared he or she will be for speaking, reading, and writing. Take the child with you whenever you can, even to the grocery store. Talk about the people and things you see.
9. Plan special trips with children. Take them on walks, go with them to the zoo or museum, visit places of interest in the area, and talk with them about these experiences.
10. When your family goes on a trip, short or long, talk about the things you see along the road or highway, the names of rivers, mountains, etc. Try to stop occasionally at historical markers along the road or at places of particular interest.

Such statements may seem too direct; you might wish instead to write a short letter to parents, embodying these or similar ideas. The point to stress is that encouraging language development is something that can be done by talking with children and providing them with experiences and that the important ingredients are time and attention rather than financial outlay. It is possible that many parents who are willing to spend the time have simply not realized this.

EVALUATING ORAL EXPRESSION

Standardized tests for measuring oral language performance are not available, but this does not mean that children's skills and abilities in speaking situations should not be evaluated. Evaluation can and should be a part of virtually every speaking situation. This does not mean formal evaluation or the testing that first may come to mind, but it does mean appraisal, determining what children can and cannot do adequately for their maturity levels. Such evaluation is a basic element in teaching if children's speaking skills and abilities are to improve from one speech activity to another.

Standards

Let's Be Good Conversationalists

1. Always be polite.
2. Only one person should talk at a time.
3. Speak clearly and listen carefully.
4. Use good language.
5. Do not intrude on the conversations of others.

Guidelines, rules, or standards for performance in oral expression can be developed for all oral language situations. These standards should be developed by you and the pupils. They should reflect the children's way of looking at things, but if they are too restrictive or are beyond the performance levels possible, some modification may be necessary. Standards should always be thought of as evolving.

Evaluation should always be made in terms of the standards developed by you and the children and, most importantly, in terms of each individual child and the amount of progress he or she has made toward achieving these goals. In addition, you should evaluate the extent of each child's capabilities in the speech skills discussed earlier in this chapter, as well as his or her efforts to make any needed improvement. The evaluation of oral expression is bound to be somewhat subjective, but it will be less so if goals are clearly understood, if progress in achieving these goals is discussed regularly by you *and* the children, and if each child is evaluated according to his individual abilities, needs, and achievements.

Checklists

Rules for Giving a Report

1. Pick an interesting topic and stick to it.
2. Have a good opening and closing.
3. Look at the audience.
4. Make your voice loud enough to be heard.
5. Organize your report carefully.
6. Use good sentences and interesting words.

Checklists are similar to lists of standards in that they also suggest appropriate behaviors. The items on a checklist are usually questions that can be answered with "Yes," "No," or a check mark. Checklists may be used by individual pupils for self-evaluation or by the teacher.

Checking Up on My Speech

1. Is my voice pleasant to hear?
2. Do I speak so everyone can understand me?
3. Do I adjust the volume of my voice for different situations?
4. Am I prepared for speaking activities?
5. Do I think before speaking?
6. Do I use good words and sentences?

A checklist may be extended to include questions about specific usage items of concern, physical mannerisms exhibited by pupils, and more details regarding the content and organization of the material.

Checklists should be used at regular intervals, and comparisons made of the responses from one time to another. And checklists, like standards, may need to be revised as children's abilities progress.

A FINAL WORD

Recognizing that children come to school with considerable speaking ability, knowledge of how language works, and much to talk about is the basis of an effective oral language program. This foundation must then be built upon for children to gain added skill in conversing, discussing, and behaving with ease in social situations. It must also be built upon for children to learn to participate effectively in meetings and interviews and in the giving of reports and announcements. This building results from direct attention to these speaking activities and from creative dramatics, the use of puppets, and choral speaking. The teaching focus should be on utilizing the many natural situations that occur in classrooms for teaching and developing the needed skills and abilities.

REFERENCES

Books

Bamman, Henry, *et al. Oral Interpretation of Children's Literature.* Dubuque, IA: William C. Brown Co., 1971.

Bauer, Caroline Feller. *Handbook for Storytellers.* Chicago: American Library Association, 1977.

Chambers, Dewey W. *Storytelling and Creative Drama.* Dubuque, IA: William C. Brown Co., 1970.

Complo, Sr. Jannita Marie. *Dramakinetics in the Classroom: A Handbook of Creative Dramatics and Improvised Movement.* Boston: Plays, Inc., 1974.

Edwards, Charlotte. *Creative Dramatics.* Dansville, NY: The Instructor Publications, Inc., 1972.

Evans, Helen. *Together We Speak: A Collection of Choral Readings.* Dansville, NY: F.A. Owen Publishing Co., 1959.

Gardner, Richard. *101 Hand Puppets.* New York: David McKay Company, 1962.

Gillies, Emily. *Creative Dramatics for All Children.* Washington, DC: Association for Childhood Education International, 1973.

Goaman, Muriel. *Judy's and Andrew's Puppet Book.* Boston: Plays, Inc., 1973.

Hawes, Bill. *The Puppet Book.* San Diego: Beta Books, 1977.

Lowndes, Betty. *Movement and Creative Drama for Children.* Boston: Plays, Inc., 1971.

McCaslin, Nellie. *Creative Dramatics in the Classroom,* 2nd ed. New York: David McKay Company, Inc., 1974.

McIntyre, Barbara M. *Creative Drama in the Elementary School.* Itasca, IL: F. E. Peacock Publishers, 1974.

Philpott, Violet and McNeil, Mary Jean, *The Know How Book of Puppets.* New York: Sterling Publishing Co., 1975.

Rasmussen, Carrie. *Let's Say Poetry Together and Have Fun: For Intermediate Grades.* Minneapolis: Burgess Publishing Co., 1963.

———. *Let's Say Poetry Together and Have Fun: For Primary Grades.* Minneapolis: Burgess Publishing Co., 1962.

Stewig, John W. *Spontaneous Drama: A Language Art.* Columbus, OH: Charles E. Merrill, 1974.

Wilt, Joy, *et al. Puppets With Pizazz.* Waco, TX: Creative Resources, 1977.

———. *More Puppets With Pizazz.* Waco, TX: Creative Resources, 1977.

Films

Fun with Speech Sounds. Chicago: Coronet Films (11 minutes; color, b/w; primary).

How to Make a Puppet. Los Angeles: Bailey-Film Associates (10 minutes; color; primary and intermediate).

Let's Pronounce Well. Chicago: Coronet Films (11 minutes; color, b/w; intermediate).

Let's Try Choral Reading. New York: McGraw-Hill Films (12 minutes; color; grades 2–6).

Parliamentary Procedures in Action. Chicago: Coronet Films (16 minutes; color, b/w; intermediate).

Storytelling: Can You Tell It in Order? Chicago: Coronet (11 minutes; color or b/w; primary).

Storytelling Is Fun. Chicago: Coronet (11 minutes; color or b/w; intermediate).

Talk About It Series. New York: McGraw-Hill (3 sets of 10 super 8 millimeter film loops; primary).

Unfinished Stories. Garden City, NY: Doubleday and Company, Inc. (series of short films; color; intermediate, upper).

Ways to Better Conversation. Chicago: Coronet Films.

Your Communication Skills: Exchange of Ideas. Chicago: Coronet Films (11 minutes; intermediate).

Your Communication Skills: Speaking. Chicago: Coronet Films (11 minutes; color, b/w; intermediate).

Filmstrips

Captain Good Speech and Mr. Mumbles. Jamaica, NY: Eyegate House (Set of 6 color-sound strips; primary).

Good Manners at Play. Jamaica, NY: Eyegate House.

Improving Communication Skills through Speech Correction. Jamaica, NY: Eyegate House (Set of 7 color strips; grades 2–6).

New Classmate. New York: Popular Science Films.

Riddle a Rhyme. Jamaica, NY: Eyegate House (Set of 8 sound strips; primary).

Talking Time Series. New York: McGraw-Hill (2 sets of 8 strips each; grades 2–6).

Thinking Imaginatively, Speaking Clearly. New York: Learning Corp. (Set of 6 strips with records; primary and intermediate).

Why Have Good Manners? Jamaica, NY: Eyegate House.

You Decide: Open-Ended Tales. Mahwah, NJ: Troll Associates (6 film strips and 3 records or cassettes; intermediate).

Recordings

Fun with Speech. Chicago: Encyclopedia Britannica Educational Corp. (One 12″ LP; primary).

Talkstarters. Chicago: Scott, Foresman (books and records; primary).

What Did You Say, Dear? Weston, CT: Weston Woods (One 7″ LP; primary).

Kits

Naturally Speaking. Irving-on-Hudson, NY: Hudson Photographic Industries (4 filmstrips, 2 cassettes, and guide; primary).

Story Starters. Holyoke, MA: Scott Education Division of Jam Handy (3 kits of 5 filmstrips, 4 cassettes, storybook prints, and guides each; primary and intermediate).

ACTIVITIES FOR PRESERVICE TEACHERS

1. Interview the speech correctionist in a school district to find out what kinds of speech problems he encounters and what kinds of remedial procedures are used.

2. During your observations of various classrooms, see if you can discover a child whose difficulty in speaking appears to stem from feelings of insecurity. Ask the teacher's permission to help work with this child. Over a period of several weeks, see if you can detect any signs of increased confidence due to the additional attention.

3. Observe a class during some oral activity and use a checklist to evaluate both individuals and the group. From this evaluation, decide which skills,

attitudes, or abilities should have teaching priority for the entire class and which children need individual help.

4. Compile a booklet of poems that would be appropriate for choral speaking. Determine which type of choral activity each is best suited for.

5. Plan a lesson utilizing creative dramatics for a grade level of your choice. Be sure to include motivation, kinds of activities that might develop, and follow-up activities.

6. Develop a file of ideas that children might like to dramatize. These ideas can be written on 3x5 cards and should include little more than the

nucleus of the idea. Identify each as to the number of children to be involved. Some ideas might be Children in the Cafeteria Lunch Line, The Family Loads the Car for a Vacation, Sitting on the Bench at a Big Game, and The School Office.

7. Preview one of the films in the preceding list (or another list of films intended for use in teaching some aspect of oral language), decide whether it is one you would want to use, and suggest ways in which it might be integrated into a program.

ACTIVITIES FOR INSERVICE TEACHERS

1. Obtain the telephone materials suggested in this chapter. Examine them carefully, select those appropriate for your class, and prepare a variety of experiences and activities using them.

2. Assist the children in your class in forming a club based on their interests. Use the information in this chapter and perhaps that in a language textbook to teach the children the parliamentary procedures needed by their club.

3. Prepare a card file of information on books of jokes, riddles, and speech games that children may use.

4. Arrange for children in your class to interview various persons around the school—custodians, clerks, bus drivers, etc. Make certain that suggestions in this chapter for preparing for interviewing are followed.

5. Develop a Drama Book Shelf. This should include books with good stories to dramatize. Criteria for selection of stories should include: simple sequences, clear-cut climax, significance of content, and possibilities of characterizations.

6. Plan a choral speaking activity with your class

that could be presented to another class, a school assembly, or a parents' night.

7. List the steps you would use when making puppets with a group of children. What problems might you encounter? How would you resolve them? Now that you've planned, try puppet making with your class. Evaluate the experience in terms of children's interest, participation, and opportunities to use language.

8. Collect and file in a small box selections for choral speaking that can be used in the small periods of time that become available daily. Use these for the minute spent waiting for the bell, for settling-down time after a physical activity, for those in the class who have finished their cleaning up, etc.

9. Develop a lesson that will use creative dramatics in a curriculum area other than language arts. Evaluate the success of the lesson and report results to the class.

10. Prepare a page that could be sent home to parents suggesting ways they might foster the development of their children's speech in various situations.

INDEPENDENT ACTIVITIES FOR CHILDREN

1. Keep a card file of topics or situations calling for oral activities. These might be filed under types (conversation, discussion, interviews, storytelling, explanations and directions, etc.) or they might be labeled simply *individual* or *group*.

When children have free time during the day, they draw a card at random and develop the activity suggested. Group activities can be enjoyed and/or evaluated by those participating; individual activities can be recorded on tape or presented to the class at odd moments—before lunch, for example. Topics should not be too specific or directive. A conversation card, for example, might say, "A new neighbor has moved into the house next door. Decide just how you might meet and carry on conversation. Be yourself, not some imaginary person."

The children themselves should be encouraged to add topics; they may also help to rotate cards so topics do not become stale.

2. Give a child a list of words that are sometimes not pronounced correctly or that are not clearly enunciated so that they are confused with other words. Have him record these and listen to himself. You may also check his recording or have him do this with another child so that they check on one another. Some words to use are *quote, quota; compile, compel; partial, parcel*; etc.

3. A child can prepare a talk to give to the class on a topic such as:
   a. How to make a kite.
   b. How to build a snowman.
   c. How to build and care for an aquarium.
   d. How to make a stamp collection.

4. Give a child a collection of pictures from magazines and have him record on tape a story based upon these pictures.

5. Children may also record original stories on tape. At a special time, such as once each week, tapes may be played to the class for listening and discussion practice.

6. Let children keep a file of pantomime ideas. Provide a mirror in a corner of the room where individual children can experiment with pantomimes and prepare to present them to the class or to small groups.

7. Individual children may prepare and present announcements at school assemblies or over the school public address system.

8. Two children may work together to plan a play to demonstrate good manners. For example, one might be a guest visiting the classroom and the other could greet and introduce him, or they might illustrate ways to disagree in a conversation without being discourteous.

9. Have a child plan a skit for a special day (Citizenship Day, the anniversary of the Boston Tea Party, United Nations Day, Washington's Birthday, Flag Day, etc.). The planning may include writing a script, getting props, researching, selecting participants, etc.

10. A child can relate to a small group an incident in a story he has read, telling it as though he had been one of the characters. (He may wish to rehearse this before a mirror or record it on tape before presenting it to the group.)

11. Allow children to select a "visitors' committee" who will greet guests to the classroom, explain activities of the class to them, and otherwise act as hosts. Ask school personnel and parents to visit regularly to provide practice for the hosts. New members should be appointed at regular intervals.

12. Children can make puppets independently if they are provided with a place and materials—paper bags, paint, scissors, socks, sticks, stapler, etc. Have a few puppet models, but encourage individual departures from copying these.

13. Stories can be made up to tell using puppets. Children may make up these stories independently and practice them in front of the mirror before telling them to the class or to a small group.

14. A child can make and use finger puppets to dramatize nursery rhymes for a friend who has been out of school for several days.

15. Paper dolls and their clothing can be cut out and used for dramatic play. One or two children may create a play with paper dolls.

7

Fostering Effective Listening

At a party, were you ever caught in the middle of two or three conversations taking place at once? How was your listening? Does the rock music coming over the radio in your home affect your listening? What about traffic noise that almost literally shakes the windows?

Most of us are concerned with screening our listening—with noise "pollution." Yet we are also concerned about receiving the newscaster's words accurately and about gaining "the message" from members of our family—incuding the children. And we want the listening skills of our children at home and at school to be effective.

Listening is more than just hearing: hearing frequently cannot be avoided because sounds cannot be screened out. However, we can do something about deciding what we listen to and how this listening can be done most effectively. Likewise, we can help children attain listening skills.

LISTENING CONCERNS AND ISSUES

By the time children come to school for the first time they have had five or six years' experience in listening. From listening they learned the language of their homes, of their neighborhoods, and possibly of much of the world (through travel and television). No one has taught them to listen, although they have likely been told many times to "Pay attention." They have probably acquired some listening habits and skills, but they have probably not developed the concern and many of the practices for learning by listening that teachers desire.

Although we sometimes say we "half listen" and although we often listen intermittently or in a somewhat passive manner to music or to someone talking, real listening requires participation. Like the reader, the listener must actively engage in the perception and recognition of words and phrases, in the comprehension of ideas and facts, and in conscious or emotional reaction to these in relation to his or her background of experience. Listening is not an activity that should be

"When the eyes are closed, the hearing becomes more acute," says a medical authority. You may have noticed students experimenting on this in class.

separated from expression. Listening to speech requires a speaker. Listening to music requires a performer. Someone or some thing is always producing the sounds heard; thus the active nature of listening is further emphasized.

The first step in listening is hearing, which involves auditory acuity, concentration, and a basic understanding of the way the language being heard works. As one author has said, listening requires "noticing sound, translating it into internal speech, . . . evoking images for the things and events named, [and] thinking of relationships."[1] What transpires in the listener after that she regards as "thinking beyond listening." This is a key point, because it means that in teaching children to be effective listeners, thinking skills as well as listening skills must receive attention.

Listening is affected by the acuity with which a person receives sound waves of various frequencies (tones) at various intensities (levels of loudness). An inability to respond to normal frequencies and intensities represents a hearing loss, which may range from minor to serious. Although a hearing loss affects an individual's ability to perceive sounds and discriminate among them, it is possible for a person to have normal hearing and yet have difficulty with sound perception and discrimination. This is particularly the case with people who have speech problems and with those unfamiliar with a language or a particular dialect. There should be, at most, only minimal problems with children who speak the language or dialect and who do not have speech or hearing problems. Many children who seem to have difficulty with perception and discrimination are probably reflecting a lack of understanding of what they are asked to do, unfamiliarity with aspects of the language (e.g., the words used), little motivation to retain (remember) what they heard, or inattention.

Hearing is also affected by fatigue and masking. Masking is simply a failure to hear because of the superimposition of sounds that interfere—the many voices at a cocktail party. Related to this, but with a physical base, is inadequate binaural hearing. Binaural hearing may be thought of as similar to depth perception in vision; that is, without adequate binaural hearing the individual cannot locate a particular speaker among several talking at once.

There are a number of factors related to hearing and listening that may interfere with reception:

- speech that is too rapid for reception (usually because the content is unfamiliar)
- slow speech, which leads to "mind wandering"
- lack of interest in the topic or speaker
- waiting for the opportunity to take issue with the speaker
- inadequate knowledge of the topic
- distractions caused by sounds, movement, or the physical surroundings
- an "over-acceptance" of the speaker and/or the topic
- inadequate development of the skills needed for listening
- poor organization of the material to be listened to
- preoccupation with personal interests and problems
- a hearing loss

Research has shown that:

- 45% of a child's school day is spent listening.
- 52.9% of a group of teachers reported doing "little" direct teaching of listening.
- Less than 1% of the content of elementary school language textbooks is devoted to listening instruction.[2]

THE LISTENING SKILLS

Listening skills have been listed by many researchers, but with the increase in the number of these lists there has arisen more and more skepticism about their validity. Obviously, though, there are factors that make reception of sounds meaningful. Possibly listening is something of a state of mind. The young child who has received no instruction in listening can listen well when he or she wishes to do so. No one has to be called twice for supper if he is hungry. A child must have listened effectively in order to have learned the many words that he knows and to have the understanding he has of many ideas and concepts.

Yet young children have generally not been required to listen for some purposes so some guidance or teaching for these purposes seems necessary. We believe that skills helpful to listening for various specific purposes have been identified. Whether or not they should be regarded exclusively as listening skills matters little. These skills, combined with those concerned with accurate perception of sound symbols, become for the elementary school teacher the listening skills.

Perception Skills

A listener's first task is perception. Like the reader, the listener must identify words. Of course, every listener has an auditory vocabulary, which corresponds in the reception act to the sight words of the reader, but both reader and listener meet unknown words and expressions that must be identified if communication is to occur. The perception skills are as follows:

- Skill in the perception of language sounds and discrimination among them. Each speech sound must be heard, identified, and recognized as different from every other speech sound.
- Skill in identifying a group of sounds as a symbol—a word—to which meaning is attached and in identifying a group of words—a combination of words, a phrase, or a sentence—to which meaning is attached.
- Skill in deducing the meanings of unknown words and phrases through context. Since in listening (as in reading) not every word is familiar, it is often necessary to get the meaning from the general understanding of the context in which it is said.

Some Purposes for Listening

1. To get the main idea.
2. To select details.
3. To establish a mood.
4. To answer questions.
5. To summarize information.
6. To separate fact from opinion.
7. To gain a visual image.
8. To appreciate and enjoy.
9. To recognize propaganda, bias, or prejudice.
10. To determine the speaker's purpose.
11. To adapt information presented to a particular need.
12. To evaluate in terms of some criteria.
13. To perceive relationships.
14. To interpret unusual or especially appealing language.
15. To show courtesy.

Comprehension Skills

Comprehension means understanding—getting the meaning. Although some of the perception skills lead to meanings of sequences of sounds or words (principally at the recognition level), getting the meaning in the sense of the total communication requires these skills:

- Skill in comprehending what has been heard by such means as the following:
   noting details and fitting them together
   determining the main and subordinate ideas
   finding the order or sequence of the communication
   summarizing
   recognizing emotional appeal and/or propaganda
   noting clues to the speaker's thoughts or opinions
- Skill in relating what was heard to previous learning in order to build new understandings. This is simply making use of what has been received; it means going beyond merely understanding and calls for making inferences and drawing conclusions.

These skills are closely related to the purposes for listening—purposes that arise throughout each day for almost everyone. For example, in the classroom children and teacher must listen to one another as they discuss topics of interest, plan activities, and stimulate each other's thinking and study. Each child needs to listen so that he or she can answer questions about social studies events, a story the class has read, or an arithmetic problem. The child must listen in order to separate fact from opinion (in a newscast, a political speech, a TV advertisement, or a talk given to the class); he or she must listen in order to summarize material (such as that given in a science report), follow directions for a game or a project, or get the main idea from a story, a TV program, or a class report. Children also listen to gain appreciation of music, a story, or a poem. They listen to establish a mood for thinking and reacting. They listen for particular words or phrases (e.g., on the other hand, my first point, in conclusion, etc.), to nonspeech sounds other than music (e.g., to start ideas flowing for a creative writing activity), or to relate words to particular gestures, voice tones, or mannerisms.

GUIDELINES FOR TEACHING LISTENING

While the importance of listening is increasingly being recognized and schools are making provision for its teaching, few if any teachers list it on their daily programs as a separate subject area. Usually listening is taught as a part of some more inclusive subject—most often English or language arts—or in relation to reading or social studies. And this is highly appropriate, since we should constantly strive for meaningful integration of subject matter.

However, if listening is taught too incidentally, the desired results may not be attained. What seems to be required is specific instruction in the listening skills, just as specific instruction is needed to teach reading skills, spelling skills, or any other skills. But this does not mean that a listening lesson may not be embedded in subject matter from another area of the language arts—or some other part of the total curriculum.

There are certain principles useful in planning a listening program. To begin with, a classroom climate that is conducive to listening avoids distracting physical and emotional conditions. This climate includes a relaxed, unhurried, nonthreatening teacher's voice, along with facial expressions that are expressive and varied but that are directed at promoting accurate listening.

Second, purposes *for* listening should be suggested or developed with the children; one should not simply demand that children listen *to* something. Listening should be done *for* information that can be gained, *for* appreciation of the language in a poem, *for* propaganda words, *for* directions, etc. Establishing standards, providing for class reactions, and discussing listening behavior will all help children discover the need for and the importance of listening.

The discovery will be further enhanced if listening activities are related to the ongoing activities of the class—this is our third guideline. These activities should be within the interest and comprehension levels of the pupils so that they become personally involved, thus avoiding "tuning out." Interest is also more likely to be maintained if the listening periods are not too long and if a change of activity is provided—questions, discussion, drawing or writing something as a result of the listening.

Listening for Sounds around Us

Street sounds—tooting horns, gears grinding, dogs barking, people talking

Sounds on a trip—getting on the bus, the bus going over a bridge, entering a pet store

Classroom sounds—footsteps, blocks falling, singing, whispering

Listening can be improved by:

Setting specific purposes for listening.

Giving directions only once.

Listening courteously to children.

Setting an example by clear enunciation and accurate pronunciation.

Organizing material presented orally to children so that it is systematic, explicit, and brief.

A Bulletin Board Idea

A Good Listener

1. Has a purpose for listening.
2. Thinks as he listens.
3. Is not distracted from listening.
4. Controls his emotions.
5. Recognizes his responsibility to the speaker.
6. Prepares to react to what he has heard.

As much variety as possible should be provided in listening experiences used for teaching the skills. For example, films, debates, individual and group reports, dramatic activities, demonstrations, music, descriptions, explanations, discussions, and conversations may all be used. Some variations in the seating arrangement will also help. That is, if you are reading a story and showing illustrations from a book the children might be grouped closely about you, while for a film they might sit in rows (with care taken to see that children at the perimeters can see well).

An effective listening program also provides for individual differences. This will include seating those children who have hearing losses as advantageously as possible, as well as providing activities of varying levels of difficulty and with varying purposes for different individuals and groups.

It is also important to help pupils form good listening habits and learn techniques for effective listening. Directions should be well organized and presented once, with pupils being encouraged to think before asking to have directions repeated. Practice is also necessary to help pupils ignore distractions. They must learn how to take notes, recognize word clues, and make use of changes in the tone of voice or manner of the speaker. Above all, the teacher's being a good listener is basic to teaching effective listening habits.

Listening and reading, which are both receptive language acts, are linked together in the same manner as are the expressive acts of writing and speaking. But for both reading and listening, receptiveness does not imply passiveness. To read well or listen well requires active engagement of the receptor in the total communication situation. A good listener is thinking, reacting, forming responses, deciding on a course of action, and so on as he or she listens. A good listener does this in all listening situations, even when participating in a conversation. The good reader does the same. The reader who does not become actively engaged is simply a "word caller"; the lethargic listener hears words but misses understanding.

Since listening and reading are receptive acts, there are many similarities between them. Both require as a first step readiness for reception. This means that interest in what is to be heard or read must have been aroused; there must be appeal or curiosity—a motivating force. Both reading and listening also require correct perception of sounds. If *build* sounds to the listener like *filled*, it may not be possible to get the message. In the same manner, the child who sees *black* instead of *blank* will have trouble understanding the sentence *"Fill in the blank spaces."* Reading and listening also both require that the words or other lexical units (e.g., rocking chair, push broom, town house) heard or read are ones whose meanings are either known or can be determined from the context or other clues.

Comprehension in both reading and listening results from understanding phrases, sentences, and statements of greater length—the paragraph, for example—rather than a single word. Therefore, both require relating what is received to past experiences, so that the content of what is heard or read can be thought about and examined creatively and critically. Furthermore, both processes require active attention to signals—punctuation marks, pauses, intonations, key words (e.g., next, for instance, perhaps, on the other hand).

Reading and listening can take place in many situations and can be done for many purposes. The closeness of their tie has been shown over and over again by the similarity of activities and exercises designed to teach their skills. In fact, since listening has begun to receive instructional attention, many reading series provide listening activities and suggest that teaching listening skills is one way to improve reading skills.

Ability to listen and ability to read do not necessarily go hand in hand, but a planned program that builds on the relationships between them should improve children's skills in both areas. For example, children may follow a story with their eyes and listen to it being read (using earphones and with the listening part of the activity on a tape cassette). Other examples include giving oral directions (they may be taped) for reading assignments, presenting material in social studies and other curriculum areas through both listening and reading, and motivating reading by having pupils listen to stories with related themes or subjects.

READINESS ACTIVITIES

Since reading and listening are both receptive communication acts, the skills children have in listening provide a foundation for reading. The sequential development of reading skills corresponds fairly closely to that of listening skills. Thus many activities useful in developing readiness for initial reading instruction also help prepare young children for the specific listening lessons and activities they will meet later. These readiness activities include listening for rhyming sounds, discriminating among speech sounds and relating them to letters, and identifying nonspeech sounds.[3] They also include listening to music and rhythms, listening to stimulate imaginative thinking, and listening for basic communication purposes. Most listening readiness activities are enjoyable to children and set the stage for teaching skills related to specific purposes. However, developing in a child the ability to listen to a speaker and get the message—including, for example, the ability to sift out the facts the speaker gives from his or her opinions—comes from direct teaching of the specific skills rather than from the development of a generalized listening ability.

Rhyming

Rhyming activities help children identify speech sounds, discriminate among them, and gain practice in auditory memory. Readiness activities include having the children listen to and repeat rhyming words (cold-told, Jill-hill, quick-stick, fast-last, cat-rat, etc.), listen for words that rhyme in stories, and listen to supply missing words in simple rhymes. (For example: We traveled far/in our new——. We saw a cat/who was very——. Go into the hall/to play with the ——.) Children may say nursery rhymes together (try Jack Be Nimble, Little Boy Blue, Hickory Dickory Dock, Little Bo Peep) or play rhyming games (I rhyme with sled. You sleep in me. What am I?). It is also fun to divide the class into teams with one team giving a word and another supplying a word that rhymes with the first one.

Discriminating among Sounds

Related to rhyming activities are those that call for discriminating among sounds and words. For example, you might say pairs of words (three-free, ship-chip, chair-share) and have the children tell if they are the same words or different ones. Or have some of the pairs begin with the same sound (mother-man, boy-ball) and others begin with different sounds (little-ball, dog-log) and let the children tell which pairs begin with the same sound. Still another variation is to say groups of words and ask the children to pick the word that begins with a different sound from that of the others in the group: mice, fish, money, mouse /fire, fact, dog, fence / top, tent, tool, cat. The children will also enjoy games such as having those children stand whose names start with the same sound as the word you say. The same game can be played with the names of the streets they live on, the cars their fathers drive, or their brothers' and sisters' names.

Simply listening for sounds is an activity often used to stimulate thoughts in a creative writing lesson, but it is also a good listening readiness activity. Have the children close their eyes for a number of seconds and then tell what sounds they heard. Or have them go on a sound hunt in the room to find the objects that make sounds—record player, water faucet, bells, clock, window closing, etc. Many of these sounds can be imitated, as well as other sounds that the children are likely to know, such as animal calls, screeching tires, etc.

Rhythms

The rhythmic activities suggested in chapter 3 provide readiness for the listening activities of the middle grades. There are many activities that will interest children. Try softly clapping a rhythm pattern and ask the children to repeat the pattern, or have them march to music, stomping when it is loud and walking quietly when it is soft. Use your tape recorder and allow the children to listen to how well they paid attention to the music.

LISTENING ACTIVITIES

The opportunities for teaching listening are unlimited. This is a speaking and listening world and every classroom is a part of it. But children must be taught to listen effectively in the many communication situations of the classroom, and this teaching can be done with varying degrees of formality. That is, you can plan lessons that focus on teaching particular skills, engage in activities that require listening for specific purposes, and use other activities of a more general nature that call for listening as a part of them.

Make the teaching of listening a part of all your classroom activities.

Since we tend to expect children to listen to everything we say, we need continually to remind ourselves that listening will not be effective unless the children understand and accept the purpose for it. To reinforce the idea that what they hear is important to listen to, give directions for something they need—and want—to do. For example, directions for making a terrarium or for drawing something should arouse interest in listening accurately. Combine an activity with using a tape recorder so that individual children can record directions that the others can listen to. Also try saying a series of short sentences and having the children count the number of times a particular word is heard.

In all classroom situations it is wise to insist on having the attention of the pupils before giving oral directions or explanations. By the same token, teachers must be attentive to what the children say, thus avoiding such catastrophes as that of the teacher who responded to a child, "Isn't that nice, dear. Now go play and have fun" after he announced that his grandfather had died last night!

You may find yourself at a loss for words when given some valuable piece of information by a pupil. If a child says, "We got new gravel in our driveway," you may find yourself wondering, "Who cares?" But the child does care; this is something to talk about. Perhaps you might begin a discussion of stone size, the difficulty one encounters in riding a bicycle on new gravel, etc. Give the child a sense of pride by truly listening and giving a positive response.

Grades K–3. Listening activities in the early grades are similar to those suggested for readiness lessons. Activities that require discriminating among sounds, associating speech sounds and letters, and rhyming are all fun and instructive for children in the early primary grades and beyond. Give the children a sentence with a word missing, but supply the first letter (letter name, not sound) of the missing word. A sentence such as "The man leaped on his h___ and dashed off" is an example of this. You might even try listen-and-rhyme games. They are silly, but they do require listening and surely help to develop sentence sense.

TEACHER: I baked a cake.

PUPIL 1:   You baked a snake?

PUPIL 2:   No, she backed into a lake.

PUPIL 3:   She baked a snake and stepped on a rake.

PUPIL 4:   My goodness sake!

Give the children the last letters of a word, and have a child supply a consonant or blend that will make a word (end-send; ead-bread), then go to the board and write and pronounce the word. Other children may say words that begin with a different consonant or consonant blend but end with the same syllable. Once the list is complete children may dictate silly rhymes to you.

> I had a hen
> Who talked with men
> As she sat in the den
> And wrote with a pen.

Listening Centers

Tape and cassette players can be wired for stations permitting individual and/or small group listening.[5]

Collect these and put them on ditto sheets which the children can make into books to illustrate and take home to read.

A completion activity that helps develop attentiveness involves simply giving the beginnings of sentences that they are to complete: "Our class is going to . . ." or "John is . . . ." At first one completion is sufficient; later, depending on the age and maturity level of the children, they may be asked to repeat what has been said and supply a new item: "John is a boy," "John is a tall boy," "John is a tall boy in a red sweater," etc.

Children, especially at this age, love to be helpful to the teacher. You can capitalize on this to help them form habits of listening, so they won't miss the opportunity to do a chore. Let them carry oral messages and run errands: "Bruce, please tell the custodian that our sink is leaking again" or "Jennifer, will you please go the the storeroom and ask the clerk for a box of chalk?" Even kindergarten children can perform such errands if they have been made familiar with the building and its personnel. As they mature, the requests can become more complicated: "Jerry, will you collect all the pictures from the children in your row and put them on my desk? Then give each person a sheet of this paper." To avoid confusion and to attract the attention of the child addressed, always say the child's name before giving directions. To involve more than one child, sometimes give directions such as this: "Has everyone finished? Will the third person in each row collect the pictures for his or her row?"

Since giving instructions is so much an integral part of the school day, there is little need to construct opportunities. It is helpful, however, to be guided by three principles:

1. Use some signal to gain attention (this might be a name, a question, possibly even a note struck on the piano).
2. Speak clearly so that those involved can hear accurately.
3. Form the habit of giving directions only once.

Plan for:

Children to listen to each
   other.
Your listening to children.
A balanced and not
   overpowering amount of
   listening.
Readiness for a listening
   activity.

Primary grade children are not too young to begin to select what is relevant to a particular listening purpose. The kinds of discrimination exercises suggested for listening readiness are a beginning. Try also giving a list of objects—for example, *cookie, muffin, fork, cake, bowl*—and asking them to name those that belong in the same category.

Activities for helping children learn to listen more effectively should of course be genuinely interesting and appealing. Carefully selected stories, read or told, have this appeal and are an essential part of the language arts program. For example, in the story *Harry the Dirty Dog,*[5] which has great appeal, the children may be asked to listen to find out why Harry ran away (main idea) or what happened after Harry ran away (sequence). Listening to a story for the purpose of retelling it is also excellent for learning sequence—as well as providing valuable oral activity.

You may need to help children ferret out the main idea, determine what the sequence really is, or actually indentify important details. Sometimes ideas that seem obvious to us are missed by children. Try asking what is important about a story or report that could be told in one sentence (main idea). Listing details on the board will help children learn to discover those that are important and to determine sequence or organization. Telling part of a story can aid in developing many skills. Children will need to listen for the main idea, for the sequence of events, and for particular information to adapt. In addition, such an activity will help them learn to draw inferences from what they hear, since the end of the story must fit the characters, the scene, and the events that have gone before. With young children, begin by using a single sentence and having the children add another: "As I was walking through the woods one dark and stormy night, I suddenly saw a flash of light. . ." If this is too difficult at first, perhaps several suggestions may be made and written on the chalkboard; the children can then decide which ones fit best with the original sentence.

A Listening Tip

Let the child who is giving a
talk observe the group and
comment on the listening
behavior of his audience
after he has finished.

Grades 4–6.   In the middle grades there are many opportunities for children to give talks and reports, all of which may be used to focus on the development of listening abilities. Again, greater success is possible if the talks and reports are on subjects of concern to the pupils. Perhaps the building of a new school might occasion special attention to some things especially desired by the children, such as basketball backboards or a listening room in the library. Some ideas included in a talk are likely to be pertinent; others are not. Listeners should have paper on which they can separate points according to whether they are fact or opinion, record details, note new words, etc. After a talk the group should discuss its content and the manner of presentation.

A natural follow-up to talks is to have the children listen to newscasts and to comments made by political figures. This listening is particularly good for practice in determining what is fact and what is opinion.

Children can tell stories or give descriptions, with their listeners responding by making drawings about the story. For example, at Halloween the ugliest monster imaginable might be described. This will surely result in drawings appropriate for the season of the year.

Activities derived from listening to your reading are also very good. Read a descriptive scene to the class; have the children draw pictures depicting what they heard. Read descriptions of well-known people—perhaps persons studied in connection with social studies—and have pupils guess who they are. Read a story or folktale to the children—perhaps one from a country the class is studying. Stop before the story is finished, and let the children guess the ending.

Children at all age levels enjoy poetry. They could listen to a poem to determine mood and feeling. A poem like Vachel Lindsay's "The Congo" is especially good for this type of listening. In addition to mood and feeling, children could also listen for pitch, stress, pauses, rhythm, and tone. In fact, both poetry and stories that are unknown to the children may be read for many purposes. Two such purposes might be to determine a title and to give practice in the development of effective use of context clues to determine word meaning.

Sentences may also be read, omitting one or more words in each, with the children supplying the missing words. Some sentences should be of the type that requires "listening on" (similar to "reading on") to determine the missing words. For example, "Last year the _____ nearly killed a man, even though the Park Rangers affectionately called him 'Old Grizzle.'"

Many television shows can be used for listening activities, including programs watched at home. For example, children who watch the cartoons can listen for and record usage "errors." These can be discussed in class. They might also record the television that they watch for a week in preparation for a class discussion on listening habits.

The use of audiovisual aids can add much to listening activities. For instance, before giving an oral report, the child can list on the board or use an overhead projector to show questions pertaining to the report. Afterward, these questions can serve as a guide for a discussion of the main ideas, details, and sequence of what was said. At first the children will need help in selecting and wording the questions.

Repeat-and-add games keep children interested and help to develop interesting sentences as well as to foster good listening habits.

PUPIL 1:   Thunder.

PUPIL 2:   The thunder roared.

A Listening Tip

Before reading to the children, write on the board words which may be unfamiliar to them. Have the children pay particular attention to gaining meanings of these words.

Write to:

National Public Radio, 2025 M St., NW, Washington, DC 20036 for information on obtaining audiotapes of educational radio programs.

PUPIL 3:   The thunder roared and the lightning
flashed.

Another activity that is fun is for the children to listen to classmates reading orally and try to determine the punctuation. They may also evaluate the reader in terms of his or her ability to read with feeling, to "capture" the audience, and to convey the author's message. Encourage questions related to specific listening skills. For example: "What did Jim talk about?" (main idea) "What did he say first, next, and last?" (details and sequence). Giving tests orally also provides useful practice in listening. That is, instead of writing questions, read them to the class (this works best for questions requiring short answers). Also try assigning various children the task of listening to and recording assignments so that they can be telephoned to a child who is absent.

An activity that is valuable in helping children understand usage problems, appreciate differences in speech, and understand various speakers is listening to different dialects. The New Englander's speech is not the same as that of the southerner or the midwesterner. Likewise, the male adult's speech often presents a different listening task from that of the female adult. Try recording the speech of friends and acquaintances who speak different dialects, have high or low voices, speak rapidly or slowly, and so on. Keep in mind, too, that music, such as the songs of Stephen Foster or modern country-western songs, offers excellent opportunities for listening to dialects.

LISTENING LESSONS

The following are examples of the types of listening exercises that may be constructed. Content for these may come from textbooks for the subject areas or it may even be adapted from reading exercises in teacher's manuals and workbooks, since the purposes for reading and listening are so closely related.

Selecting Details

Ask the children to listen for details about Virginia City and how it became a ghost town as you read the following:

Develop your listening lessons from what the children are studying in social studies, science, health, math, etc.

The miners living in Virginia City in 1860 lived in frame shanties and tents made of canvas, potato sacks, old shirts, and blankets. Two years later, however, the shacks and tents had been replaced by hotels, rooming houses, and homes—all of substantial construction. Three years after that the silver mines were closed because the silver ore began to give out. It seemed that Virginia City would become a ghost town, but new veins of silver were discovered and the life of the city revived. In 1875 a fire devoured the city, and that event combined with a decline in mining brought on the ghost town appearance of Virginia City as it is today.

Follow the reading by asking questions such as these:

What were the tents of the early miners made of?

When was the fire in Virginia City?
What was mined in Virginia City?
Why did Virginia City become a ghost town?

Finding the Main Idea

Write these sentences on the board and cover them:

The burro is a very gentle animal.
Children ride on their burros.
The burro is a favorite pet in Mexico.
The children give names to their burros.

Ask the children to listen carefully to what they are about to hear and to think of the one idea it tells about. Read the following:

Many children in Mexico have burros for pets. The burro is so gentle that a small child can take care of him. The children enjoy riding on their burros. Sometimes the children ride them in parades. They call their pet burros by name, and talk to them just as they talk to one another. Often a boy will carry sugar in his pocket. His burro will follow him, sniffing in his pocket to get the sugar.

Uncover the sentences and read them aloud. Ask the children to write the sentence that is the main idea of the paragraph.

Following Directions

Distribute one sheet of lined paper to each pupil and say something like, "Today we are going to make a terrarium. But first we need to go over the directions. I'll read them to you. Listen carefully to what we need to do. When we know exactly what we must do to build the terrarium, we will begin." The directions might be as follows:

1. Lay out the pieces of glass (except the piece for the top) on the table. Put the largest piece in the center and the smaller pieces around it, matching the smaller pieces with the sides of the large pieces.
2. Fasten the largest piece of glass (the bottom) to each of the side pieces using wide adhesive tape.
3. Make sure that all exposed edges of the glass are taped.
4. Use tape to hinge the glass for the top to the rear of the terrarium.
5. Remember that the top is taped to the rest of the terrarium only on the rear side.
6. Tape the edges of the hinged top so that no glass edges are exposed.
7. Place the terrarium on a solid surface, and cover the bottom with about an inch of fine, clean sand.
8. Place the plants in the sand, leaving them in the pots.
9. Add pieces of driftwood, rocks, and other objects to make the terrarium attractive.

Listening Skills

Everyday you receive a great deal of information by listening. You may even start your day by listening to the radio. Listening to directions and reports are part of your daily school work.

● Think why you should listen carefully in each of the following situations.

Someone is telling you how to walk to his or her house.
The coach is telling you how to play soccer.
Your teacher is telling you what you should do in case of fire.

You may be surprised to learn that listening skills are very much like reading skills. When you listen to a talk or speech you listen for the main idea. You also listen for important details that tell about or explain the main idea. You must practice to become a good listener just as you practice to become a good reader.

Here are some rules to help you become a good listener.

1. Look directly at the speaker.
2. Do not talk to others while you are listening.
3. Try to think only about what the speaker is saying.
4. Listen for the main idea. The speaker usually states the subject at the beginning of the speech.
5. Try to remember at least two important details that the speaker gives.
6. When the speaker is finished, take notes by writing the main idea and details immediately.
7. Ask questions about what you can't remember or don't understand.

174   STUDY AND REFERENCE: *Listening Skills*

Language textbooks can often help you teach listening; they suggest activities and identify the skills that need to be developed. (MACMILLAN ENGLISH, SERIES E, Book 5—Tina Thoburn, *et al.* Copyright © 1979 Macmillan Publishing Co., Inc.)

For a review of what is known from research about listening and its teaching see Thomas G. Devine, "Listening: What Do We Know after Fifty Years of Research and Theorizing?" (Journal of Reading, January, 1978, pp. 296–304).

Getting Word Meanings

Write the words "exalt" and "ravine" on the board. Ask the pupils if they know the meanings of them. Write the meanings they give on the board and then ask them to listen to this paragraph to find out if they were right.

A little way off, to the left, stood a small house; and to the right was another, before which stood the wagons belonging to his father. Directly in front was a wide expanse of rolling prairie, cut by a deep ravine. To the north, beyond the small farm, which was fenced, a still wider region rolled away into unexplored and marvelous distance. Altogether it was a land to exalt a boy who had lived all his life in thickly settled Wisconsin.

Following the reading the meanings of the words should again be discussed and looked for in a dictionary if necessary.

Distinguishing between the Relevant and the Irrelevant

Ask the pupils to listen to the following selection and to be ready to tell which sentences are needed to gain the meaning and which do not really relate to the remainder of the selection.

There were six boys beside the campfire. The dry sticks blazed and the heavy logs glowed with the heat. It was almost time to put the fish in the frying pan. The boys had poked the potatoes in their foil wrappings and already they were softening. Jim's older brother had stayed at home. He was going to college this fall. All the boys were hungry and were anxious to eat. Bill put on more wood and Bob got the frying pan.

Ask the pupils to tell why the sentences that do not relate to the remainder of the paragraph are not needed to gain the meaning.

Drawing Inferences

Tell the pupils to listen to the following paragraph in order to answer some questions that can only be answered by listening "between the lines."

The air was crisp and clear, but a wet snow had pelted the windows last night. I breathed deeply, glanced toward the snow-covered cars parked along the curb, and thought, "What a beautiful day." Suddenly I came down with a bump on the sidewalk.

Ask these questions and discuss the meaning of making inferences:

Why did the speaker fall?
Does the speaker live in town or in the country?
Had it stopped snowing?

TEACHING RESOURCES

There are many resources available to aid teachers in the development of more effective listening. As suggested in the preceding section, the content of listening lessons may come from textbooks in various subject areas of the curriculum. These should not be the only sources for lessons, however, since so many other materials are now available for providing variety and interest in the listening program.

Tape and Cassette Recorders

The increasing prevalence of inexpensive tape recorders, particularly of the cassette type, provides teachers with many opportunities to extend their teaching. Directions, tests, questions, stories, and various types of information can be recorded, leaving the teacher free to observe the children as they work, give individual help, and discover individual problems. Directions for seatwork can be placed on tape: "In row 1 put an x on the picture that begins with the sound you hear at the beginning of boy, ball, and book." Or you might tape questions to be used following silent reading of a lesson in social studies or some other subject

A group listens to a story.

area (these should be short-answer questions). Sometimes allow space on the tape for recording children's answers so that it can be kept and used by individual children or groups in studying for a test. Test questions, too, can be taped. Many teachers tape their spelling tests, for example. Then children can take their own pretests, check their spelling (correct spellings are included at the end of the tape), and, when they have studied the words misspelled, take their final tests.

Directions for games can also be taped; one like "Simon Says" is particularly suitable for listening. Another, for which the children can prepare themselves, is called "I Am a Fellow American" or "Guess the Mystery Guest."[6] For these, the children choose characters from their social studies lessons, find additional information about them in encyclopedias or other supplementary books, and tape short sketches of the persons chosen. The other children then guess who each person is. A variation of this game is to have children tape several statements about a particular person; the other children then discuss these and decide which are fact and which opinion. This can also be done with the children making statements about themselves.

Children can also be encouraged to use the tape recorder to evaluate their own performances and discover their own errors. The child who has enunciation or pronunciation problems may enjoy "playing teacher"—recording his or her own reading of a story and then listening to the tape to discover and correct errors. You will need to work with most children to help them learn this technique, but if you think children cannot hear their own mistakes, try listening to your own recorded voice and see how many speech mannerisms and habits you discover that you were unaware of. Taping is also very effective when children are preparing for a play, a choral reading presentation, an oral report, or any other activity to be presented before an audience—even if that audience is only the class itself.

You will find recording helpful for activities suggested in other chapters as well. For example, in connection with a study of interviewing, the children would enjoy taping and then listening to an opinion survey program on a topic such as the following: "Should the frog replace the bird as a decorative symbol? There could be a discussion of frog wallpaper, frog placemats, frog lampposts, frog's nest soup, frog watchers, and who knows what else to stimulate listening and stir creative thinking.

Taping chapters or portions of chapters may help children who do not read well with difficult reading in the content areas. To establish listening purposes, preface the reading with taped questions, perhaps selected from those given at the end of the chapter. As reinforcement, provide written copies of the questions to be answered, or begin the tape with an instruction something like this: "Before you listen to the tape, turn to page 46 in your textbook and read questions 1, 2, and 3. Read carefully; then reread to be sure you remember what to listen for. Keep your book open as you listen so you can check yourself. Now turn off the tape recorder until you have read the questions and are ready to begin listening."

Records

Combining the teaching of listening with music activities is helpful and enjoyable. For example, children can be given pictures of musical instruments along with information about the sounds produced by each instrument. Then, as they listen to *Peter and the Wolf,* for example, the children hold up the picture of each instrument as it is played. This may be varied by giving each child only one or two pictures; the children will need to listen carefully so that they will not miss their instruments.

A good motion activity is to play music and have the children move in time to the rhythm. They love to march to something like Sousa's "Semper Fidelis." (Older students might be stimulated to learn more about Sousa and his life as bandmaster of the United States Marine Corps band.) More creative interpretations of rhythm and mood may result from "The Dancing Doll" (Edward Poldini) or "Claire de Lune" (Claude Debussy).

Such pieces as "Claire de Lune," "Parade of the Wooden Soldiers," or "Danse Macabre" are good for drawing out what the music makes a child think of. (The children should not be told the titles.) Sometimes their interpretations might be in the form of pictures which could be displayed and discussed. The composer's purpose can also be discussed, with this discussion leading to a comparison of the composer's inspiration with their reactions.

This procedure may be reversed, of course, by telling the children the story behind a particular composition, such as *The Sorcerer's Apprentice* (Paul Dukas), and then having them listen to see how the music and the instruments reflect the theme and mood of the story.

Music is a natural corollary to social studies. Martial music of different wars, folk songs of many types and lands, spirituals—these and many other types of music will help children to truly understand the people who lived in other times and in other lands.

Books

There are many books that build interest in listening, suggesting things to listen to and for. Many others have stories that are appealing to listen to and are helpful in making children aware of listening and in teaching listening skills. Here are some:

Alexenber, Marvin. *Sound Science.* Englewood Cliffs, NJ: Prentice-Hall, 1968.
Baylor, Byrd. *Plink Plink Plink.* Boston: Houghton Mifflin, 1971.
Borten, Helen. *Do You Hear What I Hear?* New York: Abelard-Schuman, 1960.
Branley, Franklyn M. *High Sounds, Low Sounds.* New York: Thomas Y. Crowell Co., 1967.
Brown, Margaret. *Steamroller.* New York: Walker, 1974.
Brown, Margaret Wise. *The City Noisy Book.* New York: Harper and Row, Inc., 1939. (Also *The Country Noisy Book, The Seashore Noisy Book,* and *The Winter Noisy Book.*)
Elkin, Benjamin. *The Loudest Noise in the World.* New York: Viking, 1954.
Emberley, Ed. *Klippity Klop.* Boston: Little, Brown, 1974.
Guilfoile, Elizabeth. *Nobody Listens to Andrew.* New York: Scholastic Book Services, 1973.
Hanson, Joan. *Sound Words: Words That Imitate the Sounds Around.* Minneapolis: Lerner, 1976. (Also *More Homonyms: Steak and Stake and Other Words That Sound the Same But Look As Different As Chilli and Chilly;*

Homographic Homophones: Words That Look and Sound the Same.)
Johnston, Tony. *Night Noises and Other Mole and Troll Stories.* New York: Putnam, 1977.
Mayer, Mercer. *What Do You Do With a Kangaroo?* New York: Four Winds Press, 1973.
O'Neill, Mary L. *What Is That Sound?* New York: Atheneum, 1966.
Showers, Paul. *The Listening Walk.* New York: T. Y. Crowell, 1961.
Tresselt, Alvin. *Wake Up, City!* New York: Lothrop, Lee and Shepard, 1957. (Also *Wake Up, Farm!)*

EVALUATION OF LISTENING

Without some form of measurement or testing, a teacher does not know whether listening lessons and activities are achieving the desired objectives. Equally important is the fact that each child needs feedback to guide his learning. Of course, well-designed lessons provide considerable evidence to both the teacher and the children of how effective the listening was for the particular lessons. Some evidence beyond that attained by this procedure, however, is needed to determine growth.

Standards

Having pupils develop standards or guidelines for listening is one useful technique. Listening experiences can be judged by comparison with these standards.
The following is an example of a set of second grade standards:

A Good Listener

Looks at the person talking.
Doesn't talk.
Thinks about what is said.
Remembers what he is listening for.

Standards should become more specific as children mature. They should always, however, be developed with the children rather than being imposed upon them. Intermediate grade children can develop standards based upon such questions as these:

Do I keep the main idea of what I'm listening to in mind?
Am I courteous in my listening?
Do I reserve judgment until the end of a presentation?
Am I aware of transitional phrases and what they mean?
Do I recognize bias on the part of the speaker?
Do I remember what I am listening for?

Checklists

Statements of standards can be translated into checklists, such as the one below, and these can be used by pupils to keep a written record of their listening skills.

My Listening Checklist

	Yes	No
1. Could I hear and see the speaker?	—	—
2. Was I ready to think about what the speaker said?	—	—
3. Was I ready to learn?	—	—
4. Was I able to discover the direction the speaker was taking?	—	—
5. Did I determine the main idea?	—	—
6. Did I use clues the speaker provided?	—	—
7. Was I able to pick out information supporting the main idea?	—	—
8. Was I able to summarize what the speaker said?	—	—

Tests

There are a few standardized tests for measuring listening abilities. One that is sometimes used in elementary schools is the listening section of the STEP test.[7] The test is not widely used in elementary schools, but it does have forms for grades 4 through junior college that attempt to measure comprehension, interpretation, evaluation, and application of material read by the test administrator. The items on the test relate to identifying main ideas, remembering significant details, remembering simple sequences of information, seeing bias and prejudice in what the speaker says, judging the validity of information, distinguishing fact from fancy, judging the relevance of details to an idea, determining the organization of the spoken context, and recognizing what the speaker wants the listener to do and believe.

In 1967, listening tests were first included in the *Cooperative Primary Tests.*[8] There are two forms—one for grades 1 and 2 and one for grades 2 and 3. In these tests the children indicate their response to the teacher's reading by marking pictures. The tests are designed to measure recall, interpretation, and inference, as well as sound perception.

Another standardized test is the *Durrell Listening–Reading Series,*[9] which is designed to provide a comparison of children's reading and listening abilities. The several levels of the test (grades 1–3.5, 3.5–6, 7–9) seek to measure both vocabulary knowledge and comprehension ability. Essentially this test measures auditory perception and discrimination rather than listening comprehension.

Commercial materials designed to teach listening skills generally include either tests or suggestions for preparing tests. For example, the *Listening Skills Program*[10] has pretests and posttests directed at detecting rhyme; comprehending details, inferences, sequence, main ideas, facts, and purposes; understanding the listening act; and following directions. Many reading and reading readiness tests also measure some aspects of listening—auditory perception, for instance.

The various standardized and other published tests can serve as models for a teacher's own tests. Teacher-made tests can be directed at measuring achievement in specific skills. For example, to test pupils' abilities to listen for details, present material orally or by tape that contains details to listen for. In the same manner, direct test content and questions at evaluating skill in separating fact from opinion, in answering specific questions, in getting the main idea, in recognizing propaganda, or in using contextual clues to get word meanings. The listening lessons suggested earlier in this chapter provide examples of the way such tests can be constructed.

Teacher Self-Evaluation

No portion of the program will be as good as you can make it without regular self-evaluation on your part. In evaluating the listening program, begin with your own voice, speech habits, and mannerisms. Perhaps you might adapt a suggestion made earlier for the children: turn on the tape recorder while you are teaching a lesson, and try to forget that it is running. At the end of the day, listen carefully to your own voice. Is it pleasant and expressive, with sufficient variation in pitch, rate, tone? Do you tend to overuse certain expressions so that they become monotonous, to repeat excessively for the benefit of a few, or to repeat what the children say so that they do not need to listen to their classmates?

Next, think about your own attitude toward listening. Are you a good listener yourself? Do you express appreciation for and interest in what children say, show respect for their ideas and opinions, and make yourself available for listening to individuals and groups?

Finally, consider the program itself. Are its goals specific and clearly defined, or do you expect children to do too many things at one time when they are called upon to listen? Do you provide time for thinking in connection with listening activities? Does the program provide a variety of listening experiences—stories, music, games, lessons, etc.? Does it provide for individual differences by including activities of different levels of difficulty, for different purposes, and for both individuals and groups?

A Final Word

Listening occupies a baseline position in relation to speaking, reading, and writing. In a quantitative sense it is most important, since about half the average adult's or child's day is spent in listening. In a qualitative sense, listening is equally important: the "knowledge explosion" requires that information be processed as rapidly as possible—in school and out. Listening is a major means by which this may be accomplished; thus teaching listening must be a concern of every teacher.

Providing direct and regular instruction in the listening skills results in more effective listening and improved attitudes. Such teaching, however, must be based upon clear-cut purposes understood by both teacher and pupils and must be followed by evaluation of pupil learning.

ENDNOTES

1. Sara W. Lundsteen, *Listening: Its Impact on Reading and the Other Language Arts* (Urbana, IL: National Council of Teachers of English, 1971), p. 41.

2. John Warren Stewig, *Exploring Language with Children* (Columbus, OH: Charles E. Merrill Publishing Co., 1974), p. 92.

3. Commercial materials, such as *Listening Time* (Bowmar) may be very helpful, but recording your own sounds may be better.

4. There are many commercial Listening Centers available. These usually consist of a cassette recorder/player and a box with multiple jacks for headsets. Instructional/Communications Technology, for example, has 6 and 8 jack boxes and variable speeds recorder/players.

5. Gene Zion, *Harry the Dirty Dog* (New York: Harper and Brothers, 1953).

6. For many other games see David H. and Elizabeth F. Russell, *Listening Aids Through the Grades*, Second enlarged edition by Dorothy Grant Hennings (New York: Teachers College, Columbia University, 1979) and Goldie Marie Gigous, *Improving Listening Skills* (Dansville, NY: Instructor Publications, 1974).

7. *Sequential Tests of Educational Progress* (Princeton, NJ: Educational Testing Service, 1967).

8. *Cooperative Primary Tests* (Princeton, NJ: Educational Testing Service).

9. *Durrell Listening—Reading Series* (New York: Harcourt Brace Jovanovich, 1969).

10. *Listening Skills Program* (Chicago: Science Research Associates).

REFERENCES

Books

Barker, Larry L. *Listening Behavior.* Englewood Cliffs, NJ: Prentice-Hall, 1971.

Lundsteen, Sara W. *Listening: Its Impact on Reading and the Other Language Arts.* Urbana, IL: National Council of Teachers of English, 1971.

Moray, Nelville. *Listening and Attention.* New York: Penguin, 1974.

Smith, Charlene. *The Listening Activity Book: Teaching Literal, Evaluative and Critical Listening in the Elementary School.* Belmont, CA: Fearon Publishers, 1975.

Taylor, Stanford E. *What Research Says to the Teacher: Teaching Listening.* Washington, DC: National Education Association, 1964.

Films

Listening. Los Angeles: Churchill Films (14 minutes; color; intermediate).

Your Communication Skills: Listening. Chicago: Coronet (11 minutes; color; intermediate).

Most films made for children can provide worthwhile listening experiences. Companies such as BFA Educational Media, Weston Woods, Learning Corporation of America, Encyclopedia Britannica, Coronet, Stephen Bosustow Productions, International Film Bureau, and others have many appealing films available. *

Filmstrips

Adventures in Listening. Chicago: Coronet (6 filmstrips and records or cassettes; primary).

American Dialects. Jamaica, NY: Eyegate House (Color; with record).

Let's Listen. Chicago: Coronet (Set of 2 sound strips; primary).

---

* Films and filmstrips available from National Geographic Educational Services (17th and M Streets, NW, Washington, DC 20036) on such subjects as pollution, energy, cities, explorers, and government provide good opportunities for using listening skills.

Listen: There Are Sounds Around You. Pleasantville, NY: Guidance Associates (Sound filmstrip; primary).

Listening in Your Daily Life, Listening to Get Directions, etc. New York: Learning Corporation of America (Series with records).

Listening, Looking, and Feeling. Los Angeles: Bailey-Film Associates (Set of 4 sound strips).

Listening Skills Program. Chicago: Science Research Associates (3 levels—12 cassette tapes each).

Look and Listen. New York: Filmstrip House (4 filmstrips; 2 LP records; K–2).

Recordings

Countdown for Listening. Lakeland, FL: Educational Development Corp. (24 lessons on 6 cassettes with teacher's guide; 1969).

Extending Comprehension Through Listening. New York: Miller-Brody Productions (4 records with teacher manuals; intermediate).

Let's Listen. New York: Educational Record Sales (One 10″ LP).

Listening and Learning. Boston: Houghton Mifflin (20 recorded lessons; directions and space/time concepts; prereading level).

Listening Comprehension/Fluency Program. Huntington Station, NY: Instructional/Communications Technology (Cassettes; content related to science and social studies; study guides).

Listening Games. Chicago: Coronet (10 cassettes; response cards and teacher's manual; primary).

Listening Skills: Primary. St. Paul, MN: 3M Corp. (4 cassettes with worksheets).

Listening Skills Program. Chicago: Science Research Associates (Set of 36 LP's).

Listening Time. Glendale, CA: Bowmar (Three 12″ LP's; primary).

Sounds Around Us. New York: Scott Foresman (3 records).

Kits

Basic Practice in Listening. Denver, CO: Love Publishing Co. (Book of games and activities; primary).

Developing Listening Skills. San Rafael, CA: Leswing Press (Puppets; activity sheets; lesson plans; primary and intermediate).

First Talking Storybook Box. New York: Scott, Foresman and Co.

Listening–Reading Program. Lexington, MA: D. C. Heath and Co. (Minisystem series; kits for grades 1–6, each with records, response sheets, etc.).

Listening Skill Builders. Chicago: Science Research Associates.

Look, Listen and Learn. St. Louis: Millikin Publishing Co. (5 kits of transparencies, records, and duplicating pages for reading readiness stage of development).

Sights and Sounds. New York: Random House (Learning unit).

See and Say Puzzle Cards. New York: N.Y. Times Educational Service.

Skills Builder. Pleasantville, NY: Reader's Digest.

SRA Listening Skills Program. Chicago: Science Research Associates (Kit; various levels; includes 36 LP's).

ACTIVITIES FOR PRESERVICE TEACHERS

1. Make a list of pairs of rhyming words suitable for auditory discrimination activities for five- or six-year-old children. Write out a plan for their use.

2. Visit a kindergarten and listen to the records the teacher uses. Record the titles and information on the record companies of those you like.

3. Plan an activity for which you would need to give specific directions. Include in your plan the sentences you would use.

4. Examine publisher's catalogs for materials useful in teaching listening. Give particular attention to materials that relate listening to other aspects of the curriculum.

5. Collect pictures of objects children might name and categorize according to beginning sounds, etc.

6. Describe the arrangement of a classroom which would maximize attention to teaching the listening skills.

7. Add to the list of "listening books" given in this chapter.

8. Examine one of the major language textbook series for the attention it gives to the teaching of listening. Report to the class.

Activities for Inservice Teachers

1. Use a tape recorder in your class. How many different ways can you find to use it? Keep a record of the uses of the tape recorder.

2. Visit the instructional media center of your school or district to determine what materials are available for teaching listening skills in your classroom. Make notes (perhaps a card file) so that you can readily request the materials you want.

3. Experiment with the physical conditions in your classroom and their effects upon listening. Keep a record of different conditions you create and how you measure the effects on listening.

4. Prepare your own tape recordings of selections you can play for your class to help them to listen for main ideas, details, etc. Incorporate outlining and note taking into this activity.

5. Start a file of listening activities you could use with your class. Begin with activities suggested in this chapter.

6. Tape directions for games. While the children are listening and following the directions you can observe and evaluate their ability.

7. Look in the curriculum guides in the school or district professional library. Record on cards listening activities suggested in these guides.

8. Find out from other teachers in your school how they teach listening. Keep a record of what you are told.

Independent Activities for Children

1. Tape sounds of common objects such as a doorbell, electric mixer, telephone, lawnmower, water faucet, garage door, etc. Find and mount pictures of these and other objects. A child may play the recording and select the correct pictures, placing them in sequence. Be sure to space sounds just enough to allow time for selecting the pictures. Items may be named at the end of the tape so the child can check the accuracy of his listening.

2. A child may listen to a series of recorded sounds and write a word associated with each. For example:

   faucet—gurgle, drip
   rain—patter, pelt

3. Tape recordings of stories can be useful in many ways. For example, one child could listen to the story and select the "best" title from a list of possibilities provided on a card. Another could listen for the main idea or the sequence of events. A third could listen to discover the feeling or mood or to find words that bring to mind particular pictures—tall house, round face, worn shoe, etc.

4. Have a child perform an experiment or construct an object after listening to directions only once. Directions may be taped or they may be read by another child. Taped directions should be spaced to allow time to perform each step; the tasks might be simple ones such as folding

paper to make a hat. Oral directions for three to five simple tasks could be given all at once; for example, "Go to the window and raise the shade about two inches. Then come back, sit down in your chair, and fold your arms." Children will enjoy thinking up unusual directions and attempting to perform tasks accurately.

5. Record tests such as those in *My Weekly Reader* for children to take individually.

6. Have a child listen to a recorded story or description and then draw a picture of the scene described or an episode in the story.

7. A child can prepare cutouts for the telling of a flannel board story from listening to a tape recording. Listening individually permits the child to relisten to parts of the story in order to develop the sequence and to decide what illustrations he needs.

8. Have a child make a list of all the sounds he or she hears in a particular place—in the lunch line, on the playground, at a certain street corner on the way to school, etc. As an added bonus, he might use the list to write a "sound picture" of the spot, or he might try to find the best words to describe each sound.

9. As a variation of the above, a child can sit quietly in a corner of the room listening for sounds such as a clock ticking, a car going by, a whistle, a buzzer, a dog barking, or walking in the hall. He or she should write down a word or two for each sound that is heard. Or two children can listen for the same period of time and compare the number of sounds they have heard.

10. A child can listen to records such as those *Sesame Street* produces for a variety of purposes:

"Rub Your Tummy"—following directions
"A Face"—vocabulary development
"One of These"—aural discrimination

11. A child can listen to the weather report on radio or TV and be prepared to present a forecast to the class, including expected temperature range, probability of precipitation, etc.

12. Newscasts can be listened to for the major topic reported, the name of the newscaster, the name of a public figure mentioned in the newscast, etc.

13. Have a child take notes on an assembly program or a program presented to the class for the purpose of preparing a written summary for the class diary.

14. Oral presentations may be improved if a child tapes a poem or story he or she is going to read to the class and then listens to it several times to discover ways to improve the reading.

15. Children can work in pairs with one child reading a sentence and the other naming words that sound alike. Sentences such as the following might be used:

Jane knew her mother would bring a new dress. The whole class saw the hole in the fence.

16. Working in pairs, children can use simple walkie-talkie sets to give directions to one another.

17. Keeping a log or diary of listening activities for several days will help a child recognize the importance of learning to listen effectively.

8

A Focus on Written Expression

You don't need to be told that there is public concern about the need to teach writing. For several years now, the media have cited examples of students' garbled sentences, misplaced modifiers, and horrendous spellings. The National Assessment of Educational Progress has reported that samples of the writing of nine-year-olds "contained multiple misspellings and sentence fragments" and that only fourteen percent of these children could successfully write a letter requesting an item they wanted that was free.[1] Similar statements about the deficiencies in the writing abilities of youth of thirteen and seventeen have been made by this agency.

While there have been both critics and defenders of these reports and similar ones made by other groups and individuals, as well as various reasons advanced for the writing deficiencies cited, there is no disagreement about the importance of writing. The criticisms in the media are evidence of this but, more specifically, the National Council of Teachers of English has stated that writing is "an important medium for self-expression, for communication, and for the discovery of meaning" and—in rebuttal to television, computers, and telephone company advertisements—"its need [has been] increased rather than decreased by the development of new media for mass communication."[2]

Write to the National Council of Teachers of English for a copy of "Standards for Basic Skills Writing Programs."

The teaching of writing has long been an important element in the elementary school curriculum, although the emphasis given to it has varied from time to time. Regardless of the emphasis, however, the teaching of writing has too often been conducted in a framework of lessons isolated both from genuine communication purposes and the interests of children. Many teachers have sought to improve writing quality through grammar exercises while others have urged that children do much imaginative writing. In either case there has been little attention given to either the content or form of this writing. In general, it is probably fair to say that too few teachers show evidence of knowing how to teach writing, and the differences in emphasis and techniques used reflect their struggles in determining "what to do."

In this chapter we first focus on the process of writing—what children do when they write—and the classroom conditions that foster writing. Then we suggest many writing activities that children will engage in naturally and readily if there is an emphasis on expression of thought and genuine communication. Chapter 9 extends the discussion by describing teaching procedures for making children's writing more effective and suggesting how the program and products may be evaluated.

What Writers Do

Writing is the act of putting thoughts into graphic form. But it is considerably more than a mechanical act. It is a purposeful activity, a process of composing, a thinking act or series of acts that requires selecting, combining, arranging, and developing information and ideas into sentences, paragraphs, and longer units of discourse. This process occurs both before the act of putting words on paper and after this actual writing has been done, as well as during the act of writing itself. Thus, writing is a three-phase process.

Before any writing occurs there is a *prewriting phase,* a period of thinking about what to write and how to write it. While not everything about either the content of what will be written or how this content will be presented is or should be decided in this prewriting phase, every writer does need some time, some opportunity for "rehearsing" for the writing. Thus, a teacher who says "You know what to write," "Let's get busy," and so on, may be impeding rather than motivating the writer.

The prewriting phase, though, is more than a short period of time for thinking. In fact, all of a writer's experiences are a part of the prewriting phase. Thus, if a teacher assigns a common topic for everyone in a class to write about, all children will not have an equal start in the selecting, combining, and arranging of ideas and information unless attention has been given to the development of backgrounds relative to the topic. And, of course, a common background for all—even if the possibility of that could actually be achieved—does not take into account the differences in intellectual abilities and interests that bear on the selecting and arranging.

Talking about the writing, about the ideas and information, is an important element in prewriting because it is a stimulus to the thinking that is needed. The amount of talking or discussing with others, of course, varies among writers, but most writers feel the need to discuss their ideas and related words, feelings, and experiences regarding what they intend to write. Not all of this discussion is focused directly on the writing topic or content; sometimes there is a "skirting around" rather than a direct discussing of ideas. But if the writer has a genuine purpose for the writing, this "skirting around" is very much a part of the prewriting phase.

The content of a piece of writing and how this content will be presented is seldom totally planned before the *writing phase* begins. Professional writers often say that their first sentence leads them to the second sentence and so on, and they add that the sequencing does not occur easily. While these writers may not do as much pausing, scratching out or erasing, looking up of spellings, rereading, and muttering or talking as children do, they do exhibit many of the same or related behaviors. These behaviors are reflections of the searching, the trying out of both content and form, that a writer is doing. They are not, as teachers have sometimes interpreted them, evidence of delaying tactics on the part of the child—tactics that show that he or she isn't "busy writing as you're supposed to be."

The *postwriting phase* is one of contemplating what has been written and seeking to improve it. This phase includes proofreading *and* editing—which is sometimes not recognized as being more than just proofreading—and, if the writer's purpose is clear and personally important, possibly rewriting. Also in this phase—and very important to children—is the solicitation of approval for what they have written and the disposition of that writing product. If the disposition is a wire basket on the corner of a teacher's desk where it is buried for days or weeks, the writing process has been profoundly affected. It is also profoundly affected if the disposition is the one the writer hoped for—the letter mailed, the poem posted, the story put into the story book, or the report made available to the class to read.

CONDITIONS THAT FOSTER WRITING

A truly effective writing program exists only if the total language arts program is meaningful and challenging. If ideas abound in the classroom and communication is genuine, and if children are respected, a foundation is present for teaching writing. Motivating children to write will be little needed or will be very simple if there are apparent, meaningful purposes for the writing. They will write because there is a genuine need to do so—to communicate information or to express ideas or feelings. They will write because they have something to say and feel that someone will appreciate or learn from what they have written.

The Classroom Environment

Opportunities for children to write and for a teacher to help them improve their writing are gained or lost depending on the classroom conditions that exist. Throughout this book we have stressed the importance of building on children's interests, of making the curriculum in all subject areas challenging to them, of making certain that both their expressive and receptive language activities are purposeful, and of assuring each child that he or she is an important member of the class who can make worthwhile contributions to its endeavors.

A good writing environment is actually no different from the environment that should be created for any learning. Every environment consists of people, things, processes, purposes, feelings, and relationships all blended together. But a good learning environment is one in which all of these elements are brought into harmonious play with each other. Creating this harmony in a classroom is an ongoing, dynamic process—one that requires effort by both teacher and children. But it is a process that cannot be left to change; therefore, the major responsibility is the teacher's.

A Writing Corner, possibly partially screened from the class, and with paper, pencils, and places to write, will stimulate much writing.

A pleasant and attractive physical setting is important, but that is the easiest part of the responsibility to achieve. The real keys to responding to the responsibility are purpose and respect—purpose in what children do and respect for their learning efforts. Both can be achieved, though, by a well-planned, challenging curriculum in which communication is a genuinely integrated part and by understanding each child's aspirations, abilities, and potential. A child will write a report readily enough, for instance, if she feels that the information included in it is needed in the social studies class—and if that class is interesting. Another child will gladly keep a record—and do so to the best of his ability—if he is convinced that this record will actually be referred to and used later. A third will write a summary of a science experiment if she enjoyed working on it and knows that the summary will be sent to her parents. Others will write the dialog for the skit on good health habits because the skit will be presented to the second graders.

Input and Experience

As adults we know that we cannot write very effectively, if at all, about something that is largely beyond our realm of knowledge. We do not write about a chemical experiment unless we have sufficient background in chemistry to do so; we do not write about politics unless we have studied and experienced political activity. The knowledge that we have about ourselves and what we could or could not write is a most important clue to the teaching of written expression.

Children will write about subjects they know about, things that they have experienced, things that have meaning to them. Equally, they will write in forms that they have had experience with. They will write letters if they know how letters are written (and there is reason to write them). By the same token they will write reviews of books if they know the form and organization of reviews, tall tales if the purpose and form of these is understood, poetry in cinquain form if this is known and appreciated, and so on.

We have earlier pointed out that children have had many experiences before coming to school, that they continue to have many experiences outside of the classroom, and that these experiences must be respected and capitalized on in our teaching. We have also emphasized that children must have abundant and continuous opportunities for gaining new ideas and information, associating these with previous experiences, and learning vocabulary related to them. Not all experiences need to be firsthand, but as many as possible should be. Looking at pictures, listening to music and speech, talking with and watching other people all provide experiences.

Take time to observe

- The swooping of a swallow
- The chugging and blinking of a helicopter
- A bird's nest in a tree fork
- The swaying of a tall pine
- The ripple on the water caused by a fallen leaf
- Waves creeping up a sandy beach
- The bouncing run of a rabbit

Particularly important also is reading; much poor language expression—oral or written—is often an almost direct consequence of a background of little reading. Reading to children and encouraging them to read are tremendously important to a writing program. Through the reading of good literature, genuinely expressive language insinuates itself into the mind, generates thinking, awakens ideas, and gives impetus to creativeness. Reading challenges children's thinking, enriches their other experiences, and leads directly to many writing activities.

As important as direct experiences and those gained from reading and other vicarious means are, fostering writing that is genuinely effective and individually as creative as possible requires a good deal of direct teaching. Most children must be guided in being observant enough to see how the spider web seen during the walk was intricately woven—or even to see the web. They must be taught to give thought to the hardships of the southern sharecropper seen in a film or to ap-

Have you heard

- The first raindrops tapping hesitantly at the window?
- A lonely puppy wailing in the night?
- The howling wind demanding to be let in?
- The crunch of your boots on new snow?
- The conversation "levels" at different tables in the cafeteria?

preciate the artistry and craftsmanship of a wood carving from Africa. We must recognize that children may do as we often do—see, hear, read, feel, or taste at a level that leaves only vague impressions and ideas and seldom provides the base for expression that should be possible.

In addition to providing a broad range of experiences and to giving a good deal of direct guidance in helping children gain as much as possible from them, specific attention will need to be given to teaching children about a variety of forms or types of writing. Without knowledge about a particular form, a child will not be able to write effectively, if at all, in that form. Thus, children need the input of hearing and seeing the various forms of writing that you want them to use in their expression. This, of course, cannot all be given at once. As children engage in writing it can be given through models, demonstrations, and group compositions, and as with all input, it should be a continuing and recurring process.

WRITING ACTIVITIES

Many opportunities for children to write for purposes that are meaningful to them occur in classrooms every day. An opportunity may stem from a science lesson, a field trip in social studies, the information brought by a resource person to health class, the development of a story, or any of numerous other activities that are integral parts of the curriculum. This section identifies many possible writing situations and suggests the kinds of activities that can and should be planned for in a classroom where children are encouraged and helped to communicate their ideas and feelings.

Experience Stories

A foundation can be laid for much of children's later writing by experience stories that a teacher writes as an individual child or a group of children dictate. Children are eager to talk about their pets, presents they have received, places they have been, and things they have done. They are equally eager to have these accounts recorded in writing. The same is true about their school experiences if these have been appealing and challenging.

Dictation to the teacher can begin when children are in preschool or kindergarten and at first will probably consist of just one or two sentences, or possibly only a title for a picture. Individual and group dictation of stories and other forms of composition should continue in the primary grades as children are learning to make letter forms, to spell, to punctuate, and to capitalize—and even after they have achieved a measure of ability in using these skills. Since dictating frees children from handwriting and other mechanical factors, it can contribute markedly to the quality of their writing, as full attention can be directed toward the ideas being expressed and choosing the best way to express them. For this reason, experience writing—with the teacher remaining as scribe—is a valuable activity at any grade level because it makes it possible for children to focus on the organization and content of what is written—and this is where the emphasis in teaching written expression should be.

Using Experience Charts with Children by Virgil E. Herrick and Marcell Nerbovig (Charles E. Merrill Books, 1964) has many experience story ideas.

An Experience Chart

> **Our Halloween Party**
>
> We had a Halloween party.
> Our mothers sent cookies.
> Mr. Fall gave us milk.
> We played and had fun.

Stories can be written on the chalkboard, on chart paper, or, if composed by an individual pupil, on ordinary-size paper. In each case questions can direct attention toward composition and organization: How shall we start the story? Can someone think of another way? Which way do you like? What should we say next? Is this the way the story should end? Have we told the story in the proper order? Let's go back over this and decide which sentences we need to keep in the story and how they should be arranged.

Even in the very first productions, attention should be paid to the mechanical skills. At first, simply pointing out capital letters and periods will help children to become accustomed to their use. Later you could say, "How do I begin this sentence?" The same procedure can be used with other punctuation, margins, placing the title, and possibly spelling some words. However, it is not wise to introduce a great number of these skills at one time, particularly when writing a chart for young children.

To encourage young children's sense of participation in writing experience stories, copies may occasionally be made and given to children so that they can put their names on them and take them to their parents. As children begin to be experienced with stories dictated by the group they may dictate individual endings. Again, these may be taken home, or they may be posted so that children can find out how others completed the story. Stories individually dictated to the teacher might be placed in a class book of stories. Other forms of writing that children dictate should also be used—records and titles posted, for instance, letters mailed, and so on.

Our Weather

It snowed last night. The wind is blowing the snow. It is cold.

Story Writing

Story writing really begins with the first oral sharing and experience writing activities of children, even though some of these may be more similar to the reports they will write later. In the early stage of story writing, however, this distinction need not be made. To children a story is something they want to tell, and they will do this both orally and in writing when they are encouraged to do so and have the necessary skills.

Children's first stories are usually about something that happened to them or that has been read or told to them. But given their inborn imaginative and creative abilities, their stories soon become ones that they "make up" or at least embellish considerably. Teachers generally encourage children to use their imagination, "to be creative," and of course the encouragement of children's creativity—in all of their endeavors—is desirable. But creativity is more than imagination; it draws upon imagination, but it also draws on an individual's emotional resources and propensity to be curious and to think independently. It requires divergent thinking, but the expression of this thinking—the product—results only if there is some degree, at least, of convergent thinking.

Stages in the Creative Process

1. Readiness ("input" experiences, relating to other experiences and ideas)
2. Incubation (thinking, exploring, sensing)
3. Inspiration and insight (getting an idea)
4. Production (testing and verifying the idea)

We are not suggesting any diminishing of teachers' efforts to foster children's creativity. In fact, we think teachers should generally exert more effort. This effort, however, must be more than simply telling children to "write something creative." Too often this direction results in wildly imaginative pieces that have few characteristics of stories and/or creative expression—even though such a piece may contain ideas or ways of phrasing them that are indeed genuinely crea-

Planning to write about favorite hockey players.

tive. But these beginnings need guidance and direction if they are to develop into something more than merely beginnings.

Children awaken early in their experiences to the fact that a good story has an interesting beginning, is orderly in development, and has a point or climax. As the teacher reads and tells stories or relates a personal experience, they can appreciate the importance of sequence in relating events and details. And, of course, pointing out these characteristics of stories is an integral part of teaching reading and listening comprehension. Yet when children begin to write, many of their "stories" may have an appealing beginning, but then the sequence of events becomes confused, a climax is absent, and finally the "story" just stops (often with the child writing "THE END").

Too much effort to be imaginative is one cause for a story being poorly developed, but attempting too broad a scope is possibly even more often a cause. Limiting a topic—for a story or for other forms of writing—is a problem for all writers—children or adults. Help children to discover that if the scope is limited to a particular event or time span, the story can be developed more interestingly. For example, the title "Sam Got Out of the House Last Night" lends itself more readily to sequencing events and using specific details than does "My Pet Cat." Or "The First Indian I Ever Saw" is more easily handled than "Crossing the Prairie in a Wagon Train."

Helping children to plan, then, is a vital aspect of the "pre-writing" phase. The first stories children write will be much like the experience writing discussed in the previous section and can be guided in a similar manner. But by the time children reach the middle grades, it might prove helpful to formulate standards that can be posted and called to their attention each time they write. These might include such points as the following:

Our Story Formula
(one class's standards)

1. Does my story have a good beginning?
2. Does it show a reader what the story idea is?
3. Does it reach a high point or climax?
4. Do all parts of the story fit together?

Things to Think About Before I Write
1. What is the story about?
2. Where did it happen?
3. Who are the characters and what are they like?
4. Who is telling the story?
5. How will it begin?
6. What is the high point, or climax, of the story?
7. What events or actions lead up to this climax?
8. How will I end the story?

Publishers of Children's Writing:

Jack and Jill, 1100 Waterway Blvd. P.O. Box 567B, Indianapolis, IN 18431

Kids Magazine, P.O. Box 3041, Grand Central Station, New York, NY 10017

Daisy, 830 Third Ave., New York, NY 10022

Ebony, Jr!, 820 S. Michigan Ave., Chicago, IL 60605

Highlights for Children, 803 Church St., Honesdale, PA 18431

Stone Soup, Box 83, Santa Cruz, CA 95063

This may seem like a good deal for a child to think about, but children can do more than we often think—especially when they have some idea of what to do. And naturally the standards will be posted, so that children can refer to them as they plan and as they write.

Children should learn, of course, that this preplanning is not iron-clad. Sometimes plans need to be modified—possibly even abandoned. But they do help in getting started and in organizing content. The child who has some idea of where he is going is more likely to produce an interesting story than one who simply begins.

Letters

Use charts and models to show letter form.

Label the parts: heading, greeting (salutation), message, closing, and signature.

Letter writing is one of the most frequently used writing forms and therefore should receive instructional emphasis in the elementary school. Like other writing forms, it is best taught in situations where the need is genuine rather than manufactured, and such situations abound in the average classroom. The following are some examples:

A students' guide to writing letters, "All About Letters," produced by the United States Postal Service and the National Council of Teachers of English is available from NCTE for $1.50.

Occasions Calling for Letter Writing

Invitations
To friends to visit the classroom.
To parents to come to an activity.
To another class or school to come to a program.
To the principal or supervisor to observe an activity.

Replies
Of acceptance of an invitation from another class.
Of regret at not being able to come to a program.

Sympathy
To a sick classmate, teacher, or relative.
To a teacher or family of a classmate after a death or accident.

Greetings
To others at school on a holiday.
To parents at Christmas, Mothers' Day, and other special occasions.
To the principal and other teachers on birthdays.
To various friends on special occasions.

Friendly letters and postcards	To another classroom or school.
	To a former classmate.
	To last year's teacher.
	To a student in a foreign land.
	To authors of favorite books.
	To grandparents
Thank-you notes	To someone for talking to the class.
	To friends and relatives for presents at Christmas.
	To another class for the use of books or other materials.
	To a parent for the loan of materials.
	To the principal for some special favor.
Requests	To a company or individual for information.
	To a shopkeeper for materials.
	To someone for permission to visit his or her business or home.
	To the principal for permission to take a trip.
Orders	To a business for class supplies.
	To a publisher for a magazine subscription.
Applications	For a position on the school paper.
	For a job in the school office.
	For summer work.
	For after-school jobs.
Complaints	About an article in the newspaper.
	About a practice on the playground.
	About a product to a consumer agency.

Sources of Names of Pen Pals
(some have fees)

The International Friendship League 40 Mt. Vernon St., Boston, MA 02108

Student Letter Exchange R.F.D. No. 4, Waseca, MN 56093

Youth of All Nations, 16 St. Luke's Place, New York, NY 10014

The Canadian Education Association, 151 Bloor Street West; Toronto, Ontario M561V5, Canada

League of Friendship, Inc. P.O. Box 509, Mt. Vernon, OH 43050

World Pen Pals, 1690 Como Avenue, St. Paul, MN 55108

Probably you can think of other occasions for writing; textbooks may provide still more.[3] The important point is that the natural activities in a classroom provide occasions for the real practice of letter writing. If actual situations are utilized—and utilized regularly—children will develop an awareness of situations that call for letter writing. They will also see the point in making letters interesting, genuinely communicative, and courteous. They will learn when it is appropriate to write notes of sympathy or congratulations, that one should write a thank-you note to someone who has sent a gift or done a favor, that it is courteous to express respect when writing to someone older than they are, how to acknowledge invitations, and to give reasons when regrets are necessary. They should also develop the ability to select appropriate writing materials (paper, pen, typewriter) and the realization that letters should be answered and mailed promptly.[4] Like any other piece of writing, a letter should be read before it is mailed, and attention should be given to spelling and neatness. And, finally, a letter is personal; one should not read a letter addressed to someone else unless asked to. This courtesy may be emphasized by asking children's permission before posting letters or having them exchanged for correction—and respecting a child's wish *not* to have his letter read by others.

The first business letters will probably be written in the middle grades; at this point, emphasize the use of formal language and appropriate salutations and clos-

More Ideas for Teaching Letter Writing

1. Post model letters, including those written by children.
2. Show letter makeup by outlining the form with a felt pen.
3. Use dittoed work sheets, lined in such a way that the child is forced to write in correct form.
4. Keep collections of letters showing various forms.
5. Use construction-paper cutouts to show form and shape.
6. Have pupils exchange letters for correction of matters of form.

ings, and discuss the kinds of information that should be included in the body of the letter (whether money is enclosed, how to write out dollars and cents, the importance of stating exactly where merchandise or information is to be sent, etc.). Whenever children first write to an individual (rather than a firm) and request a reply, they should learn that a stamped, self-addressed envelope should be enclosed. And they should know that any letter written to a stranger—even if it is a letter of complaint—should always be courteous; rude or angry letters seldom get the desired results.

In the upper grades, introduce or reinforce any of the above items that children do not seem to be familiar with, and also bring in, discuss, and post business letters with various formats, such as block and indented styles. At this level, some pupils may also be learning to type, so they should know that it is good form to write *and* type the signature on a business letter.

Most of us do not write business letters often, but when we do it is sometimes important that they convey a particularly good impression (letters of application, for instance). Impress children with the importance of neatness, the placement of the letter on the page, and the inclusion of needed information in the body of the letter. Again, no letter should be sealed and mailed until it has been proofread. One or two inked corrections are better than mistakes left uncorrected; if there are many errors, the letter should be rewritten.

There are many matters of form that are particularly important in letter

Learning about the parts of a letter.

Notes and Summaries

Have you ever come home from school and found a message like this on the kitchen table?

My dear child,

I have to work late at the biology laboratory this evening. I must finish some experiments that have to be done today. I expect to arrive home at about 9:00 P.M. If you get hungry before then, don't hesitate to prepare yourself something.

Very affectionately yours,
Mother

You've probably never received a message quite like this one. Your mother does not need to be so formal with you. If she were going to be late, she might write this way:

Dear,

Must work late tonight. See you about 9. Fix a snack if you want.

Mom

This kind of writing is called a note. Its purpose is to give information simply and clearly.

Writing notes is an important skill with many uses. For example, you can take brief notes to help you remember things you read about or hear in class.

Different communication purposes require different language styles. (USING OUR LANGUAGE, 1977 edition; copyright © by BOWMAR/NOBLE PUBLISHERS, INC., Los Angeles, California 90039)

writing—the placement of the parts of a letter, capitalization of particular items, abbreviations of titles such as Mr. or Dr., wording of the salutation or complimentary closing, etc. Children will master these only through actual letter writing experiences. Certainly letters should not be emphasized to the exclusion of other forms of writing, but letters are often crucial, and therefore the writing of letters should not be neglected in the school program.

Poetry and Rhymes

Every child should have some experience with poetry—hearing it, reading it, speaking it individually or as part of a group, and writing it. Certainly no one class will produce many—if any—poets of great stature, but the number of children who can create a truly charming, humorous, or actually poetic bit of verse is often surprising.

Children should not be expected to write poetry unless they have heard much of it. Poetry in its various forms needs to have been read to them and they should have experienced saying it in choral speaking activities. Opening activities in a classroom provide a natural time every day for reading poetry to children, but many activities are also natural times if you have appropriate poetry ready to read (see chapter 15). There are equally many natural and fun times for children to experience speaking poetry. Important, too, as background for children's writing of poetry are experiences that have extended their language powers: finding and talking about words and phrases that create visual and sound images, words with a musical lift, new ways of saying things, and words related to their emotions.

Class composition is a good way to begin. Select a form with which the children are familiar and which they have enjoyed, read aloud several examples, and then suggest that they might compose a poem like this. With the background suggested, children should be able to suggest topics, words and phrases, rhyming words (if needed), and even entire lines. Possibly you may need to encourage such suggestions by stimulating one or more of their senses. Even a weed picked on your way to school may prompt thoughts about its structure, color, or smell and bring forth words and phrases about how ugly or beautiful it is, its uniqueness, and so on. The children can then discuss which words and phrases sound best or fit the subject or rhythm best. In this way they will learn how to go about the process of creating a poem.

It is not important to teach poetic techniques as such, but call attention to them when it is appropriate. For example, kindergarten children can not be expected either to pronounce or to remember *onomatopoeia*, but they can readily grasp that *buzz* is something like the sound that a bee makes. Upper grade pupils, on the other hand, might be extremely proud of the fact that they have used a technique called *alliteration* in creating a phrase like "the sad, silken syllables of the breeze." Emphasis should always be upon the product rather than the technique, however.

There are many forms of poetry that children may write, and some will have the desire and the ability to attempt even the most difficult of these. There are several short and rather structured forms, however, that children particularly enjoy using because the form itself creates a challenge and furnishes rather definite guidelines, thus helping them to achieve greater success with their first efforts.

Couplets and Triplets.   Reading readiness activities calling for the use of rhyming words may produce the children's first attempts at composing poems. At this point there is no need to be concerned with rhythm, although children love rhythm and they may well try to produce it. Simply encouraging them to make the second rhyming sentence relate to the first is sufficient, however.

I have a dog.
He sits on a log.

They may even be prompted to add a third line, making a triplet.

He looks like a frog!

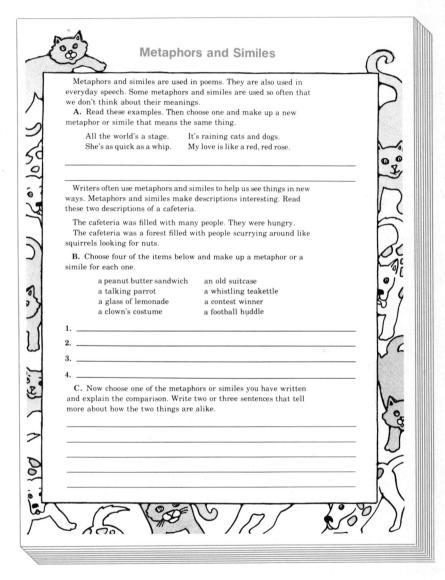

Metaphors and Similes

Metaphors and similes are used in poems. They are also used in everyday speech. Some metaphors and similes are used so often that we don't think about their meanings.

A. Read these examples. Then choose one and make up a new metaphor or simile that means the same thing.

All the world's a stage.   It's raining cats and dogs.
She's as quick as a whip.   My love is like a red, red rose.

_____

_____

Writers often use metaphors and similes to help us see things in new ways. Metaphors and similes make descriptions interesting. Read these two descriptions of a cafeteria.

The cafeteria was filled with many people. They were hungry.
The cafeteria was a forest filled with people scurrying around like squirrels looking for nuts.

B. Choose four of the items below and make up a metaphor or a simile for each one.

a peanut butter sandwich   an old suitcase
a talking parrot   a whistling teakettle
a glass of lemonade   a contest winner
a clown's costume   a football huddle

1. _____

2. _____

3. _____

4. _____

C. Now choose one of the metaphors or similes you have written and explain the comparison. Write two or three sentences that tell more about how the two things are alike.

_____

_____

_____

_____

_____

An activity for teaching about metaphors and similes. (USING OUR LANGUAGE, 1977 edition; copyright © by BOWMAR/NOBLE PUBLISHERS, INC., Los Angeles, California 90039)

For ideas see:

*Content and Craft: Written
    Expression in the
    Elementary School* by
    Dorothy Grant Hennings
    and Barbara M. Grant
    (Prentice-Hall, 1973)
*Turning Children on
    Through Creative
    Writing* by Mary Attea
    (D.O.K. Publishers, 1973)
*Language Arts Activities
    for the Classroom* by
    Sidney W. Tiedt and Iris
    M. Tiedt (Allyn and
    Bacon 1979)

Helping them to find words or phrases that sound better or improve the rhythm will help them to develop aural discrimination and to learn about sentences, capitalization, and end punctuation while they are taking their first steps toward creativity and having a great deal of fun as well.

Cinquain.   Cinquain is not difficult to write, and it is excellent for helping children to become aware of the special quality of poetry—its appeal to the emotions and the senses. It has a very specific formula:

First line: one word, giving title
Second line: two words, describing title
Third line: three words, expressing an action
Fourth line: four words, expressing a feeling
Fifth line: one word, a synonym for the title

This is too restrictive a form to stay with for very long, but it does allow some freedom in the choice of words and phrases and almost any child can achieve some degree of success with cinquain. To show how the formula works, here are two examples:

Sam

Warm, friendly,
Licks my face
To show his love.
Puppy.

Darkness

Thick, eerie;
I whistle loudly;
I fear the night;
Black.

Free Verse.   Free verse places no restrictions on total length and number of syllables or words to a line and prescribes no rhythmic pattern. The writer decides where to break lines or begin new stanzas, and when the poem is complete. In a sense, free verse may be thought of as *free thought.* The length of the thought might be one sentence by a third grader or several stanzas by a creative sixth grader.

If children experience activities in which they talk about and use words and phrases that express their feelings, that create images, about commonplace but important things to them—family, friends, fear, happiness, pain, etc.—then writing these feelings will follow.

Limericks.   Middle grade children can have a great deal of fun with limericks, and certainly children should know that poetry can be humorous as well as serious. That, in fact, is the essence of poetry—it expresses all our emotions at one time or another. Limericks have a set form with which most of us are familiar: the first, second, and fifth lines rhyme; the third and fourth lines rhyme and are shorter. Show children that the "trick" is to find a number of words that rhyme and then see if several of them suggest an idea; they will need at least three rhyming words for lines one, two, and five. Then show them how they can experiment with word order or find synonyms in order to make the meter work out correctly. The beginning couplet should be established first; then the same kind of experimentation can produce lines three and four. The final line should come rather easily after this much has been done.

> There was an old woman named Snow
> Who couldn't get flowers to grow.
> She planted some seeds
> But grew only weeds.
> What happened I really don't know!

Other Forms.   Obviously there are many more verse forms than have been discussed here, and children may be encouraged to try any that they are interested in. *Haiku* is a lovely Japanese verse form that many teachers have children try. Haiku has three lines consisting of seventeen syllables: the first line has five syllables, the second seven, and the third five. There is no rhyme or meter. The central image is usually from nature, with the final line making an observation about life. The teaching of this poetry form in the elementary school has declined, however, because of the emphasis typically given to counting syllables without enough regard for the feelings the words express. The beauty of haiku lies in the right choice of words to create the image and express the idea of the poem. Some authorities, at least, believe that elementary school children have neither the vocabulary storehouse or life experiences to create haiku. The same might be said about other Japanese poetry forms—*tanka,* which adds two lines of seven syllables each to haiku; or *senryu,* which has three lines but may add two or three syllables.

Some teachers, together with their students, have invented their own forms, such as triante and diamente. These can be structured according to the age and abilities of the children. We especially like triante, because it calls for "sense" words, as follows:

> First line: one word giving the title
> Second line: two words telling how it smells
> Third line: three words telling how it feels
> Fourth line: four words telling how it looks
> Fifth line: five words telling how it sounds

Poems can also be made in shapes; that is, a poem about a cloud might be shaped like a drifting cloud, one about Halloween might be in the shape of a pumpkin, etc. The important fact to remember is that poetry is yet another way in which ideas and feelings may be expressed. In the kind of world we live in today, it is important for children to learn to express their emotions verbally and to exercise care in selecting the words they choose to express those emotions. In addition, reading and hearing poetry can add dimension to their lives, and creating poetry will undoubtedly extend this dimension.

Reports

Teacher guidance is often needed to help a child narrow a report topic.

In the intermediate and upper grades, pupils have many opportunities to write reports. In fact, the activities in classrooms at these levels almost demand the writing of reports. Among the kinds of reports that can be written are the following:

summaries of books, speeches, articles, movies, and television and radio programs; summaries of student council, class, or club meetings or of assembly programs; research accounts based on interviews, reading on specific topics, or science experiments; accounts of personal and class experiences.

At the lower grade levels, children should begin reporting by dictating to the teacher (see the earlier section on experience stories). In the second and third grades, some report writing may be done by the children individually.

Reports can be on many topics and for many occasions. The following should suggest the unlimited possibilities:

1. Writing one-paragraph reports on famous people.
2. Visiting a museum and reporting on an object observed.
3. Writing a report on a hobby or special interest.
4. Keeping records of baseball and football games and reporting on them.
5. Explaining the organization and work of a club.
6. Describing an incident from a particular point of view.
7. Reporting on controversial issues in committee meetings.
8. Writing an account of a holiday celebration.
9. Reporting briefly on the history and derivation of a word.
10. Giving personal reactions to characters and situations in books.
11. Reporting on the steps through which a character in a story changes.
12. Reporting on the history of a custom, superstition, or place name.
13. Reporting on an interview with the principal.
14. Summarizing newspaper articles on a topic of current interest.
15. Reporting on background information relative to a current news story.

Chapters 16 and 17 contain discussions about locating information, taking notes, and correlating information for longer or more comprehensive reports. Since reporting, either orally or in writing, is important to many classroom activities, it is a good idea to initiate a class discussion aimed at formulating a set of procedures. By the time children reach the upper grades, these should probably include the following steps:

1. Decide what facts or information should be included.
2. Determine the most likely sources for this information—observation, interviews, reading.
3. Use these sources to find the information needed.
4. Recheck 1 to see whether all needed information has been found and whether new items should be included.
5. Decide on the order in which facts should be presented and the best way to present each one—illustrations, details, or reasons.

Reviews

A specialized type of report is the review. Reviews may be written about books, television programs, movies, and cultural events. A review should be a teaser, a reaction by the writer, and not a dull account of "what happened." Before children write reviews, particularly of books they have read, they should be made familiar with reviews such as those found in *Language Arts* and *The Horn Book*. Most newspapers have reviews (of varying quality) of television, movies, and local

Chapter 15 has other suggestions for book reviews.

events. Various reviews should be discussed with children so that they learn how a review differs from other kinds of reports.

Essays

Ideas for Personal Essays

I Wish I Were _____
If I Were President
Thoughts on a Rainy
   Afternoon
The Meanest Man in the
   World
If I Had a Hundred Dollars
The Day I Forgot
I Like _____
How It Feels to Be Me
On Being Ten Years Old
Walking Barefoot in the
   Mud
Skiing the Bumps
My Hockey Team

The word *essay* has fallen into disuse, except in literature classes, yet it is an apt term for a type of writing that offers endless opportunities for creative expression. In simple terms, an essay is the expression of one's own beliefs or feelings about a person, an event, or an idea. Thus much of the writing and speaking that we do, both as children and as adults, has some of the qualities of an essay—even a personal letter is a loosely organized essay, since it reflects the writer's own personality. Likewise, many of the experience stories that children write or dictate to the teacher are essays.

The essay has several advantages as a vehicle for creative expression. First, it is a form with which children have had experience; thus they can focus major attention on choosing the best way to express their ideas and feelings. Second, by its very nature the essay is creative, since it is a personal expression. Third, children want to express their own likes and dislikes, their fears and desires, so this form should appeal to them. It may even help to improve the self-image of a child who believes that his or her feelings are unimportant to others. And finally, the essay is somewhat similar in form to the kinds of writing most commonly used by children and adults—more so, at least, than are stories and poems. Thus children can learn organization and methods of developing ideas while they are also developing their creative talents.

News Articles

A classroom newspaper can be extremely challenging for motivating writing. Children will become intrigued with discovering and reporting events around the school, in the community, and in their homes. The newspaper can be published weekly, monthly, or only occasionally for special holidays and events. Frequency should be determined principally, of course, by the amount of learning and enjoyment the children gain from this activity, but other factors must be considered too. Will this frequency of publication fit into the schedule without replacing other activities that may be even more valuable? Can the paper be planned to call forth the kinds of writing practice and skills needed by the children? Is time available for typing and duplicating, or can parents and/or students be depended on for at least a part of this work?

News writing can begin in the primary grades with group-dictated news written by the teacher on the chalkboard.

The writing in a newspaper may be of many types, since newspapers ordinarily include many things—news stories, special features, letters to the editor, jokes, advertisements, poems, and comics. Organizational skills are also called into play in making decisions about what things should be placed together.

Many upper grade reading programs include material on how to read a newspaper. This may provide a starting point for a class or school newspaper. Children might read newspapers in class and analyze them, cutting out clippings of various sorts to illustrate what they have learned. Various sections of a paper (sports, world news, society news, etc.) should be noted, and special attention should be given to sources of material for these sections—syndicated columns, wire services, publicity handouts, and local reporting. Journalism has its own vocabulary, and children can learn the special meanings of words such as copy, deadline, proofreading, layout, and editor. The school newspaper should receive high priority in a program of written expression because it is a live (not book) activity, it builds class and school spirit, and it appeals to all children, regardless of creative abilities. Every child in the classroom may participate in some way, because there is such a wide variety of forms of writing. And almost every area of the curriculum may be utilized in the newspaper—social studies, science, art, health, etc.

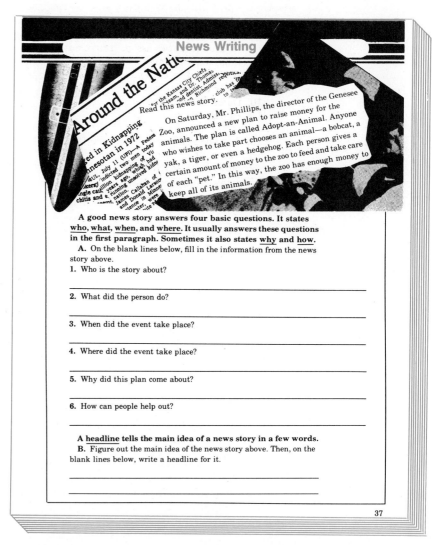

News Writing

Around the Nation

Read this news story.

On Saturday, Mr. Phillips, the director of the Genesee Zoo, announced a new plan to raise money for the animals. The plan is called Adopt-an-Animal. Anyone who wishes to take part chooses an animal—a bobcat, a yak, a tiger, or even a hedgehog. Each person gives a certain amount of money to the zoo to feed and take care of each "pet." In this way, the zoo has enough money to keep all of its animals.

A good news story answers four basic questions. It states <u>who</u>, <u>what</u>, <u>when</u>, and <u>where</u>. It usually answers these questions in the first paragraph. Sometimes it also states <u>why</u> and <u>how</u>.

A. On the blank lines below, fill in the information from the news story above.

1. Who is the story about?

_____

2. What did the person do?

_____

3. When did the event take place?

_____

4. Where did the event take place?

_____

5. Why did this plan come about?

_____

6. How can people help out?

_____

A <u>headline</u> tells the main idea of a news story in a few words.

B. Figure out the main idea of the news story above. Then, on the blank lines below, write a headline for it.

_____

_____

37

From this kind of activity move to using real news articles. (USING OUR LANGUAGE WORKBOOK, Level 5, 1977 edition; copyright © by BOWMAR/NOBLE PUBLISHERS, INC., Los Angeles, California 90039)

Records

Children's interest in nature and in everything going on about them provides opportunities for writing records of things that happen. Since most record keeping requires straightforward, factual writing, and not a taxing amount, many children who have difficulty with other forms of writing can keep records. Here are some kinds of records that can be kept:

1. The time the sun sets, recorded at weekly intervals.
2. Weather calendars.
3. Growth of plants in the classroom windows.
4. Steps followed in making pudding.
5. Spelling words missed by the class.
6. Classroom duties assigned to pupils.
7. Class diary of daily events.
8. Books read by each child. (Avoid making this too competitive.)
9. Daily temperatures, wind direction, etc.
10. Dates of appearance of first robin, ducks flying, etc.
11. Height and weight records.
12. Foods eaten for breakfast, hours slept, etc.
13. The changing appearance of the polliwogs, cocoon, etc.
14. Visitors to the classroom.
15. New words learned in various subjects.
16. Science experiments.
17. Points to remember about a film.
18. Daily attendance and daily schedule.
19. Standards or rules for class activities.
20. Events to be reported on in the yearbook.

Forms

Everyone has occasion to fill out forms. Neither children nor adults can avoid doing so; therefore children need to learn and to practice this kind of writing. There are many day-to-day activities in which children must fill out forms. These situations should be utilized to teach careful reading, the importance of legible writing (or printing), and the need for accuracy. Some school situations for filling out forms are these:

1. Enrollment cards.
2. Questionnaires regarding personal history.
3. Questionnaires concerning health facts.
4. Library loan cards.
5. Call slips for books at the library.
6. Information called for on a standardized test.
7. A money order for materials for the class.
8. An application card for an account in the school savings bank.
9. A deposit slip for a school savings account.
10. A withdrawal slip.
11. A subscription blank for a magazine.
12. Coupons for samples advertised in magazines.
13. An order to a publisher for a reference book.
14. An application blank for membership in a magazine club.
15. A book plate for use in a textbook.

Announcements, Labels, and Notices

Many school activities call for written notices, labels, titles, and announcements. This type of writing requires specificity and brevity. Moreover, such writing may not be read unless it is interesting and clear. Teaching emphasis should be upon these factors. Activities such as the following may be helpful:

1. Making oral announcements that hold to standards of brevity, accuracy, etc.
2. Giving oral directions for a game or other activity.
3. Examining the weaknesses of notices and announcements in newspapers.
4. Reporting on notices, signs, and labels seen around the school.
5. Scoring announcements and notices as to appeal, clarity, neatness, etc.

The factors to be considered can be listed on a score sheet and points assigned to each as an announcement or notice is examined.

Other Writing Activities

Many other activities can serve to stimulate children's writing. Much of what children read will particularly serve this function, with the writing also providing useful reinforcement and supplement to reading lessons as well as to reading in other curriculum areas. The following are other forms of writing that may be based on these experiences.

Character Sketches.   Sketches based on the characters in a story may be written by children. They should think about the character selected, search for details about him and the things he does, and speculate about him and his behavior. A character sketch can take any of several forms; it can be thought of as a "verbal snapshot" or an impression gained by a "first glance," a description that tells what kind of human being a person is, a combination of these, or a sketch that concentrates on an example or examples of one trait.

Biographies.   Children can research and write biographies of people in the news or ones they have learned about in social studies. They can also write "made up" biographies or autobiographies of characters in stories. These provide not only fun but also good motivation for reading. Forms of writing, such as personification, can be used if a story lends itself to such treatment. An old car, a horse, or a towering tree can write its early life through the imagination of the child.

See chapter 9 for other suggestions of writing activities.

Descriptions.   Literary selections often demonstrate how a professional writer uses composition skills. For example, at the beginning of "Rip Van Winkle," Washington Irving describes the Catskill Mountains as "swelling up to a noble height, and lording it over the surrounding country . . . when the weather is fair and settled, they are clothed in blue and purple, and print their bold outlines on the clear evening sky; but sometimes, when the rest of the landscape is cloudless, they will gather a hood of grey vapors about their summits, which, in the last rays of the setting sun, will glow and light up like a crown of glory."

In discussion, help the children to discover how the use of devices such as personification and simile adds vigor to a description, how the use of verbs as well as adjectives and adverbs gives strength, and how a few well-chosen details, instead of a wealth of them, can set scene and mood. This can be followed by thinking about a familiar setting and giving details about it. These details can then be woven into a description.

Letters.   Correspondence with an author is a way for a child to share with others some of his or her reading experiences. When correspondence is not possible, a "pretend" interview can be written. This should be based on known information and reading what the author has written, not simply made up out of whole cloth.

Children can also write letters to the librarian, to another teacher, or to children in another grade about the books they have read. These are effective whether the writer is recommending or criticizing the book.

In the middle grades, book characters may exchange letters. Have pupils write to one another as the characters might have done. For example, Henry Reed might ask Homer Price all about the doughnut machine, and Amos might be very interested in discussing French customs with Anatole.

Commentaries.   Another variation of the book report involves encouraging children to relate the most humorous incident, the most exciting happening, the part they liked best, or the saddest part of a book. This will help children learn to seek certain types of material from books and stories.

Riddles.   Children can prepare a series of clues concerning a character, a setting, an event, or an object in a story. The reader must guess who or what is being described. Sometimes it is possible to create interest by deliberately choosing ambiguous terms.

Captions and Headlines.   For children who have difficulty expressing ideas in writing, short forms of composition should be sought. Writing labels for pictures related to stories is one example. These labels should be more than simply one or a few words. Instead of writing "The Snowstorm," a child might be encouraged to write a sentence about it, such as "When I awoke everything was white and clean."

In addition to writing labels for pictures, the less able children may be encouraged to write headlines—to give in short sentences the "big idea" of a story they have read.

Diaries.   For units where stories revolve around colonial times or other periods in history, students may pretend to be living during the period and keep diaries. They can also write letters to friends telling about some of the experiences or first-person stories in which they describe events as though they had participated in the action. It is particularly important to limit the scope in this kind of writing. For example, a diary entry might cover only one day, or even a part of a day; a first-person account could be limited to a single aspect of an important historical event—for instance, what the foot soldier felt like at Valley Forge.

A Final Word

Children have a natural tendency to write. They want to express themselves, to communicate, if there are authentic reasons for doing so and the conditions for writing are encouraging. We have discussed the stages in the writing process, classroom conditions that foster writing, and activities and forms of writing children can and should engage in. In the following chapter we continue the discussion of children's writing by particularly focusing on procedures and techniques for its teaching.

Endnotes

1. The National Assessment of Educational Progress is a project of the Education Commission of the States (Suite 700, 1860 Lincoln Street, Denver, CO 80295). The project periodically assesses skills and knowledge of several age groups of Americans in various curricular areas and issues reports of its findings.

2. "Composition: A Position Statement," National Council of Teachers of English Commission on Composition, *Elementary English*, February 1975, p. 194.

3. See also Helen Jacobsen and Florence Mischel, *The First Book of Letter Writing* (New York: Franlin Watts, 1957).

4. Middle grade children will enjoy *Dear Dragon*, by Sesyle Joslin (New York: Harcourt, Brace and World, 1962), an amusing collection of improbable letters of many types.

References

Books

Brandt, Sue R. *How to Write a Report.* New York: Franklin Watts, 1968.

Burrows, Alvina T. *What Research Says to the Teacher: Teaching Composition.* Washington, DC: National Education Association, 1959.

Chase, Cheryl M. *Creative Writing: Activity Ideas for Character and Plot Development, Grades 3 and 4.* Longmont, CO: Northern Colorado Educational Board of Cooperative Services, 1974.

Hennings, Dorothy Grant. *Communication in Action.* Chicago: Rand McNally College Publishing Company, 1978.

Jackson, Jacqueline. *Turn Not Pale, Beloved Snail: A Book about Writing among Other Things.* Boston: Little, Brown and Co., 1974.

Petty, Walter T., and Bowen, Mary. *Slithery Snakes and Other Aids to Children's Writing.* New York: Meredith, 1967.

Petty, Walter T., and Jensen, Julie. *Developing Children's Language.* Boston: Allyn and Bacon, 1980.

Wolsch, Robert A. *Poetic Composition through the Grades.* New York: Teachers College Press, 1970.

Wille, Fred., *The ABC's of Creativity and Language Arts.* Carthage, IL: Good Apple, Inc., 1978.

Films

Creative Writing: A Series. Los Angeles; Churchill Films (Four films, 16 minutes each; color; primary and intermediate).

Creative Writing: A Series. Los Angeles: Churchill Films (Four films, 16 minutes each; color; primary and intermediate).

Letter Writing for Beginners. Chicago: Coronet

Films (11 minutes; color or b/w; primary and intermediate).

Let's Write a Story. Los Angeles: Churchill Films (11 min.; color, b/w; primary and intermediate).

Making Word Pictures. Chicago: Coronet Films (14 min.; intermediate).

Poems We Write. Monterey, CA: Grover Film Productions (15 min.; color; intermediate).

Poetry for Beginners. New York: Sterling Educational Films (11 min.; intermediate).

Poetry for Me. Monterey, CA: Grover Film Productions (14 min.; elementary).

Writing a Report. Chicago: Coronet Films (11 minutes; color, b/w; intermediate).

Writing Different Kinds of Letters. Chicago: Coronet Films (11 minutes; color, b/w; intermediate).

Your Communication Skills: Writing. Chicago: Coronet Films (11 minutes; color, b/w; intermediate).

Filmstrips

Getting Ready to Write Creatively. Mahwah, NJ: Troll Associates (6 color strips with records or tapes; grades 2–5).

Learning to Write Letters. Mahwah, NJ: Troll Associates, 1970 (Color; intermediate).

Stories Waiting to Be Told. New York: Learning Corporation of America (Color; with record; primary).

What's Rough? What's Soft?, etc. Irvington, NY: Hudson Photographic Industries, 1968 (Color series of ten strips and records).

Recordings

Developing Creative Ability. Freeport, NY: Educational Activities (2 records or cassettes; sound effects, incomplete stories, dramas).

Report Writing Skills. Chicago: Coronet (8 cassettes; response books; teacher's manual; intermediate).

Springboards to Writing. St. Paul: 3M Co. (4 cassettes with worksheets; intermediate).

The Writing Bug. New York: Random House (3 filmstrips, cassettes, charts, teacher's guide).

Writing Can Be Fun . . . Once You Know How It's Done. Minneapolis: Paul S. Amidon and Associates, Inc., 1969 (Tapes or cassettes with suggestions about writing letters, tales, poetry, etc.).

Other Materials

Composition Skills. Chicago: Encyclopedia Britannica Educational Corp. (268 frames; intermediate grades).

Letter Writing. St. Paul: 3M Corp. (20 transparencies; primary).

Manuals of Style. Los Angeles: Bowmar/Noble (Books for students grades 3–6).

Nice. Denver: Love Publishing Co. (Ideas for writing).

The Bowmar Creative Writing Corner. Los Angeles: Bowmar/Noble (Books; upper grades).

Write to Communicate: The Language Arts in Process. Pleasantville, NY (Records, cards, portfolio books, posters, guides; intermediate).

ACTIVITIES FOR PRESERVICE TEACHERS

1. Write something yourself—a report, essay, description—and make notes as to what you do and the order in which you do them during all three phases of your writing. What did you learn about what children may do when they write?

2. Demonstrate to the class exactly how you would go about helping a class of first graders write a group composition. Be sure to include a description of motivational activities.

3. Find a letter written by some well-known person that might be used in connection with letter writing activities. Prepare a demonstration showing how you would use it.

4. Select a unit of study for a particular grade level and plan the writing activities that might grow out of it. Include a list of skills or writing forms that might need to be introduced or reviewed at this grade level.

5. Report to the class on two of the following:

Applegate, Mauree. "After All, Mrs. Murphy—," in *When Children Write*. Washington, DC: Association for Childhood Education International, 1955, pp. 23–29.

Cramer, Ronald L. "The Nature and Nurture of Creative Writing," *Elementary School Journal* 75 (May 1975), pp. 506–512.

Goedert, William O. "The Art of Authorship: Creative Writing in the Intermediate Grades," *National Catholic Educational Association Bulletin* 60 (August 1963), pp. 397–400.

Moroney, Frances M. "The Deeper You Dig," *Elementary English* 33 (March 1956), pp. 165–168.

Murray, Donald M. "Your Elementary Pupil and the Writer's Cycle of Craft," *Connecticut English Journal* (Fall 1969), pp. 3–10.

Turner, Thomas N., and Terwilliger, Paul N. "Multi-Dimensional Creativity," *Language Arts* 53 (February 1976), pp. 155–159.

6. Plan a lesson for children at a grade level of your choice to write imaginatively something other than a story or poem (e.g., cartoon dialogue, essay, advertisement).

ACTIVITIES FOR INSERVICE TEACHERS

1. Report to the class your observations of the behavior of one child in your classroom as he or she writes. Make your observations for a period of a week and make daily notes.

2. Investigate the free materials that can be secured by writing letters. Give special attention to those that could be written for by the children. Then get the children started writing.

3. Select one child in your class to observe for a week. Record the types of writing he or she does, including all kinds of writing: titles, announcements, labels, stories, reports, letters, etc.

4. Parents often state that they have no idea what their children do in school. Plan a biweekly newsletter for reporting class activities to parents. Precede this activity by a study of newspapers and a visit to a local paper.

5. Survey your classroom as objectively as possible to determine the degree of creativity fostered by the environment. Do children's ideas abound or have they been suppressed? Is the classroom yours or does it "belong" to the entire group?

6. Try doing some creative writing yourself. Decide on a topic based upon an object, picture, etc., and give yourself a set amount of time to write your story or poem. In other words, as much as possible, put yourself in the child's position.

INDEPENDENT ACTIVITIES FOR CHILDREN

1. Provide bulletin board space for an "Announcement Center." This space can contain information or directions about daily activities that children can sign up for (if the classroom is operated as an informal or open one), special events, children's own announcements, pertinent news clippings, and school happenings. Most of the materials should be written by the children; in fact, this can be a provision for using the space.

2. Contact a local nursing or convalescent home for names of people who might enjoy receiving letters from children. A child can "adopt" one of them as a grandparent and write letters to him or her, telling about class activities, personal

interests, etc., and possibly including an occasional story or poem the child has written.

3. Suggest other persons to whom a child could write letters. For example, he or she might write to the custodian, the principal, or the school clerk, thanking this person for something he or she did; to a public figure regarding something he or she said; to a newspaper; or to an author or publisher. Model letter forms should be provided for the child to refer to.

4. Have a child collect business letters received by parents and friends and make a display of different forms, using colored pencil to point out variations in placement and to underline kinds of language appropriate for salutations, closings, and the body of the letter.

5. For the child who can't think of a story to write or who doesn't believe his experiences are worth relating (or doesn't know how to relate them), record keeping or making and observing a window garden may be the answer. Have the child bring the soil and container (paper cup, egg carton, etc.) and you furnish the seed (tomato, bean, etc.).

6. A child can write "stories" for the class newspaper (parents may type the newspaper or it may simply be a section of a bulletin board). Topics for writing might be sports, weather, local happenings, school events, world news, reviews of TV shows, etc.

7. A very capable child might plan and make up an entire single-page newspaper, writing the articles on topics of his own choosing. The single page could be a newsprint sheet or a sheet of tagboard.

8. Diaries can be kept by children for a pet, a story character, or a toy. An individual child can regularly write in the diary of one "character."

9. Individual children can write reports on topics of their choice after trips, such as a nature walk or a visit to the fire station or a construction site. Suggest possible topics:

   birds or animals seen
   the tall fireman
   building machinery
   what I saw that nobody else did

10. Have children collect "sense" words. These could be kept in a notebook in the writers' corner, where individual children could go to add words or to find words to use when they are writing.

11. Children can tape stories for others to listen to. They may also record their stories and listen to them, revising them as they listen.

12. Have a child adapt a story for dramatization, writing a script with dialogue and stage directions.

13. Suggest that children exchange stories or other writing with children in other schools. These may be children whose names were obtained from one of the Pen Pal sources or they may be children in a nearby school. Each child should write to the other child, inviting him or her to exchange and react to the writing that is exchanged.

14. Let children compile a class booklet of creative writing, with each child selecting the one piece he has written that he would like to have included. Individual children should have absolutely free choice in deciding what to include; selections may have been written as a result of a class assignment, out of school, or perhaps even in another class.

15. With children's interest in television, motivating the writing of letters to TV stars is little needed. Addresses for writing are:

(Name of star)
ABC-TV, c/o Manager,
Audience Information
1330 Avenue of the Americas
New York, NY 10019

(Name of star)
NBC-TV, c/o Vice President,
Information Services
30 Rockefeller Plaza
New York, NY 10020

(Name of star)
CBS-TV, c/o Vice President
of Press Information
51 W. 52nd St.
New York, NY 10019

9

Extending Children's Writing Abilities

Children must be taught to write. While young children have a natural interest in writing, a kind of fascination with the telling of something that they and others can read, for children to learn to write effectively requires time, encouragement, and teaching. In chapter 8 we suggested ways that children's early interest in writing can be maintained and growth in writing fostered. We stressed the importance of respecting the writing process, building children's experience backgrounds, and creating supporting classroom conditions. And we suggested and discussed the many writing activities that occur naturally or may develop in a challenging and planned language arts program.

In this chapter we discuss ways to help children improve their writing, particularly by writing better organized sentences, paragraphs, and longer pieces; by using a variety of sentence structures; and by editing and rewriting. We recognize that some children may need extra help in both starting and completing a piece of writing and suggest how they may be helped. Finally we discuss the role of evaluation in a writing program and suggest techniques to use.

MAKING WRITTEN EXPRESSION EFFECTIVE

All language expression, both oral and written, is largely effective to the extent that its sentences are well constructed, have appeal and clarity, and are arranged in such a manner that they clearly convey the thought of the speaker or writer. Because the sentence is the principal unit in communication, teaching children to form good sentences is vital. This teaching is particularly needed in the writing program (although the carry-over from speech to writing is significant) since the writer must convey his or her message without the immediate audience feedback a speaker has that prompts restatement and can be aided by gestures and facial expressions.

Extending and broadening vocabulary—important to making writing more effective—is discussed in chapter 13.

Organization is important to all expression, and the quality of the organization of a piece of writing is a reflection of the quality of thinking given to it by the writer. Children can learn to improve the organization of their written expression as we suggest in one of the following sections. They also can learn to check on themselves, to proofread and edit what they have written, seeking to make it as effective as possible before they consider it finished.

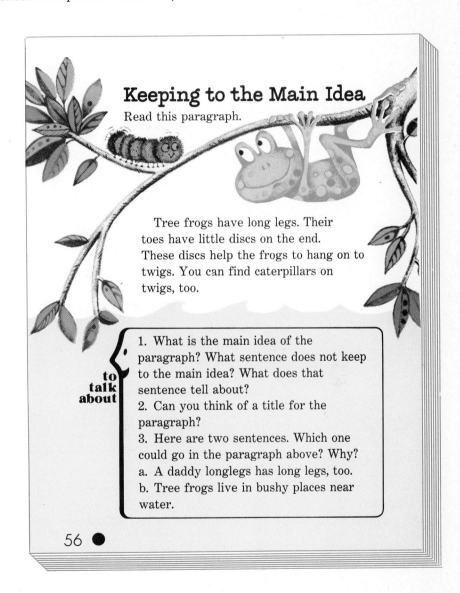

Keeping to the Main Idea
Read this paragraph.

Tree frogs have long legs. Their toes have little discs on the end. These discs help the frogs to hang on to twigs. You can find caterpillars on twigs, too.

to talk about

1. What is the main idea of the paragraph? What sentence does not keep to the main idea? What does that sentence tell about?
2. Can you think of a title for the paragraph?
3. Here are two sentences. Which one could go in the paragraph above? Why?
a. A daddy longlegs has long legs, too.
b. Tree frogs live in bushy places near water.

56 ●

Basic to both oral and written composition. (LANGUAGE BASICS PLUS, Level B. Copyright 1979 by Harper and Row, Publishers. Used by permission of the publisher.)

Developing Sentence Sense

Basically, a sentence may be thought of as a means of expressing an idea. Thus, attention should focus on the idea and on expressing that idea in a way that is clear and exact.

There are no shortcuts to skill in constructing effective sentences. Each pupil should learn that his sentences must make *sense*; that is, they must not be vague or incomplete, and they must not try to tell so much that meaning becomes confused or lost. A positive approach to the development of good sentences is the most effective procedure to use.

First, as mentioned earlier, children should have many opportunities to express themselves orally, and this is a good time to encourage them to express ideas clearly. This does not mean that every response need be a "complete" sentence in the sense that most of us have had drilled *at* us in grammar study. However, questions may be asked or issues and problems advanced that require more than a "Yes" or "No" answer.

In the primary grades, provide activities in which each child tells one thing—and only one—about some personal experience, such as a trip, a project, or a picture. Or ask questions and have children answer in sentences that tell one thing. These one-sentence statements or answers can become experience stories. As stated in chapter 8, initially you will do the writing; as understanding develops two- and three-sentence compositions may be written. Continue to act as the scribe, letting the children work together to compose sentences. By pointing out the capital letter at the beginning and the end punctuation you will help children learn to use these when they write sentences individually. By being the scribe you can also provide guidance in formulating ideas, in addition to helping them develop continuity of thought. For instance, after a trip to the zoo, questions can be designed to lead to an organized composition about the experience:

TEACHER: Tell me one animal you saw at the zoo.

CHILDREN: We saw monkeys at the zoo.

TEACHER: Now tell me one thing the monkeys were doing.

CHILDREN: They were hanging by their tails.

TEACHER: How did they look?

CHILDREN: They looked funny hanging upside down.

Of course, children will have more than one answer to such questions. Perhaps several answers to each question might be recorded and the class could choose the ones to be used—or possibly combine them into several compositions.

This kind of activity, if used often, can guide children in developing concepts about capitalization and punctuation, sentence construction, and organization of ideas. Such guidance should continue, of course, when children begin to write their own sentences and paragraphs. Care should be exercised, however, to avoid stifling originality by calling for only one possible answer or statement.

Sentence sense also develops from exposing children to hearing good sentences. This generally means that you will need to read to children in a voice that

Can you make sentences from these?

the big dog
sat in a corner
we went inside
Little Jack Horner
ran down the street
because it was raining

Be sure to use capitals and periods where they are needed.

portrays "sentence feeling." Sometimes it is helpful to have children listen to recordings of their own speech, noting how the voice tends to drop at the end of a group of words—that is, at the end of a sentence. Another way to illustrate good sentence structure is to write two stories told by children in contrasting forms—one in which good sentence sense is evident and one in which the sentences are poorly or improperly constructed. Then have the stories compared and evaluated and the poorly written one reconstructed.

Activities such as those suggested in the preceding paragraph can be used at all grade levels by simply varying the length and difficulty of the material used, as can punctuation and capitalization dictation exercises (particularly helpful after a new item has been introduced), exercises in which children match subjects in one column with predicates in another, or those requiring pupils to organize sentence elements into their proper relationships to make good sentences. At every grade level, expose children to good sentences that are read well. This means reading well-written materials frequently in a voice that clearly portrays sentence feeling.

Teaching Sentence Building

Expression becomes effective through practice. The more children write—with the focus of the teaching on the content of the expression—the more improvement they should make in the quality of the expression. However, some direct teaching is essential if children are to learn to construct sentences that say what they want to say with the impact that they desire. The suggestions that follow are for activities that provide direct teaching. They are listed in ascending order of difficulty, but many can be varied to suit different grade levels.

1. Display a large picture to the class and ask, "Who has a sentence about this picture?" A picture of a cowboy might elicit responses such as the following:

   The cowboy has a big hat.
   He sure is tall.
   I saw a cowboy on TV last night.

   Write the sentences the children give you on the board. Do not write a child's response unless it is a sentence. Don't be adamant about this. Rather, suggest rephrasing.
2. Write declarative sentences on the board. Have them read orally by pupils. Then have these sentences changed to interrogative or negative forms. For example:

   Billy is at his desk.
   Is Billy at his desk?
   Billy is not at his desk.

3. Present scrambled sentences on the chalkboard and have the children rearrange the word order so that sentences are formed.
4. Put words from reading lessons on the bulletin board. Let children use these in making sentences.
5. On charts or on the chalkboard present sentences in which parts are missing, such as the following (perhaps a word bank of spelling words can be the source of words):

   _____ went outside to play.
   Mary _____.
   Do you want to go to the _____?

Will the car _____ !

Have the children suggest words that will complete the sentences. See how many words can fit into each blank and make *sense*.

Change "the picture" by changing the sentence.

The bear came down the road.
The bear ambled down the path.
A brown bear shuffled along under the trees.
A small brown bear loped down the path.

6. Give each child an envelope containing words printed on small pieces of durable paper. These may be words taken from their reading and other class activities. Each envelope should contain nouns, verbs, adjectives, adverbs, connectives, determiners, pronouns, etc., so that sentences can be made. Have the children see how many sentences they can compose, making sure that each sentence makes *sense*.

7. Prepare phrases or groups of words on strips of tagboard. Give these strips to groups of children to use in composing sentences. A variation of this is to have like phrases on strips of like color. For example, noun phrases might be on red paper—*two boys, the black bear, a dog*—and verb phrases might be on blue paper—*walked to the store, ran rapidly, hurried*. Verb phrases can also be divided into parts—verbs, adverbs, phrases, etc.—to give extra practice in placement of sentence parts.

8. Write a sentence on the chalkboard. Ask the children to add phrases to make the idea clearer. A variation is to add adverbs and adjectives rather than phrases.

9. Write sentences involving proper names on long strips of tagboard. Then write on other pieces of tagboard pronouns that could be substituted for the nouns in the sentences. Have the children place the pronouns over the corresponding nouns.

10. Write on the board several phrases that elicit mental pictures. For example: a pile of clothes on the floor, wet leaves on the window pane, the smell of bananas. Have pupils combine and/or add to the phrases to make sentences.

11. Have the children revise "time" sentences found in their reading. For example:

> *When Edith's mother came to the door of the kitchen, all of the children were exclaiming about the dessert.*

This might be revised in one of these ways:

> *The children were exclaiming about the dessert as Edith's mother came to the door of the kitchen.*
> *Edith's mother came to the door of the kitchen just in time to hear the children exclaiming about the dessert.*

12. Write a sentence such as "He will play" on the chalkboard. Have the children add details that provide more information by answering such questions as "Who?" "What?" "How?" "When?" and "What kind?"

> *He will play with Bill.*
> *He will play baseball with Bill.*
> *He will play baseball with Bill on the school diamond.*

Remedying Sentence Faults

Children's thinking sometimes runs ahead of both their speaking and writing, resulting in the omission of some sentence elements. Children also tend to run sentences together by overuse of *and* or, in writing, by simply running them together without a conjunction or punctuation and capitalization. Other common faults include using launchers (you know, well, okay) which do not function as transition words or contribute to meaning, and the making of unnecessary repetitive and/or irrelevant statements.

Activities such as those suggested for developing sentence sense will help to remedy these faults. The idea of "making sense" causes children to realize that these faults interfere with making sense, that they make communication less effective or even impossible. But children also need to know how to proofread (see section later in this chapter) and to edit their writing to eliminate errors in the final products. Practice exercises that provide for distinguishing between fragments and sentences, correcting "run-on" sentences, adding or deleting words to make sentence meaning clear, or making sentences out of nonsentence groups of words are also needed. Here are some examples of exercises that you might make:

1. Write on the chalkboard a story composed of a series of run-on sentences. Have several children take turns reading the story, stressing the idea that they are to attempt to read it paying attention only to the punctuation they see. Following such attempts have the story read again, this time emphasizing how natural reading shows where sentences begin and end. Then have the children rewrite the story, breaking it into sentences and omitting "and" when they think it preferable.
2. Write sentence fragments (perhaps from children's own work), such as:

   Because she did not go
   After the story ended
   While the class finished the game

   Have the children decide whether these are sentences and then how each might be made into a sentence.
3. Write sentences on the board, such as:

   Linda said that it was a good story.

   The children can then try various changes to make the sentence more interesting. For example:

   Linda declared that the story was very appealing.
   "What a good story!" said Linda.

4. Have children write sentences in different ways, experimenting with the placement of parts.

   During recess she will play with her friends in the gym.
   She will play with her friends in the gym during recess.
   She will play in the gym during recess with her friends.

5. Write sentences on the board for the children to rewrite and clarify.

   He saw four live ducks on the way to the market.
   There was much action in the movie that I didn't understand.

A Bulletin Board Idea

Things We Avoid in Our Writing

1. Overworked words.
2. Inactive verbs.
3. Vague references.
4. Misplaced modifiers.
5. Stale, wornout phrases.
6. Inaccurate expression.
7. Sweeping generalizations.

Using Sentence Combining Activities

One difference between the writing of young children and adults is that adults (and older students) write sentences containing more and longer clauses than do children. Research directed at teaching students to write these more syntactically complex sentences by having them do sentence combining exercises (largely done at the junior high or middle school level or above) has shown that the students doing the exercises write more of these sentences than do students not doing them.[1] This research has led to interest in using sentence combining in the elementary school and to the inclusion of such exercises in a number of elementary school language textbook series.

The exercises in commercial materials usually have models—i.e., two (or sometimes more) sentences written separately and then combined—showing in the combining either compounding, subordinating, or substituting. Each model is then followed by a number of groups of sentences to be combined as those in the model were. While some practice like this has value, it often has the disadvantage common to many drill materials—that of being unrelated to children's own work.

Guided Writing: Paragraphs

A paragraph consists of one or more sentences with one main idea. A well-written paragraph is interesting to read because of its varied sentences.

Sentences in a paragraph work together. As you read a well-written paragraph, you sense the rhythm, or flow, of sentences that appear in a logical order. Although sentence length varies, sentences are neither too long nor too short.

As you read this paragraph, think about how it can be revised.

They gathered near the window. It was open. A creature sat there.

They stared in amazement.

A. Use the following suggestions to revise the paragraph above. Make all changes in the space left between lines.

1. Can you combine the first two sentences? Do you want to make the subject more specific?

2. The third sentence is very short. Do you want to describe the creature in greater detail? Can you add adverbs or phrases that tell *when, where,* or *how*?

3. Do you want to add any more information to the last sentence? Or do you want to keep it short? Would you like to insert a sentence in front of this one?

4. Reread your paragraph. Does it flow? Check your verbs. Do they tell exactly what is happening? Do they all refer to the same time?

B. Copy the final version of your paragraph here. Indent the first line.

Some commercial materials contain useful practice activities. (USING OUR LANGUAGE, 1977 edition; copyright © by BOWMAR/NOBLE PUBLISHERS, INC., Los Angeles, California 90039)

It usually is better to take sentences children have written or to write ones related to things they are studying and then to let them experiment with combining to achieve greater clarity, emphasis, focus on the image the writer desires the reader to have, ease of reading, or variation in style.

You might simply write two sentences on the board and ask the children *if* they can be combined into one sentence. For example:

> The fifth grade classes are having a Christmas party.
> The party will be in our room.

The children will easily find several ways to combine these sentences, so you may readily move into asking them to combine several sentences into one. Emphasize that the ideas from the sentences can be combined in different ways. For example, one might take the following sentences:

> The children got off the bus.
> John got off the bus first.
> As soon as the bus emptied the driver closed the door.
> These might be combined as follows:

> John was first as the children got off the bus, just ahead of the closing door.
> John got off the bus first, and after the other children followed him, the driver closed the door.

You may want to emphasize combining in particular ways to show how style may be changed. For example,

1. by using a connector:

> *The girl played hard.*
> *The girl won the game.*
> *The girl played hard, and she won the game.*

2. by not using a connector:

> *The girl won the game by playing hard.*
> *By playing hard, the girl won the game.*

Still another activity is to write words such as *when, after, until, there, where, if, because, then,* and *since* on the chalkboard. Then write pairs of sentences such as these:

> Everyone sat down to dinner.
> The children came in from playing.

> We will go to the airport early.
> My grandmother is coming from Syracuse.

Have pupils combine the sentences in each pair using one of the words from the board. For example:

> After the children came in from playing, everyone sat down to dinner.

There are many variations in these sentence combining activities that may be used for showing children ways that sentences may be constructed. Children usually are intrigued by the possibilities in manipulating language, and these activities have appeal if they are not used to the extent that they become boring or interfere with writing for the many purposes suggested in chapter 8.

Teaching Organizational Skill

Children need to learn that the best way to present a thought effectively is to organize the expression so that it sticks to the point and presents the information in an interesting and suitable sequence. Organization is reflected in the construction of sentences, paragraphs, and the discourse as a whole. No expression—be it one sentence or more— is effective unless it is well organized and thoughtfully composed.

When a child begins to recognize relationships, he or she is beginning to organize. Activities such as the following call for organizing skills, and are first steps in learning to organize thoughts in written form.

- Putting pictures related to a story into proper sequence.
- Putting a puzzle together.
- Classifying objects by size, color, shape, etc.
- Telling in sequence the things seen on a trip.
- Deciding what classroom tasks need doing.
- Telling how to play a game.
- Giving words that are associated with special days or events.

As suggested in earlier chapters, guidance in putting sentences into an orderly sequence may begin with children's first oral expression. This guidance is particularly important the moment that children begin to dictate stories of two or more sentences. With this kind of beginning they should be better prepared to organize when independent writing begins. Thorough preparation before children write should also help them to learn organization. However, children do tend to ramble at times, and additional practice with organizing skills may be helpful. The activities in the following list suggest ways to further organizational abilities:

1. Write a short paragraph on the chalkboard or duplicate it. Have the children tell the main idea of the paragraph in one sentence. The paragraph might be taken from a social studies or science book.
2. Have children look at and discuss the content of a picture and then state in one sentence the main idea of the picture. A variation of this activity is to choose a title (without regard to whether it is a sentence).
3. Write several sentences on the chalkboard, and have the children select the ones that could be put together into a paragraph.
4. Provide the children with paragraphs that contain one or two sentences unrelated to the idea of the paragraph. Have the children cross out the unrelated sentences.
5. Provide the children with a paragraph in which the sentences have been "scrambled," and have them rearrange the sentences in the most effective order.
6. Give children paragraphs in which the beginning or ending sentences are missing. Have them compose appropriate sentences to make the paragraphs complete.
7. Provide opportunities for pupils to discuss and list ideas and information before they begin writing. This should be done regularly at all grade levels; it is one of the most valuable ways in which you can help children learn to organize their thinking.

8. Encourage the children to watch for ways in which professional writers move skill-fully from topic to topic and use paragraphs in their writing.

The suggestions in chapter 8 for story, report, and other forms of writing focus to a large extent on the importance of organization in all communication, and these suggestions should not be overlooked as you give teaching attention to organization skill.

We discuss outlining in chapter 16 since it is a study skill as well as a skill useful to organizing expression. Outlines helpful to organizing writing need not be formal; in fact, it is probably best if they are not, for attention should be on the ideas to be presented, not upon the form of the outline. The important thing is for children to think before writing—to select ideas and determine what facts or details should be included to develop them. Used in this way, an outline can also help the writer plan the method of development best suited to his or her material—that is, whether to support ideas through details, description, or illustration; through comparison or contrast; or through argument and logical reasoning. Thus prepared, the child is more likely to write a composition that is clear, concise, and effective.

Teaching Proofreading, Editing, and Rewriting

Teaching children to proofread what they have written should begin with the writing in which the teacher is the scribe. Children should be told—and time given—to read over what they have dictated and the teacher has written. But at this stage, as well as later, saying, "Let's proofread" is not enough. Children need to learn to proofread by degrees; that is, first they need to proofread for only one or two elements—possibly, checking to see if each statement is a sentence, as shown both by its "sense" and its capitalization and punctuation. When they learn to check on one or two things, others can be added. In the various stages of developing skill in proofreading, the children should decide as much as possible for themselves what to look for. As they progress through the grades they should be encouraged to develop their own standards for guiding their proofreading.

Since the purpose of proofreading is to find errors or faults in writing, it follows that the errors—misspellings, absence of punctuation, etc.—should be corrected and the faults—in sentence structure, organization, etc.—remedied. In some instances this means a child will need to copy what he or she has written with the changes made. Other times, especially if more than looking for mechanical errors is included in proofreading, rewriting is needed.

Think about it!

Writing
is
rewriting
is
writing.

Children often dislike copying what they wrote and may well resist rewriting. This, of course, will less often be true if the writing is purposeful to them—not just something that you assigned that has little interest for them or that they know little about. Basic in convincing children that rewriting is important is development of the attitude that all writing is done for someone to read. Therefore, they need to realize that a reader may not get the idea or the information they intended to convey if the paper is messy and full of crossed-out or misspelled words or lacks clarity in many of its sentences and is poorly organized. As readers themselves they need to learn that a reader is entitled to the courtesy of a thoughtfully composed and neat and legible paper.

One way to show children the importance of rewriting is to show them one of your first drafts of a paper, a letter, or any other piece of writing that you considered important enough to edit and rewrite. Another is to find a biography of a famous author that shows reproductions of first versions of well-known works and compare these with the finished versions. Accompany this evidence that even experienced writers need to edit with exercises in actual rewriting. For example, a particularly wordy paragraph can be written on the board or placed on a transparency for use with the overhead projector, and the children can work together de-

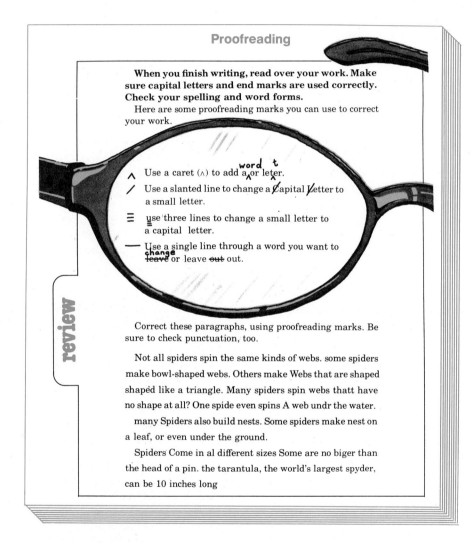

Children may be motivated to rewrite by learning basic proofreading and editing skills.
USING OUR LANGUAGE, 1977 edition; copyright © by BOWMAR/NOBLE PUBLISHERS, INC., Los Angeles, California 90039)

leting, condensing, and revising where necessary. The same thing can be done with some of the children's own first drafts—or even with presumably finished products when the need is shown. To be truly helpful, this type of editing must be done in a spirit of discovery. Questions must encourage constructive, rather than adverse, criticism: How many other ways can you think of to say this? Which one gives the best picture? Can you think of other details (reasons, etc.) that could be added? Is there any other way the same idea could be developed? Working cooperatively in this way will help pupils to discover that sometimes it is even a good idea to start over again entirely or try a different method of development.

ADDITIONAL TEACHING SUGGESTIONS

In teaching writing it is especially important to move among the children and work with them as they write. Children need encouragement, some expression of interest; they may want to ask questions or get some assurance that they have started well, or they may want a sounding board for ideas.

A child can be helped to make a connection that was missed, to find the right word or phrase, or simply to spell a word he wants to use. This kind of active participation on the teacher's part must be an essential element of any writing program if the children's efforts are to be both satisfying to them and of the quality they are capable of producing.

Furthering Children's Motivation

As we have suggested, unless there is considerable preparation through group composition activities, oral discussion, and "intake" experiences, children's

Having a typewriter to use often motivates a "non-writer."

growth in written expression will be less than desirable. Sometimes, too, children need an extra push; their experiences and desire to write about something does not quite trigger the writing process. This is particularly true for writing that does not have the specific communication purpose of a letter, report, or announcement. For some children to write stories, essays, or poetry this push or immediate

Around Again

Choose two of the subjects below to write poems or paragraphs about. Use any point of view you choose. The questions may give you some ideas, but you don't have to answer them unless you want to.

1. Mud

Do you like to feel mud between your toes? How would you feel if you fell into a mud puddle when you were wearing your best clothes? How would your parents feel if someone tracked mud onto the rug?

2. Bicycles

How would you feel if you made your living fixing bikes? How would you feel if you were a bicycle racer? How would you feel if you were a small child with a first bike?

3. Food

What is your favorite food? Has it always been your favorite? Can your point of view change?

4. Rain

Do you like rain? Suppose you're planning a picnic. Suppose you have a good book to read. Suppose you're a farmer. Suppose you're a weather forecaster.

232

Learning to write from a specific point of view needs instructional attention. (USING OUR LANGUAGE, 1977 edition; copyright © by BOWMAR/NOBLE PUBLISHERS, INC., Los Angeles, California 90039)

form of motivation may be especially needed. Some may need only a glimmer of an idea—a topic, a picture, or an object—to start their thinking and writing; others may require more to set the stage.

Specific Topics. If a teacher simply writes a topic or topics on the board and asks children to begin writing—even if he or she provides time for them to think before actual writing begins—the writing expected may not result. In fact, some children may write little or nothing.

There are several ways to avoid this. First, it is probably better to provide a choice of topics; a single topic is not likely to suit the interests and abilities of the entire group. If the general topic is one that has grown from a particular study unit, suggest different ways of treating the topic or different aspects that might be dealt with. Second, it is wise to take a few minutes to discuss the topics, suggesting—or having children suggest—ways in which they might be treated; hopefully, this will spur pupils to think of others themselves. Another possibility is to select a particular topic and list on the board, again with the children's help, some words that might be suitable to use in connection with this topic. The list need not include every word that can be dredged up—only enough to get the children's thinking started. It should, however, include nouns, verbs, and adverbs, as well as adjectives; children should discover early that adjectives are not the only words that describe. Finally, and probably most importantly, topics should be chosen with an eye toward children's interests and experience—either actual or vicarious. No one can be expected to write well about something that is uninteresting and unfamiliar.

Pictures. Using pictures as bases for ideas is another technique for getting children to write. Collect pictures of various sizes and on various subjects, mount them on heavy paper if necessary, and file them for ready reference. The filing is usually by topic (e.g., dogs, winter, children, farm animals, colors, etc.). Mounting pictures adds to the amount of filing space needed, but it also keeps them from becoming dog-eared; probably temporary mountings are best, since they may need to be changed for different purposes. (To make a temporary mount, simply fold several pieces of Scotch tape, sticky side out; attach one side to the mount and the other to the back of the picture.)

Pictures can be used in several ways: a large picture can be displayed to the entire class, smaller pictures can be distributed to individual pupils, or individual pupils or small groups can choose from a display in the chalk tray, pictures in story books, or those in readers or other textbooks. Showing a large picture to the entire class is usually good for beginning writing activities because the ensuing discussion often stimulates many ideas.

The following suggest the kinds of "thinking about" and "talking about" questions that are helpful:

1. What is happening in the picture? (Encourage various possibilities.)
2. What kind of people are these? Do they belong to the same family, are they friends, or what? Do you think you would like them?
3. What might have happened just before the time of the picture? What might happen next?
4. Think of words and phrases that describe the action in the picture. What words might describe the people or the way they feel?

Camping Topics

My Favorite Campground
Stories Heard Around a
  Campfire
Life in a Tent
Camping in the Rain
People We Met When
  Camping
Bears at the Garbage Cans

A Few Writing Topics

I Lost One Shoe
If I Could Work for the
  Circus
Morning Noises
Adventures of a School
  Desk
What I Would Do If I Could
  Fly
The Easter Egg That
  Hatched
The Lost Seagull
One Day I Went for a Walk
If I Were a Raindrop
My Life Ten Years from
  Now
The Nicest Man on the
  Block
Why I Like Red
A Day in the Life of a
  Dinosaur
The Year Santa Claus Was
  Lazy
The Day the Clocks
  Stopped

5. What are some words that describe the scenery in the picture?
6. If you were going to tell a story about this picture, how and where would you begin?

It is important that such questions be exploratory, not directive; creative writing does not result in every child turning out the same story. On the other hand, children should discuss whether or not suggestions fit the picture: a wrinkled, ragged crone might find a long-lost child, but she is not likely to marry Prince Charming or find a lucrative job unless she is in disguise or a fairy godmother has been at work!

A Story Framework.   If a topic or a picture does not give the child enough of a setting to start her or him thinking and writing, an elaboration or extension of the topic may be helpful. This extension usually provides a framework around which a story can be created. Sometimes, too, the framework stimulates thinking that leads to a story that is not directly attributable to the framework. A file of such "frames" can be useful; listed below are some that have proved successful.

1. You are a young boy who plays the drum for an army company that is part of Washington's Revolutionary Army. Tell what happens one day while you are waiting in camp for the general to arrive.
2. You are traveling on a wagon train from St. Louis to California. Many of the wagons are lost crossing the Red River. What happens the next morning?
3. Pretend you are an inanimate object such as a parking meter, a "No Parking" sign, or an object on display in the drugstore window. Describe your feelings about one of the people you "see" daily.
4. You are a famous explorer who has just returned from a trip. Tell about one of your discoveries and why it is important.
5. You wake up suddenly in the middle of the night. Everything is quiet and it is pitch dark. Suddenly you hear a clanking sound that reminds you of a TV program. Tell what happens next.
6. The chair is rocking, but no one is in it. As you watch, the rocking increases in speed and a faint glow of light travels across the room. What happens next?
7. You are lying on the bank of a lake watching your fishing line. Suddenly you hear a rustle in the bushes behind you, followed by some loud sniffing. Tell how you feel and what happens when you discover what caused the noise.
8. Describe some common happening on earth as if you were an invisible observer from another planet visiting the earth for the first time.
9. Pretend you are a statue in the park. Tell about some of the things you have seen and the changes that have occurred over the years.
10. Halloween is a time for fun. Think of some of the things you have done on Halloween, some of the ways you have dressed, some of the things you have seen and heard. Think, too, of smells and tastes and how they were related to what you did. Can you make up a story about an ideal Halloween?

A Story Beginning.   Sometimes a child cannot think of a beginning for a story but can finish one or even add more than simply the ending if the beginning is appealing. Furthermore, most children enjoy writing a story from a given beginning. One way to start stories is for the class as a group to make up an opening; then each child finishes the story individually. Magazines for teachers and for children often have story beginnings that can be used as they are or with modifications for local circumstances. Many kinds of beginnings may be used. Some actually indicate how the story should end, and only minor variations are possible. Others simply start the "wheels" turning, so that the various stories the children write reflect their creativity and individuality.

It is a good idea to have some story beginnings on hand, just as you have files of topics, pictures, and story structure statements. Here are some that teachers have used:

1. There was a strange silence along the main street of the town, even though it was only 9 P.M.
2. On the table was a stack of books; the top one was open.
3. Bulldozers began climbing the hill as the sun appeared.
4. The rain beat against the window pane as the sky darkened and lightning flashed.
5. There was a fluttering of wings, and the quail rose from the bushes.
6. He looked over the edge of the building and gasped at what he saw many floors below.
7. The door banged. Then it opened quickly and a tall, grizzled cowboy came through.
8. All the way home I kept looking at my clothes and thinking about what I might say to my father.
9. The old house looked interesting. The rocking chair on the porch had a red cushion in it and the screen door was hanging by one hinge.
10. As I passed the house I caught a whiff of . . .
11. Bill stood on the dock, his legs stiff and refusing to move. Then he felt dizzy.
12. She really was mean. She did mean things. Why, one time I remember . . .

Story beginnings that go beyond a sentence or two are also helpful. Again, it is a matter of what is needed to start children thinking of things they can write. The following are examples of types that you might try.

1. John and his younger brother were playing on the beach when they found the strange footprints. They seemed to come from the water and to go along the shore toward the trees in the distance. John started to follow his brother, who was racing after the footprints.
2. The last weak rays of the sun streaked coldly across the graying sky. Linda shivered and touched her heels gently to the horse's flanks, remembering that the field would soon be swallowed by the fog and clammy darkness. Then she heard the scream—a piercing, wailing cry.
3. George manages the family, but not always very well. He forgets that he is a dog and that there are some things a dog can't do. I remember when he tried to . . .
4. I could see the fire in the distance. The blaze danced above the tree tops and the smoke billowed away in a darkening cloud. Just then three deer burst through the undergrowth and dashed past me. What should I do? Was there a chance?
5. It's fun to watch ants. They are so busy and seem to know what they are doing. Sometimes I have fun pretending I am an ant.
6. The roar of the waterfall could be heard above the patter of the rain on the trees. I listened carefully for another sound. No, I could not hear it. I wondered why. I surely was close enough. Maybe I was on the wrong side of the river.
7. The strange sound got louder and louder until it was almost deafening. We had stopped walking when it started, and now we stared at one another. Fright began to show on John's face, and Bill's eyes were blinking. Then the sound stopped and an eerie silence ensued. We wondered what might happen next, but we still didn't talk.
8. I pounded and pounded, but the door wouldn't open. Looking around for something to use as a hammer, I spotted a large rock lying in the driveway. I ran to get it and

was hit by . . .

9. The light got brighter and brighter as the ship settled toward the earth. Then there was a slight flutter and it came to rest. I held my breath, wondering what would happen next. Suddenly a hole opened up in the bottom of the ship and a ladder came swiftly down. The figure that followed was round, spindle-legged, and silver colored—just as an "outer space" creature was supposed to look. What should I do? Should I speak? Should I run? I decided . . .

10. It was a very good movie, especially the music. It reminded me of the time we visited Yellowstone National Park and saw the geysers, although we didn't have the trouble with bears that the boy in the movie had. But wait, let me tell you about it.

Words and Phrases.   Seeing and discussing words and phrases that remind them of experiences or stir their imaginations may stimulate children to write. Often these words and/or phrases can be collected by the class and perhaps because of this they will work particularly well. Sometimes, however, pupils may need help in getting thinking started. Phrases such as these may help them to think of others:

pelting rain on the window
a prancing horse
silver-gray smoke rising
a seagull floating noiselessly above
sunlight dancing upon the blue water
the swaying, bending trees
a dewy spider web in the bush
snow blowing in waves across the field

Nothing creative is likely to result from such phrases, however, unless children have come to enjoy words and the way they are used. As you read aloud to children, comment on an unusual word or show your appreciation of an apt phrase. Talk about words; help children to enjoy the way they sound and the way they conjure up pictures. Encourage them to discover new words and learn new meanings for words they already know. Only a true appreciation of language will bring about expression that shows sparkle and imagination.

Giving Extra Help

Most children need help in making their writing ideas specific. Characters are vaguely described, or maybe simply named; details that indicate a mood or setting are skimpy; motives for actions are not given; and sequences may seem unrelated. Questioning the writer will often help. Would I recognize this character by your description of the way he looks? Or acts? Or both? What led up to Carole being lost in the woods? What things had happened? Will your reader know? Why would I think your house was scary? What is scary about it? What caused Bob to look for Carole?

Helping children to be more specific may be done as you move among them, but be careful not to interfere with their thinking. Determining how much and what kinds of help each child may need comes from experience and your relationship with the children. Often children can be helped most effectively during individual conferences. A personal conference gives the child encouragement and

Words about Weather

sunny	blustery
bright	hot
foggy	stifling
sultry	warm
snowy	humid
stormy	changeable
cloudy	windy
dry	smoggy
wet	drizzling
cold	tepid
clear	misty

incentive and you will gain a greater understanding of the child's thoughts and needs. In fact, individual conferences ought to be a part of all elementary school writing programs. Even the children who write well and readily will benefit from them. A conference does not have to be very long or very formally planned for. A few minutes with a child somewhat away from the group permits the personal exchange and a focus specifically on what he or she has written.

Another helpful arrangement is to have some of the children work in pairs or trios, with ideas coming from each child and the major task of getting them on paper delegated to the most able. Their exchanges will often result in better planning for and development of the writing product and will have carry-over into writing that they do individually.

EVALUATING WRITTEN EXPRESSION

Evaluation is one of the major elements in the total teaching–learning activity. From evaluation both you and your pupils should discover what has been learned and what has not. From evaluation you should plan your future teaching. But because evaluation is often difficult and because there is a reluctance to criticize a child's creative efforts, some teachers do little evaluation of children's writing or of their own teaching of writing.

However, evaluation need not be as difficult as it is often thought to be if its focus is realistic and instruction-centered rather than directed at giving grades, making red marks, and finding fault.

Evaluating Your Teaching

The first concern in evaluation should be the program itself—its objectives and the teaching procedures and materials used. Such questions as these should be considered:

1. What is the atmosphere in the classroom? Is it one in which each child feels free to express ideas and make contributions to projects and discussions? Is there anything that might tend to repress individual expression?
2. Does the physical appearance of the classroom reflect creativity (on the part of both teacher and children), or is it dull and unattractive?
3. Is there sufficient input of many kinds throughout the year and in all areas of the curriculum?
4. Do children have many opportunities to read and hear well-written stories, poems, etc.? Is there a real interest in words and the way they are put together?
5. Do children have enough skill in the mechanics of writing to be able to express their ideas? Is the emphasis on mechanics so great that they are afraid to try new ways of expressing themselves?
6. Are motivation and preparation for writing adequate, or are children expected to write without really having a purpose or knowing what is expected of them?
7. Is writing a genuine part of the total curriculum? Is advantage taken of the many opportunities that occur for children to do purposeful writing?
8. Do the children write in many forms and for a variety of purposes and audiences? Do they have adequate knowledge of the many forms of and purposes for writing?

9. Does each child receive constructive responses—from you and others—at various stages in the writing process? Does each child feel free to ask questions, try out ideas, and seek help?

These are questions to be asked and answered by you the teacher. In part, though, your answers must come from a consideration of the children's writing. Is the writing generally vapid, superficial, and trite? Does it neither interest nor communicate? Surely children are not like this. They are eager and sad, exhilarated and frustrated, interested and bored, possessing and giving. If their writing fails to express these feelings, if it is unimaginative and nonindividualistic, then something has happened. Something has come between the children and the papers they turn in.

Possible causes for children's failure to achieve the results desired (both by them and by the teacher) include the following:

- Lack of direction and guidance.
- Fear of teacher disapproval.
- Stifled oral expression.
- A meager vocabulary.
- Ignorance of the forms of writing.
- A deficiency of input.
- Failure to recognize the importance of the audience.
- No working knowledge of composition skills.
- Putting paper before the children too soon.
- Overemphasis on teaching mechanical skills.

Evaluating Specific Products

Evaluation of any piece of writing is largely an appraisal of its quality in terms of its purpose. From the beginning writing efforts of children, the practice of their evaluating their own work should be fostered. This may be done by providing them with models, when possible and appropriate (letter writing form, for example), for guidance and comparison. Proofreading and editing checklists or lists of standards to be observed will also help. A checklist such as the one shown may be useful to you, but it also may be modified and duplicated for children's use. That is, the spaces for the children's names could be used for a child to write in information identifying specific pieces of writing. Thus, the child could determine which areas he or she needs to work on most, where improvement is occurring, and so on, particularly if points (say from 1 to 5) are assigned to each item rather than a "yes" or "no."

The checklist can be expanded, but only if there is time available and knowledge present for using an expanded version. For example, organization can include introductions, body, conclusion, etc.; appearance can be divided into title, margins, and handwriting. Items included, of course, should vary according to grade level and standards previously established.

There are scales for evaluating written products (few available commercially) that are somewhat similar to checklists. That is, points are given for various aspects of a piece of writing—content, mechanics, style. However, a scale will have

Checklist for Written Reports	Arthur	Jean	Mary	Henry	Bill
Information					
Organization					
Vocabulary					
Sentence structure					
Appearance					
Usage					
Punctuation					
Capitalization					
Spelling					

either short examples of different levels of quality for the characteristics being assessed or will have statements upon which to base judgments, as in this example of a portion of a scale.[2]

Sequence

The order of events is clear, giving the reader a precise view of the sequence of incidents.

High   The order of events is always clear to you even if at times the author might talk about the past or the future.

Middle   A few times it is not clear which event happened first.

Low   You really cannot figure out which event comes first or goes after any other event.

Any teacher can make a scale to aid in judging a piece of writing. With guidance, children can do this too. A scale has particular value in guiding consistency in judgments about pieces of writing from the same individual or for making judgments about examples of writing of a class.

Children like their writing products to be displayed. This is satisfying to them, but it also leads to self-evaluation of their work.

Informal Records

Judgments about the writing ability of a child should not be based on evaluating one or even several pieces of writing. In order to determine a child's strong points and weaknesses various techniques should be used. One is using a checklist or scale at intervals during the year. Others include keeping folders of children's writing; anecdotal records for each child—derived primarily from individual conferences; observational records of prewriting, writing, and postwriting behaviors; and tests of knowledge and application of punctuation and capitalization skills, paragraphing, and showing variety in sentence structures.

Group Evaluation

Another valuable technique is group evaluation. This may be done in several ways. One is to have the child read his or her paper to the class and let the class evaluate it for content and organization. Another is to have children work in small groups, reading papers and making suggestions for improvement. (This is particularly helpful following the first draft of a paper; children can then use the comments in revising and formulating final drafts.) A third method is to have several children write at the board (this calls for carefully lined chalkboards) so that all the children can see several "compositions." A fourth method is to use the opaque or overhead projector to show papers and have the children make corrections and suggestions. This can be a valuable teaching technique if papers are pre-read so that those selected illustrate weaknesses common to many children in the class or especially good vocabulary, organization, or method of development.

Many teachers prefer to tell children before writing begins if there is to be class or group evaluation, to read papers themselves instead of having children read them, or—when the projector is to be used—to have each child put his or her name on the back of the paper rather than on the front, so that no child will be embarrassed. Much embarrassment can be avoided, however, if evaluation is approached in a constructive manner and if belittling others is discouraged at all times. It is probably wise, however, either to forewarn children when writing is to be evaluated by anyone other than the teacher or to give each child the right to specify that he or she does not wish to have the paper read by others—freedom of expression must not be inhibited by fear of having intimate revelations exposed.

Marking

The red pencil is too often mistakenly considered an evaluative tool. The fact is, though, that finding errors is not evaluation, and the sight of such red marks does not bring about pupil learning, since the marks usually do not supply very specific information about those things that need further learning effort. However, marking a paper—with or without red pencil—can be a means for calling attention to commendable aspects of the writing, such as a good choice of words, an apt expression, a neat margin, or good organization of thought. Every written product from every child has something about it that can be commended. Perhaps it may only be a better formed letter, fewer erasures, or greater promptness in turning it in, but, whatever it is (or, more hopefully, they are), this should be the focus of the marking. Use a positive rather than a negative approach to marking.

Standardized Tests

There are standardized tests that purport to measure ability in written expression or some aspect of it. However, these measures do not actually do what is often claimed for them. For example, a test may determine a pupil's knowledge of grammatical terminology or rules, but this kind of knowledge has nothing to do with writing ability. Identifying good and poor sentences (or fragments), choosing acceptable words and expressions (standard usage), arranging sentences in order, identifying misspelled words, and indicating where punctuation items should be placed are other activities that appear on standardized tests (although not all of these are in all tests that purport to measure writing ability). These items, of course, are all related to writing, but they simply sample the test-taker's ability to distinguish between standard and nonstandard forms and to proofread for some types of errors rather than performance in the individual's own expression.

A FINAL WORD

Teaching children to express themselves effectively by writing is one of the most complex tasks of the elementary school teacher. Ideas, organization, knowledge of forms, sentence structures, vocabulary, usage, and spelling—all these and more are inextricably bound up with written expression. When we speak, gestures, facial expressions, personal appearance, and intonation can supplement the actual words; further explanation or argument can even be added if the thought is not understood or accepted. On the other hand, written expression must often stand alone. This does not mean that the teaching of oral expression should be minimized in language arts programs, but a letter of application, a friendly note, the minutes of a meeting are often matters on which one is judged. It is important, then, that children know how to write in these and other special forms and have the skills to do so effectively. The ability to write effectively is also an aid in thinking and a means for self expression, both important in all of our lives.

ENDNOTES

1. Frank O'Hare, *Sentence Combining: Improving Student Writing Without Formal Grammar Instruction*. Research Report No. 15. Urbana, IL: National Council of Teachers of English, 1973.

2. Charles R. Cooper and Lee Odell, *Evaluating Writing: Describing, Measuring, Judging*. Urbana IL: National Council of Teachers of English, 1977, p. 22.

REFERENCES

Books

Burrows, Alvina, et al. *They All Want to Write*, 3rd ed. New York: Holt, Rinehart and Winston, 1964.

Hennings, Dorothy Grant, and Grant, Barbara M. *Content and Craft: Written Expression in the Elementary School*. Englewood Cliffs, NJ: Prentice-Hall, 1973.

Lundsteen, Sara W., ed. *Help for the Teacher of Written Composition*. Urbana, IL: National Council of Teachers of English, 1976.

Marksberry, Mary Lee. *Foundations of Creativity*. New York: Harper and Row, 1963.

Murray, Donald M. *A Writer Teaches Writing: A Practical Method of Teaching Composition*. Boston: Houghton Mifflin Co., 1968.

Films

Building Better Paragraphs. Chicago: Coronet Films (11 minutes; color or b/w; intermediate).

Filmstrips

Language and Writing. Jamaica, NY: Eyegate House (color with record).

Communication Power. New York: Filmstrip House (series; with tapes; intermediate).

Other Materials

Composition: Guided-Free Program. New York: Teachers College, Columbia University (sentence rewriting activities in booklets at 12 levels).

Working with Sentences. Newton, MA: Curriculum Associates (sentence cards).

Writing Skills Laboratory. Chicago: Science Research Associates (two series or levels with exercises in writing narration, description, and exposition).

Write On. Inglewood, CA: Educational Insights (individual writing ideas on cards; illustrated).

Write to Communicate: The Language Arts in Process. Pleasantville, NY (records, cards, portfolio books, posters, guides; intermediate).

Fokes Sentence Builder. Boston: Teaching Resources (sentence construction cards).

ACTIVITIES FOR PRESERVICE TEACHERS

1. Make a checklist to use in assessing children's writing. Include such factors as vividness of language (intensity, freshness, vigor), picturesqueness of speech, involvement of feelings, element of surprise, etc. Decide on the range of points you will assign each item. Check out your list and the points awarded for each item with someone who is now teaching.

2. Prepare several paragraphs to use in teaching organization, incorporating the suggestions in this chapter or devising ideas of your own.

3. Select a particular unit from some area other than the language arts that the class you are observing or working with will study during the year. Plan creative writing activities that might be used in connection with this unit, allowing for the capabilities and individual differences of the children who actually make up the class.

4. Select a writing topic and show exactly how you would introduce it and prepare the children for writing.

5. Begin a file of pictures that would be useful in motivating creative writing. Be sure to include some that show actions, some of single individuals, some that convey mood, etc.

6. For each of the pictures you have collected (for no. 5), jot down a list of questions that would be appropriate for starting discussion before writing begins. Or make a list of possible writing topics based on the pictures.

7. Gain permission from your supervising teacher to work with the class during a creative writing project. Make a written record of the number of children worked with, the kinds of questions they asked, and your responses to these questions. Evaluate the results as honestly as possible in terms of the following questions:

   a. Did you give assistance to many children or only to a few? Were these the less able or the more able?

   b. Which individual contacts were you happy with? Which children do you wish you had responded to differently?

ACTIVITIES FOR INSERVICE TEACHERS

1. If you are not in the practice of conferring with children about their writing, try it for a few weeks. Keep a record of changes in the children's writing that could be attributed to the conferences.

2. With the children in your class prepare a bulletin board on editing. The editing signs (sp = spelling error, lc = small or lowercase letter, etc.) will interest children.

3. Keeping in mind the abilities of your class as shown in the written work they have done, prepare a list of their needs in order of importance for a bulletin board. Hold a class discussion on proofreading; encourage the children to establish realistic criteria. Contract with each child for improvement of a weakness. Carry on this project for a month, then evaluate the results.

4. Plan a series of three-week units using various approaches to creative writing (topics, unfinished sentences, pictures, etc.). Concentrate on one approach two or three days a week for three weeks. At the end of the three weeks have the children compare their first and last stories. Discuss improvement. Continue for another three weeks with another approach. Evaluate again and so on. (*Caution:* Don't overdo this—creative writing should be fun.)

5. Make a list of factors that cause children not to

write as well as we hoped. You may want to think about your classroom as well as about the things suggested in this chapter in making your list.

6. Investigate language arts methods books, cur-riculum guides, and teacher's editions of children's textbooks for specific suggestions about teaching children to write. Evaluate these suggestions in terms of your experiences in teaching.

Independent Activities for Children

1. Prepare cards with sentences that can be rewritten without changing the meaning. Children can use these to gain practice in varying structure. For example:

   When the book fell from the table, the boy jumped.
   The boy jumped when the book fell from the table.

2. Give the child sentences to finish using simile or personification.

   I am as strong as _____
   The car sounded _____
   The tree in the front yard is as tall as _____

3. Keep an idea box where any child can place an idea for a story and any other child can use it. This could be kept in the "writers' corner," a special spot in the room furnished with a table, several chairs, paper, pencils and pens, a dictionary, and a thesaurus. Children could be allowed to go to this corner and write, just as they go to the library corner when they want to read. It may be necessary for you to begin or add to the idea box; if so, try to find ideas that may stimulate a new way of thinking. For example:

   Tell about your walk home when you were blindfolded.
   Describe the biggest dog in your neighborhood.
   Suppose you were a bear in the zoo and didn't like marshmallows.

4. A child or several children working together might do any of the following:

   Make lists of colorful phrases.
   List adjectives describing objects in the classroom.
   Find good beginning sentences for stories.
   Collect objects that provide sensory feelings.

5. Have children collect particularly good similes, metaphors, and images. They might then work in groups to compile booklets of those they like best.

6. Prepare collections of materials to spark children's writing. The collections (usually a box is needed for each) might include the following:

   Comic cartoons from newspapers
   Photographs of interesting places and events
   Cloth and other objects of different textures
   Newspaper stories
   Pictures from magazines

7. Place pictures on a bulletin board and have a child write sentences and short paragraphs describing them.

8. Cut up workbooks containing pictures that tell a story in sequence. Fasten each group together with a paperclip or rubber band, and keep them in a shoe box covered with gift wrap or contact paper. A child selects a group, places the pictures in sequence, and then writes a sentence about each, thus making a paragraph.

9. Prepare groups of sentences for a child to arrange into paragraphs. Some of the groups should include sentences that would be extraneous if included in the paragraph.

10. Prepare on ditto sheets paragraphs containing errors in spelling, capitalization, and punctuation. The child is to proofread these, making corrections as he or she finds the need. Other paragraphs may be poorly organized; instructions should then call for putting the ideas into logical order.

11. Prepare cards or dittoes containing simple sentences with verbs or verb phrases underlined. Individual children may select from these and find more colorful words to substitute for the underlined portion. For example:

Sentences	Substitutes
He *bit into* the apple.	crunched
	munched
	devoured

10

Form and Convention in Writing

Everyone who is concerned with helping children to express themselves, either orally or in writing, will agree that the vital element in any expression is the ideas that are expressed. Unfortunately, too many teachers appear to believe that the converse is also true—that matters of form and appearance are not important. Such teachers are doing their pupils a distinct disservice, particularly those pupils who have creative ideas and valid opinions but lack the skills to express them effectively.

Certainly an unpolished diamond is more valuable than a piece of glass, but most of us would pass it by without recognizing its worth. In the same way, an idea that is buried in badly worded sentences amidst errors in punctuation and spelling may also go unnoticed. Therefore, the conventions of writing—the mechanics, the matters of form and appearance, the agreed-on customs of putting language symbols on paper—must be taught. They must be seen in proper perspective, however; the conventions are aids to effective communication, not ends in themselves. With this emphasis, children will recognize that communication may well be lost if attention is not given to spelling, punctuation, capitalization, penmanship, paragraphing, etc., as well as careful proofreading of anything that is written for others to read. Good habits, established early, will stand pupils in good stead for the rest of their lives.

FORM AND APPEARANCE

A neat and attractive-looking paper, whether it is a letter, a report, an announcement, or a story, is a courtesy to the reader and helps make the expression more effective. Although there are few set rules about many matters of form, there are some generally accepted ideas about such matters as leaving margins at the top, bottom, and sides of the paper, indenting the first line of a paragraph, placing a title, avoiding crowded writing at the end of a line, and eliminating untidy erasures and messy blots. Children should learn about these.

Form and Appearance in Writing

Kindergarten	Usually little child writing, but the teacher should call attention to titles of stories and their placement, to attractive arrangements of work on paper, and to general neatness.
Grade 1	Margins at left, right, top, and bottom of page. Even spacing between letters and between words so that writing is not crowded. First word of a paragraph indented. All writing should be neat.
Grade 2	All taught in grade 1. Title centered at top, with space between it and story. No crowding of writing at ends of lines; recognition that right margin will be uneven. Name and date on all papers.
Grade 3	All taught in earlier grades. Attention to neatness.
Grade 4 and above	All taught in earlier grades. Words at ends of lines divided correctly. Use of appropriate paper for particular writing occasions. Using only one side of paper.

A Bulletin Board Idea

This Is the Way We
Head Our Papers

> name
> school
> grade
> date
> title

The above chart lists matters of form and appearance and suggested grade levels for teaching them. This list is *only* a guide and should be used the way any list of skills or learnings is used—with the recognition that not all children will progress at the same rate and that no child should be expected to master skills listed for any grade level until he or she has achieved those given for earlier grades.

Children should know what is expected of them. It is a good idea to work with them early in the year to establish standards of form and appearance for written work. These standards should be simple and should include only items needed for identification, neatness, and correctness. Items might include position of name and date on papers to be handed in, the extent of margins, regulations about writing on one or both sides of the paper, types of paper to be used for written work, etc. By all means let the children themselves participate in setting these standards. Discuss the reasons for having such standards, and then post them until habits become established, making sure that they are adhered to consistently in order to avoid confusing the children.

Form in writing can be introduced in first grade—and perhaps incidentally in the kindergarten program. At first the teacher will do much of the writing—of letters, experience stories, and charts—and should call attention to how these look, particularly with respect to margins.

When independent writing begins in grades 1 and 2, attention should again be directed to margins, neatness in writing, and the mechanical skills that have been introduced. Indenting the first word of a paragraph may be taught, as may the indentation of the closing and signature in a friendly letter, since children should be learning to write letters to friends.

PUNCTUATION

Punctuation is important, but it can be overemphasized. In any form of written expression, the content of the expression—what is said—is the most important element and should receive the principal teaching attention. Stress should be on the ideas expressed rather than on any mechanical elements used in recording them.

Many punctuation practices are arbitrary and meaningless, and the failure of many teachers and textbooks to recognize this fact results in much wasted teaching effort and unnecessary confusion for pupils.*

However, punctuation does have an important place in writing: it helps to transmit meaning. Simply stated, punctuation is a method for showing, by the use of a number of agreed-upon marks, meaning that cannot be shown—or is only partially shown—by words and arrangements given to them. In speech these meanings would usually be transmitted by the rising and falling tones of the voice, by the emphasis or stress on certain sounds, and by pauses in or the breaking off of the stream of speech.

There are, of course, punctuation items that are unique to written discourse—marks used in writing that are not meant to symbolize speech features. These include such things as a period after an abbreviation, a hyphen to show the division of a word, the underlining (or italicizing) of a book title, and quotation marks around the title of a story.

There are also features of stress, pitch, and juncture in speech that are not reflected by punctuation in written expression. Stress is usually shown by meaning. For example:

She signed the *contract* without hesitating.
As the pavement began to *contract* a crack appeared.

Pitch can sometimes be shown by punctuation, as in the sentences "He will go with us" and "He will go with us?" Although end punctuation is the most common clue to an intonation pattern, other punctuation marks sometimes indicate the need for a change in pitch. For example, "The boys without coats were very cold" will not be read orally the same way as "The boys, without coats, were very cold."

The breaks in the stream of speech, the junctures, can sometimes be signaled by punctuation marks—for example, the more pronounced juncture at the end of a sentence. However, since any sentence (The man/next to me/was laughing) has breaks in the flow of its utterance (as indicated by the /), it is a fallacy to assume that every pause requires a punctuation mark. This is particularly true with the current deemphasis upon close punctuation. We see "My friend Jim Smith will go with us" just as often as we do "My friend, Jim Smith, will go with us," and no one fails to get the meaning. Also, when one wants to indicate a pronounced interruption (a double bar juncture //, for example), there is no particular punctuation form that must be used. The sentence "My brother (actually my half-brother) will meet me in Boston" can be written "My brother—actually my half-brother—will meet me in Boston." Nothing about the way the two sentences are said indicates the difference in punctuation.

Punctuation teaching may be aided by relating the items taught to intonation patterns in speech when this is appropriate. When children read orally, opportuni-

---

*For example, a comma may or may not precede "*and*" in sentences containing words in a series. Putting a comma between independent clauses and setting off noun phrases in apposition are other examples of optional practices.

ties for calling attention to punctuation marks and what they signal often arise. Major attention, however, should be given to functional and direct teaching. That is, punctuation should be taught as it is needed by pupils in their writing, and attention given only to those items that are important to that writing.

In the Primary Grades

Punctuation teaching should begin in the primary grades. The first sentences that are put on the board, written on a chart, or met in a reader are opportunities for beginning the teaching. Although this teaching should be informal and secondary to developing fluency of expression, it can be specific and direct in a functional situation.

The Period.   The first writing children experience calls for a period *at the end of a sentence.* For example:

> We went to the park.

Call attention to the period. Point out that the little dot is a traffic signal called a period. It means that a stopping point has been reached and there must be a pause before going on to the next set of words. Later a more formal explanation may be given, such as, "A period tells us this is the end of a statement."

As children begin their own writing, remind them of the need to signal the end of a statement they write. To help them, provide charts with properly punctuated sentences as models.

Early in children's experience they will also encounter three other uses of the period. They will see it in *abbreviations of titles of persons and of place names.* For example:

> Mill St.
> Dr. Hill

They will also find it after *initials in proper names.* For example:

> H. O. Downs

Finally, they will encounter it after *numerals in lists:*

> 1.
> 2.

Each of the above four uses of the period should be introduced to pupils in kindergarten and first grade and directly taught in the first, second, or third grade as pupils begin their writing and encounter situations that require the use of the period.

The Question Mark.   First grade children should be introduced to the question mark. Since children come to school asking questions, it is natural for you to

---

A Bulletin Board Idea

Periods and Commas

John is going to the store.
Mark A. Brown
644 Mill St.
1. yes
July 16, 1970
Dear Bill,
Chicago, Illinois
red, yellow, and green

Do you know the reason for each?

place a question mark *at the end of a direct question* in a story they dictate. It is also natural for them to write questions in their first stories, and they will readily place the correct mark if it has been introduced. In fact, children probably have less trouble with question marks than with any other type of punctuation.

A second use of the question mark is *after a direct question in the context of a larger sentence,* as " 'Are you going to the store?' Billy asked." This is more difficult for children to understand and should not be introduced until the late third or early fourth grade.

The Comma.   There are many comma rules, but children should only be taught those they actually need in their writing. In the primary grades, as you write experience stories and notes to be copied by the children to take home, some uses of the comma can be introduced. These include the comma between the date and the year, between city and state, after the salutation in a friendly letter, and after the complimentary close of a letter. Children can also begin to become aware of the comma used to separate words in a series, although this use should not be directly taught until the third grade.

Quotation Marks.   Children in the primary grades will encounter quotation marks in their readers and story books and will naturally have questions about them. This is the right time, then, to introduce their use. A good way to do this is to have children take the parts of characters in stories in which the speech is set off by quotation marks. They will learn that these marks signal speech. The use of quotation marks may also be shown in group stories you write on the board as the children dictate. Use these group stories often, even after the children begin to write compositions of more than two or three sentences by themselves, for they are useful in many ways—for example, for developing vocabulary and organizational skills. As you write, point out punctuation and paragraphing, *making special mention of the placement of commas and question marks in relation to quotation marks.* Put some of the stories on charts, so the children can use them as models. And, above all, work with the children as they write; if good habits are established from the beginning, many future problems may be avoided.

Punctuation Chart

Item and Use	K	1	2	3	4	5	6	7	8
Period									
At the end of a statement	*	*	†	'	'	'	'	'	'
After initials	*	*	†	'	'	'	'	'	'
After abbreviations	*	*	*	†	'	'	'	'	'
After numerals in a list	*	*	†	'	'	'	'	'	'
After letters or numerals in an outline				*	*	†	'	'	'
In footnotes and bibliographies						*	*	†	'

*Introduction   †Suggested teaching   'Maintenance

Punctuation Chart (cont.)

Item and use	K	1	2	3	4	5	6	7	8
Question Mark									
After an interrogative sentence		*	†	'	'	'	'	'	'
After a question within a larger sentence				*	†	'	'	'	'
Comma									
Between the day of month and the year	*	*	†	'	'	'	'	'	'
Between city and state	*	*	†	'	'	'	'	'	'
After a salutation in a friendly letter		*	†	'	'	'	'	'	'
After a complimentary close		*	†	'	'	'	'	'	'
To separate parts of a series			*	†	'	'	'	'	'
To set off words of direct address				*	*	†	'	'	'
To separate a direct quotation					*	†	'	'	'
Before and after appositives					*	*	†	'	'
After introductory clauses					*	*	†	'	'
After introductory words: yes, no, interjections					*	†	'	'	'
Before the conjunction in a compound sentence						*	†	'	'
Before and after a nonrestrictive clause						*	*	†	'
Before and after parenthetical expressions						*	*	†	'
In footnotes and bibliographies							*	†	'
Apostrophe									
In contractions		*	*	†	'	'	'	'	'
To show possession		*	*	*	*	†	'	'	'
To show plurals of figures and letters				*	*	*	†	'	'
Quotation Marks									
Before and after a direct quotation		*	*	†	'	'	'	'	'
Before and after titles (other than titles of books)			*	*	*	†	'	'	'
Exclamation Mark									
At the end of an exclamatory word or sentence			*	*	†	'	'	'	'
Colon									
After the salutation of a business letter				*	*	†	'	'	'
To separate the hour from minutes			*	*	*	†	'	'	'
Before a long series or list						*	*	*	†
To denote examples						*	*	*	†
Hyphen									
At the end of a line to show a divided word		*	*	*	†	'	'	'	'

*Introduction   †Suggested teaching   'Maintenance

In the Intermediate Grades

The punctuation chart suggests grade levels for the introduction, direct teaching, and maintenance teaching of the punctuation items usually taught in the elementary school. Keep in mind, however, that these are approximations only; each class progresses at its own rate, as does each child in it. Punctuation marks—and their various uses—should be taught as they are needed in the children's writing.

In an active language arts program children will have encountered these marks in their reading, and their uses as aids to understanding meaning, as well as to reading orally, will have been pointed out. They will have participated in group writing of many kinds, and individually they will have written sentences, lists, experience stories, friendly letters, etc., by the time they reach the middle grades. If this has not been true, you may need to start virtually at the beginning, but in any case see that there is a genuine need to write letters, directions, notes, reports, reviews, announcements, news articles, and so on, and provide both the time for writing and guidance during the writing. The teaching of needed punctuation items will be a natural adjunct of such a program.

Research has shown that as children advance through elementary school they tend to make many errors in punctuation and that they show little improvement in punctuation skills. This surely means that one or more of the following are true: (1) children regard punctuation as of little importance; (2) teaching has been inadequate; (3) insufficient opportunity has been given for the use of punctuation items in genuine writing situations; and (4) evaluation has not resulted in review and further use of items needing attention. If punctuation is taught in connection with situations where there is a need to communicate and if children are shown that it contributes to this communication, there should be fewer problems.

CAPITALIZATION

Capitalization is also a mechanical element of written expression about which a great deal is known in relation to children's needs. The capitalization needs of the children in a particular class can be determined by examining their spontaneous and assigned writing. Textbooks and course guides often list recommended grade levels for introducing and teaching capitalization uses (as shown in the capitalization chart), but, as always, such lists are merely guides, not firm requirements. The best guide is the writing the children actually do.

There are a number of ways to teach capitalization skills. When children first begin to learn about letters, they discover that each letter has two forms. When they write their own names they learn to use capitals. Later, when they see words and sentences written on charts and on the chalkboard or printed in their readers and storybooks, they encounter many of the kinds of words that are customarily capitalized. The next step is experience stories, and capital letters can be pointed out as these are written on the chalkboard: "Notice that I am beginning the sentence with a capital letter" or "Bruce begins with a capital letter because that is his name."

Direct teaching begins the moment children first start to copy words from charts or the chalkboard; letters to be capitalized should be pointed out (and reasons given) so that children begin with an awareness of the need for both capital and small letters.

Capitalization Chart

Words to capitalize	K	1	2	3	4	5	6	7	8
First word of a sentence	*	*	†	'	'	'	'	'	'
First and last names of a person	*	†	'	'	'	'	'	'	'
Name of street or road	*	*	†	'	'	'	'	'	'
The word I		*	†	'	'	'	'	'	'
Name of a city or town		*	†	'	'	'	'	'	'
Name of a school or special place	*	*	†	'	'	'	'	'	'
Names of months and days	*	*	†	'	'	'	'	'	'
First and important words in titles	*	*	*	†	'	'	'	'	'
Abbreviations: Mr., Mrs., St., Ave.	*	*	†	'	'	'	'	'	'
Each line of a poem[a]		*	†	'	'	'	'	'	'
First word of a salutation of a letter		*	†	'	'	'	'	'	'
First word of a complimentary close		*	†	'	'	'	'	'	'
Initials		*	*	†	'	'	'	'	'
Titles used with names of persons			*	*	†	'	'	'	'
First word in an outline topic			*	*	†	'	'	'	'
First word of a quoted sentence			*	†	'	'	'	'	'
Names of organizations			*	*	†	'	'	'	'
Sacred names			*	*	*	†	'	'	'
Proper names generally: countries, oceans, etc.			*	*	*	†	'	'	'
Proper adjectives					*	*	†	'	'
Titles of respect and rank and their abbreviations			*	*	†	'	'	'	'

*Introduction   †Suggested teaching   'Maintenance

[a]Be sure to point out that there are exceptions to this, particularly in modern poetry.

When children begin to write independently, it is important to observe their written work, noting errors (without red-marking the papers) and planning lessons to correct the errors and to introduce new uses as they become appropriate. At this point children are fascinated with writing anything, so group and individual dictation drills can be especially helpful in emphasizing capitalization situations to which particular attention is being given or which pupils find difficult. Pupils can also compare their capitalization with that shown in models and make their own corrections. Group correction of papers, with special attention to capitalization, is possible through the use of an overhead or an opaque projector. Good habits formed at the very beginning are far more effective than any amount of corrective work.

If good habits are formed, unnecessary capitalization will probably not be a problem, but it may be necessary with some children to reteach certain usages or provide practice activities to eliminate unnecessary capitals. In particular, chil-

Good habits in the conventions of writing are like good driving habits; they become established through regular use.

dren who capitalize words for purposes of emphasis should be helped to overcome this habit.

Above all, however, teaching children to proofread their writing and then insisting that they practice this proofreading will accomplish more than most teaching activities.

PUNCTUATION AND CAPITALIZATION ACTIVITIES

As has been stated many times before, the introduction and reinforcement of skills cannot be accomplished effectively in isolation from genuine communication activities. Attention should be called to particular items of punctuation and capitalization as they are encountered in reading. As children begin to dictate, and later when directions and illustrations are written on the chalkboard, new uses can be pointed out. Then, when the time comes for direct teaching of an item, it will already be somewhat familiar.

Direct teaching should begin at the chalkboard, with a number of sentences illustrating the new use. Using colored chalk for the new item can add emphasis, as can placing illustrative sentences on charts (again using colored felt pen for the particular item) and posting these where children can see them for a few days. Following the direct teaching all the children should have immediate experience in using the item. It is a good idea to begin by writing sentences on the board and having several children use colored chalk to supply the new item; this will show quickly whether the concept has been understood and provide for immediate correction of errors. Then, as all children work at their seats, supervise closely to help avoid errors and reinforce learning. After this, activities such as those suggested in the succeeding paragraphs can be used to add variety and help establish the skill.

In the lower and middle grades, the teaching of punctuation may be enlivened by making cardboard stick puppets representing various punctuation marks. These can be given names such as Rollo Period, "Slim" Exclamation Mark, Paula Apostrophe, etc.—or let the children choose names they like. Each character can tell what he or she does and from time to time can come out and remind pupils of what they have forgotten.

Children can also play matching games, matching punctuation symbols with their uses. Make tagboard cards, printing a symbol or a use on each one. For example, make a period on a card; then on four additional cards print the words "at the end of a sentence," "after an abbreviation," "after initials," and "after a numeral in a list." A symbol card will be needed for each use. If desired, an additional set of cards can show illustrations of these uses.

Another game that can add interest is a version of "What's My Line?" The children can plan this by choosing "guests" to represent punctuation marks; the guests are then questioned by the panel about their functions and appearance. A guest might be introduced with "He is rather shy and seldom appears more than once in a sentence" (period), "Our first guest always appears in pairs" (quotation marks), or "This guest is very lively" (exclamation mark). This could make a good assembly program, with the "panel" selected from the audience. Both panel and guests should be cautioned that questions may only be answered by "Yes" or "No."

The importance of punctuation and capitalization can be shown in many ways. One is to have pupils find examples of specific punctuation and capitalization items in books, newspapers, and magazines. For instance, they might look for sentences in which commas set off words in a series, a period is used after an abbreviation, a word is divided by a hyphen, or parentheses are used to enclose matter that is not part of the main thought. These examples can be used to make wall

Titles and Brand Names

The main words in titles of books, songs, and TV shows begin with capital letters. Brand names of things like candy bars begin with capital letters.

Belling the Tiger   Cruncho bar

Fill in this chart.

My Favorite Song _____

My Favorite Book _____

My Favorite TV Show _____

My Favorite Cereal _____

My Favorite Toothpaste _____

Initials

Initials are the first letters of names. They are capital letters with periods.

Luis Ray Colon—L. R. C.

Mr. Fixler fixes watches and lockets. He sometimes adds people's initials to them. Help Mr. Fixler by writing the initials correctly on the lines.

_ _ _   1. Flora Ruth Baum's locket

2. Paul John Luce's watch

3. Sara Jane Smith's watch

4. May Lee Chen's locket

20

An example of capitalization exercises in workbooks. (From *Using Our Language Workbook*, Level 3. Copyright 1977 by Noble and Noble. Used by permission of the publisher.)

charts or a bulletin board.

Another way to emphasize the value of punctuation and capitalization is to present the children with a paragraph that has none. Choose this paragraph carefully, selecting one in which meaning is actually obscured by the lack of signals. Or let the children try reading some of Don Marquis's *Archy and Mehitabel*—this will quickly convince them.

It is fun occasionally to present "trick" sentences for pupils to punctuate. Sentences such as these can be used:

> Sixty, three, and eleven are the numbers.
> Sixty-three and eleven are the numbers.
>
> No water is coming through the pipe.
> No, water is coming through the pipe.
>
> Bill, said Joe, is very noisy.
> Bill said Joe is very noisy.

An important aspect of teaching any skill is helping children to become aware of their own errors. A good way not only to help them become aware of their errors but also to lead them to assume responsibility for overcoming them is to have pupils keep individual folders for papers that have punctuation and capitalization errors marked. From these they can compile lists of items that need to be studied and select drill materials to help them overcome their problems. Papers should be dated so that children can examine them regularly (perhaps once a month) to determine their own progress.

Actual drills are helpful in establishing a habit when it is first taught or in aiding individual children or groups who need practice on specific items. Sentences such as those below are appropriate. It is especially important that practice drills for establishing a particular habit call for the use of that skill only. For instance, a capitalization drill should not require children to supply punctuation as well.

> Write each sentence, using capital letters wherever they are needed:
>
> it was uncle jim who took me.
> we went to the zoo in glenwood park.
> will mrs. jones be at the picnic?
> last christmas we visited sarasota, florida.
>
> Write the following sentences, using commas where they are needed:
>
> Where did you get the bike Jim?
> I think Mom that I may be late.
> John come over after school and play.
> Alice aren't you going to school today?

A good variation of the above is to use the children's sentences. These can be gathered by listening and making notes as they talk or jotting down appropriate sentences from their writing. Exercises can also be made by dittoing material from reading, science, or other textbooks without capital letters or without punctuation (or the particular marks being studied). The children can supply the needed items and then compare the results with the text. (Allowance should be made, of course, for legitimate variations.)

Dictation drills can furnish variety, and they can be used in several ways. Children can dictate to each other, or recorded drills can be used by individuals who need practice on particular items. Spelling words that need review can even be included in dictation drills. Dictation can also be done by the teacher when a large group or the entire class needs practice on a specific skill or as a general review. When dictating, read the selection three times: once so pupils will know the length and get the gist of what is said; a second time, very slowly, so they can write it; a third time, more rapidly, so the writing can be checked.

Proofreading drills also add variety and can be used either for review purposes or for practice on a particular skill. They may also prove helpful in teaching children how to proofread their own work. Until children become skilled at this, it is wise to give specific directions. For example, "The following selection contains three run-on sentences. Find these and correct them. You may insert capital letters if they are needed."

A duplicated paragraph is good for a general review of punctuation and capitalization, again with specific directions as to the number of items to be supplied.

> *Directions:* Rewrite the following paragraph, using eight capital letters, three periods, and four commas.

> no one was allowed to leave boston and this could have been disastrous for paul revere had he not known the city so well in the darkness he was able to reach the charles river where he had hidden a rowboat a few days before and two friends were waiting to row him across it would be a very dangerous mission for their boat would have to pass near the enemy

It is a good idea to have a generous supply of practice materials of all types for individual children or small groups to use when they need drill and to keep these materials filed in such a way that the particular type can be found quickly. These can vary in difficulty according to the grade level and the needs of the particular children in the class. Answer sheets should be included in each folder, so children can check their own work.

TEACHING HINTS

It is a hoary adage, but it remains true: an ounce of prevention is indeed worth a pound of cure. Pupils should be required to proofread and edit all their written work, and they cannot do this successfully unless they know exactly what they are looking for. That is, they need to establish specific items to look for, such as the following:

- Look for capitalization of the first word of every sentence.
- Check punctuation at ends of sentences.
- Look for capitalization of proper names.

These (and others, depending on the maturity level of the pupils) can be placed on a chart for ready reference. In addition, proofreading drills such as those suggested in the preceding section can be used. First, let the class work together by using the overhead projector to show materials; then give the children individual dittoed copies to discover those who need additional practice.

In the middle and upper grades, the use of proofreading marks to note errors can interest children and help to avoid confusion. They will also feel less embarrassed if they know the marks used are actually those used by editors and that errors are made even by professional writers and printers—hence proofreading. These might be placed on a chart where children can see them.

A Proofreading Chart

"Why can't I go outside," I asked.	insert apostrophe ˇ / insert question mark ?/
"there isn't any- thing to do in the house, and I've finished my work.	cap capitalize / omit / insert comma / insert quotation mark

Capitalization and Punctuation Errors	Dick	Walt	Bill	Al	Roy	Nancy	Ruth
Capitals							
First word in sentence	✓	✓		✓		✓	
Proper names	✓	✓					
Titles	✓	✓		✓			✓
Abbreviations			✓	✓	✓		
Initials	✓					✓	
Others							
Periods							
End of sentence			✓	✓			
After abbreviations			✓				
After initials			✓				
Others							
Commas							
In dates	✓			✓			
In addresses		✓					
Word in list							
Complimentary close							
After salutation							

Obviously, mistakes will occur despite all efforts. Perhaps some of these can be avoided if papers are marked principally for the particular skill currently being studied. Using a colored felt pen for this marking will help children to see their errors quickly and find practice materials to work on. Note the errors and tabulate them, using them as a basis for review teaching. In addition, a brief practice period—perhaps five minutes at the end of the day—may prove helpful in correcting capitalization and punctuation errors observed during the day. (Not every day, however!) Another helpful technique is to give short diagnostic tests frequently, taking the sentences for the tests from exercise sheets used earlier, the language textbook, and the pupils' own writing. These sources will provide an excellent record of the children's achievement and their needs. Data on punctuation and capitalization errors should be placed in pupils' cumulative folders so the information can be passed on to the next teacher.

A Final Word

Fostering positive attitudes is basic to success in teaching children the conventions used in writing. These matters are not really difficult to learn if one considers them important. Help children to view the conventions as *aids* to communication. Failure to observe some—spelling, handwriting, punctuation—may result in a lack of communication. Principally, however, attention to the conventions is a matter of courtesy to the reader and is important in creating a good impression. Right or wrong, we do tend to judge people by their appearance. Since the paper he writes or the letters she sends is a child's personal representative, it should be a matter of personal pride to make it neat and attractive and as free of errors as possible.

It is important, however, not to inhibit children's desire to communicate by overemphasizing the conventions. Teacher attitude is basic here. First, set a good example by observing the conventions in your own writing—notices, records, charts, etc. Second, work with the children as they write, helping them with mechanical problems such as spelling and punctuation, so that they will not be hampered in their attempts to express their ideas. And, finally, use praise to foster positive attitudes toward doing one's best at whatever is undertaken.

References

Filmstrips

Capitalization: Don't Hide in Trees, Please. Mahwah, NJ: Troll Associates (Grades 2–6).

Punctuation: There's a Dragon in My Backyard. Mahwah, NJ: Troll Associates (Intermediate).

Punctuation Marks: Melvin Makes His Mark. Mahwah, NJ: Troll Associates (Intermediate).

The Comma. New York: McGraw-Hill (Color; 2 strips).

Using Capital Letters and Punctuation. Chicago: Society for Visual Education.

Films

Punctuation. Los Angeles: Bailey-Film Associates (6 min.; color; intermediate).

Punctuation for Beginners. Chicago: Coronet Films (11 min.; color, b/w; primary).

Other Materials

Capitalization and Punctuation: Mastery in Language Mechanics. Woburn, MA: Curriculum Associates, Inc. (Workbooks and teacher's guide).

Clues for Capitals. Baltimore, MD: Media Materials (Cassette, response books, teacher's manual, post-test; intermediate).

Lessons in Using Quotation Marks. Woburn, MA: Curriculum Associates (Workbooks; teacher's guide; intermediate, upper).

Lessons in Proofreading. Woburn, MA: Curriculum Associates (24 unpunctuated stories and letters, corrected versions, teacher's guide; intermedi-

ate, upper).

Punctuation. Wichita, KS: Learning Arts (33 transparencies).

Punctuation Power. Chicago: Coronet (6 cassettes, response books, teacher's manual; intermediate, upper).

Understanding Punctuation. San Franciso: Fearon Publishers (Transparencies).

Punctuation Skills. St. Paul: 3M Co. (5 cassettes with worksheets; primary and intermediate).

ACTIVITIES FOR PRESERVICE TEACHERS

1. Devise a punctuation or capitalization drill for a particular usage. Center the content around a story or a social studies or science lesson that might be used at the grade level at which this item would probably be introduced or reviewed.

2. Plan a bulletin board using "fun" sentences in which meaning is changed by changing the punctuation.

3. Make puppets representing the various punctuation marks and plan a play in which the various characters explain themselves. This may be as imaginative as you wish.

4. Make up a game that might be used at a particular grade level to furnish practice in punctuation or capitalization. Specify whether it is appropriate for needed drill on a specific item or for review of several.

5. Prepare a set of transparencies to be used for group practice in proofreading at a particular grade level.

ACTIVITIES FOR INSERVICE TEACHERS

1. Analyze the writing done by your class by collecting all written work for a week and tabulating both the number and frequency of punctuation items used and the capitalization and punctuation errors made.

2. Collect samples of children's writing at several grade levels. Analyze these in terms of growth in ability to capitalize and punctuate.

3. Tape individual children reading orally. Have them listen to themselves while following along in the book, noting how their reading was influenced by punctuation. Discuss the importance of punctuation to oral reading. Let the children practice for a week, then record and evaluate again.

4. Prepare a punctuation checklist for your class. Use it as a focal point for a bulletin board. Plan a series of activities based on practical, interesting uses of punctuation, and add the products of the activities to the bulletin board.

5. Prepare similar activities for capitalization. Combine these (as well as the punctuation activities) with practice in proofreading written work.

6. Report on the organizational plan for teaching punctuation skills in the series of children's language textbooks you are using. Show the sequence in which skills are introduced, taught, and reviewed.

INDEPENDENT ACTIVITIES FOR CHILDREN

1. When children need to learn about the use of hyphens to divide words at the ends of lines, turn to the newspaper. Because newspaper columns are short, they contain many hyphenated words. Have the children look for these, cut out the columns, and circle the hyphens with a red crayon. Put the articles on a chart or bulletin board. Using the display, help the children formulate generalizations about the use of hyphens to divide words.

2. Have the children make a chart showing commonly used abbreviations. The chart can be illustrated with pictures of a street, a man, a doctor, etc.

3. Record short selections on tape that a child can listen to and copy. The copying will require punctuation, capitalization, and attention to neatness and form. Dictate slowly and select material that will be interesting to a child. Various interesting facts that can be gleaned from almanacs, facts books, etc., can be put into appealing dictation paragraphs.

4. Individual children can design posters or bulletin boards on punctuation and/or capitalization for the classroom. The objective should be to make these informative, interesting, and colorful.

5. Give a child a mixture of words—names, places, dates, titles, and other words. Have him select the ones that require capitalization.

6. Individual children who need extra practice in punctuation and spelling can write sentences using their spelling words, paying particular attention to spelling, capitalization, and punctuation.

7. Make a file of sentences without punctuation written on manila strips. Have a child choose ones to punctuate with a colored crayon. Vary the sentences so that some need more than merely end punctuation and others do not. This can also be done with a strip of acetate fastened over the sentence; if the child writes on the acetate with a marking pencil that can be washed off, the sentence is reusable.

8. Two children can work together: one writes a question, using the correct capitals, spelling, and punctuation, and the other writes a statement in reply to the question. The children can check each other. (This is also excellent practice in spelling, changing person and forms of verbs, etc.)

9. One child prepares sets of sentences with different punctuation marks at the end. He or she reads them to a friend, giving the correct inflection. The second child guesses what the punctuation mark is.

   That's your dog.
   That's your dog?
   That's your dog!
   You don't know the answer.
   You don't know the answer?

10. Two children can play a game with cards bearing various types of punctuation—periods, quotation marks, exclamation marks, etc. One child draws a card; he or she must compose a sentence that uses the mark on the card, giving the proper inflection. The other child guesses which mark was on the card. Individal children can play this game by drawing cards and then writing sentences using the marks correctly.

11. Prepare two copies of several short poems—one with punctuation and the other without. Have a child read the copy without punctuation silently, and then record an oral reading. He can then listen to the recording as he reads the punctuated copy silently. Then let him record the poem again, this time using the punctuation as a guide, and compare the two readings.

11

Teaching and Maintaining Handwriting Skills

Some futurists say that the need for handwriting will disappear. This is unlikely, although the amount of handwriting adults do has undoubtedly decreased—and probably will decrease more. It does appear to be true, however, that teachers today do not give as much attention to handwriting instruction as did those of twenty years ago. How much this reduction in attention is due to a belief in the decline of the need for handwriting and how much it is due to the expansion of the curriculum (which forces teachers to give only minimal attention to some subjects) is debatable. Concern about providing for individual needs and development has also led teachers to be much less prescriptive now than formerly about forms and sizes of letters and various other factors related to handwriting.

Instructional emphasis does vary considerably from teacher to teacher and from school to school, but observation in a number of classrooms—regardless of whether or not handwriting instruction is given—will reveal children sitting in all sorts of postures at their desks, with pencils and pens clutched in various ways, and with the papers on which they are writing in many positions. It is not uncommon either to find papers with illegible or scarcely legible writing posted on bulletin boards or in the basket on the teacher's desk.

INSTRUCTIONAL OBJECTIVES

The major reason for teaching handwriting is its role in communication. Handwriting is a tool for written expression; for this reason it must be legible. Thus the principal objective of handwriting instruction is to help each child learn to write legibly. Since handwriting must be done with reasonable speed for it to be a useful skill, the development of satisfactory speed is the secondary objective.

Achieving handwriting skill is closely related to physical and mental development, and this must be kept in mind in planning the instructional program. Handwriting is a complex skill that involves both mind and muscles and the coordination of the two. Thus, evaluation of the way a child writes should be based on the degree of maturation of his or her motor skills abilities and what the child has been taught to do, not on something as artificial as grade level.

The developmental nature of the handwriting process does not mean that handwriting need not be taught. Rather, handwriting skill results from the direct teaching of forms and movements, along with adequate practice on what has been taught. Since legibility is the principal goal, recognition must be given in your program to factors that make for it, even though this may conflict with expressions of individuality. Particular attention must be given to the left-handed child.

Children's handwriting improves when they are motivated to diagnose their own handwriting needs, to evaluate their own progress, and to receive direct help with their problems. This motivation is largely based on their doing purposeful writing. Thus, handwriting should be taught throughout the day rather than being relegated only to instructional periods, although specific times should be reserved for working on problems or for teaching forms and movements.

Finally, your own handwriting, your understanding of the developmental nature of handwriting skill, the knowledge you have of effective teaching procedures, and your skill in using these procedures are important factors in creating a successful program.

Handwriting must be legible. Letters should be well formed and of the proper relative size, with adequate and uniform spacing between them. There should be uniformity of forward slant to the letters (or a lack of slant in the case of manuscript letters) and adequate and uniform spacing between words.

Good handwriting should result in a written product with a pleasing appearance; this in turn results from work that is carefully and neatly arranged and writing of an even, smooth quality.

Good handwriting is also done with ease. To write easily, the writer must have a comfortable posture (body, arms, hands), writing instruments and paper correctly positioned, free movement of the arm and hand, and a rhythm to his writing.

READINESS FOR HANDWRITING

See Maria M. Clay, *What Did I Write* (Aukland, New Zealand: Heinemann Educational Books, 1975).

Young children—even before they are of kindergarten age—are interested in scribbling and drawing, both "writing" to them. They often say that they are "writing my name," "writing a story," or "writing to Daddy." Readiness for writing in terms of interest appears early; however, even five-year-olds generally have too short an attention span to receive the direct instruction necessary to learn to write. They also need greater neuromuscular control; thus activities in the kindergarten should foster the development of this control and build readiness in other ways.

We suggested activities in chapter 3 that develop readiness for handwriting and other language skills. Kindergarten teachers, particularly, should strive to help each child achieve the ability to differentiate between the left and the right hands and the habit of left-to-right sweep in looking at charts, sets of pictures, and material on the board. At this stage, too, further development of eye-hand coordination is important, as is an awareness of likenesses and differences in sizes and shapes of objects and an understanding of space relationships—depth, height, width, distance, and comparative size. In the kindergarten it is also important for children to learn to concentrate on simple work tasks and to develop an awareness of handwriting and its purposes.

Prewriting Skills

The activities that ordinarily take place in the kindergarten should and usually do contribute to the development of the skills needed in handwriting. As children participate in a wide variety of activities that require muscular coordination and perceptual skills, note which children would benefit from specific motor control activities and which need training in careful observation of size, shape, and spatial relationships. Some of the activities related to the prewriting objectives are the following:[1]

1. Learning to differentiate between the left and right hand.
    a. Saluting the flag with the right hand.
    b. Shaking hands with the right hand.
    c. Holding up the hand called for in games.
    d. Playing games such as "LoobyLoo," "Hokey Poke," and "Simon Says."
2. Practicing left-to-right eye sweep.
    a. Noticing the left-to-right direction of a series of pictures, of writing on charts or on the board, or in counting a line of children.
    b. Watching the teacher's left hand sweep smoothly under titles of stories or under captions and signs as he or she *stands to the left* of written material on charts or on the board.
3. Becoming aware of sizes, shapes, and spatial relationships.
    a. Selecting puzzle parts and putting puzzles together.
    b. Choosing blocks of various shapes for building; putting blocks away according to size and shape.
    c. Modeling with clay or with a salt and flour mix.
    d. Arranging books on shelves according to size.
    e. Sorting shapes—triangles, squares, circles—into groups (correlate with mathematics).
    f. Sorting color chips and pictures into groups.
    g. Working with peg boards, tinker toys, etc.
    h. Recognizing the boundaries of work and play areas.
4. Becoming aware of handwriting and its purposes.
    a. Noticing and identifying one's name on name cards, art work, coat hooks, and personal possessions; on attendance, committee, and job lists. (Begin teaching with the child's name, even if the child does not speak English.)
    b. Participating in choosing captions for bulletin boards and titles for chart stories; noticing various captions, labels, and book titles.
    c. Noting signs around the school, on other buildings, and on streets.

Using Crayons

The skill a child attains in the use of crayons is an important index of the success he or she will have when handwriting instruction begins. These crayon pictures of fathers (reduced in size) made by kindergarten children show progression in the

a. Only a suggestion of form is evident; many details are missing; control of crayon is erratic (top left).

b. Lack of perception of the relationship of the parts to the whole is apparent; details are missing; some details are overelaborated (top right).

c. Keener observation of form is noticeable; significant details are included, such as ears, arms, hands; hair placement is more accurate (center).

d. An awareness of the relationship of the parts to the whole is shown; many details such as eyebrows, fingers, neck, and shoulders are included; broad strokes of the crayon are used consistently (bottom left).

e. An understanding of body proportions is revealed; a variety of details makes a realistic picture; good crayon manipulation is evident (bottom right.) [Adapted from We Teach Handwriting, *Seattle Public Schools, 1963.]*

development of readiness for handwriting instruction—the stages of mental development and motor skill achievement. Attainment of the levels shown in *d* and *e* indicates readiness for handwriting instruction. Remember that some children in the first or second grade may not have attained levels *d* and *e* and hence are not ready for handwriting instruction.

Other Readiness Activities

Readiness for handwriting instruction is also dependent on the child's ability to use language. Many children in the kindergarten and first grade need experiences that stimulate the desire for language expression and show the importance of writing. They need to listen to stories, look at pictures, dictate stories about their experiences, describe objects, play games that require speaking and listening, tell how objects are alike or different, retell stories, and play word and sound games.

Also see readiness activities in chapter 14.

There are other activities that give practice in basic movements needed for writing: making clocks, doughnuts, soap bubbles, Halloween faces, a Christmas tree with ornaments, a cat, stick figures, a square wagon with wheels, and so on.

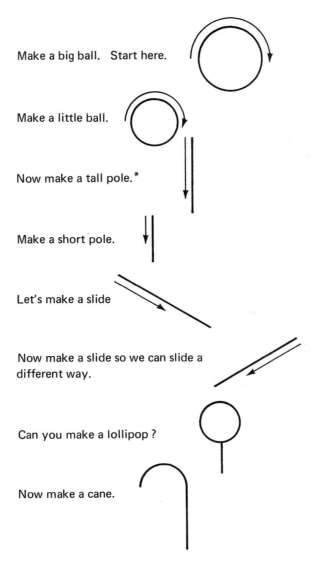

Make a big ball.   Start here.

Make a little ball.

Now make a tall pole.*

Make a short pole.

Let's make a slide

Now make a slide so we can slide a different way.

Can you make a lollipop ?

Now make a cane.

* Make certain that words such as pole, line, lollipop, slide, cone, etc., are in the children's vocabularies.

Beginning Handwriting Instruction

The first few weeks of grade 1 are important in furthering readiness for handwriting instruction. Activities with shapes, as suggested previously, will help to provide clues to the children's readiness. Usually at least two to four weeks should be devoted to a continuation of readiness activities begun in the kindergarten, but these should not be regarded as fixed limits. No instruction should be given until a child possesses the necessary muscular coordination, the emotional and mental maturity required for learning the skills, and the desire to write.

Children are first taught printscript—probably more often called manuscript. The reasons for teaching manuscript rather than cursive form include the fact that it is considered easier to learn than cursive, since only simple curves and straight lines are required to form the letters, and that the formation of letters in manuscript is similar to that of letters encountered in reading. Manuscript is also typically more legible than cursive writing, and young pupils derive great satisfaction from their rapid progress in mastering it. The use of manuscript writing thus appears to contribute to achievement in reading and spelling, as well as to help children produce more and better written language products.

Basic Objectives

Children need to be shown in school activities that the purpose of writing is to communicate. Primary teachers are doing this when they write children's dictated stories on the chalkboard or chart paper (an activity that should be continued for other values as well—see chapter 8). Thus, fostering children's natural interest in writing is basic to initial instruction and to children's learning to write well. In addition, the beginning writer should attain these objectives:

1. To write easily on lined paper in printscript, under your supervision, a two-sentence story composed by the class.
2. To write a story of similar length of his or her own composition.
3. To learn how to sit, to place the paper, and to hold the pencil correctly.
4. To follow your instructions for the beginning and direction of strokes and the size of letters.
5. To observe a two-finger margin at the left side of the paper, a one-finger space between letters, and a two-finger space between words.
6. To recognize and know the names of all letters of the alphabet.
7. To write his or her first and last name from memory by the end of the year.

Commercial handwriting materials have guidebooks for teachers which provide a sequential series of steps to be followed in introducing manuscript forms. If such a reference is available it should be used. However, you may wish to supplement and evaluate the suggestions by using some of the procedures presented here.

Writing on the Chalkboard

The chalkboard is a good place to begin handwriting instruction. A child has the space on the board to make use of the large muscles, which are better controlled

Evaluating Handwriting Readiness

Affirmative answers to the following questions indicate the child's readiness for beginning handwriting instruction.

1. Does the child show a preference for one hand over the over?
2. Does the child show good dexterity in finger and wrist movement as shown in the use of scissors, for example?
3. Does the child follow a left-to-right direction easily when viewing a series of pictures or when following your writing?
4. Is the child increasingly aware of size, shape, and spatial relationships and does he demonstrate this awareness in his art and building activities?
5. Does the child have in his or her vocabulary the terms that will be used in handwriting instruction, such as large, small, short, tall, straight, round, top, and middle?
6. Does the child listen accurately and with concentration for increasingly longer periods of time?
7. Can the child recognize his or her own name when it is written in the approved printscript form?
8. Does the child recognize needs for writing, such as a thank-you note or a message to be taken home?

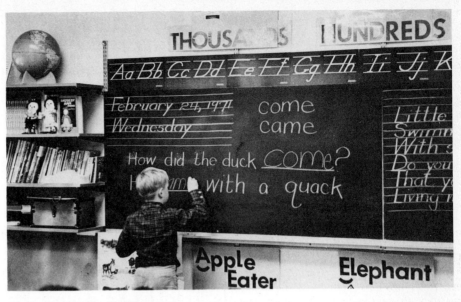

Handwriting at the chalkboard.

In your demonstrating of letter forms at the chalkboard make sure that all of the children are sitting facing the board.

than some small ones, so that corrections can be made easily. All writing should say something, so begin with a word (the children should have made the basic movements suggested earlier in this chapter as a part of the readiness program). Choose a word that is within the children's reading vocabulary and that has meaning for them. Demonstrate each letter of the word on the board. Call attention to how each letter is made. (You may want to call the vertical lines *bats* and the circles *balls*.) Write the word, say what it is, and then write it again, asking the children to tell you how each letter is made.

Demonstrate how to hold the chalk. Have each child stand directly in front of where he or she is to write, holding a half-piece of chalk with the index finger (the child may call it a "pointer") near the tip, the middle fingertip next to it, and the thumb underneath. For straight lines, children should start at the top and pull down; letters with round movements should be done according to the directions for the handwriting system being used. The pupils should learn the movements for making each letter and be corrected if they do not do as directed.

Writing at the board can be done at first without lines, but after a short time children can be asked to evaluate their attempts in terms of whether their letters are "sitting" on a straight line (use a pointer or yardstick). Later draw lines on the board and have each child stand in front of one that is at eye-level. Soon after this, attention can be given to spacing between letters, and, as more than one word is written, between words.

Writing on Unlined Paper

The first writing on paper should be on unlined newsprint 12 × 18 inches in size. Some teachers have the children use a thick-leaded pencil; others prefer a crayon or a felt-tipped pen. If a crayon or pen (may be messy!) is used, it should be held in the same manner as a pencil will be held later (see diagram on p. 255). The first writing on paper may be done without attention to letter alignment. Later the folding sequence that is shown below can help pupils learn to keep their writing within spaces. The amount of time given to learning letter forms and to practicing each stage of the sequence will vary from class to class and from child to child.

Folding 12 x 8 Unlined Paper

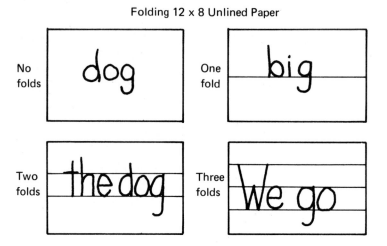

Children should continue to use unlined paper in grade 1 until they are able to comply reasonably well with these standards:

1. Know the directions for strokes (down for straight lines and usually, depending on the system, from left to right and over the top for circles).
2. Observe size relationships of letters.
3. Make letters approximately fill the spaces between folds.
4. Hold the crayon easily and move the hand freely.
5. Achieve some degree of body relaxation.

Writing on Lined Paper

After about ten weeks of instruction some children will be ready for lined paper, which also should be 12 × 18 inches in size. The first paper used should have lines spaced an inch apart. A little later, paper with narrower lines (to one-half inch apart) can be used. The use of a primary pencil (one that is not too big to be manipulated easily) with a thick black lead can begin at the same time the lined paper is introduced, or a short time before.

When writing on lined paper begins in a normal classroom, some children will still be writing at the board and some will be writing on unlined paper. Beginning handwriting instruction should proceed slowly, with careful supervision of all of the writing of each child. A slow and careful procedure will prevent the development of poor writing habits, fatigue, and loss of interest.

CONTINUING DEVELOPMENT

Practice develops habits; the habit of writing legibly and with adequate speed is needed by every child.

The teaching of handwriting does not end with teaching children the manuscript forms, even though many teachers wish it did, considering the many things they are called on to do each day. There are some school systems that teach only manuscript, but the majority have children continue using manuscript in grade 2 and then teach cursive forms in grade 3. A few schools do not introduce cursive forms until grade 4, and an increasing number of schools include a program for the maintenance of manuscript skills after cursive is introduced. Since many forms we are all called on to complete say "print," there is a need to maintain manuscript skill. Manuscript is also good for posters and other writing that is to be exhibited.

Grade 2

The program in grade 2 ordinarily consists of teaching manuscript to the few children who did not learn the forms in grade 1, providing practice in the use of manuscript to maintain and refine skills, and carefully evaluating all writing for the purpose of doing corrective teaching. The objectives include the following:

- Refining manuscript ability—keeping the letters well rounded; making firm, straight lines; spacing letters closely and evenly within words; leaving a space of one finger between words; and placing all letters properly on lines.
- Writing all the small and capital letter forms correctly by the end of the year.
- Maintaining a consistently acceptable hand position—holding the pencil about an inch from the point, keeping the hand and elbow below the base line of writing, and keeping an air space under the wrist.

Grade 3

Handwriting Reminders

1. Join all letters properly.
2. Lift the pencil only at the end of a word.
3. Slant your paper to the left (to the right if you are left-handed).
4. Dot your *i's* and cross your *t's* when you have finished writing a word.
5. Leave even spaces between words.

The major event in the third grade handwriting program is the introduction of cursive (or, as many children say, "real") writing, usually near the beginning of the second semester. Actually there is a readiness for cursive writing just as there is for beginning writing, so ideally cursive form should be taught (regardless of grade level) when *a child* is ready. Evidence of this readiness includes the ability to write manuscript letters well from memory, the ability to read cursive writing that is written well, and the desire to learn the new form.

Until cursive writing is introduced the objectives of the program are simply an extension of those for the second grade program. Letter forms should be made correctly, spacing should be improved (and done without finger measurements), and lines should be firm and made with even pressure.

Transition from Manuscript to Cursive

While there is some difference of opinion about whether the learning of cursive form should occur as a transition or changing of manuscript to cursive or result from the teaching of a system unrelated to manuscript, most authorities favor steps which show relationships. There is a shift in motor skills required, since cursive requires new movements, new proportions, and a slant to the writing. Some letters differ considerably from the manuscript styles, the pencil is not lifted from the paper between letters in a word, and the paper is placed differently.

Since commercial handwriting systems give instructions for teaching cursive forms, you should use the instructions provided with the materials you use. The following suggestions may be helpful in using the specific steps outlined for a particular system.

1. Show the relationships of cursive forms to manuscript forms by using illustrations such as the following:

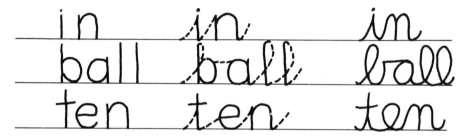

2. Move from the simple to the complex. Introduce lowercase or small letters first, starting with the ones that are easiest to make: 1, e, i, t (undercurve and slant strokes).
3. In introducing letters, use parallel slanted guidelines on the board to show how each straight line slants the same way as the others. The parallel lines will also help in showing spacing between letters, the widths of humps in m's and n's, the width of the loop in an 1, etc.
4. Introduce letters in words on the chalkboard, calling attention to the strokes, to the way the word begins, to the way the letters join, to the size of the letters, and to the ending stroke of the word.
5. Introduce new letters in several words, so that a new letter will appear in various positions—at the beginning, in the middle, and at the end of a word.

Books about Handwriting for Children

The Art of Writing (UNESCO, 1965; intermediate grades).

Gourdie, Tom. The Puffin Book of Lettering (Penguin Books, 1961; intermediate grades).

Meller, Ann. Children's Printing (Educational Development Center, 1969; intermediate grades).

Ogg, Oscar. The 26 Letters (Thomas Y. Crowell, 1971; upper grades).

Thomson, George L. Better Handwriting (Penguin Books, 1967; intermediate grades).

Dowdell, Dorothy. The Secrets of the ABC's (Oddo Publishing, 1965; intermediate grades).

Taylor, Margaret C. Wht's Yr Nm? (Harcourt, Brace & World, 1970; intermediate grades).

Intermediate and Upper Grades

After cursive form has been introduced, handwriting instruction is still very important for two reasons: (1) the skill in cursive writing acquired during and shortly after its introduction must be reinforced and maintained; and (2) the amount of handwriting done by the pupils in their school work increases at each grade level. To meet the increased demands, direct instruction toward helping each pupil achieve the following specific objectives:

1. To write all letters legibly in both lowercase and uppercase cursive forms.
2. To understand how the terms shape, size, space, line quality, and alignment apply to evaluating his or her own handwriting.
3. To maintain attention to posture, hand position, and movement in writing.
4. To evaluate his or her own handwriting in terms of class standards and commercial models and diagnostic materials.

5. To maintain previously acquired manuscript skills and to use manuscript writing in appropriate situations (making posters, filling out forms, and labeling materials).

ALTERNATE WRITING SYSTEMS

Criticism of the fact that children essentially learn two forms of handwriting (regardless of whether cursive is taught as a new form or by a transition approach) has been voiced because of the time that the learning of two forms requires and because the transition to or learning of the second form interferes with the development of children's ability in written composition. This criticism has led to advocacy for teaching only manuscript—an advocacy that runs counter to tradition and a substantial amount of public opinion.

The criticism has also led to the introduction in some schools of handwriting systems whose forms are in a sense both different from and similar to manuscript and cursive. One of these systems is known as D'Nealian. In beginning instruc-

Transition from manuscript to cursive forms as illustrated in one commercial series. From *The New Handwriting Series, Book C* (Los Angeles: BOWMAR/NOBLE, copyright © 1974. Used by permission).

tion this system calls for making letters that are oval rather than round and slanted rather than vertical. Most of the lower case letters are made in one movement instead of two. Later children are taught to connect these letters which, in effect, makes the writing similar to typical cursive.

A second system is a revived one, Italic. Italic letter forms are less slanted than D'Nealian ones and are unconnected in grade one. These letters are "modified slightly during the second grade by joining the small letters with entrance and exit strokes."[1] Capital letters are the same in both beginning and later instruction. Italic writing is attractive when done well and probably most viewers of it would first regard it as connected manuscript. However, some of the letter forms are quite different from manuscript, with early advocates of its use calling it "true cursive" and stressing its similarity to "present type faces."[2]

Whether the teaching of either of these forms will supplant the teaching of manuscript and cursive seems doubtful. The introduction of Italic writing in England more than twenty years ago caused little stir in the United States, possibly because it received some criticism.[3] Of course, manuscript writing did not attain its present wide-spread use until more than thirty years after its introduction.

OTHER INSTRUCTIONAL CONSIDERATIONS

The preceding sections discussed how handwriting should be taught at the beginning stage, at the stage of transition to cursive writing, and in the intermediate

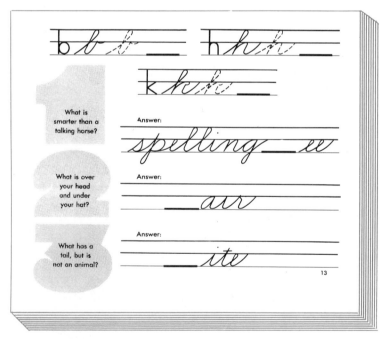

Motivate the transition to cursive form. [*Walter B. Barbe et al.* Creative Growth with Handwriting, *Grade 3. Columbus, Ohio: Zaner-Bloser, Inc., 1975, p. 13. Reprinted by permission of the publisher.*]

grades where the problem is the maintenance of skills. The issue of other systems or forms of writing was introduced. There are other issues and considerations that a teacher should give attention to. These are discussed in the following sections.

From *D'Nealian™ Handwriting* by **Donald N. Thurber.** Copyright © 1978 by Scott, Foresman and Company. Reprinted by permission.

Practice Emphasis

In addition to teaching handwriting directly and maintaining skills through the use of teacher's and pupils' guides and textbook materials, you should capitalize on opportunities to give attention to handwriting in all of the pupils' writing. Handwriting skill will diminish unless it is practiced, and this practice must include corrective work on factors that cause the writing to be illegible or cause it to be done awkwardly or in a tiring fashion.

Keep a checklist for recording individual problems that need correction. Search for the causes of handwriting faults as well as for the faults or errors—check for poor posture, improper paper position, poor lighting, a too tightly held pencil, or a writing instrument that is too large, too small, or too short. In addition to the checklist, it is a good idea to keep samples of the children's writing collected at intervals throughout the year. Supplement your analysis of the handwriting on these by asking the principal, or perhaps the next-door teacher, to rate them.

Children should also evaluate their own writing. They should make comparisons with levels of achievement shown on commercial scales as well as with their own previous writing efforts. Their efforts toward improvement may be encouraged by displaying samples on the bulletin board, holding a writing clinic with several of the best writers acting as "doctors" for specific problems, having children report on their handwriting (each child indicating his best letter, the most difficult letter to make, why his handwriting is improving, etc.), and giving emphasis to handwriting in all areas of the curriculum.

The opaque and overhead projectors are useful for looking at children's writing. In showing children's writing, emphasize improvement rather than finding fault. Do not stress details too much: dwelling on "the tail of the q is too long" or "the o is not round enough" will make handwriting improvement more difficult to achieve. Instead, have the children refer to handwriting charts that they can use to form their own judgments. Some discussion of handwriting will help focus on particular problems. For instance, one day talk about the effect of the slant of letters upon speed and legibility. On other days attention can be given to uniformity of size of letters, spacing, formation of letters, and so on.

Handwriting practice should grow out of the needs that arise as the children write stories, poetry, reports, summaries, diaries, minutes, letters, notes, announcements, signs, etc. Genuine communication will foster an appreciation of the importance of good handwriting to communication. It is usually helpful to set up one main objective for the class each week, with each pupil paying particular attention to any of his handwriting faults that relate to that objective. The objective might be maintaining parallel slant, gaining uniformity of letter size, closing letters properly, maintaining good margins, or using good posture.

Novelty can be added to practice through the use of such sentences as the following:

> Zillions of zebras zipped by.
> Well, Willie works willingly.
> Buzzy, a busy bee, buzzed by.
> A snappy turtle snapped at the stick.

To provide further variety in practice, tape a paragraph or two, speaking slowly but evenly and paying strict attention to the number of words per minute. If you have several tape recorders with listening stations, different children can practice writing different paragraphs (different content, different speeds, etc.).

Planning a handwriting project with another teacher of the same grade level can also provide motivation for practice. Pupils can write selections (without

OBJECTIVE: The student will:
write a paragraph when given sentences and a choice of phrases within each sentence.

Write this paragraph. Each time there is a choice, pick the one you like best.

| It was the | most beautiful
strangest
most horrible | thing I had ever seen. I could |

| hardly wait to | snap a picture of it.
tell my friends about it.
get as far away as I could. | The whole |

| thing was the color of | alphabet soup
rose petals
rusty water | and smelled like |

| springtime.
moldy cheese.
clouds. | Do you think other people will really | believe
like
fear |

what I saw?   Pick-a-Story
_____

Answers will vary.
_____
_____
_____
_____
_____
_____
_____
_____
_____
_____

Directions: Have students complete the page independently, then elect a friend and read stories to each other.   **47**

Handwriting practice can be more than writing words and making letters. (Walter B. Barbe et al., *Creative Growth with Handwriting*, Grade 5. Columbus, Ohio: Zaner-Bloser, Inc., 1975, p. 47. Reprinted by permission of the publisher.)

names on papers) to be exchanged between classes for other children's evaluation. A variation of this is to exchange letters with pupils in a more advanced grade or some other part of the country.

If a child's handwriting remains poor, consider the possibility that he or she may have an emotional problem. If so, it would probably be wise to forget about any intensive effort to help the child improve. Instead, try to give emotional support and look for ways to help with the problem. Persistently poor handwriting may also be caused by poor visual-motor control. Vision should be checked, of course, but sometimes readiness activities merely need to be continued.

WRITING A BUSINESS LETTER

Write this letter on the following page. Use your own address and to-day's date in the heading.

Heading {
62 Blake Road
Gary, Indiana 46405
March 8, 19__

Cory's Sporting Goods, Inc.
231 Madison Avenue   } Inside address
Chicago, Illinois 60617

Gentlemen: } Greeting

    Please send me the pitcher's glove, model 146R, priced at $13.00, including postage, shown on page 27 of your new spring catalog. I am enclosing a money order for $13.00.

Closing } Yours truly,
Signature } John Larson

Emphasize good handwriting in all writing. (From *The New Handwriting Series*, Book G. Copyright 1974 by Bowmar/Noble, Publishers. Used by permission of the publisher.)

Don't overlook children who know how or are learning to type. Some commercial handwriting programs (such as Writing Our Language, Scott, Foresman and Co., 1973) *devote some attention to typing. Typists do need to maintain handwriting skills, though.*

Paper Position for Cursive

The relaxed angle of the forearm across the desk and the maximum convenience of the forearm and fingers to the paper decide the position of the paper. Usually the angle of the bottom of the paper with the edge of the writing surface should be 30 degrees. For the left-handed writer, the paper should be angled in the opposite direction.

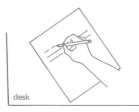

Paper Position for Manuscript Writing

For manuscript writing the paper is usually perpendicular to the edge of the desk. Some authorities suggest an angle of about 10 degrees.

Activities

Beginning pupils are always eager to learn to write. Later they are also motivated to learn cursive form. However, interest in practicing skills may lag. Special attention must be directed toward creating interest in handwriting and providing a freshness to instruction for a program to be successful. Try using some of the following activities to supplement the preceding suggestions and furnish motivation:

1. Combine spelling review with handwriting practice by having the children compose sentences using the spelling words.
2. Children can use bags or envelopes to make individual mailboxes. These mailboxes are then placed beside the pupils' desks, and the pupils may use them to send daily notes to one another. Legible notes may be read; illegible ones are sent to the dead-letter office where a committee of student postmen study the writing and report on its weaknesses.
3. Pupils may do research on the history of handwriting, kinds of paper and how paper is made, the handwriting of famous people, kinds of handwriting tools, italic writing, graphology, or the handwriting of pupils in their school.
4. Children may report on writing that they do at home—letters, thank-you notes, shopping lists, telephone messages. To help show the importance of writing, they may also report on writing their parents do.

Instruction Time

Research evidence indicates that 10 to 15 minutes of concentrated work each day should be sufficient for teaching and maintaining handwriting skills. Most primary grade teachers will find occasion and need for daily handwriting periods, whereas perhaps no more than a five-minute lesson on alternate days will be adequate at the middle and upper grade levels. The less frequent and shorter periods presuppose, of course, that attention is being given to individual diagnosis of need and practice.

In addition to having specific handwriting periods, devote attention during the day to handwriting skills in all areas of work in which writing is involved. Pupils must feel responsible for legibility in all their writing.

The way to eliminate poor handwriting is not to spend more time in handwriting periods but to better utilize the time that is devoted to its teaching and practice.

Position and Movement

A child's handwriting is affected by the fit of the desk and the child's position in relation to it. Handwriting is also affected by the position of the paper, the way the writing instrument is held, and the movements of the handwriting strokes. If attention is given to each of these factors at the proper times, much time and energy on the part of both the child and the teacher will be saved.

A child should sit comfortably, with both feet touching the floor and both arms resting in a relaxed position on the writing surface. The writing instrument should be held lightly, and the index finger should be placed nearer to the point than the thumb, with both at least one inch above the writing point. The writing movement should involve smooth coordination of the whole arm, the wrist, and the fingers.

Speed of Writing

Attention to speed is not only useless but harmful if it begins before letter formation is spontaneously good. No end is served by making letters, words, and sentences rapidly and illegibly. Speed is important when letter formation has been properly established, since we all need to write rapidly at times. However, pupils usually make their own adjustments according to the nature of the work—pressure work, personal writing, or work that needs to be particularly neat and pleasing in appearance. Speed norms (see scale samples later in this chapter) are only rough averages and should not be used as arbitrary standards for all children or for every product of a child's writing.

Differences in Letter Forms

A common instructional problem, particularly in the intermediate grades, is that different children in a class will write a number of different forms of the same symbol. These differences are particularly apparent in many capital letters, and they usually simply reflect the fact that the teachers the various pupils have been instructed by in earlier grades have used different commercial materials. Since there seems to be no conclusive evidence to demonstrate the superiority of a given letter form over other forms of the same letter, it is reasonable to permit pupils who have learned different forms to continue to use these so long as they are legible and can be made with sufficient ease and speed. However, it is a good idea for a school to adopt a single system, so that teachers will not confuse pupils further by advocating their individual ideas. Further, before adopting a system, a school may want to simplify some letter forms (removing loops and swings).

Handwriting Materials

Materials for handwriting include chalk, chalkboard, paper, crayons, pencils, pens, and usually commercial handwriting books. There is great variation in the use of these materials in different programs. Most programs call for the use of chalk and crayons in the primary grades, and many call for large beginner's pencils. As to the latter, there is less emphasis today on a larger diameter for the pencil than normal, but the lead should be thicker, since the essential requirement is that the beginning pupil be able to make a line that is easily seen.

There is also variation in the paper advocated for the various grade levels. You should insist that several types of paper be available to the children in your classroom—not all paper in grade 2 should have lines ½ inch apart, for example. In addition, there should be stationery available for letter writing. Following is a guide to practice and instruction paper:

A Guide to Practice and Instruction Paper*

Grade 1   12 × 18 inch unlined newsprint (the use of this will depend upon the attention given to handwriting in the kindergarten)
12 × 18 inch newsprint lined the long way

A Guide to Practice and Instruction* (cont.)

	12 × 18 inch (or shorter), with lines ½ inch apart alternating light and heavy
Grade 2	9 × 12 inch, with lines ½ inch apart alternating light and heavy
Grade 3	9 × 12, lined the long way with lines 1 inch apart
	9 × 12, with lines ½ inch apart alternating light and heavy
	9 × 12, with lines ½ inch apart
	8½ × 11 inch, with lines ⅝ inch apart
Grade 4	8½ × 11 inch, with lines ½ inch apart
	8½ × 11 inch, with lines ⅜ inch apart
Grade 5	8½ × 11 inch, with lines ⅜ inch apart

---

*Paper varies in size. Some beginning lined paper, for example, is 8½ × 11 inches (with the lines running the long way).

A Bulletin Board Idea

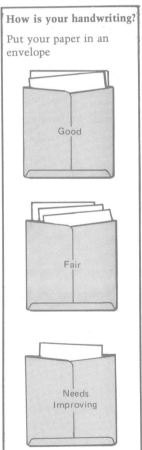

How is your handwriting?

Put your paper in an envelope

Good

Fair

Needs Improving

The Left-handed Child

Five to ten percent of the pupils in a classroom are likely to be left-handed. These pupils are in a right-handed world, and are probably taught by a right-handed teacher. If the pupil cannot imitate the teacher as the right-handed pupils do, he or she starts off with a problem. It is important, therefore, that you be aware of the left-handed pupils in your classroom, since their need for instruction is equal to that of right-handed pupils. First of all, it is necessary to recognize that left-handed children can be taught to write as well and as quickly as the right-handed ones. On the other hand, the time needed for development of particular skills is not necessarily the same for the left-handed pupils as for right-handed ones. In any case, it is important to avoid the implication that a child needs special attention because he or she is left-handed—simply pay attention to this child's individual needs as you do to those of other children.

Attention does need to be given to special instructional problems. For example, there should be much writing at the board in the early years, since when a child is writing at the board it is practically impossible to use the upside-down style some improperly taught left-handed writers use.

The best way to avoid upside-down writing is to make sure that the paper is angled in the opposite direction from that suggested for the right-handed child. In addition, encouraging the left-hander to hold the writing instrument slightly farther from the point helps, as does making sure that the top of the pen or pencil is pointed toward his or her left shoulder.

It is possible that some left-handed pupils will have developed the upside-down writing habit before they come into your classroom. Whether or not a teacher should attempt to change this habit after about the fourth grade depends on a number of factors. The pupil may not be psychologically or emotionally responsive to a change. In such cases, if the handwriting is reasonably legible and can be done with adequate speed, no attempt to change is advised.

Left-handed writers should not be expected to write with the same slant as the right-handed ones, although they may do so. However, if the paper is placed properly and the writing instrument held correctly, it is logical for the left-handed child's writing to slant in the direction of the writing movement—that is, to the right.

EVALUATING HANDWRITING

Handwriting can either be evaluated formally through the use of published scales or less formally by the teacher and the pupils. Since evaluation should lead to corrective practice and remedial teaching, the latter procedure is recommended. This evaluation should be pupil-focused, systematic, and used as the basis for further teaching.

Diagnosis and Remediation

Most publishers of commercial handwriting material can supply instruments helpful in locating handwriting faults. Some extracts from one handwriting chart—*Handwriting Faults and How to Correct Them*—are given below:[4]

> [This chart] is designed to reveal whether or not the pupil's handwriting violates one or more of the following essential qualities: (1) uniformity of slant, (2) uniformity of alignment, (3) quality of line, (4) letter formation, and (5) spacing. Three levels of quality—excellent, mediocre, and poor—are shown for each trait. In addition to illustrating these qualities, the chart contains excellent suggestions on ways to test a pupil's handwriting for each quality. The chart is particularly helpful because it enables both the teacher and the pupil to discover specific handwriting weaknesses that are in need of remedial treatment and makes helpful suggestions for correcting the defects.

How to test legibility: Make a letter finder by cutting a hole a little larger than the letter in a piece of cardboard. Place the hole of this finder over each letter in turn and mark the letters which are illegible. Have the pupils practice these letters separately, then write the word again and test as before.

How to test slant: Draw slanting lines through the letters and mark all letters which are off slant. If the slant is too great, the paper is tilted too much. If the writing is too vertical, the paper is too upright and if the slant is backward, the paper is tilted the wrong direction.

correct   incorrect

How to test for spacing: Draw parallel lines between letters (see diagram). Place the paper in front of you and mark all letters and words which are unevenly spaced.

correct   incorrect

How to test alignment: Alignment and size are closely integrated and should be studied together. Use a ruler (a diagnostic ruler is best) and draw a base line touching as many of the letters as possible. Also draw a line along the tops of the small letters. Mark the letters above or below these lines.

correct   incorrect

How to test size of letters: Draw lines along the tops of the letters. Remember the minimum letters, i, u, v, etc., are ¼ space high; d, t, p are ½ space; capitals and l, h, k, b, d, are ¾ space high. All the lower loop letters extend ½ space below the line.

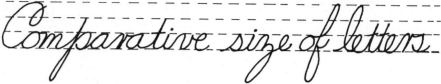

How to test for quality of line: Make a letter finder by cutting a hole a little larger than the letter in a piece of cardboard. Place the hole of this finder over each letter in turn and mark the letters which are illegible due to the quality of line.

Have pupils practice these letters from their writing books separately until the letters are perfectly legible. Then have them write the whole word again and test as before.

Handwriting Scales

Handwriting scales are often not used because of the feeling that children will attempt to copy the handwriting on the scale and thus lose their individuality in writing. However, scales do not have to be used for *grading* pupils' handwriting; they can simply be bases for the pupils to use in making their own judgments about the legibility of their handwriting.

One commercial instrument, *Guiding Growth in Handwriting Evaluation Scales*, provides five specimens of handwriting for each grade level and suggests that samples compared with these specimens be rated as good, medium, or poor. There is also a numerical score for each of the five specimens. Two of these specimens are reproduced below.[5]

Specimen 3—Medium for Grade 5.   Similar cursive handwriting may be marked 75. The standard speed for this grade is about 60 letters per minute.

> *I live in America. It is good to live where you have freedom to work and play. As an American, I support my country and what it stands for.*

Specimen 5—Poor for Grade 5.   Similar cursive handwriting may be marked 65, and writing poorer than this may be evaluated accordingly.

> *My name stands for me. I want to write it well.*

Checklists

Procedures for evaluating handwriting were suggested in the section on handwriting practice, since practice should grow from diagnosis and evaluation. You can make a legibility checksheet such as the following, but be sure to list only the letters causing difficulty for your class. The checksheet can be added to as new problems are noted.

	NOT THIS	BUT THIS
Straight back stroke for e, l	*e, l*	*e, l*
Avoidance of loop in a, i, n, t, u	*a, i, n, t, ee*	*a, i, n, t, u*
Points on r and s	*r, s*	*r, s*
Well-rounded curves on m, n, u	*m, n, u*	*m, n, u*
Carefully crossed t	*t, t, t*	*t, tt*
Open loops on b, f, h, k	*b, f, h, k*	*b, f, h, k*
Avoidance of lazy ending on h, m, n	*h, m, n*	*h, m, n*
Open loop on g, p, y, q	*g, p, y, q*	*g, p, y, q*
Dot over i, j in line with letter	*i, j*	*i, j*
Closing of f on the line	*f, f*	*f*
Careful closing of a, d, g, q	*a, d, g, q*	*a, d, g, q*

Individual pupil records, such as the one on p. 262, are useful for self-evaluation. You can modify the form for your own use by substituting pupils' names for the months; it can then be used in a periodic evaluation of the handwriting of your class.

A FINAL WORD

Handwriting instruction continues to have a place in the elementary school language arts program. There has been a shift of emphasis, however, to helping chil-

My Handwriting Progress								
KEY: S = Satisfactory Name _____ N = Needs improvement Grade _____								
	Oct.	Nov.	Dec.	Jan.	Feb.	Mar.	Apr.	May
Letter forms								
Letters to work on								
Size of letters								
Spacing within words								
Spacing between words								
Alignment of letters								
Slant								
Joining of letters								
Ending strokes of words								
Line quality								
Margins and arrangement								
Neatness								
Rate of writing								
Position and movement								

dren develop a good bit of individuality in their writing if they can maintain legibility and reasonable speed. Instruction is needed in the way letters are formed and how the movements necessary can be made smoothly. Children must also recognize the importance of slant, spacing, and letter size to both legibility and speed.

ENDNOTES

1. Charles Lehman, *Italic Handwriting and Calligraphy*. New York: Pentallic Corporation, 1973, p. 5.

2. Winifred Berry, "Italic Writing," *The Independent School Bulletin*, January 1961, p. 69.

3. Frank N. Freeman, "On Italic Writing," *The Elementary School Journal*, vol. 60, no. 5 (February 1960), pp. 258–264.

4. Zaner-Bloser Staff, *Handwriting Faults and How to Correct Them* (Columbus, OH: The Zaner-Bloser Company, 1937, periodically revised). Reprinted by permission.

5. *Guiding Growth in Handwriting: Evaluation Scale* (Columbus, OH: The Zaner-Bloser Company, 1966). Reprinted by permission.

REFERENCES

Books

Anderson, Dan W. *What Research Says to the Teacher: Teaching Handwriting.* Washington, DC: National Education Association, 1968.

Cahn, William, and Cahn, Rhoda. *The Story of Handwriting.* New York: Harvey House, 1963.

Freeman, Frank N. *Guiding Growth in Handwriting.* Columbus, OH: The Zaner-Bloser Co., 1965.

Handwriting. Urbana, IL: National Council of Teachers of English, 1965.

Myers, Emma Harrison. *The Whys and Hows of Teaching Handwriting.* Columbus, OH: The Zaner-Bloser Co., 1963.

Petty, Walter T., and Jensen, Julie M. *Developing Children's Language,* chapter 16. Boston: Allyn and Bacon, 1980.

Scott, Louise Binder. *Developing Communication Skills.* St. Louis: Webster Division, McGraw-Hill Book Co., 1971.

Stewig, John Warren. *Exploring Language with Children.* Columbus, OH: Charles E. Merrill Publishing Co., 1974, chapter 8.

Films

Between the Lines—The Story of Writing. New York: Modern Talking Pictures, Inc. (22 minutes; b/w).

History of Writing. Chicago: Encyclopedia Britannica Films (25 minutes; b/w; intermediate).

Handwriting for Beginners: Manuscript. Chicago: Coronet Films (13 minutes; color or b/w; primary).

Improve Your Handwriting. New York: Young America Films/McGraw-Hill (intermediate).

Writing Different Kinds of Letters. Chicago: Coronet films (11 minutes; color, b/w; intermediate).

Written Word. Bloomington, IN: National Educational Television Service, Indiana University (15 films, each 29 minutes; b/w). Titles include *Sign and Symbols, Between the Rivers, Keys to the Mysteries, Along the Nile, A B C's, Westward to Greece, Book Takes Form, Noble Roman Letter, Beautiful Book, Paper from China, Wood Blocks and Metal Type, Printing in Venice, The Perfect Book, New Worlds for the Book, Decline and Revival.*

Filmstrips

Correlated Handwriting. Chicago: Society for Visual Education (4 strips; primary).

Cursive Alphabet. Columbus, OH: Zaner-Bloser (2 strips; b/w or color).

Manuscript Alphabet. Columbus, OH: Zaner-Bloser (2 strips; b/w).

Step by Step Handwriting. Chicago: Society for Visual Education (2 strips; primary, intermediate).

The Story of Writing. St. Louis: Webster Publishing Co. (1 strip; intermediate).

ACTIVITIES FOR PRESERVICE TEACHERS

1. The teacher's handwriting, both manuscript and cursive, will serve as a model for the children in the class. A teacher needs to be able to write neatly on unlined surfaces such as the chalkboard or chart paper. Using the guides suggested in this chapter or in a handwriting program, practice your handwriting for five minutes each day—manuscript and cursive. Keep a folder to note progress, and continue to practice until you feel that your writing will serve as a good model.

2. Evaluate the quality of your handwriting by several of the means suggested or explained in this chapter.

3. With a colleague plan a debate for class on the *pros* and *cons* of not teaching children to write the cursive forms.

4. Observe handwriting lessons at several grade levels. Note differences in posture, hand and arm movement, quality of writing produced, handedness, etc. Note also what provisions are made for individual differences.

5. Examine samples of commercial handwriting materials for the grade level of your choice. Decide which you would like to use if you had a choice.

6. Obtain several samples of children's handwriting and try to evaluate them using a handwriting scale.

7. Plan a presentation to the class about what you would do to determine the level of readiness for one stage of handwriting instruction. This might be for initial instruction in manuscript, transition to cursive, practice after an initial learning stage, etc.

ACTIVITIES FOR INSERVICE TEACHERS

1. Evaluate your own handwriting on the scale used in your school. Locate your weak letter formations and practice daily until your writing is close to the sample.

2. Make an informal survey of the handwriting in your school. Collect papers and analyze for specific handwriting faults. Note amount of writing done, posture, types of assignments, etc., and their relationship (if you can determine any) to handwriting ability.

3. React to the article by G. Halpin, "Special Paper for Beginning Handwriting: An Unjustified Practice?" (*Journal of Educational Research*, September 1976, pp. 668–669).

4. Have all the children in one classroom write the same paragraph; then arrange these so that you can identify three or four levels of quality. In other words, see if you can construct a handwriting scale.

5. Prepare activities for children in your class to do individually to improve their handwriting.

6. Have a "Handwriting Week" in your classroom. With the children plan special lessons and displays.

7. Start a file of examples of good and poor handwriting by adults. Try to get examples that are not signatures. Later, with children, examine the examples for specific illegibilities.

8. Purchase from a bookstore descriptive books on graphology. Use the study of graphology to stimulate interest in handwriting among upper grade children.

INDEPENDENT ACTIVITIES FOR CHILDREN

1. To develop small muscle coordination, a child can snap clothespins on a clothesline or coffee can using only one hand, then remove them and try to do it faster the next time.

2. Fabric and torn paper can be pasted on paper to form designs or make houses, trees, etc. Pasting activities help develop eye-muscle coordination.

3. Children can also use the Montessori dressing forms to develop small muscle coordination. The snapping, large button, zipper, bow-tying, and shoelacing frames are all helpful.

4. The child can keep his or her own handwriting improvement record by filing dated samples in order of quality, using a standard handwriting scale to help him or her make adjustments.

5. A child can enjoy and profit from making a personal handwriting scale, using samples of his or her own writing—from weak to improved—along with dates on which they were written.

6. Encourage individual children to use a diagnostic chart such as the ones suggested in this chapter to examine their handwriting and determine what they need to practice.

7. Have a child write his or her name—first, middle, and last—and compare individual letter formations with those found on a handwriting scale to determine which letters need improvement.

8. Provide a child with a device for determining the legibility of a single letter in a word. An easy device to make is a piece of tagboard about one inch wide and three inches long; near one end punch a hole with a hole punch. The child places the hole over individual letters and practices making those that are illegible.

9. For individual practice, prepare a holder with a pocket on one side and a sheet of acetate on the other (fasten it to the folder on one long side and on the bottom). In the pocket place cards containing directions for the formation of letters and lists of words using those letters. A child selects a letter to work on and places it under the acetate. Using a marking pencil and with the card as a guide, the child first traces the letter, then writes it without tracing, and finally writes the words, comparing them with the model.

10. Some attention to speed is necessary in the middle grades, but legibility must remain paramount. To practice on this, individual children can write short paragraphs and time themselves. Prepare paragraphs that should take about a minute to copy (about 40 to 60 letters) at first. Paragraphs and sentences may be taken from handwriting scales, textbooks, or familiar books or stories.

11. As an incentive to improve, suggest that a child prepare a sample of his or her handwriting (enough so that most letters—upper and lowercase—and numerals are included) and write a letter to a pupil in another part of the country to send with the sample suggesting an exchange several times during the year.

12. Have a child find examples of early picture writing and/or other alphabets—hieroglyphics, Indian picture writing, Greek alphabet—and prepare a demonstration for the class. As a part of the demonstration, several children might develop symbols depicting an activity the class is involved with and have the other children try to "read" what they have written.

12

The Teaching of Spelling

The basis of effective spelling instruction and learning is a school program that appeals to children and provides for genuine communication activities. If writing activities are purposeful—written to communicate—then the correct spelling of the words written is important to the communication. If the writing done in school is meaningless to children and seems to have no real purpose, spelling instruction will be no more meaningful.

PROGRAM OBJECTIVES

The basic goal in spelling instruction is to teach children to spell the words they use in their writing. This means the writing that they do in school *and* the writing they will do after their school years. Of course, no one knows all of the many words a child may need to spell at some time in life. Therefore, he must be taught some specific words—the ones that are frequently written by everyone—but he must also develop attitudes, habits, and skills that will help him to spell all words correctly.

Focusing on basic objectives often prevents spending time in the spelling class on activities that have little to do with spelling, even though they may be entertaining to the children or useful to them in some other setting.

In the first place, no one really spells correctly, or seeks to, unless he or she believes that spelling is important. A good speller recognizes that incorrect spelling may cause poor communication or foster in the mind of the reader a negative opinion about the writer of the misspelled words.

Since spelling requires putting into written form words that are familiar from speaking, reading, and listening, two important abilities are needed. The first of these is the ability to recall how words look—the words that the child has studied and those that he or she has seen in reading. The second basic ability is required in order to spell words the pupil cannot recall a visual image of; it is the ability to associate letters and patterns of letters with specific sounds. For most children these two abilities work closely together. As they advance in school they gain images of many words through their reading and hence are able to recall how these look. For words that are new to them, various sound patterns bring to mind visual patterns. Thus a child is often capable of spelling a word he has not seen or has seen so infrequently that he has no visual image of it.

An effective speller needs appropriate knowledge of sound and symbol correspondences; he or she also needs knowledge of the lack of such correspondence, since many words do not fit into phoneme–grapheme correspondence patterns. And a good speller needs to know spelling rules, pattern generalizations, and the cautions that should be observed in applying them.

The fact that a relatively small number of words account for most of the words any person writes is very important. It is important because the number is not so large that the words cannot be learned through direct study in school, thus avoiding undue dependence on applying generalizations about how sounds that have many exceptions are represented.

A good speller naturally must know the letters of the alphabet and how to write them in both lowercase and uppercase forms. He or she should know how to alphabetize words and use this knowledge to find the spellings of words in dictionaries and glossaries. He or she should be able to pronounce words clearly and accurately and to use a dictionary, including its diacritical markings and key words, as well as phonetic and structural aids to help with pronunciations.

A person who spells well shows a concern for doing so by proofreading his or her writing, by looking up the spellings of unknown words, and by establishing a specific study procedure for learning to spell new words. Thus the objectives of teaching the child habits of proofreading, studying, and using the dictionary properly are very important.

These basic objectives should be kept in mind as you read the remainder of this chapter, as you plan your program, and as you select and use materials in the program.

Teaching Specific Words

A great deal of evidence has been accumulated about the words people write most often. Many commercial spelling materials provide for the teaching of these words, although some materials tend to emphasize the teaching of words that illustrate "spelling patterns" (for example: cap, cat, catch, pack, cab, cad, badge, bag, jam, pan) even though some of these words are not likely to be written—at least not frequently—after the completion of the lesson.

The commercial spelling books that seek to teach a core of important words usually present 3,000 to 4,000 (grades 1 through 8) for children to learn. Materials emphasizing spelling patterns may include a greater number of words (including many of the "most commonly written" ones) in order to illustrate the patterns and to show exceptions to them.

The following words are of particular importance. Elementary school children should be able to spell these words without hesitation by the time they reach the fifth grade (or sooner).[3]

A 1972 study showed that 1,000 words account for 83% of all words used in children's writing; 2,000 words account for 89%.[1]

Another study found these words account for over 36% of all words written:

*the
I
and
to
a
you
we
in
it
of
is
was
have
my
are
he
for
on
they
that
had
she
very
will
when*[2]

a
about
after
again
ago
all
along
also
always
am
an
and
another
any
are
around
as
asked
at
away

baby
back
bad
ball
be
because
bed
been
before
best
better
big
black
book
boy
boys
bring
brother
but
buy
by

call
called
came
can
car
cat
children
close
coat
cold
come

coming
could
country
cut

daddy
day
days
dear
did
didn't
do
does
dog
doing
doll
don't
door
down

each
eat
end
even
every

fall
far
fast
fat
father
feet
few
find
fire
first
five
for
found
four
friend
from
fun

game
gave
get
getting
girl
girls
give
glad

go
going
good
got
grade
great
grow

had
hand
happy
hard
has
hat
have
he
hear
heard
help
her
here
him
his
hold
home
hope
hot
house
how

I
if
I'm
in
into
is
it
its

just

know

land
large
last
let
letter
like
line
little
live
long

look
looked
lost
lot
lots
love

made
make
man
many
may
me
men
milk
more
morning
most
mother
much
must
my

name
never
new
next
nice
night
no
not
now

of
off
old
on
once
one
only
open
or
order
other
our
out
over

part
people
place
play
played
please

pretty
put

rain
ran
read
red
rest
ride
right
room
run

said
same
sat
saw
say
school
see
seen
send
she
should
show
side
sister
sleep
snow
so
some
something
soon
started
stay
stop
such
summer
sun
sure

take
teacher
tell
than
that
the
their
them
then
there
these
they

thing	took	walk	what	would
things	top	want	when	write
think	town	wanted	where	
this	tree	was	which	year
thought	two	water	while	years
three		way	white	yes
through	until	we	who	yet
time	up	week	will	you
to	use	well	wish	your
today		went	with	yours
told	very	were	work	
too				

Fostering Positive Attitudes

A truly good speller is one who endeavors to spell all words correctly. A good speller possesses an attitude of concern and knows how to learn to spell a new word, how to get help in spelling unknown words, and how to make the best use of the knowledge of words that he or she has. Good attitudes toward spelling may be encouraged through continuous attention to correct spelling in your own writing. Show the children that correct spelling really matters by proofreading your writing and by using a dictionary when necessary.

Showing the children that the words they are required to learn to spell are ones they consistently use in their writing and have need to spell is also useful. A simple tabulation of the words they write or of the words written by their parents and friends will show this—and will produce a list very similar to the one in the preceding section.

Requiring the children to learn only those words that spelling tests and actual writing situations have shown they are unable to spell makes sense to the children and avoids the development of the negative attitudes that often result from studying words that are already known. It is also important to make certain each child knows and uses a specific and efficient method of learning to spell new words.

Encouraging in the class a spirit of mutual pride and cooperation in spelling achievement builds good attitudes. Children enjoy helping one another study, giving proofreading help, and providing encouragement to one another. Also emphasize individual and class progress in spelling, making each pupil aware of the progress he or she has made. Records of progress should be kept by the pupils themselves, although you may want to keep supplemental ones.

Encouraging high standards of neatness and accuracy in all writing is very helpful. Standards can be developed for the class to apply and these should be referred to as often as necessary to see that they are maintained. It also helps to conduct an efficient spelling period—avoid dragging tests out too long or permitting procedures to develop which encourage dawdling and other poor habits. Negative attitudes toward spelling should be attacked immediately, although fault-finding should be avoided in favor of determining the causes of spelling failures and encouraging and stimulating the efforts children make.

Are you a good speller?

Here's how to tell:
1. Do you think spelling all words correctly is important?
2. Do you try to spell correctly every word you write?
3. Do you know how to learn to spell new words?
4. Do you know how to look up the spelling of unknown words?
5. Do you proofread for spelling errors?

Developing Desirable Habits

Although a favorable attitude toward spelling correctly is basic to a successful program, merely desiring to achieve will accomplish little unless certain basic habits are developed. The following are particularly important habits that can be developed:

- *Being concerned about the spelling of words used in written expression.* This means teaching the child that anytime he is in doubt he should think, "Is this word spelled correctly?" and "Am I sure?" This habit is established by the development and maintenance of standards in written work and by the concern about correct spelling that you show.
- *Proofreading all written work carefully.* Proofreading must be taught so that a child will not simply stare at the paper and think he or she is proofreading. To proofread for spelling errors, each word must be looked at letter by letter.
- *Checking the spelling of all words about which the child is in doubt.* This does not mean that every doubtful word must always be checked in a dictionary—though knowing how to use the dictionary is essential—since sometimes a spelling can be checked in a reading text's glossary, by asking a classmate, or by asking you.
- *Using a specific procedure for learning the spelling of new words.* Although the procedure may vary slightly from child to child (as is discussed later), there are specific steps that are important and should be thoroughly known and practiced.
- *Working efficiently during the spelling period.* Following a specific study procedure is an important part of working efficiently during the spelling period, but listening attentively to the pronunciation of words during testing, completing the spelling exercises promptly, and simply not wasting time are also important habits to be encouraged.

SPELLING READINESS

The time and effort spent on readiness training in the kindergarten and the first and second grades is most often thought of as being directed toward the reading program, but a similar level of readiness is needed for spelling. In fact, being able to recognize some words—a major step in reading instruction—is needed before spelling instruction begins. A child who looks at *ball* and *tall* and does not see that *b* and *t* are different letters is not going to succeed in either reading or spelling. The one who cannot hear the difference in the way these words are said may likewise have difficulty.

Readiness for spelling, like readiness for reading or any other school subject, differs with individuals. When children enter the kindergarten and first grade they are at various stages of development in their ability to express themselves orally. They also listen with varying degrees of effectiveness. Recognition must be given in spelling instruction, therefore, to differences in the ability to use and understand spoken language, including those differences attributable to sex and experiential backgrounds. Although language development does not proceed through distinct stages that are the same for all children, all children do pass through certain obvious phases.

Reasonable facility with oral language is certainly a necessity for development in other uses of language. Like the others, this phase of a child's total language development is extended by the proper environment throughout a child's years in school, but facility in speaking should be discernible before instruction is given that requires other abilities, such as those needed for reading and writing.

The second phase is relating spoken language to printed symbols, beginning with those symbols that represent important words in the child's speaking and listening vocabularies. The third phase is writing, which includes spelling the words written. No phase is ever completely terminated and the development within each is never the same for two individuals, but the sequence is there and must be respected if one is to achieve instructional success.

Many activities develop readiness for beginning spelling instruction. These include activities that involve auditory perception and discrimination, such as the following:

- Show pictures of objects and have the children tell which have names that begin with the same sound. For example, you might have pictures of a bear, a baby, a lion, a cat, a ball, a cup, a lamp, and a box.
- Do the same for ending sounds. For example: *sled, bread, bed, cap,* and *lamp.*
- Say a key word, followed by several others, and have the children hold up their hands for each one that begins with the same sound (or ends with the same sound or has the same middle sound). For example: *soft,* followed by *dot, sit, sing, bought, sand, song.*
- Activities similar to the ones above can be developed for consonant or vowel clusters (*st, gr, oy,* etc.), as well as for single phonemes. Further, associating similarities or identifying differences in words rather than simply in sounds calls for much the same type of exercises.
- Say pairs of words and have the children hold up their hands when the two begin with the same sound (or end the same way or rhyme with each other). For example: *big— boy; fill—ball; live—give.*
- Ask a child to name objects, and have the other children give words that begin with the same sound (or end, etc.).
- Have the children think of words beginning with the same letter *(boy, bat, bear),* say these words, and then compare the beginning sounds and letters.

Attention should also be given to visual perception and discrimination. Begin by having children match objects of the same size, shape, or color. Later, have them find like and different letters and word forms. This sort of activity can also be combined with auditory activities.

- Have the children match pictures of objects whose names begin with the same sound (or letter) as their own names.
- Write letters on the board and have the children select pictures of objects whose names begin with the same letter (or end with the same letter or have the same medial letter). This activity should be used with caution since the children may match sounds that are represented differently. For example, a picture of a bear might be readily and correctly matched with the letter *b* for the beginning letter or with *r* for the ending letter, but there might be difficulty with the medial sound representation.

The Instructional Program

In most classrooms the spelling program centers around the use of a textbook. This may be a workbook in which the child writes and which therefore is not reusable, or it may be a hardcover book containing the word lists and spelling activities (in which case the child writes on his own paper). A few classrooms have no books, but have a word list for the grade level. Some have no furnished materials; the teacher selects the words and activities from various published sources and from the writing of the children.

Basic Premises

Spelling can be taught efficiently and effectively if instruction is based upon the knowledge that research and practice have provided.[4] For example, as suggested in the discussion of attitudes, spelling should receive attention throughout the school day as well as during the spelling period. With such attention all children can learn to spell the words they write if they are ready for the instruction provided, if recognition is given to the fact that they learn in different ways and at different rates, and if teaching procedures are used that have been reaffirmed by numerous research studies.

A basic premise is that the spelling program should enable a child to use his time and energy economically. Children can and should have a part in planning the program, evaluating it, and making changes when objectives are not being achieved. With this approach the main responsibility for spelling progress will be on the child.

Correct spelling is a concern of parents. Make sure that they understand your program.

An awareness that the ability to spell is largely contingent upon the effectiveness of two processes—reception and recall—is also fundamental. Reception is made by *recognizing* letters, noting their sequence, and associating sounds and knowledge of word structure with them individually or in patterns. Recall requires *remembering* the sequence of letters and/or making associations that aid in achieving the correct sequence. Both reception and recall must be practiced if new words are to be learned and if spellings or associations helpful to spelling are to be recalled in actual writing situations.

Related to the above is the fact that spelling is closely linked to all other linguistic skills. In both reception and the application of this reception (recall) attention must be given to both the regularities and irregularities in sound and symbol correspondence in the English language. In other words, some rules and generalizations about how a sound is represented may be helpful to recall and therefore to spelling, but caution must be used in the reception of other sound representations or the recall will lead to misspellings.

Finally, the fact that the true evaluation of spelling ability is the quality of spelling done in *all* written work should be a basic factor in all program planning.

A Spelling Program Plan

As has been stated, the spelling program in a specified classroom is often largely determined by the textbook or other materials. Most commercial spelling textbooks make use of one of two basic plans. These plans are usually called the *test–study* and *study–test* plans. We believe that evidence clearly favors the test–study plan as the most efficient and satisfactory approach because it focuses on individual differences among pupils and because it fosters positive attitudes by requiring pupils to study only those words they do not know how to spell. The test–study plan consists of these features:

Children learn to spell many words from their reading; therefore, they may know how to spell many of the lesson words.

1. A test is given at the beginning of the term or month to determine the general level of spelling achievement of the class and of individuals in the class. This can be constructed by randomly selecting words from the lessons to be covered during the term or month. Select as many words as the pupils can attempt without becoming

overtired or losing interest (usually 20 to 25 words are enough).

2. Pupils may be grouped for instruction on the basis of the preliminary test, or individualized teaching may be planned. For example, high achievers may be released from spelling instruction for other activities and low achievers may be assigned other materials, given fewer words, or provided with planned, individualized study help.

3. The weekly assignment begins with a test. This permits you and each child to determine the specific words that require study. You may want to precede this test (perhaps only occasionally) by pronouncing the words and having the pupils pronounce them. If you think there are words whose meanings are not known, these may be discussed. However, this is usually not necessary if the words have been selected properly.

4. The words that each pupil misspells on the pretest are identified by the child (see the following section on the weekly spelling lesson) and become his or her study list for the lesson.

5. In studying each word the children use the steps that have been worked out by the class, or by you and individual children if modifications in the class steps seem to be necessary.

6. A final weekly or lesson test is used to determine the degree of mastery each child has achieved (a mid-week test is also usually advisable, since attempting to spell—trying to recall—for a test is a good learning procedure).

7. Each child keeps a personal record of spelling achievement on a chart or similar device.

8. To prepare for reviewing, each child records in a notebook all words misspelled on the final test. Review words are studied using the steps followed in studying new words.

9. Each child is tested on the words in his or her review list at regular intervals until these words have truly been mastered.

10. A final term or monthly test is given to measure the progress made since the administration of the first test. This test may be a sampling of the words or it may include all of the words taught during the period of time (perhaps in more than one sitting).

Research shows that no more than 75 minutes per week should be devoted to direct spelling instruction.

A good instructional plan in spelling also provides for children correcting their own tests and for giving most tests in list form. Having pupils correct their own tests makes the testing a learning experience, for pupils see exactly what mistakes they made. Having the test corrected by another pupil or by you practically eliminates the possibility of any learning occurring from the procedure.

Some variation in testing is useful. For example, you may dictate sentences, each containing a spelling word, or perhaps a paragraph containing several or all of the words in a lesson. However, the difficulty with this form of testing is that other words used may not be known by the children. Thus, the list test should be used most often because it is economical of time and focuses upon the objective of learning to spell the words in the lesson.

The Weekly Lesson

The spelling of a word important in most writing should be taught whenever the opportunity to do so occurs. However, it is also wise to have regular spelling lessons. The following describes the principal features of a five-day lesson plan. The weekly lesson might be done in three days by including the second day's activities with those given for the first day and the fourth day's activities with those of the third day. Too, some children may not need all of the visual and auditory impression activities and, as suggested in the preceding section, especially good spellers may need little or none of the weekly program.

First Day.   Administration of a pretest of the words in the lesson (pronouncing the word, using it in a sentence, and pronouncing again); checking the test (each pupil checking his or her own); making individual study lists of words misspelled; discussing the words as necessary—their meanings and use, any unusual spellings, the application of any rules, or etymological matters that are appropriate and of interest.

Second Day.   Visual and auditory study of structural and phonemic elements in the words; direct study of the words on individual spelling lists.

Third Day.   Administration of a test (usually including all words in the lesson as a means of ensuring that guessing did not account for some correct spelling on the pretest); checking the test, again each pupil checking his or her own; studying the words misspelled.

Fourth Day.   Continued practice in visual-aural analysis of the words; learning new meanings for the words; extending word knowledge through practice in using linguistic principles; studying words misspelled on the third-day test.

Fifth Day.   Administration of the final test; checking the tests, still with each pupil checking his or her own; writing words in a review list; marking achievement on a progress chart.

In addition, time may be given as it is available to practice in using the dictionary, to engaging in vocabulary building exercises, and to participation in games and enrichment activities. Some study of language, particularly of word origins, is also appropriate for inclusion in the lesson as time permits.

Grouping for Instruction

The above lesson outline indicates that much of the learning and teaching effort is individualized; for example, each pupil makes his own study list, each pupil studies the words he misspells individually, each pupil writes his own review words, and each pupil marks his own progress chart. However, the plan does not indicate how to go about grouping for instruction.

Actually, grouping is not difficult. It may be done in a manner similar to that used for reading or for mathematics instruction. The first step should be administering a quarterly, semester, or yearly pretest of 25 to 75 words (depending on the ability of the pupils to handle the mechanics of writing). The words on this test should be randomly selected from the words for the particular quarter, semester, or year. Children who misspell none or very few of these may be considered the high achievers; those who misspell 10 to 50 percent should be considered the average group; and those who misspell more than half of the words should be considered the slow group. Some teachers make the average group larger than suggested and limit the slow group to only a few pupils.

The high and average groups should be given all of the words in a lesson, though some enrichment words may be added to the list for the high group if they are carefully selected because of their need in writing.

Pupils' Study Procedures

There is general agreement among spelling authorities that the spelling of a word is learned by a series of steps involving impression and recall. The impression or image steps generally include visual, auditory, and kinesthetic impression. The recall steps usually suggest "seeing" the word in the mind and then writing from memory. Children who are very good in spelling can often learn a new word after seeing it only once; hence the other steps may not be necessary. The poorer spellers need help and encouragement in learning the steps and putting them into practice. They may also need to have the steps individualized by the addition of extra ones to help them say the words properly or to gain better visual, auditory, or kinesthetic impressions.

The following method of study is suggested as suitable for most children. You may wish to modify it in some manner for your class, but keep in mind that alternating impression and recall procedures are needed.

Learning to spell is a series of

impression

recall

impression

recall

1. Look at the word carefully and pronounce it correctly. Say it slowly, naturally, and clearly, looking at it as you say it.
2. Cover the word with your hand or close your eyes. Say the word and think how it looks. Try to visualize exactly the way the word is written as you say each letter in sequence to yourself.
3. Look at the word again to be sure that you said it and spelled it correctly. If you did not, start again at 1.
4. Cover the word and then write it, thinking carefully about how it looks.
5. Check your spelling. If you misspelled the word, begin again at 1. If you spelled the word correctly, go on to the next word.

Practices to Avoid

There are a number of practices sometimes used by teachers that should be avoided. Often these are used because the teacher is frustrated or simply does not know they are of no value or may be harmful. For example, calling attention to possible "hard spots" in words may implant a spelling difficulty that could be avoided through a positive approach to learning. The practice of "writing" words in the air is also sometimes done in an effort to give children a kinesthetic–tactile impression of words. This is not a valid procedure, since to give a true kinesthetic–tactile impression of a word, the shape of letters should be felt (in sand or on chalkboard) and the muscle movement should be approximately that used when the word is actually written.

Sometimes teachers have a child write a word ten or some other number of times without intervening attempts at recall. Simply copying a word is not likely to make a permanent impression. This practice is related to the less frequently used one of assigning the studying or writing of spelling words as a form of punishment. Neither practice does much to promote positive attitudes toward spelling, nor does reprimanding children for asking how to spell a word.

Even spelling words orally for a child is not good practice, because it ignores the importance of a visual impression to learning. Instead of spelling orally, write the word asked for on the board or on a slip of paper.

ISSUES PERTINENT TO SPELLING INSTRUCTION

There are some questions about spelling instruction that require particular attention. Some of these questions are related to activities not helpful in accomplishing the objectives of a good spelling program. The fact that they are used is frequently the result of the commercial materials in the classroom—materials that have either ignored or misunderstood research on spelling instruction.

Linguistics and the Program

The recent interest in linguistics and its relationship to spelling has centered around the extent of the correspondence between the speech sounds and the letters used to represent them in writing. Studies have shown that each sound is represented by a particular letter (or, in some cases, a group of two or more letters) more frequently than any other letter. For example, one researcher who tabulated the representations given to the sounds in a 10,000 word vocabulary reported that "the k sound is spelled with c 64.36 percent and the s sound with s 71.19 percent of the time."[5] The importance of such information to the spelling program is debatable, however. Some authorities stress the "regularity" of sound and symbol relationships (generally termed phoneme–grapheme correspondence), while others stress the exceptions to correspondence, particularly as they are present in the most frequently written words.

It is important to remember that some sounds are represented by a single letter or a cluster of letters with a great deal of regularity (the b sound, for example), but that others, particularly vowel sounds, are represented by many letters. There are certain word patterns that are important for pupils to know. For example, pupils should learn that *bed* fits a pattern like *red, fed,* and *led* and should not be spelled *bede.* They must also learn, however, that the same vowel sound occurs in *head* and *said* but is represented differently.

There is frequently confusion about phonic or phoneme/grapheme generalizations taught in reading instruction and their application to spelling. For example, teaching children that "when there are two vowels, one of which is final *e,* the first vowel is usually long and the *e* is silent" (*bake, tone, fine*) is helpful to them as they *look* at the word and seek to pronounce it as an aid to getting the meaning of what they are reading. However, in thinking of the word as they are writing, or in hearing it, there is *no clue* as to whether the word has two vowels, whether there is an *e* on the end, or whether the vowel sound is represented by a letter or letters. This is only one example; there are many others that you will want to think about as you consider reading instruction in chapter 14. The point to remember is that *reading is a language receiving* act and *spelling is a language expressing* act.

There are, though, some warranted conclusions regarding the phoneme–grapheme correspondence issue that can be useful in teaching children to spell.

1. Instruction in both the consistencies and inconsistencies of phoneme–grapheme relationships should be a part of every spelling program.
2. Instruction in generalizations or "rules" concerning spelling patterns or sound-to-letter association should focus on those that occur in a considerable number of words and have few exceptions.

Spelling Sound-Alikes

Some possessive pronouns sound exactly like other words. Although they sound alike, they are different in other ways.

- Read the following sentences.

    Jane and Eddie wrote their report.
    Now they're finished with the typing.
    The children put the report over there.

How are the underlined words different? *Their, they're* and *their* are different in two ways. They have different spellings and different meanings.

    Their shows what two people have. It is a possessive pronoun.
    They're is a short way of writing they are.
    There means in that place.
    Words like their, they're, and there are homonyms.

    Homonyms are words that sound alike but have different spellings and different meanings.

- Read the following sentences.

    Is this your magazine?
    You're welcome to read it.

Do the sentences give you a clue to their meanings? *Your* shows what you have. It is a possessive pronoun. *You're* is a short way of writing *you are*.

- Now read these sentences.

    This television has its own antenna.
    But it's broken.

In the first sentence above, *its* means *belonging* to it. In the second sentence *it's* is a short way of writing *it is*.

126   SPELLING: *Homonyms*

Knowing the meanings and spellings of homonyms is often a problem for children. From *Macmillan English,* Series E, Grade 5 by Tina Thoburn et al. Copyright © 1979 Macmillan Publishing Co., Inc. Used by permission of the publisher.

3. Instruction in sound and symbol correspondence must recognize that there are dialect differences in many classrooms and that the pronunciation of many words, even by the same individual, varies with the context in which they are used.
4. Linguistic principles should be regarded as aids to spelling rather than as substitutes for teaching pupils to study the lesson words directly.
5. Most persons have learned to make application of many phoneme–grapheme correspondences from their reading and spelling instruction. Thus it appears that generalizations which are useful are learned quite easily. Programs that rely heavily upon learning many generalizations may result in the formal teaching of rules, which may be misapplied as well as correctly applied.

Interest in using linguistic knowledge in the spelling program is not limited to phoneme–grapheme associations. For example, language study includes determining the origin and history of words. Children are interested in the way language developed, the origins of particular words, words that have traveled to English from a foreign language, etc.[6] There are also linguistic principles to be observed in forming compound words, in affixing, and in dividing words into syllables, although these are not really new and are included in most reading and spelling programs.

Spelling Rules and Generalizations

While a number of generalizations may be taught, the following have few exceptions and should definitely be learned by each pupil. They should not be taught in such a way that the child simply learns to say the rule but then has difficulty in making use of it when he or she attempts to spell a word. Rather, these rules should be presented during lessons on words to which they apply. The child then learns the pattern and internalizes the generalization. Other practices that should be observed are teaching only one rule at a time, showing exceptions to rules as they are taught, reviewing rules frequently, and being alert to opportunities to show the application of the rules previously taught.

1. Words ending in a silent *e* usually drop this *e* before a suffix beginning with a vowel (*make-making*) but keep the *e* before a suffix beginning with a consonant (*time-timely*).
2. For words ending in a consonant and *y*, change the *y* to *i* before adding a suffix, unless the suffix begins with *i* (*candy—candies; baby—babying*).
3. Words ending in a vowel and *y* do not change the *y* to *i* when adding a suffix (*play—played; enjoy—enjoying*).
4. Words of one syllable or words accented on the last syllable, ending in a single consonant preceded by a single vowel, double the final consonant when adding a suffix beginning with a vowel (*run—running; begin—beginning; need—needed*).
5. The letter *q* is always followed by *u* in common English words (*quite, quart*).
6. English words do not end with *v* (*believe; give*).
7. Proper nouns and most adjectives formed from proper nouns begin with capital letters (*France; French*).

Rules concerning the use of the apostrophe are also useful, since improper use of the apostrophe is the cause of many spelling errors. The following are helpful rules:

1. The possessive of a singular noun (including those ending in *s*, *z*, *ss*, or *x*) is formed by adding an apostrophe and *s*. *

John's idea	Congress's action
father's hat	box's top
Ms. Jones's house	Buzz's pitch

2. The possessive of a plural noun ending in *s* is formed by adding an apostrophe.

girls' coats	Matthewses' relatives
Smiths' house	states' rights

3. The possessive of a plural noun not ending in *s* is formed by adding an apostrophe and *s*.

women's hats	data's use
teeth's whiteness	children's books

4. Personal pronouns do not take the apostrophe to show possession.

his	theirs
hers	whose
its	

5. Pronouns that are not ordinarily possessive show possession by adding an apostrophe and *s*.

someone's coat	each other's dog
everyone's house	another's name

6. An apostrophe is used to indicate missing letters in contractions, letters omitted to show speech, and the missing part of a date.

'ere's to you	your 'ome
don't (do not)	we'll (we will)
it's (it is)	you're (you are)
the winter of '92	the class of '72

There are rules regarding the formation of plural forms that are also useful:

1. Plurals of most nouns are formed by adding *s* to the singular.

boy—boys   book—books

2. When a noun ends in *s*, *x*, *sh*, or *ch*, the plural is generally formed by adding *es*.

buses	bushes
foxes	churches

3. A noun ending in *y* preceded by a consonant forms its plural by changing the *y* to *i* and adding *es*. Words ending in *y* preceded by a vowel do not change *y* to *i*.

body—bodies   boy—boys

---

*It is also correct to simply add an apostrophe to singular nouns ending in *s* (e.g., Ms. Jones' house). However, it is simpler for children to learn one rule than two.

4. Plurals of a few nouns are made by changing their forms.

woman—women   mouse—mice   scarf—scarves

Integrating Spelling and Writing

Although a major objective is to teach each child to spell correctly all words that he writes, it is even more important to teach him to be *concerned* with spelling correctly. When children write imaginatively they want to get their ideas on paper before they are lost, and in their enthusiasm for writing, they frequently use—or

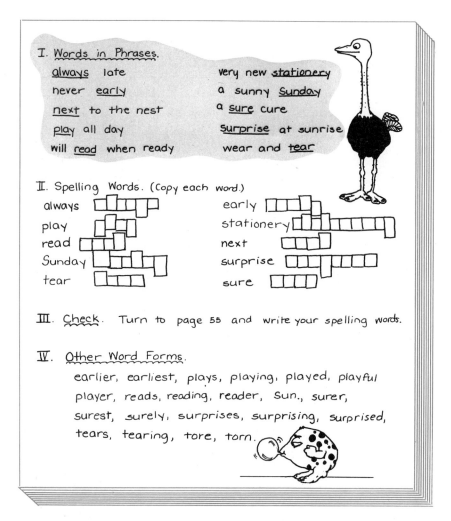

I. <u>Words in Phrases</u>.
<u>always</u> late   very new <u>stationery</u>
never <u>early</u>   a sunny <u>Sunday</u>
<u>next</u> to the nest   a <u>sure</u> cure
<u>play</u> all day   <u>Surprise</u> at sunrise
will <u>read</u> when ready   wear and <u>tear</u>

II. Spelling Words. (Copy each word.)
always   early
play   stationery
read   next
Sunday   surprise
tear   sure

III. <u>Check</u>.   Turn to page 55 and write your spelling words.

IV. <u>Other Word Forms</u>.
earlier, earliest, plays, playing, played, playful player, reads, reading, reader, Sun., surer, surest, surely, surprises, surprising, surprised, tears, tearing, tore, torn.

Children need to learn to spell derivatives of base words. This lesson also emphasizes visual impressions. (A part of Lesson 22 in *Spelling Words in Use* by G. Willard Woodruff and George N. Moore. Curriculum Associates, 1977, p. 46. Used with permission.)

want to use—words they do not know how to spell. This is a problem that every child and every teacher faces. Certainly it is more important to get the child's expression on paper than it is to have him spell every word he writes correctly. Too, since many of us do not always spell correctly in our first drafts, it makes sense to permit a child to do so as well. For example, permit children to write only the first letters of the words they cannot spell or simply draw a line to show where a word was left out. In addition, you can help forestall spelling problems by listing on the board words that the children may want to use, by permitting children to ask one another for help—if they can do so without interfering with the other child's writing—and by encouraging them to use a dictionary, pictionary, file of words, or textbook to find the word they want to use. Help children yourself with words they cannot spell if their other efforts fail or if their thinking seems to be stymied by a spelling problem.

Encouraging the children to experiment with problem spelling words by writing them on scratch paper to see if they recognize the correct spelling is also helpful. You should have the children proofread the final draft of their writing, but be careful of penalties, such as not putting a story on the board if it has misspelled words or requiring recopying. In some cases these things may work; in others the next attempt at writing will produce poorer results. The important concern in all writing is to get ideas on paper first, and then to give attention to sentence structure, vocabulary, mechanics, and spelling, so that the finished product will be as effective as possible.

Special Spelling Problems

Some words are frequently misspelled (these are the "demons" that most teachers know about) and will require persistent effort from you. There are reasons for the persistence of their difficulty, however, as discussed below.

Many words are misspelled because the children do not know or do not apply the rules that are workable, do not understand the use of the apostrophe, fail to capitalize properly, or do not have the linguistic knowledge they should have (for example, how compounds are formed). Here are some that are frequently misspelled:

Note:

Attention to "correct" pronunciation must take into account dialect differences as they are shown in pronunciations —e.g., some people give the vowels in *naughty* and *knotty* the same sound.

coming	its	Sunday
didn't	it's	that's
don't	getting	tried
I'll	sometimes	truly
I'm	studying	writing

Homonyms also often cause difficulty. For pupils to learn these requires that meanings be thoroughly taught and that visual images be gained. Spelling authorities disagree about whether homonyms should be taught together. We believe that for the first instruction they usually should not. However, since much review of them is necessary, they should be presented together in the review to emphasize the differences:

there	hear	your
their	here	you're

they're	four	write
	for	right
two		
to	buy	piece
too	by	peace
know	some	our
no	sum	are

Improper pronunciation is a frequent cause of errors. Such words as *and, going, third, ask, today, Saturday, pretty, hundred, kept, been, library, children, desk,* etc., are pronunciation and spelling problems for some children.

Phoneme–grapheme irregularity which results in misspelling because of the misapplication of a generalization is also a problem. Commonly written words that fall into this category include:

ache	believe	enough	thirty
across	birthday	friend	though
afraid	build	guess	thought
again	color	heard	tonight
among	could	one	very
answer	cousin	sure	were
beautiful	decide	the	when
because	does	they	women

The following list of spelling "demons" has been developed from studies of misspellings of elementary school children. These words are important and should be learned by every pupil.

about	because	December
address	been	didn't
afraid	before	different
afternoon	birthday	dog
again	bought	doing
all right	boy	don't
along	boys	down
already	brother	
always	brought	Easter
am		enough
an	can	every
and	cannot	everybody
answer	can't	
anything	children	
anyway	Christmas	father
April	close	February
are	clothes	fine
arithmetic	come	first
aunt	coming	football
awhile	couldn't	for
	cousin	fourth
		Friday
baby		friend
balloon	daddy	friends
basketball	day	from

front
fun

getting
goes
going
good
good-bye (good-by)
grade
guess
guest

had
Halloween
handkerchiefs
has
have
haven't
having
he
hear
hello
her
here
his
home
hope
hospital
house
how
how's
hundred

I'll
I'm
in
isn't
it
it's
its
I've

January
just

knew
know

lessons
letter
like
likes
little
lots

loving

made
make
maybe
me
Miss
morning
mother
Mr.
Mrs.
much
my

name
nice
Nov.
now
nowadays

o'clock
October
off
on
once
one
our
out
outside

party
people
play
played
plays
please
pretty

quit
quite

receive
received
remember
right

said
Santa Claus
Saturday
saw
school
send
sent
sincerely

snow
snowman
some
something
sometime
sometimes
soon
stationery
store
studying
summer
Sunday
suppose
sure
surely
swimming

teacher
teacher's
Thanksgiving
that's
the
their
them
then
there
there's
they
they're
think

thought
through
time
to
today
together
tomorrow
tonight
too
toys
train
truly
two

until

vacation
very

want
was
weather
well
went

we're	with	you
were	won't	young
when	would	your
whether	write	yours
white	writing	
will		

Enrichment Activities

Spelling programs can be enlivened through the use of the games and other activities directed at learning the words in the spelling lessons and at building vocabularies. Activities and games are useful for motivating pupils, caring for individual differences, and providing variety in the program.

Vocabulary

Vocabulary-building activities are suggested in chapter 13. For additional activities, look in commercial vocabulary and spelling materials. These can often be used at times appropriate to your program rather than at times indicated by the order in which they occur in a book.

Activities that build interest in words, help to teach spelling, and have appeal to children include finding substitutes for such overworked words as *awful, funny, scared, pretty, good, nice, real,* and *sure;* synonyms for such words as *small, cold, sad, big, work, see, happy, strong,* and *tired;* and homonyms for *blue, do, fair, great, hail, made, pain, rain, read, sew, sight, tail, whose, wait,* and *pause.* These can be found and put on charts by individual pupils or groups, or the project can involve the entire class.

In a like manner, antonyms may be collected (try finding them for *rise, new, bottom, full, empty, colder, front, never, short,* etc.), lists can be made of words that have the same root *(report, portable, import, portage, portly)*, and words that have more than one acceptable spelling can be found *(judgment, judgement; gayly, gaily; driest, dryest).*

Exercises can be made which ask pupils to build compound words from other words. Words to start with might include *day, news, hall, base, stand, light, band, paper, ball,* and *way.* Or you might have the children form plurals for irregular words, such as *wife, foot, mouse, leaf, woman, man,* and *calf.*

Children can become quite interested in words because of their origins, their forms, or changes that have occurred in them. For example, they might be asked to find the origins of such words as *braille, boycott, vandal, cologne, maverick,* and *nicotine.* They might also enjoy tracing the origins of words from other languages *(cipher, kimono, oasis, parka, pretzel)* or compound words *(warehouse, chairman, downtown, statehouse).*

Other interesting activities include seeing how many uses can be found for such common words as *run, head,* or *board;* finding words with different sounds represented by the same letter or letters *(enough, though; graph, rough; taught, taut);* discovering different ways in which the same meaning is expressed in various parts of the world where English is spoken *(lift* for *elevator, petrol* for

Tired Words and Good Ones to Use

awful—horrible, dreadful
funny—humorous, strange
pretty—considerably, fairly
good—suitable, valuable
nice—pleasant, neat
real—genuine, actual
sure—certain, steady

Be certain that you use each word correctly.

A Chart Idea

Do You Know These Compound Words?

airbus
audiotape
fastback
hovercraft
skateboard
trendsetter

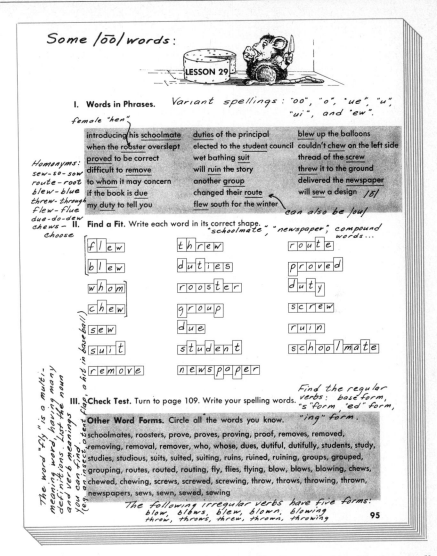

This series gives attention to building on base words. (From *Working Words in Spelling*, Level E, Teacher's Edition. Copyright 1977 by Curriculum Associates, Inc. Used by permission of the publisher.)

gasoline, *lorry* for *truck*, and *sweets* for *dessert* in England; *tap* for *faucet* in Canada, etc.); and finding new words that have been added to the language and determining why they were created.*

---

* *Compton's Encyclopaedia Yearbook* contains a list of new words and meanings for them with each year's edition.

Games

Games should not replace direct study of words, because direct study is a better use of a pupil's time in achieving the objectives of the program. However, games interest children, build class spirit, and provide a break in routine. If games are used they should be ones that call for the children to write words (reinforcement of learning) rather than spelling them orally (which is an unlife-like activity). Here are some games that might be used.

More Than One.   Say the following words. Have the children raise their hands when the word you say means more than one.

boy	*letters*	*arms*
boys	*three*	bed
toy	green	*cakes*
top	letter	flower
toys	schools	*elephants*
girl	*apples*	*trees*
school	book	table
books	rabbit	*stars*
girls	apple	*hills*
tops	horse	hole

Stand-Up.   Divide the class into three or four teams. Assign each team one of these letters: *b, f, h, t, m.* Read the following list of words. A member of each team stands up whenever a word is read that begins with that team's letter. If a team member stands when the word does not begin with the team's letter, that member and another must sit down. The team that has all of its members standing first is the winner.

kite	*toad*	cook	clothes	us	*milk*
baby	*hear*	ate	*fairy*	*mouse*	got
old	*fat*	beach	cave	yet	*feet*
face	any	*fire*	*happy*	moon	bed
hand	*bad*	grass	*two*	write	bear
top	across	*her*	arm	tiger	*fire*
get	*feather*	did	*must*	*heel*	hit
my	wing	teacher	bag	wood	met
back	*hard*	*mile*	move	won	garden
clay	very	hen	*airplane*	fed	took
	today	ten	all	*ball*	

Spelling Ball.   Spelling ball is an adaptation of baseball. Divide the class into two teams. Place a chair in each corner of the room to serve as home plate and first, second, and third bases. Select a pitcher for each team.

The team at bat lines up at home plate. The pitcher of the opposing team asks the first batter to come to the board and write one of the new words. A correct spelling is a hit, and moves the player to first base; an incorrect spelling is an out. A player on first base advances to second if a succeeding batter makes a hit, and so on until a run is scored. When a team makes three outs, the opposing team lines up to take its turn. The team with the highest number of runs at the end of the game wins. If the words become too easy for the children, have the pitcher use words from previous lessons.

Team Spelling.   Divide the class into two teams. Give each pupil a card bearing a letter used in one of the spelling words. When you say a new word, both teams spell the word by placing themselves in proper position. The team that spells the word first scores one point. Continue in this manner until all the new words have been used. The team with the most points wins. (Note: Be sure to provide two cards for each team for any letter that is used more than once in a word.)

Getting Ahead.   Arrange a group of children in random order. Pronounce a spelling word to each one in turn. Continue in this manner without correcting misspellings. If a pupil in the group recognizes a misspelling and is able to correct it, he or she goes to the head of the group. The object is for each pupil to try to remain at the head of the group.

Spelling Row.   Place the children in five or six equal rows. Pronounce a spelling word to the first row. The first child says the first letter, the second child says the second letter, and so on until the word has been spelled. The next group is asked another spelling word. The children in the second row respond in the same manner. This procedure is continued for each row. For each letter omitted or every word misspelled, a team is given one point. The team with the fewest points wins. It may be necessary to regroup occasionally in order for the children at the end of a row to have an opportunity to participate. (Or begin at one end for the first round, the opposite end for the second, and so on.)

Try having the better spellers make crossword puzzles using words from the spelling lesson or other words that they might have occasion to write. Some commercial materials can provide puzzle models.

Spelling Circle.   Have the children form a large circle. One child is "It." He or she walks around the circle, stops in front of another pupil, and asks this pupil to spell one of the new words. If the pupil spells the word correctly, he or she becomes the new "It." The spelling words can be written on a small piece of paper and passed on to each "It."

Spelling Hunt.   Write the spelling words on slips of paper. Fold these and place them in a box. Ask one pupil at a time to take a slip. The child hands the paper to the teacher, who pronounces the word and asks the pupil to write it on the board. If the child misses the word, he takes the paper and studies it.

Spelling Sitdown.   The spelling sitdown is played in the same manner as a spelling bee, except that the children who spell the words correctly take their seats. The team that has the fewest members standing wins. (The spelling may also be done by writing responses on the board. Children at their seats may write the words you pronounce on paper.)

Rhyming Words.   Have one child stand in front of the room and say, "I am thinking of a spelling word that rhymes with tack." The other children try to spell the correct word. The one who spells it correctly has the next turn. The words should be written on the chalkboard.

Pyramids.   Starting with a vowel, have children take turns adding one letter at a time so that a word is spelled with each addition.

a	o	e
at	on	be
ate	one	bee
late	tone	been
later	stone	

Children can work singly or in groups. The objective is to see who can make the longest list of correctly spelled words within a given time.

Spelling Match.   Divide the class into six equal groups. Have members of each group number off (1, 2, 3, 4, etc.). Have the 1's go to the board and write as you pronounce several words. Correct their spelling and tally the number of misspelled words. Then the 2's go to the board and write an equal number of words. These words are checked and scored. When all the members have had a chance to write, scores are checked and the group with the fewest misspelled words wins.

Think and Spell.   Have one pupil stand in front of the class and say, "I am thinking of a spelling word that ends with an *e*." (Words from a single spelling lesson should be used for this.) The children who know the answer raise their hands. One child is called on to write the word on the chalkboard. If he writes the word correctly, he becomes the leader.

Crosswords.   One child on a team begins by writing a word he or she knows on the board. This child then asks another to spell a word that begins with the last letter of his or her word. Continue this, giving a point to the opposite team when a pupil cannot think of a word or misspells one.

Spelling Play.   Have a pupil dramatize the meaning of a spelling word. The player then chooses someone to write the word. The pupil who writes the word correctly takes the next turn and acts out another word.

Guessing.   Choose one child to write a new word on the chalkboard and cover it with one hand. The child then chooses a classmate to guess which word was written. The child who is chosen says, "Did you write *m-i-s-s miss?*" "No, I did not write *m-i-s-s miss.*" Another child is chosen and the same procedure followed until the correct word is guessed. The child who guesses correctly writes the next word on the board.

Spin and Spell.   Make a large clock face with a moveable hand. Number the face from 1 to 9 (a number for each spelling word). A pupil is called on to spin the hand and read the number to which the hand points. The child then must write the word that corresponds to the number. You should have a numbered list, so children do not have to memorize the order of the words.

Word Endings.   Write on the board a number of words from which new words can be made by adding the endings *-ed, -er,* and *-ing.* See which children can make the longest lists of new words. Let the children compare their lists in order to prevent the learning of nonsense words. This may be made more challenging by including the possibility of adding prefixes as well as endings. Words that might be written include: *bring, clean, do, eat, end, grow, late, like, pen, play,* and *walk.*

Add-a-Letter.   Divide the class into several equal teams. As you pronounce a word, the first member of each team goes to the board and writes the first letter of the word, then runs back and gives the chalk to the second member. This child then writes the second letter, and so on until the word is completed. The team that finishes first gets five points, the second four points, etc. One point is subtracted for each incorrect or unreadable letter. The team with the highest score wins.

New Words.   One pupil starts the game by writing a base (root) word on the chalkboard (such as *write*) and then asks who can spell a word that has this word as a base (e.g., *writing, writer*). He or she calls on one pupil, who comes to the board and writes the new word. If the new word is written correctly, this pupil writes the next base word.

Other Activities

Dictionary Challenges

How many can you find?
1. Synonyms for smart.
2. Meanings for dark.
3. Adjectives that describe food.

- Playing word games such as Scrabble and anagrams.
- Providing riddles that can be answered with words from a list.
- Providing crossword puzzles and having children make puzzles for classmates to work.
- Finding the histories of words such as *desperado, digit, festival,* and *vocation.*
- Rewriting trite sentences using more interesting and specific words.
- Reporting on new words added to the language because of the space program, computer technology, environmental problems, etc.
- Making charts of synonyms, antonyms, contractions, abbreviations, or some other category.
- Having groups or individual children find words for various categories such as food words, TV words, words about our city, or holiday words.
- Using words in some form of creative writing. For example, children might write a story using *bronco, radar, calico, lizard,* and *desert.*
- Making individual graphs of spelling progress; making lists of words that are difficult; making lists of new words to learn to spell.
- Finding modifications of spelling in newspapers, TV advertisements, and signs.
- Making a word–picture dictionary.
- Searching for the origins of surnames (they are usually related to places or occupations).
- Writing descriptions of objects, using as many new descriptive words as possible and using them accurately.

Evaluating Spelling Achievement

Evaluation should begin with examining goals. As was pointed out earlier, the goals of a desirable spelling program are to create a number of attitudes, habits, abilities, and skills and to teach the spelling of a basic core of words. Each child's ability to spell the assigned words on the basic list can be evaluated by you during the year the child is in your classroom, but a true evaluation of many of the attitudes, habits, abilities, and skills cannot be made until after more than two or three years of spelling instruction. However, the difficulties involved in evaluating all the goals of your program completely should not deter you from making some attempt to evaluate each one. Of course, the child's ability to spell the words in the basic list in all of his or her writing is a good indication of the attainment of the other goals.

Tests

Test for

1. General spelling ability of class before teaching (a test using a few words from each lesson).
2. Study needs and achievement by giving a pretest and a final test in the weekly program.
3. Individual progress on review words.
4. Mastery of special words (from unit, other subjects, contractions, etc.).
5. Progress and achievement at end of month, semester, or year.

Children's ability to spell the words in a basic list can be measured in several ways.

- The regular teaching program should include several weekly tests, perhaps monthly tests, and a test at the end of each term. Each of these tests should include only the words the children should have learned (or a sampling of them) during the particular time period. Provision should also be made to test words learned earlier (including previous grade levels). The form of these tests should be that suggested earlier for the weekly lesson.
- A standard spelling scale can be used to compare the spelling of your class with that of children of the same grade level as reported in the scale. The only usable spelling scale today is *The New Iowa Spelling Scale* (Bureau of Educational Research, University of Iowa, Iowa City, Iowa), which lists the percentage of children in grades 2–8 who spelled each of 5,500 words correctly.
- Testing through the spelling section of standardized achievement tests provides limited measures of spelling ability. The form of most tests is one of recognition rather than recall, and there are so few words tested that the results are useful only as guides.

Checklists

A checklist or similar device can help to systematize evaluation of children's attitudes, habits, and abilities. For example:

November Name	Proof- reads spelling pages	Proof- reads other work	Uses diction- ary	Uses study proce- dure	Uses gener- aliza- tions
Bill	no	no	no	no	sometimes
Roy	✓	?	✓	no	✓
Mary	✓	✓	✓	✓	no
Julie	✓	✓	some- times	✓	✓

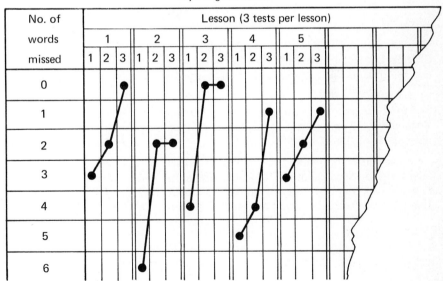

Pupil Self-Evaluation

Pupils should participate in the process of evaluation whenever possible. Some ways in which they can do so are the following:

Children like to see the progress they are making.

- Keep individual progress charts of scores made on spelling tests.
- Keep progress charts on written activities that contain misspellings. For example, the number of words misspelled per 50 or 100 words written may be recorded periodically.
- Keep a record of the proofreading of their written work.
- Correct their own spelling tests and analyze the errors made.
- Keep individual spelling lists of words misspelled in their writing.
- Participate in class discussions of spelling achievement.

A FINAL WORD

The systematic teaching of spelling remains an important part of the elementary school language arts program. However, instructional attention must also be given throughout the school day. Developing attitudes of concern for correctly spelling each word written should receive equal emphasis with the direct teaching of a basic core of important words. A carefully constructed program based upon the suggestions offered here will result in effective learning in your classroom.

ENDNOTES

1. Ves Thomas, "The Basic Writing Vocabulary of Elementary School Children," *The Alberta Journal of Educational Research* 18: 4 (December 1972), 243–248.

2. Sigmund Folger, "The Case for a Basic Written Vocabulary," *Elementary School Journal* 47 (September 1946), 43–47.

3. This list was compiled by the authors from various sources. Studies of basic words are summarized in J. Stephen Sherwin, *Four Problems in Teaching English: A Critique of Research* (Scranton, PA: International Textbook Company, 1969).

4. A recently published review of research on the teaching of spelling is Ruel A. Allred, *Spelling, The Application of Research Findings* (Washington, DC: National Education Association, The Curriculum Series, 1974).

5. Ernest Horn, "Phonetics and Spelling," *The Elementary School Journal*, May 1957, p. 431.

6. See chapter 13 for suggestions of things to do.

REFERENCES

Books

Allred, Ruel A. *Spelling, The Application of Research Findings*. Washington, DC: National Education Association, The Curriculum Series, 1974.

Boyd, Gertrude A., and Talbert, F. Gene. *Spelling in the Elementary School.* Columbus, OH: Charles E. Merrill Publishing Co., 1971.

Horn, Thomas D., ed. *Research on Handwriting and Spelling.* Urbana, IL: National Council of Teachers of English, 1966.

Lutz, Jack. *Expanding Spelling Skills.* Dansville, NY: The Instructor Publications, Inc., 1973.

Petty, Walter T., and Jensen, Julie M. *Developing Children's Language.* Boston: Allyn and Bacon, Inc., 1980, chapter 15.

Thomas, Ves. *Teaching Spelling, Canadian Word Lists and Instructional Techniques.* Toronto: Gage Educational Publishing, Limited, 1974.

Films

Spelling for Beginners. Chicago: Coronet Instructional Media (11 minute color or b/w; primary).

Spelling Is Important. Mount Vernon, NY: Macmillan Films (18 minutes; middle grades).

Filmstrips

Discovering Spelling Patterns. New York: McGraw-Hill Films (Set of 36 strips; intermediate).

New Spelling Goals. New York: McGraw-Hill Films (Set of 7 strips; primary).

Spelling. Santa Monica, CA: BFA Educational Media (2 strips; intermediate).

Words: Their Origin, Use, and Spelling. Chicago: Society for Visual Education (Set of 6 color strips; intermediate).

Recordings

Spelling. Baltimore: Media Materials (cassettes, worksheets, teacher's guide).

Spelling Patterns. St. Paul, MN: 3M Company (10 cassettes with worksheets; intermediate).

Spelling Progress Laboratory. Tulsa, OK: Educational Progress (audio tapes; identified as supplementing visual spelling programs).

Steps to Spelling Breakthrough. St. Paul, MN: EMC Corp. (3 levels; each has 8 cassettes, activities, teacher's guide).

Games

Dean, John F. *Games Make Spelling Fun.* San Francisco: Fearon Publishers, 1956.

ACTIVITIES FOR PRESERVICE TEACHERS

1. Test your own spelling ability by having someone test you on the list of spelling "demons" given in this chapter. List any you misspell and learn to spell them correctly. Continue to retake the test until you have mastered all the words.

2. Study teacher's manuals and advertising materials for several sets of spelling books to find answers to the following questions: How were the spelling words selected? What is the total number of words for each grade? Does the series use the test-study or study-test method? Are provisions made for good spellers and for poor ones? What activities are provided other than tests and direct study of words? Are study steps suggested?

3. Outline a spelling readiness program for a first grade. Include in your outline references to commercial or teacher-made materials you would use.

4. Select a spelling book for a grade of your choice and plan the spelling program for a week, basing it on one of the weekly lessons in the book. Show how you would provide for upper, average, and slow groups; in what ways you would use individualized instruction; how you would use activities in the book; what enrichment activities you would add; and how the lesson might be integrated with other subject areas or other areas of the language arts. Be sure to stay within suggested time limits, except possibly when integrating spelling with other areas.

5. If you were a fifth grade teacher and had several requests from parents that their children be given spelling homework, what would be your response? Plan what you would do in some detail and report this to the class.

6. Select several pages from a paper you have written and a letter or some other piece of personal writing you have done. Tabulate all the different words written and the number of times for each. Of the total number of different words, what percentage appear on the list of 300 basic words given in this chapter? What percentage of those used more than twice appear on the list?

ACTIVITIES FOR INSERVICE TEACHERS

1. Work out a plan—and then put it into operation—for improving the attitudes of pupils in your class toward spelling correctly all the words they write. Base your plan upon suggestions in this chapter.

2. Start a file of spelling games. The ones in this chapter can be the first ones in your file. Ask other teachers and look in other textbooks and in magazines for others.

3. Prepare a variety of materials for children who find spelling difficult. Letters cut out of wood, stiff paper, sandpaper, or felt are useful for a child to trace. A box of wet sand in which the child can write words also helps.

4. Prepare a notebook for yourself of materials designed to carry out the readiness activities suggested in this chapter. Index your notebook for speedy reference.

5. Prepare a card file of spelling puzzles, exercises, and games that children may do during free time.

6. Review the reading levels of children in your class. For example, list their names, reading scores (word attack, vocabulary, comprehension, total), and your observations on their reading so that the picture is before you. Then think of each child's spelling problems. Is there a relationship to reading ability? Do you need to modify or individualize the spelling tasks you have been giving some children?

INDEPENDENT ACTIVITIES FOR CHILDREN

1. Each child should keep his or her own list of spelling "demons"—words missed in writing activities or consistently misspelled in review lessons. He or she may study these during free time and practice using them in sentences.

2. Sheets can be prepared with questions, directions, and space for the child's responses. Such entries as the following might be on the exercise sheets:

   a. Change the first two letters of *fright* and write the new words (*bright, slight, flight*).
   b. Put prefixes before these words so that antonyms are formed:

   _____ clear   _____ true
   _____ spell   _____ correct
   _____ patient   _____ sense

   c. Write synonyms for these words:

   | *throw* | (*hurl, cast, pitch, toss*) |
   | *shut* | (*close, bar*) |

   d. How many compound words can you make by adding words to these words?

fire	(*fireman, fireplace, fireside*)
ball	(*baseball, football, basketball*)
man	(*fireman, chairman, mailman*)

3. Have the child prepare a chart for the bulletin board that lists the most commonly used contractions (*don't, aren't, can't, I'll*, etc.).

4. Prepare sentences with blanks that children can fill in with appropriate words from the spelling lesson—or several lessons.

5. Exercises can be prepared for children to work on independently. For example:

   a. Underline the silent letters:

knife	*gate*	*below*
jelly	*lock*	*pie*

   b. Underline the short vowels:

grant	*bred*	*sample*
rain	*basement*	*appoint*

   c. Write homonyms for these words:

creak	*herd*	*pour*
hole	*pleas*	*feat*
boll	*led*	*waist*

6. Prepare a number of cards, each with an interesting activity on it, from which children may select and do an assignment. Cards might have the following activities:

   a. Write the plurals of these words:

wolf	*woman*	*fish*
leaf	*sheep*	*church*
shoe		

   b. Rearrange the letters in each group and write the words:

lrig	*pllse*	*drow*	*eerd*

   c. Combine these words into compound words:

ball	*way*	*net*
fish	*door*	*foot*

   d. How many words can you write that begin with these letters?

cl	*st*	*gr*	*tr*	*bl*

7. A child can categorize words according to spelling patterns. Various patterns can be used. For example:

   a. words with a certain sequence of vowels and consonants (vcv—begin, major, music; vccv—summer, dollar, filled)
   b. words ending in -*ing* or -*ake* (sing, bring, thing; cake, lake, take); two-syllable words (later, truly, pilot)
   c. words that begin with a two-symbol consonant cluster (*br*—brother, bring, bright; *sl*—slip, sleep, sly).

8. Have a child write words that rhyme with these words:

bone	test	take
tent	car	clock
wrong	sing	pan

Various lists of words for this activity can be put on separate cards. For example, a set of such words could be prepared for each spelling lesson.

9. Prepare cards, each with a word that has several fairly common meanings. The child is to find as many meanings as possible and to write sentences illustrating them. Words to use might be common ones such as *left, right, train, dress,* and *ship* or less well-known ones such as *bond, idle, type,* and *trim.*

10. Put a series of compound words on cards—one word on each card. The child may add as many other compounds as possible that include one of the words in the given compound word. Some compound words to use are *cowboy, mailman, background, football,* etc.

11. Have the pupil develop a file of words that are most often misspelled in the writing the class does. He or she may secure these words from reports of other pupils (reporting the words they misspelled themselves). The words can be put on cards. Later pupils may select cards and write sentences using the words.

12. The slow learner may be helped by the use of crossword puzzles made up of words from the spelling list for the week or a list of words that have caused special difficulty. If desired, the puzzle may even be used in conjunction with a list of the words to be used, so that the child may learn the correct spelling as he or she copies the words from the list.

13. In a shoe or boot box, place letters cut from tagboard and backed with flannel, making sure to provide duplicates of vowels and the frequently used consonants (a Scrabble board makes a good guide to the number needed). Line the top of the box with flannel. Two or more children may take turns drawing letters; as soon as a child can form a word with his letters, he places them on the flannel lid, each child keeping his words in a separate column. The first child to form a predetermined number of words is the winner.

14. The letter box suggested above can also be used

in other ways. A single child may draw letters and see how many words he or she can make; or several might play a sort of modified Scrabble, building from the original word in all directions, with each child getting one point for every letter in a new word. The score should include not only new letters added, but also any already on the board which are used to make the new word.

III

*Reading,
Literature,
and
Study*

Teaching children how to read has far too often been separated from teaching other aspects of the language arts. There has also been a tendency to divorce the teaching of reading skills from a consideration of the importance of reading, the use of reading to gain knowledge and pleasure, and the development of life-long reading habits. This separation is not supported by evidence; therefore, this section stresses the fact that reading is one of the language arts and must be taught in relation to that fact.

Learning to read is a major task for many children. The chapters in this section should afford much guidance for you in providing the necessary instruction. We suggest, however, that you may need to read one or more of the references listed in chapters 14 and 16 for further teaching suggestions.

We want children to learn to read, but we also want them to read; we want them to use their reading skills. Therefore, this section is about children's literature, study skills, and using the library, as well as teaching reading skills and developing the vocabulary needed for understanding and appreciating what is read.

13

Attention to Vocabulary Development

Ours is a world of words. Individuals who possess vocabularies of substantial breadth and depth can communicate their ideas, desires, and needs, and are aided in gaining understanding and appreciation of the language used by others. The knowledge each of us has of words and how to use them comes largely from simply living in this world of words—from all the activities that involve language, are described by language, or provide a reason for speaking, listening, reading, and writing. This is the basic means for developing vocabulary.

While experience and individual learning efforts are the means by which we as adults strengthen our vocabularies, direct teaching of vocabulary—plus the providing of many experiences—is needed if children's vocabularies are to develop to the point where they will be fully equipped to meet their life needs, both in school and out.[1] Words important to a subject area, a unit of study, or any class activity need to be understood if children are truly going to learn the concepts, attitudes, and skills which are a part of that study or activity. And they must learn the skills and attitudes needed for gaining the meanings of new words or new meanings for known words that they meet in independent reading and listening.

SOME BASIC CONSIDERATIONS

Most children entering the first grade understand several thousand words. Of course they do not use all of these in their speaking, nor can they explain the meanings of many. But they have encountered such a large number of words so frequently in their preschool years that they "know" them with varying degrees of understanding. Certainly "knowing" a word does not necessarily mean that one is confident in using it (or even willing to try), nor does it mean understanding all of the multiple meanings possible for most words. Regardless of these limitations, however, children do understand and use a large number of words, and this means that an amazing foundation is present for further vocabulary development.

Kinds of Vocabulary

By age 2½ the vocabulary of the average child is about 400 words; by first grade some children understand as many as 20,000 words.

Every person has several vocabularies; we tend to use one group of words for speaking, another for writing, another for reading, and still another for listening. There is usually considerable overlap among these vocabularies, but all evidence indicates that they are not the same.

Our listening vocabularies are usually larger than those we have for reading, speaking, and writing. This is especially true for young children since they have not learned to read or write, or are just learning to do so. Children's speaking vocabularies are generally their second largest, but this is often not true for adults because adults are able to read, to write, and to spell the words they need in their writing.

The teaching of beginning reading skills is discussed in chapter 14.

In the early stages of learning to read, gaining an adequate vocabulary for reading tasks is difficult for some children. This is not because most children do not know many of the words in the reading materials; it is because they have the task of determining what they are in graphic or printed form. As reading abilities approach or reach considerable maturity, reading vocabularies become very large, and the average person understands many words he or she is unlikely to use in either speaking or writing.

Speaking vocabularies are somewhat more informal than those needed for reading or writing. However, every person has several speaking vocabularies: one for home and among friends, one for working hours (including, perhaps, professional or other specialized terms of one kind or another), and one used in formal social situations—among strangers, at meetings, and so on. People who are effective communicators have learned to use the vocabulary appropriate for the various occasions. These vocabulary differences and the importance of using appropriate vocabulary should be recognized by everyone (especially teachers), since the traditional tendency has been to teach formal language and to attempt to insist on its use. This point was discussed in earlier chapters and will be reemphasized in those that follow because of its major importance.

Preschool Vocabulary Development

As we have stated, children's levels of language development are determined both by their experiences and by their innate intellectual abilities. The words children have learned prior to coming to school are those that they have needed in the environments in which they have lived. How they pronounce these words and put them together in utterances reflect these environments. By the time you meet these children they will have learned a great deal of language; their vocabularies will be of considerable size. Naturally the sizes of the vocabularies will vary from child to child, and this fact must be recognized and planned for. It is also important that as much as possible is known about each child's knowledge of words as you plan your vocabulary teaching.

The meanings preschool children give to words that they "know" is particularly significant to teachers. Anyone who has associated with children of age five or under knows that these children do not use some words to mean the same things that adult usage of them would. This does not mean, of course, that the words preschool children use are without meaning to them. In fact, "they are typically used with consistent meanings that bear systematic relations to the adult meanings."[2] A teacher does have the responsibility, though, for helping children learn the adult meanings.

In addition to attaching meanings that are somewhat "skewed" to some words, young children often do not know that most words have more than one meaning. Even in grades four and above some common meanings of frequently used words are not known by large numbers of children.[3] Yet many words that children meet early in their school days (e.g., *bed, fire, hard, table*, etc.) may be used in ways unfamiliar to the children.

While teaching young children new words and new meanings—or clarifying and extending the understandings that they have—must be a concern of teachers, Dale points out that "It is easy to be impressed by the magnitude of the differences in semantic sophistication between child and adult" and not properly respect the semantic abilities of young children.[4] The key is to build upon the knowledge and abilities that the children have.

Of particular concern to teachers and to all of society is the education of children from underprivileged environments. Children who have not had the educational, social, and economic experiences of the middle class—to which school curriculums are so frequently tied—naturally will not have vocabularies comparable to those of children from homes that do not have these deprivations. Of course there are many exceptions, but, for whatever reason, different environments usually result in somewhat different needs, including language needs. A child from an educational, social and economic background that is different from the norm will have a vocabulary that is different from that norm. He or she will not necessarily be "poorly" languaged, nor will that language be either superior or inferior to any other; it will simply be different.

On the other hand, there are often conditions attached to poverty and restricted social and economic opportunities that affect a child's vocabulary development in ways other than those related simply to a different experiential background. These include such factors as self-image, expressional freedom, and the persons who most affect children's development. Numerous writers who have studied children whom society tends to label as disadvantaged have stated that these children often suffer from a negative self-image and limited opportunities for language exchange with adults due to the pressure on the adults they are associated with simply to accomplish the tasks required to provide basic life needs. There is an emphasis on the immediate: getting the meal, getting to sleep in order to be rested for the next day's work, caring for the food, shelter, and clothing problems of a family under crowded physical conditions, and so on. All these concerns tend to restrict a child's use of language. The child learns to do what he or she is told to do and to avoid situations that might interfere with the pressing tasks. The words learned are those that are needed, but there is a good deal of sameness to the tasks and hence a sameness to the words.

The child of poverty also has a restricted environment in the physical sense. There is no money for travel; the traveling that is done is usually connected with the adult's job and with getting groceries and other necessities. There may be no easy means of transportation to the country, the park, or even other neighborhoods within the city. Poor children's travel is often limited to going to school, to church, to neighborhood stores, and to the homes of friends. It is not unusual to find children in ghetto areas of cities who have never been more than a few blocks from their homes (and rural children who may never have been on a highway or to a city).

Children from economically deficient backgrounds are not nonverbal; they are nonverbal about things they don't know about. This is natural. All of us keep quiet in strange surroundings. The surroundings may be strange because we are in a foreign country, at a meeting of nuclear scientists, or observing a construction crew at work on a building. Certainly the advent of television has increased the knowledge of the deprived child—and of other children as well. Doubtless it has also added to his store of words. But television alone cannot provide the exchange of ideas and the experience in using language that are needed to prepare the child for the school environment.

It is not only poor children, however, who suffer from a lack of verbal exchange with adults. Increasingly, schools are finding that children from comfortable homes in attractive neighborhoods lack vocabulary and concepts that many of us consider commonplace. One first grade teacher found that some children could not give any name to cocoa or hot chocolate, although every child had tasted it. This phenomenon may be an outgrowth of today's social and economic milieu, in which parents may be divorced or separated or both parents may hold jobs and have many other interests outside the home. The "poor little rich girl" of yesteryear may well be found at any social level in today's world. It becomes even more important, then, for the teacher to help each child to acquire the kinds of experiences, and to learn the concepts and words to describe them, that will make the evolving school environment—including its language—a familiar one, one in which the child can function successfully.

EXPERIENCES AND VOCABULARY GROWTH

Vocabulary development may occur from

1. Making a mural.
2. Planning and giving a puppet show.
3. Looking at and discussing pictures.
4. Drawing pictures of objects, people, and places.
5. Writing stories.
6. Planning for and making an exhibit.
7. Viewing films and television programs.
8. Talking with classroom visitors.

While the experiences children have had prior to their coming to school—experiences significantly responsible for the learning they have gained and the habits, attitudes, emotions, and interests that make up their personalities—the building of further background is important to all children. This background should be built as much as possible by experiences that place the children in direct contact with concrete objects and real-life situations and those that permit words to be associated specifically and meaningfully with objects and concepts. Opportunities for direct, firsthand experiences may be provided in many ways and in all areas of the school program.

Experiential Opportunities

A creative instructional program provides endless opportunities for vocabulary development. Each day is filled with experiences, and every experience holds the possibility of teaching at least one child a new word or a new meaning. There is no end to the activities that may be carried on in a classroom: cooking Indian food, constructing an aquarium, making adobe bricks, building a simple generator, etc.

Each activity will lead to new words. For example, building a terrarium might lead to the Latin base word *terra;* to charcoal, peat moss, and drainage; and to the names of the plants placed in it. The real issue is in making these experiences worthwhile for as many children as possible and in as many ways as possible, including that of further developing the children's vocabularies.

Manipulative activities that involve handling various materials, tools, and equipment bring children into direct contact with objects and ideas and provide opportunities to learn new words and concepts, to understand directions, to gain ideas of how things work, and to relate the objects to things read and talked about. Included in such activities are those which use blocks, art materials, science instruments and models, construction tools, and audiovisual equipment.

Many types of experiences develop the vocabularies of young children.

Social experiences within the classroom, such as the Show and Tell period, the daily news or current events period, small-group committee work, free conversation periods, and class discussions provide opportunities for new words to arise, for their meanings to be learned, and for the words to be put to immediate use. Emphasize vocabulary in these experiences. For instance, if a boy tells about his dog barking in the night and awakening the household, you might promote a discussion about what the bark sounded like (was it a yip, a yelp, a growl, or what?), how he felt when he was aroused from sleep (drowsy, alert, curious, frightened?), or what others in the household did.

Direct observations of people, things, and processes through trips away from the classroom are particularly conducive to vocabulary development. These may be extended field trips to a museum, a farm, a factory, city hall, etc., or they may be excursions to places close by such as to see the nests in the shrubs at the back of the school ground or to the principal's office to learn what records are kept. Each trip requires planning, observation, and follow-up discussion. Many trips will require practice in observing, writing letters and charts, and giving some preliminary attention to the vocabulary that will be encountered on the trip.

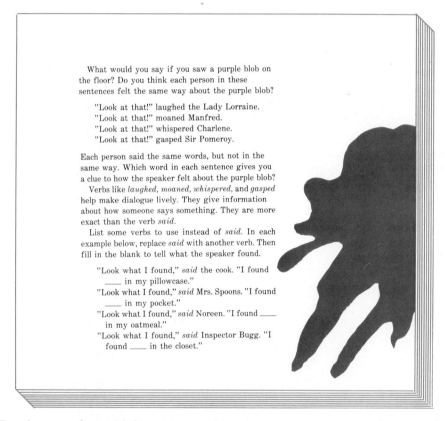

What would you say if you saw a purple blob on the floor? Do you think each person in these sentences felt the same way about the purple blob?

"Look at that!" laughed the Lady Lorraine.
"Look at that!" moaned Manfred.
"Look at that!" whispered Charlene.
"Look at that!" gasped Sir Pomeroy.

Each person said the same words, but not in the same way. Which word in each sentence gives you a clue to how the speaker felt about the purple blob?

Verbs like *laughed, moaned, whispered,* and *gasped* help make dialogue lively. They give information about how someone says something. They are more exact than the verb *said.*

List some verbs to use instead of *said.* In each example below, replace *said* with another verb. Then fill in the blank to tell what the speaker found.

"Look what I found," *said* the cook. "I found ____ in my pillowcase."
"Look what I found," *said* Mrs. Spoons. "I found ____ in my pocket."
"Look what I found," *said* Noreen. "I found ____ in my oatmeal."
"Look what I found," *said* Inspector Bugg. "I found ____ in the closet."

Experiences can be provided in many ways. (From *Using Our Language,* Level 5. Copyright 1977 by Noble and Noble. Used by permission of the publisher.)

Any oral or written expression that occurs spontaneously in a classroom, as well as all expression that may be considered of an "assignment" nature, provides opportunity for vocabulary development. Encourage children to make a conscious effort to select words that express thoughts exactly. Children tend to overuse a small stock of verbs, adverbs, and adjectives, but they can be successfully led away from repeated use of such omnibus words. One teacher led children to discuss words that might be used instead of *said.* Her fourth grade class discovered 104 words that could be used. You can generate a great deal of interest in finding better choices in particular contexts for such words as *nice, real, pretty,* etc. Even a word like *ran* may not be as accurate as *scurried* or *dashed.* As is suggested later in this chapter, the emphasis should be on the image to be gained by the listener or reader. Help children to see that the choice of words affects the picture or image received, and thus communication hinges upon the vocabulary that is used.

Simply observing things brought into the classroom or seen from the window produces ideas and words. You and the children can bring in rock samples, tree leaves, insects, growing plants, seeds, etc. The classroom may have its rabbit, gerbil, hamster, duck, or whatever. Observing the growth of a plant from a seed may lead to learning the words *chlorophyll, carbon dioxide, stem, dissolve, blossom, respire,* and *ecology.* If attention is not directed to learning new words, however, a

Children learn new vocabulary from their experiences, from doing things and talking about them.

seed can be planted, the soil faithfully watered, and growth observed and measured, without any vocabulary development taking place.

Visualizing and Listening

Since there are always some limitations in the degree to which actual experiences can be depended on to develop children's vocabularies as much as is desirable, the use of visual and auditory materials and reading are the practical substitutes. Reading as a means for providing experiences in which new vocabulary is learned generally has been a part of school programs, as has the development of vocabulary as a way to improve reading abilities. However, in spite of the abundance of audio-visual equipment and the often first-rate materials (software) available to use with it, not enough recognition is given in school programs to the value of other-than-print media for giving breadth and depth to children's experiences and the consequential development of their vocabularies. Even the general awareness of the public that the television experiences of preschool children foster vocabulary development has not had the use impact on the school curriculum that might have been expected.

Write to the Television Information Office, 745 5th Ave., New York, NY 10022 for a free schedule of quality programs.

Through television children have seen the volcano Irazu erupt in Costa Rica, Olympic events, animals of all types, and the devastation caused by hurricanes. They have explored ocean floors, climbed mountains, walked on China's Great Wall, laughed at Fat Albert, and lived with the Waltons. But they have also seen war almost at first hand, become absorbed by the unrealistic activities of "private eyes," and witnessed adult fights. The TV watching that children do in their homes can't be controlled by teachers, but a teacher can be knowledgeable about the programs they watch, discuss these with them, help them evaluate story lines and make fantasy-reality distinctions, and suggest programs that would be good for them to watch. And, of course, words that the children learn from their watching can be discussed and perhaps the concepts they represent clarified.

Television can also be used in classrooms, and this viewing can be planned for. But television is not the only means for the visual and auditory building of experiences. Film, filmstrips, phonograph and cassette recordings, photographs, and drawings and paintings can all substitute to some extent for field trips, interviewing resource people, and handling objects, and many of these materials provide experiences that go far beyond the direct experiences possible for a school to provide.

The Role of Reading

Reading has been and is the principal means that most of us have used in developing whatever breadth and depth of vocabulary we have. However, reading as a means for developing children's vocabularies is sometimes limited by their reading skills, by the interest they show in a particular reading activity, and by the availability of reading materials that provide the depth and breadth of vocabulary development desired. Also, much reading material is written with an expectation of vocabulary development—particularly with respect to knowledge of several meanings for words—that requires vocabulary teaching before the selection can be read. Therefore, a teacher must discuss these new words as well as use direct experiences, films, filmstrips, models, dramatizations, and so on to supplement the discussion.

Even after aids have introduced new words, meanings, and concepts, reading needs guidance—no less for its vocabulary development aspects than for the learning of word recognition skills. It is particularly important to remember that the context in which a word appears often does not provide a satisfactory clue to its meaning. For example, in the sentence "The ship set sail for the tropics," there is no clue to the meaning of *tropics* if this word is unknown. Even if *sail* is known, there is nothing to show whether it was actually a sailing vessel that departed or some other kind of ship. And, of course, a child might have absolutely no difficulty "reading" this sentence. This sentence and the many similar ones a child encounters illustrate that what the context of any reading material reveals to a particular reader depends on that reader's previous experience and on the clarity of the relationship between an unknown word and the other words near it.

Teach the children to note and make use of clues to meaning that are provided by the context. Such clues include an example in the context that explains an unknown word, a restatement of an unknown word in a form that is in effect a definition, or the presence of a modifying phrase or clause that reveals meaning. The best way to teach children to use these clues is through selecting paragraphs and sentences that contain one or more of these types of context clues and using them for illustration and practice.

> *Example:* He was truly *vicious;* for instance, he never had a kind word for his children and he beat his dog cruelly for no reason at all.
> *Restatement:* She recited her story *monotonously;* her voice droned on and on without change in tone or rate of speaking.
> *Modifying:* People looked at him as if he were a *leper,* whom everyone was afraid to approach for fear of catching the dreaded disease.

Provide practice in making inferences; that is, in reading between the lines. This practice is possible with much material used in reading lessons, including that in basal readers, if questions asked require making inferences rather than simply giving factual answers. For example, this quotation might be useful for such practice:

> The house had a lonely look. Its paint was peeling, the front gate hung by one hinge, and a forlorn rosebush struggled for existence among the weeds.

Questions might include:

> What kind of people do you suppose lived in this house?
> Were they neat, orderly people?
> Did they like flowers?
> If the yard was not cared for and the rosebush was being choked out by weeds, what do you think *forlorn* might mean?

Teaching punctuation items that are particularly relevant to understanding the meanings of words can also be helpful. One example of such an item is the use of commas to set off words used in apposition:

New Words

Do you know their meanings?

Afro
cassette
fallout
flipside
hovercraft
minibus
paramedic
update

A Bulletin Board Idea

> **What is the difference between:**
> • a cheetah, a bobcat, and a lynx?
> • odor, fragrance, and stench?
> • tall, high, and lofty?

The *pachyderm*, a huge bull elephant, was an awesome sight.

Words set off by parentheses or dashes also frequently give clues to word meanings:

His *unkempt* appearance (he surely hadn't shaved for at least a week) startled us.
He was protesting *vociferously*—I'm sure everyone in the building could hear him.

Basic to word study is the ability to use the dictionary effectively (see chapter 16). Children should be encouraged to use the dictionary to verify their inferences about words, to find meanings of words for which no context clues are given, or to discover variant meanings.

Use of the thesaurus, too, should be introduced and encouraged as soon as children have the reading ability and facility in dictionary skills to use it effectively. It may be introduced when children are writing—possibly a group composition—or searching for synonyms or a "better word." Middle and upper grade children should turn to the thesaurus as readily as to the dictionary.

Giving special attention to particular categories of words can broaden the children's understandings and add to their skills in both the receptive and expressive language arts. For example:

- Words often used figuratively, such as *face, leg, arm, table* (e.g., *face* of *the cliff, tableland*).
- Relationship words, such as *over, under, among, between, across, first, second.*
- Judgment words, such as *great, heavy, long.*
- Indefinite words, such as *some, several, most, few.*
- Common idioms, such as *clear up, hold out, bring down, close out.*

In order to be ready for reading and other first grade activities, a child must understand relationship words, such as those listed above. The concepts associated with these words are important for every child to learn through direct experience. Children can find things that are *over* other things, *under* the table, *across* the street, and so on. They can discuss whether one jump rope is as long as another and whether one child is as heavy as another. They can also consider what is meant by the *arm* of the chair and the *face* of the clock. Children in the middle grades can have fun competing to see who can compose the greatest number of sentences using "body words" figuratively: *heart, throat, body, foot,* etc. They can also make charts of words that belong in particular categories. These can be used in the children's writing and can be searched for in reading materials. The most successful procedure, however, is to teach the meanings of these words as they are encountered in reading and other activities in the classroom.

In Other Words, A Beginning Thesaurus (Grades 3 and 4) and *In Other Words, A Junior Thesaurus* (Grades 5 and up) are available from Scott, Foresman and Co.

How many meanings can you think of for:

ball?
bank?
iron?
head?
pass?
turn?
string?
sweep?

A Bulletin Board Idea

Sound Words	
buzz	hum
bang	ping
crunch	zing
chirp	tick
clatter	smack

OTHER TEACHING/LEARNING ACTIVITIES

New words and their meanings can be brought to the attention of children through many activities which have appeal for them and which are inherently interesting or can be made so. Much can be done somewhat indirectly (as has been suggested) if you are alert to the possibilities. More teaching should be done directly, however. Some activities that can be used in a direct way and the kinds of experiences related to them are given in the following pages. These are only suggestions; they should be modified and added to according to the needs of a particular class.

Word Activities

A major kind of vocabulary-building activity involves giving special attention to words. This activity is not a vocabulary exercise in the ordinary sense that we all remember, nor does it call for procedures related to teaching the meanings of words directly. The idea is to make the activities focus upon the appeal of words and the many interesting facts that can be learned about them. One such activity is to list on the board or on charts new words found in daily classroom activities. These may be words from social studies, science, or other subject areas; words used by the children in the classroom or on the playground; or words they heard on TV, saw on a sign on the way to school, or heard used by a visitor to the classroom. Little learning will result, of course, unless these lists appeal to children. For example, lists might include places that have retained Indian names, science terms derived from people's names, slang expressions and their origins, or foreign words that have been assimilated into our language.

Charts may be made of words in particular categories, such as "quiet" words, "sad" words, or Christmas words; these can be related to many activities. Charts may also be made of words to use instead of commonly overworked ones (*real, nice, pretty,* etc.) and of words for special occasions or special interests, such as football, camping trips, or art class. Charts of synonyms and antonyms can also help in building vocabulary. One class found 30 words that were better in various contexts than *mad* to describe the incidence of *anger*. Finding synonyms and antonyms for such words is also an activity that could be on a task card in the language arts center of your classroom. Chart making can be an activity for the entire class, for individual pupils, or for small groups, and the charts can be made in final form or planned so that they may be added to.

Children are interested in figures of speech, and good writers and speakers use these to get their ideas across. Figures of speech include personification, simile, metaphor, hyperbole, and euphemism. Children may be interested in collecting and categorizing these, keeping charts of good ones to use, finding their meanings, or deciding which are clichés to be avoided.

Personification is the giving of human or personal qualities to anything that is not human: in terms familiar to most children, the speaking in "Bugs Bunny" TV cartoons or "Little Toot." A simile makes a direct comparison: "as slow as molasses in winter" or "He fought like a tiger." A metaphor also compares, but it is not introduced by *like* or *as*: "He became purple with rage" or "She has a finger in every pie." Hyperbole is an exaggeration for effect, a figure of speech in which the truth is stretched: "I was scared to death" and "He can throw the ball a mile."

The above figures of speech are based on similarity; euphemism is based on contrast. We use euphemism to express an unpleasant fact indirectly. For instance, in referring to someone who has died we say "passed away" or perhaps "gone to the happy hunting ground." We also *perspire* instead of *sweat, withdraw* instead of *retreat,* or have a tooth *extracted* instead of *pulled.*

Children can be encouraged to keep individual lists of words they have

---

A Classroom Chart

Be a Word Detective

These words came into our language from Spanish. Can you add others?

rodeo
tornado
Colorado
peon
Nevada
mesa
mosquito

A Classroom Chart

Do you know these prefixes?

dis-	pre-
ex-	pro-
im-	re-
in-	sub-
mis-	un-

Find the meanings of the ones you don't know.

Try questions on bulletin boards; for example:

1. How many words can you think of to name a stream of water?
2. What are two meanings of *tear?*
3. How do you pronounce these words?

    bow
    read
    lead

learned and want to use. For this to succeed the children must really be interested in the words; an assignment of so many words a day becomes drudgery. This means that each child keeps his or her own list and that you help each one find words which appeal, show interest in their words, and make learning new words an important part of classroom activities. Some provision should be made for having a child tell about these words—perhaps in spare moments throughout the day different children can tell about words they have added to their lists.

Campaigning for the adoption of new words is fun, but it should continue for only a few weeks or interest will lag. Such a campaign may take the form of intro-

28

Goodbye Now!

"Isn't that just *great!*"
"Something wrong with the *grate?*"
"No—something terrible. I just invited the wrong *guest.*"
"You *guessed* wrong?"
"Oh, leave me *alone!*"
"You want a *loan?*"

Giving special attention to words can be fun. (From *Would You Put Your Money in a Sand Bank?* by Harold S. Longman. Copyright 1968 by Harold S. Longman. Published by Rand McNally & Co.)

ducing one or more new words daily by showing pictures and drawings that give the meanings; by putting questions on the bulletin board asking "How is it pronounced?" "Can you find it in the dictionary?" "Have you heard anyone use it?" or "Can you use it in two sentences?"; and by providing situations in which the new word can be used. Or possibly each day a different pupil might select a word and present it to the class. Some teachers like to supervise this selection; others prefer to let children exercise their ingenuity in finding words, even though some

Making New Words

A compound noun is a word formed from two smaller words. You can also make new words by adding a letter or letters to the end of some words.

● Look at each word. What letters were added to form new words?

| listen | listener | farm | farmer |
| direct | director | report | reporter |

The letters *er* and *or* were added. They usually mean *a person who*. A *listener* is a person who listens. A *director* is a person who directs. A *farmer* is a person who farms. A *reporter* is a person who reports. The letters *er* and *or* are called *suffixes*.

A **suffix** is one or more letters added to the end of a word.

● Look at these words. Notice the spelling.

drive operate
driver operator

If a word ends in *e*, you must drop the *e* before you add the suffix *er* or *or*.

You will find that most words add the suffix *er*. Only a few words add the suffix *or*.

● Look carefully at the spelling of each word below.

visitor operator inventor sailor

54 VOCABULARY: *Noun Suffixes*

Expand children's activities in word building from those suggested in textbooks. (From *Macmillan English*, Series E, Grade 4. Copyright 1979 by Macmillan Publishing Co., Inc. Used by permission of the publisher.)

turn out to be less than useful.

There is also value in teaching words and word elements directly, including the meanings of important root words, prefixes, and suffixes. The teaching may develop the meaning of a root (for example, *port*) with as many prefixes and suffixes added as possible: *report, import, deport, portage, portable, porter, reporter, export*, etc. Learning the meanings of commonly used suffixes and prefixes—along with the various forms some of them can take (*in,* for example)—can help children to unlock the meanings of many new words they meet. Give them active practice in looking for familiar elements in words, such as prefixes, suffixes, Latin or Greek roots, and English base words. For instance, the child who knows the word *limit,* the suffix *-able,* and the *il* variation of *in* should have no difficulty in arriving at a reasonable definition of *illimitable.* Other direct teaching might include listing words and phrases that prompt images (e.g. "shimmering snow," "rolling waves," "shattering blast," etc.), discussing the meanings, and suggesting other phrases that create images. Children may also be encouraged to notice and discuss alliteration and rhyme in slogans. Similarly, many opportunities can be capitalized upon for noting words whose meanings have shifted or for which new meanings have been added. Consider the "space" words: *junk, clean, stage, capsule, pad, bird.* Other categories for word study include manufactured words (*rayon, dacron*), words with multiple meanings (*pitch, fall, lean*), and "loaded" and emotional words (*time-tested machine, loved ones*).

Learning and reinforcing the learning of new words through expressional activities that do not use language has great appeal. Children can make cartoons or drawings to illustrate word meanings and accurate word choices; they can dramatize meanings of words in specific contexts; and they can even play charades, using new words they have learned.

Vocabulary Exercises

Although the major emphasis in vocabulary building should be upon teaching new words in natural and meaningful situations, exercises that focus upon specific words can also be valuable. These exercises use paper and pencil and require filling in blanks, writing a numeral or letter to indicate the answer, or circling or underlining a word or number. Such exercises smack heavily of "busywork" and are too often used in such a way that little genuine learning occurs. However, the shortcomings of such exercises can be overcome if they are selected with care and not overused.

Many vocabulary books, workbooks that accompany reading textbooks, and dictionary and spelling workbooks offer vocabulary exercises. The following exercises, typical of those found in such sources, may be used to reinforce learning of particular words. Exercises modeled on the ones below can also be constructed by the teacher to suit the needs of a particular group.

1. Write the word for the young of each animal family.

bear	cub	horse	_____
dog	_____	lion	_____
duck	_____	sheep	_____
cow	_____	goat	_____

Roots and Words

color	circle
colorful	circus
discolor	circular
colorless	circumference
Colorado	encircle
telephone	move
microphone	remove
saxophone	movable
phonics	movement
symphony	moving

What do they mean?

shoulder the burden
put your back into it
cog in the wheel
get things rolling
none of your lip
elbow grease
put the finger on him

Children can make their own thesaurus. Have them find words that describe a particular smell, taste, kind of weather, noise, texture, emotion, etc., and then list synonyms for each of their words.

2. Circle the definition of *huff*.

hurry	fit of anger
excitement	anxiety
moment's time	

3. See how many different meanings you can find for each word. Write a sentence to show each meaning.

pool	running
rock	picking
blank	cutting
strike	feeling

Here are some examples:

Blane's favorite game is *pool*.
The swimming *pool* is my favorite spot in summer.
Connie drives in a car *pool*.

4. Write each word in Column 1 next to its antonym in Column 2.

1	2	
present	broad	_____
victory	civilized	_____
smooth	retreat	_____
dull	absent	_____
advance	tight	_____
barbaric	bright	_____
narrow	defeat	_____
loose	rough	_____

5. Write a synonym for each of these words.

swift	_____	journey	_____
error	_____	wane	_____
mend	_____	depart	_____
rich	_____	huge	_____
visitor	_____	dress	_____

6. For each word choose the prefix that will make its meaning become the opposite of what it is without the prefix. Write the words you make, and use each in a sentence.

im   dis   il   un   in

clean	_____	legal	_____
like	_____	definite	_____
cover	_____	honest	_____
mature	_____	possible	_____

7. Choose the suffix that will make each sentence read correctly. Be sure to make necessary spelling changes.

For fun with words see:

If You Talked to a Boar by Michael Sage (Lippincott)
Nailheads and Potato Eyes by Janet McCaffery (Morrow)
Pick-A-Riddle by Ennis Rees (Scholastic)
Word Twins by Mary White (Abingdon)

ness   ment   less   ed

a. Happy___ is spending holidays together.

b. We are waiting for the announce___ to tell us when the plane will leave.

c. It seems hope___ that our team will go to the Super Bowl.

d. We are please___ to see you ski so well.

e. You must be kind or you will be friend___.

8. Choose the right word.

a. I _____ Bob when we were in the third grade.
   (new, knew)

b. She walked down the _____.
   (isle, aisle)

c. We drove _____ the school.
   (by, buy)

d. Chris, please _____ me at school.
   (meat, meet)

e. I will _____ for you.
   (weight, wait)

f. Tim is _____ years old.
   (to, two, too)

g. Yes, I _____ he is.
   (know, no)

9. Make three headings: Food, Weather, and Places. Put each of these words under the correct heading.

corn   hail   bank   school   dry   snow
shed   cloudy windy   cake   park   barn
storm   berries beans   soup   forest clams

10. Add words to the ones below to make compound words.

snow_____   base_____   sun_____
class_____   arm_____   mail_____

11. Find the correct words for these sentences.

a. A desk has a _____ but cannot spin it.   (top)

b. A chair has an _____ but cannot raise it.   (arm)

c. A rug has a _____ but gets no rest.   (nap)

d. A clock has a _____ but cannot smile.   (face)

Pick out words from what children are studying in social studies, science, etc., and what they talk and write about when you make exercises like these.

12. How many words can you write to rhyme with the words below?

meat   flame   book   slow

_____   _____   _____   _____

_____   _____   _____   _____

_____   _____   _____   _____

13. Write homonyms for these words.

haul	_____	role	_____
our	_____	wait	_____
tale	_____	sent	_____
road	_____	hole	_____

14. Underline the word that does not belong in each group.

good	slow	real
decent	idle	false
corrupt	lazy	proven
honest	active	true

15. Write the meaning of each expression.

The idea overwhelms me.
She was the understudy to the actress.
The disease is incurable.

16. Draw a line from the word in column 1 to the word in column 2 that makes you think of the word in column 1.

1	2
narrow	thin
marrow	bone
tired	attempted
tried	weary
angle	corner
angel	wings
trial	path
trail	test

Games

Word games can be fun, and they can be used to provide variety in vocabulary-building activities. They can involve all the children, small groups, or, in many cases, individuals. Games are not an adequate substitute for direct attention to broadening vocabularies or providing the depth of understanding needed to use words comfortably, but they can be a useful part of the total program. Below are some to try; many will give you ideas for variations.

Also see

The Arrow Book of Word Games by Murray Rockowitz (Scholastic)

Guess the Rhyming Words.   Make up sentences and have children supply the missing words to complete the rhymes. For example, "My brother *Bill* sits on the window _____" and "We looked into the *hall* when we heard a loud _____." Discuss the meanings of words the children give, particularly those with more than one more meaning, and help them to find as many words as possible that rhyme and also make sense.

What's the Answer?   Ask children riddles, such as "What has four legs, one head and one foot?" (bed) or "What has a heel but only one toe?" (shoe). This game can be extended into an interesting investigation of the use of figurative language, with the children finding examples of words used figuratively.

Tom Swifties.   This game calls for completing a sentence with the adverbial form of a word that has already been used. For example:

> He showed his anger by shouting _____. (angrily)
> "There's a bright sun today," she said _____. (brightly)

More Swifties.   There are many variations of the above game. For example, children may compose sentences containing homonyms (This is the *tale* of a dog without a *tail*) or two different meanings for the same word (The *lean* man *leaned* against the door.) These can make delightful bulletin board displays, particularly when illustrated by imaginative drawings.

Hinky-Pinky.   The object of Hinky-Pinky is to find a pair of rhyming words where the first describes the second: motion–ocean, tasty–pastry, cook–book, fleeting–greeting.

Add-a-Letter.   Have one child start with a letter. Each has to add one letter, in each case making a word. For example:

a	i
an	in
ran	tin
bran	thin
brand	think
brandy	

Little Words.   Put a long word on the board—often it can be a word associated with a special event, such as Christmas, Halloween, vacation, or graduation. Challenge the children to find as many "little" words in it as they can. Vary the rules from time to time; for example, the rules can specify whether the letters of words must be in the order found in the long word or whether they must simply be included in it.

Word Jump.   Start with a word and have a pupil think of a new word that begins with the last letter of the first word—for example, *book, kite, elephant, table, egg, gym, money, yardstick,* etc. Continue until you get to a stickler. Generally it is best to make all words nouns, but this can vary. Rules regarding use of the dictionary can vary but should be established before the game starts.

Just the Opposite.   Have one child use a word in a sentence. For example:

> *young:* He is a young man.

A second child should reply with something like,

> He certainly isn't very *old.*

The second child then chooses another word and uses it in a sentence, a third child responds with an antonym, and so on. Children must drop out of the game if they fail to give a sentence or choose a correct antonym. Dictionaries should be available for checking the antonyms. (This game can also be played with teams.)

Pairs.   Divide the class into teams, and assign each team a pair of letters. The objective is to make a list of words that contain these letters as a pair. For example, one team might be assigned the dipthong *oy* and the other *oi*. One team might list *employ, alloy, coy, decoy, envoy*, etc., and the other team might list *soil, boil, coin, poison, voice*, etc. Pupils may use their dictionaries and the team with the longest list wins. Discuss the meanings of words listed.

Give a Synonym.   The class is again divided into teams. A member of one team gives a word and a member of the other team must give a synonym. For example, *ran–dashed*. Have the teams take turns giving the first word.

A FINAL WORD

Like any other portion of the curriculum, vocabulary can be dull and stereotyped when it is presented for a certain number of minutes each day in isolation from any other part of the curriculum. It is doubtful whether much learning takes place in such a setting; certainly little excitement about words will be generated. Many of the activities suggested in the preceding pages might be used in such a program, as might any activity that seeks to build a skill or present a concept. The secret lies in planning and organization.

It is important to reiterate here what we have said or will say about every area of the language arts curriculum. *Effective instruction must have objectives and it must have a plan for accomplishing these objectives.* If these objectives and these plans are meshed, motivation for learning needed skills will probably result. For example, if learning prefixes is one of the vocabulary skills your class needs, plan to coordinate this with a reading lesson in which a number of new words contain prefixes, a spelling lesson that includes words with prefixes, or a social studies unit in which this learning is meaningful.

In short, this is what we mean when we speak of an *integrated* curriculum: needed skills are combined with acquiring concepts or knowledge to create a meaningful experience.

ENDNOTES

1. The importance of a specific, planned vocabulary development program is substantiated by research. See, for example, Edgar Dale and Joseph O'Rourke, *Techniques of Teaching Vocabulary* (Chicago: Field Educational Publications, Inc., 1971).

2. Philip S. Dale, *Language Development, Structure and Function*, 2nd ed. (New York: Holt, Rinehart and Winston, 1976), p. 192.

3. Edgar Dale and Joseph O'Rourke, *The Living Word Vocabulary, The Words We Know* (Chicago: Field Enterprises Educational Corporation, 1976).

4. Dale, *Language Development*, p. 192.

REFERENCES

Books

Dale, Edgar. *The Word Game: Improving Communications.* Bloomington, IN: The Phi Delta Kappa Educational Foundation, 1975.

Dale, Edgar, and O'Rourke, Joseph. *Techniques of Teaching Vocabulary.* Palo Alto, CA: Field Educational Publications, 1971.

Deighton, Lee C. *Vocabulary Development in the Classroom.* New York: Teachers College Press, Columbia University, 1959.

Petty, Walter T., and Bowen, Mary E. *Slithery Snakes and Other Aids to Children's Writing.* Englewood Cliffs, NJ: Prentice-Hall, 1967.

Pilon, A. Barbara. *Teaching Language Arts Creatively in the Elementary Grades.* New York: John Wiley and Sons, 1978, Chapter 5.

Tiedt, Sidney W., and Tiedt, Iris M. *Language Arts Activities for the Classroom.* Boston: Allyn and Bacon, 1978.

Children's Books about Words

Alexander, Arthur. *The Magic of Words* (Prentice-Hall, 1962), grades 4–6.

Asimov, Isaac. *Words from the Myths* (Houghton Mifflin Co., 1961), grades 6–8.

Churchill, E. Richard, compiler. *The Six-Million-Dollar Cucumber* (Watts, 1976), grades 3–6.

Fadiman, Clifton. *Wally the Wordworm* (Macmillan, 1964), grades 2–5.

Ferguson, Charles. *The Abecedarian Book* (Little, Brown), grades 3–5.

Funk, Charles. *Heavens to Betsy* (Harper and Row, 1955), grades 5–7.

Funk, Charles E., and Funk, Charles E., Jr. *Horsefeathers and Other Curious Words* (Harper and Row, 1958), grades 5–7.

Gwynne, Fred. *The King Who Rained* (Dutton, 1970), primary.

Hanson, Joan. Synonyms (Lerner Publications, 1972).

Hefter, Richard. *Yes and No: A Book of Opposites* (Larousse, 1975), kindergarten–grade 1.

Kohn, Bernice. *What a Funny Thing to Say* (Dial, 1974), grades 4–7.

Lambert, Eloise. *Our Language* (Lothrop, 1955), grades 4–6.

Mathews, Mitford. *American Words* (World Publishing Co., 1958), grades 6–9.

O'Neill, Mary. *Words, Words, Words* (Doubleday and Co., 1966), grades 5–7.

Radlauer, Ruth S. *Good Times with Words* (Melmont Children's Press, 1963), grades 3–6.

Rand, Paul, and Rand, Ann. *Sparkle and Spin* (Harcourt Brace Jovanovich, 1957), grades K–3.

Reid, Alastair. *Ounce, Dice, Trice* (Little, Brown and Co., 1968), grades 3–5.

Sage, Michael. *Words Inside Words* (J. P. Lippincott Co., 1961), grades 4–6.

Schwartz, Alvin. *Tomfoolery—Trickery and Foolery with Words* (Lippincott, 1973), grades 2–6.

Tremain, Ruthven. *Fooling Around with Words* (Greenwillow Books, 1976), grades 1–4.

Shipley, Joseph. *Playing with Words* (Prentice-Hall, 1960), grades 5–8.

Waller, Leslie. *Our American Language* (J. B. Lippincott Co., 1960), grades 4–6.

Films

Fun with Words: Word Twins. Chicago: Coronet Films (11 min.; color, b/w; primary grades).

Fun with Words: Words That Add Meaning. Chicago: Coronet Films (11 min.; color, b/w; primary grades).

Fun with Words: Words That Name and Do. Chicago: Coronet Films (11 min.; color, b/w; primary).

Improving Your Vocabulary. Chicago: Coronet Films (11 min.; color, b/w; intermediate grades).

Wordwise: Suffixes. Los Angeles: Bailey Film Associates (12 min.; color; intermediate).

Filmstrips

Discovering New Words. Mahwah, NJ: Troll Associates (6 color strips; 3 records or cassettes; K–4).

Fundamentals of Vocabulary Building. Jamaica, NY: Eye Gate House (Set of 9 color strips; intermediate grades).

How to Develop a Good Vocabulary; Importance of Vocabulary in Communication. Tujunga, CA: Herbert M. Elkins Co. (Color).

Our Language. Chicago: Coronet (6 filmstrips; records or cassettes; intermediate).

Making Words Work. Chicago: Coronet (6 filmstrips; records or cassettes; intermediate).

Words, Media and You. Chicago: Coronet (6 filmstrips; records or cassettes; intermediate).

Word Meaning. Boston: Houghton Mifflin, 1956 (2 color strips).

Word Study Series. New York: McGraw-Hill Films (Set of 6 strips; intermediate).

Words and Writing. New York: Popular Science Publishing Co. (Set of 6 strips; primary).

Words: Their Origin, Use, and Spelling. Chicago: Society for Visual Education (Set of 6 color strips; intermediate).

Recordings

Building Verbal Power. Freeport, NY: Educational Activities, Inc. (4 albums each for primary and upper grades; includes word games, similes and analogies, homonyms, multi-usage words, etc.).

Building Word Power. Chicago: Coronet (9 cassettes; response books; teacher's manual; intermediate and upper).

Vocabulary Building. Saint Paul, MN: 3M (10 cassettes; workbooks; intermediate).

Vocabulary Enrichment. Saint Paul, MN: 3M (8 cassettes; worksheets; intermediate).

Wordplay. Chicago: Coronet (6 cassettes; response books; teacher's manual; primary).

Kits

Deighton, Lee C. *Vocabulary Development.* The Macmillan Reading Spectrum. New York: The Macmillan Company, 1964 (A series of six programmed workbooks for intermediate grades).

Evans, Bergen. *Wordcraft.* Chicago: Vocabulary Incorporated, 1969 (Multimedia approach; records, tapes, or cassettes, and color filmstrips; middle and upper grades).

Hodkinson, Kenneth. *Wordly Wise,* Book 1; and Ornato, Joseph G. *Wordly Wise,* Book 2. Cambridge, Mass.: Educator's Publishing Service, 1967 (Exercises and puzzles for grades 4 and 5).

Picto-Cabulary Series. Baldwin, NY: Barnell Loft (Sets for different levels; booklets, teacher's manual; tests, etc.).

+10 *Vocabulary Booster.* New York: Webster Division, McGraw-Hill (Five levels grade 4 and above; cassettes; student notebooks; tests; books; etc.).

ACTIVITIES FOR PRESERVICE TEACHERS

1. Develop lists of words that will interest children of the ages you plan to teach. For example, you might include words borrowed from the American Indians *(moose, squash, pecan)* or the French *(boulevard, chalet, envoy)*; words that have become generalized *(kleenex, ghetto, coke)* or specialized *(maid, corn, city)*; and words derived from mythology *(Achilles heel, cupid, Pandora's box)*.

2. Investigate books about words and language written for children. Develop a file indicating where these can be obtained and how you would use each.

3. Investigate new words and how they originated. One good source to examine is Clarence L. Barnhart, Sol Steinmetz, and Robert K. Barnhart, *The Barnhart Dictionary of New English Since 1963* (Bronxville, NY: Barnhart/Harper and Row, Publishers, 1973). Be prepared to report some of your findings to the class and to show how the information you found could be used in elementary school teaching.

4. Plan a field trip for a grade level of your choice. List the new vocabulary the children should have the opportunity to learn.

5. Prepare a bulletin board designed to help build vocabulary. Have in mind a specific grade level and a particular lesson or unit of study with which this bulletin board would be used.

6. Make a list of words with multiple meanings and collect pictures to illustrate the various meanings—e.g., *park* the car; play in the *park*.

7. Obtain as many different texts as you can for the grade level you prefer (language, social studies, spelling, science, etc.). Prepare ten different vocabulary development worksheets for this level based on material from these texts and the suggestions in this chapter.

8. Read a chapter in an intermediate grade social studies or science book. Establish objectives for teaching the vocabulary in the chapter, and plan how you would go about accomplishing your objectives.

ACTIVITIES FOR INSERVICE TEACHERS

1. Using the media resources in your school, preview materials that might be appropriate for building vocabulary in connection with content areas. Add these to your media file, along with notations concerning vocabulary to be developed and methods for developing it. Be sure to include call numbers or other markings (color codes, etc.) to assist you in locating materials.

2. Use your content texts to plan specific vocabulary development lessons before the children read assignments. Introduce new words and concepts as you do in reading—using new words in a context that will assist the reader in gaining meaning.

3. Using the method suggested in no. 1, select books from your school and local libraries that will be useful supplementary reading for specific units of study in content areas. Be sure to check glossaries as well as text for vocabulary words to introduce.

4. Prepare charts for vocabulary development similar to those illustrated in this chapter. As you plan and perhaps illustrate these charts, remember that they must be interesting, stimulating, and fun and that they must be a part of your total curriculum (not apart from it).

5. Work with the children in your class in developing charts of interesting words on different subjects. For example, a list of words dealing with the American Revolution, the human body, the history of mathematics, or regional dialects should make good charts.

6. Preview as many of the films and filmstrips suggested in this chapter as possible, and discuss whether they would be of use in your classroom.

7. Visit the instructional resources center in your school district. Look through catalogs for vocabulary development materials that are not presently available in your school but would be desirable and appropriate for the age and ability levels of the children you work with. Meet with your principal or immediate supervisor and explain why money should be allotted for these in the next budget.

8. From the independent activities for children suggested in this chapter, select those that would be suitable for enrichment or remediation for the children in your class. Adapt and expand these to fit individual needs.

9. Map reading calls for a specialized vocabulary. In connection with an appropriate social studies or science lesson, develop a plan for teaching the vocabulary needed to understand and use the various kinds of maps found in an atlas.

INDEPENDENT ACTIVITIES FOR CHILDREN

1. Make a vocabulary bulletin board featuring a large tree with many branches. (This could be a mobile, if space is limited.) Have children cut leaves, flowers, fruit, birds, nests, or even monkeys or other animals that could be found in a tree from colored construction paper; place these in an envelope or box nearby. When a child meets a new word in any curriculum area, he writes it on one of the cut-outs and hangs it on the tree. During free time, children practice reading the words on the tree and using them in sentences. As children master words, they can be replaced by others. Or, periodically, old words can be removed and each one awarded to the child who is first to use it correctly in a sentence.

2. Let each child keep a word file or dictionary of interesting new words that he meets. Have him look up the correct pronunciation and meanings of each word he decides to "keep," and fix it in his memory by using it as many times as possible, both in speech and in writing.

3. Word exercises for children to do in their free time can be prepared on cards (3 × 5 cards, for example). The cards might contain one of the following:
   a. A large word (hippopotamus) in which small words can be found (hip, pop, pot) or letters rearranged to make words (must, top, pit, ship, post, shop).
   b. A word category (for example, sports) for which the pupil writes all the words he can think of (goalie, quarterback, basket, glove, football, bat, net, foul, puck, dribble).

4. Prepare lists of words for which a child can find homonyms. For example:

1	2	3
know	too	new
feat	sale	weight
our	peace	roll
hole	led	knight
grate	fair	do

5. Using a list of homonyms which have been identified, a child writes one sentence using each word, placing these on separate 3 × 5 cards. When enough cards have been accumulated, children can use them to play games similar to Old Maid or Rummy.

6. Children can also develop lists of homographs—words that are spelled alike but pronounced differently (bow, live, read). They can then write sentences demonstrating how the context determines the pronunciation:

Chip has a bow tie.
Please bow when you meet the king.

These can also be used in matching games.

7. For practice with synonyms put sentences on cards, each containing an underlined word for which a child may find synonyms. Here are some sentences:

The thunder breaks the silence.
Rain pelted the window glass.
The snow fell steadily.
He ran across the road.
The engine started when he stepped on the starter.

8. Prepare a file of cards containing lists of words with multiple meanings. For example, on one card might be such words as bank, store, shop, park, and box, along with directions to the child to write sentences showing different meanings for each word.

9. Individual children can prepare lists of "food words" by categories. The categories might be Cereals, Meats, Dairy Products, Vegetables, and Fruits. Encourage children to be observant at home and in stores so that lists will be long.

10. Have a child make a list of words that have taken on new meanings in recent years. Start him with capsule, pad, stage, and rock.

11. Provide lists of "special" words whose origins a child can trace. For example:

From proper names—braille, cologne, ampere
From other languages—veto, exit, vacuum, nest
Recently coined—helicopter, amplifier, laser, missile
Names of states—Connecticut, Wisconsin, Oregon

12. Have a child make a list of words heard on TV during a particular week that he would like to add to his vocabulary. He can enlist the aid of parents in writing them down, or he can jot down the context in which the word was used and spell it phonetically, checking the dictionary later for correct spelling and meaning.

13. A child can use crayon, fabric, clay, or any other available material to make an object, then make a list of all the words he or she can think of to describe it. For example: Mud—squishy, dirty, oozing, fun.

14. Have a child look in a full-length mirror and try to think of an adjective to describe each feature or part of his or her body. This can be followed by writing a self-description or drawing a self-portrait.

15. Put pictures on a bulletin board and have individual children look in magazines for words, phrases, and sentences to describe them. These can be cut out and placed around the pictures to make a word bulletin board.

16. Two children can play a game using antonyms. One child reads words (adjectives and adverbs) from a list he or she has made, or simply says words he thinks of. The other child must furnish an antonym for each. After the second child misses, he or she reads words and the first child supplies antonyms.

17. Individual children can make lists of incomplete sentences to share with the class at a later time. Other children then try to think of words and/or phrases that fill the blanks and make interesting sentences.

I looked out the window and saw _____ .

Sitting on the front doorstep was _____ .
He _____ the cake _____ .

18. Have a child prepare a chart for the bulletin board of words that can be used instead of such "tired" words as *awful, pretty, big, nice, fun,* etc.

19. Place small pictures from magazines or ones that you draw on 3 × 5 cards. Print the name of what is pictured on each card. With enough of these cards children can make up their own games—for example: matching pairs of homonyms, homophones, antonyms, or synonyms. After you get them started children can make or find pictures for cards to add to the set.

20. Have children talk about their hobbies or favorite sports using, and perhaps illustrating or explaining, the specialized vocabulary of the hobby or sport.

21. Decorating words to look like their meanings can help individual children think more creatively about language. For example:

22. At holiday time, a child might list all the words he or she can think of to describe the holiday and customs associated with it. These might be verbs, nouns, adjectives, and adverbs—or they could be limited to one of these categories.

23. When children study and discuss careers in the upper grades, they might make charts of words used by people in particular occupations. For example, a person selling automobile insurance might use such terms as *no-fault, assigned risk,* and *mass marketing.* The help of parents and other adults might be enlisted for this activity.

14

Teaching Children to Read

Children bring all of their experiences—those with language, those of thinking and emotion, and those with people and objects—to the challenging task of learning to read and to the development of skills needed by maturing readers after initial learning has occurred. Reading is not something that can be separated from these experiences, nor from the other language arts or other parts of the school curriculum.

Practically all children come to school eager to learn to read. They usually have had experiences with books; they've been read to and have looked at and handled books—although too often they may not have had enough of these experiences. In spite of this general eagerness, however, many children become frustrated in their learning efforts, so that after only a year or so at school they have lost much of their curiosity and their desire to know; they may even ignore the appealing books that are available to them.

The causes of this change—which happens to far too many children—are many and varied. Differences in learning abilities, in experience backgrounds and readiness to learn what teachers seek to teach, and in adjustments to the school setting may not have been recognized and considered in instructional programs. Sometimes, too, the classroom instruction is contrived and forced; it does not focus on natural communication; it does not recognize that the reading act depends on the other language arts and is intertwined with them. Probably most of all, there are too many teachers not sensitive enough to each child as an individual and not enthusiastic enough themselves about the wonders of learning.

Less than 1% of children readily learn to read prior to grade one.

READING: AN OVERVIEW

A child does not learn to read suddenly or after only a short period of time, as one might learn to ride a bicycle. Of course a beginning reader may struggle with learning to remember what sounds certain letters represent or what word a series of letters stands for and then suddenly be able to remember these so that he or she can recognize a word or several words. But this is not reading.

Most adults are continuing to learn to read. The ability any person has as an adult is not the same ability he or she had in grade 2 or grade 3. Most adults have learned to skim, to draw inferences from content, to be expressive in oral reading, and to adjust their reading rate to the material being read and the purposes for reading it. Learning to read does not end with grade 3, with the elementary school, or with formal schooling at any level; as a developmental process it continues to develop as the individual's life changes.

What Is Reading?

Reading is not a simple act; it is a complex one that involves a series of mental processes. But the fact that reading is complex does not mean that it is difficult to learn. Speaking is a complex act, yet children learn to speak, apparently without great difficulty.

Defining reading is not easy. Try to think of a one-sentence definition. What do you include? Is it attaching a sound to each squiggle that we call a letter so that putting the sounds together forms a word that the reader knows? Is it getting a clue to what several squiggles represent by any means possible—from pictures, from the shape of the pattern of squiggles, or by guess and inference? Is it saying each word either audibly or silently? Is it recognizing the meaning of a word, a phrase, or a sentence? Is it relating one's experiences to those of the writer? Is it a process of thinking that is stimulated by a special kind of object?

Perhaps reading might be defined in terms of what it does. Is it a means by which a person's life is enriched, his personality developed, or information gained that is vital to his life activities? Is he given a way to escape from reality?

The fact is, of course, that reading defies a glib definition. It is an act that must be viewed from many perspectives. It is an act that has many stages. It is more than visual perception of letters; it is more than simply decoding or translating these letters into known sounds and words—a point of view apparently held by teachers who are satisfied that they have taught a youngster to read if he or she can "call words" accurately. Reading is also more than simply receiving meaning in a literal sense. It involves bringing an individual's entire lifetime of experience and all of the individual's thinking powers to bear on understanding what the writer has encoded.

Factors Affecting Reading

Differences in Children That Affect Learning

1. Intellectual abilities.
2. Mental maturity levels.
3. Experiential backgrounds.
4. Verbal facility.
5. Emotional adjustment.
6. Attitude toward learning.

The extent to which any reading act is successful is affected both by the reader and the material he or she is seeking to read. The reader must be ready for the specific reading effort. That is, he or she must have the mental capacity, experience background, language maturity, and skill development required, as well as an interest in doing the reading. These factors are not unique to reading, however; none of us is successful in anything we attempt to do without readiness for doing it. If we have not had some related experiences, an understanding of what is involved and what we need to do, and either the physical or mental—or both—

ability required, our effort will not be successful. And, of course, we would not even try it if we weren't interested in doing it.

Reading readiness is often defined as that stage in a child's development at which he or she can fairly readily begin to learn to read. In school programs reading readiness activities are planned for the five- and six-year-old child. The definition is likely not to disappear, and the activities certainly should not. But it is important for every teacher to remember that readiness is an ongoing and ever-present concept. Every child must develop the readiness for each successive step in learning to read. Every person, regardless of age, must have the required readiness for any reading effort if reading is actually to occur

Reading is also affected by the material. Its language structure may be so abstruse, awkward, or unfamiliar that a reader is unsuccessful even with the experience background, skills, interest, and intellectual ability to read it. A reader may reject material also if its appearance does not appeal—even if the content does. This is particularly true in the case of children. Style and size of print, spacing, length of lines, and number of illustrations are among the factors in reading material that may influence the interest of the reader and the ability to use the skills he or she posesses.

Of course, the content of the material and the vocabulary used are factors affecting reading, but these are more directly related to a reader's experience and ability. Because of this, though, they are especially important factors in reading instruction. Children can go a long way toward reading material whose content is generally familiar to them, especially if the content does not contain too many words and language structures that they have heard infrequently or do not use.

Objectives of Reading Instruction

The overall objective for teaching children to read is to develop in them the attitudes, abilities, and skills needed for securing information, fostering and reacting to ideas, developing interests and tastes, and deriving pleasure by reading. This fundamental objective may be met by a program which:

1. develops in each child skill in
   a. recognizing many words at sight.
   b. gaining meaning quickly upon meeting unknown words and expressions by using one or a combination of the following:
      analysis of structure,
      phonics,
      configuration of the graphic symbol,
      contextual analysis,
      the dictionary.
   c. comprehending and interpreting the meanings of words, phrases, and sentences.
   d. reading silently at speeds appropriate to the content and purpose.
   e. reading orally with fluency, suitable speed, expression, correct pronunciation, and attention to enunciation.
   f. evaluating the content of what is read.
   g. using books efficiently—locating information, using the library, etc.
2. provides many opportunities for rich and varied experiences through reading.
3. develops a lasting interest in reading.
4. fosters the resourceful and creative use of reading to meet particular needs and interests.

Reading in the Curriculum

Reading is an all-day, all-life activity; wise teachers are aware of this and use it to their advantage in teaching reading skills as well as building children's under-

24

How to Read a Science Book

Do you ever think about all the different kinds of things you read? You read stories and poems and cereal boxes and street signs. You also read books that give information. Do you read all of these things in the same way?

Here are some paragraphs from a science book. As you read them, see if you think about them in exactly the same way you would think about a story. After you finish reading, you will be asked to find the main idea, so look for it as you read.

254

Knowing how to read means having the ability to read in all areas of the curriculum. (From *Using Our Language,* Level 3. Copyright 1977 by Noble and Noble. Used by permission of the publisher.

standing that reading and the other language arts are communication skills that are important in virtually all of their activities.

The more the various areas of the language arts and other subjects are meaningfully related in instruction, the greater the possibility that learning will be enhanced and interest developed. The following chapters on study skills, library skills, and children's literature add to the instructional suggestions in this chapter. The interrelatedness of all of the language arts and the need to use language skills and abilities in all areas of study also make the teaching of reading easy to relate to vocabulary study, spelling, and handwriting, as well as to science, mathematics, and social studies. Because sharing personal experiences orally or through writing is highly motivational, the sharing can also be related to reading instruction. In many ways the interrelating of the various instructional areas is easy, but careful planning is required for the objectives to be achieved. Numerous aids to such planning have been suggested in earlier chapters, and others will be discussed in the chapters that follow. However, an alert teacher will find many more ways throughout each day to relate his or her instruction in reading and the other language arts to all the other areas of the curriculum. These natural occurrences usually top suggestions in any book, because they relate activities to real people in a genuine situation.

Children have not been taught to read until they can read their social studies, science, and mathematics books with an understanding of concepts, directions, and questions.

READINESS FOR BEGINNING READING

Many of the reading problems of concern to teachers (and, less directly, to the entire public) are a direct result of improper attention to children's readiness for the teaching effort directed at them. If readiness for the particular learning is absent, a cycle of frustration and failure is being thrust upon a child. Readiness for any learning can be encouraged and guided; it can never be rushed.

Determining Readiness

Before instruction in reading begins the teacher needs to look at many factors in a child's development to determine which areas must receive attention prior to the initial instruction in actual reading skills. Once this determination has been made, attention can be given to building readiness in those factors needing it. There may be some children, of course, who do have the readiness for initial reading instruction when they come to school, but most will range from "nearly ready" to needing both time and considerable attention to most of the factors. It is important to remember that at any stage of development every human being is ready to learn something, but readiness is not static nor does it proceed in regular cadence for all individuals. Two children might both be ready for the first steps in initial reading instruction, but they both may not be ready for the next steps. You must continually seek to elevate a child's readiness and know what the readiness level is for instruction to be most successful.

Factors that are generally in need of assessment to determine the readiness strengths and weaknesses of the child before reading instruction begins are indicated by the following questions:

A. Background experience: Has the child
1. been on shopping trips to the market, department stores, etc.?
2. visited a zoo, farm, office building, etc.?
3. gone on trips to other parts of the country?
4. been to the library?
5. been read to at home?
6. looked at picture books, etc. at home?
B. Verbal facility: Does the child
1. have the ability to describe experiences to others so that they enjoy listening?
2. understand many concepts and vocabulary—e.g., a peach is a fruit, a cow's baby is a calf?
3. know the meanings of most common prepositions—*over, under, between, above,* etc.?
4. use and understand the language of the school—*library corner, talking time, bring your chairs to the circle,* etc.?
5. have the ability to understand and repeat oral directions?
C. Intellectual and perceptual ability: Does the child
1. have the general intellectual ability and maturity of other children of the same chronological age?
2. have the ability to discriminate visually among shapes, words, and letters?
3. recognize and name the letters of the alphabet?
4. identify words that rhyme or begin alike?
D. Physical condition: Is the child
1. in general good health?
2. sufficiently rested and nourished each day?
3. able to hear and see adequately?
4. coordinated as well as others of the same age?
5. able to articulate sounds and pronounce words normally?
6. established as to eye, hand, and foot dominance?
7. able to use crayons, pencils, and scissors adequately?
E. Emotional-Social stability: Does the child
1. modify behavior to adjust to changing situations?
2. work independently?
3. have the desire to learn and complete tasks?
4. work and play with other children?
5. listen to and react to others?
6. have a positive self-image?

These are not all of the questions that might be asked, nor is a negative answer to one or even several of these evidence of possible failure in the beginning stage of learning to read. But such questions do get to the heart of the abilities, attitudes, and skills that are important to first instruction, and therefore many "yes" answers are needed. "No" answers indicate the readiness program that should be planned for the child.

The child's level of readiness for initial instruction with respect to many factors may be determined by commercial tests—of which there are many. Caution needs to be exercised in using some of these materials, however, since they are often not as diagnostic as is claimed. Also, there are differences among the tests as to what should be evaluated as evidence of readiness. If a commercial test is used, its use should be followed by informal assessment of various aspects of readiness as the initial teaching is being done.

See Roger Farr and Nicholas Anastasia, Tests of Reading Readiness and Achievement *(Newark, DE: International Reading Assoc., 1969) for reviews of readiness tests.*

Developing Readiness

Readiness instruction requires ingenuity and creativeness (as does all teaching), since no list of activities can suggest everything that might be needed nor can any number of commercial materials provide adequately for each child. Careful judgment should be exercised in selecting and using commercial materials since they have been developed for a hypothetical classroom rather than yours. While you may modify these materials or the suggestions as to how they should be used, they often include many more worksheets and dittoing exercises than are needed or should be used.

Building Experiential Backgrounds.　Although children's experiential backgrounds vary greatly, all children need opportunities to have experiences that relate to school activities. These are some ways that may be used to build experiential backgrounds:

1. Do a great deal of reading to the children and have them discuss what was read.
2. Encourage children to tell about things they have done, to make up stories, and to share information. Let them bring objects to show and explain to the other children and to you.

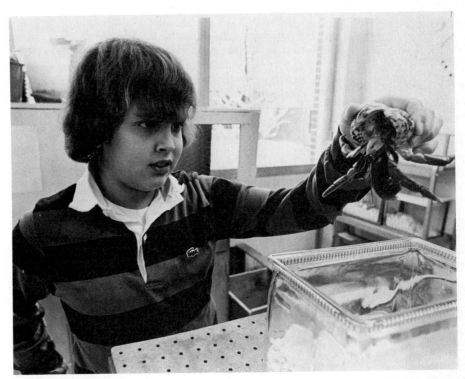

Building children's experiential backgrounds is an important part of developing reading readiness.

3. Provide opportunities for dramatic play, for experimenting with clay, finger paint, and cold water paint, and for creative expression through music and rhythm.
4. Have places within the room for displaying interesting materials—leaves, flowers, rocks, etc. Show pictures—still, motion, filmstrip, slide—and encourage the children to talk about them. Conduct experiments with seeds, flowers, and plants. Observe animals, fish, etc. (have a classroom pet, an aquarium, or a terrarium).
5. Take many excursions—into the schoolyard and neighborhood, around the building, and to stores. Plan these with the children and discuss them afterwards.

Developing Vocabulary.   Many opportunities to develop children's vocabularies will present themselves during discussions, reading by the teacher, and sharing periods. These should be utilized whenever they occur. For example, in discussing something that Mary told in Show and Tell, have the children substitute words with the same meaning: Can you give us another word that tells how Mary felt? From Mary's description, can you tell what kind of day it was?

In other instances, dramatic activities can be used to develop word meanings. As children play at being firemen, mechanics, housewives, etc., they can be told new words (by other children as well as by you). Also simply talking about words with the children—discussing meanings, variations, the way words sound, etc.— is interesting and helps develop vocabulary.

Understanding Relationships.   Experiential backgrounds are also built through activities that focus on teaching new concepts and developing understanding of relationships among known concepts. For example, have the children tell what they would wear on a hot day, on a rainy day, etc. Have one describe how he or she would dress and the others guess the time of day. Fold a paper in half; then have children make and cut out pictures of objects that belong together and paste the pairs in the "boxes." Set up a play street of cardboard store fronts, with picture cutouts of items the children can pretend to buy in these stores. Many of the activities suggested in this section and in other chapters can be directed at showing relationships.

Visual Skills.   Children need the ability to perceive and discriminate visually. Again, there are many activities for building these skills. For instance, give a child pieces of paper of different shapes to be sorted according to shape. Start with two shapes and increase the number (they may also be sorted according to color). After forms have been matched, the child can check his or her work by placing them side by side on the flannel board. You might also have form boards or puzzles to assemble, beads to string, pictures to color, and blocks to build with. Pictures can be classified for scrapbooks (dogs, cats, pets and not pets, types of food, etc.). Arrange objects on a table, cover them, and have the children recall the objects. Show a sample form (square, triangle, circle, etc.), remove it, and have the children draw what they saw. (This will also provide a check on eye–hand coordination.)

Also, begin giving attention to likenesses and differences in words. For example, *red* and *yellow* are words in which the general configuration is helpful. Be sure, however, that these early exercises include only gross differences; make no attempt to teach words. Point out that words that "sound short" often look short and those that "sound long" look long.

Move as quickly as you can into activities that involve seeing likenesses and differences in words—even before the child can tell what the words are.

Discriminating visually among shapes of objects and drawings is not the same as discriminating between words.

Auditory Skills.   Because children have learned to speak, they obviously are able to perceive sounds reasonably accurately and can discriminate between similar ones. Beginning reading instruction may be aided, though, if children practice these skills. Activities for their development and practice include identifying and distinguishing among the sounds produced when different objects are struck; listening to music for high, low, soft, and loud sounds; identifying rhyming words (out in the snow/sat a black crow); finding the missing word in two-line rhymes (we went so far/in Daddy's new _____); and making charts using pictures of objects whose names rhyme or begin with the same sound.

Children should also listen for and give words that rhyme or begin with the same sound. This can be done on a pupil-teacher or child-to-child basis. It can also be a team activity, but be sure that children who "drop out" early have a way to participate. In other words, do not make this an activity for those who already have good ability.

It is helpful, too, to vary regular classroom activities in which responses are asked for by rows or in some other ordinary way by using skill-building activities instead. For example, "All children whose names begin with the same sound as 'Mary' may collect the crayons and put them away."

Other activities include giving several words, some of which rhyme (or begin alike), and having the children tell which ones belong together and which do not; making different sounds in sequence and having the children tell which was first, middle, and last; having the children take turns imitating sounds of animals or machines while the others try to identify them (sometimes it may be desirable to determine *why* a particular response—right or wrong—was made); and using jingles or rhymes that repeat sounds or words (Jack Be Nimble, Hickory Dickory Dock, etc.).

Listening.   Listening ability requires particular attention and its teaching can be related to other activities in the classroom (see chapters 3 and 7 for specific suggestions). In relation to reading readiness, it is particularly helpful to develop standards for listening, sharing, and being courteous. (Each child should be taught self evaluation in terms of these standards.) It helps to limit the size of the group in which the child who needs help with listening is working; the size of the group can be increased gradually. When reading or telling a story, stop occasionally to ask questions that test attentiveness and listening ability.

Following Directions.   As indicated above, reading instruction requires the ability to pay attention to directions. Directions should be clear and simple, and at first there should be only one thing to remember. It is also important to check to see that directions are understood, particularly in respect to any sequence involved, and then see that they are followed. Variation in teaching can be provided by follow-the-leader games or games in which the children give the directions.

Expressing Ideas Verbally.   You can best help children learn to express themselves simply by giving them many opportunities to talk. Introduce new words as they are needed in these speaking activities. Explain the meanings of the words using concrete objects or pictures when possible to give additional substance to the explanation.

Invite parents to learn about your reading program.

Be prepared to give them suggestions for helping their child become ready for your first instruction and for helping as the child is beginning to read.

Hearing and listening are not the same thing. Listening requires thought and often some action.

For Parents

(Available from the International Reading Association)

Why Read Aloud to Children? by Julie M. Chan.

How Can I Encourage My Primary Grade Child to Read? by Molly Kayes Ransbury.

What Books and Records Should I Get for My Preschooler? by Norma Rogers.

In addition to naturally occurring speaking activities, try these:

- Have children create new endings for stories read.
- Provide for sharing experiences and showing objects—toys, pets, etc.
- Have art work interpreted orally.
- Encourage the dramatization of words like *walked, ran, crept, raced.*
- Use play activities, such as playing house, store, etc., to induce speaking.

Sensing Sequence.   Many activities are useful for helping children to learn the importance of sequence and to use sequence in stories they tell and later write. These include discussing the day's or week's program and other activities and experiences in terms of sequence; using dramatic play with dialogue or pantomime to tell a story; utilizing art work (a series of pictures, a class movie, etc.) to show the importance of order; and having the children retell a story heard or seen on a film or filmstrip or finish a partially told story.

Eye–Hand Coordination.   Dramatic play activities, building with blocks, using tools, working with pegboards and puzzles, and playing on outdoor equipment are all useful for developing eye–hand coordination. A sand box is also helpful; the children can write letters and names in the sand. Other activities include cutting and tearing, pasting, coloring, easel and finger painting, and working with clay.

Large plastic boats, wading pools, and tubs make good sandboxes.

Left-to-Right Movement.   Since reading requires left-to-right movement, it is necessary to teach this to children. This can be done both directly and incidentally. For example, when reading to the children, hold up the book and run your finger under the words as you read. To teach more directly, you may have them arrange a series of pictures on the chalk tray to tell a story. Make sure that the pictures must be looked at from left to right to tell the story in proper sequence. Another activity is a directional game in which the children tell each other to go to certain places or perform certain actions, using the words *left* and *right.*

Extending the Attention Span.   Reading instruction is hampered and perhaps nullified if children do not pay attention to instructions. A young child has a short attention span, but it is possible to develop his ability to pay attention without unnecessary forcing. For one thing it is helpful to begin and end activities at systematic and logical times. Planning with the children will also be useful, since they will better understand what they are to do if they contribute to the planning. Children can also be given jobs that require paying attention, such as housekeeping and other classroom chores. Observe children's actions at these times, and make sure not to give responsibilities only to those who are well-behaved or who do things well.

Teaching a Child to Read by Roger Farr and Nancy Roser (Harcourt Brace Jovanovich, 1979) suggests in chapter 3 many readiness activities.

Above all, give purposes for doing things. Give the children something specific to watch for, listen to, or find out.

Differentiating among Colors.   Visual discrimination also calls for distinguishing colors. Activities you may find helpful include placing colored objects in the chalk tray and directing children to "find something red" (later these may be differentiated by shape as well as color); having objects of a certain color found in the classroom; and giving oral directions for coloring pictures (let the children participate in deciding what color each object should be). Colored beads and shoelaces can also be used in teaching colors (and in teaching children to follow directions). Work with small groups and say, "I will string one red bead, two blue beads, and one yellow bead on my shoelace. Now you do it." Variations of this are easy to imagine. After the children have completed each task, ask them to tell what they did.

With the wealth of beautifully illustrated picture and story books now available, there should be little difficulty in teaching children about colors. The principal ingredient needed is awareness of the importance of being able to recognize colors and their names.

Adjusting to the School Setting.   It is essential to help each child become acquainted with the school environment—the classroom, the building, the grounds, the people—since this environment is usually strange and perhaps even frightening.

Providing opportunities for expression and creative work, giving encouragement and praise, directing the child's attention to something outside the self, and helping each child achieve success are all useful in helping him or her make the adjustment to school. In all of these activities be friendly, calm, relaxed—and not overcritical of mistakes. Especially, be fair in all your dealings; give the child an extra smile or a pat on the back to show he or she is liked and wanted.

Practices more specifically related to reading are making a special point of introducing children to the books they will use, demonstrating how books and other reading material should be used, and giving practice in their use (see chapter 17).

Furthering the Desire to Read.   As suggested at the beginning of this chapter, most children are anxious to learn to read and are curious about books. This interest should be encouraged through the following techniques:

Provide private places to read.

In an old bathtub full of pillows.
In a papier-maché cave (with a light inside).
In a large box.
Under a long table on a rug.
In a carrell.

- Make liberal use of labels on objects and pictures—name cards on desks; labels for articles made by children, paintings, drawings, science collections, and other materials and equipment.
- Make and use signs: "We are outside," "Gone for a walk," "Save."
- Maintain a library corner with many books available for children to examine. Time should be allotted for the use of the corner.
- Read stories, informational materials, and poems to the children. Be sure not to do all the selecting yourself; let the children choose what they would like to hear.
- Read other materials to and in front of the children. For example, when a notice comes to your room, make a point of the fact that you are reading it. Point out the importance of reading as a means of communication. When appropriate, print a notice on the board to serve as a reminder of what the note said.
- Write charts of the children's experiences. The children can "read" (tell) what these say.

ORGANIZING FOR INSTRUCTION

For proper attention to be given to instructional procedures and techniques, use of materials available, and, most importantly, the differences in the abilities and achievement levels among the children, it is necessary to plan the organizational pattern of the teaching/learning program. Essentially, this planning must begin with decisions about the extent to which all of the children in a classroom will be taught as a group, in smaller groups, and individually. This planning must be of a continuing nature, since the factors influencing decisions will change.

Looking at Individuals

To make organizational plans it is necessary to learn a good deal about each child: various measures of his or her reading ability or readiness for instruction, intelligence, health or emotional problems, previous school achievement, home factors that may affect learning, experiences he or she has had, and any other factors that may influence achievement in reading.

Beginning as well as experienced teachers frequently have difficulty organizing the instructional program. One of the reasons is that often not all of the information suggested above as being important is available—or at least not readily. There is also the problem of systematically looking at the information that can be garnered and making decisions based upon it. We suggest that you record information about each child on a 5 x 8 card. Then, from the cumulative folders of the children, record standardized test scores (not simply cumulative scores, but those of the subtests: word recognition, comprehension, etc.), I.Q., last reading book or program completed (including test information on these), age, various teachers' comments, information about the child's background and interests, etc. With the information condensed in this fashion, basic needs may be identified and organizational ideas can be more readily explored.

Most teachers find rather quickly that planning to teach the entire class as a group of individuals with comparable abilities, potential, and interests simply will not provide effective teaching for many of the children. They also discover frequently that, although there are wide individual variations among the children, there are some common needs that suggest the use of groups for a good deal of instruction.

The card technique suggested above aids primarily in finding common or related abilities, backgrounds (including books read in earlier grades), and interests, but it is also useful in helping you understand the tremendous differences among the children in your class. We recently worked through a set of cards with a first-year fifth grade teacher and found a range in I.Q.'s from 75 to 145 and a range in reading levels (based on standardized test scores) from grade 2 to grade 11.

Although there is much to be said for individualized programs, particularly if the conditions suggested for them are met, experience tells us that, for best use of time, much instruction can and should be done in small groups.

Grouping Plans

The objective of most grouping plans is to narrow the range of differences so that a single set of materials and common objectives are appropriate for all the children in the group. Thus, in a classroom in which children are reading from first grade

Reading Levels

Children "read" on three basic levels:

1. *Independent Level:* Very few words are unknown; content is related to experiences. Children read for enjoyment at this level, which is about one year below the instructional level.
2. *Instructional Level:* About 90% of the words are recognized independently, with about 75% to 80% comprehension. This level is about one year below the frustration level.
3. *Frustration Level:* The child demonstrates great difficulty in word recognition and comprehension. This is often identified as the reading level according to standardized test scores. You may find the social studies and science books for a grade are at this level for many children.

level to sixth grade level (which is not at all uncommon in third and fourth grade classrooms), four groups might be formed, each with its own materials and objectives. The children in one group might all be reading at about the third grade level; they could all use the same reading textbook and be given instruction in many of the same skills. Another group might be those reading at a second grade level; they would use materials that they could read without frustration or boredom. A third group might be the few children who were still struggling with beginning reading skills; perhaps the reading materials for these children might be individualized as much as possible to meet their specific needs. The fourth group might be the more capable readers, who would generally read independently but would be taught needed skills as a group.

Other plans for instruction include grouping on the basis of interests rather than ability and grouping on the basis of social preferences. Interest grouping can be based on differences in the interests children show as they study social studies or science, play games, and read independently. Social preference grouping simply means that children are put in a group because they are "special" friends, live on the same street, have birthdays in the summer, have moved to the school from another town or city, etc. Both of these plans permit teaching fewer children at a

A reading group may work in the library.

time, just as ability grouping plans do, but they widen the range of reading abilities in the group considerably.

Grouping can take still other forms. The entire class may be a reading group when they watch classmates dramatize a story or report on a project. Other variations include putting two ability groups together when they are working on a particular skill or when both are reading about something related to another area of the curriculum (e.g., both reading about peoples of the Far East).

Grouping may also involve the entire school. For example, at a given time of day all classrooms may have reading instruction, and each child moves to the classroom whose teacher is working with the children on his or her reading level. (This is known as the Joplin Plan.) This plan permits the narrowing of the range of differences to a greater extent than is possible in a single classroom but does present the potential problem of having some children taught by a teacher who does not know them as well as their regular teachers do.

A modification of this plan involves all teachers in a school who work with the same grade level. The teachers, acting as a team, discuss each child's strengths and weaknesses as discovered through observation and reading tests and agree on the group each will instruct, as well as on a common time for instruction. During the given period of time, each teacher works with about twenty-five children who are at approximately the same level. Teachers who have used this plan have found that they still need to do further grouping among those coming to their classrooms, although the range of abilities is certainly much less than in the ordinary self-contained classroom. The plan may be particularly difficult for the teacher who takes the slowest children, since even an excellent teacher will have difficulty in teaching reading to a class of twenty-five slow children in 60 to 90 minutes. These children have the greatest academic needs and are commonly the greatest behavior problems. Thus the teacher working with them should have fewer children—perhaps fifteen—along with an aide and a parent volunteer. A teacher with more able students can take a larger class, because these children are more likely to be independent workers.

Pupil-team grouping is being used in some schools. In this plan, superior readers give assistance and extra practice to groups of three to five children who need extra help. In fact, there are so many variations in how instruction can be organized for a particular class that the only limitation is usually the flexibility of the individuals involved.

Working with Groups

Although the effectiveness of an organizational plan depends to a great extent on the teacher's personality and the characteristics of a particular group of children, there are other factors that influence how well a plan meets instructional needs. The principal factor is the operation of the plan itself. That is, the operational scheme—the schedule—must be workable for the plan to be effective.

Any grouping plan will permit variation in the schedule or operational scheme. The following is an example of one way of scheduling three groups. A similar schedule could be made for four or any other number of groups. However, the management of more than four groups is difficult.

Examples of Seatwork Activities

1. Practicing handwriting.
2. Studying spelling.
3. Working in a reading workbook.
4. Writing a story.
5. Reading for fun.
6. Working on a science experiment.
7. Working on a social studies project.
8. Doing learning games and puzzles.
9. Practicing visual discrimination activities.
10. Classifying objects.
11. Listening to tapes and records.
12. Following suggestions on task cards.

Giving the same seatwork to all children is an injustice to them. Make sure that all seatwork has a purpose and is not something just to keep a child "busy"!

Time	Group		
	A	B	C
9:20–9:50	Work with teacher on guided reading and skill development	Other language arts activities (story writing, spelling, etc.)	Preparatory seat-work for guided reading lesson
9:50–10:20	Follow-up seatwork	Prepatory work for guided lesson	Guided work with teacher
10:20–10:30		Rest or recess period	
10:30–11:00	Other language arts activities	Guided work with teacher	Follow-up work and other language arts activities

Notice that this type of schedule keeps some of the children busy working independently while the teacher is teaching the others. For this to work, there must be meaningful independent or group activities that do not require much direct teacher attention. Listening to children read is not teaching, especially if the teacher is giving a substantial amount of attention to the other children in the room. Without planning, careful scheduling, and an adequate supply of materials for children to use, a teacher is "keeping school" rather than teaching.

Planning for the Limited Reader

Some of the children at any grade level have very limited reading ability. These children and those who have learned to read very well are the major reasons for grouping and individualizing instruction. The child who can read the material assigned to his or her classroom—the social studies books, the science materials, and the reading textbook for the grade level—well or fairly well presents few problems. The child who has an instructional reading level considerably below the grade level to which he or she is assigned is a major problem for most teachers. And these children are found in most classrooms.

A teacher must accept the fact that these children do exist and that they are in most classrooms, and must ask, "What can I do?" The answer is not simple—it must vary with every teacher and every classroom. First, as suggested earlier, a teacher should take a look at the child's record. What do other teachers say about him? What is his mental ability? A pattern should be looked for in tests—a weakness that can be pinpointed. For example, if enough information is available, it may be noticed that this child has low scores on the word recognition portions of reading tests and quite consistently has trouble with vowel digraphs (two vowels together that represent a single sound—*boat, meat, beet*) on spelling tests. Perhaps this is the pattern. If further investigation confirms the pattern, attention

Recently many materials have been produced for the limited reader. Investigate, for example, Bowmar/ Noble materials, Clues to Reading Progress *(Educational Development Corp.), and* The New Open Highways Program *(Scott, Foresman).*

should be given to working on vowel digraphs.

Whatever the search for the cause or causes of a reading problem reveals, realistic action must be taken. This means finding something at which the child can succeed—something that will build ego and provide a sense of achievement. Begin with reading at a very easy level; perhaps a sixth grader may very easily read a book written at second or third grade level. Look, too, at the other books he or she has. Surely the sixth grader who reads at third grade level will have difficulty with the sixth grade spelling program; not only the words themselves but also the practice activities are likely to present a reading problem. Yet this child might find success in—and benefit from—a third grade spelling program. In other words, avoid the all-too-common mistake of placing a child at the correct instructional level for reading but at the same time expecting him or her to spell words or read social studies and science books at a reading level two or more grades above that level. After all, integrating curriculum areas means just that—providing each child with suitable materials in every area.

TEACHING READING SKILLS

We have suggested factors—skills and abilities—important for children to have developed when the first instruction in reading is given. As this instruction begins there is an immediate need for children to have other skills. Teaching these does not take place all at once, even for the child who possesses a high level of development in all of the initial readiness factors. Rather, instruction in these skills is woven in over a period of time—usually two or three years—as children need them in order to read.

In this section we suggest procedures and activities for teaching and developing these skills. However, you may want to seek further descriptions of procedures and more extensive suggestions of activities in reading methods books, in educational journals, and in reading materials published for use with children.

Word Recognition

The ability to recognize, recall, or otherwise identify or determine a word is basic to reading. There are several intertwined skills involved in word recognition. No one of these "always works," nor do all children need an equal amount of instruction in all or any one of them. Some activities related to gaining these skills are discussed in the following sections.

Sight Recall.   Adults generally recognize "at sight" most of the words they encounter in their reading. We simply know the words and do not have to stop to figure out what they are. We have gained this ability by our experiences. We have heard many words, seen them often in written form, and possibly have written most of them ourselves. In other words, how they appear in graphic form has been memorized. Of course, we sometimes "look up" a word in a dictionary, ask someone what it is, or possibly stop long enough to see a clue in it that we relate to a word that we do know.

Children who are ready for beginning reading instruction also recognize some words by simply seeing them. These words are ones they have seen frequently in stories that were read to them or that they helped "write" in experience stories. Young children are great at pretending to read, and much of their pretending is recalling. Sometimes their identification of specific words is inaccurate, but often they actually do recognize some words and almost always have a genuine sense of the meaning of a group of words even if they don't know what all of them are. The first reading instruction builds on this knowledge and focuses on teaching a small number of words that a child will readily recognize by sight. These words are introduced slowly and with a heavy reliance on pictures, actual objects, or the experiences of the child so that meaning immediately becomes a part of the reading process. These words provide the foundation for future learning of other words and for learning ways to determine words that are known in speech but are unknown as graphic symbols. Not only do these words need to appear in context meaningful to the child, but they also need to appear frequently so that they can be learned.

Context Clues.   The most important skill for determining the meanings of unknown words is that of using context clues. These clues are available to a reader because of some degree of shared experiences with the author of the materials and because of the reader's knowledge of how the language works. While most of the clues are verbal, since pictures generally relate to the content, they also provide clues to meaning. Thus, a reader using context clues to determine the meaning of a word that he or she does not recognize at sight draws information from the remainder of the sentence, other sentences in the context, pictures that appear to be related, and experiences that he or she has had with related ideas. In a sense this is a guess (as, actually, are all word recognition techniques other than using a dictionary), but it is an informed guess.

Children's skill in using context clues is closely related to the breadth and depth of their vocabularies (see chapter 13). Knowledge of the multiple meanings of many words is necessary, as is knowing that many words have synonyms, figures of speech and idioms have special meanings, modifying phrases and clauses serve specific purposes, and particular words suggest the author's pattern of thinking (e.g. *first, also, on the other hand*, etc.). Activities such as the following can help develop this skill:

1. Write sentences in which one word has been omitted and have pupils supply as many words for the blank as possible. Vary this procedure by writing different first letters in the blank:

   John _____ to the store.
   John w _____ to the store.
   John r _____ to the store.

2. Write homographs (*bear, stick, fleet, flat, fair*, etc.) and illustrate their meanings with sentences:

   I cannot bear *to see you suffer.*
   The bear *ran down the road.*

3. Think of all the possible descriptive words that could be related to a particular object or action.
4. Write as many sentences as you can showing different meanings of common words.

Try words such as *run, walk, back,* and *step.*

5. Write synonyms for words in a story. Will all synonyms for a word always fit the context?

6. Circle the clues to the meanings of the underlined words in these sentences:

The submarine is a reliable underwater craft.

After Bob bought the groceries for his mother, he purchased candy with the change.

Structural Analysis.   Structural analysis involves looking for known parts within unknown words. Determining if a part of a word is known by the reader— that is, that it has meaning that is understood—often leads to identifying the unknown word. Many words are compounds, and a reader may know the meaning of one of the words forming the compound. This may be enough of a clue (especially if other word recognition skills are used) for the reader to get the meaning of the compound. In the same way clues may be provided by other word elements: inflectional endings—*s, ed, ing, ly,* etc.—prefixes, suffixes, and roots. Knowledge of how contractions work, plurals are formed, and words may be divided into syllables is also helpful in structural analysis.

Various teaching procedures or approaches are used for teaching structural analysis, as well as varying emphasis given to each of the elements. The following are examples of activities that are useful:

1. Write inflected and derived forms of words and have pupils underline the root word of each (e.g., *happier, making, shorter, carries, flies,* etc.).
2. Have pupils find the root common to all (or a certain number) of a group of words (e.g., *reporter, portable, portage,* etc.).
3. Make lists of words that have the same ending (suffix) and have the pupils see if they can determine the meaning of the suffix (e.g., *helpful, tearful, hopeful, fearful*).
4. Have pupils make lists of compound words or put words together to make compounds.
5. Provide lists of words to be divided into syllables.
6. Write prefixes on cards and place them in a box. Then have each pupil draw a card and give a word that has the prefix as a part of it.
7. Have children classify words in a list by common suffixes, prefixes, syllabication rule, or root.

Phonics.   Phonics is the relating of graphic symbols (one or more letters) to sounds (also one or more). The objective is to help a reader identify unknown words by putting together sounds associated with the graphic symbols, thus saying a word that is known. Various "systems" or approaches to teaching phonics have been advocated, each with varying numbers of generalizations or rules about the sound or sounds that are represented by a letter or groups of letters and suggestions for blending of sounds so that a "sounding out" approximating the pronunciation of a word is produced.

Children should not be taught to depend exclusively—or even largely—on phonics for recognizing unknown words. There are simply too many exceptions to many of the rules or generalizations to be as helpful as some people state. Too, combining sounds does not always result in approximate pronunciations. Finally, the process may slow the reader down excessively. This slowing down causes a reader to lose the sense of the context and language structure and thus not use the

Dictionary skills are discussed in chapter 16.

clues these provide. On the other hand, phonics used in combination with structural analysis may be helpful in enabling a reader to gain enough sense of the context to make better use of clues it and the language structure provide. The key is not to "over dose" children with phonics but for them to have the phonics knowledge that may genuinely be useful at times.

There are many activities for developing phonics skills. Here are some ideas:

1. Change the beginnings and endings of words to make new words (*man—can; meat—meal; walk—talk*).
2. Underline the common elements in a series of words (the *cl* in *clouds, climb, clap, clang*).
3. Make charts of pictures illustrating words that begin with the same blend (or letter, prefix, etc.).
4. Have children come to the board and point to the letter (or blend or digraph) that begins the word you say.
5. Substitute vowels to form new words (*cap—cup—cop; big—bag—beg—bug*).
6. List "families" of words (*cake, take, lake, make, sake, rake, bake, snake, shake*).
7. Have pupils sort cards with words on them into groups with the same vowel sound (or same beginning sound, ending sound, beginning blend, etc.).
8. Match words with specific sounds at the beginning to words with the same sounds at the end.
9. Add letters to beginning blends to make words (*cr—crash, creek, crazy, creep*).
10. Make lists of new words that contain a part from a familiar word (*shoe—shop, ship, show, shine,* etc.).
11. Pronounce pairs of words (*pay—pat; head—said; cap—hat*) and have the pupils tell in which pairs they hear the same vowel sound.
12. Match cards to make words. Initial consonants may be matched with phonograms (*an, ink, eat,* etc.); suffixes may be matched with bases; or two words may make a compound.
13. Match pictures whose names rhyme (or begin with the same sound).
14. Write words with medial vowels omitted (r__d, t__n, p__n) and have children insert as many different letters as possible.
15. Have the children write the first letter or first two letters of the words you say.

The Dictionary.   The most reliable way to determine the meaning (and pronunciation) of an unknown word is to look it up in a dictionary. While words in the listening/speech vocabularies of a reader can often be recognized by the other means suggested, some words frequently cannot; thus, the ability to use a dictionary is also important for word recognition.

Decoding Independence.   Independent readers use combinations of both pronunciation and meaning clues, reflecting the fact that all learning involves associating the unknown with the known. Thus, in helping children develop independence in reading, all avenues for relating what they know to the unknown symbols should be used. They must be taught to associate sounds with individual letters and combinations of letters (blends—*bl, tr,* etc., and digraphs—*ch, sh,* etc.); to divide words into syllables (to aid in pronunciation or determining meaning); to understand the meanings of many prefixes, suffices, and root words; to use the dictionary skillfully; to gain an accurate visual image of words; and to relate their experiences to the content of what is being read.

Throughout the period of learning to identify word symbols and to interpret their meaning, the skills should be used in purposeful situations. The skills should be taught as a means for helping pupils secure information, get enjoyment from their reading, and achieve genuine understanding of what is read. During this instructional period much reading material must be available and used so that children can develop the independence they need. Thus, attention must be directed to stimulating and expanding reading interests, to showing the children that reading is a part of many classroom activities outside of reading class, and to building upon the success each child has in developing his or her reading independence.

Reading carefully is important. (From *Wide-Eyed Detectives Skill Book*, Level 8, of the Laid-law Reading Program, copyright by Laidlaw Brothers, Publishers, 1976. Used by permission of the publisher.)

A Focus on Comprehension

The ability to read is more than identifying the words that graphic symbols represent. The basic element in reading is comprehension, and comprehension is an active mental process. To comprehend, a reader has to relate his or her experiences and knowledge of how language works to the words that have been decoded. Comprehension occurs when the reader has enough background experience to relate to the content of the reading material and thinks about what he or she both knows and wants to know regarding this content.

As we pointed out in chapter 13, knowledge of words and skill in using language comes from experience. Thus, if children are to comprehend what they will be called on and want to read, their experiential backgrounds must be continually broadened and strengthened—not only at the "readiness" stage but throughout their days in school.

In addition to extending their experiences and to providing opportunities for them to gain in language ability, children must be taught a number of specific skills that will aid them in comprehension; they must know how to read for the main idea, for details, for the organization of the content; they need to be able to skim, to read critically, to outline, to use the dictionary, and to vary the reading rate (these skills are discussed in chapter 16). Children must also be taught to go beyond the literal interpretation of what they read. They must learn to do cause-and-effect reasoning, to draw inferences, to arrive at conclusions, and to make generalizations.

Comprehension teaching should begin even before the first reading instruction. In many ways stories listened to as well as the first stories read require the skills of the mature and highly effective reader. While not all of the skills stated here can be taught at once, attention can always be given to purposeful reading, the experience backgrounds of the children, and their use of reason at all levels of instruction. Unfortunately, though, some teachers end their teaching of reading when the children are reasonably skillful at identifying and recognizing words and fail to give attention to the comprehension skills as the curricular requirements of teaching social studies, science, and the like bear down upon them. Wise teachers (including those who teach in middle schools, junior highs, and high schools) recognize that effective teaching of subject specialities requires that reading skills also be taught.

All classroom activities that aid the development of children's thinking powers help to improve their reading comprehension. To encourage thinking, of course, the activities must be purposeful, relate to the children's experiences and interests, and require some degree of reasoning or the testing of ideas. Here are a variety of activities to use or adapt to your class:

1. Have individual conferences with pupils to help determine comprehension and to aid it by the exchange that takes place.
2. Have children illustrate favorite events in a story by drawing a picture or by dramatizing.
3. Question children about cause-and-effect relationships in things that they talk about as well as read.
4. Encourage pupils to volunteer for oral reports on definite topics of special interest to them.
5. Aid pupils in constructing their own questions to be answered from their reading.

6. Have many projects going on around the classroom (science experiments, games, seatwork exercises, etc.).

7. Take time to point out and discuss figurative, idiomatic, and picturesque language. Encourage children to find other examples of these forms.

8. Have children describe a place or activity in one word and tell why the word is an appropriate description.

9. Use seatwork activities such as matching:
   • questions with answers in lists.
   • paragraphs with titles.
   • words with their synonyms (or antonyms).
   • pictures with sentences (or words or paragraphs).

10. Other seatwork activities include using selections in which the main idea is to be found, details related to the main idea listed, directions followed, an inference that is justified stated, or a conclusion written.

11. Have children prepare short oral or written summaries of science experiments or social studies units.

Reading Rates

Not all reading must be done as rapidly as possible. The type of thinking the content requires should determine the rate of reading. Thus, much of the problem in developing effective reading rates centers upon having the child recognize the type of reading required—appreciative, critical, or informative. Talking with the children about how different materials, such as newspaper articles, cartoons, science experiments, arithmetic problems, and social studies books, should be read will help. This kind of discussion gives focus to reading purposes.

In addition, direct attention should be given to increasing reading rates. Try timed reading activities. Pick selections with words the pupils are likely to know, and have them read for one or two minutes (gradually increasing the amount of time). Then have the pupils count the number of words read and divide by the number of minutes to get their reading rate per minute. Some testing of comprehension should accompany these exercises.

THE READING LESSON

The basis of effective reading instruction is the reading lesson. The lesson is the focal point on which a teacher brings his or her instructional knowledge and ability fully to bear. This requires careful planning for specific purposes and for individual children. We suggest that there are certain essential features involved in lessons—in planning for them, teaching them in a total class setting, modifying them for children with limited reading ability, and integrating them with the remainder of the curriculum. These features are discussed in the following sections.

Lesson Essentials

Naturally, a teacher must be flexible in the techniques used from day to day and from one particular teaching situation to another. Not every lesson should follow the same format; a teacher should show initiative in planning lessons. However, the focus should always be on reading to gain meaning and to interpret and use the ideas presented in print. (Most methods or approaches to teaching reading have this kind of emphasis, the principal exception being those that focus almost exclusively on decoding.) Hence the plan suggested here for daily instruction may be regarded as an outline. The essentials are the following:

I. Developing readiness for the reading activity
    A. Through a discussion of experiences that are related to the material to be read.
    B. Through the introduction of new words and new concepts and the relating of these to known words and concepts.
    C. Through relating children's interests to what is to be read and establishing purposes for the reading.
II. Guiding the first or survey reading of the selection
    A. By asking questions and by responding to children's questions so that the child is motivated to read for the purpose or purposes of the lesson.
    B. Through noting the organization of the selection.
III. Rereading for specific purposes, such as
    A. Answering specific questions.
    B. Doing interpretive oral reading.
    C. Finding specific words or explanations of particular concepts.
IV. Developing important habits and skills
    A. Through direct instruction and practice in using word recognition techniques, comprehension skills, and so forth.
    B. Through the use of workbook and teacher-prepared materials.
    C. Through evaluation of progress and the establishment of further instructional goals.
V. Providing for enrichment
    A. By following up on activities during rereading.
    B. By relating what has been read to interests and needs in other curriculum areas.
    C. By suggesting supplemental readings and other activities.

Planning a Lesson

Even an experienced teacher makes plans; these include writing out reminders of things to do during the lesson, planning the probable sequence of activities, and gathering together needed materials prior to the lesson. An inexperienced teacher should make rather detailed plans—even if the teacher's edition of the children's reader has extensive suggestions. The following indicates the general outline of a reading lesson plan, along with some suggestions regarding each point.

Objectives.   Write out the objectives in terms of what you want the children to know or to be able to do as a result of teaching the lesson. Think about how you will be able to observe what each child has learned. An objective is of value only to the extent that its achievement can be determined. For example, if an objective is to teach the children the meanings of certain words, whether or not they have learned these words can easily be determined.

Materials.   List everything that you will need for the lesson: books, word cards, sentence strips, objects illustrating new words and concepts, pictures, etc.

Time.   How much time must be spent on this lesson? Is it a lesson that should extend over more than one day?

Readiness.   What will you do to get the children ready to do the reading and to learn the new words and skills? If you are going to have a discussion of previous stories in the unit, what will you do to relate the discussion to this particular story? Readiness for the skills to be introduced or practiced must also be considered. Perhaps you will need to list words that can help provide configuration (shape) clues, illustrate a phonetic or structural principle, or teach a principle that can be used to determine meaning.

Reading the Story.   How much of the story do you plan to have read at a time before discussing it—a paragraph, a page, or some other unit? Or do you want the children to read the story in its entirety before it is discussed or otherwise reacted to? (Beginning readers should read no more than one page before discussing and responding to questions.) How are you going to use the pictures? Will you have the class discuss them to help build readiness? Reading should usually be done silently first, and then orally, but not every line needs to be read aloud. You will need to think about the purposes for specific reading acts. For example, you may list purposes such as the following: Read to find out why everyone in the picture is laughing. Now find out what happened next. See what the story tells about this picture.

Skill Development.   The portion of your lesson devoted to skill development should include structural analysis and phonics activities, vocabulary building exercises and activities, and work on comprehension skills. Some of this can be done before the story itself is read. However, you may want to see if the children can independently identify or determine the meanings of words that are new to their reading experiences. If they cannot, this may mean that a phonics principle (for example) needs to be discussed, examples given, and the relation to known words and other principles shown after the actual reading is completed. Workbook activities are usually closely tied to this portion of the lesson and should be used. The workbook activities should be examined as you plan the lesson, however, to determine their suitability to your purposes and their relationship to the teaching procedures you must plan for yourself.

Evaluation.   Don't wind up your lesson by asking, "Did you like the story?" Instead, discuss the mood or plot of the story, how the story relates to real life, etc. Plan evaluation in terms of the objectives. Are you going to give the children a worksheet in which they match words and definitions? Are you going to ask questions that require answers that show understanding of the story read? What are these questions?

Enrichment.   There are usually enrichment suggestions in the teacher's editions of reading textbooks at the end of either a story or a unit. Typically these suggestions include books that are related to the story or unit, films or filmstrips that extend understanding and build further interest, and dramatic activities that relate to the reading. These enrichment suggestions should always be considered. While possibly not all of them will be possible to use, the ones that could be used should be. Sometimes, too, the suggestions will cause you to think of other things to do.

Materials and Instructional Approaches

Reading instruction has been of educational concern for so long that a great quantity of reading materials has been developed, along with many procedures, methods, and approaches. Yet many teachers are faced with the task of caring for the needs of individual children without adequate materials. It is not unusual either for a school or district to purchase an excess of "packages" or "kits" of limited scope, rather than books, and then to have all children "put through" this material, which some or all of them don't need; thus many learn little or nothing from the experience. However, a teacher sometimes does have a choice of books and other materials (possibly from a district or school resources center) and always has a good bit of freedom regarding their use.

At the present time there are many approaches to teaching beginning reading. The most commonly used of these advocate similar fundamental procedures. Differences are often in the sequence of the teaching of specific skills, the stress placed upon the use of particular skills, the rate of introduction of new words, the amount and kinds of grouping for instruction, and the supplemental activities advocated. There are, however, rather large differences in the materials used in the approaches.

Seek the help of your reading and curriculum specialists in selecting and using materials.

The following sections describe several approaches to teaching beginning reading (and beyond the beginning stage for several of them) that are widely used. There are variations in all of these depending upon the material or some author's or advocate's description of the approach.

The Basal Reader Program

Reading in the Elementary School by George D. and Evelyn B. Spache (Allyn and Bacon, 4th edition, 1977) thoroughly discusses the major approaches to reading instruction.

The large majority of schools use one or more sets of books called a basal reader series. One source has identified 33 "major basal reading series," which indicates the quantity of materials published, the market for reading materials, and differences in points of view as to how best to teach reading (although, as suggested above, procedures are quite similar to one another). The principal premise for using a basal reading series is that systematic grading or sequencing of the reading skills is possible and necessary. That is, a basal series seeks to control the manner in which various skills are introduced, the sequence of their introduction, and the extent and timing of the reinforcement practice given for each skill. In addition, a basal series controls the vocabulary the child meets and the practice given on this vocabulary.

The first materials in a basal series are readiness workbooks, picture cards, and sentence and word strips that can be used to build the first stories and to teach the first sight words. Readiness materials are followed by preprimers, which use the words introduced in the readiness materials and which often contain stories with the same characters as those in the readiness materials. (Some of the more recently published basal books do not use the same characters and story line and introduce words and concepts not taught in the readiness materials.) A typical preprimer may have from 20 to 50 or 60 different words in it, which generally means that each word is repeated frequently, giving the child practice in recognizing it. Most basal series have three or four preprimers.

The preprimers are followed by a primer (usually the first hardcover book in the series), which continues to introduce new words and to give practice on those previously introduced. After the primer comes the graded series; usually one book is identified as level one (in schools with grade levels, the readiness materials, the preprimers, the primer, and the level-one book would ordinarily be completed by a child in grade 1), and there is a first-level and second-level book for each higher grade.

A Pair of Problems

There is a mill with seven corners.
In each corner stand seven bags.
Upon each bag sit seven cats.
Each cat has seven kittens.
When the miller and his wife come into the mill,
how many feet will there be in the mill?

Answer
Four. The cats have paws.

234

Children's reading textbooks today have great appeal. (From *Thundering Giants,* Level 10 of the Laidlaw Reading Program. Copyright by Laidlaw Brothers, Publishers, 1976. Used by permission of the publisher.)

Since the competition among the companies publishing basal reader series is very keen, there has been a great increase in the number of materials available to complement and supplement the core program found in the children's books and teacher's guides. Most companies have workbooks to aid in the development of specific skills, along with duplicating masters of practice exercises, pretests, and posttests. Most companies also have filmstrips, records and cassettes, and supplemental books (some are paperbacks) as part of the program.

The teacher's guides or manuals tend to be less prescriptive in their teaching suggestions than those of a few years ago. However, they do suggest how to organize the class and how to use the materials to develop skills, vocabulary, and related attitudes and abilities. A teacher using a basal program would be wise to follow the suggestions in the guide, making adjustments in terms of the needs and capabilities of specific children.

Particularly noticeable in the newer basal programs is the emphasis given to eye appeal. The pictures are colorful and interesting. There is also a good deal of attention paid to picturing people of different races and ethnic groups and to variety in the reading content (including more than only middle class families).

Although the instructional plans of various basal series are not alike, they do generally provide for the preparational activities (introduction of new vocabulary, setting purposes for reading, establishing experiential backgrounds), silent reading to get the sense of the story, oral reading to check on the use of specific skills, the introduction to and practice of specific skills, and enrichment activities (supplemental reading, related arts, building additional experience backgrounds, etc.).

As has been stated, basal reading programs have been the subject of a great deal of criticism. Yet many teachers have used them quite successfully, and they are not likely to be replaced as the major resource for teaching reading. There is simply too much to be said for a systematic program that does not leave the teaching of skills and vocabulary to incidental encounters. We believe that the values of organized and planned teaching outweigh the criticisms directed at basal series. Fortunately, though, the bases for much of the past criticism have been eliminated.

The best practice, in our opinion, is to use the basal program but not to be limited by it. It can be supplemented in many ways—experience stories, other books, and materials related to all areas of the school curriculum. The basal program should not be used in all its elements by every pupil. Some children simply do not need as much vocabulary repetition as others do. Other children will need additional reinforcement of particular skills. For still other children the fare may need to be changed in order to gain or maintain their interest in reading.

The Language-Experience Method

Regardless of the method or approach used in teaching reading, kindergarten teachers should write many experience stories each week with the children.

The language-experience method utilizes the experiential backgrounds of the pupils and their abilities to express themselves orally for the content and form of the reading materials. The basic premise of this method or procedure is that children need to see the relationship between speaking, writing, and reading. The procedure also stresses the idea that reading is for communication and that children want to tell about, write about, and read about their experiences. The feeling is strong among advocates of this approach that children will be successful in reading what they have actually written themselves and that the experience of failure will then be avoided.

There is no attempt to specify the content of stories by any means except the children's experiences. Thus, although a story in a basal reader might tell about an experience of a suburban family or an event in the life of a city youngster, an experience story can be about anything the children (or an individual child) want to tell about and then read. There are no vocabulary controls in the method, although a teacher may help to see that certain words are repeated in the content of the stories children dictate and some words will be repeated simply because they are used so frequently in everything that is said or written. There is no attempt to structure the sequence of skills taught from one reading experience to another.

Most teachers have always written stories that children dictated and have used them in their instruction. These are usually called experience stories or chart stories. The uniqueness of the language-experience method when it is used to the exclusion of a basal program is that the reading skills are taught as they emerge from the story writing and reading. The responsibility for the program thus rests heavily upon the teacher.

This method is generally recognized as having limitations in terms of providing the kind of extensive experience in reading needed to teach all of the reading skills. However, using experience stories (and not just in the beginning reading stage) is a good way to teach vocabulary, to maintain interest in reading, and to individualize instruction. The language-experience method is also particularly useful with children who need remedial treatment, who speak a nonstandard dialect, or who have had experiential backgrounds that are difficult to relate to the content of the reading series textbooks.

Experience charts can be written about

Daily classroom plans.
The "news."
Individual experiences of
    the children.
Group exercises.
Classroom helpers and
    tasks.
School or playground rules.
Stories and poems that have
    been told or read.
Directions for doing
    something.
Sensory experiences—
    feeling, tasting, seeing,
    hearing.
Classroom pets.
The weather.

The Individualized Approach

Since children differ in ability, background, and interests, and since they learn at different rates and in different ways, there is reason to believe that each one should be allowed to progress at his or her own pace and to the extent of his or her own capacity. Many critics of basal reading programs maintain that it is difficult, if not impossible, for proper attention to be given to such differences if basal reading materials are used, particularly if they are used exclusively. Thus there is a strong feeling among some of these critics that individual children should select for themselves the books they want to read and be permitted to set their own pace and to follow their own interests. This is the essence of the individualized approach.

This approach requires that many books be available for the children to choose from and that the selection be of a wide enough scope (in terms of the difficulty of the reading materials) that children can read extensively at whatever level of development they have achieved. The approach also requires that the teacher determine whether all the skills are being taught. In successful individualized programs, the teacher spends a great deal of time conferring with pupils individually—listening to them read orally, talking about what they have read, helping them attempt a book of greater difficulty, and teaching skills directly.

What appears to some critics of this approach to be an unstructured program is, in fact, a highly organized way to teach reading. A classroom teacher who uses the individualized approach should be a skilled diagnostician, able to determine quickly which skills the child needs additional help with and which ones have been mastered. The teacher must also be familiar with activities that develop skills and have available a wealth of prepared work materials to aid in the teaching.

Some teachers give their initial instruction in a language-experience format and then move into the individualized approach. Still others begin with the first books of a basal series. From the beginning, skills are developed on the basis of needs (the development might actually be done in small groups), with the teacher keeping records of each child's progress. Good record keeping is an integral part of effective individualized programs.

Two widely used individualized programs are published by Random House and Scholastic. Examine these—and others.

The individualized concept has been seized upon by many commercial concerns, resulting in many sets or packages of materials. This development is understandable, since the key to an individualized approach is that a large number of books be available for the children to choose from in their reading. Thus, companies have produced packages containing a wide variety of books (most often paperbacks) of varying levels of reading difficulty about many subjects of interest to children. In addition, the commercial materials provide forms for the record keeping an individualized program calls for, suggestions to teachers for using the program, and synopses of the stories.

Reading authorities who advocate individualized reading suggest that at least 100 books be available to children at the primary level and as many as 500 to those in the intermediate grades.

In many ways the packaged individualized programs resemble the basal programs. The guide materials for teachers are not unlike basal readers' teacher's manuals, and there are cassettes, records, filmstrips, and tests with some programs. They are unlike basal programs, however, if the child is truly free to select what he or she reads.

The most effective individualized programs in our view are those in which there are many books available and the teacher is very competent. He or she must know the books thoroughly, be a well-organized individual, and be a keen observer of children. Without such a teacher, packaged materials will not solve all of the instructional problems, although they are likely to produce results far better than those produced by a less effective teacher with an inadequate number of suitable books.

Programmed Approaches

Programmed instruction provides for the presentation of subject matter in small units, with each presentation calling for a response from the pupil. In true programmed instruction, each response is followed by an indication to the pupil of whether his or her response was correct or incorrect and what he or she should do next. The theoretical base for programmed reading materials is that the process of learning to read is a sequential one, the elements of the process are identifiable, and the order of their presentation is determinable. The objective of the programming is to permit each child to learn at his or her own rate—learning each skill before going on to a new one.

Commercial materials most recently put on the market attempt to combine elements of the individualized approach described in the preceding section with the sequential and feedback aspects of programmed instruction. The System 80 program, for example, is a diagnostic–prescriptive system which utilizes a machine for the presentation of both sounds and visuals. The child views a television-type screen, moving the filmstrip frames by pushing a button according to recorded directions. There are various ''kits'' in the program, which has elements titled ''Beginning Language Concepts,'' ''Letter Names through Sounds,'' ''Reading Words in Context,'' etc.

Many of the commercial materials are advertised as being of a supplemental and individualized nature, suitable for use with basal materials. The principal feature of these materials is the individualized testing and the presentation of decoding and comprehension skills. They generally give a great deal of the responsibility for determining weaknesses and recording progress to pupils.

Proponents of these programs stress the importance of following the program exactly and completely. They also emphasize the value of reinforcing learning, which the sequential steps provide for, and of giving pupils the opportunity to correct mistakes and remedy weaknesses immediately. Critics of programming are generally disturbed by its impersonal approach. They also question whether the skills necessary for effective reading can be taught by a machine, whether the programs are really used in an individualized manner, and the cost factor. There does seem to be evidence that some schools attempt to justify the cost of materials by putting all pupils through the program.

However, the advantages of programmed instruction should not be overlooked because of a reluctance to accept its mechanical type of teaching. Too often in traditional programs specific skills are neither well taught nor reinforced. Often, too, pupils do not have much feedback concerning what they are learning or how well they are learning it. And, of course, a great deal of teaching is unsystematic and without defined objectives. Programmed instruction at least attacks these faults.

Other Approaches and Materials

There are various other approaches and materials, some of which resemble those described. Programs that stress phonics to a large extent or almost exclusively have some supporters. There are also modified alphabet programs—Initial Teaching Alphabet (i/t/a), Words in Color, etc.—that seek to simplify the symbol-sound problem caused by English spelling. Some materials are labeled ''linguistic'' and most of these emphasize the gradual introduction and numerous repetition of sound-symbol relationships.

EVALUATION

Evaluation in reading is more than administering standardized reading and general achievement tests. Evaluation in reading involves making judgments about teaching procedures and pupil performance—judgments that are based both on children's performances on commercial and other types of tests and on observations made of children's reading behavior. Evaluation should *not* be a once- or twice-a-year activity; it should be a continuing process—a process that is very much a part of teaching.

Observations

A teacher should make observations systematically, recording the results so that they may be recalled. Results may be recorded on progress charts and checklists and through notations made during or following interviews, reading children's autobiographies, and regular lessons. Examples of these means for recording information about children's learning based on their performance, as well as a teacher's reaction to what has been observed, are given in other chapters. Records need not be very elaborate or complicated. Simply regularly writing notes about how a child is progressing in reading is often all that may be needed. Using checklists and charts, of course, may simplify the noting. That is, a checklist may list children's names and provide spaces for checking how each one is achieving in using various decoding skills or in reading for details, main ideas, etc. Teachers often have two or three types of checklists in order to note items related to all of the program objectives.

Informal Reading Inventories

Another informal but systematic procedure for determining children's reading abilities and problems they may have is to have them read selections from basal readers (other than those used in the instructional program) of different difficulty levels. If the focus in this reading is on word identification skills, the selections can be read aloud, with the teacher marking on duplicated copies of the selections the errors made—substitutions, omissions, inversions of word order, miscallings, repetitions, etc. More important to assessing children's reading ability, however, is to have the selections read silently and followed by questions directed at determining how well they comprehended the content.

Standardized Tests

Most standardized tests are group tests that provide quantitative data as to how a child compares with either the achievement of a norming sample of children or a preestablished standard of performance. Standardized reading tests do not tell a teacher what he or she needs to do about improving the reading performances of individual pupils. They do provide a teacher with information as to the general level of achievement of his or her pupils in comparison with other pupils with whom logically they might be compared.

Helpful references on reading testing include the International Reading Association's Tests of Reading Readiness and Achievement: A Review and Evaluation *(1969) and* Measuring Reading Performance *(1974).*

There are many standardized reading readiness and achievement tests on the market. Selecting a test appropriate for a particular group of children, the program objectives, and the procedures used is a substantial task. Attention should be given to the standardizing procedures the test-maker used, the population of children used for determining norms, the ease of administering and scoring the test, what the test purports to measure, and so on. Also, a teacher and others concerned about the testing (school administrators, for instance) should know what the test results really show and have clearly in mind how the results will be used.

A FINAL WORD

Teaching children to read is a very important task for teachers. As we stated at the beginning of this chapter, teaching reading is complex and deserves more attention than our space permits. Therefore, for further help look at books that are devoted exclusively to the teaching of reading and at professional journals. However, because of the interrelatedness of the language arts, you can refer to almost any other chapter in this book for additional activities useful in developing skills needed for reading.

REFERENCES

Books

Allen, Roach, and Allen, Claryce. *Learning Experience Activities.* Boston: Houghton Mifflin, 1976.

Durkin, Dolores. *Teaching Them to Read,* 3rd ed. Boston: Allyn and Bacon, 1978.

Farr, Roger, and Roser, Nancy. *Teaching a Child to Read.* New York: Harcourt Brace Jovanovich, 1979.

Griese, Arnold A. *Do You Read Me? Practical Approaches to Teaching Reading Comprehension.* Santa Monica, CA: Goodyear Publishing, 1977.

Heilman, Arthur W. *Principles and Practices of Teaching Reading,* 4th ed. Columbus, OH: Charles E. Merrill Books, 1977.

Hill, Walter R. *Secondary School Reading: Process, Program, Procedure.* Boston: Allyn and Bacon, 1979.

McCracken, Robert A., and McCracken, Marlene J. *Reading Is Only the Tiger's Tail.* San Rafael, CA: Leswing Press, 1977.

Spache, George D., and Spache, Evelyn B. *Reading in the Elementary School,* 4th ed. Boston: Allyn and Bacon, 1977.

Stauffer, Russell G. *Directing the Reading-Thinking Process.* New York: Harper and Row, 1975.

Film

Ready Set Read! New York: Learning Corporation of America (36 8mm. film loops; 3 to 4 minutes each; lesson plans and activity loops).

You'll Find It in the Library. Chicago: Coronet (13 minutes; color or b/w; intermediate).

Filmstrips

Basic Primary Phonics. Chicago: Society for Visual Education (Set of 18 strips).

Better Reading Series. Pasadena, CA: Still Film Inc. (70 strips on word and phrase recognition).

Bookmark Reading Filmstrips. New York: Harcourt Brace Jovanovich (6 sound strips; color; and 6 cassettes for each grade 1–6).

Consonants: How They Look and Sound. New York: Filmstrip House (16 strips and records; primary and intermediate).

Look, Listen and Read. New York: ACI Films, Inc. (Two sets, each containing 4 sound strips, 4 cassettes, media and teacher's guides, spirit masters, a poster, and flash cards).

Phonics Practice. Chicago: Science Research Associates (2 strips).

Reading. Berkeley, CA: Pacific Productions (Sets of color strips on phonics, structural analysis, comprehension, etc.; total of 41 strips).

Reading for the Fun of It. New York: Guidance Associates (word recognition and comprehension skills; intermediate).

Words to Work With. Boulder, CO: Learning Tree Filmstrips (3 strips; recognition and comprehension skills; primary and intermediate).

What's the Word? Boston: Houghton Mifflin Co. (12 strips on contextual aids, phonics, and structural analysis).

Recordings

Pathways to Phonic Skills. New York: Audio-Education (3 LP albums).

Phonics for Children. New York: Audio-Education (4 records for primary children).

Phonics and Word Development. Freeport, NY: Educational Activities (tapes or records).

Read Card Program. Huntington Station, NY: Instructional/Communications Technology (5 sets, each having 5 cassettes, READ cards, and story and activity sheets; filmstrips).

Reading Records. Los Angeles: Educational Recording Services (4 LP albums on phonics).

Kits

Behind The Bright Lights. Palos Verdes Penninsula, CA: Educational Materials (paperback biographies; cassettes; teacher's guides; upper grades).

Bridge: A Cross-Culture Reading Program. Boston: Houghton Mifflin (booklets; cassettes; teacher's guide).

EDL Study Skills Libraries. Huntington, NY: Educational Developmental Laboratories (Grades 3–9; materials on science, social studies, library skills).

Firefly Reading Fun Libraries. Pleasantville, NY: Reader's Digest (35 books and records).

Fuzzies. Los Angeles: Argus Communications (paperbacks; filmstrip; cassette; intermediate).

Individualized Reading Instruction. Denver: Love Publishing Co. (games and activities).

Listening–Reading Program. Lexington, MA: D. C. Heath (Records of completed and unfinished stories, response sheets, and teacher's manual; kits for grades 1–6).

Reader's Digest Science Reader. Pleasantville, NY: Reader's Digest (6 books; grades 4–6).

Reader's Digest Reading Skills Media Centers. Pleasantville, NY: Reader's Digest Educational Division (Skill-builder magazines and cassettes).

Reading Skills Practice Kit. Newton, MA: Curriculum Associates (primary and intermediate).

Reading Readiness Kits. New York: Webster Division, McGraw Hill (comprehension; thinking; phonics; writing practice).

Reading-Time Library. New York: Holt, Rinehart and Winston, Inc. (40 books for first and second grade children in arithmetic, literature, science and social studies).

SRA Reading for Understanding. Chicago: Science Research Associates (400 groups of graded paragraphs designed to promote inferential thinking).

SRA Reading Laboratories. Chicago: Science Research Associates (Kits of graded reading selections and exercises for comprehension, speed, and listening for each grade level 1–6).

Silver Edition Skill Builders. Pleasantville, NY: Reader's Digest (supplemental readers; 4 at each level 1–6).

Specific Skills Series. New York: Barnell Loft (booklets; teacher's manual; test package; etc.; several levels).

Other Aids

Basic Word Sets. Baldwin, NY: Barnell Loft, Inc. (36 titles; teacher's manual, tests, record sheets, and spirit masters).

Blanton, William, et al. *The Power Reading System.* Minneapolis: Winston Press, Inc., 1973 (A diagnostic/prescriptive program with criterion-referenced assessment elements, lesson plans, and record-keeping system).

Bloomer, Richard H. *Skill Games to Teach Reading.* Dansville, NY: F.A. Owen Publishing Co., 1964.

Boning, Richard A. *Using the Context.* Rockville Centre, NY: Barnell Loft, 1962.

Dolch Basic Sight Cards; Dolch Basic Phrase Cards; Consonant Lotto; Vowel Lotto; Group Sounding Game; Sight Syllable Solitaire, etc. Champaign, IL: Garrard Publishing Co.

High Interest/Low Readability Activity Program. Pound Ridge, NY: Sunburst Communications (25 books, 25 activity cards, and teacher's guide).

Johnson, Ida Mae, et al. *Letters and Sounds.* Chicago: Scott Foresman, 1974 (Phonics workbooks for middle grades).

ACTIVITIES FOR PRESERVICE TEACHERS

1. Observe a group of kindergarten or beginning first grade children for differences in verbal facility, social–emotional stability, and physical coordination. Consult the list of questions suggested in this chapter as you watch the children.

2. There are many more reading aids—kits, filmstrips, records, etc.—than are listed in this chapter. Check with your instructional materials center for aids that could be added to these lists.

3. Design exercises for children (grade level of your choice) to practice finding the main idea, selecting details, and determining the organization.

4. Report to the class on reading approaches or materials only mentioned in this chapter (i.e., i/t/a, Words in Color, "linguistic").

5. Examine commercial reading readiness tests. Do they determine the child's readiness in the factors listed in this chapter?

6. Outline a plan for teaching reading to a hypothetical class for one week. Show in the outline how you would include elements of individualized, basal, and language-experience approaches.

7. Examine two or three series of basal readers. Compare the vocabulary loads, linguistic emphases, story content, illustrations, and teacher's manuals.

8. Present arguments in favor of using an individualized approach to reading instruction rather than a basal program.

ACTIVITIES FOR INSERVICE TEACHERS

1. Identify the reading levels and some of the interests of your class. Then, accompanied by two children acting as teacher aides, go to the library and borrow for one month as many books (or more) as there are children in your class. With the children's help set up a reading interest center and begin an individualized, free-time activity which stresses reading for relaxation and enjoyment.

2. Using the readiness evaluation list in this chapter as a guide, prepare a checklist for your class. Duplicate this checklist, and fill one out for each child. Then discuss with the child's parents your observations, how they might help him to develop reading readiness, and what you plan to do in the classroom.

3. From your school's curriculum library or the public library obtain teacher's manuals for teaching reading (other than the ones you use). Nearby school systems might also lend you manuals. Examine these to determine how they might aid you in doing a better job of teaching each child in your class to read. Try out ideas from other manuals.

4. Examine your present system for grouping. Does it meet the needs of your children? Work out a way to improve your group organization based on suggestions in this chapter. Write to nearby schools requesting information on the organizational patterns that they use. Visit another school to examine a different organizational pattern, such as the open classroom. Apply what you have learned to your situation.

5. Secure copies of reading tests, such as the California Reading Test, the Developmental Reading Tests, the Gates MacGinitie, and the Iowa Silent Reading, and consider the possibility of using them in your class. Before examining them, decide what you want to determine by testing.

6. Examine recent publications of the International Reading Association—including copies of the journals. Report to the class about your examination. How valuable are these publications?

INDEPENDENT ACTIVITIES FOR CHILDREN

1. Assemble reading games and toys for children to use individually and in small groups. Card games, puppet games, and puzzles can be made or obtained from companies such as Garrard Publishing Company, Creative Playthings, Inc., and Instructo Corporation.

2. The best "independent reading" activity for children is reading. A section of the room where a child can go to find a book or to read alone is very important. The fare from which he or she may choose must be varied and appealing, and time must be provided for "just" reading.

3. Type descriptions of items pictured in catalogs or magazines, making sure the language is appropriate for the abilities of the children. Cut out the pictures and have pupils match them with the descriptions.

4. Activities such as the following can be done by individual children or small groups for structural analysis practice:

   a. Match cards with root words written on them with others cards containing prefixes or suffixes.

   b. Write in the missing inflectional suffixes in sentences. For example:

      We are go _____ to town.
      This is the small ____ of the three balls.

      Put the sentences on cards and place them in a file.

   c. Prepare cards containing various words with common base forms. Have the child separate the cards into base-word categories. Words might be *green, greener, greenest; report, portal, portage, import;* etc.

   d. Word cards can be sorted into those with particular endings (*-ed, -ing, -ness,* etc.), particular combinations of letters (*ake, ime,* etc.), or particular beginnings (*b, gr, str,* etc.).

5. Similar activities can be constructed for auditory discrimination and letter–sound association practice.

   a. Prepare sets of unlabeled pictures. A child can then group them according to the initial or final sound of their names.

   b. A child can sort words on cards according to the number of syllables in the words, words containing syllables that begin with a particular letter, those that rhyme, etc.

6. Prepare a bulletin board (one the children can reach) in which each section shows a letter or combination of letters. Under each section thumbtack a box. Children can find pictures of objects whose names begin with the letters and place them in the correct boxes. This activity can be varied. For example, instead of showing letters the bulletin board sections can contain pictures. Another variation is to find pictures with names whose ending sounds match the letters on the board.

7. To give individual children reading practice, prepare material on cards that children can read and then respond to by:

   a. Writing answers to questions about the selection.

   b. Following directions.

   c. Listing particular details given in the selection.

15

Literature for Children

Teaching a child the basic reading skills is necessary if the child is to succeed in school since such a large portion of the learning that takes place in school involves reading; but if that teaching also results in the child's learning to *enjoy* reading, that learning will aid the child in becoming a more complete person throughout life. The reading program, then, should be two-pronged. First, it must give each child the skills he or she needs to read well, for if these skills are not learned there will be little or no seeking of the knowledge, pleasure, and insights that reading can provide. Second, if a child is to discover these things, there must also be specific provision for the kinds of literary experiences that will encourage and develop appreciation of the written word and the desire to read.

VALUES OF LITERATURE

The principal value of literature is surely the pleasure and enrichment it brings to the individual. A child who loves to read will never be at a loss for something to do and will spend many pleasant hours with books as companions. This reading will enlarge and extend the reader's world and, hopefully, will result in his or her gaining greater appreciation of the beauty and power of language—the way words can stir the imagination, arouse the emotions, and develop new insights.

Books can also help children to understand both themselves and their relationships with other people, and this understanding can often help an individual child to improve his or her self-concept. This is a central theme of an increasing number of books written for primary children. For example, there is Pat Hutchins' *Titch*, which exemplifies the frustrations of innumerable small children, for Titch is the youngest and smallest member of his family. *Emily and the Klunky Baby and the Next Door Dog*, by Joan Lexau, will strike a response not only from children of divorced parents but also from those whose parents are very busy or who

Bibliographies Helpful for Building Social Awareness

American Potpourri: Multi-ethnic Books for Children and Young Adults. Washington DC: U. S. Office of Education, 1977.

Baker, Augusta. *The Black Experience in Children's Books.* New York: New York Public Library, 1971.

Griffin, Louise. *Multi-Ethnic Books for Young Children.* Washington, DC: National Association for the Education of Young Children, 1970.

We Build Together. Urbana, IL: NCTE, 1967.

must help to care for younger brothers or sisters. The illustrations in this book will bring gleeful giggles as the huge, shaggy next-door dog steals rides on Emily's sled, making it heavier and heavier for her to pull until she finally decides not to run away from home after all. Similarly, a fourth grade girl who feels that she is different from others might find solace in *The Hundred Dresses*, by Eleanor Estes, as she reads of Wanda, the poor Polish girl who is ridiculed by her classmates because she must wear the same faded dress to school each day. And the sixth grader who is beginning to feel independent can surely empathize with Dave, in Emily Neville's *It's Like This, Cat*, who wants a cat simply because his father thinks he should have a dog. There are books about old age, death, the problems of adolescence, and so on. In short, there are innumerable opportunities for children to discover that they are not alone in their problems, to find inspiration for setting and seeking goals, and to learn how they can adjust to situations and personal problems.

Children need not only to understand their own problems, but also to recognize that other people have problems not unlike their own. Hopefully, this may

Reading is total involvement.

lead to the realization that people are not so different after all. For example, the white child who reads Ezra Jack Keats' *Whistle for Willie* will not be able to help identifying with this black boy who cannot whistle for his dog; likewise, the child of divorce—or of poverty—must surely feel kinship with Rafer in Joan Lexau's *Me Day*. Progressing to such books as *Stevie* by John Steptoe, *Watch Out for the Chicken Feet in Your Soup* by Tomie de Paola, *Zia* by Scott O'Dell, and *The Turning Point* by Naomi Karp can help children to a better understanding of other cultures and other races.

Equally important in these days of mainstreaming and the struggle for equality by the handicapped are books that help to develop an awareness of those who are physically or mentally different. There are many of these, even at the primary level—for example, Joe Lasker's *He's My Brother* (slow learner), Bernard Wolf's *Anna's Silent World* (deafness), or Ezra Jack Keats' *Apt. 3* (blindness). Thus reading can help children to gain a greater understanding of people and the world in which they live. This understanding can be further increased by reading literature of and about the past. It has long been recognized that literature is a major avenue for transmitting to the present the values, ideas, and experiences of past generations. Knowing about the past can provide a new perspective on problems of the present and increase children's appreciation of both their own heritage and that of others.

There can be little doubt that wide experience with books increases a child's vocabulary. The children whose parents have bought them books and have read to them frequently are better prepared for the language of the school. Likewise, those who plan kindergarten and primary programs advise teachers to use many books and to read and tell many stories to help the children learn new words and acquire new meanings for words they already know. As children advance in school, reading can continue to enrich vocabulary in these ways.

Reading is also an important way to build and extend concepts. For example, a common word like *home* may have different connotations for different children. One may think of home as a two-story frame house in a typical suburban neighborhood, another may think of it as a crowded apartment in a city tenement, and possibly neither has ever heard of a home called an *igloo* or *hogan*. Books may introduce these and many other words that hold the concept of *home,* along with the emotional factors with which this word may be associated. And as they advance in reading skills and experience, children can acquire and broaden many concepts and ideas.

In addition to providing vocabulary and ideas, books can help children learn to express their own thoughts and to become familiar with the language patterns they meet in reading and in listening to others. The child who comes to school with a limited language background is especially helped by having heard many stories both read and told, but all children need to become acquainted with many types of sentence structure, the use of figurative language, the language of poetry, the formal language of research, and so forth, if they are to learn to use language effectively. And perhaps one of the most valuable corollaries of reading is that it stimulates the child's imagination and helps to stir creative talents. There is no child who cannot write something creative with the proper encouragement and a wealth of models.

Finally, any program that is tied to a single textbook is almost bound to be both narrow and uninteresting. Resource materials are invaluable, but why not add a third dimension through the use of imaginative literature? Benjamin

Franklin becomes a real person, not just a character in history, when viewed through the delightful *Ben and Me*; a story like *The Cabin Faced West* helps children to experience vicariously the loneliness and hardship of pioneer life; Mike Fink, Paul Bunyan, and Davy Crockett add color and humor to a study of the expanding frontier. Pupils with a scientific bent might enjoy reading science fiction and trying to decide whether the events depicted could really happen; a letter-writing unit can be enriched by the addition of letters written by famous people; and, of course, biography can be useful in any area. Finding just the right materials to make best use of literature in the total program may take a little time, but the rewards are immeasurable.

CREATING THE CLIMATE

Just as you are the model for children's speaking, so will you be a model in their attitude toward books and reading. Thus a cardinal requisite for guiding children toward a love for reading is to enjoy books yourself. Even an avid reader of adult

Here, Archie and his dog Willie search frantically for the cat, who has disappeared on the day of the pet show. [Reprinted with permission of Macmillan Publishing Co., Inc. from *Pet Show* by Ezra Jack Keats. Copyright © 1972 by Ezra Jack Keats.]

books may find it difficult to communicate this enjoyment to children; it is there-fore vital that you become widely acquainted with books written expressly for children. A good first step is to take a course in children's literature, if this is possi-ble. In addition, books written about children's literature (such as those by Arbuthnot, Huck, or Glazer and Williams), book reviews, and bibliographies of var-ious types can serve as guides to specific titles. (See list of aids to book selection at the end of this chapter.) But these are only guides. Simply knowing *about* books or knowing specific titles and authors is only the beginning; to really *know* children's books, it is necessary to read them. Spend time regularly in the children's section of the library making notes of books that would be good for reading aloud, those that would be good additions to the room library, those that would interest a particular child in your class, those that would be useful as supplementary reading for a par-ticular unit of study, etc. This should not be an onerous task; the world of children's books is a delightful and colorful one.

Demonstrating Interest in Books

Ideas

Children's Book Week in early November is a good time to promote children's books. Write to The Children's Book Council, 67 Irving Place, New York, NY 10003.

Also remember Library Week. Write to National Library Week, 58 West 40th St., New York, NY 10036.

For a Book Fair write to The Children's Book Council and to Scholastic Teacher, 50 W. 44th St., New York, NY 10036.

See sources such as Charlotte Huck, *Children's Literature in the Elementary School*, for other ideas.

The daily activities of the classroom provide many opportunities to demonstrate to the children your own interest in and dependence on books. First, make it a point to show your own reliance on books. Let the children see you reading, use stories and poems to illustrate situations and show how ideas have been expressed by others, and use quotations when they are appropriate—perhaps putting a daily or weekly quotation on the bulletin board. This can be overdone, however; quotes should be used naturally and only when they are suitable to the occasion or chil-dren will become bored with them.

Second, make time in the schedule to read aloud to the children at least once every day. This practice should be continued even after children have acquired the skills to read on their own. In fact, it is perhaps more important in the upper grades, since young children are ordinarily eager to read and to be read to, whereas the expanding interests of older children may tend to diminish this interest unless it is carefully nurtured. The reading may be only a short poem, or it may be a story, a chapter in a book, or something interesting and informative that you wish to share with them. Learn to read well, and let the children see that you enjoy reading.

Third, discuss books with the children. Ask them questions about books they are reading or have read, let them recommend selections to be read aloud to the class, help individual children to find books that are suited to their interests and needs, and seek their opinions about books that you have especially liked—or perhaps even ask them to evaluate a book you did not like and see if they can decide why you didn't. Your attitude should show that you value their opinions and that not everyone has to like the same book, even if it it supposed to be "good."

And, finally, although reference materials are not, strictly speaking, "litera-ture," you can foster the idea that books are friendly helpers by turning to books regularly for information and assistance. Children need to learn that not even the teacher knows everything—that it is the most natural thing in the world to turn to the dictionary to check a spelling, to seek out additional information on a sub-ject they are studying, or to look up something they do not know.

The Room Library

The corner of the room devoted to the room library is an important factor in creating an atmosphere that encourages reading. If it is nothing more than simply a corner where there happen to be some bookshelves and perhaps a table and a chair or two, it will do little to reinforce the attitude that reading is a pleasant and satisfying experience. The reading corner should be warm and bright—one of the most attractive spots in the room—and should have enough light so the children can read comfortably and can see to find books on the shelves. Chairs arranged invitingly in groups around a low table on which books are attractively displayed will provide motivation.

Some teachers like to obtain children's lounge or rocking chairs or to construct chairs from wooden boxes, foam rubber and some colorful remnants—perhaps adding a lamp and a plant or two as an extra touch. Others produce an even more informal atmosphere by strewing large cushions on the floor or perhaps filling an old bathtub or rowboat with pillows so that children can truly relax as they read. And, of course, now that so many filmstrips and cassettes of children's stories are available and the "hardware" for seeing and hearing them can easily be operated even by primary children, a filmstrip machine and a recorder should be a part of the library corner. If space is limited, plan to have the listening–viewing center nearby and be sure to allow children free access to both materials and machines.

Provide for places to read informally.

A bulletin board devoted exclusively to books is also an important part of the book corner. The children themselves can help to make displays and see that they are changed regularly. Here are a few ideas:

1. Place at the top a caption reading "Can You Match These?" On one side put pictures of well-known authors of children's books, and on the other put either actual book jackets or some that have been drawn by the children for books that were written by these authors. Provide lengths of colored yarn which the children can use to connect each writer with his book as they discover which ones belong together.
2. Use the same type of setup as above to match characters and the books they are in or quotations and the characters who said them (Chicken Little—The sky is falling; The Little Engine—I know I can, I know I can; etc.)
3. To create interest in a particular book, cut pictures representing characters and scenes in the book from publisher's advertisements, book jackets, or magazines, mount them attractively, and arrange them around a replica of the book.
4. Let children write captions for pictures or draw their own illustrations for stories they particularly like. These can be used to make a bulletin board about a particular book or about several books with a common theme, the same author, the same setting, etc.
5. Let the children write "advertisements" for books they particularly like and post them on the bulletin board. This would be excellent in connection with a study of advertising techniques.
6. Regularly center a display around a particular ethnic or national group. This might include authors, illustrators, or even favorite characters in books.
7. Cut a large tree from construction paper and place it in the center of the bulletin board. At the lower corners tack envelopes containing apples, oranges, or whatever, also cut from construction paper (it could even be a magic tree, bearing many different kinds of fruit). As each child finishes reading a book, he writes his name and the name of the book on one of the pieces of fruit and fastens it to the tree.
8. Have the children write letters to their favorite authors, and make a display of the answers received so that all the children can enjoy them.
9. Many of the activities suggested in the later section on book reports can provide attractive and interesting bulletin boards.

Of course, there is no point in making an attractive book corner unless the children are allowed to use it. The schedule should provide daily time for children to read, listen to stories, work on book reports, and discuss the books they have enjoyed, and they should be allowed and encouraged to browse when they arrive at school early or when they have finished assigned work and the other children are still busy. There is no need for absolute quiet in the room library—if the children enjoy books, they will want to share their pleasure. The classroom atmosphere—not just during the library period, but at all times—should be one in which children feel free to ask questions, share information, and help each other. However, they should at the same time recognize that consideration for others demands that they do this without disturbing others or disrupting the activities of the class.

Naturally, the most important furnishings for the room library are the books themselves. Beginning with the very first day of school, the library should be well stocked with books, records, and tapes, including both fiction and nonfiction of many types and covering many areas. Books should have eye appeal—attractive illustrations and easy-to-read type—and there should be a few books for advanced readers that are above grade level, as well as a good number with high interest and simple vocabulary for the reluctant and poor readers, who are especially difficult to entice. Books should also be changed regularly so that no child will be unable to find something of interest to him that he has not already read.

Knowing the children, their interests, and their abilities is the best aid in selecting books and other materials that will be particularly suitable for them. Another aid is the children themselves. Allowing several (not the same ones each time) to go along on trips to the library will help them to become familiar with the library and library procedures. They can help not only in selecting books, but also in "taking orders" for particular kinds of books from the other children, thus freeing you to browse among new additions and find those suitable for children with special interests or needs. In the middle grades (if this is permitted in the school or library) two or three children might occasionally go by themselves to select books, again taking orders from the others. To avoid confusion and the "bandwagon" effect that might result from taking oral orders, these could be written on slips of paper and placed in a box kept on the table in the library corner or in a colorfully decorated envelope thumbtacked to the bulletin board. Pupil selection, however, should be an addition to, not a substitute for, teacher selection, since pupils cannot have a total picture of class needs.

Reading Aloud

Unless you are one of the few who read dialect well, use a recording of a story which makes extensive use of dialect—but be sure it's a good one!

As suggested earlier, providing time during each school day for reading aloud to the children will do much to stimulate interest in books. Sometimes this reading will be spontaneous (a particular situation simply demanding the reading of a certain selection), but most of the time reading should be planned. There are two reasons for this: first, it is not possible to have at hand every selection that you might want to read; second, reading aloud requires preparation and planning.

Many selections are now available on records or tapes; both the quality and quantity of these are increasing almost daily. However, allowing individual children to select and listen to these—or playing them for the entire class—should supplement, not supplant, reading aloud. This is a time for sharing an enjoyable experience with the children, for building rapport, for discovering their interests and tastes, and for broadening interests and improving tastes. Sometimes, of course, you may wish to use a recording in order to free your hands for manipulating visual aids or in order to join the children in enjoying an especially well-read story or poem. But this should be the exception rather than the rule; the avenue of pleasure for children should be your own voice, not that of an unseen actor.

Becoming a good reader may require practice. Even an experienced reader should not read a selection without going over it first. It is a good idea to borrow a tape recorder from the school and listen to your own voice as you read. This will provide an opportunity to make sure that the pitch is pleasant and loud enough to be heard, check speed and enunciation, or listen to an entire selection to see if it gives the desired impression.

In general, select for reading aloud only those stories or poems that you personally enjoy. Just as you would probably do a poor job of teaching something that you don't really think the children need to learn, so you will not read well a story you do not particularly like. The pleasure the children get from listening is in direct proportion to the pleasure you have in reading.

Be constantly on the alert for selections that would be appropriate for reading aloud. Making a card file is one way to be sure you will find the right story for the right time. Cards might be organized according to the particular units or areas the class will be studying, or they might simply be under rather general headings, with the possible addition of special categories such as Christmas, Personal Problems, or Stories for a Dreary Day. Each card should contain enough information to aid you in deciding which particular story to use and to help you find it quickly. It might include the following items:

- Title and author.
- Where it may be found—Is it in a collection? In what library? Call number?
- Audiovisual possibilities—Are the illustrations suitable for showing; are filmstrips, slides, etc., particularly good; is there a record or tape that might be used with visual aids?
- Time required for reading.
- Brief summary—only as much as is needed for a reminder.

With the exception of poetry, which in most cases is meant to be read aloud, there is no point in reading something the children could just as easily read for themselves. Reading time is precious; it should be reserved for those things which children might find difficult to read for themselves or which they might not appreciate as thoroughly. For example, humor—particularly subtle humor—is sometimes not evident to children when they read silently, although they respond delightedly when it is read well to them. Dialect, too, poses a problem, as may stories containing foreign words and names, because the words do not *look* familiar. And many children's classics contain a number of words that children can understand in context but have difficulty in reading for themselves. Marguerite Henry's *King of the Wind*, for instance, is neglected by many middle graders until the teacher selects it for reading aloud. Thus, reading aloud is an excellent way to improve children's tastes and increase their perception. Reasons for reading aloud, then—or for using records and tapes—might include one or more of the following:

1. The selection is high in interest level, but vocabulary and/or sentence structure are difficult for the children. (This might apply to anything read to kindergarten or first grade children, but should be particularly considered at higher levels.)
2. The selection is of particular interest, but not enough copies are available for individual reading.
3. The selection is of high interest, but print in available copies is difficult to read and illustrations are poor.
4. The selection is particularly suitable for reading aloud. Sounds of the words and phraseology add markedly to enjoyment, and/or appreciation is particularly heightened by oral interpretation.

Not everything that is of value is suitable for reading aloud. Check by asking yourself these questions:

1. Is the action (of a story) fast moving and easy to follow?
2. Is the length suitable for reading at one sitting (the length of a sitting should depend on the age and maturity level of the children)? If it is long, could it be satisfactorily divided—e.g., chapters in a novel?

3. Is the vocabulary such that children will understand what is happening even if there are a few words they do not know?
4. Will it be of interest and value to all the children?
5. Is the content pertinent to something that the children are studying or that they are interested in?

The atmosphere for reading or storytelling should be pleasant and informal. If at all possible, gather the children around you in such a way that they can see illustrations easily without delaying the reading unduly. Illustrations are often important to enjoyment (it would be a shame to read *Where the Wild Things Are* without letting the children see those marvelous "wild things"), so they should be large enough to be seen by all the children. If not, consider other possibilities: larger pictures placed on a flannel board, transparencies made for the overhead projector, or perhaps a filmstrip. In such cases it might be helpful to tape the story or to use a commercially produced tape, thus freeing your hands to manipulate the aids. This is useful also when realia are being used, as, for instance, when reading is being used to develop vocabulary for primary children. It is not necessary, however, to use visual aids every time a story is read. In fact, with some children (such as educationally disadvantaged children, whose attention spans may be short) visual aids may prove to be a distraction. A child may become more interested in what makes the figures stick on the flannel board or how the projector works than in the story and interrupt the reading to investigate. Thus discretion is needed in deciding when and how to use visual aids. Certainly good illustrations should always be shared, and aids can add variety. They can also be incorporated into the discussions that precede or follow the reading of a selection when this seems appropriate.

Successful reading or storytelling is an act of sharing. Hold the book away from your face so the children can see your expression as you read, and maintain eye contact by looking up at them occasionally. The reading should move along smoothly or interest will lag, but children should be allowed to see illustrations, to laugh at a humorous line or situation, or even to ask a question that can be answered in one or two words. Other questions can be answered with a friendly smile and "Let's find out" or some similar remark. Too many interruptions may mean that you are not reading well or loudly enough or that the children find the story uninteresting. In the latter case, it may be best simply to put the book away until another time. The possible cause of the inattention should then be considered. Possibly the story was too difficult in concepts or language, there was too little action, or the characters did not seem believable. If so, look for another story that will serve the same purpose but have more appeal for the children. However, if you consider the story suitable and wish to try it again at a later time, perhaps the visual aids could be changed or omitted entirely, the story told instead of read, or some other variation applied.

Storytelling

A good storyteller is always in demand. None of us ever grows too old to enjoy a well-told story, but this ability is particularly useful with young children, since their attention span is short. Telling a story instead of reading it also frees your hands for illustrating it with flannel-board figures or some other aid. More important, it permits you to maintain eye contact and makes you seem closer to the children—there is not even a book between you. Further, storytelling permits the insertion of synonyms or appositive phrases to explain an unfamiliar word or a definition of a foreign term (*hombre*—that means *man* in Spanish) without interrupting the story.

The criteria for selecting a story to be told are much the same as those for choosing one to read, with one important addition: it is important that the story does not lose by being translated into your own words. For example, *The Elephant's Child* without Kipling's "great, gray-green, greasy Limpopo River," or *The Wonderful O* in any language but Thurber's own would surely be less effective. Of course, it is possible to memorize a story, but this is not advisable except in very special cases. Memorization takes a great deal of time, and a story can be ruined if you forget something at a crucial point.

A good storyteller has a great fund of words at his command. He does not need to memorize, because he can find exactly the right way to describe a character or an event. He loves words, he loves stories, and his enthusiasm is contagious. And, with only rare exceptions, *he has planned carefully*. There are few "born storytellers"; thorough preparation is the key to success.

Like reading aloud, storytelling is an act of sharing, but it is even more intimate than reading. Therefore, the experience should be truly enjoyable for both the teller and the listeners. Select for telling only stories that you particularly enjoy and that are suited to the age and experiential backgrounds of the children. Study the characters thoroughly and decide what kinds of voices and mannerisms they would have. Visualize the setting and think of words that will convey this image concisely. Determine the mood of the story and what vocabulary, phrasing, and tone of voice will best express it. Examine the wording of the story to see whether retaining some of the author's words or phrases will heighten enjoyment, either because they are particularly colorful or because they form a repetitive pattern. Decide where gestures would be effective and whether visual aids are needed, such as pictures, flannel-board figures, puppets, a filmstrip, or realia. Remember, however, that a well-told story often needs no embellishment. And finally, make sure that you know the exact sequence of events, including any details that are important to appreciation or to later events. Certainly the effect is lost when important information is omitted and has to be inserted at a later time.

Practice and rigid self-evaluation are essential to good storytelling. Using a tape recorder, experiment with pitch, intonation, phrasing, and use of pauses; practice telling the story before a mirror to judge the effect of gestures and facial expressions; time several tellings so you will know how much time is needed to tell the story effectively. All this will seem very time-consuming at first, but it will prove to be time well spent. And a story once learned can be told again and again—possibly even to the same children. In this connection, it should be noted that even a story that has been told many times before should be mentally reviewed to make sure of details and sequence. A set of cards containing names of characters, important details, the sequence of events, and useful visual aids can help you to review. These cards can be filed with those containing information about stories for reading aloud.

For many helpful ideas about storytelling see:

Bauer, Caroline Feller, *Handbook for Storytellers* (Chicago: American Library Association, 1977).

Ross, Ramon R., *Storyteller* (Columbus: Charles E. Merrill Publishing Co., 1972).

Sawyer, Ruth, *The Way of the Storyteller* (New York: Viking Press, 1970).

Wagner, Joseph A., *Children's Literature through Storytelling* (Dubuque, IA: William C. Brown Co., 1970).

Using Media

Much has already been said in this chapter about using audiovisual aids, and many of these will and should be products of your own ingenuity or that of the children. However, school libraries are increasingly becoming treasurehouses of many materials other than books. A well-stocked library may contain files of book jackets, pictures, flannel-board figures, overhead transparencies, realia of many kinds, films, filmstrips, tapes, records, and cassettes, as well as the equipment for utilizing all of these. Often information about such aids is included in the library catalog on color coded cards so that particular types of material can be identified and located quickly. That is, a card for a filmstrip might have a strip of red tape across the top edge, a cassette card might have a green tape, and so on. Use these materials wisely.

Do preview all audiovisual materials before using them. There is great variety in these; even some authors do not read their own works as well as professional actors—and vice versa!

Plan carefully, so that they will enhance the literature program, *not* replace it. Plan for variety as well; use flannel-board figures one day, a filmstrip and/or cassette another, and simply tell or read a story when that seems to be the best method. And by all means, try to use the method best suited to the material you are presenting. Keeping media information in your book file can be helpful here; memories are short, and this will be a valuable asset in planning. For convenience, cards may be color coded in a manner similar to that used by libraries (see above). Cards can be marked with colored tape, crayon, or felt-tipped pen.

An almost endless number and variety of commercial materials are available for use as aids in presenting literature to children. Many children's stories have been made into movies that are available to schools at low cost. Well-known actors have recorded stories and poems; authors have recorded their own works. Nearly all of the Newbery Award books are available in filmstrip/cassette or filmstrip/record form, as are interviews with many well-known authors and illustrators. In fact, most companies are now producing these combinations of filmstrips and records or cassettes, thus using both audio and visual means of telling a story. These often can be purchased—and certainly can be used—separately if desired. In addition, multimedia kits include multiple copies of a book, plus a filmstrip, a cassette, or both, as well as a teacher's guide and sometimes even duplicating masters for children's responses. Such materials can be used by the entire class, by small groups, or by individual children in the library corner or media center.[1]

HELPING CHILDREN SELECT BOOKS

Developing an understanding of each child's interests, expanding those interests, and helping the child to develop new interests is the responsibility of each teacher. In order to help a child select books, it is vital to know the child and his or her interests. This is one reason for staying with the class when they go to the library. The librarian can offer suggestions and help children find books, but the librarian cannot be expected to know individual interests and abilities as a teacher does.

Begin by reading the cumulative records for your class before school starts. These records will furnish background information on age, sex, health problems, family structure, abilities, and perhaps interests. Knowing that Lily Jones hates her name or that the biggest child in your fifth grade has first grade reading ability, for example, will be helpful in selecting books for the class and for individuals.

Interests by Age and Sex

Naturally children differ in reading interests just as they do in every other respect. Children in general, however, appear to show certain preferences at certain age levels, and these are discussed below. They should not be thought of as absolutes, but only as guidelines to be used in conjunction with a knowledge of the interests of the specific children in a class.

Primary Grades. Primary children select books principally by their pictures; therefore the illustrations are of primary importance. Bright colors are preferred over pastels, and pictures should occupy a major portion of the space, with only a few words on each page. Illustrations may be fanciful, but objects should be readily recognizable. Young children love animal stories, like *The Surpise Party* and *The Happy Lion;* stories about mechanical objects, like *Little Toot through the Golden Gate;* and stories about those who have problems they can identify with, like Jim in *Will I Have a Friend?* who wonders apprehensively if he will find a friend on his first day at school, or the boy in Marchette Chute's poem, who says,

> I told them I didn't WANT mittens
> And they've given me mittens again!*

Folk and fairy tales are perennial favorites, and children love fantasy as long as the characters have human feelings and reactions. For example, Horton may sit on the egg without breaking it, but he must shiver when the winter winds blow and grow lonely sitting there on the nest alone.

Middle Grades. Middle grade children continue to like fantasy and folk tales, but as their knowledge and experiences broaden, so do their reading interests. They are interested in the world around them, both near and far, today and yesterday. Many books appeal to the middle grader—histories, biographies, stories of other lands; adventure tales about pirates, cowboys, and frontiersmen; books that explain the wonders of the world about them. Boys, particularly in the upper middle grades, begin to be interested in sports and science and both sexes continue to enjoy animal stories. As a rule, these children are interested in a wide variety of subjects and types; their principal criterion, as far as fiction is concerned, is that the plot move fast and have plenty of action.

Upper Grades. Most of the interests pupils have in the middle grades continue into the upper grades. At this level, however, the sexes begin to differentiate. The boys often prefer sports, action, adventure, and mystery, whereas many girls begin

---

*"Presents" by Marchette Chute. Copyright, 1932, 1960 by Marchette Chute. From the book *Around and About* by Marchette Chute. Copyright © 1957 by E. P. Dutton & Co., Inc., publishers, and used with their permission.

to enjoy a bit of love interest. It might be said that the girls' interests are broader, since they often enjoy the same books as the boys, while boys scoff at love and tend to avoid books in which the principal character is feminine.

At all ages, children enjoy and should be exposed to humor as well as to stories about those who have problems to which they can relate. Humor is a safety valve for emotions, and it is important that children learn to laugh—at themselves as well as others. By all means encourage the enjoyment of humor: problems at which we can laugh grow small enough to attack. Similarly, children need to be exposed to stories about both personal and social problems. The important factor here is to make sure that the problem is not too great for the children's experience and is one to which they can relate.

Another factor to be considered at all levels is the size of print and general attractiveness of the books. As mentioned earlier, young children select books primarily by their illustrations. Appearance continues to be important, even in the upper grades; children will seldom select a book that has very small print and no illustrations. Naturally, the size of print can decrease as children mature, as can the amount of space devoted to illustrations, but it is important that books be attractive and not too difficult to read. This is especially true for children who do not read well.

Reading Ability

It is relatively easy to find books for good readers, but a major problem for most teachers is helping those children who have limited reading ability select books that will interest them and that they can read. This is not an easy task; it is one that will require a great deal of patience and ingenuity. A few guidelines may prove helpful:

1. Determine the child's independent reading level. If you don't know how this is done, consult a diagnostic reading book or the reading consultant in your school or district.
2. Determine the child's interests by observing and listening.
3. Use the knowledge you have gained about the child's interests and particular characteristics to guide you in the library in selecting material for that child.
4. Branch out in the use of resources. Perhaps magazines rather than books can furnish the necessary stimulus.
5. Help the child maintain self-respect by finding easy-to-read materials that are not beneath his or her age level. Help the child gain standing in the other children's eyes. Make the most of other abilities the child has.

Children have been known to extend themselves in reading ability if they are sufficiently motivated. For example, a thirteen-year-old with third grade reading ability and an interest in fast cars might be successfully tempted by Lerner Publications' series about racing. This series includes books about the Indianapolis 500, race-car drivers, drag racing, motorcycle racing, and even snowmobile racing. Watts has a similar series, written by E. and R. S. Radlauer, which has great appeal to children in the middle and upper grades. Both have middle grade reading levels and are amply illustrated with actual photographs filled with action and excitement. Such materials might also be utilized to improve reading skills so that re-

Children's Newspapers and Magazines

Cricket (Open Court Publishing Co., 1058 8th St., LaSalle, IL 61301).

Children's Digest (Parents' Magazine Enterprises, Bergenfield, NJ 07621) 1–3.

Ebony Jr.! (Johnson Publishing Co., 820 S. Michigan Ave., Chicago, IL 60605) 4–8.

Young World (Saturday Evening Post Co., 1100 Waterway Blvd., P. O. Box 567B, Indianapolis, IN 46206) 5–8.

Calling All Girls (Better Reading Foundation, Inc., 52 Vanderbilt Ave., New York, NY 10017) 4–8.

Ranger Rick's Nature Magazine (National Wildlife Federation, 1412 16th St. NW, Washington DC 20036) 4–6.

Stone Soup (a magazine by children; Children's Art Foundation, P. O. Box 83, Santa Cruz, CA).

Sesame Street (P. O. Box C-10, Birmingham, AL 35283) 1–4.

World (National Geographic Society, P. O. Box 2895, Washington, DC 20013) 4–8.

luctant readers can advance to higher levels of ability and appreciation.

Children are no different from adults when it comes to reading. Age, sex, environment, interests, and ability all influence what a person selects to read. A wise teacher knows each child and guides each child in the selection of books.

Again, a useful aid is a set of file cards. In this case, the cards can be used to record the children's interests so that you can help them to discover books that they will enjoy and profit from. Let the children start the cards themselves; at the beginning of the year, have each child fill out a card, giving his or her name and age and the answers to a few simple questions, such as:

- Of all the books you have read (or stories you have heard), which did you like the best?
- What was one you didn't like very well?
- What is your favorite TV show?
- What do you like most to do after school or at recess?
- If you could go anywhere you wanted to, where would it be? Why?

Other questions may be more suitable for a particular class or grade; the important thing is to keep to a few that can be answered briefly. Use the cards as a beginning and add to them as you talk to the children, jotting down names of books they seem to enjoy, hobbies, problems, etc. Thumb through the cards before going to the library, making notes of particular types of books, authors the children have enjoyed, special problems, etc., to guide you in the selection of books for the room library or for reading to the class. In addition, a "request box" might be kept in the library corner, where individual pupils could place requests for particular books or books about particular subjects. And, whenever possible, several children might go along to help make selections.

Book Lists

Although you and the children will make the final selection of books for the room library, the librarian can be extremely helpful in making suggestions. Most librarians will go to great pains to help find exactly what is wanted, if they are only asked. In addition, a librarian usually has a number of book lists to guide him or her in book selection. Such lists are generally annotated and arranged by subject areas, with age or grade levels indicated. The librarian will also have lists of Newbery and Caldecott award winners[2] these are excellent both for the children and for reading aloud.

Naturally you will want to read or skim all the books you select for the room library, but these lists and the librarian can save you a considerable amount of time by leading you to specific titles and authors.

THE INSTRUCTIONAL PROGRAM

"There are no values in knowing how to read, only values which are derived *from* reading," says Charlotte Huck. "As teachers recognize the values that result from wide and varied reading, they will see the need for a planned literature program in the elementary school."[3]

If children are exposed to a wide variety of good books, have a teacher who

For Special Events

Children's Books for the Holidays (National Council of Teachers of English). An annotated list of books for Christmas and Hanukkah, K-7.

Light the Candles (The Horn Book, Inc., 585 Boylston St., Boston, MA 02116). An annotated bibliography of books for the Christmas season.

Purdy, Susan, *Festivals for You to Celebrate* (Philadelphia: J. B. Lippincott, 1969).

Shapp, Martha and Charles, *Let's Find Out about New Year's Day* (New York: Franklin Watts, Inc., 1968).

Booth, Edna, *Turkeys, Pilgrims, and Indian Corn* (New York: The Seabury Press, 1975).

We Learn About Special Days (Kankakee, IL: Imperial Productions, 1968). Tapes, manual, posters, etc.

Larrick, Nancy, ed., *Poetry for Holidays* (Champaign, IL: Garrard Publishing Co., 1966).

Morrow, Betty, and Hartman, Louis, *Jewish Holidays* (Champaign, IL: Garrard Publishing Co., 1967).

The Crowell Holiday Books (New York: Thomas Y. Crowell Co. These include books about St. Valentine's Day, Hallowe'en, Thanksgiving Day, Passover, and others).

enjoys reading, and are given the time to become acquainted with literature, they may very well develop a taste for reading and some discrimination in selecting what they read. If literature is integrated with other areas of the curriculum, there is little doubt that both the curriculum and individual children will be enriched. And if the kinds of activities discussed in later sections result from reading, children's language skills will surely improve. But if careful planning of literary experiences coordinates all of these, the benefits will be even greater.

Planning, however, does not mean that children's reading should be circumscribed, nor that they should be limited to a specific reading list. Experience with this type of approach in the secondary school has shown that it does little to inspire enthusiasm for reading. Rather, the program should include both planned

---

2 Preparing a Book File

To Read and Think Over

Ramona's class wanted to put in one place all the books they had shared together. They decided to make a book file. Here is a card that Ramona wrote for the file.

O'Dell, Scott

The Island of the Blue Dolphins

What would you do if you had to live all alone on an island — without food, tools, books, or radio? Could you learn how to do everything? Karana, a twelve-year-old Indian girl, did all these things. She lived on the island for eighteen years.

I like this story because it's based on a real person who was very brave. It's very exciting to read, particularly the part about the fight with the octopus.

Ramona Arnez

● Write the answers to these questions on your activity paper.

1. Where did Ramona put the author's name?
2. How did Ramona capitalize and mark the title?
3. What kinds of sentences did she use to begin her summary?

156

Sharing books should be a part of literature programs. (From *Language for Meaning*, Level 5. Copyright 1978 by Houghton Mifflin Company. Used by permission of the publisher.)

Book Clubs for Children

Arrow Book Club, Scholastic Book Services, 904 Sylvan Ave., Englewood Cliffs, NJ 07632. Ages 9–11.

The Bookplan, 921 Washington Ave., Brooklyn, NY 11225. Ages 8 months–11 years.

Catholic Children's Book Club, 260 Summit Ave., St. Paul, MN. Ages 6–16.

Junior Literary Guild, 177 Park Ave., New York, NY 10017. Ages 5–16.

Lucky Book Club, Scholastic Book Services, 904 Sylvan Ave., Englewood Cliffs, NJ 07632. Ages 7–9.

Parents' Magazine Book Club for Little Listeners and Beginning Readers, 52 Vanderbilt Ave., New York, NY 10017. Ages 3–8.

See-Saw Book Club, Scholastic Book Services, 904 Sylvan Ave., Englewood Cliffs, NJ 07632. Ages 5–7.

Weekly Reader Children's Book Club, Education Center, 1250 Fairwood Ave., Columbus, OH 43216. Ages 4–10.

Young America Book Club, 1250 Fairwood Ave., Columbus, OH 43216. Ages 10–14.

Young People's Book Club, 226 North Cass Ave., Westmont, IL 60559. Ages 4–10.

Young Readers of America (Division of Book-of-the-Month Club), 345 Hudson St., New York, NY 10014. Ages 9–14.

experiences and free choice, and it must be built around the interests, needs, and abilities of the particular children for whom it is planned. There should *not* be a specified reading list for each grade, which all children are expected to follow, but there should be specific planning for the *kinds* of literary experiences that will be included in the program, not just at one grade level but at all levels. With planning, one experience builds upon and relates to another. Without it, children may have many valuable and enjoyable experiences, but they may also wind up being "introduced" to haiku (for example) in the fifth grade, again in the sixth grade, in the seventh grade—and even again in the secondary school.

Instructional Considerations

A number of factors need to be considered in planning, both for a single grade level and for the entire program. These are discussed in the following sections.

Variety.   Selections chosen for the entire group—to be read either by or to the children—should include a variety of kinds and styles. This variety should embrace genre (stories, poems, plays, etc.), theme, tone, humorous selections as well as serious ones, and type (fantasy, folklore, adventure, history, biography, etc.). In addition, there should be some older classics and some new ones. Not all of these are suitable at every grade level, of course, but every effort should be made to see that children at all levels become acquainted with many kinds of writing and many styles.

Experience Level.   Like any other area of the curriculum, the literature program must begin where the children are. If the language and sentence structure are too difficult for them, they will probably find a selection boring. Further, the concepts must be ones to which they can relate. For example, the first grader who has never seen snow is less likely to respond to *A Snowy Day* than is one accustomed to wintry weather. This is not to say that children can only relate to that which is within their immediate experience—part of the value of literature lies in the vicarious experience it provides—but there must be a basis for relating. Primary children, for instance, can enter readily into a story in which animals speak, especially since they themselves frequently carry on lengthy conversations with pets, dolls, and even imaginary playmates. This is "pretend," and they understand that, as long as there is some other basis for relating. Thus they delight as Roald Dahl's "Fantastic" Mr. Fox outwits Farmers Boggis, Bunce, and Bean, because they recognize the parent's role as provider for his family and also because the three obnoxious farmers represent the adult world which so often circumvents their own desires.

Integration.   If literature is to be an integral part of the curriculum, consideration must also be given to how this integration is to be accomplished. Just as overall planning requires decisions about experiments, field trips, and audiovisual aids, so it requires decisions about literary experiences that may enrich and be supplemented by other curriculum areas and that are suited to the particular children involved. Should a social studies unit include the tall tales of the expanding frontier? If so, should this be balanced by a realistic story of life in the early days?

Does a group of reluctant readers need a story to "spice up" their interest in the American Revolution, such as *A Spy in Williamsburg* by Isabelle Lawrence? How can poetry be used? What kinds of literary experiences have these children had, and what kinds do they need?

Flexibility.   If the literature program is truly to be adapted to the needs of the children and if it is to supplement and enrich their experiences as well as the curriculum, it must be flexible. No plan is so good that it cannot be changed. Suppose, for example, you had planned to have the children read a particular book as a group, but, as the year progresses, you discover that it is too difficult for a number of them. Possibly you might read it aloud if it is suitable for oral reading; perhaps the substitution of another book that is easier to read but has a similar theme or setting would be desirable; or the class might be divided into several groups, each reading a different book and preparing some sort of report on it for the rest of the class. The important fact to remember is that the interests, needs, and abilities of the children are at the heart of any successful program.

Growth.   In order to provide for the needs of *all* the children, the program must include both group and individual experiences. Some selections can be read to or by the entire class, so that they develop understandings and broaden concepts through guided discussions and shared reactions. Sometimes small groups may read different selections to accommodate differing interests and abilities. Above all, the program must provide opportunity and encouragement for each child to explore in the area of his own interests, to discover new ones, and to grow in understanding and appreciation through individual reading.

Objectives of the Literature Program

Underlying all of the considerations discussed above is the most important element in planning—consideration of the objectives of the literature program. First, of course, are the underlying objectives, embodied in the earlier section on the values of literature as well as in the preceding paragraphs. These must be the overriding considerations in planning for both group and individual reading. Second are the immediate objectives—what are the specific outcomes desired from reading? These will be discussed in the following sections.

Since we have grouped the language arts into two categories—receptive and expressive—let us consider the specific objectives of the literature program in the same way. Those having to do with reception involve understanding and appreciating what is read; those having to do with expression involve both oral and written responses to what is read, including creative responses.

Receptive Abilities.   In considering the objectives of the literature program, it is vital to remember that elementary school children should *not* engage in critical analysis—this should be reserved for university students and possibly some secondary students. However, some understanding of genre, theme, plot, setting, characterization, and point of view can be developed gradually during the elementary and secondary years, and these will lay the foundation for greater perception and appreciation. Children need not know the meaning of a word such as *genre*, but they will understand the concepts all these terms embody if they have been exposed throughout the elementary years to a program that has provided many experiences with them. For example, the primary child can certainly understand that Nonny Hogrogian's *One Fine Day* is a story, while the book that tells about the weather or how to feed the fish in the class aquarium is not. Perhaps factual material might even be kept on a different shelf in the room library to further this concept. This child also begins to realize that some stories are about people who could be real (*A Snowy Day*, for example), while one like *Where the Wild Things Are* is pure make-believe. Thus the child is laying the foundation for understanding the difference between fiction and nonfiction and between fantasy and realism, although none of these words are known.

The child can also begin to recognize that poetry is different from prose, particularly if rhyme and rhythm are pointed out. Much is done with both rhythm and rhyme in readiness activities (see chapters 3 and 14), and many children's stories are written in rhyme. Primary children will enjoy clapping their hands softly to the rhythm of a poem or song, and they may even attempt to write simple poems if poetry has been made a vital part of their reading experiences.

Talking about things is an important part of language development, especially at the primary level. Suppose you interrupt the reading of a story to ask, "What do you think will happen next?" You are giving the children an opportunity not only to express themselves and to think critically, but also to understand a basic element of plot construction—the way a story turns out is built upon the events that have gone before and the kinds of characters involved. Having children recap the sequence of events in a story builds organizational skills and also helps to develop the concept of plot. "Why did Horton keep sitting on the egg when he was so cold and miserable?" "What kind of boy is Archie?" "What did you learn from this story?" Questions like these are concerned with theme and characterization and will help children learn to think about and evaluate what they read.

In the middle and upper grades these concepts can be further developed. Children who are going to use the library independently need to know the difference between fiction and nonfiction and to understand what biography is. To write reports and stories they must understand sequence and organization. Some direct instruction will be needed, but the best teacher is example. Certainly no child should be asked to write a story without having heard or read many stories. In addition, discussions can point out sequence in plot development and the need for *cause* to be established before *effect* is reasonable.

Children of this age should also be aware of figurative language. They can talk about phrases like "the *heart* of the problem" and "matters came to a *head*." They can compose similes and metaphors (note that they should compose these, not just identify them in someone else's writing); they may even experiment with personification, describing an event from the viewpoint of an old house, a pet, or a piece of furniture. Dealing with figurative language, however, requires many examples and much familiarity with both written and spoken language.

As children discover the thought and work that goes into writing well, their appreciation for good writing will grow. This appreciation and the understandings that effect it develop slowly, and only as a result of wide acquaintance with books over a long period of time. Children cannot be told to understand a concept or to appreciate a poem—the foundation for understanding and appreciation must be carefully laid through experience.

Expressional Abilities.   If literature is truly made an integral part of the activities and program of the classroom, it will be inextricably interwoven with the use of language in all its aspects. Children may develop both oral and organizational skills as they plan the dramatization of a scene from a favorite story (see chapter 6 for suggestions). Shy children who have difficulty in making oral presentations may tell a story through the use of puppets, thus taking a first step toward developing oral abilities (chapter 6 gives directions for making several kinds of puppets). Children may read aloud stories or poems they particularly like, or they may participate in choral reading activities.

A good literature program should also stimulate creative writing of many kinds: children can write stories, poems, accounts of incidents that might have occurred before or after the action of a particular story, letters from one character to another, etc. (see also suggestions in chapter 12). Book reports, too, can take both conventional and creative forms; this will be discussed in the next section.

In doing any kind of writing or talking about a book (other than merely recounting the plot), the child must do some evaluation. If he or she is going to write a different ending for a story, it must fit the events that have gone before and the characters who are involved. If a poem is written, it should capture the mood of the story. If an illustration is drawn, the setting must be accurate. Discussions of common reading are a good way to help children see the considerations that must enter into this kind of expression. Such evaluation, in turn, should help them to make their own writing and speaking more effective.

In planning the literature program, then, you should take into account the kinds of expressional activities the children need to engage in. Naturally, not all oral and written expression must result from literature, nor is it necessary that expressional activities result from everything read—this would be proselytizing in the worst way. However, reading *may* stimulate expression, and it certainly can and should provide models, particularly for creative writing.

Book Reports

The book report has been used and abused for years. Too often it is dull to read or hear and consists of little more than a recounting of the plot. This type of report has some value; it gives practice in using the skills of writing or speaking as well as in selecting important details and arranging events in sequence. But a good book report can do this and much more.

To begin with, not every book read needs to be reported on. If you wish to keep a record of the children's reading—and this is a good idea for many reasons—each child might keep a card on which he or she records the names and authors of the books read, along with the date on which each was finished. As an added bonus, the children might use a numerical system to evaluate books:

   1—Excellent. I recommend it highly.
   2—Very good, but not everybody would like it.
   3—Not bad, but I wouldn't particularly recommend it.
   4—I didn't like it much.

These cards could be kept in a room file; children could glance through them for recommendations and they could serve as an extra check before the regular trips to the library.

However, most books read should be reported on, because a pleasant experience should be shared and because books make excellent springboards to both oral and written expression. Some suggestions follow, and both you and the children can probably think of more.

Oral Activities.   Oral activities may take a variety of forms. A few suggestions are these:

Make book reports—like science reports or those in any other curriculum area—an integral part of your oral language program.

1. A child might read a particular incident from the book to the class. This requires preparation so that it will be read well; also, the incident selected should be complete in itself or listeners will lose interest.
2. Several children who have read the same book could dramatize a scene.
3. Children who have read books about the same period of history could have a panel discussion comparing the information learned—or developing different aspects of life during the period.
4. An individual child could demonstrate skills learned from a book—card tricks, a sports skill, etc.
5. A child could pretend to be one of the characters in a book giving an interview to a reporter or TV newsman. Another pupil would act as interviewer and would be given a list of questions to ask.
6. A child could prepare a speech explaining why a particular character would make a good friend.

Written Activites.   These should vary according to the age and abilities of the children; some of the following might be appropriate:

1. An imaginary letter written by one character to another at a particular point in the story.
2. A TV script based upon the book.
3. An estimate of what kind of people might enjoy the book and why.
4. A review or advertisement for the class or school paper.
5. A first person description of a particular event in the story, told as though the writer had been an onlooker. (This observer could even be a dog or some inanimate object rather than a human being.)
6. A character sketch of one of the people in the book. This should include both a physical description and a discussion of the kind of person this character was (using specific actions to prove points).
7. A description of the setting of the book, telling why this was or was not important to the story.
8. Book reviews. As children reach the upper grades, they should learn how to write a good book review. Prepare for this by bringing in sample reviews from magazines and papers.

Other Activities.   Nonlanguage activities can be useful in two ways: they create an opportunity for children who are not highly verbal to make something the other children will admire, and they can add interest and color to the library corner. Such activities might include the following:

1. Making models, dioramas, or maps. For example, one child might use sand, twigs, and other items to show the setting for the battle at Little Big Horn, another might make a scale model of the Kon Tiki, a third might draw a map showing Huck Finn's trip down the Mississippi, etc.

2. Drawing illustrations for a particular story. These can make excellent bulletin boards.
3. Drawing a cartoon strip showing the action in a certain event (also good bulletin board material).
4. Dressing a doll in a costume that might have been worn by a character in a story.
5. Making a mobile depicting characters or objects in a book. This can be hung in the library corner.

Activities such as these can be used to encourage a shy child to speak before the group. For instance, the child who drew the map might be asked to explain briefly where various incidents took place, or the one who made a model could explain what it represents. These explanations can be done very informally with the children grouped around and looking at the object being shown rather than at the one who is speaking.

POETRY IN THE CLASSROOM

Many adults think they do not like poetry, but children love rhythm, rhyme, and the sounds of words. Mother Goose has remained in good standing for years, and Dr. Seuss is an undisputed favorite with young readers. Unfortunately, teachers and textbooks must take a large share of the blame for this shift in values. Selections inappropriate to the age, experience, and interests of children have made poetry dull; teachers have read beautiful poems badly; forced memorization has placed poetry in the same category as multiplication tables; and an overemphasis on analysis has made poems seem like scientific data to be studied rather than an experience to be enjoyed.

Poetry offers a way to express ideas and feelings, it stimulates the imagination and provides an outlet for the emotions, it motivates children to express their own creativity, and it furnishes a way of showing children the beauty and expressiveness of language. What better reasons can be offered for using poetry with children?

Guidelines

Poetry had its birth in song and, like song, its aural qualities are among its chief assets. Thus, with a few rather obvious exceptions, poems are meant to be heard, not seen. This does not mean that the children may not have copies to follow as a poem is read—in fact, this may sometimes increase their enjoyment—but it should be read aloud, not silently, and it should be read in such a way that the greatest appreciation is obtained. This means preparation; attention must be given to the speed at which individual lines should be read, what the cadence is, which words should be emphasized, and what tone and pitch will best express the poem's meaning. Reading poetry well requires even more practice than reading stories well; again, the tape recorder can be a valuable ally.

Poetry should become a natural part of the ongoing activities of the classroom. Opportunities are endless; children love Indian chants, folk ballads, songs of the riverboatmen, etc. Many of these are available on records or in filmstrip-record packages, or, when possible, arrangements could be made to have someone come in to play and sing some of these for the class. Older children will particularly enjoy this.

The use of poetry might be occasioned by a holiday, a change in the weather, a circus in town, or animals or insects brought in by the children. There have been poems written about every imaginable subject or situation, for poetry is truly a natural form of expression. For example, sixth graders struggling with fractions might find a moment of relaxation with Carl Sandburg's "Arithmetic," or on a dreary day when the schoolyard is a sea of mud, you might say to the children, "Do you know what? I know a poem about mud."

Mud

Mud is very nice to feel
All squishy-squash between the toes!
I'd rather wade in wiggly mud
Than smell a yellow rose.
Nobody else but the rosebush knows
How nice mud feels
Between the toes.*

Select poems carefully and choose only those you and the children will enjoy. Probably too few children have regular exposure to enjoyable experiences with poetry after they have passed the nursery-rhyme stage. Therefore, at any grade level it is important to start with poems that the children understand and like. Children will not learn to love poetry or any other type of literature by being forced to read particular poems simply because they are reputed classics or because they are in a particular textbook. There are plenty of good poems; it requires only a little time and effort to find those that appeal to the children in a particular class.

Studies have shown that children prefer humorous poems to serious, meditative ones and that they like narrative poems and poems about animals or about experiences that are familiar and enjoyable to them. They respond to rhythm, rhyme, and sound in poems, but they reject those that rely heavily on imagery and figurative language, finding these difficult to understand. Such findings would seem to indicate that children need to have much experience with poetry and language before they are exposed to the more subtle types of figurative language and imagery.

This does not mean, however, that even very young children cannot respond to the language of poetry—simply that it should be presented in small amounts, as an aid to appreciation rather than as something to be studied and learned. For example, if you should read the poem quoted above, perhaps you might ask, "What are a rosebush's toes? Do you suppose it can really feel the mud?" Or possibly "I like the words 'squishy-squash,' don't you? Isn't that just the way mud feels?" Certainly children can enjoy Carl Sandburg's fog that comes "on little cat feet" or James Reeves' picture of the wind that can "carry a house-top or the scent of a pink." Simply point out such images, and of course encourage children to experiment with their own word pictures and colorful language when they write.

An excellent way to spoil poetry is to require memorization. This does not mean that children should never memorize poetry—it simply means that memorizing should not be required. Just as you learn certain poems through re-

*"Mud," by Polly Chase Borden. From *Child Life,* Copyright 1930.

peated reading or because you particularly like certain lines, so will the children. Sometimes they may decide themselves that they ought to memorize lines for a choral reading or for presentation to the class, but little purpose is served by requiring the memorization of certain lines simply because they are famous or because you recall having had to learn them.

Neither should poetry be spoiled by being overanalyzed like a specimen under a microscope lens. This does not mean that attention may not be called to rhythm, a specific rhyme pattern, or the use of alliteration, onomatopoeia, metaphor, or any other techniques that make a particular poem effective, but it is important to remember that these techniques are aids in creating the total effect of the poem, not ends in themselves. These devices may be pointed out particularly when children are preparing to write poems, but they should be taught as writing aids, not as information to be memorized for tests.

Poetry File

The file in which you keep records of stories to be told or read should also contain poems. A file is probably even more important for poetry than for stories, since

Find time for poetry and you will give yourself the privilege of seeing before you dozens of eyes light up in recognition of an experience they too have shared—a love, a hate, a fear, a fantasy, a joke, a riddle, a dream. Watch these eyes as they are interpreting, identifying, and *living*.

For those who might say, "There just aren't enough minutes in the day!"—try using those "loose-end" five-minute periods, like:

Waiting for the recess or noontime bell.

During quiet rest periods.

Following a reading lesson when a new story can be related to or illustrated by a special poem.

During sharing time when a poem relates to an experience a child has had.

During language, mathematics, science, or social science periods when a poem will help develop a concept.

And your reward will be even greater if you select the poem that illustrates a special occasion, like:

A holiday, birthday, May Day, first day of each season.

A rainy day, when the wind is blowing, or the sky is full of clouds, rainbows, lightning.

A character-learning day, involving truthfulness, honesty, happiness, sadness, cheerfulness.

A day when a new brother or sister has arrived, a relative has come to visit, a pet has been added to the household.

As May Hill Arbuthnot has said, "Poems can take experiences of the child's world and give them a new importance, a kind of glory that they did not have when they were just experiences." *Find Time for Poetry* and share this glory with the children.

Good advice! (Oakland Unified School District. *Find Time for Poetry*, Grades 5 and 6. Hayward, CA.: Alameda County School Department, 1966, p. 28.)

poems are short and it is virtually impossible to remember exactly where to find a particular one. Very short poems may simply be clipped or copied and placed in the file; other entries might show only where the particular poem is to be found. It is also a good idea to keep at least one good anthology (preferably several) in the classroom so that poems are quickly available. These should not be the only sources of poems, but they should be selected with great care.

Another possibility is to clip a card with titles and sources of poems to pictures in your picture file. These can provide a quickly assembled—and effective—bulletin board for some special occasion.

Suggested Activities

Primary children should participate in rhythmic activities to help them develop coordination and aural discrimination. Select poems with a strong, regular beat, preferably ones the children know and like, and let them clap out the rhythm as you read. They will also enjoy acting out nursery rhymes as you read them; try simple ones first, such as "Humpty, Dumpty," "One, Two, Buckle My Shoe," "Jack and Jill," and "Three Little Kittens."

Children love familiar poems just as they love to have the same story read again and again. When they ask for particular poems, you can begin to develop appreciation by asking questions such as the following: Why do you like this poem so much? Which words do you like the best? Does this line make you see a picture? When the three little kittens say "Mew, mew, mew," does it sound as though they're crying? How do they feel when they say "Purr, purr, purr"?

Such questioning should not be overdone, however. The important goal is to have the children enjoy the poem. Let the questions come as a spontaneous expression of your own appreciation; use them to increase pleasure, just as you point out illustrations in a book to make the story more enjoyable.

Young children love rhythm and rhyme. Seek out opportunities to capitalize upon and develop this interest whenever you can. For example, when you talk about rhyming words in developing reading skills, let the children make couplets using the words that rhyme. You be the scribe, furnishing spelling, punctuation, and capital letters. They will enjoy this and learn to put a thought into a few words:

> The sky is black
> Because night came back.
>
> See what I found!
> A ball that's round.

Primary children can also participate in simplified choral reading—that is, you might read the verse, while they recite the refrain. Intermediate children can progress to more complex types of choral reading; in fact, students of all ages will enjoy this activity if poems are carefully selected.

Intermediate and upper grade children also enjoy reading aloud poems they particularly like. This is an excellent way to introduce a poetry unit. It is important here to accept any poem a child selects, even if it is not a very good one. The selections children make can serve as a guide to discovering other poems that they can understand and enjoy.

As middle grade children expand concepts and vocabulary and begin to feel more at ease with writing and spelling, they should also be increasing their appreciation of the ways words are used. Choosing exactly the right word to use is important to all writing, but it is especially vital to poetry. This is a time for emphasizing the fact that the sound of a word, as well as its meaning, contributes to the effect of a poem. An excellent vehicle for this is a sampling from Mary O'Neill's *What Is That Sound!* For instance:

Growl?

When a surly dog
Complete with scowl
Goes rumbly-grumbly
That's a growl.
Growl's sound is surly
Snarly-gray,
And when you hear it
Back away. . . .*

Talk about the sound of words like *rumbly-grumbly, surly,* and *snarly:* Do they sound unpleasant? Why do you suppose she called a snarl *gray* instead of some other color? Certainly it rhymes with *away,* but is that the only reason?

The introductory poem from the same volume is excellent for building vocabulary as well as for talking about the images words create.

Sound of Water

The sound of water is:
Rain,
Lap,
Fold,
Slap,
Gurgle,
Splash,
Churn,
Crash,
Murmur,
Pour,
Ripple,
Roar,
Plunge,
Drip,
Spout,
Slip,
Sprinkle,
Flow,
Ice,
Snow. †

*Text copyright © 1966 by Mary O'Neill. From *What Is That Sound!* Used by permission of Atheneum Publishers.
† Text copyright © 1966 by Mary O'Neill. From *What Is That Sound!* Used by permission of Atheneum Publishers.

Experiment with reading this poem in such a way that each word sounds like its meaning, and be sure to point out the rhyme if children have missed it. Then let them try to create a similar poem about the sound of food, paper, the classroom, etc. Be sure to give several choices.

Almost every child can be inspired to be creative in some way. Perhaps the extent of this creativity is merely to find and cut out pictures from magazines that will illustrate a particular poem for a bulletin board display, but even this is a beginning and should be praised. Many children can write surprisingly good poems if they are motivated. Free verse may be good for some children because they can concentrate on choosing the best words instead of on form. However, free verse is not as easy as it seems, and many children prefer poems that rhyme. Middle and upper grade children like limericks and would consider it fun to try writing them. They will also meet with success in forms such as cinquain (see chapter 12 on creative writing).

As with any writing, children should begin with short poems so they can concentrate on excellence rather than length. Praise for their efforts and constructive criticism will encourage further efforts with other types of poetry. If sufficient interest is displayed, they might work in groups to create a class poetry book, with some children doing the major portion of the writing, while others draw illustrations, develop a format, plan organization, design a cover, etc. It is vital to remember, however, that, before being asked to write, children should see and hear many models and that they should thoroughly understand the particular characteristics of the kind of poem they are going to write; *this* is the time for talking about poetic techniques.

EVALUATION OF THE PROGRAM

Since the principal value of literature is the pleasure and enrichment it brings to an individual, some people oppose evaluating the literature program. Our viewpoint throughout this book, however, is that evaluation is an integral part of teaching. Without evaluation how does a teacher know what he or she has done well or needs to do? Also, with regard to evaluation of literature programs, there is a special need for a teacher to evaluate since literature so frequently receives only peripheral attention in the crowded school curriculum.

Because what one gains from literature is a very personal matter, we do not advocate giving tests over literature selections. Such tests usually measure reading comprehension and reflect an adult's point of view as to what should have been gained from the reading. We do believe, however, that you should ask yourself a number of questions:

1. Do the children show interest in reading beyond that assigned?
2. Do I read to the children and in reading introduce them to various genre and content?
3. Do the children share their reading with me and the other children?
4. Is the reading corner or center a busy place when children have "spare" time?
5. Do the children use the library or media center?
6. Is there evidence that children with personal problems have been affected by their reading?

These are not the only questions that you might ask, and the answers to them may be more reminders to you than measures of your program in any objective sense. On the other hand, you may make notes about what the children talk about, the interests that they show, who goes to the library or reading corner and how often, and how much sharing of reading there is.

A FINAL WORD

Teaching children the skills necessary for reading and helping them learn to use the library to find books have both been discussed in other chapters of this book. Both are directed at giving children the skills needed to discover the pleasure and knowledge that books can bring. The rewards that reading gives are immeasurable and invaluable. There is nothing the school can do that will be of more permanent worth than giving a child the ability and the desire to read widely and wisely.

ENDNOTES

1. These materials are being produced in such quantity that selecting wisely is very difficult. Consult with your school librarian and refer to such sources as these:

Greene, Ellin, and Schoenfeld, Madalynne. *A Multimedia Approach to Children's Literature* (Chicago: American Library Association, 1972).

Iarusso, Marilyn, and Nicholaou, Mary. *Recordings for Children* (New York: New York Library Association, 1972).

Miles, Josephine, *Multimedia for Children's Literature* (Danville, NY: Instructor Magazine).

2. The Newbery Medal is awarded annually to the best children's book published during the preceding year. The Caldecott Award is given to the book with the best illustrations, also annually.

3. Charlotte S. Huck, "Planning the Literature Program for the Elementary School," *Elementary English*, 39: (April 1962), 307–313.

REFERENCES

Books

Arbuthnot, May Hill. *Children and Books.* Glenview, IL: Scott, Foresman and Company, 1964.

Boyd, Gertrude A. *Teaching Poetry in the Elementary School.* Columbus, OH: Charles E. Merrill Publishing Company, 1973.

Carlson, Ruth K. *Literature for Children: Enrichment Ideas.* Dubuque, IA: Wm. C. Brown Co., 1970.

Cullinan, Bernice E., and Carmichael, Carolyn, eds. *Literature and Young Children.* Urbana, IL:

National Council of Teachers of English, 1977.

Georgiou, Constantine. *Children and Their Literature.* Englewood Cliffs, NJ: Prentice-Hall, Inc., 1969.

Glazer, Joan I., and Williams, Gurney, III. *Introduction to Children's Literature.* New York: McGraw Hill, Inc., 1979.

Huck, Charlotte S. *Children's Literature in the Elementary School.* New York: Holt, Rinehart and Winston, 1976.

Hughes, Rosalind. *Let's Enjoy Poetry.* Boston:

Houghton Mifflin Co., 1966.

Jacobs, Leland B., ed. *Using Literature with Young Children*. New York: Teachers College Press, Columbia University, 1965.

Lonsdale, Bernard J., and Mackintosh, Helen K. *Children Experience Literature*. New York: Random House, 1973.

Reasoner, Charles F. *Releasing Children to Literature*. New York: Dell Publishing Company, 1968.

———. *Where the Readers Are*. New York: Dell Publishing Company, 1972.

Shapiro, Jon E., ed. *Using Literature and Poetry Affectively*. Newark, DE: International Reading Association, 1979.

Whitehead, Robert. *Children's Literature: Strategies of Teaching*. Englewood Cliffs, NJ: Prentice-Hall, 1968.

Guides for Selecting Books for Children

Bibliography of Books for Children. Washington, DC: Association for Childhood Education International, 1977.

Children's Books of the Year. New York: Child Study Association of America, published annually.

Cianciolo, Patricia, ed. *Adventuring with Books*. Urbana, IL: National Council of Teachers of English, 1977.

Growing Up with Books. New York: R. R. Bowker Co., 1977.

Growing Up with Paperbacks. New York: R. R. Bowker Co., 1977.

Haviland, Virginia, ed. *Children's Books of International Interest* (Second Edition). Chicago: American Library Association, 1978.

Haviland, Virginia, and William J. Smith, eds. *Children and Poetry: A Selective, Annotated Bibliography*. Washington, DC: Government Printing Office, 1970.

Matthews, Judy, and Lillian Drag, eds. *Guide to Children's Magazines, Newspapers, Reference Books*. Washington, DC: Association for Childhood Education International, 1974.

Reid, Virginia, ed. *Reading Ladders for Human Relations* (Fifth Edition). Washington, DC: American Council on Education, 1972.

Rollock, Barbara, ed. *The Black Experience in Children's Books*. New York: New York Public Library, 1974.

Smith, Dorothy B. Frissell, and Eva L. Andrews, eds. *Subject Index to Poetry for Children and Young People*.

Spache, George D., ed. *Good Reading for the Disadvantaged Reader: Multi-Ethnic Resources*. Scarsdale, NY: Garrard Publishing Co., 1970.

Spache, George D., ed. *Good Reading for Poor Readers*. Scarsdale, NY: Garrard Publishing Co., 1972.

Subject Guide to Children's Books in Print. New York: R. R. Bowker Co., 1977.

Sutherland, Zena, ed. *The Best in Children's Books: The University of Chicago Guide to Children's Literature 1966-1972*. Chicago: University of Chicago Press, 1973.

Children's Books Referred to in Chapter 15

Cohen, Miriam. *Will I Have a Friend?* New York: Macmillan, 1967.

Dahl, Roald. *The Fantastic Mr. Fox*. New York: Alfred A. Knopf, 1970.

de Paola, Tomie. *Watch Out for the Chicken Feet in Your Soup*. Englewood Cliffs, NJ: Prentice-Hall, 1974.

Estes, Eleanor. *The Hundred Dresses*. New York: Harcourt Brace Jovanovich, 1944.

Fatio, Louise. *The Happy Lion*. New York: McGraw-Hill, 1954.

Gramatky, Hardie. *Little Toot through the Golden Gate*. New York: G. P. Putnam's Sons, 1975.

Henry, Marguerite. *King of the Wind*. Skokie, IL: Rand, McNally, 1945.

Hogrogian, Nonny. *One Fine Day*. New York: Macmillan, 1971.

Hutchins, Pat. *The Surprise Party*. New York: Macmillan, 1969.

———. *Titch*. New York: Macmillan, 1971.

Karp, Naomi. *The Turning Point*. New York: Harcourt Brace Jovanovich, 1976.

Keats, Ezra Jack. *Apt. 3*. New York: Macmillan, 1971.

———. *The Snowy Day*. New York: Viking Press, 1962.

_____. *Whistle for Willie*. New York: Viking Press, 1964.

Kipling, Rudyard. *The Elephant's Child*. Chicago: Follett, 1969.

Larrick, Nancy, ed. *Poetry for Holidays*. Champaign, IL: Garrard, 1966.

Lasker, Joe. *He's My Brother*. Chicago: Albert Whitman, 1974.

Lawrence, Isabelle. *A Spy in Williamsburg*. Skokie, IL: Rand, McNally, 1955.

Lawson, Robert. *Ben and Me*. Boston: Little, Brown, 1951.

Lexau, Joan. *Emily and the Klunky Baby and the Next-Door Dog*. New York: Dial, 1972.

_____. *Me Day*. New York: Dial, 1971.

Neville, Emily. *It's Like This, Cat*. New York: Harper and Row, 1964.

O'Dell, Scott. *Zia*. Boston: Houghton, Mifflin, 1976.

O'Neill, Mary. *Hailstones and Halibut Bones*. Garden City, NY: Doubleday, 1961.

Sendak, Maurice. *Where the Wild Things Are*. New York: Harper and Row, 1963.

Seuss, Dr. *Horton Hatches the Egg*. New York: Random House, 1940.

Steptoe, John. *Stevie*. New York: Harper and Row, 1969.

Thurber, James. *The Wonderful O*. New York: Simon and Schuster, 1957.

Wolf, Bernard. *Anna's Silent World*. Philadelphia: Lippincott, 1977.

Books about Authors and Illustrators of Children's Literature

de Montreville, Doris, and Hill, Donna, eds. *Third Book of Junior Authors*. New York: H. W. Wilson, 1972.

de Montreville, Doris, and Crawford, Elizabeth D. *Fourth Book of Junior Authors and Illustrators*. New York: H. W. Wilson, 1978.

Fuller, Muriel, ed. *More Junior Authors*. New York: H. W. Wilson, 1969.

Kunitz, Stanley J., and Haycraft, Howard, eds. *The Junior Book of Authors*. New York: H. W. Wilson, 1951.

Something About the Author. (A 14 volume series containing facts and pictures about contemporary authors and illustrators of books for young people.) Detroit: Gale Research Book Tower, 1971–78.

Filmstrips

American Folk Heroes and Tall Tales. Mahwah, N.J.: Troll Associates (6 color filmstrips, including tales of Paul Bunyan, Rip Van Winkle, Pecos Bill, Johnny Appleseed, John Henry, and Ichabod Crane; K–5).

Beloved Fairy Tales. Troll Associates (6 strips; K–4).

Best Stories Ever. Learning Corporation of America, 1970 (5 strips; color; kindergarten and primary).

Charlotte's Web. Santa Monica, CA: Stephen Bosustou Productions (18 color–sound filmstrips with narration by E. B. White).

Enrichment Filmstrips. NY: Enrichment Teaching Materials (Also records; based on Landmark Books).

Favorite Poems to Read. Troll Associates (6 strips; elementary grades).

Myths and Legends of Ancient Greece. Mahwah, NJ: Troll Associates (5 color filmstrips including such myths as *Prometheus and the Gift of Fire* and *Theseus and the Minotaur*; upper grades).

Pick a Peck O' Poems. New York: Miller-Brody Productions (6 color filmstrips with cassettes or records; lower elementary).

What Is Poetry? New York: Caedmon Records (Includes 10 color filmstrips with accompanying records, teacher's guides, and duplicating masters; elementary).

Weston Woods has sound filmstrips of a great many Caldecott Medal winners and other favorite children's stories; they are also available in multimedia kits.

Films

Millions of Cats, *Whistle for Willie*, *The Foolish Frog*, *Harold's Fairy Tale*, and many others are available from Weston Woods. This company also has a number of films featuring authors and illustrators such as Robert McClosky, Maurice Sendak, and Ezra Jack Keats.

The Rabbit Who Wanted Red Wings. New York: Miller-Brody Productions (Color; 12 min.; K–3).

Tale of the Lazy People. New York: Miller-Brody Productions (Color; 15 min.; based on a story from a Newbery Medal winner, *Tales from Silver Lands*).

Encyclopedia Britannica, Coronet, McGraw-Hill, and others also have many literature films.

Cassettes and Records

The National Council of Teachers of English distributes many recordings. Write to the NCTE, 1111 Kenyon Road, Urbana, IL 61801.

Best in Children's Literature. Mahwah, NJ: Troll Associates (20 cassettes; K–3).

Best in Children's Literature. Los Angeles: Bowmar/Noble (4 series, 374 selections; records or cassettes; teaching guides).

Pippi Longstocking, and others. New York: Viking Press (Available with accompanying books).

Great Legends of Ancient Greece. Mahwah, NJ: Troll Associates (10 cassettes; 5–8).

Golden Anthology of Children's Verse. Kankakee, IL: Imperial Productions, Inc. (8 tapes with 70 poems; K–3).

My Favorite Fairy Tales. Mahwah, NJ: Troll Associates (8 cassettes; K–3).

Scholastic Record and Book Companion Series. Englewood Cliffs, NJ: Scholastic Records.

Treasury of Classroom Poetry. Mahwah, NJ: Troll Associates (7 6-min. cassettes; K–4).

Ten Tales of Mystery and Terror. Mahwah, NJ: Troll Associates (Includes *Dr. Jekyll and Mr. Hyde, Pit and the Pendulum*, and others; 5–8).

Caedmon Records (New York) has many recordings of both prose and poetry suitable for every grade level and read by authors or well-known actors. For example, Carl Sandburg tells the Rootabaga Stories, Carol Channing reads *Madeline*, Boris Karloff reads *The Reluctant Dragon*, and Ed Begley tells tall tales.

Miller-Brody Productions has nearly all of the Newbery Award-winning books on both records and cassettes. A great many of these are available also in sound filmstrips and in multimedia kits which include paperback or hardcover copies of the book.

ACTIVITIES FOR PRESERVICE TEACHERS

1. Read several research studies about children's interests in literature and compare the results. Report your findings to the class.

2. Check with the audiovisual or instructional materials center for children's literature films, filmstrips, and records. Preview several of these, making notes to remind you of them later.

3. Learn a story to tell to children. Review the section on storytelling and read some of the suggested references before you begin.

4. Begin a collection of pictures of authors of children's books.

5. Visit the children's section of a public library. Inquire about the most popular books, the frequency of children's visits, and the method used to select books for the collection.

6. Visit a library or bookstore and investigate collections of poetry for children. Select at least one that you would like to have as a part of your personal collection of children's literature.

7. Begin a collection of poems about holidays that occur during the normal school year. Confine your selections to those suitable for a particular age group (primary, middle grades, or upper grades), and try to include as many poems and as many holidays as possible.

8. Begin a file of stories for reading or telling to children. Concentrate on primary, middle, or upper grades.

9. Plan an activity designed to aid sixth grade children in understanding and using figurative language. Use a story or poem as a motivating device. Outline carefully each step you would use in teaching the concept.

10. Visit a public library during the storytelling hour. Observe and report to the class on storytelling techniques used, choice of stories, and the children's reactions.

ACTIVITIES FOR INSERVICE TEACHERS

1. Instead of, or in addition to, providing comfortable spots for readers in the library corner, some teachers like to set up "quiet areas" where children can sit on chairs or recline on mats while they enjoy their books. Experiment with this, and, with the children, set up standards for behavior in these areas.

2. Listen to a record such as Ruth Sawyer's *Storyteller* (available from Weston Woods). Relate her comments about storytelling to the stories she tells on the record. Play the record for your class, using this as a first step in a study of storytelling.

3. Investigate the availability of paperback books for children. Where can they be obtained? How durable are they? What do they cost?

4. Add to the independent activities for children suggested in this chapter.

5. Compile a file of poetry appropriate for particular days, such as the first day of spring, the first snow, a foggy day, Christmas, Valentine's Day, etc.

6. With your class make a bulletin board about a favorite author.

7. With the children, organize a book fair and book swap. The children can bring favorite books, books they want to trade, and books obtained from neighbors (watch these for appropriateness). Assemble the books in an attractive and organized manner in an area of the room where children can easily go to browse and to make selections. Bulletin boards, book displays, mobiles, posters, and the children's own book-sharing devices (a card file of reactions to books that have been read, dioramas, art work, objects that have been constructed or collected, etc.) may also be used to enhance the appeal of the book area.

8. List the stories, poems, and books you have read to your class this year. Are you reading a variety of literature, presenting new authors, and introducing new literary forms?

INDEPENDENT ACTIVITIES FOR CHILDREN

1. Encourage children to make their own poetry anthologies and illustrate the poems with their own drawings or pictures cut from magazines. These should not be collected or graded (although they may be shared if the children wish). Poems might be written by the children themselves, might be ones they especially like, or both.

2. Have individual children select favorite poems and record them on tape. They can then use the tapes to judge their own reading for speed, expression, enunciation, etc. After a child feels that an effective reading level has been achieved, he or she may read the poem to the class.

3. Allow a child to go to the library and select books about a topic being studied by the class. This child may then be responsible for helping other children select from them either for personal enjoyment or for reporting to the class.

4. Have the child interview classmates and other children in the school about their favorite books. Urge the child to find out *why* each book is a favorite. He or she may report the results of the interviewing to the class, and show copies of some of the books.

5. One or several children might stage a puppet show based on an incident in a story or book.

6. Have a child look through magazines for pictures to illustrate a favorite story for telling to the class.

7. A child can prepare a bulletin-board display advertising a favorite book. A colorful jacket, sketches of characters, and a biography of the author might be included. Lists of "good" words, appealing passages, and chapter titles may also be prepared for the display.

8. Have the child select a character from a story that he or she knows well and finds especially appealing. The child then lists words, phrases, or sentences (either those used in the story or ones selected from his or her own impressions) that describe the character.

9. In the upper grades many children are beginning to play the guitar. Such a child may prepare for the class a program of ballads or folk songs from a particular era or locality in conjunction with a social studies or literature unit.

10. Mobiles illustrating a story or several stories may be made. These might show principal characters, location of action, or anything else the child wishes to express.

11. Many opportunities for independent activities are presented by audiovisual aids. Individual children or groups can listen to taped or recorded stories and poems, view filmstrips, prepare flannel-board stories to tell, etc. Sometimes this individual activity can lead to class viewing or listening. A child may wish to write a comparison of a filmstrip and a recorded version of the same story, or children may simply view or listen for pure pleasure.

12. A child may write a letter to an author or illustrator of a book that he or she has particularly enjoyed. Make sure that the letter includes particular reasons for liking the book (or the illustrations) or points out parts that were especially enjoyed. As an alternative, some piece of creative writing or art work that resulted from the reading might be sent to the author or illustrator.

16

Reading and Study Skills

Study skills are not the exclusive domain of the language arts program. They are an integral part of teaching—and learning—in every curriculum area and at every grade level. When a kindergarten teacher asks, "When we go out to peek at the nest in the big mulberry bush, what are we going to look for? How will we have to behave?" he or she is laying the foundation for good study procedure by helping the children to set both purpose and method. In the fourth grade, a teacher may say, "Before you start to write your paragraph, make a list of the things you want to include. Then decide what should come first, second, and so on." This teacher is helping children to organize. Both are guiding children toward techniques that will aid them in learning effectively and independently. This guidance is one of a teacher's most important tasks.

LEARNING TO STUDY

Academic success or failure is often determined, or at least strongly influenced, by a student's knowledge of how to study—his or her ability to use the study skills. Time and again parents are told by a teacher, "Marie would do better if she worked harder." But "working harder" may not be very meaningful to Marie or her parents. They may well assume that it means she needs to spend *more time* studying—and possibly it does—but it may also mean that what she really needs is to learn *how to study.*

There is no reason to believe that children enjoy being failures any more than the rest of us do. It is the school's job to give them the tools with which they may achieve success. Important among these tools are the study skills, and they must be systematically and carefully taught, not left to incidental learning. This chapter will discuss particular skills needed and suggest ways in which they may be taught.

Assignments

Properly made assignments are an important part of teaching children how to study. Suppose, for example, that you write on the chalkboard a notation something like this:

Homework
> Social Studies—read pages 140–145.

If this is the extent of the assignment, most children will probably read the pages because they are supposed to, but how much real learning will take place? What will the individual child remember from what has been read? On the other hand, such a notation may merely be a reminder to the children after you have thoroughly introduced the assignment. In fact, a visual reminder of page numbers, questions to be answered, etc., is good reinforcement. This may be written on the chalkboard (preferably with more than simply page numbers) or dittoed and given to the children as a study guide, or pupils may keep notebooks in which they jot down page numbers and other pertinent information about assignments. This is a good habit for them to form, particularly in the upper grades.

To be truly meaningful, an assignment must guide study so that the desired learnings will occur. It should tell the child *what* he or she is supposed to do, *why* it is to be done, and *how* it is to be done. This requires more than simply assigning page numbers; it includes motivation, filling in necessary background, and giving specific purposes for the lesson. Suppose, for example, that pages 140–145 in the social studies text concern the colonial Southeast. The assignment might involve three steps.

Well-made assignments are an integral part of planning for instruction.

I. *Motivation:* This could take the form of discussion centered around questions such as the following:
   A. When we talked about the colonization of the New World, we discussed how the different colonies were founded. Do you remember how Virginia and the Carolinas began? What about Georgia and Florida?
   B. Do you suppose life in the southern colonies was the same as that in New England or different? In what ways might it have been different?
   C. What is the climate like in the South? Might this have anything to do with the crops they raised and the way they made their living?
   D. We know that slavery developed in the South rather than in the North. Can you guess why?
II. *Background:* This might include briefly reviewing pertinent facts that the children may have forgotten, possibly listing the names of the southern colonies, and introducing new terms and vocabulary.
III. *Specific Purposes:* No assignment is complete until the children have specific things to look for as they read. You might duplicate or write on the board several questions to guide their reading, you might use some or all of the questions that are found at the end of a section or chapter in the text, or you might suggest the following procedure:
   A. As you read, notice the headings in dark print. Turn each of these into a question and see if you can answer it in one or two sentences. For instance, on page 141 you see the heading "Important Money Crops in the Southeast." Turn this into a question: What were the important money crops in the Southeast? Read the paragraph and see if you can answer the question in one sentence.
   B. As you read, try to discover one particular topic that you would like to find out more about and report on to the rest of the class. A list of suggestions is on the

Useful Books for Students

Steps to Beginning Research by Faye J. Buttle (Extension Publications, Division of Continuing Education, Brigham Young University, Provo, UT 1967).

Study Skills Library by H. Alan Robinson, Stanford E. Taylor, and Helen Frackenpohl (Educational Development Laboratories, 1965).

The First Book of Facts and How to Find Them by David C. Whitney (Watts, 1966).

board, but you may be able to think of another topic that would make a good report.

The example above not only illustrates one way of making an assignment meaningful but also shows how the language arts can be integrated with other curriculum areas. As previously stated, study skills should be taught in all areas; this particular assignment may lead to a need for library skills (see chapter 17), skimming and locational skills, organizational skills, and speaking or writing skills. In addition, this assignment gives practice in the linguistic activity of turning headings into questions; the reading skills required to find details, discover the main idea, or answer specific questions; and even vocabulary, spelling, and handwriting skills. Needed review should be a part of reading, spelling, handwriting, and language periods, and certainly the preparation for oral or written reports should be the subject matter of the language arts class.

The three steps listed above—providing motivation, furnishing needed background, and outlining specific purposes—are vital to every type of assignment and every grade level. Even in the primary grades, where study is largely supervised, it is important to remember that children learn more readily when they know what they are doing and why they are doing it. For example, suppose a group of third graders are preparing to read "Carmen's First Day."* Both motivation and background might be provided by talking about moving and the problems of making new friends. Perhaps you and the children might look at the pictures of Charlie, the orange cat, and speculate as to whether pets can be helpful in making friends. New words can be discussed, pronounced, and looked up in the glossary (background). Then the children are ready to read and find out whether Carmen made a new friend and whether Charlie was a help or a hindrance (purpose).

These steps can be adapted to suit almost any kind of assignment or activity, whether it be solving an arithmetic problem, planning a field trip, or preparing for a science experiment. Obviously, variety may—and should—be introduced; nothing could be duller than to have every lesson, even for only one subject area, presented in exactly the same manner. Motivation, for example, might include reading a story or poem, bringing in a group of pictures, showing a film, or simply reminding the class that "We decided that we ought to write for some materials for our science experiment" (more opportunities for integration). Similarly, specific assignments must be varied; converting topic headings into questions is a valuable study technique for children to learn, but they would soon lose interest if they were asked to turn every topic heading in a textbook into a question.

Study Steps

In addition to the guidance provided in assignments, attention should also be given by the time a child is in the middle grades to learning certain study steps to use either in reading a textbook or in doing independent reading. A number of systems for reading and retaining written material have been advanced, and in keep-

Prisms (Lexington, MA: D. C. Heath and Company, 1975), pp. 19–25.

Discourage reading only to find answers to specific questions through thought-provoking questions which call for more than factual information and discussions centering around why, how, what was the result, *etc.*

ing with current fashion, most are known by their acronyms—e.g., PQRST, POINT, EVOKER, PANORAMA. The number of steps in these may vary, but for most purposes good study procedure boils down to four basic points:

1. *Preview:* Read the introduction if there is one. Look at section headings, pictures, maps, graphs, etc. This will help you to get an idea of what the chapter (selection, unit, story) is about.
2. *Purpose:* Read the questions at the end of the chapter (and/or questions prepared by the teacher as a part of the assignment) *before* reading the chapter itself. This will help you to know what kind of information you are looking for—it establishes a purpose for reading.
3. *Read:* Read the chapter carefully, keeping in mind the questions to be answered.
4. *Review:* Read the questions again, and see if you can answer them. If not, review necessary sections. Or, look at section headings again, turn each into a question, and try to answer it in one or two sentences. For some assignments or for particularly difficult material, you may wish to use both of these methods.

When these steps are first introduced, children will think they are time consuming and therefore not worth using. But if you can persuade them to try this method, they will discover that they read faster because they know what information they are looking for, and that they are better prepared to take part in discussions or to report on their reading.

Children should also be shown that, like the assignment techniques suggested previously, these steps can be adapted to many kinds of assignments and activities and can help them in many ways. The "preview" technique can be adapted for selecting a book for pleasure reading—a child might read the first few paragraphs, look at chapter headings and illustrations, and perhaps skim a page or two here and there to get a fairly reliable impression of whether he or she would enjoy reading the book. Or the child might use this technique to discover whether a particular article or book contains the information needed for a report. In this way, children may learn how to avoid wasting time in reading something that is not suitable to their particular purposes.

In a similar way, children may learn that establishing purposes for reading—that is, beginning with specific questions in mind—is also time saving. The child who knows what he or she is looking for and who uses the preview method will be able to prepare a better report because the time spent will be devoted to fruitful efforts.

Further, the review step furnishes an excellent way to study for tests. Far too many students, even in high school and college, spend the night before an exam trying frantically to reread all the material covered; using the suggested review method will not only refresh one's memory, but will reveal those sections that do need to be read more closely.

LOCATING INFORMATION

In addition to learning how to study, children need to learn certain skills that will help them to locate information quickly and easily. Library skills are discussed in the following chapter; those presented here are alphabetizing, using the dictionary, and note taking. Many of the activities suggested are directly related to reading, reading and spelling readiness, and handwriting; some involve using picture dictionaries, learning initial consonants for reading, and learning visual and auditory discrimination skills helpful to reading and spelling. Learning is more meaningful when curriculum areas are interwoven, and constant reinforcement of skills is necessary for lasting learning. Keeping these two principles in mind, as well as the needs of the individual children in your class, will aid you in planning a program and selecting activities that provide real learning situations for the children.

Alphabetical Order

Children must know the alphabet thoroughly to use a telephone directory, a card catalog, a book index, an encyclopedia, or a dictionary both rapidly and efficiently. Activities for helping children learn letter names and alphabetical order are used principally in the primary grades, but the intermediate grades teacher should not ignore them, since it is possible (and in some situations even probable) that some fifth and sixth grade children will not have this skill.

In the early grades the letters of the alphabet should be visible to the children throughout the school day. You might want to sing the ABC song as part of your opening exercises. Stress left-to-right order at the same time, using a pointer or yardstick to indicate each letter as it is sung.

Primary children can also make their own ABC books, using pictures cut from magazines or catalogs. Assigning children to locate a picture of something that begins with B or some other letter can make them feel very important. Judgment should be exercised about using a picture of bread or a block; some teachers prefer not to use these "blend" pictures.

Large sheets of paper can be used to make a class ABC book, either before the children make individual books or at the same time. Use any available wall space to post the individual pages, being sure to keep the letters in alphabetical order and to show both the capital and lowercase forms for each letter. As the children bring in pictures to paste on the pages, they will be practicing pronunciation, learning to work cooperatively, and gaining skill in finding the letters quickly. An activity such as this will add color to the room and will promote interest among parents if it is started before "Open House" time.

Many ABC books should be kept on the library table in the primary classroom. Read to the children from these, encourage them to "read" along with you, and allow pupils to look at them individually. A few are listed here; the librarian can suggest others.

Crews, Donald. *We Read: A to Z* (New York: Harper and Row, 1967).
Federico, Helen. *ABC* (New York: Golden Press, 1974).
Feelings, Muriel. *Jambo Means Hello: Swahili Alphabet Book* (New York: Dial Press, 1974).
Fujikawa, Gyo. *A to Z Picture Book* (New York: Grosset and Dunlap, 1974).
Low, Joseph. *Adam's Book of Odd Creatures* (New York: Atheneum, 1962).
Miller, Barry. *Alphabet World* (New York: Macmillan, 1971).
Munari, Bruno. *Bruno Munari's ABC* (Cleveland: World, 1960).
Oxenbury, Helen. *ABC of Things* (New York: Watts, 1971).

Ruben, Patricia. *Apples to Zippers* (Garden City: Doubleday, 1976).

Scarry, Richard. *ABC Word Book* (New York: Random House, 1971).

Shuttlesworth, Dorothy. *ABC of Buses* (Garden City: Doubleday, 1965).

Tobias, Hosea, and Baskin, Lisa. *Hosie's Alphabet* (New York: Viking Press, 1972).

Wildsmith, Brian. *Brian Wildsmith's ABC* (New York: Watts, 1963).

Select ABC books with more in mind than the purpose of teaching letter names and their sounds in words. Certainly this is their primary purpose and should be uppermost in your mind, but there are other purposes as well. *Brian Wildsmith's ABC* could be selected for its illustrations alone; *We Read: A to Z* uses the letters of the alphabet to introduce concepts which primary children need to understand (*Ii* is for *inside*, *Ll* is for *left*); while Miller's *Alphabet World* stimulates imaginative viewing of the world about us by using photographs with overlays showing how letter shapes can be seen in all kinds of commonplace objects. *Jambo Means Hello* adds still another element: softly painted illustrations and words in the Swahili language introduce children to another culture. The latter two might prove especially useful in second or third grade if reinforcement is needed or with children who are still having problems with letter names and sounds since their vocabulary and content make them somewhat different from the usual alphabet book.

You can help children become familiar with letter names by such a simple procedure as having them line up for lunch, to make teams for a game, or for some other real purpose by calling letter names: "If your name begins with T, line up." Use either first or last names, or vary for different purposes. An alphabet-soup party can also add spice; some children may not know about alphabet-soup and they will have a great deal of fun with it. This might be combined with a health unit in which the children plan a lunch and make their own butter and applesauce to go with the soup—another opportunity for combining areas of the curriculum.

An alphabet procession game, using old shoe boxes, can help children to associate the letter name with its written forms. For this, put a letter (both capital and lowercase forms) on each box. The children then bring from home inexpensive articles to place in the boxes. For example, the C box might have a comb, a toy car, and a candle in it. During free time children can empty two or three boxes, mix up the contents, and then place the articles in the boxes according to beginning letters. Articles placed in the boxes should not be valuable or expensive, and it is important to stress that everything in a box belongs to someone and may not be taken by another person—children are often like crows and have a tendency to pick up bright objects!

Keep the "room alphabet" on display during all alphabetizing activities.

From the very beginning, children should be made aware of the difference between capital and small letters. At the primary level they should begin to learn that their names, the names of the streets they live on, and the name of the school begin with capitals, while the names of most of their possessions begin with small letters. Also, as you write sentences on the board, point out that each sentence begins with a capital.

A number of activities can be devised with a pack of 3×5 cards and a magic marker to write the letters—one set of capitals and one set of lowercase letters. Begin with something simple, such as distributing the cards and then designating a pupil who stands and says, "I am capital D. Where is small d (or capital S, or any other letter)?" The child who has this letter identifies himself and asks for another, and so on. Later the children can place their cards in the chalk tray in alphabetical order as they are called. Another game with cards calls for holding up a card and asking a child to name an object that begins with that letter. For example, a small b might produce *bear, bunny,* or *box,* and a capital D could result in *Dorothy* or *Dr. Dolittle.*   An activity of this type is good to use just before lunch or before children go home. Once they have the idea, they can play in small groups when they first come to school in the morning or when they have free time during the day.

These cards can also be useful in teaching letter sequence. Shuffle them and pass them around the room until the entire deck has been distributed. Then say, for instance, "Capital S, go to the front of the room." As soon as this child has

Using a Picture Dictionary

Can you tell what kind of book this is? How do you know?

live : to be alive; to make your home
lives George Washington <u>lived</u> two hundred years ago.
lived I <u>live</u> on Elm street.
living

load: what someone or something is carrying
loads The train has a <u>load</u> of coal.
load to fill; to get ready to carry
loading They are <u>loading</u> the truck.

loaf: the shape bread is baked in
loaves Cut two slices of bread from this <u>loaf</u>.

lone·some : being alone and feeling sad about it
The boy is <u>lonesome</u> for his dog.
I feel <u>lonesome</u> for my friends.

to talk about
1. What word comes first on the dictionary page? Why does <u>load</u> come after it?
2. Does the dictionary page show two meanings for the word <u>load</u>?
3. Does it show another form of the word <u>loaf</u>?
4. Are there two sentences that use the word <u>lonesome</u>?

36 ●

Using a dictionary may begin in the primary grades. (From *Language Basics Plus,* Level B. Copyright 1979 by Harper and Row Publishers, Inc. Used by permission of the publisher.)

done so, ask the children with the two letters that go before S to go to the front, then the two that come after. This could be varied by dividing the class into teams, one using the capitals and the other using the small letters. Points could be given for completing the sequence first.

The teaching of alphabetical order can also be combined with practice in handwriting. On the chalkboard or a chart, place rows of letters, with one letter missing at the beginning or end of each row. The children copy these, filling in the missing letters:

abcde—
—bcdef

This can also be done with uppercase and lowercase letters:

A—B—C—D—
—a—b—c—d

After the children become proficient at this, let them work with only one letter as a cue—for example, —g and g—. Later they may move to —k— and — —c, — —z. The "room alphabet" should remain visible during this activity so that children can check themselves if they are not sure of the correct order. Incorrect habits should not become established.

Exercises such as those suggested above can also be placed on ditto sheets to furnish practice for children who need recurring experiences with alphabetical order. Actually writing all the letters in order provides reinforcement for the learning and gives more handwriting practice, but it is more time consuming for both teacher and pupils. Thus it might be wise to keep a box of dittoed exercises that those children who need extra practice may use at odd moments during the day.

Alphabetical order and handwriting can both be combined with other areas of the curriculum. Perhaps in health class children might make a list of green vegetables. The next day for handwriting they could copy this list from the board, placing the words in alphabetical order. This activity is meaningful, and it will keep those who are working on it busy, freeing you to work with small groups or individuals.

Most of the activities suggested in the preceding paragraphs are principally intended for the early primary grades, though, as mentioned before, if children have not learned alphabetical order, practice is appropriate at any grade level. To supplement those suggested previously—or variations of them—a few more exercises suitable for the later primary or middle grades are listed below.

1. Have each reading group keep a dictionary to which individual children add their new words daily, placing each word neatly under the correct letter. These words will serve as a reading review and as a beginning dictionary for a child to refer to for the spelling of a word needed in writing. Or, if you prefer, each child may keep a personal dictionary.
2. When teaching about the telephone, make a class directory in connection with a handwriting lesson. Children can copy the names and numbers from the board in alphabetical order, probably doing only a few each day until the directory is completed. Addresses may or may not be included, depending on the age of the children.
3. From the picture file, select pictures showing things whose names begin with a vari-

ety of letters. Hold up a picture, and let children tell you the name of the picture, the letter the name begins with, and whether that letter is found at the beginning, the middle, or the end of the alphabet. A card with this information on it can be stapled to the back of each picture so that children can play the game when they have free time. Or cards can be separate, and children can match them with the pictures.

4. After children know letter names and sequence, begin having them alphabetize words by second letters, and later by third letters. Using reading, vocabulary, or spelling words for this exercise will make it more meaningful and help to fix words in the children's minds.

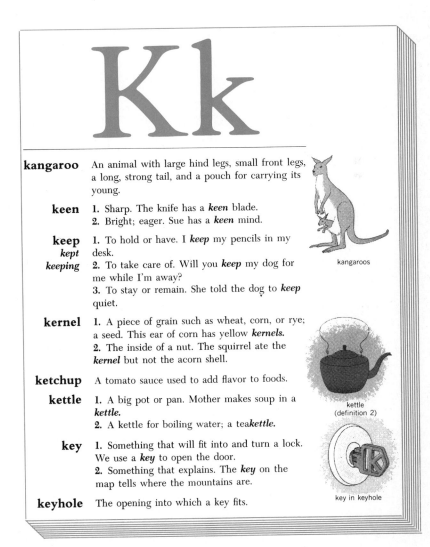

Kk

kangaroo An animal with large hind legs, small front legs, a long, strong tail, and a pouch for carrying its young.

kangaroos

keen 1. Sharp. The knife has a *keen* blade.
2. Bright; eager. Sue has a *keen* mind.

keep 1. To hold or have. I *keep* my pencils in my
kept desk.
keeping 2. To take care of. Will you *keep* my dog for me while I'm away?
3. To stay or remain. She told the dog to *keep* quiet.

kernel 1. A piece of grain such as wheat, corn, or rye; a seed. This ear of corn has yellow *kernels.*
2. The inside of a nut. The squirrel ate the *kernel* but not the acorn shell.

ketchup A tomato sauce used to add flavor to foods.

kettle 1. A big pot or pan. Mother makes soup in a *kettle.*
2. A kettle for boiling water; a tea*kettle.*

kettle
(definition 2)

key 1. Something that will fit into and turn a lock. We use a *key* to open the door.
2. Something that explains. The *key* on the map tells where the mountains are.

key in keyhole

keyhole The opening into which a key fits.

Some beginning dictionaries show more than the base forms of verbs. [William Morris, ed. *The Weekly Reader Beginning Dictionary*. Middletown, Conn.: Xerox Education Publications, 1973, p. 157. Reprinted by permission of the publisher.]

Dictionary Skills

Although dictionary skills are usually taught in the fourth grade, children should begin in the first grade to learn the uses of this valuable tool. Every primary classroom should have at least one picture dictionary, and children should have specific instruction in its use. Begin by making certain that they understand the relationship between the illustration and the printed word, as well as the arrangement of the words in the book. As they begin to write, help them to discover how the arrangement helps them to find words quickly and how the dictionary can help them to find the correct spelling of words they want to write.

As children progress through school their knowledge and use of the dictionary increases. In other words, dictionary usage is a developmental activity in which skills are taught, reinforced, and added to as children move through the elementary grades. These skills and understandings fall into four general categories.

The first category is that discussed in the preceding section—alphabetical order. Children should recognize early that not only dictionaries but nearly all other references they will use are arranged in alphabetical order by the first, second, third, etc., letters in the words. Thus efficient use of a dictionary requires a virtually automatic familiarity with letter sequence, as well as with the relative positions of letters (the *d*'s come in the first third of the dictionary, the *y*'s in the final third, and so on).

The second category involves understanding the particular characteristics of the dictionary that aid in using it efficiently. Children should learn to use guide words to locate the page on which a word may be found and that words are listed by their base forms (*come* is listed but *coming* is not).

The third group consists of pronunciation aids provided by the dictionary: accent marks, phonetic respellings, diacritical markings, and key words. In this connection, children also need to understand how syllabication is shown and how it is useful to pronunciation and to division of words in writing.

Finally, there is much information other than definitions and pronunciations that the dictionary can provide. It may give abbreviations, synonyms, antonyms, variant meanings of words; it may show related forms, irregular plurals, principal parts of irregular verbs, meanings of prefixes, etc.; and it may contain many special features, such as tables of weights and measures, a gazetteer, a list of foreign words and phrases, and so forth.

Beginning Dictionary Activities

The activities suggested here are intended for several levels of dictionary users. There is a general progression from the general and simple skills to the more specific, although many of the activities can be used in varying ways and at varying levels. Select those which appear suitable for the children in your class, and supplement them with others of your own devising as they are needed.

1. Make a large, chart-size classroom picture dictionary by having the children bring in pictures, which are then pasted on the chart with the name of the picture (cat, house, etc.) written below. Both capital and lowercase letters should appear at the

---

Test Yourself:

Can *you* turn quickly to the portion of a dictionary where a specific letter is located?

Picture Dictionaries

Clemons, Elizabeth. *Pixie Dictionary.* New York: Holt, Rinehart, and Winston, 1961.

Monroe, Marion, and Greet, W. Cabell. *My Little Pictionary.* Glenview, IL: Scott, Foresman and Company, 1963.

Monroe, Marion, and Greet, W. Cabell. *My Second Pictionary.* Glenview, IL: Scott, Foresman and Company, 1964.

Moore, Lilian. *The Golden Picture Dictionary.* New York: Western Publishing Company, 1976.

Parker, Bertha Morris. *The New Golden Dictionary.* New York: Western Publishing Company, 1977.

Scarry, Richard. *Storybook Dictionary.* New York: Western Publishing Company, 1966.

Charlie Brown Dictionary. New York: World Publishing Company, 1973.

top of each page. Refer to this picture dictionary throughout the day when talking to the children about words.

2. Have the children make individual picture dictionaries. Since they will need help writing the words, it would be wise to limit this in some way. For example, each child might bring only one picture per day—or he or she could bring several, but select one to be used for the dictionary. An orderly way of organizing the activity is to progress through the alphabet, with each child bringing an A picture the first day, B the second, and so on. Each day the words are written on the chalkboard as the children name their pictures (undoubtedly there will be many duplications), and then copy them from the board. It is a good idea to have a supply of old magazines for those who have not been able to find a picture or have forgotten to bring one. Be prepared to improvise, too—help a child to draw a large question mark for Q, color a yellow flower for Y, or draw a picture of a zebra.

3. Individual picture dictionaries are also helpful to older children who do not know letter names or alphabetical order or who are having difficulty with reading.

4. Word and picture associations can be strengthened by using words from reading lessons. Have the children find pictures named by the words, paste them on 5 × 8 cards, and print the words below. Children can shuffle the cards and then arrange them in alphabetical order.

5. Some picture dictionaries have category words together—farm, city, people, animals, etc. The children may want to bring in pictures for categories they select. Although this does not involve alphabetical order, the activity does help promote early organizational skills.

6. Select a word from a picture dictionary and ask one child to find it for you. This child then gets to select a word and ask another to find it.

7. From the picture file, select several pictures of objects whose names are in the picture dictionary. Show a picture to the class and say, "I can't spell the word for this picture. Who can find it for me in the picture dictionary?" After doing this a few times, leave the pictures out so that children can play the game in small groups.

8. Point out the glossaries in books the children are using. Help children to develop the habit of looking up the word meanings needed for comprehension in reading.

9. As children progress in their dictionary skills they may begin using a dictionary such as those listed on this page. Such dictionaries usually have sections explaining their use. *The Thorndike-Barnhart Beginning Dictionary*, for example, not only has an introduction showing how to use it, but also includes a series of exercises to give the children practice in dictionary skills.

10. Teach new vocabulary words associated with the dictionary itself. Show and explain *entry words, guide words*, and *definitions*. It might be helpful to make a bulletin board showing a sample page from the dictionary, with the guide words, entry words, and definitions labeled.

11. Have the children write on 3 × 5 cards questions that can be answered by using a dictionary and then exchange questions. Each child finds the answer, writes it on the back of the card along with the number of the page where the answer was found, and then reads it to the class. (Encourage good sentence formation, handwriting, capitalization, and punctuation on the cards.) Make a tree of knowledge on the bulletin board with these cards. The following are a few sample questions:

> Does a badger wear a badge?
> Does a foothill wear a shoe?
> Could a person play an oboe?

12. Select a list of words from your readers. Have the children divide the words into syllables and place the accent marks where they feel they should go. Then have them check their answers in the dictionary.

Beginning Dictionaries

Ginn Beginning Dictionary. Lexington, MA: Ginn and Company, 1973.

Weekly Reader Beginning Dictionary. New York: Grosset and Dunlap, 1973.

Webster's Elementary Dictionary. Cincinnati: American Book Company, 1977.

Macmillan Beginning Dictionary. New York: Macmillan Publishing Company, 1975.

Macmillan Dictionary for Children. New York: Macmillan Publishing Company, 1977.

Scott, Foresman Beginning Dictionary. Glenview, IL: Scott, Foresman and Company, 1979.

Thorndike-Barnhart Beginning Dictionary. Garden City: Doubleday and Company, Inc., 1972.

13. Randomly select a guide word from the dictionary and say the word. The first child to find that word gets to say a guide word for the others to locate.

14. Write phonetic spellings of several words on the board. Children are to determine what each word is and then write a sentence using it. Allow them to use the dictionary to check their answers.

15. Children can make their own glossaries of library, social studies, health, or science words.

16. Have the children learn a word a day, with each child getting a turn to select the

---

jackknife / Japanese

box that a doll pops out of when the lid is opened.
jack-in-the-box (jak′in′thə boks′) *noun, plural* **jack-in-the-boxes.**
jackknife A large pocketknife with blades that fold into the handle.
jack-knife (jak′nif′) *noun, plural* **jackknives.**
jack-o'-lantern A pumpkin that has been hollowed out and carved to look like a face. Jack-o'-lanterns are used at Halloween.
jack-o'-lan·tern (jak′ə-lan′tərn) *noun, plural* **jack-o'-lanterns.**
jackpot The top prize in a game or contest. That quiz show has a *jackpot* of $100,000.
jack·pot (jak′pot′) *noun, plural* **jackpots.**
jack rabbit A hare that has a thin body and very long ears. Jack rabbits use their strong back legs for leaping, and are one of the fastest of all animals.

Jack-O'-Lantern

jade A hard, green stone that is used for jewelry and carved ornaments.
jade (jād) *noun, plural* **jades.**
jagged Having sharp points that stick out. Eagles build their nests on high, *jagged* cliffs.
jag·ged (jag′id) *adjective.*
jaguar A large animal that belongs to the cat family. The short fur of a jaguar is golden with black spots. Jaguars are found in the southeastern United States, Mexico, and Central and South America.
jag·uar (jag′wär) *noun, plural* **jaguars.**

Jaguar

jail A building where people who are waiting for a trial or who have been found guilty of breaking the law are kept; prison. *Noun.*
—To put or keep in jail. The police *jailed* the men they caught robbing the bank. *Verb.*

jail (jāl) *noun, plural* **jails;** *verb,* **jailed, jailing.**
jam[1] **1.** To press or squeeze into a tight space. Ed tried to *jam* all his clothes into one small suitcase. People *jammed* onto the bus to get to work. **2.** To become or cause to become stuck so as not to work. The soldier's gun *jammed* when he tried to fire it. Rust and dirt *jammed* the lock on the gate. **3.** To push hard. Jim *jammed* on the brakes to stop the car. **4.** To bruise or crush. The girl *jammed* her hand when she closed the drawer on it. *Verb.*
—**1.** A mass of people or things so crowded together that it is difficult to move. Bill was three hours late because he was stuck in a traffic *jam*. **2.** A difficult situation. The man was in a real *jam* when the police found the stolen money in his room. *Noun.*
jam (jam) *verb,* **jammed, jamming;** *noun, plural* **jams.**
jam[2] A sweet food made by boiling fruit and sugar together until it is thick. Jam is used to spread on bread or other foods. Helen's grandmother makes strawberry *jam* every summer.
jam (jam) *noun, plural* **jams.**
janitor A person whose job is to take care of and clean a building.
jan·i·tor (jan′ə tər) *noun, plural* **janitors.**
January The first month of the year. January has thirty-one days.
Jan·u·ar·y (jan′yōō er′ē) *noun.*

▲ The Romans named **January** after *Janus*, their god of doors and gates. A holiday in his honor was held during this month. Janus was shown with two faces that looked in opposite directions. His holiday was probably held in January because this month looks in two directions—back on the year that has passed and ahead to the year to come.

Japan An island country in the Pacific Ocean. It is off the eastern coast of Asia. Its capital is Tokyo.
Ja·pan (jə pan′) *noun.*
Japanese 1. A person who was born or is living in Japan. **2.** The language of Japan. *Noun.*

at; āpe; cär; end; mē; it; īce; hot; ōld; fôrk; wood; fōōl; oil; out; up; turn; sing; thin; this; hw in white; zh in treasure. ə stands for a in about, e in taken i in pencil, o in lemon, and u in circus.

341

The dictionary is a useful and fascinating tool. [William D. Halsey, editorial director. *Macmillan Beginning Dictionary.* Copyright © 1975 by Macmillan Publishing Company. Reprinted by permission of the publisher.]

word. The others locate it in the dictionary, discuss it, record the meanings and part (or parts) of speech it may be, and write a sentence or two using it.

17. To develop speed in locating letters in the dictionary, give a letter name such as *I*. The child who opens to the letter *I* or closest to it gets to say the next letter.

18. Children in the upper intermediate grades should be taken to see the different dictionaries in the library. Allow them sufficient time to look through these and discover their special features.

19. Have children compare a dictionary with a thesaurus and list differences and similarities in both format and use.

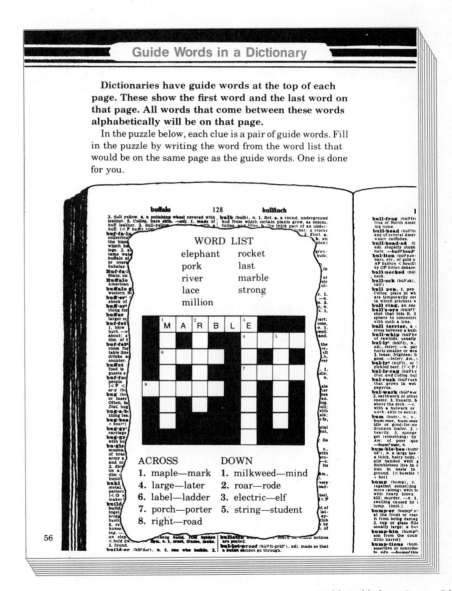

Guide Words in a Dictionary

Dictionaries have guide words at the top of each page. These show the first word and the last word on that page. All words that come between these words alphabetically will be on that page.

In the puzzle below, each clue is a pair of guide words. Fill in the puzzle by writing the word from the word list that would be on the same page as the guide words. One is done for you.

WORD LIST

elephant   rocket
pork   last
river   marble
lace   strong
million

ACROSS

1. maple—mark
4. large—later
6. label—ladder
7. porch—porter
8. right—road

DOWN

1. milkweed—mind
2. roar—rode
3. electric—elf
5. string—student

56

Using Our Language Workbook, Level 4. Los Angeles: Bowmar/Noble Publishers, Inc., p. 56.

Other Activities and Exercises

Children who have had a great deal of practice in using the dictionary from the time they first began to read should not need much teaching of dictionary skills in the middle and upper grades. However, some children have not learned to use this valuable tool—and all may need occasional refresher practice. Many of the activities suggested in the preceding section can be used in, or adapted for, the middle and upper grades; in addition, language texts often contain units on the use of dictionaries and other reference tools. But it may also prove helpful to keep a file of dictionary exercises to be used by one, several, or all of the children when specific skills need to be learned or reinforced. The suggestions below can be adapted to fit the needs of particular classes.

1. *Guide Words.*
   a. You might run into the words below when studying about airplanes. Find each of the words in your dictionary and write the two guide words that are on that page.

Word	First Guide Word	Second Guide Word
propeller	_____	_____
runway	_____	_____
aviation	_____	_____
jet propulsion	_____	_____
wing	_____	_____
beacon	_____	_____
radar	_____	_____
ceiling	_____	_____

   b. *Nest* and *new* are the guide words on page 268 in a certain dictionary. Underline the words in the following list that would be found on this page.

lake	nerve
net	neither
neutral	nail
neglect	nettle
nestling	next

2. *Syllabication and Accent:*
   a. Divide the following words into syllables and place accent marks where they belong. Use your dictionary if you are not sure. When you are finished, use the dictionary to check *each word,* even if you are sure you were right.

galaxy	geography
atmosphere	mountainous
lunar	continent
astronaut	ocean

   b. Sometimes two-syllables words are accented on the first syllable when they are nouns and on the second when they are verbs. Look up the following words.

and write three sentences for each, using a different meaning in each sentence. In each underline the syllable which should be accented.

conduct   compress   project   contrast

3. *Diacritical Markings and Key Words:* After each of the following words, write the phonetic spelling you find for it in the dictionary. Be sure to show the accent and the diacritical marks above the vowels. In the third column write the key words that will help you to pronounce each word. Be prepared to pronounce each word correctly.

Word	Phonetic Spelling	Key Word(s)
menace		
vegetation		
mammal		
locust		
debris		
swarm		
rubbish		
larva		
mesquite		
retrieve		

4. *Selecting Appropriate Meanings:* In front of each sentence below put the number of the meaning which fits that sentence. Use the word in four other sentences, one for each of the four meanings.

sup-port(sup-port′),v.1) To hold up; to keep from sinking or falling; as, pillars support the porch roof. 2) to bear; to endure; as, he could not support the pain any longer. 3) to take sides with; to back up; as, to support a candidate. 4) to provide with food, clothing, shelter, etc.; as, he supports his mother.

     1. He could not support the suspense any longer.
     2. Many people must support a man to get him into office.
     3. He helped to support his family by working after school.
     4. The shelf was supported by braces.

5. *Finding Correct Spellings:* Below you will find the phonetic spellings of a number of words. Using your knowledge of the way various sounds may be spelled, find these words in the dictionary and write their correct spellings. [For this exercise be sure to use the phonetic spellings that are found in the particular dictionary that your children use. Select words that have appeared in reading they have done or that might appeal to them. Begin with simple words that the children know and work up to those which might be spelled in a number of ways—pneumonia, physical, pylon, heather, etc.]

These exercises are intended, of course, as examples only. Wherever possible, practice in using the dictionary—or any other reference tool—should be done in connection with actual needs. For example, new words in a science unit might be used for finding diacritical markings and phonetic spellings—and meanings, too, of course.

Note Taking

The abilities required for taking effective notes are essentially those required for reading comprehension—getting the main idea, selecting supporting facts or important details, putting ideas into sequence—plus the ability to skim. These skills are discussed in later sections of this chapter. Even at the primary level, however, there are many activities that can help children to develop the habit of organized thinking which is so necessary to these skills. For example, children can compose titles for pictures. Discuss the pictures first, then let them suggest various titles and select the most appropriate one. They can also help to make charts showing what to do during a fire drill, who is responsible for various housekeeping chores during the day or week, or what activities are planned for the week. Following a trip, have the children dictate while you write an experience chart that lists what was observed and learned. After a story, ask them to recall the events; list these on the board in sequence. Or read a short description to the class and have them draw pictures, supplying as many of the details as they can. (You may need to read the description more than once.)

As children advance in reading and writing skills, group activities can be used to help them learn how to take notes. Before such an activity begins, however, the children should be helped to develop standards for note-taking. At first these may be quite simple.

TIPS FOR NOTE TAKING

1. Decide exactly what you want to find out.
2. Write down only important facts on the particular information you are looking for.
3. Use your own words. *Do not copy.*

With the standards firmly in mind, try these activities:

1. Choose several paragraphs that are particularly easy to take notes on from one of the class texts. (This is an opportunity to integrate; don't simply select at random, but choose material that you had planned to assign anyway and that the children will be expected to understand.) Have all the children read the material and take notes, reminding them of the standards that have been established. After all have finished, select several to go to the board and write what they have written. Compare these and compile a composite, letting the children decide which facts to include and add any important information they think has been omitted.
2. Use an opaque or overhead projector to show a brief article from a magazine or book. Again, this should be something that pertains to the curriculum. Follow the procedure suggested above, or use the projector to show individual children's notes. (Papers should be handed in without names, so no child will be embarrassed.)
3. Have children take notes as a film is shown. Before showing the film, write on the board a list of questions for which they should find answers. After the film, have each child use his notes to write answers to the questions. The questions should include some that call for specific information and some that require drawing inferences.

Note-taking skills facilitate independent learning.

4. Use films and tapes frequently to give children practice in noting only important details or finding answers to specific questions. This will help them to avoid the usual tendency beginning note-takers have to write down everything they read or hear, since the time will be controlled. Do this regularly throughout the year in connection with units of study in content areas, making sure always to provide guidance by giving children specific information to look for.

5. Have children watch specific television shows or particular kinds of shows at home and take notes on advertising techniques, use of dialects, new vocabulary words, etc. Let children who have seen the same show compare information and prepare a group report for presentation to the class.

6. Let individual children who need practice work with tapes in the listening center, making sure that they have questions to guide their listening. Allow them to stop the tape or replay portions in order to find the information they need, just as one would reread a portion of a book or article.

In the middle and upper grades, children will be preparing reports to give to the class, and for these they will need to use reference materials obtained from the library. Since the individual child will be using several sources and will be investigating different sources to discover material, standards will need to be more refined and inclusive:

Point out to children that these steps are really only an adaptation of the study steps suggested on page 396.

1. Skim. Glance through the article to see whether it contains information that is important to the report.

2. Write down the name of the book, author's name, and page numbers on which the information is found. For encyclopedias, write the name of the encyclopedia, vol-

ume number, subject heading, and page numbers.

3. Write down only the important facts or the particular information you are looking for. Use your own words; *do not copy.*
4. If you do wish to use the author's words for some particular reason, use quotation marks and *write down the exact page number.*
5. Check names, dates, and figures for accuracy.
6. Skim once more to see if you have missed anything important.

Taking Notes

Angela took notes as she read the whale book. She wrote her notes on a 3-inch-by-5-inch card.

Whales: Their Life in the Sea, Faith McNulty
Phoenicians called whales Lord of the Fish
Blue Whales - over 100 feet long, 20 feet high -
two-story house
largest creature ever lived - bigger than
dinosaur; very powerful
cruise at 6 to 8 mph; frightened, 20 mph

to talk about   What did Angela write at the top of the card? Did she put all the information from the book into her notes? Did she write in full sentences? Why is it important to take notes as you read?

▶ When you are taking notes, remember to do these things.

- Write the name of the book and the author at the beginning of your notes. A 3-inch-by-5-inch index card is good for notetaking.
- Read for facts. Look for the main idea of each paragraph. Write it down.
- Add the details that you want to remember.

220 ●

Good advice! (From *Language Basics Plus,* Level E. Copyright 1979 by Harper and Row Publishers, Inc. Used by permission of the publisher.)

When children first start making individual reports based on notes they have taken from several sources, teacher guidance is particularly important so that they learn to locate materials quickly and to select the important information, as well as to avoid the pitfalls of unintentional plagiarism and forgetting to write down sources.

ORGANIZING AND REPORTING INFORMATION

The skills required to write the actual sentences and paragraphs of a report are essentially those required for any writing; these are discussed in chapter 8. Of particular concern to the total report are organization, language level, and giving credit to sources of information.

Outlining

Perhaps the most difficult point in preparing a report comes when a child has collected the information needed and is ready to begin writing. Faced with what seems to be a welter of disorganized facts, the child must somehow put them in order. The solution is to use an outline.

Actually, all writing should begin with an outline. Even before beginning to collect information for a report, either oral or written, a child should make a tentative outline; this will serve as a guide in deciding what information to look for. The outline may be quite brief and certainly it may need to be revised in light of the information found, but it does provide guidance. In the same way, the child who is going to write a business letter should jot down ideas about what items to include and the order in which they are to be placed. In writing a story, there is need to plan the sequence of events and provide for the inclusion of those details that will be important to plot development and reader interest. Such outlines can be very informal, but children should learn that preplanning not only saves time but results in better organization and thus more effective writing.

Not only written activities but all the activities of the classroom at every grade level need organization. Children should learn at an early age that they cannot even have a successful class picnic without planning what they will need and who will provide it. Later, they should be shown that a written outline can help keep a speaker from omitting important points, that outlining study notes can be helpful in studying for a test, and so on.

Readiness Activities.   The following activities are suggested for helping primary grade children develop the ability to find the main idea, locate supporting details, and determine the sequence of events in what is read or heard.

I. Main idea
  A. Readiness books contain many pictures, most of them designed to assist children in gaining the main idea. Use these for discussions of "what the story is about."
  B. Using picture books such as John Peterson's *Tulips*, have children tell what is happening.

C. Bring in pictures and ask the children to tell the main thing each one shows.

D. Show a picture and have the children dictate a story about it. Write it on chart paper and evaluate it with the class as to its accuracy and completeness in telling about the picture.

E. When you have finished reading a story to the class or when they have finished reading one, select one child to pretend to be a mother or father and another child to play himself. The child comes home from school and tells a parent the story.

F. A variation of this is to have the child tell the parent the major things done in school that day.

G. Select an animal every week. Have the children dictate daily stories about the made-up adventures of David Donkey or Harry Hippopotamus, for example. When the daily story is completed on the experience chart, children select a title (main idea) for that story.

II. Details

A. Take the children for a walk in the schoolyard or to another room in the school (gymnasium, principal's office, another classroom), first telling them that they will be asked to describe what they saw. On returning, list on the chalkboard all the details they can recall. Use questions to elicit specifics: What was on the principal's desk? What did the principal look like? Were there pictures on the wall?

B. Before reading a story to the class, tell them that when the story is finished they are to draw a picture of their favorite part. Remind them to listen carefully so that they can include every detail they need.

C. Homework for a primary grade child could be to study something in his or her home, paying particular attention to details such as size, shape, color, and texture. The next day the child may describe the object in detail, with the other children trying to guess what is being described.

D. Ask one child to stand up, walk around the room, and then stand at the back. Have children describe his or her appearance without turning around to look. Include details such as color of eyes, type of shoes, etc.

E. Help the children make a mural of something they are studying, such as different types of homes for humans. Details will be important in the pictures. When the mural is completed, the children may dictate experience chart stories describing the houses. Children may also draw their own pictures of the different houses and copy the experience stories. Both can be put into individual books which may be taken home.

F. Use lines or sentences from nursery rhymes that describe something, such as "Jack jumped over the candlestick." Each child draws a picture for this line. Use these for a bulletin board in which the line or sentence serves as a caption.

III. Sequence of events

A. After reading a story such as "The Three Billy Goats Gruff," ask children what happened first, next, and last.

B. In connection with teaching children to tell time, make up ditto sheets of clocks or have children draw clocks. Help them to place the hour and minute hands on the correct numbers to show what time they come to school, what time they have lunch, and so on throughout the day. The children can then draw pictures of themselves performing a particular activity underneath the clock that shows when that activity takes place. Start with the early morning hours and do one clock a day. It is possible that some children may come from homes where no one pays much attention to time. Be patient and consistent in your efforts to teach time sequence.

C. Questions of a cause-and-effect nature help children to understand the importance of sequence. Use such questions as listening purposes: "As I read this story, listen for the one event that caused Harry to get into trouble. Listen and remember what happened to him because of that."

D. Teaching the days of the week and months of the year helps children to become aware of sequence.

E. Tape or staple comic strips to cardboard. Cut them apart and place in envelopes. During free time children can place the comics in correct sequence.

F. Ask children to name all the holidays that occur during the school year and then put them in the order in which they occur.

Primary Grades.   Children can become familiar with outline form in the early grades. The outline below entitled "Our Trip" illustrates the type of outline that might be put on the chalkboard or on a chart for pupils to see. They should participate in preparing it, although they may need help in putting the statements into the correct form.

I. On the bus
  A. Stay in seats
    1. Talk quietly to neighbors.
    2. Keep hands inside.
  B. Do not eat.
    1. Keep food in a bag.
    2. Don't trade food or bags.
II. At the zoo
  A. Find the animals that live an a warm climate.
  B. Find the animals that live in a cold climate.
III. Return to school
  A. Write a report about the zoo.
  B. Draw pictures.

Opportunities for using outlines in planning and reporting class activities are numerous. For instance, directions or plans for a class picnic or luncheon can be outlined on the board. Or, when children have completed reading or listening to a story, ask them to dictate the first main idea, details, and sequence, then the second main idea, and so on. Write these on the board or on chart paper; then reread the story to check the outline form. This kind of activity will help demonstrate to children how their own stories can be improved if they jot down their ideas and organize them into a meaningful sequence. As a follow-up, have them suggest several story ideas; then, with you as scribe, they can decide on a series of events and select the supporting details for each. At first, simply list the suggestions; then work with them to organize these into an outline for the story. Several of these might be written on charts to serve as models. The final step is to use one of them as the basis for a class story. You might divide the class into groups, having each group either develop one of the outlines or make their own outline and write a story from it.

Middle Grades.   Outlining must have a purpose to have value to children. Many children will outline simply because they are told to, but it is important to convince them that outlining has value whenever they sit down to write or whenever they plan for something they are to talk about.

Outlining form can best be taught through use of a chalkboard, chart, or overhead projector. Although the use of an outline is the most important point for a child to learn, some attention needs to be given to outline form and why such form is followed. The following should be taught:

    I. Use Roman numerals for main topics—the most important points.
       A. Indent and capitalize letters for subtopics.
         1. Use Arabic numbers for the details.
         2. Because you have one, you need at least one more detail about subtopic A.
       B. This is another subtopic of Roman numeral I.
         1. Give one detail about B.
         2. One B detail needs a second.
   II. List another main topic.
       A. Subtopic.   Details may or may not be needed here.
       B. Subtopic.   Again, if there are two or more parts or details, there will need to be a division of the subtopic.

A common experience such as a movie is excellent for teaching outline form. The movie should be carefully selected with a view toward its suitability for outlining, and preparation should be thorough so the children will not be frustrated in selecting important points. Before the movie begins, the class should be instructed to take notes so that they can outline the content when it is over.

Once the movie is over, ask the children to tell what they saw or learned, and write everything they say on the board. The next step is to organize the information—select the first main idea, then the details, the next main idea, details, and so on until everything has been covered. As the children select the main ideas and details, help them to make the outline, using the overhead projector or chart paper. When the lesson is completed the children can copy the outline and file it in a booklet of "Movies I Have Learned From" or with pictures, reading notes, etc., from the same unit. Naturally, the outline and movie should be an integral part of a particular unit of study—there is no point in showing a film or making an outline that does not pertain to anything that the class is doing.

The discussion of content area subjects in class also provides good opportunity for teaching the value of outlining. As discussion takes place, write in outline form any information that you want the class to remember. The children can copy this in their notebooks and use it as a basis for study.

Upper Grades.   Continue to give upper grade children practice in outlining skills if they appear to need it and to insist that outlining precede both oral and written activities. Show your own reliance on this skill by outlining important facts on the board as you discuss them, by distributing written outlines of a projected plan for a unit of work, etc.

At this level, children may need help in correlating information from several sources for an oral or written report. If they do, the following procedure should prove helpful:

1. Using an overhead projector, show three different articles about the same subject. All should contain some common information, but each should include facts not found in the others.
2. Have the children take notes on each selection. This may be a group effort, with

notes being taken on the chalkboard.

3. With the children's help, outline the notes from each selection.
4. Make a composite outline, including important points from all three. You may wish to have the children place numbers (1, 2, 3) in parentheses after each point, both to illustrate how the material is correlated and to help them locate information quickly if they need to refer to the articles in writing their summaries (step 5).
5. Have each child use the outline to write an individual summary of the information obtained from all three selections.

Preparing Footnotes and Bibliographies

Writers spend long, hard hours preparing the material that is found in books and magazines; they need to be given credit for their work, and children must understand this. As soon as children are ready to use reference materials to gain information, they are also ready to add bibliographies to reports compiled from these sources. First, develop the understanding that borrowing words or ideas is like borrowing books. People do not write their own names in books borrowed from friends or from the library; neither should they pretend that other people's words and ideas are their own. Second, help children to recognize that if a writer has authorities to back up what is said, readers will know that the subject has been studied and that the writer knows what he or she is talking about. Further, appending a bibliography gives readers the opportunity to find out for themselves if they doubt the information or wish to learn more about the subject.

Children love big words, and there is no reason why they should not use the word *bibliography* to show their sources. In the beginning, form should be simple. A chart may be used to help with the punctuation and with the spelling of *bibliography*.

Bibliography

Adams, Richard. *The Story of Canada*, pages 21–26.
The World Book, Vol. C, pp. 1166–1195.

By the time children reach the sixth or seventh grade, they should be ready to include slightly more information in bibliographies. For example, the items given below should probably be included. Again, charts should be used to help with punctuation and order of items; children should not be expected to remember these, especially since various authorities suggest different punctuation. We suggest that the punctuation items and order given in the language text the class uses be the guide.

Trade Books	**Encyclopedias**	**Periodicals**
author	title	author (if named)
title	most recent copyright date	title of article
publisher	volume number or letter	title of magazine
copyright date	pages	date
page numbers		pages

In the upper grades some children may learn how to use footnotes. Generally in the elementary grades there is little need to require the use of footnotes, particularly for anything other than direct quotations. In a short paper the source of a particular item of information can be found, if needed, by checking the bibliography or the pupil's notes. They will later learn that in longer papers it is sometimes desirable to footnote certain types of information that are not directly quoted; however, elementary school children should *never* be assigned to write long "term papers." The important learning involved is the ability to correlate information from several sources and to organize it into a well-written report; if subjects are sufficiently limited in scope, children can concentrate upon organization and good form in writing rather than sloppily throwing together a great volume of information.

Work with the children as they take notes. Emphasize that they should *never* copy directly from a source without putting quotation marks around the words that are copied and jotting the exact page number immediately following the quotation. In this way they will both avoid unintentional plagiarism and have the necessary information for footnotes if they decide to quote directly. Introduce the word plagiarism, explain its meaning, and invoke severe penalties if it should occur, however unintentionally—they will thank you for it later. Take the time to check sources if you are suspicious—the formation of bad habits negates the positive aspects of note taking and reporting.

Help children to learn that a paper should be more than simply a series of quotations strung together, however well organized, and that it is "dirty pool" merely to transpose a few words or phrases and consider the writing original. The ideas and information in a report are gathered from other sources, but the organization and wording should be original. Quoting is done when it will strengthen the report in one of two ways. First, the writer may wish to use an author's own words to illustrate a point. For example, in discussing a poet, one might well quote from one or more poems; or a paper about a famous person might be enriched by the use of that person's own words. Second, it is sometimes desirable to use a quotation to show a particular person's opinion, especially if he is a well-known authority.

Footnotes may be in simple form. Author, title, and page number are sufficient; anyone who wishes more complete information can check the bibliography. There is no need to add the extra burden of learning about specialized forms, such as ibid. and op. cit. The important facts for children to learn are that they may not copy someone else's words without giving credit and how this credit may be given. Footnote form, like bibliography form, can be illustrated on charts to help children with punctuation and order of items. There is no need for them to memorize these, since, as mentioned earlier, forms vary. Point this out and explain that they should use whatever form is required by a particular teacher or school.

USING READING SKILLS

There are many skills needed for effective reading. Foundational skills are dealt with in chapter 14; those discussed here are the ones particularly associated with the study skills—skimming and critical reading.

Skimming

Children should be taught how to skim in the intermediate grades, as this important skill will help them to study and to locate information more efficiently. Skimming is not a skill that is simply acquired as children grow in reading abilities; it must be specifically taught. Habits to be developed are discussed in the following sections.

Reading the First and Last Sentences of a Paragraph.   Both you and the children should be aware that the topic sentence of a paragraph is not always first or last, but it is frequently in one of those positions. Even when it is not, these sentences should give clues to the general content. In longer selections, the first and last paragraphs might be read quickly.

Looking for Cue Words.   Cue words are of two types. First, if a child is looking for a specific piece of information, he or she should watch for words related to that information. For example, if a child only wants to find out where a particular tribe of Indians lived, then place names—California, Northern plains, Mississippi River valley, etc.—should be looked for. Second, there are general cue words. The way they are used is illustrated in this paragraph. The heading has given the main idea. The first sentence uses the words *two types;* the words *first* and *second* lead immediately to these two types. Number words (or the numbers themselves) are perhaps the most helpful of all cue words. If these had been omitted, however, *For example* in sentence three should send your eyes back to the preceding sentence to discover one of the two types. Other cue words that can help children to locate ideas are words like *causes, reason, however, principal*, and *furthermore* and phrases such as *in addition, on the other hand, in conclusion,* etc.

Using Format Clues.   As was suggested in the section concerning study steps, one of the quickest ways to discover the general content of a long selection is to glance through it and read the various types of section headings, as well as captions for pictures, graphs, maps, etc. A child who is preparing a report can be led immediately to the information needed by using this technique, particularly if it is used in conjunction with the card catalog, table of contents, index, etc. (see chapter 17).

Materials used for teaching skimming should be selected carefully if these habits are to be established. This does not mean that they should not be related to the subject matter of content areas—only that you must select them with an eye to their suitability in developing a particular habit or skill.

Try dividing the class into teams for skimming practice. Award points for finding a correct answer first, but subtract points for incorrect answers.

Begin with short selections that clearly illustrate the habit you are developing. The first few times you may wish to underline the parts that are important—beginning and ending sentences, cue words, or topic headings. Give the children specific questions to answer and discuss what procedures might be used to find the answers. At first, simply ask them to decide what the selection is about. Later, proceed to more detailed questions, such as "What kind of homes did the Indians live in?" or "Find three reasons why the colonists came to America."

Using an overhead or opaque projector to show practice exercises makes it possible to control the time more easily. Another method is to write the selection on the chalkboard in a spot where it can be covered by a pulldown map or screen.

The time allowed can be cut as the children become more skilled in using clues. Regular, brief practice will supply speed. For example, say to the class, "Turn to page 142 in your text and find the name of the Indian who guided the Smith family through the forest. As soon as you have found it, close your book and hold up your hand. Remember, find the name of the Smiths' Indian guide."

To help children who have difficulty in scanning, some teachers have tried drawing a vertical red line through the middle of a paragraph. The children are to look only at the words that touch this line as they look for clues instead of letting their eyes go across the line horizontally. Or you might try two vertical lines, dividing the page approximately into thirds. The idea is to help children learn to move their eyes quickly *down* the page, looking for clues, rather than looking *across* each line horizontally.

Observe children as they study and work on reports from supplementary reading. Guide individual children by reminding them of clues to look for, and provide reinforcement exercises when the need is indicated.

Studying together is often helpful to children.

Critical Reading and Thinking

Children show a tendency to believe everything they read. Most people eventually learn that not everything in print is true, but often they do not learn this well enough or soon enough. Thus, thinking critically about issues, listening critically to what is heard on radio or television, and reading information critically need to be taught. Many of the ways words are used to give a false impression are well known. For example, a newspaper reports that a large number of young people attending a music festival were treated at the medical center for overdoses of drugs, upset stomachs, and cut feet. This is a fairly unadorned statement of fact, yet some readers might conclude from it that the use of drugs at the festival was widespread and that the principal cause of treatment at the center was drug overdose. This conclusion could be due (perhaps largely) to the readers' own preconceptions, but it is encouraged by the use of the term *large number*, the placement of the drug item in first position in the list, and the lack of specific numbers or percentages. Even numbers can be misleading, of course. Let us presume that 10 percent of those who came to the center were treated for drug overdose; this percentage is still not meaningful unless the reader knows the total number treated and how this number relates to the total number attending the festival.

It is important not only that we teach children to read but that we teach them to read critically. To develop into critical readers, children must learn to approach the printed words with inquiring minds, to evaluate what is read in the light of known facts or objective evidence, to examine the logic of the presentation, and to distinguish between fact and opinion. All learning, of course, is related to previous knowledge and experience, but the critical reader learns to suspend judgment and personal opinion until the total selection has been evaluated and assimilated, to seek out other knowledge and opinions, and to draw inferences from what has been read.

Reading materials designed for classroom use commonly provide children with the opportunity to make inferences or "read between the lines." This kind of reading can be encouraged by asking questions: Why do you think _____? Could this be true? What do you think really happened? It is important to stress that answers must be based on information given or knowledge gained from other sources, not simply upon opinion or personal preference. One way to help children develop this kind of thinking is to begin with sentences from which inferences can be drawn.

- It is a beautiful day for a walk, but there is a sharp wind blowing. (Perhaps we will need jackets when we go out.)
- Bruce Smith has been practicing running and passing all summer. (He wants to go out for football this fall.)
- Mrs. Jones puts on her glasses the minute she gets up in the morning. (She can't see well without them.)
- Ordinarily, we have frequent showers in the summer, but this year the grass is brown and the trees look thirsty. (This has been an unusually dry summer.)

Another way to help children learn to draw inferences and base their thinking on known facts is to read or have them read part of a story and then ask them to write or tell a possible ending. This need not be the same as the ending used by the writer of the story, but it should be logical in terms of what is known about the characters and the events that have gone before. Begin with something short and fairly obvious, like "The Boy Who Cried Wolf," and advance to stories in which character might decide the outcome.

As in developing other language abilities, it is wise to begin teaching critical thinking with group activities so the children may learn from each other. This can be done even at the kindergarten level with activities such as the one suggested in the preceding paragraph. Be sure to ask not just "What do you think happened next?" but also "Why do you think so?"Try to get a number of responses, examine them critically (in a constructive way), and decide together which ones fit best with the known facts.

Besides supplementary reading materials, there are also filmstrips and cassettes designed to further critical thinking. These are useful because they are more readily associated with television, which influences so much of our thinking these days. They also provide variety, and they can be used with the entire class, with groups, or by individual children who need additional experience.

Closely allied to drawing inferences is distinguishing fact from opinion. Activities such as these can help children to develop this ability:

1. Have the children select famous personalities and write opinions about them: "I think Laura Ingals Wilder must have lived in South Dakota because she wrote about life there so realistically" or "I think Reggie Jackson had more hits during the 1979 season than any other player on the Yankees." Then have them use their library skills to show whether these are opinions only or actual facts.
2. Cut from magazines several full-page color advertisements, clipping off all printed material pertaining to the product. Show the pictures only to the children and ask them to write statements of fact and opinion about them. For example:

Fact

    a. A woman is sitting on a patio with a collie.
    b. The woman is smiling.
    c. There are flowers and trees surrounding the patio.

Opinion

    a. The woman is smiling because her new toothpaste got her teeth so white.
    b. She is smiling because the flower seeds she bought made her yard so beautiful.
    c. She is smiling because a particular fertilizer made her garden grow especially well.
    d. She is smiling because her dog likes that new dog food.

Check to make sure the facts are really facts, and lead the children into a discussion of whether such statements as "The woman is beautiful" or "The collie is a thoroughbred" are fact or opinion. Then show the printed material that was cut from the picture so children can find out which of their opinions were correct (at least according to the advertisement!)

3. Help children evaluate newspaper accounts by looking for key words that indicate opinion rather than fact. Here are some statements of the type to look for.
    a. There is *probably* more snow here than any other place in the country.
    b. The remains just discovered *may* be the missing link.
    c. This *appears* to be the driest spot in the nation.
    d. Doodling Dad's paintings show the *precision* and *forcefulness* of a great artist.

4. A variation of the above is to have children separate fact from opinion.
   a. Yesterday's rain, which lasted for five hours, was probably the worst downpour in our history.
      Fact: It rained yesterday. The rain lasted five hours.
      Opinion: It was the worst downpour in our history.
   b. Jim Simmons, who is exactly six feet tall, must be the tallest boy in school.
      Fact: Jim Simmons is six feet tall.
      Opinion: He is the tallest boy in school.
   c. Mrs. Gotrocks, often said to be the wealthiest woman in the country, was shopping yesterday in Zayre's.
      Fact: Mrs. Gotrocks was in Zayre's yesterday.
      Opinion: Mrs. Gotrocks is the wealthiest woman in the country.
5. Have the children listen to television newscasts for several days and make a collection of phrases that are used to introduce statements that are not definitely known to be true, such as "It has been reported that," "Reliable sources inform us," "One witness said that," "Rumor has it," etc.
6. Children should also be shown how the choice of words can sway opinion. Let them try showing opposing views of the same event:
   a. Congressman Wilkins smirked sardonically, then snapped, "I have nothing to say at this time."
   b. The weary Congressman attempted a smile, then said simply, "I have nothing to say at this time."
7. As a follow-up to the above, have the class compare newspaper accounts of the same event written by different writers. A football game between teams from two cities, for example, would be written up quite differently by sports writers from each of those cities. Follow by having them attempt to sort out facts and opinions.

We are bombarded daily by propaganda of various sorts; those who have learned the skills of critical thinking are better prepared to make decisions based on reason rather than emotion. By the time children reach the middle grades, they should begin to draw conclusions from what they read or hear, distinguish between fact and opinion, and recognize that words have connotations as well as denotations. At this point they are ready for a more direct study of the ways in which people attempt to influence our thinking. Perhaps a good place to begin is with advertising techniques, since advertising is the most obvious type of propaganda. Begin with the most common categories:

1. *Plain folks:* The president of the company started as a janitor. He still enjoys pitching horseshoes with the boys during the noon-hour break. (He understands ordinary people and wouldn't try to cheat them.)
2. *Bandwagon:* More doctors recommend this pill than any other. (Notice that it doesn't say any other *what.*)
3. *Repetition:* Sticky goo holds your false teeth so you can munch, munch, munch for your lunch, lunch, lunch. (A more common type of repetition currently appears to be the use of frequently repeated slogans or "spot" ads which appear so often on TV that even small children can repeat them.)
4. *Testimonial:* The star pitcher for the Oakland A's eats Ironies for breakfast. (If you eat Ironies, you can be a big leaguer too.)
5. *Snob appeal:* Come out and see this executive house in an exclusive neighborhood. (Buy here and you can be part of an exclusive group.)
6. *Emotional words:* Good mothers buy Junkie sneakers for their children. (If you don't buy your child Junkie sneakers, you aren't a good mother.)
7. *Rewards:* Buy at Smith Brothers' Store and get Pink Stamps. (You can use Pink Stamps to get beautiful gifts for your family or home.)

A bulletin board might be a starting point. Ask children to bring in examples of the various advertising techniques and let them judge which ones are the most representative and therefore the best to post. They may also enjoy collecting phrases commonly found in advertising. These might include the following:

Huge savings.	For better mileage.
This week only.	Discount prices.
Buy with confidence.	Money back guarantee.
Service with a smile.	For preferred customers.

An extension of this study that will appeal to children is to have them watch television commercials and decide which groups they are directed at—small children, women, teenagers, etc.—and which techniques are used for each group. They will be fascinated to discover that variations of the same technique may be used for every age level: the four-year-old demands a certain cereal because there is a toy in the box, and the child's father buys a particular car because the company pays him a cash bonus.

As the children become expert in detecting the techniques, have them watch for overlapping ones. For example, "All responsible parents buy Dryer raincoats for their children. Your children deserve the best," includes the bandwagon, emotional, and snob appeal approaches.

As a concluding activity for the unit, divide the class into small groups and let each group select an item to shop for in the advertisements. Each group should collect all the advertisements they can locate about their item. Then they should evaluate each one, write reactions to it, and report their findings to the class, including the reasons they decided to buy a particular brand or shop at a particular store. Items might include automobiles, a swimming pool, a pool table, an auto racing set, a motorcycle, a snowmobile, or a sewing machine.

A Bulletin Board Idea

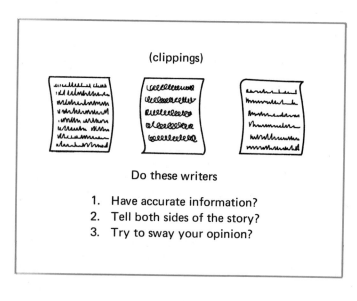

If it is valuable to recognize the advertising ploys used by those who are trying to sell their products, it is even more important to recognize that virtually the same techniques are used by those who want to sell us *ideas*. During every political campaign, for example, we are bombarded by the same spot announcements on TV and radio to keep candidates' names before us, film stars and other entertainers endorse their favorites, and so on. In fact, we are surrounded daily by propaganda of many types.

Children should learn to recognize propaganda, but they should also learn that it is not necessarily bad. Rather, it is a part of our way of life. TV stations, for instance, commonly telecast what they sometimes term "public service announcements," warning young people against the use of drugs, advertising public clinics that give immunizations against various diseases, etc.; prominent athletes plug not only shaving cream but also fund drives against multiple sclerosis or heart disease. No one is completely without bias; therefore, what a person writes or says is colored by his own beliefs. This "slanting" may be intentional, or the writer may make every effort to present an objective view. But the important thing is that children should learn to search for bias or motive, to distinguish fact from opinion, to examine opposing views, and to draw their own conclusions. The following are some of the types of activities that can help them to recognize and evaluate propaganda.

1. Use reading exercises that call for making inferences and for distinguishing fact from opinion, as suggested earlier.
2. Begin even in the early grades to help children find themes in stories they read, for these are a type of propaganda—they represent the writers' beliefs. Begin with simple questions: Do you think the man who wrote this story likes dogs? What makes you think so? As children mature, they can grasp more subtle and complicated themes.
3. To help children think about the purposes and qualifications of writers in evaluating what they have to say, show a variety of articles from newspapers and magazines by means of an opaque or overhead projector. Then discuss such questions as the following:
   a. Did the writer simply want to sell more newspapers or magazines? (New Clues Uncovered!)
   b. Is the writer encouraging you to vote for a candidate or an issue? (Mr. Christopher is an all-around family man who lives in a neat, modest suburban home.)
   c. Is the writer qualified and competent to write on this subject? (Has the writer studied his subject sufficiently or had enough personal experience with it to know what he or she is talking about?)
   d. Does the writer present both sides of an issue or only one? (Those who oppose this issue base their objections on emotion alone; there can be no valid objection.)
4. Have children bring in accounts of a political speech appearing in newspapers with opposing political views. Compare these and note the ways in which each supports its point of view.
5. Have the children write papers either supporting or opposing a particular school or community issue on which opinions are strongly divided. Then have the class research the subject through whatever means are available—guest speakers, reading, etc.—and write new opinions based on what they have learned, telling why they have or have not changed their minds.
6. Bring in several articles concerning a current problem or issue. Show these on the opaque or overhead projector and have the children evaluate them in terms of propaganda techniques used, presentation of facts rather than opinions, use of "loaded" or emotional words, and use of logical reasoning.

Developing critical readers takes time and effort. Broaden the children's reading through the use of multiple texts, children's newspapers such as the *Weekly Reader*, local newspapers, and national magazines. Help them to question what they read and to use library reference materials to check facts. Storybooks and biographies also widen their horizons and help them get other views of facts and events. Remember, too, the many nonfiction books available for classroom use which give added insight into areas of study. Avoid single-text teaching when your goal is to develop critical readers.

A FINAL WORD

Children who have learned how to study, how to use efficiently the tools of learning that are available to them, how to evaluate the information they hear and read are well on the way to mastering the skills of communication. Before anyone can communicate effectively either orally or in writing, he or she must have something to communicate. The child who knows how to use the kinds of study skills discussed in this chapter and the library skills that are the subject of the following one will have something to communicate. Thus the skills needed for spelling, handwriting, and composition will be both useful and meaningful because he or she has something to say.

REFERENCES

Books

Crawford, Marion. *Teaching Study Skills.* Dansville, NY: The Instructor Publications, Inc., 1973.

Fry, Edward B. *Skimming and Scanning.* Providence, RI: Jamestown Publishers, 1978.

Karlin, Robert. *Teaching Elementary Reading.* New York: Harcourt Brace Jovanovich, Inc., 1971, Chapter 7.

Robinson, H. Alan. *Teaching Reading and Study Strategies: The Content Areas.* Boston: Allyn and Bacon, 1975.

Sanders, Norris M. *Classroom Questions: What Kinds?* New York: Harper and Row, 1966.

Simpson, Dorothy M. *Learning to Learn.* Columbus, OH: Charles E. Merrill, 1970.

Films

Building an Outline. Chicago: Coronet Films (11 min.; color, b/w; intermediate).

Dictionary for Beginners. Chicago: Coronet Films (11 min.; color; primary).

We Discover the Dictionary. Chicago: Coronet Films (11 min.; color, b/w; intermediate).

Your Study Skills. Chicago: Coronet Films ("How to Use a Textbook," "Taking Notes on Reading," "Reviewing for a Test"; 11 to 14 min. each; intermediate).

Filmstrips

Alphabetical Order. Chicago: International Film Bureau, 1970 (Color filmstrip; other related strips from same company).

Alphabet Library. New York: Miller-Brody Productions, Inc. (three sets of four filmstrips each, with teacher's guides).

Basic Study Skills I, II, III. New York: Miller-Brody Productions, Inc. (three sets of four filmstrips each, with two cassettes each, plus teacher's guides; intermediate).

Constructing Reports. Chicago: Encyclopedia Britannica Educational Corp. (Set of 6 strips; intermediate).

Developing Your Study Skills. New York: Guidance Associates, Harcourt Brace Jovanovich (Record, filmstrip, and guide).

Dictionary Skills. Chicago: International Film

Bureau (10 filmstrips and spirit masters; intermediate).

Fundamentals of Thinking. Jamaica, NY: Eyegate House (Set of 9 strips; intermediate).

Good Study Habits. Mahwah, NJ: Troll Associates (4 filmstrips and 2 records or tapes; intermediate).

How to Find It; How to Take Notes, etc. Hollywood, CA: AIMS Instructional Media, 1969 (Color filmstrips and records; intermediate and upper).

Learning to Use the Dictionary. Berkeley, CA: Pacific Productions (Set of 8 strips).

Library Series. New York: McGraw-Hill Films (Strips on using dictionary and other books).

Thinking Skills. Mahwah, NJ: Troll Associates (6 filmstrips and 3 records or tapes; 1–4).

Using a Dictionary. St. Louis: Webster Publishing Co. (Intermediate).

Your Dictionary and How to Use it. Chicago: Society for Visual Education (Set of 6 strips; intermediate).

Transparencies

Basic Dictionary Skills. St. Louis: Milliken Publishing Co. (12 frames, 24 duplicating masters, and a teacher's guide; intermediate).

Learning "Look It Up" Skills with a Dictionary. Chicago: Field Enterprises Educational Corp. (4 frames; intermediate).

Reference Tools and Study Skills. St. Louis: Milliken Publishing Co. (12 frames, 24 duplicating masters, and a teacher's guide: intermediate).

Other Aids

Dictionary Skills. St. Paul, MN: 3M Corporation (3 cassettes with worksheets).

Dictionary Skills, Books A, B, C. Englewood Cliffs, NJ: Scholastic Book Services (3 workbooks; grades 2 to 6).

Kaplan, Sandra Nina, Madsen, Sheila K., and Gould, Betty Taylor. *The Big Book of Independent Study Games and Activities.* Englewood Cliffs, NJ: Prentice-Hall, Inc. (Activities and games for use by individuals or groups; grades 3 to 6).

Look-It-Up-Books. Chicago: Field Enterprises Educational Corporation (3 levels, grades 3 to 8).

McDanield, Michael A., Janson, Kathleen A., Forest, Robert G., and Sullivan, Richard J. Jr. *Aaron Zwieback and His World of Words: Thinking Through the Dictionary.* Englewood Cliffs, NJ: Prentice-Hall, Inc. (skills book to accompany *Webster's New World Dictionary;* grades 4 to 8).

Minisystems. Lexington, MA: D. C. Heath and Co. (various levels; each contains a cassette, teacher's guide, and pupil activity sheets; lessons include dictionary, outlining, skimming, note taking, etc.).

Exploring Language with the Dictionary. Englewood Cliffs, NJ: Prentice-Hall, Inc. (workbooks on four levels, including teacher's editions, plus pre- and post-tests).

Strategies in Study Skills. Springfield, MA: Milton Bradley, Inc. (self-instructional cassette program in dictionary, reference skills, etc.).

Study Skills. Baltimore: Media Materials, Inc. (10 lessons, including cassettes, response booklets, teacher's guides, tests; primary).

Study Skills for School Success. Baltimore: Media Materials, Inc. (15 lessons, including cassettes, response booklets, teacher's guides, tests; intermediate).

ACTIVITIES FOR PRESERVICE TEACHERS

1. Plan the assignment for a specific lesson at a grade level of your choice. Show exactly how you would prepare the children for this assignment. Include motivation, background, and specific purposes.

2. Begin a picture file that would be useful for teaching alphabetical order (and for many other purposes as well). See if you can find a picture suitable for each letter of the alphabet.

3. Visit the curriculum library or the children's area of a public library. Examine ABC books and/or dictionaries suitable for a grade level of your

choice and decide which ones you would like to have in your classroom. Give reasons for your selections.

4. Using a textbook for a grade level of your choice, plan a dictionary exercise to be used in connection with a particular story, lesson, or unit.

5. Select or compose three paragraphs that might be used in teaching note taking by the method suggested in this chapter. Be sure to integrate them in some way with the ongoing activities of

a particular class or grade level.

6. Plan a lesson in drawing inferences for a grade level of your choice.

7. Find a selection that would be particularly useful for teaching skimming, and show how you would use it in a demonstration lesson.

8. Make a bulletin board display that could be used in connection with a lesson on advertising techniques or propaganda.

ACTIVITIES FOR INSERVICE TEACHERS

1. Evaluate the way you assign homework. When you begin a new unit in social studies or science, experiment with the techniques suggested in this chapter for helping children learn how to study. Include in your experimenting an assessment of the effectiveness of the study procedures in terms of how well the children learned.

2. Plan dictionary activities for your class that are coordinated with other activities the children are involved with throughout the day. Suppose you are studying vibrations in science; for vocabulary development you might plan a bulletin board of vibration words, such as *sandpaper—harsh,* and *sponge—soft.* Then have the pupils use the dictionary and thesaurus to look for synonyms and antonyms for these words.

3. Examine filmstrips, transparencies, cassettes, and other materials designed to teach skills discussed in this chapter and select those that you would like to have added to the materials center in your school. Present your list to the person who orders such materials, along with your reasons for believing that they are needed.

4. Select three movies from your school media center, or send for some that fit well with your curriculum. Use these to teach your outlining

lessons. Plan carefully. You may need to show the movie two or three times when you first start this project.

5. With your class, select a topic for a report, perhaps one from social studies. Help the children to locate material in the library, take notes, outline and correlate information from several sources, write a rough draft, prepare a bibliography, and then write a final copy. Do this as a class project, using this and other chapters along with appropriate sections from the class language text to guide you. Plan this for early in the year so that children will be proficient by year's end.

6. Collect a number of pictures from magazines. Have children write sentences identifying fact and opinion. Have them search headlines and newspapers for further evidence of fact vs. opinion.

7. Develop critical listening and reading skills through a study of propaganda techniques used in television and magazine advertising. Begin with a class discussion of favorite commercials and magazine advertisements. Select one topic and develop a series of lessons on it. Conclude by having the children invent a product and prepare the advertising.

INDEPENDENT ACTIVITIES FOR CHILDREN

1. Put lists of words on cards—on the front in any order and on the back in alphabetical order. Vary the difficulty to provide for differences in the abilities of the children. An individual child can select a card, put the words in alphabetical order on paper, and check by looking at the back of the card.

2. A child may prepare a bulletin-board display showing parts of the dictionary—guide words, entry words, pronunciation key, syllabication, etc.

3. Dictionary exercises for individual children may include the following:

   a. Circle the words that come between *club* and *enough* in the dictionary.

clown	easy	draw	country
family	dust	cover	evening
oval	cloth	egg	explore
desk	close	ever	could

   b. Write the entry words for each of these dictionary respellings.

   bütz _____   kül _____

   mün _____   tüth_____

4. Prepare specific questions related to the content being studied in social studies, science, etc. The child will utilize the study skills in locating answers to these questions.

5. A child can look in a thesaurus to find synonyms and antonyms for each word in the spelling list for the week.

6. A child who needs practice in putting items in sequence or selecting details can draw a picture sequence of everything he or she did between getting up and arriving at school. The pictures might then be put into a sort of comic strip, with dialogue added where appropriate.

7. Practice in finding the main idea can be gained by having a child read articles in a certain section of the school newspaper or one such as *My Weekly Reader* and put the main thought of each article into a single sentence.

8. To aid the child who has difficulty with organizational skills, prepare several outlines with main topics listed in order on one side of the page and subtopics in jumbled order on the other side. Have the child select appropriate subtopics for each main idea and place them in logical sequence.

9. Encourage individual children to use note cards in giving oral book reports, putting one principal idea on each card and listing important details they want to include under each main point.

10. A child can preview filmstrips and recordings in order to determine their value for use in a social studies unit, taking notes and preparing a brief summary or list of material covered. He or she may then compare this with the topics covered in the text to decide which ones would add or relate to the material there.

11. Be sure that your listening center is well supplied with tapes and/or records designed to build skill in finding main ideas, putting items in sequence, using the dictionary, etc. Children who need practice with specific skills may use these during free time.

12. Let an individual child (or a group) select a brief article from a current newspaper—possibly an account of a sports event or whatever else is of special interest to the children. Then have them list facts and opinions stated in the article.

13. Select articles such as those suggested above and place them in plastic envelopes or folders. Individual children can use these to practice many types of study skills—e.g., to make an outline, to separate fact from opinion, to find words or phrases which denote order of items or events (then, in the final two minutes, etc.).

17

Children and the Library

Of all the facets of language arts instruction, none is more important than providing children with the ability and desire to read and use books. Children should look at the library as a storehouse of pleasure and information. And the key to this storehouse is the ability to find the knowledge that is wanted or the particular book that will bring pleasure. This chapter is concerned with teaching children the skills that will enable them to get the most in both pleasure and information from books. It is important to remember, however, that these skills are valuable not in and of themselves, but only if they help children to unlock the storehouse.

GUIDING PRINCIPLES

The most valuable ally to enlist in teaching the library skills is the librarian, since most librarians have chosen their profession because they like books and want to share them, just as most teachers like children and want to help them grow. Naturally not all of the teaching can or should be turned over to the librarian. To a great extent, motivation for using library skills must come from the classroom activities, and children will need a great deal of individual help and reinforcement both in the library and in the classroom. But an enthusiastic librarian who believes that books should be off the shelves and in children's hands will do much toward providing a stimulating and interesting environment in which children may learn.

Library skills must be taught directly and completely if they are really to be learned and used. Like any other skills, they are best learned in a situation where they are being used for a meaningful purpose. Therefore they are best introduced when children need to locate information, find a book about something of interest, or simply explore what this room full of books is all about.

A spirit of discovery must exist in a classroom for library skills to be needed.

As children explore, seeking to satisfy their curiosities, motivation for learning the library skills will be provided. The major task, then, is introducing children to ideas, to information that appeals to them, and to new thoughts. Reading frequently to children—and this should be a habit exercised daily—is a good way to introduce them to the world beyond their experience and at the same time show the importance of books.

An attractive and well-supplied room library that children are allowed and encouraged to use can supply the initial focus for teaching beginning library skills. A multimedia and a multitext approach to teaching in all curriculum areas will also help children learn to look beyond a single source for information. This does not mean that every child must have several texts for each subject, but rather that additional resources of many kinds should be available to children and should be a part of their daily activities.

Your own attitude is a vital factor. Even a simple act like looking up the correct spelling of a word in the dictionary or turning to the atlas for a specific fact will demonstrate to children the usefulness of library tools. Bringing in additional resources, showing your own interest in books, and encouraging (and helping) children to look up information will provide motivation for acquiring library skills.

A final *must* is knowing the children, their interests and abilities, and what they do outside school. A child who doesn't know how to use the card file or take notes is ill-prepared to go to the library alone to find information for a report. Neither can a reluctant reader, whose only interest in life is football, be expected

Children need to have reason to use the library as well as to know how to use it.

to become enthusiastic about learning library skills in order to find out about the history of ballet—but he might do surprisingly well at finding out about the career of Terry Bradshaw or how and when football was first played. Thus knowing when individual children are ready to take the next step and building upon the knowledge they already have are as vital to teaching library skills as they are to any other learning activity.

Introductory Activities

At the primary level, the most important thing is for children to learn to know and use books. As they are first beginning to look at and read books, they can also learn how to use and handle them, how to talk about them, how to locate the ones they want, and how to check them out and return them.

These learnings can begin in the room library, which should contain as many books as possible.[1] The teacher's first job, then, is to know the books suitable for children and make many of these known to the children. There are numerous aids available for this purpose: books on children's literature, such as those by Arbuthnot and Sutherland, Huck, Glazer and Williams, or Stewig; lists published by professional organizations and publishers; reviews of children's books which appear regularly in magazines such as *Language Arts, School Library Journal, The Horn Book,* and *The Reading Teacher;* and special lists, such as those of the Newbery and Caldecott Award Winners.[2] The school librarian, if there is one, or the children's librarian at the city or county library should have many of these and should also be helpful in making recommendations. In addition, you should be familiar with many children's books, particularly those which you select for the room library.

Books in the room library should be changed often so that no child will be unable to find one that interests him or her, although special favorites may be retained or brought back, since young children particularly love to "reread." Books should vary in level of difficulty and be of many types. The following list may serve as a guide.

Picture or "Easy" Books
Brown, Marcia. *Felice* (Scribner's, 1958)
Carroll, Ruth. *What Whiskers Did* (Walck, 1965)
Edmondson, Madeleine. *The Witch's Egg* (Seabury, 1974)
Hutchins, Pat. *Rosie's Walk* (Macmillan, 1968)
Keats, Ezra Jack. *Pet Show* (Macmillan, 1970)
Lionni, Leo. *Swimmy* (Pantheon, 1963)
Lobel, Arnold. *Frog and Toad Together* (Harper and Row, 1972)
Matsuno, Masako. *A Pair of Red Clogs* (World, 1960)
Rey, Hans A. *Curious George* (Houghton Mifflin, 1941)
Scarry, Richard. *Best Mother Goose Ever* (Western, 1970)
Seuss, Dr. *The Cat in the Hat* (Vanguard, 1957)
Wildsmith, Brian. *Brian Wildsmith's Birds* (Franklin, 1957)

Ideas or Theme Types
Alexander, Martha. *Nobody Asked Me If I Wanted a Baby Sister* (Dial, 1971)
Burningham, John. *Seasons* (Bobbs-Merrill, 1970)

Cleary, Beverly. *Ramona the Pest* (Morrow, 1968)

Cohen, Miriam. *The New Teacher* (Macmillan, 1972)

de Paola, Tomie. *Watch Out for the Chicken Feet in Your Soup* (Prentice-Hall, 1974)

Gramatky, Hardie. *Little Toot through the Golden Gate* (Putnam's, 1975)

Hutchins, Pat. *Titch* (Macmillan, 1971)

Johnson, Johanna. *Speak Up, Edie* (Putnam's, 1974)

Lexau, Joan. *Me Day* (Dial, 1971)

Steptoe, John. *Stevie* (Harper and Row, 1969)

Viorst, Judith. *Alexander and the Terrible, Horrible, No Good, Very Bad Day* (Atheneum, 1972)

Wolf, Bernard. *Anna's Silent World* (Lippincott, 1977)

Zolotow, Charlotte. *The Hating Book* (Harper and Row, 1969)

Animal Stories

Barrett, Judi. *Animals Should Definitely Not Wear Clothing* (Atheneum, 1970)

Du Bois, William Pène. *Bear Circus* (Viking, 1971)

Freeman, Don. *Corduroy* (Viking, 1968)

Gag, Wanda. *Millions of Cats* (Coward-McCann, 1928)

Northrup, Mili. *The Watch Cat* (Bobbs-Merrill, 1968)

Oxenbury, Helen. *Pig Tale* (Morrow, 1973)

Schatz, Letta. *A Rhinoceros, Preposterous* (Steck-Vaughn, 1965)

Tresselt, Alvin. *The Beaver Pond* (Lothrop, 1970)

Ward, Lynd. *The Biggest Bear* (Houghton Mifflin, 1952)

Many other types should also be included: ABC books, picture and beginning dictionaries, stories of other lands, poetry, and so on. The point is to have books suitable for every child in the class, so that motivation will be provided for acquiring the beginning skills.

Even in as small a place as the room library, books should be arranged on the shelves in some sort of logical way so children may understand that there is a pattern to the way libraries are set up and that the purpose of this pattern is to help them find books. This arrangement may be by type, by level of difficulty, or perhaps alphabetical (this would give meaningful practice with alphabetical order). Whatever the arrangement, explain it to the children, show them how to look for particular books, and teach them to return books to their proper places so that others will be able to find them.

When children first begin to handle books, they should also learn how to take care of them and, as in other matters, they should help to formulate the standards themselves. Perhaps they will come up with something like this:

Taking Care of Books

1. Always have clean hands.
2. Don't write in a book that isn't yours.
3. Protect books from rain or snow.
4. Keep books away from younger brothers or sisters who don't know how to handle them.
5. Be careful not to tear pages.
6. Return books as soon as you are through with them.

Show children also how to open a new book and have them practice doing it. A good time for this might be just after a set of new textbooks or dictionaries or a box of new library books has been delivered to the room. This is also a good time to teach the vocabulary for talking about books—children are curious about everything, and they will take pride in knowing the right words to use and how a new book should be handled. Try something like the following, making sure to illustrate each step:

1. Lay the book on its *back.*
2. Open the *front cover* and press it down gently.
3. Put the *back cover* down and press it down.
4. Take six or eight *front pages* and run your finger along the *spine.*
5. Repeat with an equal number of *back pages.*
6. Do another six to ten pages, then go to the back again, and so on until you reach the *middle.*

The most important terms (and the concepts they represent) that primary children can learn to use when talking about books are *title, author, illustrator,* and *table of contents.*

The concept of *title* is not a difficult one for children to grasp. They are already aware of their own names and those of their pets, the school, and so on. It is a simple matter, then, to explain that the name of a book is called a title and that this often helps to tell what the book is about—for example, *Curious George, My First Pictionary, Millions of Cats.*

Author and *illustrator* can also be related to the children's own names. Just as a child puts his name on his papers, the person who writes a book puts his name on it. Most children know Dr. Seuss, for example, and can understand that if they liked *Horton Hatches the Egg* they might also like other books by the same author. Several authors the children are familiar with might be used to illustrate this point, thus laying the foundation for using the card catalog and the alphabetical arrangement of books by author to find books they will enjoy.

The illustrator is of great importance to a book for young children, who usually select books by the pictures alone. Again, just as children put their names on their own drawings, a person who draws in a book has his name on the cover. And just as an author may write more than one book, so he may sometimes illustrate his own book. Show the children books by such author–illustrators as Beatrix Potter, Maurice Sendak, Ezra Jack Keats, Lynd Ward, Ed Emberly, and Robert Lawson and discuss ways in which the illustrations add to the books. Having copies of the same story—a fairy tale, for example—with pictures by different illustrators can add much to this discussion. Children will also enjoy drawing pictures about stories that are read or told; these can be posted, with captions showing the name of the story, the author, and the phrase "Illustrated by_____."

At the primary level there is little need for children to be concerned with publication information, but they should know that they can find the title of a book and the names of the author and illustrator on the title page. If they are curious about the other items found on this page, these can be explained simply, but they should not be emphasized, nor should children be required to know them.

Children ought to know that books contain more than stories and poems. The selection of books in the room library will demonstrate this, as will the regular use of resource materials. When discussing weather, for example, bring from the library books that contain factual material at the children's level, including at

Factual Books for Young Children

Asimov, Isaac. *ABC's of the Ocean* (Walker, 1970)

Froman, Robert. *Less than Nothing Is Really Something* (Crowell, 1973)

Gross, Ruth Belov. *A Book about Pandas* (Dial, 1972)

Rinkoff, Barbara. *A Map Is a Picture* (Crowell, 1965)

Selsam, Millicent, and Joyce Hunt. *A First Look At* Series (Walker)

Shuttlesworth, Dorothy. *The Story of Ants* (Doubleday, 1964)

Simon, Seymour. *Science on Your Street* Books (Holiday)

Tresselt, Alvin. *How Far Is Far?* (Parents', 1964)

least one that has a table of contents. Point out again that the title gives a general idea of what the book is about; then turn to the table of contents and show how this gives much more specific information. Further understanding and competence in using this aid can be gained by writing the name of the daily story on the chalkboard and having the children look up the page number in the table of contents.

The important concern at this level—or any other—is not the terminology of books, but the concepts related to the terminology and the understanding that books may provide not only pleasure but also knowledge of many kinds.

As soon as possible, arrange to take the class to the school and community libraries. Involving parents in the latter trip may encourage them to help their children to obtain library cards as soon as this is permitted in the particular library or to get cards for themselves and check out books for their children. Many parents are probably unaware of the vast array of beautiful children's books that are now available. These visits should be prearranged so that the librarians will be available to talk to the children. It is important for children to know the librarians' names and to look on them as friends and helpers.

Before making these trips, teach library behavior and explain the reasons for library rules. If, as suggested in the preceding paragraphs, children have learned how to handle and care for books, they will not be unwelcome guests in the library. If they have learned consideration for others, they will understand the need for quiet. The librarian can explain rules about checking out books, how long they may be kept, and so forth.

In some schools library rules forbid checking out books to young children. If this is true, it is still possible to schedule regular trips to the library to let the children help select books for the classroom. The librarian can explain the fun of browsing, help in selecting books, and show them where the various kinds of books may be found and how they are arranged. And children should be allowed to explore for themselves as well.

Card that is in the pocket inside the cover

Call Number	JE D	2 · Copy Number
Author Title	Daugherty Andy and the Lion	

Date Due	Borrower's Name
Feb. 19	David George

Date Due · · Your Name

Date due is found inside the book on a slip like this

JE Daugherty			
Andy and the Lion			
Date Due			
Jan. 14 Apr. 29			
Library Name City, State			

As soon as children are old enough to check out books, they should be taught borrowing procedures. Here again it is a good idea to enlist the aid of the librarian. Actually checking out books is the best way to learn the procedures, but reinforcement and clarification of library terms may be provided by a bulletin board designed around a favorite book, showing the book card and the date due slip as they are found in your particular library. At this level, call number and copy number, like the publication information on the title page of the book, need not be stressed; if the children ask questions about these items, explain simply that they help to identify the book and show the librarian where it belongs on the shelves.

Children should be shown the importance of placing their names—in their best printing—in the correct space on each book card. This can be illustrated by making sample cards for the books in the room library. Let the children select a different librarian daily and practice checking out and returning the books in the room library.

Skills and Activities for the Middle Grades

Intermediate grade children's knowledge about books and libraries will vary widely. Hopefully, a child entering the fourth grade will have visited libraries, will know where to find picture and story books, and will have had some experience in checking out books. By this time, too, most children will have had experience with filmstrips, cassettes, picture files, and various types of displays in the classroom; they should learn that libraries also have these items (in fact, in many schools the library is the media center) and that they can be checked out or used in the library just as books can.

Factual Books for Older Children

Asimov, Isaac. *How Did We Find Out about Germs?* (Walker, 1974)

Brenner, Barbara. *A Snake-lover's Diary* (Young Scott, 1970)

Gallob, Edward. *City Rocks, City Blocks and the Moon* (Scribner's, 1973)

MacClintock, Dorcas. *A Natural History of Giraffes* (Scribner's, 1973)

Murphy, Barbara Beasley, and Norman Baker. *Thor Heyerdahl and the Reed Boat Ra* (Lippincott, 1974)

Rahn, Joan Elma. *Seeing What Plants Do* (Atheneum, 1972)

Again, learning to use a public library is crucial since it is a public library that is used or not used by adults.

During the intermediate grades children will be embarking on more and more independent study and preparing both oral and written reports. Therefore, no later than about the fourth grade you should have a series of lessons and activities specifically designed to help children learn about the many kinds of materials to be found in libraries and how to locate them. It goes without saying, of course, that these lessons should be planned in conjunction with actual needs for finding and using information. Most language arts textbooks for the intermediate grades contain one or more units on using the library. If these are suitable to the children, their needs, and the particular library or libraries they will be using, by all means use them. Be very sure, however, that the materials you select are both adequate and suitable, for this is one of the most valuable lessons you will teach. There is little point in teaching children to read and enjoy books and the knowledge to be found in them if they are unable to find the books and other materials they want and need.

Basic Library Skills

As suggested previously, children should be exposed to books from the very beginning of the school year. Make sure that the library corner is stocked with a variety of books—stories, poems, factual books; humor, fantasy, stories about problems children face, etc. Read some of these to the children; then talk about the library, mentioning shelf arrangements (left to right), shelf labels, and different classifications (easy books, juvenile, etc.).

Ask the librarian to give the class a tour of the library, explaining where different books, magazines, and newspapers are located and why they are located in these places. Comparing a library with a supermarket may help children to understand that, just as all the fruits and vegetables are located near each other, all the books on similar subjects are located together: stories are together, biographies are together, and nonfiction books on topics such as conservation, hobbies, sports, and archaeology are grouped.

Intermediate children should have in mind the concepts related to book vocabulary, such as *title, author, illustrator, cover,* and *spine.* These may need review. To aid them in studying efficiently and in gathering and reporting information, they also need to understand the purposes and uses of the various parts of a book. This knowledge can be developed over a period of time, as children have need to use various kinds of books and refer to various sections of them. They should become familiar with the following terms:

Publisher	The company that printed the book and put it together.
City	Place where the book was published.
Copyright date	When the book was published
Title page	The title, author, and publisher.
Dedication	Special page in the book where the author thanks people, often special friends or members of his family.

Introduction, Preface, or Foreword	Any one of these names can be used for the section in the front of the book that tells briefly what the book is about or why it was written.
List of illustrations	A list usually found in a book with many pictures, maps, or charts.
Table of contents	A list of stories or chapters. [Refer to this throughout the school year in all subject areas so that children may become familiar with it. If you are using a basal reader, have children use the table of contents to find their story.]
Glossary	A small dictionary that defines words used in this particular book. [In elementary grades this is often found in the back of a basal reading, social studies, or science book. Basal series frequently provide experiences in using the glossary. Capitalize on these.]
Index	A list of subjects found in the back of most books. It is the principal means for locating information. [Several lessons will be needed so that children develop an understanding of the arrangement of indexes, their location, the symbols and pronunciation keys used, any subtopic arrangements, and the relationship to the table of contents in amount of detail.]

Ideally, before children are asked to use the library to prepare an oral or written report, they should have visited it many times and checked out books; they should have had opportunities to browse among the different kinds of materials to be found there and to know the librarian as a friend and helper. Try to see that the children in your class have as much preparation of this kind as possible. Improvise where necessary (some suggestions are included in the following sections), but try to avoid simply having available in the classroom everything that they will need to prepare a report. Children need to learn how to locate information for themselves; they cannot forever be dependent on the teacher.

However, children should not be expected to learn all at one time both the skills of organizing material from several sources and those of using the library to locate information. Using the room library, give them practice in taking notes and correlating information from two or three sources;[3] then let them advance to using the school library for further information. Using the library to locate information involves using the card catalog, knowing the difference between fiction and nonfiction, understanding what call numbers signify, and perhaps even knowing the basic elements of classification systems. These skills are interdependent. There are many things to be learned at the same time; thus some practice exercises may need to be provided. If the need for the skills is real, however—that is, if children are preparing reports to be used in connection with a particular unit of study—practice exercises will be more meaningful.

The skills discussed in the two following sections are interrelated and must be presented at the same time. They are separated here for purposes of organization; for the same reason, practice exercises may also need to be presented separately. But library skills should never be taught in isolation from any real need for their use.

Using the Card Catalog

On their initial visit to the library, the librarian will undoubtedly show the children the card catalog and explain its use. Later, when the opportunity arises, this learning can be reinforced. Perhaps a child may say, "This was a good book. I would like to read another one like it." This is the time to suggest that he look in the card catalog to see if there is another book by the same author or on the same subject. Perhaps another child might report, "Someone told me the name of a good book, but I don't know how to find it in the library." Thus the use of title cards can be introduced. Then when children are ready to prepare reports, the catalog will not be entirely unfamiliar to them. Before they can be truly independent in using it, however, they will need a lesson or series of lessons demonstrating the various kinds of cards and how they can be of help.

CHART OR BULLETIN BOARD

Juvenile A	Juvenile F-Foo	Juvenile L	Juvenile Pi-Q	Juvenile S
B-Boy	For-Gov	Mc-Mix	R	T

Begin with the physical setup of the catalog. In most libraries, author, title, and subject cards are all filed together in alphabetical order. Some, however, file subject cards separately from those for authors and titles; this might be mentioned in the upper grades, but libraries that middle grade children use are likely to file all cards together. A helpful technique is to check the school or community library and sketch the outside of the card catalog, including the outside guide letters. Make a chart or bulletin-board display showing this and use short oral drills to provide practice. Stress the alphabetical arrangement, point out that even the books listed under an author's name are in alphabetical order, and call attention to the fact that articles *(a, an,* and *the)* are not considered in alphabetizing titles.

Ask questions such as these:

In which drawer would you find:
Julie of the Wolves?
information about fire-fighting?

Children should learn to use a card catalog by using one.

how to make puppets?
basketball stories?
a cassette recording of *And Now Miguel?*
a biography of Abraham Lincoln?
a Halloween poem?

Continue this type of exercise only as long as seems necessary, making sure to include a variety of topic headings, as well as many that might be found under more than one heading. And help children learn to explore all possible headings—for example, a Halloween poem might be located under *Halloween*, *holidays*, or even *poetry* or *poems;* and the cassette could be listed in the general file or in a special one.

Children who are ready to use the card catalog will have had much experience already in using other materials that are alphabetically arranged—dictionaries, indexes, telephone directories, etc. Therefore, they should have little difficulty in understanding the alphabetical nature of the catalog. The important part of this learning is understanding the different kinds of cards in the catalog and how to use them to find books and information. In conjunction with teaching about the physical setup of the catalog, then, explain the cards themselves. A bulletin board showing enlarged drawings of actual cards from the catalog of the school or community library is almost a must. (See pages 440–441 for types of cards that should be included.) These can be placed below the chart showing the outsides of the drawers. Both color and meaning can be added by putting explanatory notes on colored cards and attaching each to the item it refers to with a piece of colored yarn. Be sure to include all types of cards and to keep the display up until after the children have had actual experience in using the catalog to find information for a report.

Children will have many questions about the cards and the items on them: Is a book listed only once in the catalog? What does the call number mean? These questions should be answered as thoroughly as possible to help children feel competent and at ease in using library aids. Some questions may not have particularly logical answers; when this is true, simply say so. For example, why are an author's first *and* last names capitalized when only the first word of the book title is? Why does one card contain more complete information than another card on the same book?

If children have had a limited amount of library experience, they may need practice exercises to ensure that they know exactly how to use the card catalog. For example, they might report on how many books the library has by Lois Lenski, Beverly Cleary, or some other author they like; they could begin with a list of book titles (both fiction and nonfiction) and find the names of the authors and where the books are located in the library; or each child could select a subject and find three books containing information about it, what subject headings they are listed under, and where they are located on the shelves. Again use only as much of this kind of drill as seems necessary; if some children are already fairly adept at using the catalog, let them work on special reports or serve as "assistant teachers" for those who need practice.

As soon as possible, each child should select a topic and go to the library to find information for a brief oral report; purposeful activities will provide greater reinforcement than any number of practice drills. Frequent opportunities to use the library in connection with units of study in all areas of the curriculum will both enrich the curriculum and help learnings to become well established.

Teaching activities related to cards should be designed to make sure the children learn the following:

1. Author, title, and subject cards are all arranged in alphabetical order.
2. Titles beginning with *A, An,* or *The* are alphabetized according to the second word.
3. A number in the title is always spelled out.
4. Abbreviated words are listed as if they were spelled out. For example, for U.S. Government, the alphabetical arrangement would have this entry as if it were spelled out—United States Government. The same would apply to such abbreviations as Dr., Mrs., Mr., St., etc.
5. Author cards for books by the same writer are filed according to the alphabetical order of the titles of the books: Politi, Leo, *Butterflies Come, The* comes before Politi, Leo, *Song of the Swallows.*

If your school library does not have a card catalog or if your school does not have a library make a card catalog for the books in the room library so that children will have an opportunity to learn how to use this valuable aid. Use shoe boxes or metal file boxes for the drawers, making author, title, and subject cards for each book. Set up the library corner as much like a real library as possible, and allow children to take turns being the class librarian, checking out books and see-

Catalog Cards
Dewey Decimal System—Simplified for Children's Catalog

Author Cards

j shows that book may be found in juvenile fiction

j	Carpenter, Frances	author
	Wonder tales of dogs and cats;	title
	illustrated by Ezra Jack Keats	(sometimes publisher and date are also given here)

book is located in juvenile non-fiction

j595.7   Lemmon, Robert Stell

All about moths and

butterflies; illustrated by

Fritz Kredel. N Y Random House

1956

illus. (All about books)

book is illustrated and is one of the All About series

Title Cards

Wonder tales of dogs and cats

j   Carpenter, Frances

note that cards are alphabetized by first letter at top of card, regardless of indentation

All about moths and butterflies

j595.7   Lemon, Robert Stell

Subject Cards

Cats, Stories

j   Carpenter, Frances

    Wonder tales of dogs and
cats; illustrated by Ezra
Jack Keats

Butterflies

j595.7   Lemmon, Robert Stell

    All about moths and butter-
flies; illustrated by Fritz
Kodel   N Y Random House 1956

illus.   (All about books)

See and See Also Cards

there is nothing
catalogued under
this heading; look
under woodcarving
for information
about whittling

WHITTLING   see

WOOD CARVING

some information can
be found under this
heading; you may find
additional information
under the second heading

AIRPLANES   see also

AERONAUTICS

ing that they are returned to their correct places on the shelves. Even though this catalog will be small, children will have fun "playing library" while they learn that the catalog can help them:

- Find a book quickly when they know the title but not the author.
- Find out whether the library has another book by an author whose work they have enjoyed. (It could be checked out and therefore not visible on the shelf.)
- Find out whether the library has a book on a particular subject.

Another possibility is to enlist the cooperation of one or two other teachers in making a cooperative catalog. The call number for each book could show which room the book is in and where it can be found in that room, and children would be allowed to check books out from any of the several rooms. Thus many more books would be available to each child. This would entail a great deal of work initially, but it would be well worth the time spent, particularly in a small school or with children who, for one reason or another, do not have the opportunity to use a large library regularly.

Locating Media Information

Many schools are now keeping filmstrips, tapes, records, and other audiovisual materials in their libraries so that they may be used by pupils as well as teachers, instead of housing them in a center available only to teachers. If your school library has such materials, children should learn how to locate these as well as books. They may be listed in a media file similar to the card catalog, or their cards may be included in the general catalog along with those for books. In the latter case, they will be identified in some way—possibly by a simple notation at the top of the card or by a color code.* Familiarize children with these materials; show them where and how they are used and how to locate them in the library.

Using Call Numbers

Children should learn about call numbers while they are learning to use the card catalog. They should also learn the difference between fiction and nonfiction and understand the meaning of biography. Middle grade children can understand that fiction is a story that someone made up, even though some characters may be real people and some incidents true; that nonfiction contains true information, which the author has tried to verify, and which may or may not be in story form; and that biography is the true story of the life of a real person.

---

*Color coding is especially useful, since it helps you and the children to discover quickly and easily whether the library has a filmstrip, cassette, etc., that might be useful in presenting a report or teaching a particular unit. With this system, cards for all types of material (including books) are filed together and each type has a particular color assigned to it. That is, cards for filmstrips might have a strip of green tape across the top, records a blue one, films a red one, etc.

The following understandings should be developed:

1. Books of fiction are shelved together and arranged in alphabetical order according to the author's last name. Just as children's books and adult books are in different sections, sometimes picture books and books for older children can be found in separate sections—in fact, many libraries have added a third group that includes books for children in the upper grades. A fiction book for young readers will have *j* on its spine, possibly followed by a capital letter indicating the first letter of the author's last name. These letters constitute the call number of the book. If the library has a special section for older children, books shelved there will be marked *y* (young adult) rather than *j* (juvenile). Cards for both groups, as well as those for picture books, will be found in the children's catalog.

2. Biographies are usually shelved together and arranged alphabetically, but in most libraries they are alphabetized by the name of the person the book is about rather than that of the author. Thus all the books about the same person can be together, so that if a child is looking for a biography of Abraham Lincoln, for example, there will be only one place to look instead of several. A biography will have on its spine the letter B, and underneath it the first letter of the subject's last name.

3. Other nonfiction books (biography is nonfiction) are arranged in numerical order according to numbers that indicate what each book is about. Thus, as with biographies, all the books about the same subject can be shelved together. Call numbers are assigned according to a classification system that has been worked out to include all subject areas. There are two of these systems; one or the other is used in almost every library of any size. General reference books such as encyclopedias and dictionaries which contain information about many subjects are another special category of nonfiction. These usually have the letter R on their spines, are kept in a special area, and can seldom be checked out of the library.

Children who understand how to use the card catalog and what the call numbers mean are well on their way to being able to find what they are looking for, even in the large libraries they will encounter later. It is important to help them understand that this is not simply a complicated system set up by adults to try to confuse them. Rather, the card catalog is like a telephone directory; just as a child can look in the telephone directory to find out where a friend lives, so the card catalog indicates where a particular book—or information about a particular subject—can be located. The call number is the book's "address"; it shows where the book is in the library and it helps the librarian to put it away quickly so another child will be able to find it.

Children should *never* be required to memorize either the Dewey Decimal or Library of Congress system of classification; there is no more point in this than in memorizing the call numbers of individual books. The important concept to learn is that the numbers will guide them in locating the books they want. If they are curious about what the numbers mean, a simple explanation can help them to understand why books about the same subject have the same or similar numbers and to recognize that there is order in the arrangement.

Although most university and other large libraries now use the Library of Congress system, many small libraries—including those in schools—find the Dewey Decimal system better suited to their needs. Begin with whichever is used in libraries available to the children, although it would be a good idea to point out that this is not the only system. If neither is used, teaching should be postponed until it can be meaningful.

Dewey Decimal System.   In the Dewey Decimal System, books are arranged numerically on the shelves; thus anyone who can count and knows the call number of the book he wants can find it easily—the call number, of course, is found by looking in the card catalog. The numbers represent ten general subject areas, as follows:

000–099 Reference books, such as encyclopedias, and books about books (bibliographies). These books usually have *R* on the spine and can seldom be checked out of a library.
100–199 Philosophy, psychology, ethics (conduct).
200–299 Religion, including mythology and religions of all peoples.
300–399 Social Sciences: law, government, education, vocations, civics, economics.
400–499 Language: dictionaries and books about the study of all languages.
500–599 Science: mathematics, physics, chemistry, biology, zoology, botany.
600–699 Useful Arts: medicine, engineering, agriculture, aviation, manufacturing, etc.
700–799 Fine Arts: painting, music, photography, recreation.
800–899 Literature: poetry, plays, novels, and criticisms of these.
900–999 History, geography, travel, biography.

Each of these general areas is divided into many subtopics, each of which has its own number. For example, the 630s are devoted to agriculture, and a book on forestry will be numbered 634, probably with a decimal to indicate a further subdivision.

Library of Congress Classification.   The Library of Congress classification may also be explained if it is used in your library. By the time children reach the upper grades, they should at least be aware that there is more than one system of classification, since they may be using more than one library.

A—General Works—polygraphy
B—Philosophy—religion
C—History—auxiliary sciences
D—History and topography (except America)
E & F—America
G—Geography—anthropology
H—Social Science
J—Political Sciences
K—Law
L—Education
M—Music
N—Fine Arts
P—Language and Literature
Q—Science
R—Medicine
S—Agriculture—plant and animal industry
T—Technology
U—Military Service
V—Naval Service
Z—Bibliography and library science

By the time children reach the junior high school level they should be able to use all the aids of the library to locate information they want or need without

Catalog Cards
Library of Congress System

Author Card

call number   * jRA   Shay, Arthur   author
     965   What happens when you go   title
     S4   to the hospital. Chicago,
publisher   Reilly and Lee [c. 1969]
and date

     31 p.   illus.   29 cm.

     1. Hospitals   1. Title   there are two
other cards for
this book under
the headings given

Subject Card

     HOSPITALS
     * jRA   Shay, Arthur
     965   What happens when you go
     S4   to the hospital. Chicago,
     Reilly and Lee [c. 1969]

the book   31 p.   illus.   29 cm.
has 31 pages
and is
illustrated   1. Hospitals   1. Title

Title Card

     What happens when you go to
the hospital. [c. 1969]

     * jRA   Shay, Arthur
     965   What happens when you go
     S4   to the hospital. Chicago,
     Reilly and Lee [c. 1969]

     31 p.   illus.   29 cm.

     1. Hospitals   1. Title

(Children will be interested to know that 29 cm. means that this book is 29 centimeters tall; the asterisk before the call number also indicates that this is a tall book. These items are intended to help the librarian in shelving it.)

READING CATALOG CARDS

There are three kinds of cards in the card catalog: author, title, and subject.

The Author Card

> F
>
> Blanchard, Miriam
>   The little toy horse;
>   New York: McGraw-Hill,
>   1964

The Title Card

> F
>
>   The little toy horse
> Blanchard, Miriam
>   The little toy horse;
>   New York: McGraw-Hill,
>   1964

The Subject Card

> F
>
>   TOYS - STORIES
> Blanchard, Miriam
>   The little toy horse;
>   New York: McGraw-Hill,
>   1964

The "F" in the upper, *left-hand* corner tells us that this is a fiction book. On the *Author Card*, where is the author's name placed?

____ at the top ____

What four other pieces of information are there on the *Author Card*?

____ book title ____   ____ publisher ____

____ city where published ____   ____ date of publication ____

Now look at the *Title Card*. Is the "F" there? ____ Yes ____   What else is at the top?

____ the book's title ____

Where is the author's name?

____ under the title ____

The *Subject Card* gives us a clue to the contents of this book. What is this book about?

____ It is a story about a toy. ____

The "F" lets you know that the book is fiction; the word "stories" just reminds you.

What is after the subject heading?   ____ the author's name ____

Where is the book title?   ____ under the author's name ____

Notice the *last three* items. Are they the same or different on the three cards?

____ the same ____

What kind of card would you choose if you know a book's title but do not know its author?

____ a title card ____

If you want to find out how many books by a certain author are in the library, which kind of card will you use?   ____ an author card ____

If you are writing a report on Norway, which kind of card will you use?   ____ a subject card ____

_____

55

Teaching the use of a card catalog in a library setting may be supplemented with commercially prepared exercises. [From *Study Skills for Information Retrieval* by Donald L. Barnes and Arlene B. Burgdorf. Copyright © 1970 by Allyn and Bacon, Inc.]

teacher guidance. They should know where the card catalog is and how it is used; where to find the Dewey Decimal Classification (or Library of Congress) Wall Chart; where newspapers are kept; where current magazines are and where to find old magazines; where records, tapes, cassettes, filmstrips, etc., may be found; where indexes, atlases, dictionaries, and other reference books are; and—most particularly—how to go about finding what they want in any library they may use (this includes asking the librarian for assistance).

SPECIAL REFERENCES

The use of an encyclopedia, atlas, almanac, biographical dictionary, fact book, or similar reference involves many of the same skills as those needed for effective use of a dictionary or a library card catalog. In addition, skillful use of most reference books requires the ability to locate the particular section, paragraph, or sentence within a topic or a book that gives the specific information sought,[4] and some familiarity with each of the reference sources—familiarity gained through practice in using them.

Reference Books for Elementary and Junior High School Libraries by Carolyn S. Peterson (Scarecrow Press, 2nd ed., 1975) reviews reference books for children.

Encyclopedias

An encyclopedia such as *Childcraft* can provide the primary grade child with good experiences in seeking and locating information in an encyclopedia. The first work in encyclopedia use should be by your demonstrating that you use the index to find where to look for information, and that you can then turn to the correct page and read the information you were looking for. Do this frequently as things are discussed and more information on them is needed. Tell and show the children what you are doing, and read what you find. Primary grade children should be permitted to browse in the encyclopedias available to them, and as soon as they have learned to read with sufficient skills they may be assigned simple facts to look up.

Intermediate grade children should receive more direct instruction, which should include the following skills and understandings:

- The form in which material in an encyclopedia is arranged, and differences in arrangement in the encyclopedias available for their use.
- Knowledge of the location of the index and the meanings of guide letters on the covers of volumes. Particular attention should be given to boldface type, parentheses, italics, etc.
- The use of pronunciation keys, cross reference listings, bibliographies at the close of articles.

Compton's Encyclopedia has Fact Indexes—each volume has its own—that will be most helpful when they are used correctly. If *Compton's* is available to your class, practice in using the index can be provided by picking a subject related to something the class is studying, deciding which facts to look up, and using the index to help find these facts. For example, a subject like "waterfalls" will give the class an opportunity to explore and have experience with the arrangement of an encyclopedia, the use of an index, cross references, guide words, and the help given by pictures, charts, and their captions. The number of times instruction in using the encyclopedia is given will depend upon the particular class; they may need daily exposure in a meaningful setting for some time.

Many good encyclopedias for children are available—*The World Book, Collier's, Compton's, Americana, Britannica Junior,* and *Merit Student's Encyclopedia,* to name a few—and most school libraries have several of these. Children

Using the Card Catalog

Three people in the class were looking for the same book. Each had different information about the book. Here is how they found the book listed in the card catalog.

Lee knew that the person he wanted to read about was a silent movie comedian. But he couldn't remember the comedian's name. Lee went to the card catalog and found this **subject card** under *C.*

```
791.43      COMEDIANS
JAC       Jacobs, David
          Chaplin, the movies, and Charlie.
        New York: Harper & Row, 1975
```

Jackie knew that David Jacobs had written a book about a silent movie comedian. She went to the card catalog and found this **author card** under *J.*

```
791.43      Jacobs, David
JAC          Chaplin, the movies, and Charlie.
         New York: Harper & Row, 1975
```

Nina knew the title of the book she wanted was *Chaplin, the Movies, and Charlie.* She went to the card catalog and found this **title card** under *C.*

```
791.43      Chaplin, the movies, and Charlie.
JAC       Jacobs, David
          Chaplin, the movies, and Charlie.
        New York: Harper & Row, 1975
```

How many different ways are there to look up a nonfiction book in the card catalog? How are the cards in the catalog arranged? What information appears at the top left-hand corner of each card?

to talk about

● 143

Newer language textbooks give attention to library and study skills. (From Language Basics Plus, Level F. Copyright 1979 by Harper and Row Publishers, Inc. Used by permission of the publisher.)

should have experience with all that are available to them. In connection with learning to take notes, each child might select a topic and look for information about it in all of the encyclopedias available. Comparing the information found can help children to discover the importance of looking in several sources for information. This should be done a number of times with a number of subjects; repeated lessons under guidance are essential for effective use of these materials.

Children can work both individually and in groups to gather information for oral reports. A group report can be valuable in several ways: the children can learn organization through planning what information each will look up and report, they can help each other in both finding and organizing material, and together they can present a more complete coverage of material than if each child were working individually.

Opportunities should also arise in an activity of this sort for children to discover that different sources sometimes present conflicting or different facts. Discuss how this might happen and emphasize the importance of using several sources to try to verify facts insofar as is possible. It is also helpful to point out that the copyright date of a book may have a bearing on the accuracy of certain facts—population figures and scientific data, for example. In other words, information might not have been wrong—or known to be wrong—at the time that it was printed.

Children enjoy working with encyclopedias and other reference tools, and this type of experience provides opportunities for learning to locate information; to read critically; to take notes on, summarize, and outline what they have read; to prepare an oral or written report; to use handwriting, spelling, and punctuation skills; to compose with specific information and an audience in mind; and to do proofreading and editing. Thus learning to use the encyclopedia is not only valuable in itself, but also involves practice in a wealth of related language skills.

Atlases

Use of the atlas is frequently taught in connection with social studies, but, as with most social studies and other subject matter teaching, the tools and skills are those of the language arts.

Like the encyclopedia, use of the atlas should be taught first through demonstration. If the atlas includes a section which tells how to get the most out of it, this should be used as an aid. *The World Book Atlas,*[5] for example, has at the beginning a section called "How to Get the Most out of *The World Book Atlas,*" which explains how to find places, directions, and distances; how to understand symbols and population figures; how to pronounce names of cities; and how to understand abbreviations and foreign geographical terms. This atlas is also color keyed to help the user find quickly sections such as the United States, Asia, Africa, the index, etc. Children using this atlas to learn about the United States can find both physical and political maps of the entire country, as well as maps of regions and individual states. There are historical maps showing colonial America, the U.S. at the time of the Revolution, territories opened up by 1800, westward expansion from 1800 to 1850, maps showing positions and routes of the forces during the Vicksburg, Chattanooga, and Atlanta campaigns of the Civil War, plus two maps of the Eastern theatre in 1862–1863 and 1864–1865.

Other maps show principal air routes, railroads, and highways; and charts give populations and areas of states and major cities and distances between these cities. In addition, the student can learn that New York is the largest city in North America, that the highest elevation is Alaska's Mt. McKinley at 20,320 feet, and that the lowest spot is California's Death Valley, 282 feet below sea level. And this is only a part of what the atlas can reveal; there are maps and charts showing weather, population density, average income, available medical care, and so on. Children will be truly amazed at the variety of information that can be gleaned from a single book.

To give children experience with the atlas, have each child choose a city in the United States that he or she would like to visit. Help to direct selections so that each city will be large enough to be shown on maps and listed in at least some tables. Then have each child see how much information can be found about the city chosen and write this information on a small card. Perhaps the class could discuss the kinds of facts it would be desirable to know and formulate a list of questions such as the following:

- How far is the city from where we live?
- What route would I take to get there by plane? Train? Car?
- What kind of weather does the city have?
- What is its population?
- How many miles above sea level is the city?
- Is it located in an agricultural or industrial area?

The information gained through such an activity can be used to make a very attractive bulletin board—a map of the United States surrounded by the cards the children have made, each connected with a piece of colored yarn to a pin showing the location of the city. A map can be made very easily by taping a piece of white shelf paper or tagboard to the chalkboard, using the opaque projector to focus a picture of the map on the paper, and then drawing the outline with a felt pen. The children can color the states and locate their cities and other points of interest.

Once the children have learned to find places through the use of the index and map searching, teach them about directions and aids to pinpointing places. Parallels of latitude and meridians of longitude should be explained and discussed. Ask the children questions: Which is farther from our city—Houston, Texas or Tallahassee, Florida? If you were traveling from Louisville, Kentucky to Memphis, Tennessee, which direction would you travel?

Other atlas activities include these:

1. The reading of map symbols is necessary for understanding a map. The children can make a bulletin board showing the common map symbols and their meanings. Allow the children to copy these symbols from actual maps in an atlas. Perhaps the class could make up a game that involves identifying map symbols.
2. Determining distances on maps can and should be taught as part of the arithmetic class. It will take the pain out of arithmetic for some.
3. Abbreviations and foreign geographic terms become understandable to children once they are able to read and understand the tables where these are listed. When children are aware of the tables, they will enjoy looking for their new-found words or abbreviations on the maps.
4. An atlas also gives a great deal of information about a country—the area in square miles, the population and population density, the form of government, the capital

and the largest cities, official and major languages—all on one easy-to-read table. It also gives information about the world as a whole—the largest countries of the world in population and in area, climates, rainfall, etc. Give the children questions that require them to find such information: What is the coldest it ever got in North America and where was this? Where was it the warmest in North America and what was the temperature? In what countries—or on which continents—do most of the people in the world live?

5. Teaching about relief maps found in an atlas can be related to the making of salt-and-flour maps. Salt-and-flour maps can be made of a state, of a country, or of areas to help develop concepts such as peninsula, gulf, bay, or plateau. A child who uses an atlas as a guide in making a salt-and-flour map of a plateau will have solid knowledge of that term. Activities of this type are particularly beneficial for children who have difficulty with reading. (Make the salt-and-flour mixture with one cup each of salt, flour, and water, plus one tablespoon of powdered alum. The mixture can be stored in old coffee cans until you are ready to use it. If it dries out, add more water.)

Other References

Children will be fascinated with the many kinds of one-volume references to be found in the library. Here are a few; let them see how many others they can find.

Guinness Book of World Records
Webster's Sports Dictionary
Encyclopedia of Animals
Dictionary of Synonyms
Geographical Dictionary

A library contains a wealth of other reference materials that children should become familiar with; the following may be of particular interest. In addition, permitting children to browse in libraries and encouraging their reporting on interesting things they discover may suggest other things to study.

Almanacs.   The best way to teach children what an almanac contains and how to use it is to provide them with copies for exploration. Once they have done some browsing, a few specific lessons should be sufficient to acquaint them with this interesting tool. Following are a few suggestions:

1. Ask each class member to write the name of a magazine or newspaper that is in his home. Then let each one use the almanac to find what the circulation of that magazine is.
2. Have each child select a city and use the almanac to find out what its population is, how high the tallest building in that city is, etc.
3. Let each child look for a famous person with his last name. The class might even like to make a *Who's Who* of these famous "relatives."
4. Have children make up questions for which answers can be found in the almanac—for example, "Who won the National League batting championship in 1971?" These can be placed on cards and exchanged, perhaps with children divided into teams and competing to see which team can find all the answers first.

Famous First Facts.   Intermediate grade children have been known to get into a "He did"—"He didn't" type of argument. Many times such an argument can be settled by the use of *Famous First Facts*. The index in this book is different from others children may be familiar with. Each child might use this index to make a list of all the important events that occurred on his birthday or on a particular holiday. These could be incorporated into a bulletin board entitled "Famous Days," which would include a picture of each child, the date of his birthday, and a list of the events that happened on that date written by the child concerned. A similar bulletin board might show famous events of a particular year—the year most of the children were born, the year they started attending school, etc. This type of activity can stimulate conversation and lead to other language activities.

Books of Quotations.   Books of quotations may be introduced in a manner similar to that used to introduce almanacs and *Famous First Facts*. The primary objective is for children to become aware that there are books like this and to understand how they are organized and in what ways they are helpful. Again, a bulletin board can be useful. It might be entitled, "I Wish I'd Said That," with each child selecting an author—perhaps just because the name appeals—and then finding a quotation from the author selected. These may be written on cards, along with credit to the author and the source, and placed on the board. To extend this activity, children might check for facts about the person in an encyclopedia, take notes, and give orally or write a brief report.

The references mentioned above are intended as suggestions only—so many excellent books are available that it would be impossible to teach about all of them. The important thing is for children to become aware of the many resources to be found in libraries and to become familiar with ways to use them. Plan lessons around those that are of special interest to your class or that may be used in conjunction with class activities or units of study.

The Reader's Guide to Periodical Literature

Children in the seventh or eighth grade who have become adept at locating and using materials may be ready for an introduction to *The Reader's Guide.* It should be stressed, however, that the child who has not learned to use an encyclopedia easily, who does not readily use the table of contents or index of a book to locate information, or who has not learned to organize materials from two or more sources is *not* ready for this more complicated source. Generally speaking, children in the upper elementary grades—and beyond—are still struggling with the skills of note taking and organization and still working at becoming conversant with the many aspects of the library already mentioned in this chapter. If, however, you do have a few children who seem ready, select a time when the children are working on group or individual reports to introduce these few to this valuable research tool. Bring in a volume of *Reader's Guide*—or if this is not possible, copy a few pages on one of the machines now available in most libraries. Show the children how to find out what periodicals are included and how to interpret the entries; then let them practice looking up sources of specific information. (Very little instruction or practice should be needed if they are truly familiar with other references.) Then arrange a trip to the library, either for these children or for the entire class, so they may have actual experience in using the *Guide* and finding magazine articles listed there.

The Media Center

As mentioned earlier, the elementary school library now usually contains many materials other than books. A well-stocked library may have pictures, graphics of various kinds, films and filmstrips, slides, records and tapes, programmed mate-

Media equipment and materials are a part of modern elementary school libraries.

rials, kits and games, models, dioramas, maps, etc.; and most libraries will have at least some of these. Children will have had experience with these in the classroom and they should learn to find and use them in the library, as a source of both pleasure and information. Further, they should learn to use such aids to supplement and/or add interest to reports, just as you do in preparing your lessons for the class.

Plan for reports in several subject areas for which children may use various types of audiovisual aids, and make sure that these are included in the organizational plans for the reports. Point out that if a particular filmstrip, for example, cannot be included in the outline for a report, then it should not be a part of that report, however interesting it may be.

Upper grade children should be aware that the city, county, or university library is a veritable treasure house of records, tapes, picture files, films, micro-recorded materials, and equipment to use them. In addition, there are pamphlet files, newspaper files, bound volumes of innumerable periodicals, art objects, dioramas, and exhibits of many kinds. There are soundproof rooms where one may go to listen to recordings and machines for copying pages from books. If there is such a library in your area, upper grade children should visit it. Possibly you could arrange a guided tour by the children's librarian or someone else who knows and understands children. This may help them to be less awed when they are ready to take advantage of the library's resources.

A FINAL WORD

The library is truly an exciting place, and children should be helped to discover this. There is little doubt that the child who knows how to use library aids can prepare a better report and will, in all probability, be a better student. But the greatest reward will come not just during school years, but when the child reaches maturity, for then he or she will be able to find information needed and to locate books and many other materials that enrich life and aid personal fulfillment.

ENDNOTES

1. See pp. 365–367 for a more complete discussion of room libraries.

2. A more complete list of aids to book selection is found at the end of chapter 15.

3. Refer to chapter 16 for suggestions on teaching children to take notes.

4. See the section on study skills in chapter 16 for teaching suggestions.

5. *The World Book Atlas* (Chicago: Field Enterprises Educational Corporation, 1970).

REFERENCES

Books

Arbuthnot, May Hill, and Sutherland, Zena. *Children and Books*. Chicago: Scott Foresman and Co., 1972.

California Association of School Librarians. *Library Skills*. Belmont, CA: Fearon Publishers, 1973.

"Getting Kids into Libraries—and Vice Versa." *Learning*, 5 (April, 1977): 60–63.

Glasser, J. F. *The Elementary School Learning Center for Independent Study*. West Nyack, NY: Parker Publishing Co., 1971.

Holstrop, R. W. *Education Inside the Library Media Center*. Hamden, CT: Shoestring Press, 1973.

Margrabe, Mary. *The New Library: A Stations Approach*. Washington, DC: Acropolis, 1973.

Filmstrips

How to Use the Card Catalog. Chicago: Society for Visual Education (intermediate).

How to Use a Library. Niles, IL: Moreland-Latchford (4 filmstrips, 2 cassettes; intermediate, upper).

How to Use Maps and Globes. Mahwah, NJ: Troll Associates (6 color strips, 3 records or cassettes; intermediate, upper).

Look It Up: How to Get Information. Mahwah, NJ: Troll Associates (4 color strips, 2 records or cassettes; intermediate).

Multimedia Center. Wichita, KS: Library Filmstrip Center (strip with record or cassette; intermediate).

Quickwick: Your Library Guide. New York: Miller-Brody Productions (5 strips with records or cassettes, teacher's guide, activity sheets; grades 2–5).

Using the Elementary School Library. Chicago: Society for Visual Education (6 sound color strips; intermediate).

Transparencies

Basic Library Skills. St. Louis: Milliken Publishing Co. (12 transparencies, 24 duplicating masters; intermediate).

Learning "Look It Up" Skills with an Encyclopedia. Chicago: Field Enterprises Educational Corp. (4 frames; intermediate grades).

Library Science Project-Aid Transparencies (for use with *Compton's Pictured Encyclopedia, World Book,* and *Encyclopedia Britannica*). New York: General Analine Film Corp.

Library Skills. Atlanta, GA: Colonial (2 sets of transparencies; intermediate).

Library Skills. Holyoke, MA: Technifax (30 transparencies and teacher's guide).

Using the Library. Jamaica, NY: Eyegate House (10 transparencies).

Other Aids

Barnes, Donald L., and Burgdorf, Arlene B. *Study Skills for Information Retrieval.* Boston: Allyn and Bacon (series of workbooks on locational skills; middle and upper grades).

Cleary, Florence Damon. *Discovering Books and Libraries.* New York: H. W. Wilson Co., 1977 (a handbook for middle and upper grades).

Getting to Know the Library, Books A, B, C. Englewood Cliffs, NJ: Scholastic Book Services (3 workbooks; grades 1–6).

How to Use the Reader's Guide to Periodical Literature. New York: H. W. Wilson Co., 1978 (Pamphlet; free in reasonable quantities).

The Library Skill Box. Mahwah, NJ: Troll Associates (10 cassettes, 50 duplicating masters, and teacher's guide; intermediate, upper).

Library Skills. Minneapolis: T. S. Denison and Co., n.d. (workbooks and teaching guides on how to use the library; grades 4–6).

ACTIVITIES FOR PRESERVICE TEACHERS

1. Investigate the possibility of involving parents as librarians or library helpers. Be prepared to report to the class.

2. Gather materials on book fairs. What does a school need to do to get a traveling exhibit?

3. Survey several classrooms to determine how many pupils have public library cards. Inquire how often those with cards use them.

4. Plan a lesson for a particular primary grade that would necessitate looking up information in a beginning encyclopedia. Be sure to find out whether this information can be found in an encyclopedia that would be available to a class at this grade level.

5. Visit the library to obtain lists of Newbery and Caldecott award winners. Familiarize yourself with as many of these books as possible, and begin a card file of annotations for primary, middle, or upper grades.

6. Select a fifth grade text for a subject area of your choice. Using the text as a base, make a unit lesson plan that would require children to go to the library for added information. Be sure to provide for differences in library experience and language ability.

7. Familiarize yourself with at least one set of encyclopedias, one atlas, and one of the other references listed in this chapter. Note particularly organization, teaching aids provided, types of information included, and grade levels for which each might be suitable.

8. Plan an activity designed to familiarize children with the use of a reference tool other than the encyclopedia. Demonstrate to the class exactly how you would present this.

9. Plan a unit for a subject area and grade level of your choice. Include at least three different types of media aids and tell how you would use them.

ACTIVITIES FOR INSERVICE TEACHERS

1. Visit libraries in your area. Discuss with librarians the ages, interests, and reading abilities of your class. Find out what each library has to offer of a special nature for children. Find out what the librarian would like children of the ages of those in your class to know about the library.

2. Prepare a bulletin board designed to teach the use of the card catalog. Make large sample cards, similar to those in this chapter, with explanations (including pictures) of the various entries on the cards.

3. Plan a library skills unit for your class. Include visits to libraries in your plans.

4. Prepare activities for children that require particular library skills—for example, finding several references about a topic, using an atlas, finding fiction books by a particular author, or locating a specific issue of a magazine.

5. Make a survey of the amount of library-use teaching done in your school. Report the results of your survey.

INDEPENDENT ACTIVITIES FOR CHILDREN

1. Arrange a filmstrip viewer, filmstrips, and other practice materials in a corner (see the references at the end of this chapter for suggestions) where individual children may review procedures as needed.

2. A child might go to the library for the purpose of reporting back to the class about the different kinds of atlases (or almanacs, encyclopedias, fact books, etc.) that the library has. The report should be complete enough for the pupils to really see differences among the references in a category. Possibly permission could even be obtained to bring one or more of these references to the classroom at the time of the report for purposes of illustration.

3. Have the child find the title and call letters for a book by each of these authors:

Lois Lenski   Robert Lawson
Eleanor Estes   Laura Ingals Wilder
Ludwig Bemelmans   Maurice Sendak

4. Prepare sheets containing various types of information, some true and some false. Individual children who need additional practice in locating information can use library and study skills to find out whether or not the information is true. Sample statements might be as follows:
   a. *Henry and Ribsy* was written by Roald Dahl.
   b. *Hailstones and Halibut Bones* is a book of poems about holidays.

c. Chicago is approximately 850 miles from Boston by air.

d. The piranha is a flesh-eating fish that is found in the Amazon River.

5. At the beginning of the football (or baseball, ice hockey, etc.) season, a sports-minded pupil might prepare a bulletin board about the sport, using pictures cut from magazines and newspapers along with information gathered from almanacs and other sources to give interesting information about the game.

6. Have a child prepare a report on the library to present to another class. This should include the use of visual aids—for example, reproductions of various types of cards from the card catalog, a floor plan of the library, books with different types of call numbers, etc.

7. A child can use an atlas to plan an imaginary trip, plotting the route to be taken, places of interest to visit, time necessary for traveling, method of travel, kinds of clothing needed, etc.

8. An individual child can prepare a report for the class about the Caldecott or Newbery Award. This might include such items as when the award was first given, what factors enter into the selection, and which books and authors that the class is familiar with have won it. Several books that have received the award might be used to illustrate the report.

9. When the class is working on a project for which supplementary material is needed (this will occur often in a program that is vital and broad), a child—or several children—could go to the library to locate and examine materials that might be useful. They could then check out these materials for class use (arrangements will need to be made with the librarian for this) or prepare a list to be placed on the bulletin board, giving title, author, a few words about content, and the call number or location for each item.

INDEX

A